Neuropsychology
A Clinical Approach

To Francis Patrick Bowler

Neuropsychology
A Clinical Approach

Kevin Walsh
BA, MB BS, MSc, FACRM, FBPsS, FAPsS
Reader in Psychology, University of Melbourne;
Director, Department of Neuropsychology,
Austin Hospital, Melbourne

SECOND EDITION

CHURCHILL LIVINGSTONE
EDINBURGH LONDON MELBOURNE AND NEW YORK 1987

CHURCHILL LIVINGSTONE
Medical Division of Longman Group UK Limited

Distributed in the United States of America by
Churchill Livingstone Inc., 1560 Broadway, New
York, N. Y. 10036, and by associated companies,
branches and representatives throughout the world.

First edition 1978
  Reprinted 1982
Second edition 1987

ISBN 0-443-03858-9

British Library Cataloguing in Publication Data
Walsh, Kevin W.
  Neuropsychology: a clinical approach.
  — 2nd ed.
  1. Brain — Diseases — Diagnosis
  I. Title
  616.8′0475   RC386.5

Library of Congress Cataloging in Publication Data
Walsh, Kevin W.
  Neuropsychology: a clinical approach.
  Companion v. to: Understanding brain damage/
Kevin W. Walsh. 1985.
  Bibliography: p.
  Includes index.
  1. Brain — Diseases.   2. Neuropsychology.
3. Psychology, Pathological.   I. Walsh, Kevin W.
Understanding brain damage.   II. Title.   [DNLM:
1. Neuropsychology.   WL 102 W225n]
RC386.W29   1987   152   86–29948

Produced by Longman Singapore Publishers (Pte) Ltd.
Printed in Singapore

Preface to the Second Edition

The preparation of this edition proved more difficult than it might appear. With the almost explosive growth in neuropsychological knowledge since the first edition, the author had to resist making the text more advanced, since the earlier version appeared to have served a purpose in providing a broad background to the clinical knowledge of brain-behaviour relationships at an intermediate level. It is hoped that the fairly extensive bibliography will allow those interested in particular topics to extend their knowledge. The publication of the small companion volume, *Understanding Brain Damage*, late in 1985 allowed certain material to be omitted to allow for review of some more recent studies without a measurable increase in the scope of the work. The anatomical format has been retained despite acknowledged deficiencies. It is pleasing to note that the neurological brand of neuropsychology, as distinct from the psychometric, is alive and flourishing and that we are beginning to lose the undue emphasis on the cerebral cortex in favour of the systemic notion, with due importance being given to subcortical structures and intracerebral connections.

Melbourne, 1987   K. W.

Acknowledgements

I would like to express my thanks to the medical staff and neuropsychologists at the Austin Hospital for their continuing support and helpful discussions, in particular Dr Peter Bladin, Dr Geoffrey Donnan, Dr David Andrewes, Dr Michael Saling, Danny Moglia, Toni Miles and Mary Kotzmann. Library service provided by Medical Librarian Ann McLean was the backbone of the enterprise. Academic support to facilitate the work was freely given by Professors of Psychology, Gordon Stanley, Alexander Wearing and Roger Wales. Present and former graduate students provided cases for Chapter 10 and helped with the proof reading. Much of the burden of the latter fell on Dr David Darby, who has my thanks. The manuscript was ably handled by Kathleen Wood and Laurie Hassall. Medical artist Vivienne James upgraded many of the figures from the first edition and provided new ones. The Departments of Radiology and Clinical Photography provided several of the plates. To all of these, my gratitude.

K. W.

Contents

1. History of neuropsychology   1

Ancient civilization   1
    Craniotomy   4
Classical Greece   6
The ventricular localization hypothesis   6
    Vesalius   11
Search for the cerebral organ   13
Faculty psychology and discrete localization   14
Lesion studies of the 19th century   15
    Broca and the localization of speech   16
    Wernicke and the beginning of modern neuropsychology   17
    Memory disorder and the brain   18
The cortical map makers   19
    Cytoarchitecture and myeloarchitecture   19
Modern neuropsychology   20
    Neuropsychological syndromes   21
    Functional systems   23
    Double dissociation of function   24
    The disconnection syndrome   27

2. Basic anatomy of the brain   32

Anatomical terms of relationship   32
The coverings of the brain   34
    Dura mater   34
    Arachnoid mater   35
    Pia mater   35
The cerebrospinal fluid system   35
    The subarachnoid space   35
    Ventricular cavities   36

Gross topography of the brain   39
  The cerebral hemispheres   39
The cerebral cortex   49
  Cellular layers of the cortex   50
  Functional areas of the cortex   51
The brain stem   52
The internal structure of the hemispheres   59
  The white matter   59
  The basal ganglia   66
Blood supply of the brain   67
The internal carotid arterial system   68
The vertebrobasilar arterial system   72
Venous drainage   73
The cerebral arterial circle   73

3. Elements of neurology   78

Methods of investigation   78
  The neurological examination   78
  Radiological investigation   79
  Electrical investigation   85
Common neurological disorders   88
  Cerebral trauma   88
  Intacranial tumours   92
  Cerebrovascular disorders   94
  Epilepsy   98
Disruption of higher cerebral functions   103
  Aphasia   103
  Agnosia   107
  Apraxia   111
  Amnesia   113
  Dementia   116

4. The frontal lobes   117

Anatomy and functional organization   117
The frontal lobe controversy   122
The frontal lobe syndrome   126
  Confabulation   127
  Lesion studies and cognitive change   128
Psychosurgery   158
  Prefrontal lobotomy and its congeners   158
The frontal lobes and personality   161
Cognitive changes with modified leucotomy   164
Frontal lobe syndrome: one or many?   168

5. **The temporal lobes**   169

Integrative functions of the temporal lobe   169
Anatomical features   170
   Functional organization   172
   Visual perception   182
   Olfactory function   183
Complex partial seizures (temporal lobe epilepsy)   184
   Behavioural change   184
   Hallucinations and illusions of the temporal lobe   185
Electrical stimulation of the temporal lobe   187
Temporal lesions and cognitive change   189
   Unilateral lesions   189
   Bilateral lesions and the general amnesic syndrome   195

6. **The parietal lobes**   201

Anatomical features   201
Sensory and perceptual disturbances   204
   Somatosensory discrimination   204
   Disorders of tactile perception   207
   Disorders of intersensory association (cross-modal integration)   209
   Symbolic (quasi-spatial) syntheses   210
Disorders of spatial orientation   212
   Disorders of location and orientation   212
   Impaired memory for location   215
   Topographical disorientation and loss of topographical memory   216
Route finding difficulties   219
Constructional apraxia   221
   Status of the concept   221
   Laterality of constructional apraxia   224
   Qualitative differences and laterality   225
   Constructional apraxia and locus of lesion   227
   Resolving the confusion   227
   Associated disabilities   228
   Frontal apraxia   229
   Constructional apraxia as a disconnection syndrome   230
Spatial dyslexia and dyscalculia   231
   Spatial dyslexia   231
   Spatial dyscalculia (acalculia)   231
Spatial disorders: general comments   233
Unilateral spatial neglect (USN)   233
   Testing for neglect   233
   Laterality of lesion and USN   233

Locus of lesions causing neglect   236
Unilateral neglect and perceptual disorders   237
Nature of the defect   238
Unilateral neglect and recovery of function   239
Motor neglect   239
Disorders of the body schema   239
Anosognosia   239
Lack of awareness of body parts   241
Right-left disorientation   242
The Gerstmann syndrome   243
The parietal lobes and short term memory   244
Postural arm drift   246

7. **The occipital lobes**   247
Anatomical features   247
Visual pathways   249
Cerebral blindness   253
'Blindsight'   254
Denial of blindness (Anton's syndrome)   254
Hysterical blindness   257
Visual perception   257
Visual location   257
Visual orientation   258
Stereopsis and depth perception   258
Achromatopsia   259
Visual agnosia   260
Visual object agnosia   260
Simultanagnosia   262
Prosopagnosia   263
Colour agnosia   267
Status of the concept of visual agnosia   269
Alexia without agraphia   269
Reversible alexia   273
Visual hallucinations   273
Electrical stimulation   273

8. **Hemispheric asymmetry of function**   276
The concept of cerebral dominance   276
Hand preference and language dominance   277
Unilateral lesion studies   280
Visual perception and asymmetry   281
Tactile perception   285

Auditory perception 287
Temporal order 287
The right hemisphere and communication 288
Memory and learning 289
Emotional functions 289
Motor impersistence 291
Bilateral effects from unilateral lesions 291
Attention and the right hemisphere 292

Hemispherectomy 293
Infantile hemiplegia 293
Adult hemispherectomy 296

Cerebral commissurotomy 298
Visual perception 301
Tactile perception 306
Auditory Perception 307
Language 308

Agenesis of the corpus callosum 312

Functional asymmetry in normal subjects 314

Dominance revisited 315

9. The interbrain 318

The diencephalon 319
Diencephalic amnesia 320
Amnesic syndrome: one or many? 324
Unilateral thalamic damage 327
Thalamic aphasia 328
Thalamic neglect 329

10. Neuropsychological assessment 330

General considerations 330
Roles for neuropsychological assessment 331
Symptoms and syndromes 332
Face validity and the seductive inference 334

The neuropsychological syndrome 338
The method of extreme cases 339
Selecting the tools 339

Case examples 340

References 375
Index 421

1

History of neuropsychology

Ancient civilization   1
Classical Greece   6
The ventricular localization hypothesis   6
Search for the cerebral organ   13
Faculty psychology and discrete localization   14
Lesion studies of the 19th century   15
The cortical map makers   19
Modern neuropsychology   20

ANCIENT CIVILIZATION

The earliest written information we possess on localization of function in the brain is contained in the Edwin Smith Surgical Papyrus. The copy acquired by Smith in Luxor in 1862 is thought to date from the 17th century BC, while orthographic and other evidence would place its origin some 1000 years earlier, somewhere between 2500 and 3000 BC. It contains the earliest known anatomical, physiological and pathological descriptions and has been described as the earliest-known scientific document.

The papyrus contains reports of some 48 cases of observations and description of treatment of actual cases, many of them suffering from traumatic lesions of various parts of the body including many injuries to the head and neck. Translation of the papyrus was undertaken in 1920 and the detailed examination of the text and commentary was published by Breasted in 1930. It is in this papyrus that a word for brain appears for the first time. The papyrus 'opens the door on cortical localization of function with its description of injuries to the brain' (Gibson, 1962).

The material of the papyrus may be divided into two parts, namely, the original text and the explanatory comments (glosses) which have been added at a later date to expand and clarify the text. That these glosses which appear on the back (verso) of the manuscript are of a much later date, is witnessed by their explanation of terms in the texts which had, by the time of our extant copy, apparently become obsolete.

1

Of the 48 cases the first eight deal directly with injuries to the head and brain. Though some of the injuries may have been sustained in civilian occupations, it is more than likely that many of them, as well as wounds described in other parts of the body, were sustained in war. If so, this would be the earliest recording of the contribution of the study of war wounds to the study of brain-behaviour relationships, a source which has been of paramount importance in more recent times.

The following cases serve to illustrate the careful observations made by the ancient medical practictioner. The direct quotations are from Breasted (1930). Thirteen cases of most interest to the neurological scientist have been reprinted in Wilkins (1965).

1. The examination of case four reads in part:

> If thou examinest a man having a gaping wound in his head, penetrating to the bone, (and) splitting his skull, thou shouldst palpate his wound. Shouldst thou find something disturbing therein under thy fingers, (and) he shudders exceedingly . . .

The shuddering which occurred upon the surgeon's palpation may refer to convulsive movements produced by pressure upon the exposed brain. It is reminiscent of the extraordinary case described by Gibson (1962).

2. Case six described a skull fracture with rupture of the coverings of the brain.

> If thou examinest a man having a gaping wound in his head, penetrating to the bone, smashing his skull, (and) rendering open the brain of his skull, thou shouldst palpate his wound. Shouldst thou find that smash which is in his skull (like) those corrugations which form in molten copper, (and) something therein throbbing (and) fluttering under thy fingers, like the weak place of an infant's crown before it becomes whole — when it has happened there is no throbbing (and) fluttering under thy fingers until the brain of his (the patient's) skull is rent open — (and) he discharges blood from his nostrils, (and) he suffers with stiffness in his neck, (conclusion in diagnosis).

The commentator has written two glosses in clarification:

> *Gloss A*
> As for: 'Smashing his skull, (and) rendering open the brain of his skull,' (it means) the smash is large, opening to the interior of his skull, (to) the membrane enveloping his brain, so that it breaks open his fluid in the interior of his head.

> *Gloss B*
> As for: 'Those corrugations which form on molten copper,' it means copper which the coppersmith pours off (rejects) before it is forced into the mould, because of something foreign upon it like wrinkle.

Here is a clear description of the meninges and an awareness of the cerebrospinal fluid which bathes the brain, together with a picturesque but apt description of the appearance of the brain's convolutions.

3. In a further example (case eight) we are introduced to statements which obviously relate brain injury to disordered function, that is, the earliest recorded findings in neurophysiology or functional neurology.

> If thou examinest a man having a smash of his skull, under the skin of his head, while there is nothing at all upon it, thou shouldst palpate his wound. Shouldst thou find that there is a swelling protruding on the outside of that smash which is in his skull, while his eye is askew because of it, on the side of him having that injury which is in his skull; (and) he walks shuffling with his sole, on the side of him having the injury which is in his skull . . .

The ancient Egyptian has noted that injury to the brain may affect other parts of the body, here the eye and the lower limb. The shuffling of the foot presumably refers to the weakness of one side of the body produced by damage to the motor pathways from their origin in the cortex of the brain, what would now be termed hemiparesis. The manuscript had been written so long before that the commentator had to explain the obsolete word for shuffle. The physician who wrote the manuscript also appears to have been aware that the effects of brain injury varied according to the side of the brain receiving the injury.

Breasted notes that the physician has reported weakness of the limb on the same side as the head injury and suggests that the physician may have been misled by a *contre-coup* effect. If so, this could be the first of innumerable occasions in the history of neurology where an incorrect inference has been made on the basis of accurate observation through lack of sufficient information. The contre-coup effect refers to the fact that trauma to the head may produce injury to the brain either beneath the site of external injury, (*coup*) or to an area of brain opposite to the external injury (*contre-coup*). Examples are depicted in Figure 3.14. Since damage to the motor region of the brain produces weakness or paralysis of the opposite side of the body, a contre-coup injury may give the appearance of weakness on the same side as the scalp or skull wound.

Apart from these examples of effects resulting from brain injury the papyrus also describes several effects of spinal injury, e.g. seminal emission, urinary incontinence and quadriplegia as a result of injury to the cervical portion of the spine. However, there appears to be no evidence that the author considered the brain and spinal cord to be part of a single system.

While the Edwin Smith Surgical Papyrus described head injury there was no reference to common behavioural manifestations such as post-traumatic amnesia. Another work, the Papyrus Ebers (Ebell, 1937) contains a general recognition of organic causes of forgetfulness.

Turning from Egypt to the other ancient cradle of civilization in the Tigris and Euphrates valleys we find evidence that medical and surgical practice was well organized and legally regulated in this region in the latter part of the third millennium BC. However, information from this civilization was recorded on fragile clay tablets which have largely perished and even the few surviving fragments from a much later period provide us with no evidence of knowledge of brain-behaviour relationships possessed by these great peoples. It is unfortunate that no surgical treatise, if such existed, has survived from ancient Assyria and Babylon to compare with the Egyptian papyri.

Craniotomy

No history of the brain and behaviour, no matter how brief, would be complete without reference to the neurosurgical procedure of craniotomy or surgical opening of the skull. This serious and difficult surgical intervention was carried out with extraordinary frequency from late Paleolithic and Neolithic times and has continued without interruption down to the present century. Whether such procedures also included operation upon the brain itself is open to conjecture. Some of the interventions show associated skull fractures but many do not. It is likely that only a relatively small proportion of operations was undertaken for traumatic injury.

The widespread use of craniotomy is evidenced by the discovery of prehistoric trepanned skulls from Europe (Italy, France, Austria, Germany, the Netherlands, England), Africa (Algeria, Rhodesia), South America (Peru, Bolivia, Colombia), North America and numerous islands of the South Pacific region. In some places such operations continued in their primitive form into the 20th century. Apparently no skulls showing prehistoric trepanation have been reported from China, Vietnam or India (Gurdjian, 1973).

Early instruments were made of obsidian or stone while, with the development of later civilizations, metallic instruments of iron and bronze were employed. Hundreds of examples of trepanation have been reported from the Peruvian civiliations beginning with the Paracas culture around 3000 BC and extending up to the end of the Inca civilization in the 16th century AD. In their examination of these pre-Columbian craniotomies Graña, Rocca and Graña (1954) have provided us with illustrations of (i) operations in every part of the human skull; (ii) operative openings of different shapes: circular, oval, rectangular, triangular, and irregular; (iii) sets of craniotomy instruments from different eras which include chisels, osteotomes, scalpels and retractors as well as bandages and tourniquets.

That many patients successfully survived such major cranial surgery is amply attested by skull specimens which show more than one surgical opening and having evidence (such as the bony changes around the opening) of different dates of operation in the same individual's lifetime.

As many as five separate craniotomies have been discovered in a single specimen.

In 1953 Graña and his colleagues successfully employed a set of these ancient instruments for the relief of a subdural haematoma (a large clot of blood pressing on the brain) in a patient who had suffered a head injury resulting in aphasia and right hemiplegia.

An elegant example from the Peruvian collection of instruments is shown in Figure 1.1. Known as a tumi, it depicts on its handle an operation on a patient where the surgeon is employing a similar instrument.

One can only speculate about the reasons for many of these early operations. Gurdjian lists as possible indications for operation headaches, the releasing of demons from the cranial space, for certain religious and mystical exercises and also 'the fact that some of the openings in the skull have been repaired with silver alloy suggests surgical treatment for the possible skull wound caused in battle.' (Gurdjian, 1973, p. 3).

How much evidence regarding brain functions was brought to light by these ancient operations is lost to us because of the absence of a written language among these various early peoples.

Fig. 1.1 Ancient Peruvian tumi.

CLASSICAL GREECE

The most frequently referred to writer from this period is Hippocrates. As Clarke and O'Malley (1968) point out, the Hippocratic writings were clearly the product of a group of physicians between the latter part of the fifth century BC and the middle of the fourth century BC. These physicians probably had little familiarity with the human brain because of the aversion for dissection of the human body which existed in Greece at that time although they did open the skulls of certain animals. Despite this lack of anatomical knowledge they considered that the brain was the seat of the soul or of mental functions and offered comments which showed that they had made very careful observation of their patients. Many would agree with McHenry (1969) that the Hippocratic tract *On The Sacred Disease* contains antiquity's best discussion of the brain and demonstrates the care with which a number of epileptic patients were studied. Another of the Hippocratic writers observed that damage to one hemisphere of the brain produced spasms or convulsions on the other side of the body though little was made of this observation and it appears to have been forgotten in the period which followed.

Hippocrates also 'warned against prodding blindly at a wound of the temporal area of the skull lest paralysis of the contralateral side should ensure' (Gibson, 1969, p. 5).

THE VENTRICULAR LOCALIZATION HYPOTHESIS

This theory of localization of function postulated that the mental processes or faculties of the mind were located in the ventricular chambers of the brain. The cavities were conceived of as cells, the lateral ventricles forming the first cell, the third ventricle the second cell, while the fourth ventricle made up the third cell. Hence this doctrine is often termed the Cell Doctrine of brain function.

In its almost developed form the ventricular doctrine was first put forward by the Church Fathers Nemesius and Saint Augustine around the turn of the fourth century AD and it was to remain very much the same for well over 1000 years, that is, well into the beginning of the Renaissance. Outlines of the doctrine together with excellent pictorial representations are given in Magoun (1958) and Clarke and Dewhurst (1972).

The ventricular theory had its roots in a number of earlier ideas particularly those of Aristotle and Galen. Aristotle had discussed the separate sense modalities and their contribution to perception. To account for the unity of sense experience he proposed a mechanism of integration which he called the common sense or *sensus communis*. Aristotelian psychology divided mental activity into a number of faculties of thought and judgment, e.g. imagination, fantasy, cogitation, estimation, attention and memory. These faculties were to become allotted to the ventricular chambers in the Cell

Doctrine. Even as early as 300 BC, Herophilus of Alexandria had localized the soul in the fourth ventricle.

Galen, in the second century AD contributed his theory of the psychic pneuma or gas and, though he himself did not propound the ventricular theory, he contributed to it in no small way. The reverence with which the writings of the 'prince of physicians' were held in the centuries which followed helped to set the doctrine in a form which was to remain unchanged for the next millenium. Unfortunately, Galen's followers were to copy his ideas slavishly without developing further his knowledge of the brain's anatomy and his careful and detailed observations of behavioural change.

As Gibson (1969) has it, Galen's 'brand of orthodoxy overcame medical science for a thousand years so that it required a Leonardo and a Vesalius to overcome it.'

With the intellectual ascendancy of the Arabic speaking peoples around the eighth century all the important Greek medical works were translated into Arabic and preserved in this way for some 500 years until re-translated into Latin, where they formed the basis of medical science at the beginning of the Renaissance and, indeed, long after. The anatomy of the great Arabian medical writers, Avicenna, Hali Abbas, and Rhazes around the 10th century depended to a great extent on translations of Galen.

Galen had incorporated into his system the knowledge of the anatomy of the ventricles already present in Alexandrian medicine. He described the ventricles in detail and, though he laid the foundation for the final form which the Cell Doctrine was to take, did not himself do more than hint at the association of the ventricles with intellectual functions preferring to locate the faculties of the brain substance itself.

Magoun (1958) gives the following concise account of Galen's theory of the 'psychic gas'.

> Nutritive material passed from the alimentary canal through the portal vein to the liver, where natural spirits were formed. These ebbed and flowed in the veins, taking origin from the liver, to convey nutriment to all parts of the body. A portion of these natural spirits passed across the septum, from the right to the left side of the heart, and joined with material drawn from the lungs to form the vital spirits. These ebbed and flowed to all parts of the body through the arteries, taking origin from the heart, to provide heat and other vital requirements. A part of these vital spirits passed to the base of the brain, to be distilled there in a marvellous vascular net, the rete mirabile, and to mix with air inspired into the cerebral ventricles through the porous cranial base, for, at this time, the pulsing of the brain in the opened cranium was conceived as an active process, much like that of thoracic respiration. As a consequence, animal spirits were formed, and 'animal', in this use, was derived from the Latin 'anima' and Greek 'psyche', meaning soulful, and was not animal in any lowly sense. This psychic pneuma, stored in the brain ventricles, passed by the pores of the nerves to the peripheral organs of sense

and to the muscles, to subserve sensory and motor functions. Its equivalently important role in managing central functions of the brain was affected either within the ventricles themselves or in the immediately bordering substance of their walls.

Sherrington pointed out how the movement of the brain which is a passive or transmitted pulsation misled Galen and his followers by apparently supporting their notion of the ventricular system as pumping the fluid to the different parts of the body. Sherrington supposed that Galen had not only seen it in the scalp of the young child before the vault closes but that he had observed that 'war and the gladiatorial games were the greatest school of surgery' (Sherrington, 1951).

It was as cells to contain the animal spirits that the ventricular chambers took on their great significance. A number of writers have pointed out that, of course, the ventricular cavities are the most striking features on gross dissection of the untreated brain.

Sherrington comments. 'It is interesting to speculate how much this concentration on meninges and ventricular cavities, an obsession that was to dominate thought about the brain for nearly two thousand years, was due to the simple fact that, unless fixed and hardened, the brain resembles an amorphous gruel, of which one of the few distinguishing features is that it possesses cavities'.

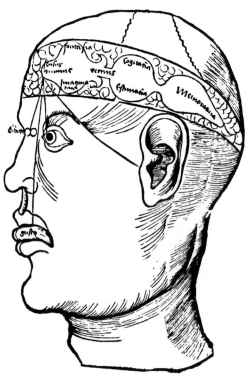

Fig. 1.2 Cell doctrine. Gregor Reisch (1504).

After Galen there was no significant development of anatomical knowledge for many centuries and Galen's influence can be most clearly seen in the slavish copying by those who followed of the *rete mirabile*, a network of blood vessels at the base of the brain. This network which appears in ungulates such as the pig and the ox is not found in man and those who followed Galen's findings for so long were apparently unaware that, although the master had knowledge of the human brain and that of the Barbary ape, his neuroanatomical descriptions were mainly derived from the ox. This also explains how his descriptions of the ventricles seem erroneous for man while they are highly accurate for the ox.

Two early 16th century woodcuts serve to illustrate the Cell Doctrine. Because of its clarity, Figure 1.2 has been reproduced very frequently. It is from an encyclopedia produced by the Carthusian monk, Gregor Reisch about 1504.

It shows the senses of smell, taste, sight, and hearing connected to the *sensus communis* at the front of the first chamber. This chamber is the seat of fantasy and imagination, the second of cogitation and estimation and the third memory. There is also a possible depiction of part of the cerebral convolutions.

The label vermis or worm would seem to refer to the choroid plexus which passes through the opening which connects the lateral ventricle (first cell) with the third ventricle (second cell) (see Fig. 1.3).

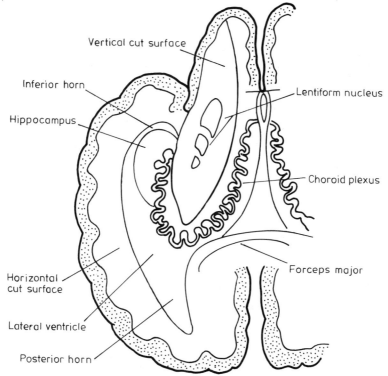

Fig. 1.3 Worm like appearance of the choroid plexus.

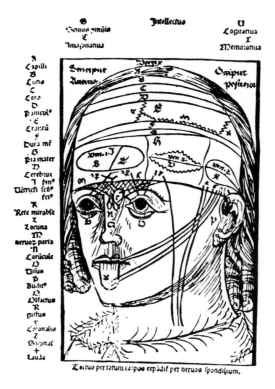

Fig. 1.4 Cell doctrine. Magnus Hundt (1501).

The second illustration is noteworthy for its reproduction of the rete mirabile at this late date. It is taken from Magnus Hundt, 1501 (Fig. 1.4) and illustrates not only the Cell Doctrine but also the cranial nerves according to Galen's classification together with the skull sutures and the different layers of the scalp. Magoun (1958) gives us a liberal interpretation of the Cell Doctrine.

> On passing to the brighter functional aspects of these early views, they first proposed that incoming information from a peripheral receptor was conveyed to a sensory portion of the brain, where it could be interrelated with other afferent data. Activity was thence transmitted to a more central integrative region, equivalently accessible to internal impressions related to sense and to general memory. Last, activity was capable of involving a motor portion of the brain, so as to initiate movement or behaviour. The sequential ordering of these Aristotelian faculties from the front to the back of the brain conveyed an implication that central neural function normally proceeded through such successive stages. Such conceptualization is not excessively different from that reached by Sherrington in his founding studies of modern neurophysiology nor from that which confronts us continually today.

This interpretation may be overgenerous but the crudity of depiction should not be taken as the only measure of the state of development of ideas. In reviewing such ideas from antiquity, Woolam (1958) warns of the danger of imputing too much knowledge to our predecessors:

> The great scientific names of the ancient world, Aristotle, Democritus, Galen and Hippocrates have received so much tribute, that it is easy to fall into the belief that all our modern scientific belief already existed in embryo as it were in the ancient world . . . Hippocrates described how a blow on the head could produce paralysis on the opposite side of the body. It is not too difficult to fall into the trap of reading backwards from our knowledge of the anatomy of the brain and see in this statement the first reference to the crossing of the pyramidal tracts. The study of the knowledge of the anatomy of the brain displayed in the Hippocratic Corpus proves a salutary corrective to this view.

Vesalius

With Andreas Vesalius (1514–1564) came the era in which careful scientific observations began to triumph over the dogmatic statements which had been handed down from the time of Galen.

His anatomical masterpiece, the *De humani corporis fabrica* and its companion volume the *Epitome* were published at Basle in 1543. This work has been called the embodiment of the spirit of the Renaissance and many have considered it the most influential factor in establishing the modern era of observation and research.

Vesalius was a pupil of Sylvius (1478–1555) who was known as a great follower of Galen. Vesalius was instructed in the ventricular hypothesis and recounts how he and his fellow students were shown the illustration from Gregor Reisch's *Margarita Philosophica* (Fig. 1.2) which they had to copy as an adjunct to their lectures on the functions of the ventricular chambers. The teaching of the time is well preserved in the following extract which records what Vesalius learned at the University of Louvain (Clarke & O'Malley, 1986, p. 468)

> Indeed, those men believed that the first or anterior, which was said to look towards the forehead, was called the ventricle of the sensus communis because the nerves of five senses are carried from it to their instruments, and odours, colours, tastes, sounds, and tactile qualities are brought into this ventricle by the aid of those nerves. Therefore, the chief use of this ventricle was considered to be that of receiving the objects of the five senses, which we usually call the common senses, and transmitting them to the second ventricle, joined by a passage to the first so that the second might be able to imagine, reason, and cogitate about those objects; hence cogitation or reasoning was assigned to the latter ventricle. The third ventricle (our fourth) was consecrated to memory, into which the second desired that all things sufficiently reasoned about those objects be sent and suitably deposited.

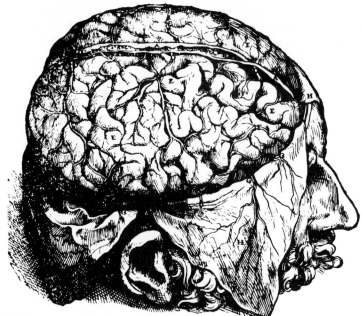

Fig. 1.5 Brain anatomy. Vesalius.

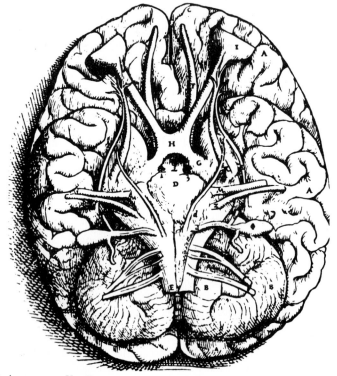

Fig. 1.6 Brain anatomy. Vesalius.

The detail of Vesalius' anatomy (Figs. 1.5 and 1.6) is in sharp contrast to the crudity of the earlier 16th century woodcuts. However, despite their artistic excellence and their dependence upon actual observation of anatomical specimens, the influence of his early Galenical teaching can be seen in the perpetuation of errors which cannot have been present in dissections. Though later commentators have stressed his anti-Galenism and though he was attacked by his contemporaries for his departure from their slavish following of the Galenical teachings, Vesalius himself was at pains to point out his respect for the greatness of the 'prince of physicians and preceptor of all'. What he would not condone was an indiscriminate acceptance of every one of Galen's teachings. His greatness lay in using the observational method to confirm earlier postulations and to note where the observations were at variance with accepted dogma.

Unfortunately, this sudden increase in knowledge of structural neuro-anatomy was not paralleled by an increase in knowledge of the brain's functions and this discrepancy between anatomy and physiology continued well into the 20th century.

SEARCH FOR THE CEREBRAL ORGAN

During the second half of the 17th century and the early part of the 18th a number of separate investigators attempted to find the one part of the brain that was the seat of the mind or soul. The essential feature of these attempts is the fact that they were based on speculation not on clinical observation or experimentation.

The most well-known of the theories was that of Descartes, who in selecting the pineal gland as the seat of the soul argued that it was so strategically situated with regard to the ventricular chambers that it could influence and be influenced by the flow of the spirits between them — 'a certain very small gland situated in the middle of its (the brain's) substance and so suspended above the channel by which the spirits in its anterior cavities have communication with those of the posterior, that the slightest movements which take place in it can greatly alter the course of these spirits; and reciprocally that the least changes which occur to the course of the spirits can greatly alter the movements of this gland' (from Clarke & O'Malley, 1968, p. 471).

Descartes reasoned that since our experience of the world is unitary despite the multiple organs of sense, each of which is double, there must be some place where these separate sense impressions could come together 'before they reach the soul'. 'It can easily be conceived how these images or other impressions could unite in this gland through the mediation of the spirits that fill the cavities of the brain. There is no other place in the body where they could be thus united unless it be in this gland' (Clarke & O'Malley, 1968, p. 472).

Other writers thought that this cerebral organ or organ of the soul might be represented by such structures as the corpus striatum (Willis), the white matter (Vieussens), or the corpus callosum (Lancisi). The fact that many were preoccupied with the search for a single vital structure does not mean that excellent observations and inferences were not made during the 17th and 18th centuries. However, they were greatly overshadowed by the search, and the clues to the nature of brain organization found in such fine examples as those cited by Gibson (1962) seem to have been overlooked when interest in the problem of localization blossomed some two centuries later.

FACULTY PSYCHOLOGY AND DISCRETE LOCALIZATION

In the period which followed, the notion of the unity of conscious experience gave way to the 'faculty psychology' which divided mental processes into a number of separate, specialized abilities and this was to precipitate the search for the neural substrate of such faculties or powers of the mind. In founding the system which came to be known as phrenology, Gall leaned heavily on the lists of faculties provided by the Scottish philosophers Thomas Reid (1710–1796) and Dugald Stewart (1753–1828). Gall's was not the only attempt to relate separate mental functions to discrete parts of the brain but it was certainly the most influential, its influence persisting for a century.

For all its drawbacks phrenology proved a more fertile notion than the earlier search for 'the single organ'.

Gall taught his doctrine in Vienna from 1796 onwards, and was soon joined by Spurzheim who, in fact, coined the term 'phrenology' and was to develop a moralizing version of Gall's ideas which was to become as keenly supported as it was contested. The essence of this movement is simply stated. The brain is composed of a number of separate organs each of which controls a separate innate faculty, i.e. there are as many cerebral organs for mental processes as there are faculties. The location of the faculties according to Spurzheim is shown in Figure 1.7.

The development of the cerebral organs led to prominences in the individual's skull so that by the process of 'cranioscopy' or palpation of the prominences the practitioner of phrenology could divine the nature of the person's propensities.

Gall stressed the role of the cortex in which he located his faculty organs. This was an advance since the cortex had been considered relatively unimportant up to this stage. Gall made a number of important discoveries in neuroanatomy but these have been greatly overshadowed by his speculative physiology.

When one reads the original work one is struck by the extraordinary lack of evidence given in support of what seem today strange and sweeping claims. Nevertheless, it certainly stimulated the scientific thought of the period. Boring (1929) called it 'an instance of a theory which, while essen-

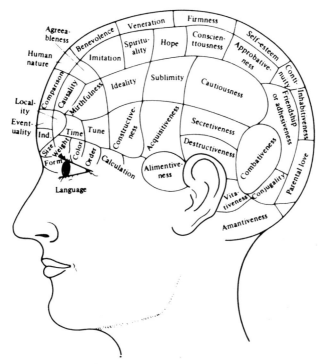

Fig. 1.7 A phrenological map (from Miller G A & Buckout R Psychology: The science of mental life, courtesy Harper and Row).

tially wrong, was just enough right to further scientific thought'. Although not providing proof it established the belief in many minds that the localizationist position was a tenable one.

The most powerful and influential opponent of phrenology was Flourens (1794–1867). He is commonly credited with beginning the movement that resulted in the holistic theory of brain function which held that mental functions are not dependent upon particular parts of the brain but, rather, that it functions as a whole.

Flourens experimented mainly with birds and demonstrated that animals may recover after ablations of part of their central nervous systems and that the same recovery takes place irrespective of the site of the ablation. This work anticipated the notion of equipotentiality, the ability of other parts of the brain to take over the functions of damaged neural tissue. Flourens stated quite clearly that he did not believe that the nervous system was a homogeneous mass but he did believe that it operated in a concerted, integrated fashion, unlike the theory of discrete localization.

LESION STUDIES OF THE 19TH CENTURY

During the long controversy between the supporters of Gall on the one hand and those of Flourens on the other, what one writer refers to as the controversy between the skull palpators and the bird brain ablators, numerous clinicians were making valuable observations on brain-behaviour relationships. In fact, clinical observations of language disturbance with brain trauma had been recorded for at least two centuries before aphasia become a major focus of attention. Many examples are provided in the fine historical paper of Benton and Joynt (1960). Unfortunately, even the more important of these were not seen in their true light because of their association in people's minds with one or other side of the controversy, e.g. Bouillaud in 1825 pointed out the frequent association of loss of language with lesions of the anterior or frontal lobes but clouded the contribution by stating that this could be taken to support Gall's contention that the faculty of language lay in this region.

It was quite some time later that Broca was to publish his well known dictum. Even when Dax read a paper in 1836 clearly relating the left half of the brain with aphasia it remained unpublished until his son brought it forward 25 years later. A number of factors may have conspired to bring about this delay, not the least of which may have been Dax's political unpopularity in the region at the time he delivered his paper. It is clear that Dax understood the specific role of the left hemisphere in the production of aphasia since he searched for cases of right-handed aphasics with right hemisphere lesions but was unable to find one such case.

Broca and the localization of speech

Broca's role in this history of functional localization is a particularly complex one which has been discussed in many places. Joynt's (1964) paper provides a brief but clear outline of the main contentions. Broca himself made no claim for priority in the discovery of the relation between the frontal region and language disturbance. He acknowledged more than once the contributions of Bouillaud. His sustained and systematic observations did, however, greatly advance the cause of the localization of function in the brain.

In 1861 Broca exhibited the brain of his patient 'Tan' who had died only the day before and who had in life lost the power of speech so that the only word which he was able to utter was 'Tan'. The lesion lay in the posterior part of the left frontal lobe. Later in 1861 Broca exhibited a similar case which confirmed his notion that the lesion in cases of aphasia was situated in the frontal lobes of the brain. At this stage, like the cautious observer he was, Broca posed the question as to whether a more exact localization was possible, leaving the question open for further investigation.

> It is a much more doubtful question to know if the faculty of articulate speech is dependent upon the whole anterior lobe or particularly upon one of its convolutions; in other words, to know if the localization of cerebral faculties

happens by faculty and by convolution, or only by groups of faculties or by groups of convolutions. Further observations must be collected with the object of solving this question. It is necessary for this purpose to indicate exactly the name and place of the diseased convolutions and, if the lesion is very extensive, to seek, wherever possible by anatomical examination, the place or rather the convolution where the disease appears to have begun (Clarke & O'Malley, 1968, pp. 496–497).

However, he did consider that even his first observations were more consistent with the system of localization by brain convolutions than the phrenological notion that he termed the 'system of bumps'. Even with the further accumulation of cases over the next 2 years he was still restrained in his statements: 'Here are eight cases where the lesion is situated in the posterior portion of the third frontal convolution . . . and, a most remarkable thing, in all of these patients the lesion is on the left side. I do not dare to make a conclusion and I await new findings' (Benton, 1965). At this time Broca also speculated on the possibility of localizing other functions than speech. Finally, in 1885 Broca published his famous dictum which was to become such a landmark in the history of brain function: 'Nous parlons avec l'hémisphère gauche'.

Broca's work stimulated a good deal of clinical research into the anatomical basis of language and numerous workers published findings in his support and soon others began to report observations which supported the view of localization in other areas of functioning.

Broca himself noted, with other workers, that exceptions to the location of language in the left hemisphere appeared to occur in left-handed individuals and from such observations began the notion that a crossed relationship existed between hand preference and hemispheric dominance for language, a notion that has bedevilled us ever since and one that is only now beginning to be clarified (see Ch. 8).

Wernicke and the beginning of modern neuropsychology

In 1874, several years after Broca's demonstration of the importance of the left posterior frontal region for spoken language Wernicke described a case where a lesion of the left superior temporal gyrus caused difficulty in the comprehension of speech. The addition of this finding to that of Broca meant that at least two separate functions could be affected by lesions in two separate locations. This could not fail to reinforce the ideas of those leaning towards a theory of localization and the search for similar 'centres' for other mental functions was greatly stimulated.

Wernicke's place in the history of brain function has been overlooked by most writers. Even the comprehensive and thoroughly documented work of Clarke and O'Malley does not mention him while other writers see him as merely subscribing to the notion that the 'discovery of a lesion in a particular area of the brain in an individual with a concomitant definite type of disturbance (signifies) that the area containing the lesion is the "centre" for the function that had been impaired' (Luria, 1966, p. 12).

Geschwind (1966, 1967) considers that Wernicke's contribution was very much greater, pointing out that his paper on receptive aphasia provided a potentially productive theoretical approach which made possible scientific method in the study of aphasia.

> 'On the basis of this theory it was possible to predict the existence of syndromes not previously seen and to devise experimental means of testing hypotheses'. Wernicke's reasoning was simple. He applied Meynert's teaching on the fiber tracts of the brain to the problem of aphasia. The phrenologists, he argued, had been wrong in their attempt to localize such complex mental attributes as magnanimity or filial love; what was actually localizable were much simpler perceptual and motor functions. All the complex array of human intellectual attributes must somehow be woven from these threads of different texture. The cortex could at its simplest provide two means of achieving this higher integration, it could store sensory traces in cells for long periods of time and, by means of association fiber tracts, it could link together different parts of the system' (Geschwind, 1966, pp. 4, 5).

Subsequent workers such as Lichtheim (1885) and Dejerine (1892) used this method both to predict and explain specific defects of psychological processes with localized brain lesions. Geschwind summarizes Wernicke's position in the following way.

> Wernicke was one of the first to see clearly the importance of the connections between different parts of the brain in the building up of complex activities. He rejected both of the approaches to the nervous system which even today are often presented as the only possible ones. On the one hand, he opposed the doctrine of the equipotentiality of the brain; on the other, he rejected the phrenological view which regarded the brain as a mosaic of innumerable distinct centers. He asserted that complex activities were learned by means of the connections between a small number of functional regions which dealt with the primary motor and sensory activities. Although this third view dominated research on the neurological basis of behaviour for a period of nearly 50 years, it has been omitted almost entirely from the discussions of the higher functions in recent times (Geschwind, 1967, p. 103).

Wernicke's point of view has been fully developed in Geschwind's logical analysis and development of the notion of 'the disconnexion syndrome' described later in this chapter (Geschwind, 1965a, b, c). In a very real sense Wernicke could be considered the father of neuropsychology.

Memory disorder and the brain

In a series of reports from 1887 to 1891, Korsakoff reported the association of various mental disorders with polyneuritis. Sometimes the patient retained clear consciousness but was agitated while in others the agitation was part of a confusional state. In most of the patients an amnesic disorder was a prominent feature. Soon after these observations Korsakoff, along with others, noted that the amnesic syndrome could be seen without the polyneuritis. The most common factor in the overwhelming number of cases was heavy indulgence in alcohol. It was some decades before the neuropathological basis began to be established (see Victor, Adams & Collins, 1971) and even today the necessary and sufficient lesions are still not settled.

Even before the classical papers of Korsakoff a recent review (Levin, Peters & Hulkonen, 1983) reminds us that Ribot (1839–1916) was the first to develop a systematic theory of memory and its derangement and a classification which incorporated important distinctions still is used, e.g. amnesia with forward extension (anterograde amnesia) and extension into the past (retrograde amnesia).

THE CORTICAL MAP MAKERS

From the era of Broca and Wernicke until well into the 20th century there were numerous reports of the discovery of similar localized centres in the cortex so that maps of the brain surface with functional labels attached to different areas appeared frequently in the literature. The cortical cartographers were aided by the widespread acceptance of associationism in the new science of psychology which was beginning to assert its independence. They were also in tune with the discoveries on the finer anatomical detail of the cortex and its physiology. The diagrams of the cortical map makers began to relate these latter findings such as the location of primary sensory and motor functions (mainly derived from ablation and stimulation experiments in animals) to the human brain and to add possible sites for higher mental processes, many of which were as speculative as the assignment of functions to particular areas by the phrenologists.

Cytoarchitecture and myeloarchitecture

Cytoarchitectonics refers to the study of the architecture of cells or the disposition of cells and their type and density in the layers of the cortex. This study was dependent on the discovery of methods for fixing and staining the nerve tissues so that adequate examination of cell populations could be made. Soon after the early development of these techniques of neurohistology by Ramon y Cajal and others it became apparent that the composition of the cortex was not everywhere the same and the discovery that the cortex could be subdivided into differently composed areas invited the possible inference that differences in structure might mean differences in function. Again the relationship between morphology and function could be demonstrated for the sensory and motor areas of the cortex which left the tantalizing possibility that the same might hold for higher functions. Though few such relationships have been found to date this story is not yet concluded.

The corresponding study of the fibre structure of the brain is known as myeloarchitectonics and Flechsig (1849–1929) had quite early related the time of development of the myelin covering of fibres to the development of different areas of the cortex. This suggested that the neural bases of higher functions might lie in cortical-subcortical systems rather than being restricted largely or wholly to the cerebral cortex.

The first major work in this new field by Campbell (1905) *Histological Studies on the Localization of Cerebral Function* shows in its title the avowed aim of the author to correlate function with histological structure. His map divided the cortex into some 20 regions. Shortly after, Brodmann (1909) produced his map with the separate zones now numbering around 50. This map has been widely reproduced and referred to ever since (see Fig. 7.3). Still other workers increased the number of subdivisions until 200 or more separate areas were differentiated in some systems. Milner comments: 'The difference between many adjacent regions in these later maps were so small as to be imperceptible to all but the anatomists who first described them. This problem was pointed out by Lashley and Clark (1946), who found only a few regions of the cortex that they could recognize from anatomical sections alone *if they did not know beforehand what part of the cortex the sections had come from*' (Milner, 1970, p. 109).

The earliest subdivision of the cortex related large areas of the brain's surface to the name of the overlying bones and this division into frontal, temporal, parietal and occipital lobes remains with us today. It has been stressed very often that these are artificial abstractions. However, 'as far as the psychologist is concerned the acid test of (any) such subdivisions is whether or not they can be shown to mean anything behaviorally. Does a lesion of an anatomically or physiologically defined area produce a more isolated and clear cut behavioral disturbance than a lesion that ignores such boundaries?' (Milner, 1970, p. 112). A century of lesion studies has demonstrated that these abstractions, the 'lobes' of the brain, are still more useful at this stage in discussing brain-behaviour relationships than those based on the finer subdivisions of cytoarchitecture.

MODERN NEUROPSYCHOLOGY

The past three decades have seen an accelerated growth in the new or re-awakened science called neuropsychology as lines of evidence converge from the parent disciplines of neurological medicine and psychology and as the special methods of each are modified for use in the new field. As with other areas where scientific endeavours overlap, new conceptions and formulations arise which not only advance the new science but also provide useful stimulation for the progenitors. The two principal aspects of clinical neuropsychology are clearly outlined by Luria, one of its ablest practitioners and developer of an influential theory whose principal features are outlined below:

> The study has two objectives. First, by pinpointing the brain lesions responsible for specific behavior disorders we hope to develop a means of early diagnosis and precise location of brain injuries . . . Second, neuropsychological investigation should provide us with a factor analysis that will lead to better understanding of the components of complex psychological functions for which the operations of the different parts of the brain are responsible (Luria, 1970a, p. 66).

This twofold nature of neuropsychology means that by utilizing appropriate tools and concepts to examine brain-behaviour relationships we may be in a position to further our knowledge of the nature of the psychological processes themselves. Neuropsychology has already given us greater insight into some of the processes of perception, memory, learning, problem solving and adaptation. The sophisticated techniques and methodology of modern psychology have also allowed a more detailed analysis of higher nervous disorders than was previously possible.

Leaving aside the psychological measures themselves since they are dealt with in some detail in Chapter 10, there seem to be a number of concepts developed only in recent years which are proving very fruitful. Among these the following four are chosen as they provide a basis for what follows: (i) the adoption of the syndrome concept as against the unproductive 'unitary' concept of brain damage; (ii) a re-evaluation of the concept of 'function' and the development of the concept of functional systems as the neural substrates of psychological processes; (iii) the use of 'double dissociation' of function to strengthen the certainty with which statements may be made concerning the relation between anatomical lesion and behavioural disturbance, and (iv) the development of the notion of the 'disconnection syndrome' to explain neuropsychological findings and to predict others.

Though these notions are interrelated with each other and with other ideas in the field they will be outlined separately.

Neuropsychological syndromes

The general failure of psychological tests to provide suitable measures of 'brain damage' was one of the key factors in moving neuropsychologists in the direction of describing the effects of cerebral malfunction in terms of syndromes. Those with a background in medicine and neurology are already familiar with the utility of the syndrome as a conceptual tool in everyday practice. More and more psychologists have moved in the direction of syndrome analysis at least in clinical diagnostic practice. Piercy (1959) and McFie (1960) favour this approach: 'a patient's performance should be described not so much in terms of extent of deviation from statistical normality as in terms of extent of approximation to an established syndrome or abnormality' (McFie, 1960). The use of psychological test methods in the appraisal of the patient's preserved abilities as well as deficits has helped to clarify the definition of some syndromes and is already beginning to describe new ones. The syndrome concept has allowed the more realistic use of psychological test procedures aimed at gauging patterns of impairment on appropriately selected measures. In discussing the objections to the syndrome method in clinical research as opposed to practice, Kinsbourne (1971) reminds us that the association between the constellation of signs and symptoms which we term a syndrome and the presence of a disease, is a probabilistic not an invariant one. 'Partial syndromes abound, and it is often not clear how many ingredients have to be present to justify the diagnosis. This is particularly true since not all ingredients of a syndrome are of equal importance, their relative valuation being unformulated outcome of the interaction of medical instruction and clinical experience, and thus a somewhat individual process' (Kinsbourne, 1971b, p. 290). On the research front he points out that correlative studies between lesion and syndrome need to employ valid experimental designs and that appropriate statistical procedures such as cluster analysis should prove useful in the validation of clinical syndromes. 'Pending validation by appropriate testing, the clinically observed "syndrome" represents an educated guess at a relationship which has value in generating hypotheses and experimentation' (Kinsbourne, 1971b, p. 291). One of the major tasks of present day neuropsychology is to increase the degree of confidence with which such probabilistic statements can be made.

Strub and Geschwind (1983), in their discussion of the Gerstmann syndrome (see Ch. 6) point out that some neuropsychologists have a basic misunderstanding of the medical use of the term syndrome. All would agree that a syndrome may be considered as a constellation of signs and/or symptoms which indicates the presence of a disease or lesion. It is not necessary for there to be a high correlation between the elements, though this would strengthen the diagnosis were it to occur. What should be characteristic is the uniqueness conveyed by the total *Gestalt*, and statistical techniques such as cluster analysis might be relevant in distinguishing syndromes from pseudosyndromes.

Closely related to the interpretation of signs and symptoms as a syndrome is the medical concept of differential diagnosis. This means the awareness that similar constellations may be seen in several different diseases or disorders. Ignorance of some of the possibilities will result in a proportion of incorrect diagnoses. This may occur in two directions. Either the pattern of signs and symptoms may be ascribed to the wrong cause or the pattern may not be recognized as a result of a particular disease, or both. The seriousness of the error will depend on the implications for prognosis and treatment.

One of the principal advantages of the differential diagnostic approach is that it allows hypotheses to be set up both to confirm the presence of one disorder and to disconfirm the possibility of others. This approach using psychological tests is exemplified with clinical case examinations in the final chapter. Unfortunately, in neuropsychology there are fewer pathognomonic signs than there are in medicine. The term pathognomonic refers to a sign or symptom which is specifically characteristic of a particular disease. Most symptoms and signs in neuropsychology have multiple significance.

The syndrome approach is close to the distinction made in recent years between monothetic and polythetic classification in biological taxonomy. 'The ruling idea of monothetic groups is that they are formed by rigid and successive logical divisions so that the possession of a unique set of features is both sufficient and necessary for membership in the group thus defined' (Sokal & Sneath, 1963, p. 13). With regard to the description and classification of brain damage such a system is not applicable in the light of present knowledge. On the other hand, the notion of 'polytypic' (Beckner, 1959) or polythetic groups is very much of value since no single attribute or set of signs and symptoms defines the group. A polythetic classification would place together in one group or syndrome all those cases which share a sufficient number of common characteristics. However, 'no single feature is either essential to group membership or is sufficient to make an organism a member of the group' (Sokal & Sneath, 1963, p. 14). The first major attempt to apply a taxonomic key approach to the problem of assessment of brain lesions was that of Russell, Neuringer and Goldstein (1970).

The description of syndromes in neuropsychology is of the polythetic type and is of undoubted value in the preliminary allotment of a patient to a diagnostic category which may then be checked further in the process of differential diagnosis.

Functional systems

The idea of a functional system as the neurological underpinning of a complex psychological function has been developed over a long period by Luria and is clearly outlined in his textbook (Luria, 1973b). At the outset he draws attention to the fact that the term 'function' may be used in at least two principal ways. Firstly, one may describe the function of particular cells or organs, e.g. one of the functions of the liver is to produce bile, the function of the islet cells of Langerhans is to produce insulin. This usage is readily understood. On the other hand, the term 'function' is widely used to describe more complex processes involving the integrated participation of a number of tissues and organs in a functional process, e.g. the function of digestion, circulation, and respiration. Such organizations are termed systems and though the final result, such as the absorption of nourishment or the provision of oxygen to the tissues, remains constant, the way in which the system performs the function varies considerably according to a wide variety of factors. 'The presence of a constant (invariant) task, performed by variable (variative) mechanisms, bringing the process to a constant (invariant) result, is one of the basic features distinguishing the work of every functional system' (Luria, 1973b, p. 28).

The systemic approach has a second advantage which proves useful in topical diagnosis. While it is true that damage in any part of a functional system may lead to disruption of a psychological process it is also true that damage to different parts of a system will impress a different character on the complex of symptoms and signs which result from the damage. Thus it is of paramount importance to establish not only that there is an alteration in a particular psychological function following a brain lesion but also what qualitative features this loss of function has. It was principally for this reason that psychological tests, particularly some of the more widely used psychometric measures proved of such limited value in diagnosis since they did not allow this difference in the quality of performance to be brought out or psychologists were too impressed with the scores or level of performance to see the significance of qualitative changes. Indeed, workers like Goldstein were roundly attacked because of their lack of norms, standardization and other features of the epitome of psychological assessment, the intelligence test. This overgeneralization is easy to make with hindsight and it is true, particularly of the British clinical psychologists that they quite early realized the shortcomings of dependence upon test scores alone. Shapiro (1951) expressed it pithily when he commented 'the test scores do not communicate the responses in full'.

The notion of functional systems is a marked advance on the notion of strict localization of function in discrete areas of the cortex. The functional system has as its anatomical basis a number of cortical and subcortical areas working in concert through the action of fibre pathways and it is for this reason that a working knowledge of the gross anatomy of the brain will be indispensable for the neuropsychologist. This becomes apparent in the understanding provided by the disconnection model discussed below.

Double dissociation of function

This concept was put forward by Teuber (1955, 1959) and has been widely accepted and quoted by other workers. In discussing whether certain visual discrimination difficulties described after temporal lobe ablations in animals were specific to those particular areas Teuber commented:

> To demonstrate specificity of the deficit for visual discrimination we need to do more than show that discrimination in some other modality, e.g., somesthesis, is unimpaired. Such simple dissociation might indicate merely that visual discrimination is more vulnerable to temporal lesions than tactile discrimination. This would be a case of hierarchy of function rather than separate localization. What is needed for conclusive proof is 'double dis-

sociation', i.e. evidence that tactile discrimination can be disturbed by some other lesion without loss on visual tasks and to a degree comparable in severity to the supposedly visual deficit after temporal lesions (Teuber, 1955, p. 283).

A more general statement appeared a few years later in discussion of Teuber's findings in his extensive studies of human subjects with wounds to the brain: '. . double dissociation requires that symptom A appear in lesions in one structure but not with those in in another, and the symptom B appear with lesions of the other but not of the one. Whenever such dissociation is lacking, specificity in the effects of lesions has not been demonstrated' (Teuber, 1959, p. 187).

Numerous examples of double dissociation of function appear in the later chapters. The concept has proved extremely useful but care must be exercised in transposing the word 'symptom' in the above quotation to mean the patient's performance on a psychological test. Kinsbourne has discussed the application of the concept to *groups* of individuals with damage in different parts of the brain.

> If a patient group with damage centered at location A is superior to one damaged at B in respect to task P, but inferior in task Q, a double dissociation obtains between these groups. This permits the inference of at least one difference between the two groups specific to location of damage, for P may be a nonspecific task, relating, say, to general intelligence or some other variable in which the groups are imperfectly matched. But then it must be admitted that function Q must have been selectively impaired by a lesion at location A; since the inferiority in performing Q cannot be accounted for by failure of matching on the other task. The search for double dissociation is a valid means towards progress in neuropsychology (Kinsbourne, 1971b, p. 295).

This author warns that the converse situation, namely the failure to find dissociations, should not lead us to conclude that specific relationships do not exist between performance on specific tasks and particular anatomical sites or structures since performance on a particular task may be affected by a number of factors. The recognition of the multiple determinants of the performance on many psychological tests should lead to the design of more 'discrete' tasks which are tied to single factors which might then be studied for their association with or dissociation from particular brain structures.

With the double dissociation paradigm Weiskrantz (1968) points out that

> the maximum information is conveyed when two treatments are alike in all but one oritical aspect (e.g. for brain lesions — same mass, same damage to meninges, but different in locus) and that the two tasks similarly are alike in all but one critical aspect (e.g. same training procedure, same cue-response contingencies, but difference in sensory modality). This is simply to restate

the essence of analytical control procedures, and the double dissociation paradigm is simply a way of combining two control procedures into a single pattern. But there are also great risks of reifying a dissociation between tests into a dissociation between functions and arguing that the affected function has been isolated by a single instance of dissociation.

Finally, the principle of double dissociation is proposed by Luria and others. 'The initial hypothesis in this line of work is the assumption that in the presence of a given local lesion which directly causes the loss of some factor, *all functional systems which include this factor suffer, while, at the same time, all functional systems which do not include the disturbed factor are preserved*' (Luria, 1973b, pp. 13–14). As one of numerous examples he points to the different effects of damage in the left temporal region in man as opposed to the effects of damage in the parieto-occipital region. Temporal damage leads to disturbance of acoustic analysis of that class of acoustic stimulation which we term phonemes and this leads to disturbance of any function which depends to any marked extent on this analysis and the greater the dependence of any function on the analysis of phonemes the greater will be the secondary disturbance of the function, e.g. repeating what another person has said or writing to dictation will be markedly affected. On the other hand, functions such as spatial perception which do not depend to any extent on phonemic analysis will be unaffected. Conversely, parieto-occipital damage will spare all those functions dependent upon phonemic analysis but disrupt all functions which have a dependence on spatial orientation.

Congruent dissociations

Since naturally occurring lesions are liable on most occasions to affect portions of functional systems which are geographically adjacent, the establishment of two or more 'double dissociations' will render the location of the causative lesion more and more certain. In other words the establishment of one dissociation may suggest application of an appropriate test in the form of a 'crucial experiment' in single cases. We might term such situations *congruent dissociations*. Table 1.1 depicts one 'such possible situation' based on data given in Chapter 5.

Table 1.1 An example of congruent dissociation

Tests	Lesion Site		
	Left Temporal	Right Temporal	Non-Temporal
Verbal Memory	Poor	Normal	Normal
Meaningful Sounds	Poor	Normal	Normal
Non-Verbal Memory	Normal	Poor	Normal
Meaningless Sounds	Normal	Poor	Normal

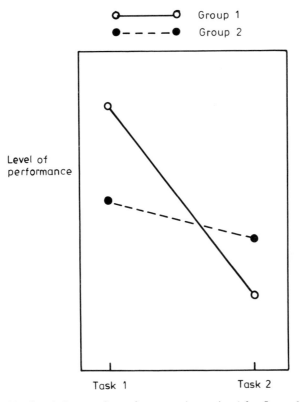

Fig. 1.8 Double dissociation as a form of crossover interaction (after Jones, 1983).

Jones (1983) points out that the paradigm of double dissociation is essentially a type of crossover interaction and, viewed as such, it is not absolutely essential for each group to perform at a normal level as in the example cited above on one of the two tasks in each dissociation. The performance on the tasks may be lowered by non-specific factors as well as by the specific factors involved in the dissociation. This opinion is shared by Shallice (1979) in his analysis. The representation of the relative performances of the two groups on the tasks is shown in Figure 1.8.

The disconnection syndrome

The notion of the disconnection syndrome dates back to the classical neurologists of the latter half of the 19th century. With their conception of specialized sets of cells disposed over the cerebral cortex and the emerging knowledge of the fibre pathways connecting the various parts of the cortex with nearby and distant structures, a distinction arose between 'cortical' and 'conduction' syndromes. Wernicke, for example, knowing the effects of damage to the motor speech area and the quite different effects of damage to the sensory speech area which he himself described, was able to predict what would result if these areas were disconnected or isolated from each other. Though his anatomical assumptions about the pathways involved were not correct the value of the concept of disconnection was validated by the discovery of the so-called 'conduction aphasia' (see Ch. 3).

The late 19th century and the early years of the present century produced a number of findings consistent with the disconnection theory particularly those of Liepmann whose analysis of apraxia was in terms of disruption of connections. He was also aware that 'disconnection' symptoms or syndromes could be brought about by interrupting connections between the hemispheres, interhemispheric or callosal disconnection (Liepmann & Maas, 1907), as well as interrupting connections between different parts of the same hemisphere.

However, the disconnection theory for all its factual support gradually lost ground in the first three decades of the present century under the impact of holistic theories espoused by such neurologists as Head, Marie and von Monakow. When Akelaitis and his group published their findings on sectioning of the corpus callosum for the relief of epilepsy in the early 1940s, the apparent absence of any of the predicted interhemispheric disconnection effects in their patients seemed to sound the death knell of the disconnection theory (Akelaitis, 1940, 1941a, b, c, 1942a, b, 1943; Akelaitis, Risteen, Herren & Van Wagenen, 1941, 1942, 1943; Smith & Akelaitis, 1942). It was only much later that it became obvious that the negative findings were due to lack of appropriate techniques for eliciting disconnection signs. Another 10 years was to pass before the elegant experimentation of Myers and Sperry (1953) in animals demonstrated convincingly that such callosal effects do in fact occur and the 'split-brain' techniques which they developed were soon applied to the small number of commissurotomy operations being performed on human subjects for the relief of epilepsy. The detailed findings of these hemisphere disconnection operations and their contribution to our understanding of the asymmetry of function in the two halves of the human brain are discussed in Chapter 8.

The split-brain work in animals also stimulated Geschwind and his colleagues both to re-examine the older clinical literature and to reassess their patients with disturbances of the higher functions. They were soon to find excellent examples (Geschwind, 1962; Geschwind & Kaplan, 1962; Howes, 1962).

The following brief summary is condensed from the extensive treatment by Geschwind (1965b, 1965c).

1. Disconnection syndromes are those produced by lesions of association pathways (see Ch. 2).

2. These pathways may be within the same hemisphere (intrahemispheric) or between the two hemispheres (interhemispheric or commissural).

3. Following 'Flechsig's principle' primary receptor areas of the cortex

have neocortical connections only with adjacent 'association' areas.

4. The association areas on the other hand receive information, i.e. have connections with several other cortical areas and send their outgoing connections to other areas at a distance.

5. Flechsig's principle also applies to linkages between the two hemispheres. There are no direct connections between the primary receptor areas of one side and the primary receptor areas of the other, only commissural connections between 'association' cortex. The effects of such an anatomical arrangement are summarized by Geschwind:

> These anatomical facts imply that a large lesion of the association areas around a primary sensory area will act to disconnect it from other parts of the neocortex. Thus, a 'disconnexion lesion' will be a large lesion either of association cortex or of the white matter leading from this association cortex. The specification of the association areas as way-stations between different parts of neocortex is certainly too narrow, but it is at least not incorrect. This view, as we shall see, simplifies considerably the analysis of effects of lesions of these regions. Since a primary sensory region has no callosal connections, a lesion of association cortex may serve both to disconnect such an area from other regions in the same hemisphere and also to act in effect as a lesion of the callosal pathway from this primary sensory area (Geschwind, 1965b, pp. 244–245).

This notion of a disconnection syndrome has been expressed in several ways in recent years depending upon the theoretical background of the author and is closely related to the notion of a functional system, a concept which is widely used in electronics and other sciences where the 'systems approach' has proved useful in pinpointing the site of lesions or faults in the system.

> The brain may be considered as a communication network, incorporating multiple information transmitting channels which lead to and from decision points. A limitation of function, namely the impairment or abolition of the ability to make particular decisions, may result from damage to the decision point and from interruption of input to or output from that point. Those points of the system which are most closely aggregated in cerebral space will be most vulnerable to selective inactivation by focal cerebral injury. The extreme example is the corpus callosum, division of which reliably induces a pure disconnection syndrome (Geschwind & Kaplan, 1962; Myers, 1956) without damage to decision points in either hemisphere . . . *The neurons that constitute a decision point are widely diffused over the cerebral cortex. But their distinctive function depends on their mode of linkage rather than on physical features of individual neurons, and this is not necessarily reflected in morphological differentiation* (Kinsbourne, 1971b, p. 287) (emphasis added)

Because midline surgical commissurotomy forms such a clear and dramatic example of disconnection, many students fail to appreciate that many naturally occurring lateral lesions must, of necessity, produce discon-

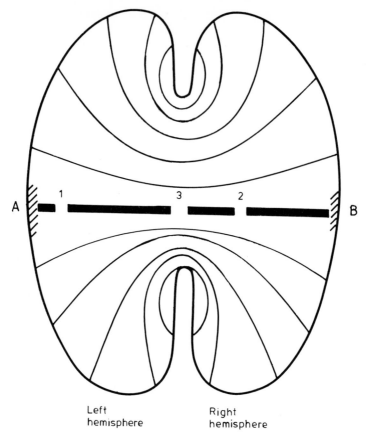

A   1   3   2   B

Left hemisphere   Right hemisphere

Fig. 1.9 Disconnection produced by a lateral lesion. Horizontal section through the corpus callosum.

nection effects. If one considers the hypothetical case shown in Figure 1.9, it becomes apparent that for the purposes served by the functional link A-B, disconnection is essentially the same whether the interruption takes place laterally in the left hemisphere (1), the right hemisphere (2) as shown or if it is surgically divided in the midline (3). Gazzaniga reminded us that cortical lesions also have the same effect: 'Hemisphere disconnection can also result, of course, from the degeneration of the callosal fibers normally innervating a region of extirpated or damaged cortex. Such lesions produce a partial commissurotomy much like those produced surgically and they result in the same behavioural characteristics' (Gazzaniga, 1970, p. 146).

We might summarize by observing that there are two major sets of connecting fibres, namely those which link areas within the hemisphere (intrahemispheric, often termed association fibres) and those which link the two hemispheres (interhemispheric or commissural fibres). This allows for three basic forms of disconnection: (i) intrahemispheric disconnection (see Conduction aphasia, Ch. 3); (ii) interhemispheric disconnection (see Callosal or left-sided apraxia, Ch. 3 and Commissurotomy, Ch. 8); and (iii) compound disconnection where both types of connection are conjointly interrupted (see Alexia without agraphia, Ch. 7).

2

Basic anatomy of the brain

Anatomical terms of relationship   32
The coverings of the brain   34
The cerebrospinal fluid system   35
Gross topography of the brain   39
The cerebral cortex   49
The brain stem   52
The internal structure of the hemispheres   59
Blood supply of the brain   67

ANATOMICAL TERMS OF RELATIONSHIP

Because some readers may be unfamiliar with anatomy while still wishing to gain a basic knowledge of the structure of the nervous system, it will be worth while to explain a few commonly used terms. In particular, one of the difficulties which students of anatomy encounter is in learning the manner in which the various structures are disposed in relation to each other. When, as is too often the case, students learning neuropsychology have little or no opportunity to attend demonstrations of dissection of the brain, it is of paramount importance to be clear about the terms which follow. Some confusion is also likely to arise in reading different texts unless equivalent terms are explained.

In lower animals the head-to-tail direction has been described by the Latin-derived terms *rostral* and *caudal* and the belly-to-back direction by the terms *ventral* and *dorsal*. These axes are often at right angles to each other. However, in man, the nose and belly point in the same direction so that the terms *anterior* and *posterior* may substitute for rostral and caudal while the terms *superior* and *inferior* stand for dorsal and ventral. Sometimes when speaking of the inferior aspect of the brain, one also uses the term base or *basal* aspect. A third set of directional terms relates to whether the structures are near the mid-line (*medial*) or away from it (*lateral*) (Fig. 2.1).

The terms *proximal* and *distal* are used to refer to the portion of the structure near to or away from its origin, e.g. the proximal part of an artery is

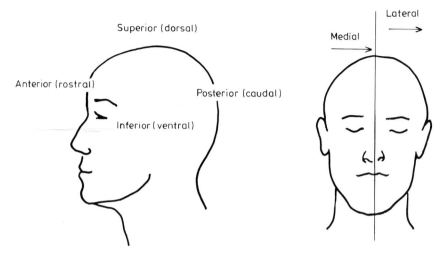

Fig. 2.1 Terms of relationship in neuroanatomy.

near its origin, the proximal part of a nerve is near the brain or spinal cord. Finally, an appreciation of the relative position of structures within the nervous system can be gained from studying series of sections cut through the brain after it has been hardened. There are three principal planes of reference: (i) *Coronal* or frontal sections are parallel to a vertical plane through both ears; (ii) *Sagittal* or longitudinal sections are at right angle to the coronal plane in a vertical direction. A median or midline sagittal section would divide the brain into its two hemispheres; (iii) *Horizontal* sections are at right angles to the other two (Fig. 2.2).

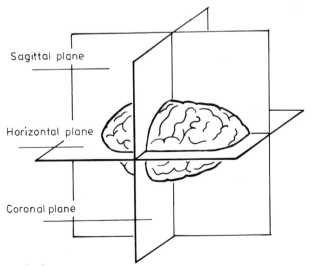

Fig. 2.2 Planes of reference.

Where there is no opportunity for dissection, brain models may help in gaining an understanding of spatial relations.

Some appreciation of the basic structure of the brain is essential for (i) an understanding of the literature, (ii) understanding relevant details communicated in patients' hospital files, and (iii) the development of the neuropsychologist's thinking about brain-behaviour relationships in the understanding of individual cases.

THE COVERINGS OF THE BRAIN (MENINGES)

Dura mater

The tough outermost layer, called the *dura mater*, is closely attached to the inner surface of the skull and also provides several partitions which divide the skull cavity into relatively separate compartments. Since these partitions are anchored to the skull, they help to prevent the very soft and fragile brain tissue from excessive movement which would result in tearing of the brain substance whenever the head was suddenly accelerated, decelerated, or rapidly rotated. Even this protection breaks down when such movements are very violent.

The two major partitions of the dura mater are the *falx cerebri* and the *tentorium cerebelli* (Fig. 2.3).

The *falx cerebri* provides a partition between the major divisions of the cerebrum, the left and right cerebral hemispheres. It is a vertical partition,

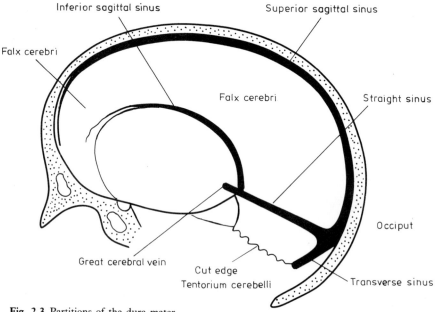

Fig. 2.3 Partitions of the dura mater.

shaped like a sickle with its narrow end attached to the base of the skull anteriorly. Its upper edge is attached to the vault of the skull in the midline while its lower edge arches over the upper edge of the *corpus callosum* to join on to the other major partition, the *tentorium cerebelli*, just posterior to the *splenium* of the *corpus callosum*. The *falx cerebri* becomes deeper as it sweeps backwards.

The *tentorium cerebelli* is a sharply arched or tent-like structure which is attached to the falx cerebri above, while the lower edge of the tent is attached to the periphery of the posterior skull depression which houses the *cerebellum*. Thus the tentorium serves to separate the posterior part of the cerebral hemispheres (the occipital lobes) above from the cerebellum below. The tentorium and falx cerebri are stretched taut while the free margins of the front of the tentorium provide an opening through which the mesencephalon or mid-brain passes.

In the outer layer of the dura mater are embedded arteries which are termed meningeal arteries though their main purpose is to provide blood supply for the bones of the skull as well as the relatively avascular dura mater. The dura also forms the walls of the large channels or sinuses which drain the venous blood from the brain. The narrow space between the dura and arachnoid mater is termed the *subdural space*.

Arachnoid mater

The second meningeal membrane is also avascular but, unlike the dura, it is very thin and delicate. It is separated from the dura only by a very thin layer of fluid and is attached by cobweb-like strands of tissue to the third membrane which closely follows the conformation of the outer layer of the brain and spinal cord. This latter layer is known as the *pia mater*, and the fluid-filled space which separates the arachnoid from the pia mater is termed the *subarachnoid space*. The blood vessels of the brain are distributed in the *arachnoid mater* and send branches through the pia mater to supply the outer layer of the cerebral hemispheres known as the *cerebral cortex*.

Pia mater

The inner membrane, the pia mater, closely follows the convolutions or *gyri* of the cerebral hemispheres and dips down into the fissures or *sulci* which separate them.

THE CEREBROSPINAL FLUID SYSTEM

The subarachnoid space

The subarachnoid space is filled with cerebrospinal fluid (CSF) which is a crystal clear, colourless fluid composed largely of water. The subarachnoid space is narrow over the cerebral hemispheres but is expanded around the base of the brain particularly around the brain stem. These expansions are known as cisterns and the *cerebellomedullary cistern* is important for our understanding of this fluid system since it is here that the subarachnoid space communicates with the ventricular cavities within the brain. The cerebrospinal fluid acts as a buffer to protect the brain and spinal cord. It also helps to provide a constant pressure within the bony cavity under normal conditions. The numerous other functions of the cerebrospinal fluid are beyond the scope of the present outline.

Ventricular cavities

There are four ventricular cavities within the brain. These are continuous with each other and the central canal at the upper end of the spinal cord. Each cerebral hemisphere contains a *lateral ventricle*. Each of these communicates with the midline *third ventricle* which in turn communicates with the *fourth ventricle* (Fig. 2.4).

The lateral ventricles are cavities with an arch-like or C-shaped contour which conforms to the general shape of the brain. They are filled with cerebrospinal fluid and may be divided into five parts: (i) the anterior (frontal) horn, (ii) the body, (iii) the collateral trigone, (iv) the inferior (temporal) horn, and (v) the posterior (occipital) horn.

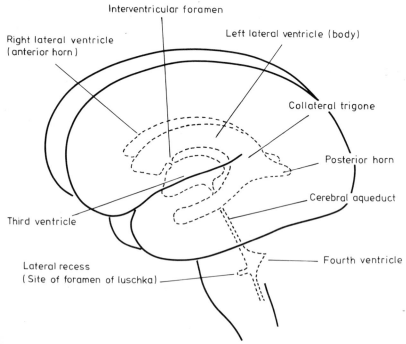

Fig. 2.4 Outline of the ventricle projected onto a lateral view of the brain.

Each lateral ventricle opens by means of an opening termed the *interventricular foramen* into the third ventricle which is situated in the midline.

The frontal horns are anterior to the interventricular foramina ending in the substance of the frontal lobe.

The body extends posteriorly from the foramina to the region of the splenium of the corpus callosum. It is narrow and slightly arched in form.

At the posterior end of the body there is a widening into the region termed the collateral trigone which is confluent also with the posterior horn, which extends into the occipital lobe, and with the inferior horn, which turns downwards into the substance of the temporal lobe.

Since we will have cause to mention conditions which may impair brain functions as a result of alteration in the CSF system, it will be of value to outline in a gross way the characteristics of the circulation of this fluid. Figure 2.5 provides a schematic diagram of the main anatomical features while Figure 2.6 sketches the fluid dynamics.

The cerebrospinal fluid is largely produced by the *choroid plexuses* of the lateral ventricles which are paired cavities, one in each cerebral hemisphere. These lateral ventricles are connected to a single narrow midline cavity, the *third ventricle*, by the *interventricular foramina*. From this third ventricle the cerebrospinal fluid passes by way of the cerebral aqueduct into the fourth ventricle which has one median aperture and two lateral apertures through

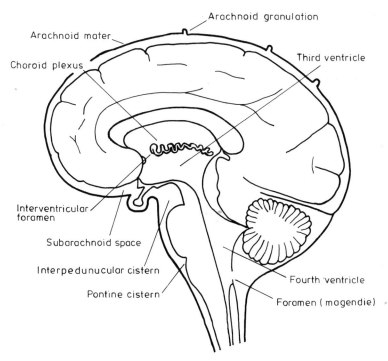

Fig. 2.5 The subarachnoid space and cerebrospinal fluid system.

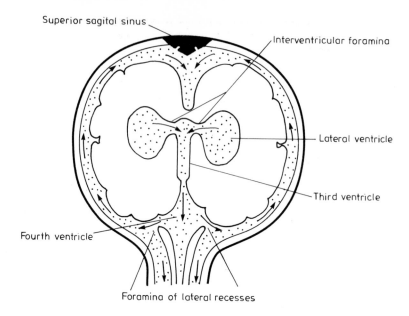

Superior sagital sinus

Interventricular foramina

Lateral ventricle

Third ventricle

Fourth ventricle

Foramina of lateral recesses

Fig. 2.6 Schematic view of the cerebrospinal fluid circulation.

which the CSF passes into the subarachnoid space to bathe the whole of the brain and spinal cord.

Finally, the circulation is completed by the drainage of the fluid into the venous system via the *arachnoid granulations*. In the region of the great venous channel termed the *superior sagittal sinus*, the closely related membranes, the pia and the arachnoid, send prolongations through openings in the dural wall of the venous channel and these permeable granulations allow the fluid to drain into the blood stream (Fig. 2.7).

The cerebrospinal fluid is produced by the plexuses of blood vessels principally in the lateral ventricles and, to a lesser extent, elsewhere. Two main theories have been put forward for its production: (i) a process of filtration or dialysis or (ii) a process of secretion. Whatever the mechanism, some 600 or 700 ml may be produced each day which needs to be passed into the blood circulation. Such disposal may be prevented by a failure of the fluid to be filtered away or by an obstruction in such sites as the interventricular foramina, the aqueduct, or the apertures in the roof of the fourth ventricle. These obstructions may lead to local or general ventricular dilation with increased intracranial pressure and wasting of the surrounding brain tissue. This condition, known as *hydrocephalus*, may occur in the young infant or in the adult and lead to severe cerebral impairment if some surgical method is not employed to restore a free circulation to the cerebrospinal fluid. In adults, an insidious onset of dementia may signal the presence of often unsuspected acquired hydrocephalus.

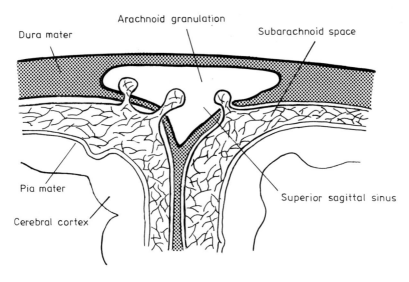

Fig. 2.7 Drainage of the cerebrospinal fluid into the venous system.

GROSS TOPOGRAPHY OF THE BRAIN

The brain has three major divisions, the cerebral hemispheres, the brain stem, and the cerebellum. Our main concern will be with the cerebral hemispheres and, to a lesser extent with the midbrain. Description of the cerebellum will be omitted since it is little concerned with man's higher functions. The cerebellum is concerned primarily with motor co-ordination and the control of muscle tone and equilibrium.

The cerebral hemispheres

The paired hemispheres appear to be mirror images of each other. They are covered by a convoluted layer of grey matter, the *cerebral cortex* (Fig. 2.8) which covers the internal white matter and deeply placed collections of grey matter or neuronal masses collectively known as the *basal ganglia*. The grey matter represents nerve cell collections while the white matter represents cell fibres which unite the various regions of the brain with each other (Fig. 2.9).

The two hemispheres are separated by the *longitudinal fissure* which completely separates them in the anterior (frontal) and posterior (occipital) regions (Fig. 2.10). The falx cerebri forms a partition between the two sides. In the central region the two hemispheres are united by a thick band of white matter, the *corpus callosum* which is the chief functional link between them.

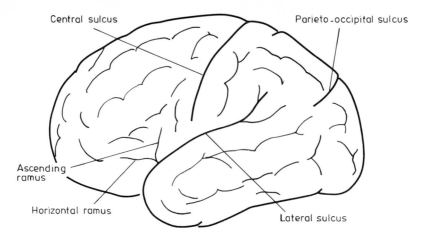

Fig. 2.8 Lateral view of the left cerebral hemisphere.

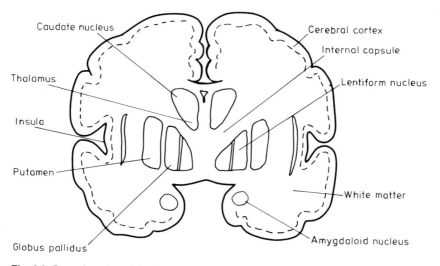

Fig. 2.9 Coronal section of the hemispheres.

Superolateral surface

Each cerebral hemisphere has three surfaces, the large convex superolateral surface, the flattened medial surface in contact with the falx, and the inferior surface which lies on the floor of the anterior and middle cranial depressions (fossae) in front and on the tentorium cerebelli behind.

The convoluted portions of the cerebral cortex are known as *gyri*. They are separated from each other by fissures or *sulci*. Some of these sulci and gyri are relatively constant features of most human brains and form the

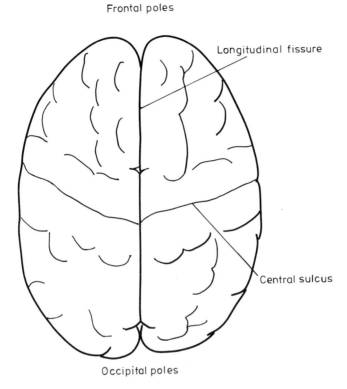

Frontal poles

Longitudinal fissure

Central sulcus

Occipital poles

Fig. 2.10 Superior view of the hemisphere.

basis for describing the general external topography of the brain. On the lateral surface three prominent sulci are used as a basis for dividing each hemisphere into four major areas or lobes. A fifth 'lobe', the limbic lobe, will be described separately. The three sulci are (i) the lateral sulcus, (ii) the central sulcus, and (iii) the parieto-occipital sulcus.

The *lateral sulcus* is a very deep division between the frontal and temporal lobes anteriorly and portions of the parietal and temporal lobes posteriorly. Towards the anterior end two small branches (rami), the *anterior horizontal ramus* and the *anterior ascending ramus* run for about 2 cm into the lower part of the frontal lobe while the terminal *ascending ramus* extends into the inferior part of the parietal lobe.

Buried within the lateral sulcus is a cortical area known as the *insula*. This can only be seen when the lips of the fissure are drawn apart (Fig. 2.11).

The areas of cortex overlying the insula are called the opercula (lids). The superior surface consists of the *frontal operculum* which lies between the anterior horizontal and ascending rami, and the *frontoparietal* operculum.

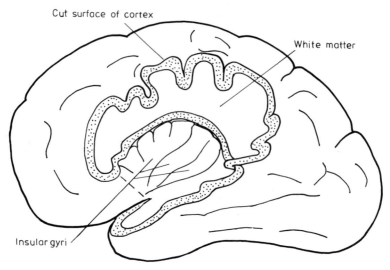

Fig. 2.11 The insular gyri with overlying cortex removed.

The *temporal operculum* is below the posterior ramus and is made up of the superior temporal gyrus and the transverse temporal gyri.

The *central sulcus* is less easy to find. It runs from the superior margin of the hemisphere downward and forward towards the lateral sulcus separating the frontal from the parietal lobe. The central sulcus is variable in form and runs only a little way over the superior border of the hemisphere to the medial surface.

The *parieto-occipital sulcus* is a fairly constant deep sulcus which cuts into the superior border of the hemisphere some 5 cm anterior to the occipital pole and runs on the medial surface in an anterior and inferior direction to intersect the well marked *calcarine sulcus* about midway along its length.

Lobar divisions. The arbitrary boundaries of the lobar divisions are shown with respect to the major sulci in Figure 2.12.

The *frontal lobe* is that part of the hemisphere above the lateral sulcus and in front of the central sulcus.

The *parietal lobe* is bounded in front by the central sulcus and below by the lateral sulcus before it turns upwards to the line which forms the posterior boundary of the lobe. This line runs from the point where the parieto-occipital sulcus crosses the superior border of the hemisphere to a small notch (pre-occipital notch) some 4 cm in front of the occipital pole.

The *occipital lobe* lies posterior to the vertical boundary line on the convex surface and, on the medial aspect, to the parieto-occipital sulcus and a line joining the junction of the parieto-occipital sulcus with the preoccipital notch.

The *temporal lobe* is bounded by the lateral sulcus and the artificial line of demarcation described above.

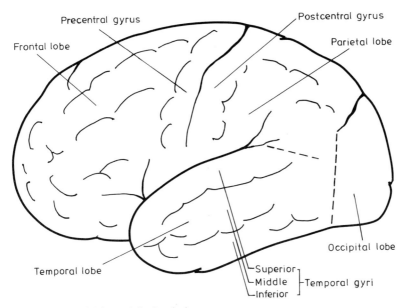

Precentral gyrus

Postcentral gyrus

Frontal lobe

Parietal lobe

Temporal lobe

Occipital lobe

Superior
Middle   Temporal gyri
Inferior

Fig. 2.12 Lobar divisions of the hemisphere.

Further details of the frontal, temporal, parietal and occipital lobes are described in the separate chapters devoted to each lobe.

Apart from the major divisions into lobes, certain gross features of the external topography of the brain may be described on the three surfaces of the hemispheres, the superolateral, medial, and inferior surfaces.

The superolateral surface is divided into more or less constant gyri as depicted in Figure 2.12.

Medial surface

The medial surfaces of the hemispheres are seen after cutting through the corpus callosum which joins them (Fig. 2.13). The corpus callosum is some 8 cm in length. The anterior curved portion is known as the genu of the corpus callosum and this tapers posteriorly and inferiorly as the *rostrum*. The corpus callosum ends posteriorly in a blunt enlargement termed the *splenium* which lies over the pineal body and the midbrain. The corpus callosum is separated on its upper surface from the *cingulate gyrus* by the callosal sulcus. Posteriorly this gyrus curves around the splenium of the corpus callosum to enter the temporal lobe as the *parahippocampal gyrus*.

Above the cingulate gyrus is a well marked fissure which runs from a position just below the genu (*the sub-callosal area*) to a point just in front of and vertically above the splenium where it turns upwards as the *marginal sulcus* (or marginal branch of the cingulate sulcus), above the splenium. Usually the cingulate sulcus gives off a prominent branch, the *paracentral*

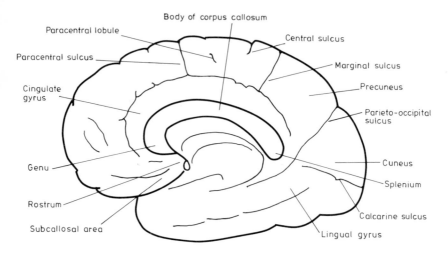

Fig. 2.13 Medial view of the right hemisphere.

sulcus which crosses the upper medial border of the hemisphere vertically above the middle part of the body of the corpus callosum. The area between the paracentral sulcus and the marginal sulcus is the *paracentral lobule*. The lobule is divided by the small part of the central fissure which just reaches the upper medial surface of the hemisphere so that the paracentral lobule contains the extension over on to the medial surface of the *precentral and postcentral gyri*. The area between the marginal sulcus and the parieto-occipital sulcus is the *precuneus*. This is the extension medially of the superior *parietal lobule*. The *calcarine sulcus* runs forward from the occipital pole to divide the occipital lobe into the cuneus above and the lingual gyrus below.

Inferior surface

The inferior surface of the hemisphere consists of two parts (Fig. 2.14). The smaller anterior portion is the inferior or orbital surface of the frontal lobe while the larger posterior portion represents the inferior surfaces of the temporal and occipital lobes.

The orbital surface of the frontal lobe has a deep straight sulcus, the *olfactory sulcus*, with the *olfactory bulb* and *tract* lying on it. Medial to this sulcus lies the gyrus rectus while lateral to it lie the *orbital gyri*.

The inferior surface of the occipital lobe and the posterior part of the temporal lobe lie on the tentorium cerebelli while the anterior portion of the temporal lobe lies in a depression in the skull, the *middle cranial fossa*. The gyri in this posterior portion are the *lingual gyrus* medially, the *para-hippocampal gyrus* and *uncus*, and the *occipitotemporal gyri* laterally.

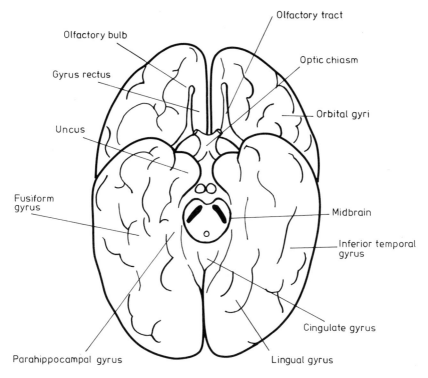

Fig. 2.14 Inferior surface of the hemispheres.

The limbic lobe and limbic system

On the medial surface of each cerebral hemisphere there is a ring of structures which surrounds the anterior (rostal) part of the brain stem and the
commissures uniting the hemispheres. The major portion of the limbic lobe
is made up of the *cingulate gyrus* above and the parahippocampal gyrus
below (Fig. 2.15). It also includes the smaller *subcallosal gyrus* and the
hippocampal formation and dentate gyrus.

  The term limbic system refers to a much more extensive complex of
structures which includes not only the structures of the limbic lobe but also
the temporal pole, anterior portion of the insula, posterior orbital surface
of the frontal lobe and a number of subcortical nuclei. These subcortical
nuclei include thalamic, hypothalamic, septal and amygdaloid nuclei, and
there is also evidence of a close relationship with the midbrain reticular
formation and the reticular nucleus of the thalamus. The term limbic
system includes so many structures and pathways that the general usefulness of the concept of a unified system is open to question. Certainly, it
is a region where a large number of circuits relating to different functions
come together. Since they lie generally towards the middle axis of the brain
mass we will later refer to them as axial or medial structures (Fig. 2.16).

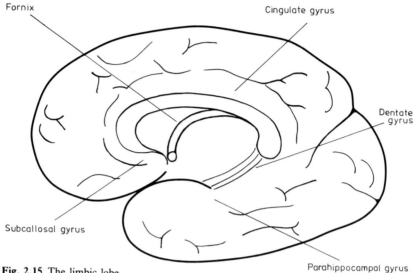

Fig. 2.15 The limbic lobe.

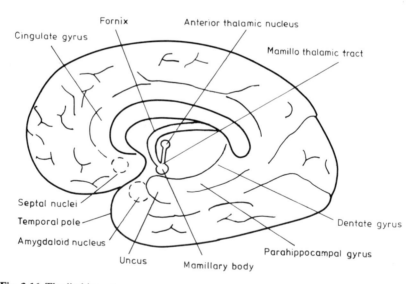

Fig. 2.16 The limbic system.

As early as 1937 Papez defined a recurrent or 'closed' part of the system, now known as the 'circuit of Papez' as the substratum for controlling emotions and emotional expressions. The Papez circuit forms the following linkage: hippocampus-fornix-mamillary bodies-thalamus-cingulate cortex-hippocampus. A good deal of evidence has also accumulated in recent years to associate lesions of the hippocampal-fornix-mamillary body connections with a disorder of memory of the type known as the Korsakoff amnesic syndrome. The importance of the limbic system in emotional experience and expression has also been demonstrated by bilateral removal of the limbic structures in the temporal lobe, amygdaloid nucleus, hippocampus and parahippocampal gyrus as well as the temporal neocortex overlying these structures.

Despite the general use of the terms *limbic lobe* and *limbic system* there are those who see dangers in grouping structures under such headings:

> It is difficult to see that the lumping together of these different regions under one anatomical heading, the limbic lobe serves any useful purpose . . . It is even less justifiable to speak of a 'limbic system' . . . the 'limbic system' appears to be on its way to including all brain functions. (Brodal, 1980, pp. 537–538)

The hippocampal system

The *hippocampal system* (Fig. 2.17) is one of the more primitive parts of the cerebrum and has an extremely simple three-layered cortex, the *archipallium*. The hippocampal system is made up of the *parahippocampal gyrus* and *uncus*, the *hippocampal formation, dentate gyrus, gyrus fasciolus, indusium griseum, fimbria* and *fornix*. These structures form a pair of arches extending from the region of the interventricular foramina to the tip of the inferior horn of the lateral ventricle (Fig. 2.16, 2.17). The *parahippocampal gyrus* and *uncus* have been seen on the inferior surface of the brain towards the midline. The *hippocampus* is a slightly curved elevation in the floor of the inferior (temporal) horn of the ventricle. Its broader anterior end is just posterolateral to the uncus and the hippocampus diminishes rapidly as it moves posteriorly. The structure of the hippocampus and its relation to neighbouring structures can be further appreciated in a transverse or coronal section through the temporal lobe (Fig. 2.18).

Fibres on the medial surface of the upper convexity of the hippocampus form a flattened band, the *fimbria*, which increases posteriorly as the hippocampus diminishes and, as the pair of fimbria curve dorsomedially the fibres become the *crura of the fornix* which then pass forward beneath the corpus callosum. Figure 2.19 shows the corpus callosum cut away to reveal these structures.

Ventral (inferior) to the fimbria, there is a narrow notched band, the *dentate gyrus*. It lessens posteriorly accompanying the hippocampus, curves around the splenium of the corpus callosum having separated from the fimbria and passes on to the superior surface of the corpus callosum in the form of the delicate *fasciolar gyrus*. It then spreads out into a thin grey sheet termed the *indusium griseum* or *supracallosal gyrus*.

The fornix forms the principal efferent fibre system of the hippocampal formation. It has both projection and commissural fibres. The commissural

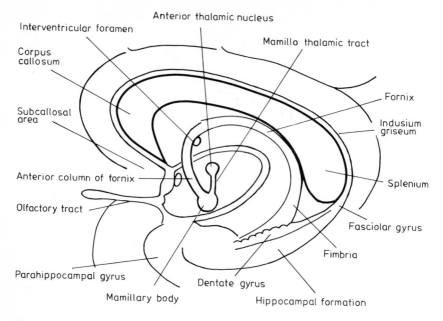

Fig. 2.17 The hippocampal system.

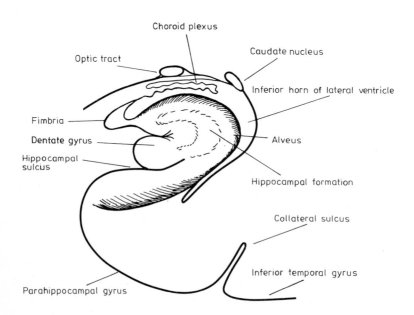

Fig. 2.18 Coronal section through the hippocampus.

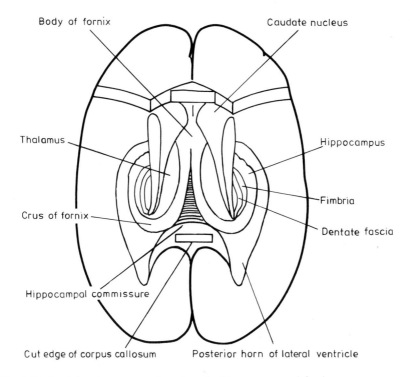

Body of fornix

Caudate nucleus

Thalamus

Hippocampus

Crus of fornix

Fimbria

Dentate fascia

Hippocampal commissure

Cut edge of corpus callosum   Posterior horn of lateral ventricle

Fig. 2.19 Overlying tissue removed to show the hippocampus and fornix.

fibres of the fornix (*hippocampal commissure*) are described below. As the crura of the fornix come together under the ventral surface of the corpus callosum, they form the *body of the fornix* which travels forward to the rostral margin of the thalamus where they separate again into bundles forming the *anterior columns of the fornix*. The bundles again diverge from each other, arch in front of the *interventricular foramina* and posterior to the *anterior commissure* and incline slightly posteriorly to terminate in the mamillary bodies.

Further detail about the anatomical connections and functional contributions of the hippocampus and related structures can be found in the extensive reviews in the books edited by Isaacson and Pribram (1976) and Seifert (1983).

THE CEREBRAL CORTEX

The cerebral cortex is the most recently elaborated structure in the central nervous system. It is only in the mammal that it takes on special significance and it reaches its greatest size relative to other structures in man.

The notion of architectonics was mentioned in Chapter 1. Though the cellular arrangement of the cortex varies in different areas of the brain, it is customary to describe a sample of 'modal' or 'typical' cortex made up of six layers. This six-layered pattern distinguishes the *neocortex* or new cortex from the *paleocortex* which predominates in lower animals and is largely concerned in them with olfaction. Though a certain amount of more primitively structured cortex has been preserved in man, it has become displaced to deeper parts of the brain where it is almost completely covered by the neocortex which comprises the major part of the cerebral cortex in man. The stages of development of the different types of cortex from primitive animal to man is well described by Romer (1955). The paleo-cortical structures, because of their earlier association with smell, are some-times termed collectively the *rhinencephalon* or nose brain. In man, as in other higher mammals, the functions of these structures have little to do with olfaction. They might best be described as being made up of (i) olfactory components and (ii) the limbic components described else-where.

Cellular layers of the cortex

The six layers or strata are typically described as follows:

I. The *plexiform* or molecular layer is usually quite distinct; it is made up mostly of apical dendrites of cells in lower layers with a few horizontal cells;

II. The *external granular layer* made up of small pyramidal and granule or stellate cells;

III. The *outer pyramidal layer* made up of medium sized pyramidal cells;

IV. The *internal granular layer* made up of small granule cells (stellate cells) and a few small pyramidal cells;

V. The *inner pyramidal* (ganglionic) *layer* made up of a large number of large, medium, and short pyramidal cells;

VI. The *polymorphic layer*, so called because it contains cells of many different shapes. Many of the cells in this layer are spindle-shaped so that the layer has been called also the layer of spindles.

Milner (1970) points out that it is customary for neuro-anatomical texts to state dogmatically that there are six basic layers. Nevertheless, few inexperienced observers will spontaneously recognize six layers in sections of the cortex. During the 19th century, before the figure six had been decided upon, various eminent histologists estimated the number of layers as between five and eight, and there was no general agreement on where one layer stopped and the next began.

It was Brodmann who somehow managed to raise the idea of a six-layered structure almost to a law of nature, but the layering differences in different regions of the cortex are so great that his idea can be sustained only by sub-dividing layers in some places or making arbitrary distinctions where in fact there is a gradual and smooth transition (Milner, 1970).

Certain areas of the cortex, such as the precentral region of the frontal lobe, show very poor development of the granular layers II and IV and are called agranular. The 'typical' six layers are more characteristic of the post-central lobes, i.e. the parietal, temporal, and occipital lobes.

Within and between the layers of the cortex there are complex sets of connections between nerve cells. These, connections are beyond the scope of this chapter and work in clinical neuropsychology at the moment is more concerned with connections made by the fibres of cortical cells which leave the cortex and travel short or long distances to link cortical areas together.

Functional areas of the cortex

Functional areas of the cortex have been defined in a number of ways including the study of electrical potentials evoked in the cortex on the presentation of different stimuli and the stimulation of the exposed cortex in conscious human subjects undergoing neurosurgery (Ch. 5). The *motor area* is situated in the precentral gyrus and the *sensory area* in the post-central gyrus, both having somatotopic representation. The *visual area* is situated in the cortex of the occipital lobe on either side of the calcarine sulcus mainly on the medial and partly on the superolateral aspect of the hemisphere. The *auditory area* is situated in the *transverse gyri of Heschl* and is largely concealed in the depth of the temporal cortex in the lateral fissure just extending on to the lateral surface of the hemisphere (Fig. 5.4). The remainder of the post-central cortex of the parietal, temporal, and occipital lobes is concerned with the integration and elaboration of incoming sensory information.

Cortical zones

Luria (1973b) has divided the whole area of the brain behind the central sulcus into three types of cortical region. He describes how disruption of these different functional types of cortex, known as cortical zones, may confer characteristic properties on the deficits observed. The following brief description scarcely does credit to the elegance of the conception nor the great value which this system has for the understanding of the individual case and for its usefulness in gaining a deeper appreciation of the psychological processes themselves. The principal features of Luria's system have been sketched in Chapter 1. Here a brief relation will be made to the cortical structure itself.

The *primary zones* of Luria are what are commonly termed primary projection areas. They possess high modal specificity, i.e. each particular area responds to highly differentiated properties of visual, auditory, or bodily sense information. They are also topologically arranged so that specific aspects of the stimulus are located systematically in order in the cortex, e.g. sense information from different parts of the body projects to particular sensory cortical areas, specific tones project to specific areas of the auditory cortex, and specific parts of the visual field to specific areas of the visual cortex. These primary zones consist 'mainly of neurons of afferent layer IV' of the cortex and their specificity and topological organization may be of considerable help in neurological diagnosis.

Each primary zone is made up largely of cells which respond only to a specific sense modality but also possess a few cells which respond to other modes of stimulation and may be concerned with the property of maintaining an optimal state of arousal or alertness in the cortex, or what Luria terms 'cortical tone'. Cortical tone is regulated by the reticular formation of the brain stem. Information on cortical arousal may be found in textbooks of physiology and physiological psychology.

The *secondary zones* are the areas adjacent to the primary projection areas where the modality specific information becomes integrated into meaningful wholes. In a general sense the primary zones may be said to be concerned with sensation while the secondary zones are concerned with perception or gnosis. In the secondary zones 'afferent layer IV yields its dominant position to layers II and III of cells, whose degree of modal specificity is lower and whose composition includes many more associative neurons with short axons, enabling incoming excitation to be combined into the necessary functional patterns, and they thus subserve a synthetic function' (Luria, 1973, pp. 68–69). Disruptions of these secondary zones will give rise to gnostic or perceptual disorders restricted to a perceptual modality, e.g. auditory or visual or tactile agnosia.

The *tertiary zones* serve to integrate information across sense modalities. They lie at the borders of the parietal (somatosensory), temporal (auditory), and occipital (visual) secondary zones. In these *zones of overlapping* of the P-T-O association area, modal specificity disappears. The tertiary cortex is typified by a predominance of cells from the upper cortical layers and this type of cortex is seen only in man. These are the last portions of the brain to mature in ontogenetic development, not reaching full development until around 7 years of age. Disruption of the tertiary zones gives rise to disorders which transcend any single modality and hence may be thought as as *supramodal* in character (see Ch. 6).

Luria's concept of the post-central cortical territory (or retrofrontal cortex) is thus a hierarchical one which moves from regions of high modal specificity to those which are supramodal.

The nature and connections of the frontal cortex are dealt with in Chapter 4.

THE BRAIN STEM

Although neuropsychology is little concerned with the brain stem, a general familiarity will be useful in reading the neurological literature and patients' case histories.

The brain stem is divided into four parts, the medulla oblongata, pons,

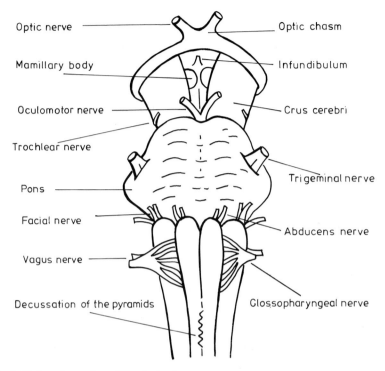

Optic nerve

Mamillary body

Oculomotor nerve

Trochlear nerve

Pons

Facial nerve

Vagus nerve

Decussation of the pyramids

Optic chasm

Infundibulum

Crus cerebri

Trigeminal nerve

Abducens nerve

Glossopharyngeal nerve

Fig. 2.20 Anterior surface of the brain stem.

mesencephalon or midbrain, and the diencephalon. It is an extension upwards of the spinal cord. The brain stem contains nuclei and nerve circuits which control important bodily functions such as respiration, cardiovascular function and gastrointestinal function. It also contains the nuclei for the cranial nerves concerned with the special senses.

In the intact brain the lateral and posterior surfaces of the brain stem are hidden by the cerebral hemispheres and cerebellum but, on the anterior surface, parts of the inferior surface on the floor of the hypothalamus (part of the diencephalon), midbrain, pons, and medulla can all be seen (Fig. 2.20).

The uppermost portion of the brain stem, the *diencephalon*, is surrounded by the hemispheres on all sides except for a small region between the mamillary bodies and optic chiasma. The diencephalon is one of the most complex regions of the central nervous system and any real understanding of its structure requires detailed study. It extends from the region of the interventricular foramen to the posterior commissure above and is continuous with the midbrain (mesencephalon) below (Fig. 2.21). The superior surface of the diencephalon forms part of the floor of the body of the lateral ventricle. The internal capsule and optic tract form its lateral boundary. The floor includes the following structures on the inferior surface

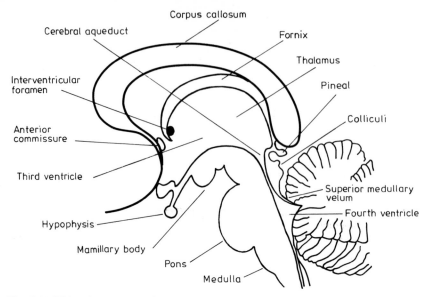

Fig. 2.21 Mid-sagittal section of the brain stem.

of the brain: mamillary bodies, infundibulum, neurohypophysis and the optic chiasma. Anteriorly, it passes into the basal olfactory area of the anterior perforated substance and posteriorly is continuous with the posterior perforated substance of the midbrain. The diencephalon encloses the third ventricle. Its principal components are the epithalamus, the thalamus and metathalamus, the hypothalamus, and the subthalamus.

The *epithalamus* contains a number of structures which can be recognized macroscopically, in particular the *pineal gland* and the *posterior commissure*. The pineal gland begins to calcify from early adult life so that it forms at times a useful midline marker in radiographs and its deviation may indicate a space-occupying lesion within the skull cavity.

The *thalamus* is an oblique mass of grey matter on either side of the midline at the rostral end of the brain stem. It is separated on the medial aspect of the hemisphere from the hypothalamus by an indistinct groove called the *hypothalamic sulcus*.

These paired nuclear masses are separated by the third ventricle. The somewhat more pointed end of the ovoid forms the posterior wall of the interventricular foramen. The more rounded blunt end of the ovoid projects over the midbrain and is termed the *pulvinar*.

The thalami have been divided into a number of nuclei whose classification and nomenclature varies somewhat from one authority to another. Some classifications include more than 20 nuclei but a simpler division is used here (Fig. 2.22). This is related below to the projection of fibres to the cortex.

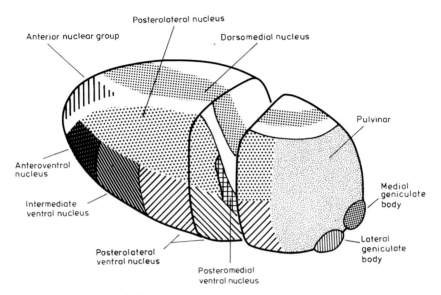

Fig. 2.22 Nuclei of the left thalamus.

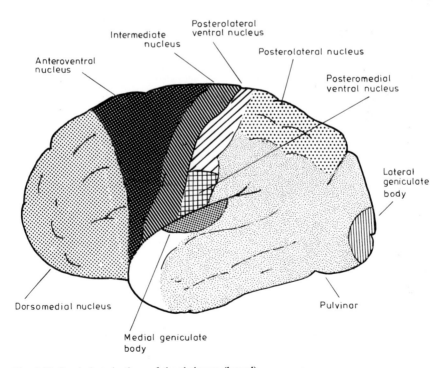

Fig. 2.23 Cortical projections of the thalamus (lateral).

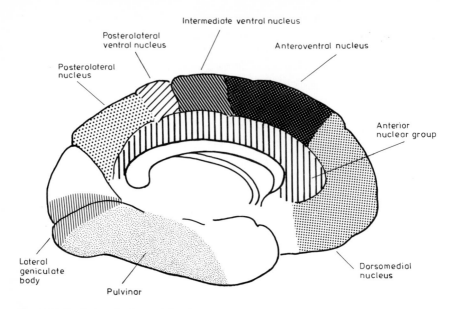

Fig. 2.24 Cortical projections of the thalamus (medial).

Bowsher (1970) points out that 'with the exception of certain areas in the temporal lobe, the whole neocortex and the corpus striatum receive specific fibres from the thalamus' (p. 125).

> Thus the whole telencephalon (cerebral hemisphere) except some of the neocortex of the temporal lobe, can be regarded as an umbrella cover, whose hub is the thalamus and the spokes of which are the specific thalamo-telencephalic projections . . . It can be seen from this that the true definition of a functional cortical area depends not upon the fortuitous folding of its surface into sulci and gyri, nor upon its cytoarchitecture (though this is related), but upon its specific projection from a particular thalamic nucleus. For example, the primary somatosensory cortex (roughly defined as the post-central gyrus) is, in precise terms, only and entirely that area of cortex which receives its specific projections from the ventroposterior nucleus of the thalamus (Bowsher, 1970, p. 125).

The thalamic nuclear complex lies between the interventricular foramen and the posterior commissure and extends laterally from the third ventricle to the posterior limb of the internal capsule (Fig. 2.30). Sometimes the medial surfaces of the thalami are joined across the midline of the third ventricle by a mass of grey matter termed the *interthalamic adhesion* or *massa intermedia*. Though it crosses the midline it is certainly not to be considered as a commissure.

Apart from its role in projecting sensory information, the thalamus also plays a part in controlling the electrical activity of the cortex and helps in the integration of motor functions by providing relays through which the cerebellum and parts of the basal ganglia can influence the motor cortex.

The *metathalamus* is the collective name for the medial and lateral geniculate bodies which lie underneath the pulvinar (Fig. 2.22). From the *medial geniculate body* fibres of the acoustic radiation pass to the auditory area in the temporal lobe while the *lateral geniculate body* gives rise to the optic radiation.

The *hypothalamus* forms the inferior and lateral walls of the third ventricle. The hypothalamus is divided into medial and lateral groups of nuclei by fibres of the fornix which terminate in the mamillary bodies. These nuclei are concerned with a wide range of functions, e.g. emotion, sleep, temperature regulation, hunger, and thirst.

The *subthalamus* is a small transitional region lateral to the hypothalamus and ventral to the thalamus. It contains a large lens-shaped discrete nucleus (subthalamic nucleus) on the inner aspect of the internal capsule.

Midbrain. The midbrain is the smallest part of the major divisions of the brain and the least differentiated. It passes through the opening in the tentorium cerebelli and it is traversed by the narrow cerebral aqueduct which joins the third and fourth ventricles (Fig. 2.21). The thinner part posterior to the aqueduct is known as the *tectum* of the midbrain and is made up of the *superior* and *inferior colliculi* (Fig. 2.25). The superior colliculus is concerned with eye movements and reflexes while the inferior colliculus receives auditory impulses which it relays to the auditory cortex of the temporal lobes. The thicker portion of the midbrain anterior to the aqueduct is made of two lateral masses, the *cerebral peduncles.* In turn, each cerebral peduncle is divided into an anterior and a posterior portion by a broad, deeply pigmented band of grey matter, the *substantia nigra* (Fig. 2.26). The anterior portion, the *basis pedunculi (crus cerebri)* contains collections of fibres originating in the cerebral cortex which pass through the internal capsule. These fibres pass to the lower brain stem, pons, and spinal cord. The two trunks of the cerebral peduncles converge from the undersurface of the hemispheres and are close together as they enter the pons. The deep triangular area thus formed is the *interpeduncular fossa.*

The substantia nigra, which is the largest single nuclear mass in the midbrain, has connections with the basal ganglia and the thalamus and is thought to subserve motor function.

Pons. The pons is well delimited as a mass of fibres arching transversely around the anterior aspect of the brain stem and is separated from the cerebellum posteriorly by the fourth ventricle. The pons is divided into a large anterior part and a smaller posterior part or *tegmentum.* The tegmental portion contains a central core of nerve cells and fibres with an open structure known as the *reticular formation.* This reticular formation is continuous into the midbrain above and the medulla below and is concerned with the state of alertness or arousal of the organism. The tegmentum also contains the nerve nuclei of the fifth, sixth, seventh, and eighth cranial nerves. The

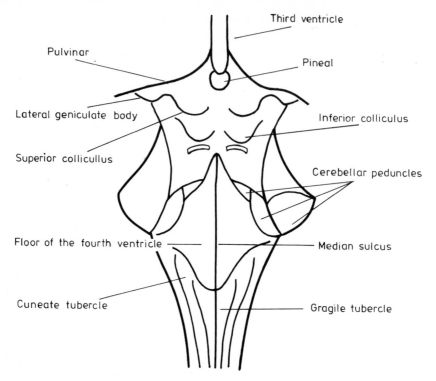

Fig. 2.25 Posterior aspect of the brain stem.

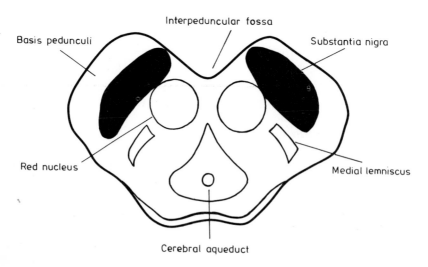

Fig. 2.26 Cross section through the midbrain.

larger ventral portion of the pons contains (i) longitudinal descending fibres, (ii) transverse fibres projecting to the cerebellum, and (iii) pontine nuclei.

Medulla oblongata. The medulla is the gradual transition from the spinal cord, expanding in a conical fashion to the lower border of the pons. The transition from spinal cord to medulla is a gradual one and shows a number of features: (i) the midline anterior fissure of the spinal cord disappears; (ii) the *decussation of the pyramids* or decussation of the cortico-spinal tracts takes place. Here bundles of fibres interdigitate as they cross the midline anteriorly carrying impulses for motor control of one half of the body from the contralateral cerebral cortex; (iii) posteriorly, the gracile and cuneate tubercles appear; (iv) the spinal nerves give way to the cranial nerves; (v) the fourth ventricle appears.

As the medulla continues upwards the fourth ventricle widens on the posterior aspect, the inferior cerebellar peduncle becomes more prominent, the eminence of the olivary complex appears dorsolaterally, the medullary pyramids medially. The fourth ventricle is a shallow, rhomboid shaped depression overlying both the pons and medulla posteriorly. One point of the rhombus continues superiorly into the cerebral aqueduct while the inferior point extends into the central canal of the upper cervical spinal cord. The roof is formed by the cerebellum and the *superior* and *inferior medullary vela*. The superior medullary velum forms the roof of the pontine part of the ventricle while the inferior medullary velum forms the roof of the medullary part. At its widest part the fourth ventricle develops two tubular recesses which curve laterally over the inferior cerebellar peduncles. There is an opening in each recess, the lateral apertures (foramina of Luschka). The third or median aperture (Magendie) is found at the lowest point of the roof. It is through these apertures that cerebrospinal fluid escapes into the subarachnoid space (Fig. 2.4).

THE INTERNAL STRUCTURE OF THE HEMISPHERES

The principal structures within the hemispheres are (i) the white matter, (ii) the basal ganglia, and (iii) the lateral ventricles.

The white matter

The white matter or medullary substance is made up of millions of fibre processes or axons of nerve cells. The white colour is conferred by the myelin sheaths which coat the fibres and act as an insulating layer around the fibre as it transmits nerve impulses from one spot to another. The fibres may be divided into three categories.

1. The *association* or intracerebral fibres which connect various regions within one hemisphere. These may join areas which are close together or the fibres may be very long.

2. Intercerebral or *commissural* fibres unite homologous or equivalent areas or structures in the two hemispheres.

3. *Projection fibres* that convey impulses from deeper structures to the cortex or from the cortex to deeper structures. These deeper structures include the thalamus, hypothalamus, brain stem, cerebellum and spinal cord. An understanding of the pathways linking the various parts of the brain is of paramount importance in understanding one of the central concepts in neuropsychology, that of the disconnection syndrome, i.e. many symptoms and signs can best be understood as the result of a break in the normal connections between brain areas or systems. It is possible only to outline the major sets of connections here. Those interested in a more thoroughgoing treatment may consult references such as Krieg (1963) and Wright (1959).

Association fibres. Association fibres may be divided into short fibre groups and long association groups. The short fibres lie beneath the cortex and arch around the bottom of the sulci to join adjacent convolutions or gyri. The long fibres lie more deeply and may be gathered into rather indefinite bundles or tracts which connect the different lobes. A number of the tracts are sufficiently circumscribed to warrant description (Figs. 2.27 and 2.28).

The superior longitudinal fasciculus courses backward from the frontal lobe to the occipital lobe and this tract sends some fibres to the posterior part of the temporal lobe. Fibres at the bottom of this fasciculus sweep

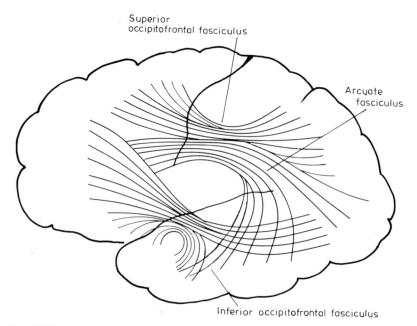

Fig. 2.27 Long association tracts. Lateral view.

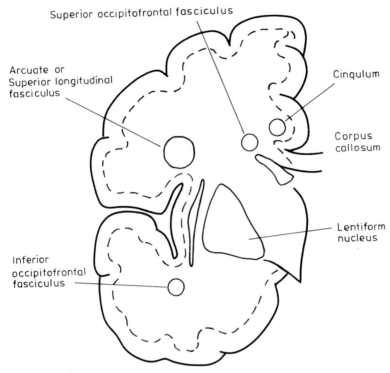

Superior occipitofrontal fasciculus

Arcuate or
Superior longitudinal
fasciculus

Cingulum

Corpus
callosum

Lentiform
nucleus

Inferior
occipitofrontal
fasciculus

Fig. 2.28 Long association tracts. Medial view.

around the region of the insula connecting the superior and middle frontal gyri with parts of the temporal lobe. These fibres, known as the *arcuate fasciculus*, are important for an anatomical understanding of the aphasias.

The *inferior longitudinal fasciculus* runs from the occipital to the temporal poles.

The *uncinate fasciculus* connects the anterior and inferior parts of the frontal lobe with parts of the temporal lobe by a bundle which is fan-shaped at either end and drawn together in a compact bundle as it arches sharply around the stem of the lateral sulcus.

On the medial aspect the principal association tract is the *cingulum* which lies within the cingulate gyrus. Like the cingulate gyrus the cingulum runs an arched course over the corpus callosum beginning below the rostrum and terminating in the uncus. The cingulum contains fibres of different length and it connects regions of the frontal and parietal lobes with parahippocampal and adjacent temporal regions. The tract is much reduced in the parahippocampal gyrus and uncus.

A coronal section through the hemisphere shows that in certain locations certain of the long association bundles are gathered together discretely, so that a relatively small lesion could produce a major disconnection (Fig. 2.29).

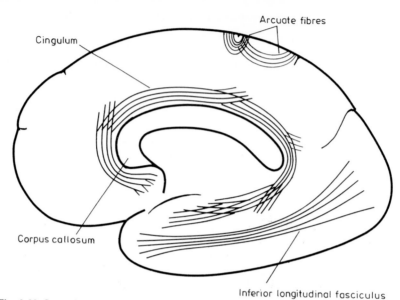

Fig. 2.29 Coronal section with association tracts.

Commissural fibres. Interhemispheric fibre systems have three well marked commissures, namely the corpus callosum, the anterior commissure, and the hippocampal commissure or commissure of the fornix.

The *corpus callosum* is the largest mass of connecting fibres in the nervous system. It joins corresponding areas in the neocortex in the two hemispheres. Fibres enter it from practically every part of the cortex (Fig. 2.30).

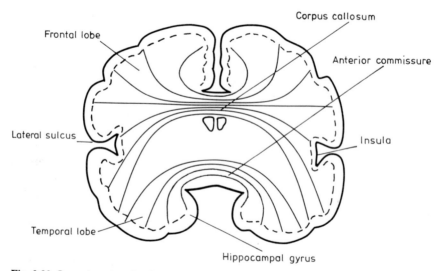

Fig. 2.30 Coronal section showing the two main commissures.

The degree of development of the corpus callosum in animal species is proportional to the degree of development of the neocortex in itself, hence its prominence in the human brain. The major named portions of the corpus callosum, i.e. the rostrum, genu, body and splenium have already been mentioned (Fig. 2.13).

Sunderland (1940) described the distribution of the fibres in the corpus callosum of the macaque. The distribution can be considered essentially similar in man. Fibres from the frontal lobes occupy the genu and the anterior third of the body. Other frontal fibres, together with fibres from the parietal and temporal area, occupy the middle third of the body. The posterior third of the body contains fibres from the parietal, temporal, and occipital lobes, those from the parietal regions being more numerous. The splenium is given over to fibres from the occipital regions.

Partial transections of the corpus callosum in man have confirmed that the posterior portion is principally concerned with the transmission of visual information while the central portion transmits somatosensory information (Ettlinger, 1965; Myers, 1961; Sperry, 1964). In 1953 Hoff put forward the interesting hypothesis that the different portions of the corpus callosum had different roles. The posterior parts were thought to integrate information, the anterior portions to separate functions, e.g. the independent functions of the two hands, while the middle parts of the corpus callosum were thought to allow 'for joint or independent activities of the hemispheres, as need for joint or independent operations may arise' (Gloning & Hoff, 1969, p. 36).

The effects of commissure section or commissurotomy are detailed in Chapter 8.

Callosal fibres from the frontal and occipital poles and the medial aspects of these lobes take curved pathways known as the *anterior* and *posterior forceps* (Fig. 2.31). Where the fibres cross the floor of the interhemispheric fissure they form the roof of the lateral ventricles. Although most of the fibres in the corpus callosum unite corresponding or homologous areas there are a small number of non-homologous fibres (Crosby, Humphrey & Lauer, 1962) (See Fig. 3.31).

The *anterior commissure* is a rounded compact bundle of fibres which crosses the midline just anterior to the anterior column of the fornix and just below the interventricular foramen. Its shape has been likened to bicycle handlebars (Carpenter, 1972). Its main part connects regions of the inferior and middle temporal gyri while a smaller portion interconnects olfactory regions on the two sides (Fig. 2.30).

The *hippocampal commissure* is composed of transverse fibres which join the posterior columns of the fornix. Fibres arising in the hippocampus pass into the posterior columns of the fornix which sweep around the splenium of the corpus callosum approaching each other as they pass forward to join in the body of the fornix. The transverse fibres of the hippocampal commissure become shorter as the columns converge and the appearance

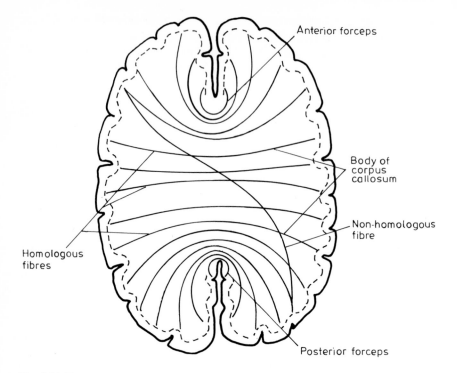

Fig. 2.31 Horizontal section showing commissural fibres.

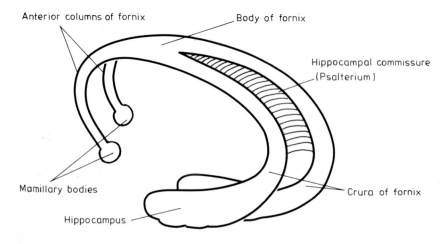

Fig. 2.32 Hippocampal commissure *psalterium*.

of this portion gave rise to the name *psalterium* because of the resemblance to an ancient stringed instrument (Fig. 2.19 and 2.32).

Projection fibres. The projection fibres are of two types, afferent and efferent. Afferent fibres convey impulses to the cortex while efferent fibres carry impulses away from it. The projection fibres are arranged as a radiating mass, the *corona radiata* that converges towards the brain stem (Fig. 2.33). Near the upper part of the brain stem the fibres are arranged in a narrow area between medial and lateral nuclear collections and are known as the *internal capsule*. The *caudate nucleus* and *thalamus* flank the capsule on the medial side while the *putamen* and *globus pallidus* flank it laterally (Fig. 2.9 and 2.34). A horizontal section through the brain shows the internal capsule has an anterior limb and a posterior limb.

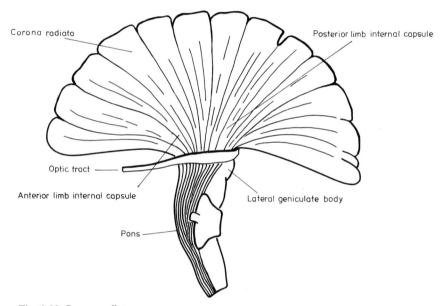

Fig. 2.33 Corona radiata.

The most posterior portion of the posterior limb of the internal capsule contains fibres of the *optic radiation* travelling from the lateral geniculate body to the calcarine sulcus in the occipital lobe.

The afferent fibres in the internal capsule arise mainly from the thalamus and project to nearly all areas of the cortex. Efferent fibres arise from various parts of the cortex. Among these are the important motor pathways which innervate the musculature of the opposite side of the body and whose disruption gives rise to contralateral paralysis since the fibres cross the midline lower down in the decussation of the pyramids.

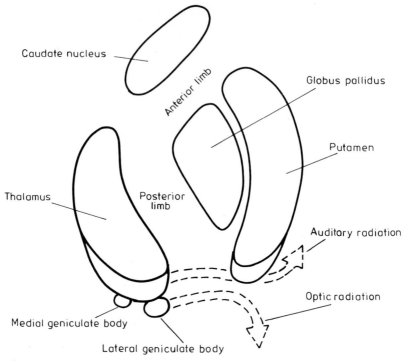

Fig. 2.34 The internal capsule.

The basal ganglia

The basal ganglia are subcortical nuclear masses. The principal structures are the putamen, the globus pallidus, the caudate nucleus, and the amygdaloid complex. The putamen and globus pallidus are sometimes referred to collectively as the lentiform nucleus.

Putamen. The putamen is the largest and most lateral part of the basal ganglia and its anterior portion is continuous with the head of the caudate nucleus (Fig. 2.35).

Globus pallidus. The globus pallidus forms the medial portion of the lentiform nucleus. It consists of two separate sections and is paler in colour than the putamen, hence its name. The medial border of the globus pallidus is formed largely by fibres from the posterior limb of the internal capsule.

Caudate nucleus. The caudate nucleus is a long, arched mass of grey matter which is closely related throughout its length of the lateral ventricle. Its enlarged anterior part is termed the head of the caudate nucleus and this portion protrudes into the anterior horn of the lateral ventricle. The body and tail of the caudate nucleus lie dorsolateral to the thalamus near the lateral wall of the lateral ventricle. The tail of the nucleus follows the same curvature as the inferior horn (or temporal) of the lateral ventricle and

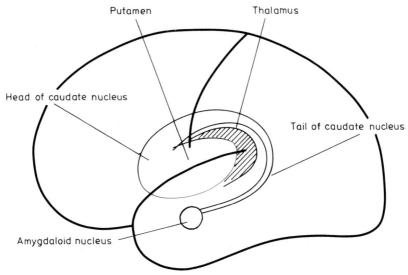

Putamen

Thalamus

Head of caudate nucleus

Tail of caudate nucleus

Amygdaloid nucleus

Fig. 2.35 Basal ganglia.

enters the temporal lobe to terminate in the region of the amygdaloid complex (Fig. 2.35).

Amygdaloid complex. The amygdaloid complex is a mass of grey matter in the dorsomedial part of the temporal lobe. It is dorsal to the hippocampal formation and in front of the tip of the temporal horn of the lateral ventricle.

BLOOD SUPPLY OF THE BRAIN

Since the central nervous system is one of the most metabolically active tissues in the body it requires a rich supply of oxygen. Some estimates put the nervous system's utilization of oxygen as high as one-fifth of that of the whole body. If there is serious diminution in blood supply to nervous tissue for even a relatively short period, there is tissue death or necrosis. The importance of understanding the rudiments of the circulation can be seen when it is realized that impairment of blood supply is the most common cause of lesions in the central nervous system.

Apart from the physiology of the cerebral circulation, it is important to understand the distribution of the blood via the various branches, since regional interruption to the blood supply is often associated with characteristic neuropsychological signs and symptoms, and a careful examination of the higher functions in such cases may allow inferences to be made about the nature and location of vascular blockages, insufficiencies, haemorrhages or the like. As yet, insufficient investigation has been given by neuropsychologists to this field.

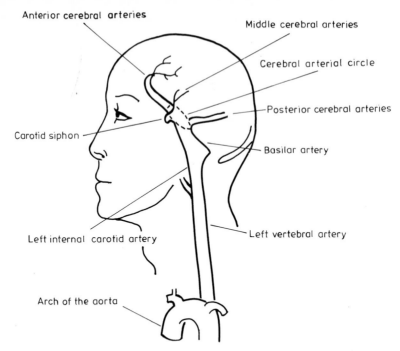

Fig. 2.36 The two arterial supply systems.

The blood supply to the brain comes from two pairs of arterial trunks; (i) the internal carotid arteries and (ii) the vertebral arteries (Fig. 2.36).

The internal carotid arterial system

The *internal carotid artery* enters the skull and, after making several sharp curves which form the *carotid siphon*, ascends lateral to the optic chiasm and breaks up into its major branches — the smaller anterior cerebral artery, and the larger middle cerebral artery. The latter is often considered as the direct continuation of the internal carotid artery. On its way to this major bifurcation, the internal carotid artery sends off three important branches, one anterior and two posterior. The anterior branch is the *ophthalmic artery* which passes forward through the opening in the optic orbit to supply the eye. The two posterior branches are the *anterior choroidal artery* and the *posterior communicating artery* (Fig. 2.36).

The *anterior choroidal artery* is usually of small calibre and passes backward across the optic tract and then laterally toward the anteromedial portion of the temporal lobe. The artery enters the inferior or temporal horn of the lateral ventricle where it supplies the choroid plexus. As well as the choroid plexus, the anterior choroidal artery supplies the hippocampal formation and other deeply placed structures such as parts of the

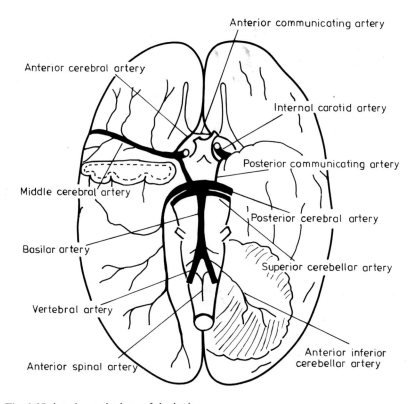

Anterior communicating artery

Anterior cerebral artery

Internal carotid artery

Posterior communicating artery

Middle cerebral artery

Posterior cerebral artery

Basilar artery

Superior cerebellar artery

Vertebral artery

Anterior spinal artery

Anterior inferior cerebellar artery

Fig. 2.37 Arteries at the base of the brain.

amygdaloid complex, caudate nucleus, thalamus, globus pallidus and internal capsule. As mentioned later, recent evidence has strongly implicated this hippocampus in the process of memory and for this reason a knowledge of the blood supply of this region becomes relevant to the neuropsychologist.

The *posterior communicating arteries* run backward to become joined to the proximal portions of the posterior cerebral arteries.

Anterior cerebral artery. The anterior cerebral artery (Fig. 2.38) passes dorsal to the optic nerve and approaches the anterior cerebral artery of the other side and is soon joined to it by the *anterior communicating artery.* The artery then enters the fissure between the two hemispheres, curves upward over the anterior portion (genu) of the corpus callosum and courses backwards on the medial surface of the cerebral hemisphere on the superior surface of the corpus callosum. It has a number of named branches: (i) orbital branches which supply the orbital lobes, (ii) the frontopolar artery which supplies medial parts of the frontal lobe and extends on to the convexity of the hemisphere, (iii) the callosomarginal artery which supplies the paracentral lobule and parts of the cingulate gyrus, (iv) the pericallosal

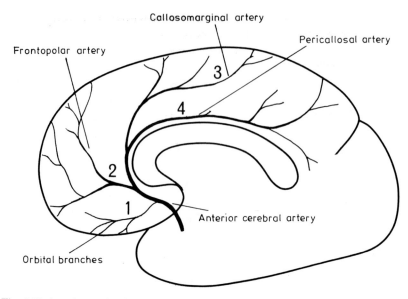

Fig. 2.38 Anterior cerebral artery.

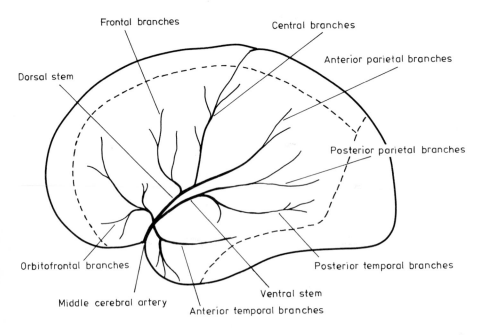

Fig. 2.39 Middle cerebral artery.

artery lies along the dorsal surface of the corpus callosum which it supplies to provide branches to the medial surface of the parietal lobe (e.g. the posterior parietal). The anterior cerebral artery also supplies the anterior columns of the fornix.

Middle cerebral artery. The middle cerebral artery passes laterally to enter the lateral cerebral fissure between the temporal lobe and the insula. It often breaks up into two stems which lie superficially in the lateral fissure (Fig. 2.39). The middle cerebral artery gives by far the largest supply to the cerebral hemispheres, accounting for some 75% or more of the blood going to the hemispheres. It supplies branches not only to extensive areas of the cortex but also to the internal nuclear masses and internal capsule (Fig. 2.40). One of these branches, the lenticulostriate artery has been known as 'the artery of cerebral haemorrhage' because of the frequency with which it is involved in spontaneous haemorrhages or 'strokes'.

The cortical branches from the dorsal portion or stem of the middle cerebral artery supply the area above the lateral fissure, i.e. orbitofrontal, precentral and anterior parts, while the ventral stem provides anterior temporal, posterior temporal and posterior parietal branches.

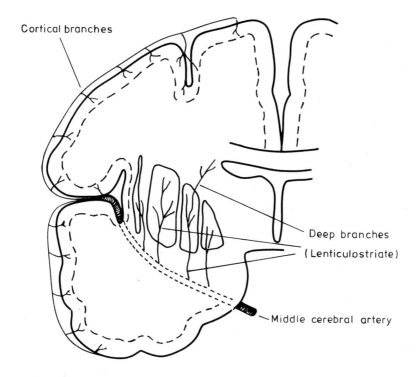

Fig. 2.40 Middle cerebral artery. Lenticulostriate branches.

The vertebrobasilar arterial system

The *vertebral arteries* enter the skull through the large opening, the *foramen magnum* through which the spinal cord becomes continuous with the brain stem. The two vertebral arteries rise along the anterolateral surfaces of the medulla and unite in the midline at the lower edge of the pons to form the basilar artery. Thus this major supply is often termed the vertebrobasilar system. The vertebral arteries give branches to the spinal cord before their entry into the cranial cavity while the intracranial branches of the vertebrobasilar system supply the spinal cord, brain stem (medulla, pons, midbrain), cerebellum, posterior diencephalon, and towards the termination of the system, the basilar artery bifurcates to form the two posterior cerebral arteries which supply parts of the temporal and occipital lobes of the cerebral hemispheres.

The *posterior cerebral arteries* pass around the lateral aspect of the midbrain and then pass dorsal to the tentorium cerebelli on to the inferior and medial surfaces of the temporal and occipital lobes (Fig. 2.41). The posterior cerebral artery has three main branches: (i) the anterior temporal which supplies all the inferior surface of the temporal lobe with the exception of a small area of the tip which is supplied by the middle cerebral artery, (ii) the posterior temporal which supplies the posterior part of the inferior surface of the temporal lobe, and (iii) the largest or occipital which runs in the calcarine fissure and gives branches which supply the whole of the medial and a large portion of the other surfaces of the occipital lobe including the visual cortex (see Ch. 7).

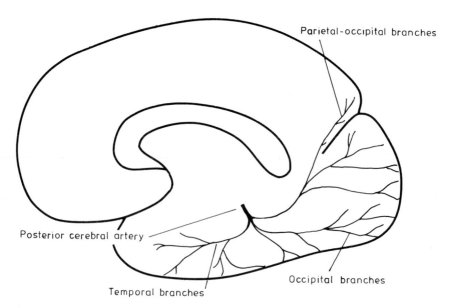

Fig. 2.41 Posterior cerebral artery.

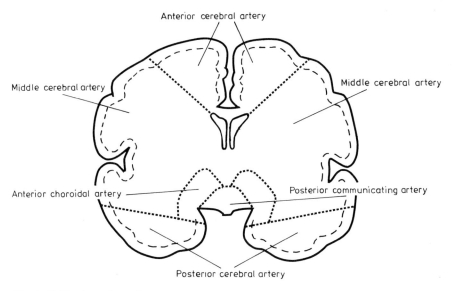

Anterior cerebral artery

Middle cerebral artery

Middle cerebral artery

Anterior choroidal artery

Posterior communicating artery

Posterior cerebral artery

Fig. 2.42 Blood supply to deep structure.

As the posterior cerebral artery passes around the cerebral peduncle it supplies adjacent structures and provides the posterior choroidal branch which supplies the choroid plexus and the larger, posterior part of the hippocampus that is not supplied by the anterior choroidal. The arterial supply of the deeper structures of the brain is shown in Figure 2.42.

Venous drainage

The venous drainage is effected by three sets of vessels: (i) the superficial veins which drain the lateral and inferior surfaces of the hemispheres, (Fig. 2.43), (ii) the deep veins which drain the whole of the internal area of the brain, and (iii) the venous sinuses.

The deep veins converge on the great cerebral vein (Galen) (Fig. 2.44) which is a short wide vein just below the splenium of the corpus callosum. It runs a short course to the junction of the sagittal and straight sinuses.

The various cerebral veins empty into the venous sinuses (Fig. 2.45). These are channels formed between two layers of the dura mater. They converge at the *confluence of sinuses* in the region of the occipital bone and the bulk of the venous blood finally enters the large *internal jugular vein* though a small amount is drained through other channels.

The cerebral arterial circle

The cerebral arterial circle (Circle of Willis) is a ring of connecting blood vessels which encircles the optic chiasm and the region between the cerebral

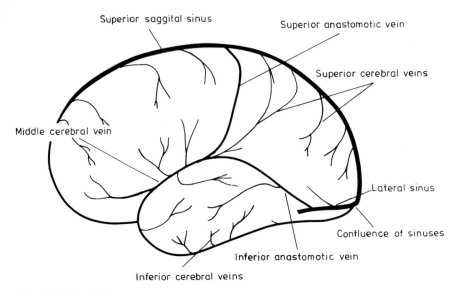

Fig. 2.43 Superficial cerebral veins.

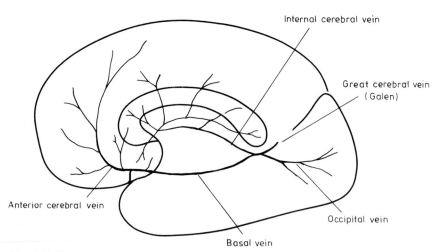

Fig. 2.44 Deep cerebral veins.

peduncles (Fig. 2.46). The circle is formed by vessels which link the two great arterial systems, the internal carotid and vertebrobasilar. In front of the optic chiasma the two anterior cerebral arteries are joined by the usually short anterior communicating artery while the whole of the internal carotid system is joined to the basilar system by the pair of posterior communicating arteries which run back from the internal carotid arteries to join the proximal portions of each posterior cerebral artery.

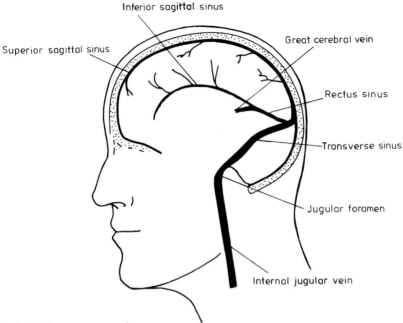

Inferior sagittal sinus

Superior sagittal sinus

Great cerebral vein

Rectus sinus

Transverse sinus

Jugular foramen

Internal jugular vein

Fig. 2.45 The great venous sinuses.

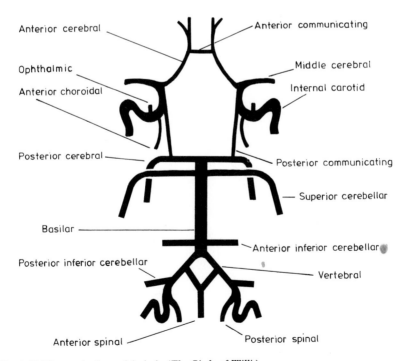

Anterior cerebral

Anterior communicating

Ophthalmic

Middle cerebral

Anterior choroidal

Internal carotid

Posterior cerebral

Posterior communicating

Superior cerebellar

Basilar

Anterior inferior cerebellar

Posterior inferior cerebellar

Vertebral

Anterior spinal

Posterior spinal

Fig. 2.46 The cerebral arterial circle (*The Circle of Willis*).

There are variations both in the disposition and the size of vessels which enter into the arterial circle in individual cases. The circle has been thought to equalize the distribution of blood flow throughout the brain but, with an equality of blood pressure, there is normally little or no exchange of blood either between the two sides of the circle or between the internal carotid and posterior cerebral vessels. However, when a blockage occurs at any portion of the circle, this may be bypassed through the other portions of the circle. The adequacy of this process will depend both on the calibre of the vessel occluded, the size and nature of the alternative circulation, and the rapidity or otherwise of the occlusion. Such 'alternative' pathways are known as *anastomoses*. They are defined by Zülch as 'intercommunications of a network character in one or between two or more functionally separate systems, allowing the possibility of draining blood from them. An auxiliary supply may result, usually after widening of the channel, and flow may result in any direction' (Zülch, 1971, p. 107). Thus, the slow narrowing which occurs due to the thickening of an artery (arteriosclerosis) may allow an anastomotic circulation to develop while a rapid occlusion by an embolus may not.

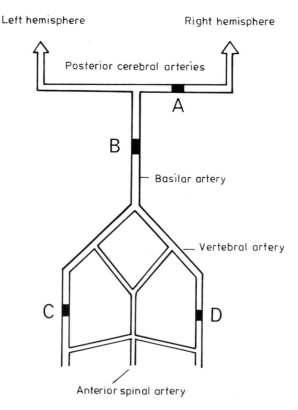

Fig. 2.47 Occlusions and alternative routes in the vertebrobasilar system.

Figure 2.46 provides a schematic representation of several possibilities of alternative supply with blockages in the vertebrobasilar system. Alternative routes for the flow of blood may be worked out for the points of occlusion indicated. For example, blockage of the right posterior cerebral artery at A will deprive the right occipital and basal temporal regions of their blood supply. Blockage at B will cause a loss of supply to the territory of both posterior cerebral arteries. Occlusion at such a 'bottleneck' will have serious consequences. On the other hand, even where both vertebral arteries are occluded (C and D) the effects may not be nearly so pronounced since an alternative supply may reach the brain via the patent branches which connect the anterior spinal artery with the vertebral arteries.

This oversimplified version of the supply pattern of the cerebral circulation can be expanded by the more extensive treatment by Zülch (1971), Kaplan and Ford (1966) and others. The arterial supply of the principal structures may be summarized as in Table 2.1.

Table 2.1 The arterial supply of the principal structures.

Frontal lobe	
Lateral surface	— middle cerebral artery
Medial surface	— anterior cerebral artery
Inferior surface	— middle and anterior cerebral arteries
Temporal lobe	
Lateral surface	— middle cerebral artery
Medial surface	— middle cerebral, posterior cerebral, anterior choroidal, and posterior communicating arteries
Inferior surface	— posterior cerebral artery
Parietal lobe	
Lateral surface	— middle cerebral artery
Medial surface	— anterior cerebral artery
Occipital lobe	
All surfaces	— posterior cerebral artery
Corpus Callosum	— anterior cerebral artery
Hippocampus	— anterior choroidal artery, posterior choroidal branches of posterior cerebral artery
Fornix	
Anterior columns	— anterior cerebral artery
Body and crura	— posterior choroid branches of posterior cerebral artery
Mamillary bodies	— posterior cerebral and posterior communicating arteries.

3

Elements of neurology

Methods of investigation   78
Common neurological disorders   88
Disruption of higher cerebral function   103

The neuropsychologist is most often a psychologist by primary training. Whether he is engaged in research or acting as a consultant concerning the patient's higher cortical functions, he brings to his collaboration with other workers in the neurosciences a rather different background. Tallent (1963), points out that 'the psychologist and his associates are members of considerably different cultures'. These cultural differences may bring fresh information and orientations which will prove helpful but they also create barriers in understanding and communication. The present chapter is aimed at providing the psychologist with the barest background to neurology including some of its terms and methodology, so that he may begin to understand, albeit in a very rudimentary fashion, the majority of neurological conditions he is likely to encounter in the literature and in practice. Absorption of some of the medical culture along with a sensible expression of his own is likely to prove mutually rewarding. Perhaps the greatest contribution in any cultural interchange is an understanding of the other culture's language.

The selection of topics is biased in the direction of the issues which have concerned neurology and neuropsychology in common in recent years.

Standard textbooks of neurology (e.g. Adams & Victor, 1981) will be needed to expand the psychologist's understanding of the field. A comprehensive source is the *Handbook of Clinical Neurology* (Vinken & Bruyn, 1969–1982) the first volume of the new series having already appeared (Vinken, Bruyn & Klawans, 1985).

METHODS OF INVESTIGATION

The neurological examination

Neurological examination consists firstly of the taking of a detailed history from the patient and, often of paramount importance, from those around him. Much valuable information about the types of neuropsychological tests to employ may be gained from a perusal of the patient's neurological case notes though, regrettably, many patients are still referred to the psychologist with a request 'for psychometric testing'. Where the anamnesis is insufficiently detailed, e.g. in questions relating to the patient's higher cortical functions, the psychologist should develop a routine of careful questioning.

A clinical neurological examination in itself is often an extensive, careful record of the patient's sensation, reflexes, movement and muscle tone, and clinical neuropsychologists will need to familiarize themselves with the details of the neurological examination and with the traditional interpretation of neurological symptoms and signs. Disturbances of integrative cerebral functions and the terminology in common use are described below.

Neurology has developed special methods in the investigation of disorders of the nervous system and a neuropsychologist will be better equipped to assist in the solution of neurological problems if he understands them. The remainder of the book is concerned with the most recently developed method, namely neuropsychological investigation, which is aimed at obtaining information on the changes in specifically human functions which occur with lesions in the nervous system so that this information may be added to the methods already in use for the diagnosis of the nature and location of the lesions. 'In this respect neuropsychology is merely the most complex and newest chapter of neurology, and without this chapter, modern clinical neurology will be unable to exist and develop' (Luria, 1973b). Clinical neuropsychology will be useful to the extent to which it provides added information to the data base on which decisions regarding diagnosis, management, and rehabilitation are made.

Radiological investigation

Progress in neuroradiology has been rapid over the past decade and the new methods have had a considerable impact on the practice of clinical neurology and neuropsychology. Some earlier methods, particularly pneumoencephalography, have practically disappeared in most centres. Neuropsychologists, particularly those whose practice includes patients with acute neurological disorders will need to be familiar with the basic nature of neuroradiological methods and the types of information which they are capable of providing.

Most radiographic methods rely on the detection of differences of electron density between the tissues for a differential effect on X-ray attenuation which is then used to create a visual image.

Computerized tomography (CT scan)

This technique has become universally accepted as standard for studying

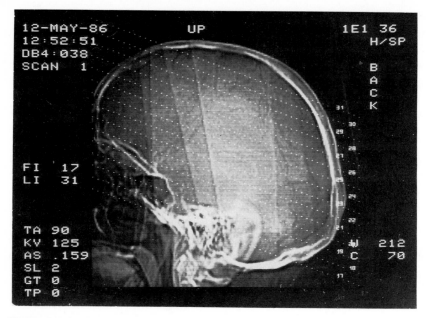

Fig. 3.1 Planes of sections with computed tomography.

morphological changes in the brain. It is safe and easy to carry out both on in-patient and out-patient cases.

In essence, the procedure consists of scanning the head with a narrow beam of X-rays which allows the transmission of X-ray photons in the layer to be measured. A number of standard 'cuts' are made at successive levels (Fig. 3.1). The photon data is processed by a computer and the density information is converted to a visual image of the internal structure of the brain. Pathological processes are indicated by alterations of normal density and by deformation of brain structures. Several examples appear throughout the text.

The sensitivity of computerized tomography can be enhanced by the intravenous injection of iodine-containing material. Where there is a defect in the blood-brain barrier or increased vascularity, retention of the high density element will result in increased contrast between the normal and abnormal tissue (Fig. 3.2).

The great value of CT scan to neuropsychology lies in a clear delineation of the morphology of neurological lesions in vivo against which to correlate behavioural indices. In its first decade CT scan information has confirmed and greatly clarified the anatomical basis of neuropsychological disorders (e.g. see Kertesz, 1983).

It must be remembered, however, that CT scan provides a static picture at the moment of evaluation. Serial scans provide further information but are still restricted to demonstrating structural change. It is apparent from

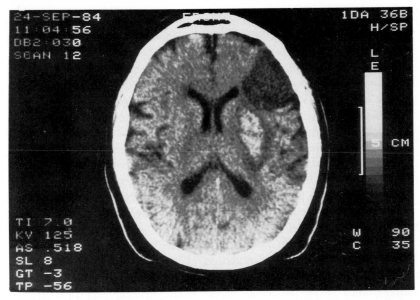

Fig. 3.2 Computed tomograph (CT scan) showing old frontal infarct (dark area) and new striatocapsular infarct (deep light area).

assessment of function, e.g. by neuropsychological examination, that disruption of brain function may extend considerably beyond the changes seen on static scanning. Several new methods are being developed to inform us about this non-functioning (or malfunctioning) but structurally intact neural tissue.

Positron emission computed tomography (PET scan)

The use of PET scanning in the study of neurobehavioural disorders is still in its early stages. Like CT scanning, it provides a cross-sectional image of the brain, but, unlike the static nature of the former, PET scanning is capable of providing dynamic information on a wide range of cerebral functions such as local cerebral perfusion, local cerebral glucose utilization (LCMR glc) and others.

PET is a scanning method for producing an image of brain radioactivity following the intravenous injection of a labelled indicator. One of the principal factors restricting its use is the need for a cyclotron to produce the appropriate short-lived radioactive isotopes. It has already proved useful in demonstrating altered cerebral function of a lasting nature in tissues which appear normal with computed tomography (Kuhl et al, 1980a; Kuhl et al, 1980b). Some examples of the potential of PET investigation in neuropsychology are described by Benson and his colleagues (1983).

Arteriography

This is the technique for outlining the circulation by means of a rapid series of radiographs taken during the passage of radio-opaque material which has been injected into the blood stream. The term cerebral angiography is used to refer to the radiological investigation of both the arterial and venous channels of the brain and is often used interchangeably with the term arteriography. Formerly, the injection was made directly into the artery, most commonly the internal carotid artery, but it is now customary to pass a catheter via the femoral artery. This allows injection of material into the arch of the aorta to display the origins of all vessels or selective catheterization of chosen vessels to study the extracranial and intracranial circulation. With the catheter in situ, separate injections can be made to visualize the circulation from lateral or antero-posterior orientations (Fig. 3.3). Presenting symptoms will determine whether the injection is made into the anterior (internal carotid, anterior and middle cerebral arteries and their branches) or the posterior circulation (vertebral, basilar, and posterior cerebral arteries).

Angiography is of particular value in the investigation of structural abnormalities of the blood vessels themselves, e.g. narrowing or ulceration of one or more vessels, intracranial aneurysms or arteriovenous malformations. On the other hand, alteration in the shape and position of vessels may indicate the presence of a space-occupying lesion such as a cerebral tumour.

In the Wada technique of sodium amytal ablation described in Chapter 5, an arteriogram may often be carried out to check the circulation prior to the injection of the drug.

Arteriography is not without risk, much of which has been associated with sensitivity to the injected radio-opaque materials. These reactions have been greatly reduced in recent times with the introduction of more physiologically compatible contrast materials.

Digital subtraction angiography

This newer form of angiography consists of scanning the output from an X-ray image intensifying tube with a video camera. This video signal is then amplified and stored in digital form in the imager's memory. Further images are taken after the arrival of contrast material at the site. The first set of data, termed the 'mask image' is then subtracted by the computer to produce the final image.

The contrast material can be introduced intravenously so that it is possible to visualize either the extracranial or intracranial circulation on an out-patient basis with relative safety, avoiding the risks associated with intra-arterial injection. The technique can also be utilized with the intra-arterial injection of a much smaller quantity of material than traditionally

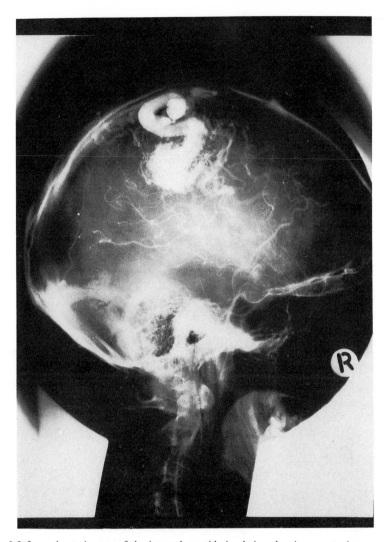

Fig. 3.3 Lateral arteriogram of the internal carotid circulation showing an arteriovenous malformation.

used in cerebral angiography with reduced risk (Little et al, 1982). The method is of particular value in detecting extracranial vascular pathology such as stenosis, occlusion and ulceration and thus performs a valuable role in the prevention of stroke.

Magnetic resonance imaging (MRI)

This newest technique, also known as nuclear magnetic resonance (NMR) imaging, differs fundamentally from conventional radiographic techniques.

It does not employ X-rays and does not require the injection of contrast media. Palmer (1985) gives the following succinct summary.

> When the nuclei of certain atoms — usually hydrogen protons — are placed in a high magnetic field, they align with the axis of spin in the direction of the field. A radio frequency, applied at right angles to the field, changes the angle of spin and the return to equilibrium when the radiofrequency pulse ceases is associated with the emission of a radiofrequency characteristic of the element and its physicochemical environment. In MRI, gradient magnetic fields in the three directions allow spatial detection of signal data and a two-dimensional image to be formed (Palmer, 1985, p. 3. See also Pykett, 1982; Tress Stimac & Brant Zawadski, 1985).

It is now possible to obtain images of the brain of outstanding quality (Fig. 3.4). In some cases, these are even superior to those obtained with the latest conventional CT scanners and the greater sensitivity of MRI in

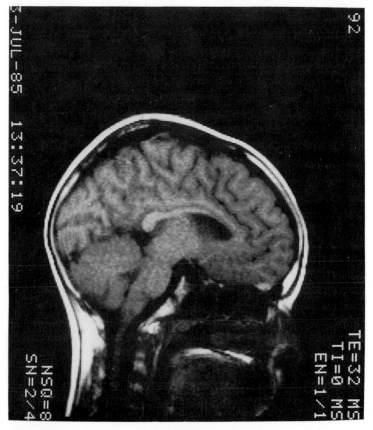

Fig. 3.4 Magnetic resonance image (MRI, NMR) showing agenesis of the anterior portion of the corpus callosum (By courtesy of Professor Valk, Amsterdam).

many neurological conditions coupled with its ability to produce images in all planes (horizontal, coronal, sagittal) may soon make it the investigation of choice, subject to the availability of what is at present an expensive installation. This possibility is enhanced by the great potential of MRI for accurate evaluation of physiological changes such as blood flow.

Electrical investigation

Recording

One of the most widely used investigative techniques in neurology is *electroencephalography*. This is the technique of recording the electrical activity of the brain through the skull by means of electrodes placed on the scalp. The potential differences between two points on the skull produced by brain activity are very small and have to be amplified many times before they can be used to drive a recording device such as a pen recorder. The mean amplitude of the brain's electrical activity is about one hundredth that of the heart. The brain potentials are recorded in wave form from 1–100 Hz with an amplitude ranging from about five to several hundred microvolts.

The scalp electrodes are usually placed in a standard pattern (Fig. 3.5) and the activity between any pair of electrodes recorded as a single channel

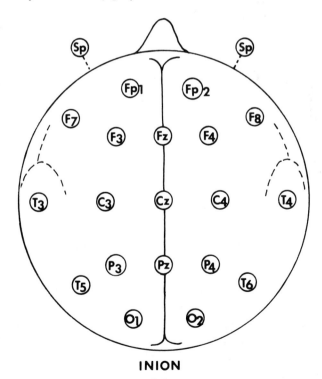

INION

Fig. 3.5 Electrode placement in electroencephalogram.

of which there are usually about eight. The various areas being analysed at any one time may be varied by switching the outputs between pairs of electrodes, e.g. in one period of examination eight channels might be devoted to the potential differences between Fp2–F8, F8–T4, T4–T6, T6–02, and the corresponding areas on the left side of the head. In a subsequent 'run' differences might be examined in the transverse direction, e.g. T3–C3, C3–Cz, Cz–C4, C4–T4 and other areas. In this way, a thorough coverage of the brain can be achieved and the activity of the various areas compared. Interpretation depends on an analysis of the principal characteristics of the wave activity, namely the frequency, amplitude, form and distribution (see textbooks such as Niedermeyer & Lopes da Silva, 1982).

For some time after the invention of the electroencephalograph it was hoped by many that it would provide the tool to unlock many of the brain's secrets. The study of the relation between the EEG and higher mental functions has been singularly disappointing though increasing sophistication in recording and analysing equipment, including computer analysis, may yet prove of value. However, the technique is often valuable in neurological diagnosis. It is a safe and relatively simple procedure routinely used in most larger hospitals.

The EEG is of particular value in the investigation of epilepsy. Here abnormal electrical activity may be recorded in the period between the patient's clinical seizures — the interictal period. The observed abnormalities may be apparent in many of the channels or may be restricted to a clearly defined focus such as over one temporal lobe.

Unfortunately, any one EEG record taken from an epileptic patient may prove to be normal and serial recordings often need to be taken. Latent abnormalities may be brought out by using various activation procedures which may be effective in evoking the epileptic discharges so that they appear on the record, though the patient may not have any clinical manifestations. Commonly-used activation techniques are: (i) recording during sleep; (ii) overbreathing for 2 or 3 minutes; (iii) photic stimulation in the form of repetitive light flashes and (iv) administration of drugs.

Recent advances in electronic technology have made it possible to record EEG activity in ambulatory patients in their normal environments for periods of 24 hours or more. The electrical signals are recorded from a small pre-amplifier attached to the scalp between a pair of silver-chloride electrodes. With care in electrode application satisfactory recordings can be obtained even during vigorous activity or major seizures though movement artefact may prove troublesome. The method can be used for reliable quantification of seizure activity and frequency in the absence of an observer. Four channels have commonly been used but commercially available products now include eight or more. 'The technique has sufficient positive yield to be applied to any patient with epilepsy or a question of epilepsy in whom routine EEG has not provided sufficient information' (Bridgers & Ebersole, 1985).

Recording from depth electrodes forms an essential part of the in-patient investigation in patients with intractable epilepsy in whom surgical treatment is projected. The electrodes may remain in situ over many days while recording is made from cable or radiotelemetry with concurrent video monitoring of the patient's behaviour.

Apart from its primary role in the study of epilepsy, the EEG is also of diagnostic value in the localization of organic lesions of the brain such as cerebral tumours, abscess, or infarction (see below) but is of much less value in determining the nature of the pathological process. It should also be borne in mind that negative findings do not rule out the presence of even major pathology since in some proven pathological lesions EEG recordings sometimes appear entirely normal. The more superficial the lesion, the more reliable is the localization.

Like evidence from other specialized diagnostic procedures the findings at electroencephalography must be examined in the light of the patient's history and clinical examination.

Stimulation

Electrical stimulation of nerve tissues is historically older than electrical recording techniques and, in many respects, is complementary to it. The value of both techniques has increased with the advance in sophistication of electronic equipment.

Modern electronic stimulators permit investigators to control such parameters of stimulation as the frequency, duration, shape and intensity of the pulses used.

Opportunities for study of human beings are restricted to patients undergoing neurosurgical procedures under local anaesthesia. Quite surprisingly, very few *positive* responses have been evoked with stimulation outside the primary motor and sensory areas. The major exception is the evocation of complex experiences from the temporal lobe described by Penfield and reported in Chapter 5. There is also great variability of response from patient to patient and in individual patients over time (e.g. Ojemann, 1979).

On the other hand *negative* responses, i.e. the disruption of functions is much more common. A typical example would be the disruption of language functions, such as the ability to name objects when certain areas of the cortex are stimulated (Penfield & Rasmussen, 1950; Penfield & Jasper, 1954; Penfield, 1958; Penfield & Roberts, 1959; Fedio & Van Buren, 1974; Ojemann & Mateer, 1979a, 1979b; Ojemann, 1980, 1981) (Fig. 3.6). Less common are the reports of interference with non-language functions with cortical stimulation (Fedio, 1980; Fried et al, 1982).

The early work was largely associated with the neurosurgical treatment

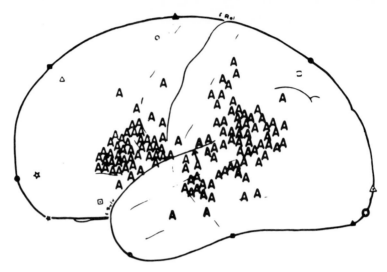

Fig. 3.6 Points at which stimulation produced aphasic responses (Fig. XIII–II: Penfield W & Roberts L 1959 Speech and brain mechanisms. Courtesy of Princeton University Press).

of epilepsy and thus was much concerned with the cerebral cortex. More recently, stereotaxic operations in subcortical regions, particularly the thalamus, for the treatment of dyskinesias has revealed a specific dissociation of effects according to the side of stimulation. It is also clear that the timing of stimulation is crucial, e.g. stimulation at the time of input of information may actually enhance retrieval whereas stimulation in the same sites at the time of retrieval may worsen performance compared with the normal state (for details see Ojemann & Fedio, 1968; Ojemann, 1971; Ojemann, Blick & Ward, 1971; Fedio & Van Buren, 1975; Ojemann, 1977, 1979; Mateer & Ojemann, 1983).

COMMON NEUROLOGICAL DISORDERS

Cerebral trauma

The functions of the brain can be seriously disturbed by physical injury. The effects of penetrating wounds of the brain resulting from high velocity projectiles such as bullets and shrapnel fragments have been studied intensively in large series of military cases, some of which have been followed up for one or more decades. These studies have contributed greatly to our understanding of neuropsychology. It is unfortunate that the drawings of such lesions often pictured as a small dot on a map of the brain, tend to leave the reader with the impression that one is dealing with a small circumscribed lesion which affects only the cortex at the point of entry. The nature of the fibre connections severed and the effect of the shock wave produced in the very soft brain mass by the penetrating missile are seldom known with any degree of accuracy. These wounds are, of course, relatively uncommon in studies of civilian subjects.

On the other hand, craniocerebral injury from the rapid acceleration and deceleration of the head in motor vehicle accidents is an ever-increasing problem. Even where the skull is not fractured, the brain may sustain a wide variety of pathological lesions. These include generalized lesions scattered throughout the brain with or without localized damage such as contusion, laceration or haemorrhage. With this complexity of pathology, clinico-anatomical correlation might seem to be an unproductive exercise. However, the presence of residual neuropsychological deficits of memory and adaptive behaviour in many so-called recovered patients and the proven relationship between lesions of the frontal and temporal regions of the brain and these disorders tempts one to draw a causal relationship between the major locus of damage in closed head injury and such deficits. Before considering this possibility readers should consult sources which convey the complexity of the pathology (Strich, 1969; Adams, 1975; Gurdjian, 1975).

The advent of the CT scan offers an opportunity to correlate the major focus of localized pathology and behavioural change in the individual case. So far no systematic study of this kind has been reported. The role of the CT scan is summarized well by Levine et al (1982) but even this is unlikely to be sensitive to the diffuse microscopic lesions which occur in severe head injury. Nevertheless, the CT scan often provides dramatic confirmation for the local character of some lesions.

Briefly, cerebral damage may be defined as primary or secondary. Primary lesions are associated with the trauma itself. The principal forms are contusion, laceration or haemorrhage although there is often a mixture of all three and contusion and laceration cannot be distinguished on clinical grounds. Secondary lesions arise from ischaemia, anoxia, oedema and intracranial haemorrhage.

Mechanism and sites of cerebral contusion

The exact mechanism of production of contusional lesions is still debated though there is general agreement about the use of two descriptive terms. 'Coup' injuries refer to damage beneath the site of impact while 'contre coup' injuries refer to lesions at some distance from the site (Fig. 3.7). The mechanics of head injuries have been the focus of numerous studies using inert models, animals and man (Holburn, 1943; Lindenberg & Freytag, 1960; Rowbotham, 1964; Gurdjian et al, 1966; Ommaya & Gennerelli, 1974).

Though there is disagreement about what mechanical stresses produce the damage there is no such disagreement about their location. Courville (1942) observed that the greatest zone of brain contusion following head injury was not invariably opposite to the impact: 'Essentially identical lesions of the subfrontal and anterior temporal regions result from contact

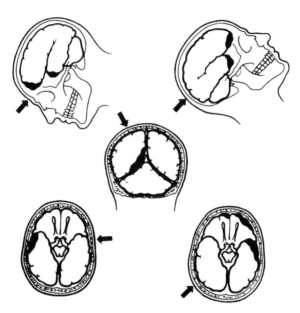

Fig. 3.7 Mechanism of cerebral contusion (Fig. 137: Courville C B 1945 Pathology of the nervous system. Courtesy of Pacific Press Publications).

of either the frontal region or the occipital region of the moving head . . . and the fact that neither gross coup nor contrecoup lesions occur in the occipital region . . . suggests that the anatomic relation of the brain and the portion of the skull proximate to it is essentially responsible for the nature and distribution of the lesion.' Speaking of the sudden deceleration of the head in motor vehicle injuries Jamieson (1971, p. 31) likened the movement of the brain within the skull to the movement of objects within the motor vehicle: 'The soft brain then travels onward and crashes into the built-in dashboard that each of us owns, the knife-like sphenoidal ridges (complete with anterior clinoid projections), together with an unyielding fascia of front wall of middle fossa and a windscreen of rough orbital plates and frontal bone'. In modern motor accidents with high velocity deceleration the damage to the anterior portion of the temporal lobe and sometimes the frontal lobe may be so great that it produces sub-dural haemorrhage, brain contusion, laceration and intracerebral bleeding that has been termed the 'exploded pole' (Bottrell & Stewart, cited in Hooper, 1966). The frontotemporal concentration of contusional injury has been confirmed frequently (Gurdjian et al, 1943; Courville, 1945; Gurdjian et al, 1955; Lindenberg & Freytag, 1957; Hooper, 1966, 1969). Figure 3.7 provides a composite sketch from these sources.

An understanding of the mechanism of cerebral contusion is important for neuropsychology and it helps to explain why some patients after head injuries have psychological deficits which suggest damage to localized areas

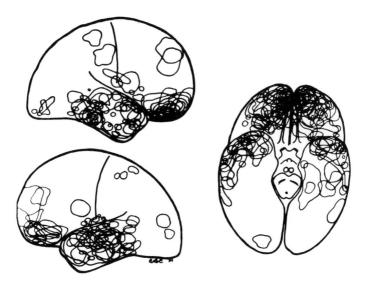

Fig. 3.8 Sites of cerebral contusion (Fig. 138: Courville C B 1945 Pathology of the nervous system. Courtesy of Pacific Press Publications).

distant from the site of impact, e.g. the very frequent occurrence of 'frontal lobe' signs such as uninhibited behaviour and lack of planned initiative in patients who have sustained head injuries. The tendency to consider all cases of closed head injury as suffering only from the effects of diffuse brain insult is not supported by the evidence and careful neuropsychological assessment may give valuable information about the location and extent of the damage which should prove useful in rehabilitation programmes.

Concussion

Prominent among the symptoms of head injury is impairment of consciousness. In a simple concussion there may be only a brief clouding of consciousness or a temporary loss. This temporary loss of consciousness is probably due to injury to the brain-stem reticular formation. The patient cannot remember the incident causing the concussion and has a loss of memory for events just preceding it. This is termed retrograde amnesia. There may also be a period of memory loss for the period subsequent to the injury which is termed *anterograde* or *post-traumatic amnesia*.

Measures of severity

Coma. The usefulness of employing length of coma as a measure of severity against which to correlate clinical and social sequelae was lessened by the variable and uncertain ways in which coma was defined in the early studies. This situation has been improved by the widespread adoption of the Glasgow Coma Scale, a simple standardized chart of eye opening, motor response and verbal response (Teasdale & Jennett, 1974).

Post-traumatic amnesia. This measure was introduced by Russell & Nathan (1946) following an earlier study by Russell (1932). This used the length of time from injury to the time the patient became aware that he had regained consciousness. It corresponds to the time when the patient begins to retain a stable record of ongoing events. The definition of Russell and Nathan (1946) and the minor modification of Russell and Smith (1961) combines the length of unconsciousness with the period when the patient is awake and responding but not consolidating memories, i.e. coma plus the period of anterograde amnesia. Recently, Artiola i Fortuny et al (1980) have attempted to provide an objective assessment of PTA. This simple quantitative procedure correlated well with independent estimates made by experienced neurosurgeons. Newcombe (1982) warns that the complexity of factors involved means that there will be no simple relationship between PTA and severity of defect. While a convincing general trend may be apparent in group data there are bound to be exceptions in both directions, some individuals with lengthy PTA having little impairment with others having shorter PTA being left with considerable deficit.

Traumatic haemorrhage

While small haemorrhages may occur in virtually any part of the brain after any form of head injury, more extensive haemorrhages occur from the laceration of blood vessels inside the skull, e.g. a fracture of the skull may tear the middle meningeal artery which, by bleeding under considerable pressure into the space outside the covering of the brain, greatly compresses the cerebral hemisphere and later the basal portions of the brain. This *extradural* haematoma is a neurosurgical emergency and has little relevance for neuropsychology.

On the other hand, bleeding from blood vessels beneath the dura mater, produces a *subdural* haematoma (Fig. 3.9), which may be less dramatic and, in elderly patients, may follow an injury so trivial that the patient does not even recall the incident. This condition may produce changes which develop over days or even weeks after the injury often simulating the picture of dementia with loss of concentration, episodes of confusion and memory loss.

Intracranial tumours

The word tumour literally means a swelling. When referring to intracranial tumours 'often erroneously labelled cerebral tumours' (Escourolle & Poirier, 1973) the term usually means a *neoplasm* or new growth. Such of neoplasm has been defined as a 'mass of cells . . . resembling those

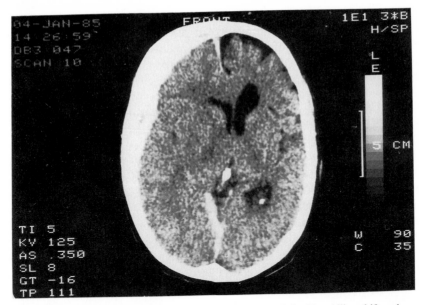

Fig. 3.9 Right subdural haematoma extending over falx cerebri with midline shift and compression of right lateral ventricle.

normally present in the body, but arranged atypically, which grow at the expense and independently of the organism without subserving any useful purpose therein' (Handfield-Jones & Porritt, 1949, p. 86).

These neoplasms in the brain may be benign or malignant. Benign neoplasms most frequently grow from the coverings of the brain. These coverings are termed *meninges* and tumours arising from them, *meningiomas*. Such benign tumours may grow slowly and attain a large size before they cause symptoms from their pressure effect on the brain or they may be symptomless and only be discovered at autopsy. They can be successfully removed in their entirety as they do not invade the brain substance.

Unfortunately, benign tumours are much less frequent than the malignant type which invade the tissue of the brain. The latter can rarely be removed fully by surgery because of the extent to which they infiltrate the surrounding tissue.

Most malignant brain tumours arise from the glial or supporting cells and not from the cells or fibres themselves. They are termed *primary neoplasms*. The most common type, the *glioma*, which accounts for some 40% of adult brain tumours is also the most malignant. A smaller proportion of brain tumours are called *secondary neoplasms* since they multiply from cells of malignant tumours in other parts of the body. These cells of origin of cerebral secondary neoplasms have become detached from their parent tumours and been carried by the blood stream to lodge in the brain to begin independent growth there. Tumours of the lung or breast often give rise to such *metastatic* or secondary tumours.

Sometimes conditions that are not neoplastic may give rise to very similar signs and symptoms, e.g. an abscess in the brain. Though these may be diagnosed from signs which signal the presence of infection their nature may not be discovered until an exploratory operation is carried out. For this reason tumours, abscesses and other mechanically similar conditions are given the title of 'space-occupying lesions'.

It can be seen from this short description that tumours within the skull may produce a multitude of symptoms which depend on their nature, location and growth. While most space-occupying lesions will produce a set of general symptoms, each particular case will have specific features which depend on the interruption of connections between different parts of the brain. Thus, a small lesion in a strategic situation may have disastrous early effects because it interferes with vital centres or cuts a large number of interconnections between different areas of the brain while a large lesion in another area may be almost silent for a relatively long period.

It is this failure to take into account the nature and location of cerebral lesions which defeated many of the earlier attempts to draw conclusions from psychological studies of heterogeneous populations of 'brain-damaged' people.

Cerebrovascular disorders

The term cerebrovascular disorder can be taken to mean any disruption of brain function arising from some pathological condition related to the blood vessels. These produce an array of disorders of great complexity.

The vascular pathology may take many forms, e.g. lesions of the walls of the blood vessels themselves in the form of deposited material (atheroma) with or without ulceration, rupture of the vessel wall itself, narrowing (stenosis) or total occlusion of the lumen from thickening of the vessel wall or the presence of an obstructing clot (thrombus) or embolus, or changes in the characteristics of the blood itself.

While the types of cerebrovascular disease are numerous the majority of cases are due to cerebral *ischaemia* or haemorrhage. Ischaemia may be transient with symptoms that recover. Any prolonged ischaemia will lead to death of tissue or *infarction*. The most common cause of infarction is thromboembolism and this accounts for two-thirds of all cases of cerebrovascular disability. Some 15–25% of cases are due to intracerebral or subarachnoid haemorrhage, while the remaining 5–10% are due to less common causes.

Cerebral ischaemia

Transient ischaemic attacks (TIAs). This term refers to recurrent attacks of short-lived local neurological deficit produced by temporary ischaemia. By accepted definition, recovery should take place within 24 hours but is often complete within a much shorter time. Although the episodes take many forms they are often rather similar, even stereotyped, in the one individual. The patient experiences sudden loss of neurological function. This may be loss of power which often begins distally but may progress to affect the whole limb or an entire side. There may be sudden sensory loss, particularly loss of vision in one eye (amaurosis fugax, fleeting blindness) or loss of speech, memory or the functions referable to the cerebral hemisphere territories supplied by the internal carotid system. It is unusual for the brain and the eye to be affected simultaneously in one attack. Where the vertebrobasilar system is compromised there may be symptoms such as ataxia and vertigo signalling dysfunction in the cerebellum or brain stem. The attacks vary from infrequent (e.g. less than one a month) to very frequent (several times a day). During the attack the neurological signs will be indistinguishable from a developing infarct but examination between the episodes will be normal.

Approximately one-third of patients do go on to suffer obvious infarction. In keeping with the higher incidence of atherosclerosis in males than females and in hypertensive patients, some two-thirds of those suffering from TIAs are male or hypertensive or both. Another third will continue to have attacks without any apparent permanent disability, while the remainder will have attacks which cease spontaneously. It is impossible to predict the outcome.

In transient ischaemic attacks it is generally assumed that ischaemia has occurred without actual death of neurones though this may not necessarily be the case and the apparent absence of findings may represent the insensitivity of functional measures as well as the relatively 'silent' location of the affected territory. Careful neuropsychological examination sometimes reveals that lasting deficits of higher function are present in some of these cases even where they appear to be neurologically intact between episodes.

Surgical treatment. Two major types of surgical procedure have been devised to prevent strokes and ischaemic attacks by reconstituting the arterial blood flow. The most common is the operation of *endarterectomy* which aims at correction of stenosis, removal of atheromatous plaques, removal of an organized thrombus and other conditions compromising the circulation. It is sometimes necessary to totally remove a diseased segment of artery and replace it with a vein graft. The operations are carried out at the sites of predilection for atheroma formation, e.g. at the origin of the internal carotid artery. The indication for operation is usually the presence of transient ischaemic attacks in the territory distal to a radiologically demonstrated stenotic or ulcerated lesion.

Occlusive lesions not accessible from the neck may be approached surgically by some form of bypass operation, e.g. where a branch of the external carotid artery such as the superficial temporal is grafted via an opening in the skull to a portion of the middle cerebral artery, the so-called *transcranial anastomosis*.

Cerebral infarction

The basic pathological process. The most common basic pathological process in infarction is *atherosclerosis.* This is not a uniform process but one which affects certain parts of the arterial system more than others. The deposition of material, mostly cholestrol, causes plaques which narrow the artery and thus restrict the flow. This may progress to complete occlusion of the affected vessel. Whether infarction occurs depends upon whether there is a collateral source of supply for the affected region (see below). However, in general, the size of an infarct depends to a large extent on the size of the vessel occluded. This may range from the minute to massive death of a large part of the hemisphere due to sudden occlusion of an internal carotid artery.

There are certain sites of predilection in the formation of atheromatous plaques mostly where arteries branch or bifurcate. The most common sites are the origin of the internal carotid artery, the upper end of the vertebrals and the lower portion of the basilar, the stem of the middle cerebral, and the posterior cerebral though other vessels are also commonly affected. The plaques may ulcerate and the debris which collects, e.g. platelets, fibrin and cholesterol, may detach in the form of emboli and travel further afield to block smaller vessels.

The other common cause of cerebral embolism is from thrombi forming in the heart due to arrhythmias or myocardial infarction.

A dramatic embolic phenomenon is *amaurosis fugax.* The term literally means fleeting blindness and is most commonly due to emboli blocking retinal arterioles. The sudden transient loss is unilateral and often takes the characteristic form of a blind or curtain coming down (or ascending) over the visual field. The ensuing blindness may last up to five minutes but is often much shorter. Full vision is usually restored within 5–15 minutes often in a reverse manner from its onset. The emboli come most frequently from ulcerated plaques in the internal carotid artery (Glaser, 1978).

Cerebral haemorrhage

Bleeding within the cranial cavity may be due to a large number of causes (see Adams & Victor, 1977, p. 536). However, three conditions account for the majority of cases. In each condition the severity may vary from a small, almost symptomless bleed to a massive haemorrhage leading to sudden death.

1. *Hypertensive intracerebral haemorrhage.* This is the most common form of haemorrhage with extravasation or bursting out of blood into the substance or parenchyma of the cerebral hemisphere. The bleeding destroys brain tissue and if it continues, causes pressure effects on neighbouring tissue by compression or displacement. Large haemorrhages may so displace vital centres that they lead to death. Less serious pressure may

disrupt the function of adjacent or nearby tissue without destroying it and this accounts for the partial, though often considerable recovery of function after the acute stages. While the onset of symptoms is rapid, hence the term 'stroke', the full development of the clinical picture may take an appreciable time, sometimes hours, depending on the rate of bleeding and its final cessation. When bleeding stops there is no recurrence from the same site, a situation unlike that of bleeding from aneurysms. While the bleeding may commence in the brain's substance, it breaks into the ventricular system and thus into the cerebrospinal fluid in a high proportion of cases.

The brunt of symptomatology with intracerebral haemorrhage tends to be on neurological rather than behavioural features since the cortex is often relatively spared. Sites of primary haemorrhage in order of frequency are the basal ganglia, thalamus, cerebellar hemispheres, pons and subcortical areas. Haemorrhages arise mainly from the penetrating branches of the middle cerebral, posterior cerebral and basilar arteries.

2. *Ruptured aneurysm.* These thin-walled protrusions are most common on the vessels which form the arterial circle (circle of Willis) or their major branches. They are assumed to be developmental defects in the arterial walls and are prone to rupture. Over 90% are found on vessels of the internal carotid system, only a few on the vertebrobasilar system. The most frequent sites of rupture are the anterior communicating region and the middle cerebral bifurcation, accounting for nearly half the cases. Sometimes the aneurysms are multiple.

In rupturing, blood may be spurted into the subarachnoid space or into the adjacent brain substance producing an intracerebral haematoma. Bleeding into the cerebral substance is particularly prone to occur at the two most common locations mentioned. The territories of vessels in the areas often show infarction and this is possibly related to arterial vasospasm since at autopsy the vessels may be patent.

The clinical symptoms and signs are those related to blood under pressure in the subarachnoid space, usually excruciating headache and collapse followed in survivors by those of local disruption of function due to local pressure from extracerebral blood clot, intracerebral haemorrhage and infarction.

3. *Ruptured arteriovenous malformation (AVM).* These developmental malformations vary from a small localized abnormality of a few millimetres to a large mass of vessels occupying considerable space often in the form of a wedge extending from the cortex to the ventricle. The blood vessels forming the mass interposed between the feeding arteries and the draining veins are pathologically thin-walled and liable to rupture. Rupture of the larger malformations may produce intracerebral as well as subarachnoid bleeding. Like saccular aneurysms AVMs have a tendency to recurrent bleeding. Hydrocephalus is a complication in some cases. Symptoms and signs will thus be extremely varied.

Epilepsy

The term epilepsy means a seizure, i.e. a sudden disruption of the patient's senses and, because it manifests itself in a great variety of ways, it is difficult to define more clearly in a short space. The problem is aggravated by the vast array of terms which has been used to define the same or very similar conditions.

Clinical classification

In 1969, The Commission on Classification and Terminology of the International League Against Epilepsy introduced a classification which has received widespread though by no means universal support (Gastaut, 1970). More recently (1981) the Commission attempted to further refine this generally useful classification though there are those (e.g. Parsonage, 1983) who feel that the newer classification is premature and that the 1969 system should stand until we have considerably more knowledge.

The Commission recognized a distinction between *epileptic seizures* (Table 3.1) and *the epilepsies* (Table 3.2). For further detail readers are referred to general reviews (Gastaut & Broughton, 1972; Aird et al 1984).

Table 3.1   Types of epileptic seizures (Condensed from the international classification)

Generalized seizures (bilaterally symmetrical and without local onset)
  Tonic-clonic seizures (*grand mal*)
  Absences (*petit mal*)
  Other forms (includes akinetic, atonic, tonic, clonic, bilateral myoclonic etc.)
Partial seizures (seizures beginning locally)
  Partial seizures with elementary symptomology (generally without impairment of
    consciousness)
  With motor symptoms
  With sensory or somatosensory symptoms
  With autonomic symptoms
Partial seizures with complex symptomatology (generally with impairment of consciousness,
    temporal lobe or psychomotor seizures)
  With impairment of consciousness only
  With cognitive or affective or psychosensory or psychomotor symptomatology
Unilateral seizures
Unclassified

Table 3.2   International classification of the epilepsies

Generalized epilepsies
  Primary (includes petit mal and grand mal seizures)
  Secondary
  Undetermined
Partial (focal, local) epilepsies (includes jacksonian, temporal lobe and psychomotor
    seizures)
Unclasssified epilepsies

Generalized seizures

The principal feature of many generalized seizures is disordered muscular contraction. The term *tonic-clonic seizure* describes the two main phases of the paroxysm which were previously termed *grand mal* seizures. In the *tonic* phase the muscles contract and the subject falls to the ground. Contraction of respiratory muscles may produce a grunt or cry. Swallowing is lost and the patient becomes cyanosed from lack of oxygen. Contraction of muscles often produces incontinence of urine and, less commonly, of faeces. The *clonic* phase follows after a brief time (a few seconds to a minute) and is marked by rhythmic contractions of limb and trunk muscles. After a variable time the clonic phase ceases and the patient passes from stupor, then confusion to a normal conscious state. On some occasions one generalized seizure may follow another in rapid succession, the so-called *status epilepticus*.

Generalized seizures may be primary or may be precipitated from a localized focus. The primary form of epilepsy was often referred to as *centrencephalic* epilepsy. The term *centrencephalon* was introduced by Penfield to refer to those neural systems which are centrally placed in the upper brain stem and symmetrically connected with both cerebral hemispheres and which serve to co-ordinate their functions.

The second form is the *absence* formerly termed *petit mal* seizures. This is largely a disorder of childhood, its prolongation into adult life being rare. The attacks are characteristically brief, usually only a few seconds with an abrupt onset and termination. The patient's ongoing activity is disturbed

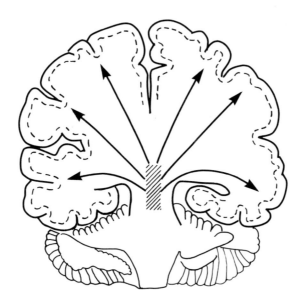

Fig. 3.10 Schematic representation of the spread of excitation from the centre of the brain.

with interruption of mental functions and sudden resumption of activity after the absence. The EEG shows a characteristic 'spike and wave' pattern both during the attacks and often bursts of such activity can be seen in the record even when no disturbance of ongoing activity is to be seen clinically. About one-third of children with absences also have tonic-clonic seizures.

Partial seizures

These seizures have also been termed focal seizures since they reflect a neuronal discharge which is more or less localized to one area of the brain. They are divided into two main types: those with elementary and those with complex symptomatology. The former type characteristically occur without any loss of consciousness while some impairment of the conscious state is found with complex partial seizures.

Simple partial seizures. Motor symptoms may take many forms and point to the localization mainly in portions of the region in front of the central or *rolandic fissure* though the focal abnormality may lie in the temporal or parietal region, e.g. when *dysphasia* is brought about by the epileptic or ictal discharge.

Sensory symptoms may take the form of any of the sense modalities, i.e. somatosensory phenomena or sensations referable to the special senses of vision, audition, and olfaction in particular. There may be a fine line between the designation of a symptom as a simple sensory seizure, a sensory illusion or even a sensory hallucination but a careful examination may be of value in localization. Patients differ a good deal in their ability to describe their symptoms and carefully phrased questions will help.

Symptoms of autonomic disturbance. These rarely occur without other symptoms.

Complex partial seizures. Since these seizures present so frequently with symptoms of disruption of higher mental functions, they have become of increasing interest to neuropsychologists.

Certain characteristics of the seizure may suggest that the focus of abnormal excitation lies in one of the neocortical association areas and so may be used as localizing signs. Frequently, the onset of the seizures or *aura* as it is usually called, is signalled by a subjective feeling or behaviour referable to a particular area and tables of the relation between the clinical type of seizure and localization have been in use for some time.

Though many attacks may recur frequently in the same manner in some patients, there are other cases where the initial warning symptoms or auras vary from one seizure to the next, so that care must be taken in using the signs and symptoms associated with any single attack as localizing indications.

Where the lesion is fairly well circumscribed, it may lend itself to surgical removal. This has been particularly successful in certain cases of lesions restricted to the temporal lobes where the removal of the temporal lobe (temporal lobectomy) may completely cure or greatly ameliorate the condition. The very frequent reference in the past two decades to studies of various higher functions in populations of temporal lobe epileptics before and after lobectomy makes it mandatory for the psychologist to have a clear understanding of the complex symptomatology of this group of seizures of which temporal lobe epilepsy forms an important part.

The portions of the cortex which may be involved in complex partial seizures are the frontal, temporal and parietal neo-cortex, and the subcortical structures associated with them. The clinical features which distinguish the subgroups mentioned below are often present in the same patient, either in the one attack or at different times and may be accompanied by impaired consciousness which may obscure the picture. The main types can be grouped as follows:

1. Cases where impairment of consciousness is the principal or even the sole symptom

2. Psychomotor attacks where the principal symptoms are confusion and automatic behaviour. Confusional automatisms may be merely a 'mechanical' prolongation of the behaviour in which the patient was engaged at the onset of the attack, or the automatisms may represent new behaviour beginning during the attack. Many forms of automatisms have been given descriptive labels, e.g. ambulatory automatisms in which the patient may carry out co-ordinated movements of some complexity during the attack and for a varying time after the seizure, verbal automatisms, gestural automatisms and the like.

3. Seizures with sensory illusions or hallucinations. The nature of these seizures varies with the region of cortex which is the site of discharge. Where the primary projection areas of the cortex are mainly affected, the phenomena are simpler sensory experiences or alteration of the perception of present stimuli, while excitation of the association areas appear to give rise to integrated perceptual experiences which, since they occur in the absence of appropriate stimuli in the environment, have earned the title hallucinations.

Once again, a careful examination of the patient's experience may point to the affected area. The illusions may be related to a specific sense modality, i.e. visual, auditory, olfactory, somaesthetic illusions, or, when the discharge affects the borderland between the parietal, temporal and occipital areas, compound illusions may result.

A special form of alteration in sense experience occurs with some temporal lobe seizures so that present experience is interpreted in a manner quite different from usual. New situations or objects may be perceived as having been seen or heard before (deja-vu, deja entendu) or familiar ones as not having been experienced before (jamais-vu, jamais-entendu).

An early description of an olfactory hallucination associated with a temporal lobe lesion was given by Hughlings Jackson (1890). The following account was provided by the patient and her sister.

The patient was a cook. In the paroxysm the first thing was tremor of the hands and arms; she saw a little black woman who was always very actively engaged in cooking; the spectre did not speak. The patient had a very horrible smell (so-called 'subjective sensation' of smell) which she could not describe . . . She had a feeling as if she was shut up in a box with a limited quantity of air . . . She would stand with her eyes fixed . . . and then say, 'What a horrible smell!'. The patient did not, so her sister reported, lose consciousness, but remembered everything that happened during the attack; she turned of a leaden colour. The patient told us that she passed her urine in the seizures. There was no struggling, and the tongue was not bitten. She never believed the spectre to be a real person.

After leaving her kitchen work she had paroxysms with the smell sensation but no spectre. At autopsy a tumour 'the size of a tangerine orange' was found occupying the anterior portion of the temporal lobe.

4. Some partial seizures may produce sudden alteration in the emotional state usually in the form of fear.

5. Disturbances of memory and thought processes may occur during temporal lobe seizures.

Finally, it is common for simple symptomatology to be followed by the more complex or there may be an admixture of both. Temporal lobe epilepsy is discussed in more detail in Chapter 5.

Partial seizures may at times progress to generalized seizures (Fig. 3.11).

Unilateral seizures

In this type of disorder the discharge, while spread over a wide area, is restricted to one hemisphere and demonstrates itself by clinical phenomena

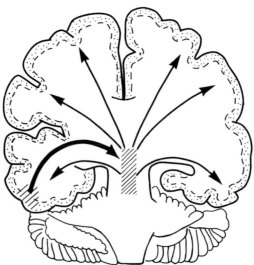

Fig. 3.11 Temporal lobe focus giving rise to a generalized seizure.

on the opposite (*contralateral*) side of the body. The excessive neuronal discharge causing the seizure, may arise in the (*centrencephalon*) whence it spreads exclusively or mainly to the hemisphere on one side or the discharge may originate in a local region of the cerebral cortex of one hemisphere and spread to the centrencephalon from which it projects in turn to the whole of that hemisphere.

The reason for considering these unilateral seizures as separate from partial seizures, is that there are no signs in the periods between the seizures of clinical or EEG features of localized brain damage and such seizures may alternate from side to side from one attack to another, or even during the course of a single attack. As with generalized seizures, unilateral seizures have been classified into a number of subtypes according to the symptomatology.

DISRUPTION OF HIGHER CEREBRAL FUNCTIONS

The following section presents an outline of the disorders of higher mental functions which have formed the focus of the bulk of recent neuropsychological studies in man. They are reviewed here in general terms only, each topic being dealt with in greater detail in the remainder of the text. The localization of lesions which produce aphasia is covered in detail in several chapters of Kertesz (1983) while a concise and very clear account of the various forms of language disorder can be found in Benson (1979).

Aphasia

The term aphasia refers to an impairment in the reception or manipulation or expression of the symbolic content of language due to organic brain damage. Such definitions normally exclude perceptual, learning and memory difficulties and purely sensory or motor deficits unless they specifically involve language symbols.

Speech difficulties due to interference with the peripheral speech mechanisms, larynx, pharynx, and tongue are termed *dysarthria*.

In general, the various forms of aphasia develop as a result of lesions in the so-called dominant hemisphere.

The importance of aphasia lies in its great localizing value in diagnosis and no neuropsychological examination is complete without a careful examination of the patient's language functions. More recently, and perhaps more correctly, the term *dysphasia* has been used to denote any disorder, however mild, of the patient's normal symbolic function.

Aphasic disturbances have usually been classified under two principal headings: (i) Expressive or motor aphasia, and (ii) Receptive or sensory aphasia.

Expressive aphasia or Broca's aphasia generally results from a lesion in the posterior part of the inferior frontal convolution (Fig. 3.12) though

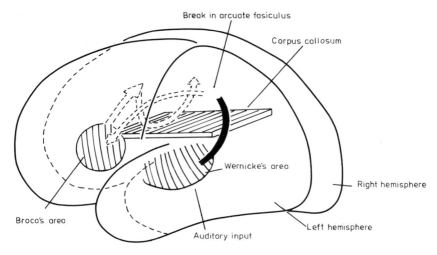

Fig. 3.12 Conduction aphasia due to a lesion disrupting the arcuate fasciculus.

cases have been reported where complete removal of Broca's area has led to only transient dysphasia. The disability may vary from a complete loss of speech to a mild deficit in which the patient's sole difficulty may be in finding the appropriate word. Where the difficulty is great, the patient may become extremely distressed and the examination of the aphasic patient is never an easy task. With the less severe disability, the patient's language may be characterized by a restriction in the range of his vocabulary, and he may use words repetitively with long pauses between words or phrases.

The dramatic quality of certain symptoms in individual patients has led some authors to give a variety of different descriptive labels to a large number of aphasias. More systematic study in recent decades has emphasised the fact that aphasia may show itself in various guises but that pure forms of any of the many aphasias described in the earlier literature are extremely rare, and some may be a function of the author's abstracting an entity and giving it a name. This is not to imply that a careful detailed analysis of the language disturbance should not be carried out, rather that we should not continue to multiply labels which have little or no implications for the nature or location of lesions which produce the disabilities or the types of treatment that might be employed to assist patients with these difficulties.

Since it is true only in the broad sense that in expressive aphasia understanding of language through the auditory and visual modalities is retained, it follows that careful examination will often demonstrate that such patients will have difficulty in understanding language as well as expressing it.

Patients with expressive aphasia often have difficulty with grammatical construction and tend to use sentences of very simple structure with a predominance of nouns and verbs and a paucity of adjectives and adverbs which gives their speech a telegraphic style. This disorder is referred to as *agrammatism*.

It has been commonly believed that in persons who have learned more than one language, the more recently acquired patterns of speech are more readily disturbed than speech in their native tongue. While this may occur on some occasions it is usually true that in aphasia all the patient's languages are equally impaired. This misconception rests in many cases on the examiner's own lack of fluency in the other language so that he fails to recognize the extent of the deficit. The use of an intelligent interpreter in doubtful cases is essential since the alterations of language may be of a subtle nature and thus may not be evident in simple conversation.

The expressive difficulty may also extend to written language where the expressive aphasic patient will show the same difficulty he shows in verbal expression. On rare occasions this *dysgraphia* has been described in cases with no obvious difficulties of verbal expression. The second frontal gyrus has been implicated in some of these cases (Aimard, et al., 1975).

Receptive aphasia (Sensory aphasia) generally results from a lesion in the region of Wernicke's area of the dominant hemisphere (Fig. 3.12). The prime difficulty is a loss of understanding of the spoken word and often of the written word as well. Thus, two major forms of sensory aphasia may be separated, an auditory-receptive aphasia usually related to lesions in the superior temporal convolution, and a visual-receptive aphasia related to more posteriorly placed parietotemporal lesions.

Patients with *auditory receptive aphasia* have trouble in understanding what is said to them. The problem is due to a failure in comprehension since auditory acuity as tested by audiometry remains adequate. The common presence of expressive difficulties as well in these patients again points to the undesirability of retaining rigid categories of classification.

Unlike the patient with expressive aphasia, the sensory aphasic's verbalizations may be fluent and, in fact, he may be unusually voluble. However, he uses language ungrammatically and often unintelligibly. Since he is not capable of monitoring his own verbal expression due to his difficulty in auditory comprehension, he may be unaware of the inappropriateness of his utterances. Verbal confusion and the substitution of wrong words or phrases (*paraphasia*) may result in a very disjointed form of speech disorder termed *jargon aphasia*.

In *visual-receptive aphasia* the understanding of written language is impaired. This difficulty is referred to as *alexia* (or *dyslexia*), or sometimes word blindness. While the patient may be able to identify individual letters, he is unable to perceive words as meaningful wholes. Alexia may occur together with difficulty in recognizing objects under the syndrome of *visual object agnosia*. On the other hand, a syndrome of alexia without agraphia has long been recognized. Sometimes the alexia is also accompanied by a failure to name colours (*colour anomia*) and the ability to read numbers may be preserved while the ability to read letters and words is lost. Geschwind's

(1965a) masterly analysis of the syndrome of alexia without agraphia forms a fine example of the use of the concept of the disconnection syndrome in analysing disorders of higher ortical processes (Ch. 7). It utilizes Wernicke's notion of the importance of the connections between different parts of the brain in the building up of complex activities. An example of the disconnection syndrome as the anatomical basis of the aphasias concludes this section.

Global or mixed aphasia refers to cases where there are both expressive and receptive elements present. These cases are usually severe in their symptoms and present extensive lesions on pathological examination.

Amnestic, amnesic, or nominal aphasia is characterized by the patient's inability to identify people or objects by their proper names. If shown a hairbrush the patient will be unable to evoke the name 'brush' though he will demonstrate both with words and actions that he is well aware of the nature of the object and will recognize the correct word when it is given to him. This ability to recognize the correct word when it is provided is not seen in patients with receptive aphasia. This form of aphasia is quite different from expressive aphasia. It does not have a precise localization though the lesion is usually behind the central sulcus.

It is the association between the object and its particular noun that is lost. If the deficit is marked, speech may be greatly reduced. When unable to find the correct word the patient may substitute colloquialisms and employ circumlocutions and periphrastic expressions to convey his meaning.

Some authors consider amnestic aphasia to be essentially a form of sensory or receptive aphasia and the responsible lesion is usually found in the posterior region of the superior temporal convolution on the dominant side.

The anatomical disconnection model. Geschwind (1969) has extended the anatomical model, first put forward by Wernicke, to provide understanding of the various forms of aphasia.

1. With a lesion in Wernicke's area, incoming auditory information will not be understood and since a lesion in this region interrupts the passage of visual information travelling forward from the visual association cortex, isolating this information from the anterior speech area, the patient will be unable to describe in words what he sees. Furthermore, since visual forms no longer arouse auditory ones because of the disconnection he no longer understands written language.

2. A lesion in the principal connecting link between the comprehension area and the expressive area, the *arcuate fasciculus*, leads to abnormality in speech with the preservation of comprehension of both written and spoken speech. Such a disorder is termed *conduction aphasia* (Fig. 3.12). Since Wernicke's area is intact the patient can understand what is said to him. On the other hand with Broca's area also intact he will be able to speak spontaneously. The speech is often copious but is abnormal because of the isolation between the two major areas. However, since the connection has

been broken between the receptive area and the motor speech area he will be unable to repeat what the examiner says to him. This disproportionate difficulty in repetition is said to be the principal characteristic of this disorder.

Furthermore, in order for the patient to carry out movements on command the information needs to go forward from Wernicke's area to the motor area and so the patient is unable to carry out such commands. As the pathway in the diagram shows, a lesion in the arcuate fasciculus will lead to bilateral difficulty in carrying out verbal commands since these are prevented from reaching the appropriate motor areas of either hemisphere.

3. When a lesion damages the left visual cortex and the posterior portion of the corpus callosum known as the splenium, the patient is still able to see stimuli in the left visual field corresponding to the intact right visual cortex though not in the right visual field. However, the information perceived by the right hemisphere can no longer reach the left hemisphere language areas so that the patient cannot understand written language though, with the preservation of both Broca's and Wernicke's areas he can both comprehend and speak spontaneously. This disorder is termed pure alexia or agnosic alexia.

4. Sometimes even extensive lesions in the hemispheres may spare both Broca's and Wernicke's areas, isolating them from the rest of the brain. Speech production and comprehension are both impaired but the ability to repeat spoken words is preserved. Such a disability is termed *transcortical aphasia*.

Further examples of the use of the anatomical model are given elsewhere and despite limitations this model 'most closely meets the criteria of efficiency in explaining the known data, efficiency in predicting new phenomena, or in design of important experiments and susceptibility to refinements that can be checked by observation or experiment' (Geschwind, 1969). Modern imaging techniques have lent support to the 'classical' anatomical theory (Kertesz, 1979, 1983).

Agnosia

It is a useful generalization to consider all the cortical territory behind the central sulcus as being concerned with getting to know the world around us. In line with the early name for the central sulcus — the fissure of Rolando — lesions in this region are still frequently referred to as retro-rolandic lesions. In Luria's terms (Luria, 1973b) this is the second major unit of the higher nervous system, the one concerned with the reception, analysis and storage of information. It is divided into three major types of cortex. Firstly, primary projection areas which are modality-specific, i.e. serve only one sense modality such as vision, audition, or bodily sensation. Each of these areas is laid out in a somatotopic manner as described in Chapter 2. Secondly, projection-association cortex which is adjacent to a

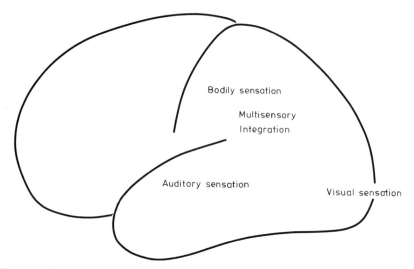

Fig. 3.13 The posterior or *retrorolandic* cortex and sensory systems.

primary projection area and, while still concerned with only one sensory mode, organizes the incoming information with the integration of information from all sensory channels and, in this integrative sense, is supramodal. This cortex, which is specific to man, is found at the confluence of the parietal, temporal, and occipital areas in the region of the supramarginal gyrus. The major divisions of the postcentral or retrorolandic cortex are shown in Figure 3.13.

Lesions of the postcentral area will give rise to simple or complex sensory or perceptual disturbances, and will affect one or more modalities, according to their location. Since, with the possible exception of some penetrating missile wounds, cerebral lesions are seldom discrete, individual cases will usually show a mixture of symptoms.

Agnosia refers to a failure to recognize familiar objects perceived via the senses where the inability does not rest on sensory impairment, intellectual deterioration or other cause. Where it is associated with only one modality, e.g. visual agnosia, an object may be recognized through other senses such as touch, or a person may not be recognized until he speaks.

The many types or forms of agnosia reported in the medical literature are probably not separate entities and the difficulties raised by the multiplication of labels mentioned above with regard to aphasia applies equally well here. The very concept of agnosia has been attacked by a number of workers. However, the term is so common that the following notes on the various described forms may familiarize the beginning student with the terminology likely to be encountered.

Auditory agnosia is the term used to refer to the inability to recognize speech. The failure to recognize melodies is referred to as *amusia*. A careful analysis by Vignolo and others of patients' difficulties with different types of auditory material has led to a valuable distinction between semantic-associative difficulties on one hand, and auditory discriminative difficulties on the other (Ch. 5). As these difficulties show double dissociation with respect to the left and right temporal lobes, they should prove of value as a diagnostic aid. Both forms of auditory agnosia occur without audiometric loss.

Visual agnosia has been classified according to the class of visual perceptual material with which the patient has difficulty. There may be *visual object agnosia* where the patient without disturbances of visual acuity or visual field defects fails to recognize the object for what it is, or he may be unable to recognize pictorial representations of objects. The patient can see individual features but he 'cannot combine these individual features into complete forms' (Luria, 1973b, p. 116). Visual object agnosia is a rare clinical entity. However, the careful examination of a case by Taylor and Warrington (1971) showed clear-cut dissociation between primary apprehension of the object via the visual modality (apperception) and the association of the object with meaning. This is close to the distinction made by Hebb some years ago between figural unity and figural identity (Hebb, 1949).

A particular difficulty in recognizing familiar faces is referred to as *prosopagnosia*. The patient may not only fail to recognize familiar faces such as those of his wife and children, he may be unable to recognize his own reflection in the mirror. There may be *agnosia for colours* which, when associated with dyslexia has special localizing significance. These and other visual agnosias are treated in Chapter 7.

Spatial agnosia. This form of disorder is sometimes referred to as visual or spatial disorientation. The patient is unable to find his way around in a familiar environment such as his own district or even his own home though he may recognize separate objects in the home quite well. There may also be defects in visual and topographical memory so that patients with this disorder are unable to find their way on a map or if asked to draw a map will produce one with topographical distortions and omissions.

Tactile agnosia or *astereognosis* refers to inability to recognize objects by feeling them. The relation of tactile agnosia to sensory defects is discussed in relation to lesions of the parietal lobes in Chapter 6.

The neglect syndrome

Subsumed under this term are a number of clinical presentations which have received increased attention in recent years (for review see Heilman et al, 1985). 'A patient with the neglect syndrome fails to report, respond, or orient to novel or meaningful stimuli presented to the side opposite a brain lesion' (Heilman, 1979a).

Four major forms can be distinguished:

1. *Unilateral spatial neglect*, also termed *hemispatial neglect, hemispatial*

agnosia, and *visuospatial agnosia*. When asked to perform tasks in space patients neglect the half of space contralateral to the lesion, e.g. when asked to bisect a line they may neglect the presence of one side and thus move their bisection point some distance to the side of the lesion or they may fail to cross out lines on one side of a page which has lines scattered randomly over it (Albert, 1973). In everyday life patients with neglect may fail to eat food on one side of the plate and bump into objects to one side which they appear not to notice. This topic is dealt with in Chapter 6.

2. *Hemi-inattention* overlaps with the former description and refers to a failure to report stimuli of various kinds presented unilaterally. Obviously it may be difficult to distinguish unilateral inattention from hemianopia or hemianaesthesia (i.e. loss of the visual half field, or loss of sensation on one side of the body). However, the subject with hemi-inattention may be able to detect the stimulus with relative ease if attention is directed specifically to its presence.

3. *Sensory inattention*, *sensory extinction*, *sensory suppression*, or *perceptual rivalry* denotes a failure to appreciate a stimulus when a similar stimulus is applied to a corresponding part of the body or to both halves of the visual field simultaneously. The patient is quite able to see and recognize things in any part of the visual field when they are presented alone or to report a tactile stimulus from either side of the body. It is only when the stimuli are presented simultaneously that the disorder comes to light. The method is termed *Double Simultaneous Stimulation*. The inattention is for the stimulus opposite the side of the lesion. This phenomenon has been reviewed by Critchley (1949), Bender (1952) and Denny-Brown, Meyer and Horenstein (1952) and has the object of numerous studies in the past decades. These attest to the existence of the phenomena in a wide variety of sense modalities, e.g. vision, audition, pain, touch, temperature, pressure, taste, kinesthesis and vibration. The range of explanations is almost as wide ranging as the phenomena themselves.

4. Some patients with unilateral lesions may show a slowing of movement or an inability or delay in initiating movement of the limb contralateral to the lesion a condition called *akinesia*. Attempts at bilateral movement may worsen the contralateral limb akinesia a condition akin to sensory extinction and actually termed 'motor extinction' by Valenstein and Heilman (1981).

Body agnosia

Body agnosia, corporeal agnosia, or *autotopagnosia* is a lack of awareness of the body's topography, an inability to recognize or localize parts of the patient's own body. A special form of autotopagnosia is *finger agnosia* where the patient cannot point to, or show the examiner the various fingers of each hand. It forms one of the four classical features of Gerstmann's syndrome which, because of its important bearing on the notion of cerebral dominance or lateralization is discussed at length in Chapter 8. Body agnosia is also often associated with lack of awareness of disease or disability known as *anosognosia*, e.g. the patient fails to perceive or denies that his arm and leg are paralysed.

Discussion of other disorders of the body schema may be found in Frederiks (1985).

Apraxia

Apraxia is the inability to carry out purposive or skilled acts due to brain damage and which does not result from the numerous other reasons which may result in imperfectly executed movements, e.g. failure to comprehend what to do, weakness or paralysis, or sensory loss. Prior to the work of Liepmann, this disorder was thought to be secondary to agnosia. It is now recognized as a pure entity with a number of subsidiary forms, the principal ones of which are (i) motor or kinetic apraxia, (ii) ideomotor or ideokinetic apraxia, (iii) ideational apraxia and (iv) constructional apraxia. Perhaps nowhere else in the realm of neuropsychological disorders has classification been so confusing (see Heilman, 1983; Geschwind & Damasio, 1985). Apraxia is seen most often with lesions of the left hemisphere and is therefore often associated with aphasia. Furthermore, two or more forms of apraxia may co-exist in the same patient.

Motor apraxia is believed to be due to loss of the kinesthetic memory patterns or engrams necessary for the performance of the skilled act. This form of apraxia usually affects the finer movements of one upper extremity, movements such as doing up buttons, opening a safety pin, placing a letter in an envelope. Where there is associated weakness, the clumsiness of the movement is out of all proportion to the loss of power. This form of apraxia usually results from a lesion of the precentral gyrus contralateral to the side of the body affected.

Ideomotor apraxia is a condition in which the patient finds it difficult to carry out an action on verbal command with either hand but may do so automatically or almost fortuitously. He is usually unable to imitate actions that are demonstrated to him. The kinetic engram is preserved but is not available to the patient's voluntary recall. This form of apraxia is usually associated with a lesion in the posterior part of the left or dominant hemisphere particularly in the region of the supramarginal gyrus.

The concept of the disconnection syndrome is also useful in understanding the anatomical basis of the apraxias. In the case of carrying out a skilled movement on verbal command there is a complex chain of events. Firstly, the auditory information is organized in Wernicke's area, i.e. the left superior temporal region if we are considering a right handed patient. From here the information travels to the motor association cortex in the frontal lobe and thence to the motor cortex which sends impulses to the appropriate muscle groups on the right side of the body to execute the command. If the patient is asked to carry out the action with his left hand,

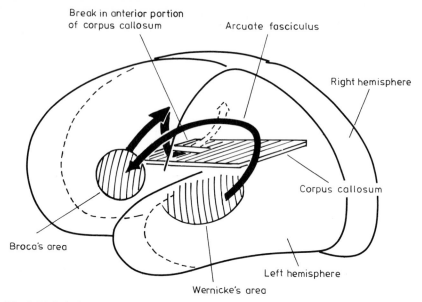

Fig. 3.14 Left-sided or callosal apraxia produced by an anterior lesion of the corpus callosum.

the sequence will have to be the same with the important addition that the information will have to travel from the left motor association area to that on the right since the right motor region commands the left hand. Consequently, a lesion of the anterior part of the corpus callosum, which carries these fibres between the left and right hemispheres, will render the patient incapable of carrying out verbal commands with his left hand while he is still able to carry them out with his right (Fig. 3.14). This disorder has been termed *left-sided apraxia, unilateral limb apraxia,* or *callosal apraxia.* In essence it is a unilateral ideomotor apraxia.

Ideational apraxia is the difficulty in executing the correct sequence of steps which makes up a complex act though the individual component acts may be carried out successfully. It is a disruption of the total programme of the required acts. Patients may show no difficulty in imitating sequences, i.e. where the programme is provided for them. The disorder may look like an extreme absent mindedness. It is often associated with difficulty in using objects correctly. The patient seems to be unaware of what the object was designed to do, akin to an agnosia of utilization. Ideational apraxia is associated with widespread bilateral lesions.

Constructional apraxia is a disorder of praxis which has received much more attention from neuropsychologists in recent years than the three major forms already outlined. Perhaps the major difference between constructional apraxia and other forms of praxic disorder is that special tests, albeit simple, are usually necessary to elicit it, while other forms are clinically apparent. With constructional apraxia the patient is unable to put together parts to make a whole. A detailed account of methods of testing for constructional apraxia is given by Critchley (1953) and recent reviews by Warrington (1969) and Benton (1969a) examine all aspects of the disorder and its implications for localization. The deficit is discussed later in relation to parietal lobe dysfunction (Ch. 6). A few examples of the patient's difficulties will suffice here.

On block design tests such as that of the Wechsler Adult Intelligence Scale (Wechsler, 1958) patients often have difficulty with the earliest and simplest designs and generally perform at a much lower level than other patients on this test. A poor level of performance on block design tests is not pathognomonic of the disorder since many patients with lesions in various parts of the brain will perform poorly on this test for a variety of reasons. However, an examination of the quality of performance shows that patients with constructional apraxia have a greater number of constructional deviations in their attempts (Ben-Yishay, Diller & Mandleberg, 1971). Simple drawing tests such as copying geometric designs of varying complexity (Benton, 1962) or drawing common objects such as a house will elicit the difficulty though more complex tasks such as constructing a copy of a three dimensional model with blocks may have to be employed (Benton & Fogel, 1962).

Dressing apraxia denotes the condition where the patient is unable to clothe himself properly, more commonly leaving the left side partly or wholly unclad. It appears to be a reflection of the patient's neglect of part of his body mentioned above and is seen more frequently with parietal lesions of the non-dominant hemisphere. It should be considered as part of the neglect syndrome rather than as a disorder of skilled movement.

Though apraxia may be seen in isolation it often accompanies other defects such as agnosia, dysphasia, and impairment of memory, and, despite the separation used here it may be difficult to decide in individual patients how much the defect of action is due to a lack of awareness, a lack of skilled movements, or some degree of weakness or ataxia of the affected limb.

Amnesia

Memory disorders are a frequent accompaniment of cerebral disorders and have given rise to countless studies reported in the literature. An overall review such as that of Whitty and Zangwill (1977) can be updated from the major specialist journals in neuropsychology.

Terminology

Clinical reports often refer to two principal terms which have derived from the study of memory disorders following cerebral insult. *Anterograde amnesia* is characterized by an inability to retain (or at least report spontaneously) ongoing events. It is synonymous with a new learning difficulty. Material which is clearly apprehended as measured by the ability of the patient to repeat it immediately cannot be reported a short time later. It is common after cerebral trauma for this condition to improve with the passage of time but lesions in certain anatomical sites may lead to a lasting memory impairment. *Retrograde amnesia* refers to the difficulty in recalling events which occurred, prior to the injury. With the passing of time retrograde amnesia shrinks so that while a few days after the injury patients may not recall events that happened weeks or even months before, they may be able to recall events much closer to the injury some time later so that the gap left in their memory may be very short.

Post-traumatic amnesia (PTA) is the period from the time of injury to the time when the patient begins to report ongoing events, i.e. when anterograde amnesia stops. Its duration has been used as a guide to the severity of the damage, the longer the period of PTA the more severe the damage is likely to be although there are some striking exceptions (for further discussion, see Walsh, 1985).

Types of memory disorder

Amnesic syndromes may accompany neurological or psychological disorders, they may be transient or lasting, and they may be specific or general.

Two major forms of memory disturbance of a non-organic nature are *hysterical fugue* and *psychogenic amnesia*. A hysterical fugue consists of a series of events whereby the patient often may remove himself from his current situation, *which is almost invariably disagreeable*, and move to another. This may involve travel to distant parts and even a change from a customary occupation. The behaviour is often described as a dissociation and the patient may appear to be unaware of his past while in the fugue state, i.e. he has a total amnesia and on return to his 'former self' will be amnesic for the period occupied by the fugue. Behaviour appears to be fairly well integrated and consistent in each of the states.

Less striking memory disorders may appear as the sole complaint in other neurotic disorders particularly those termed sick role enactments (Walsh, 1985). Such *psychogenic amnesias* or pseudoneurological amnesias may mimic those of a neurological aetiology but will be differentiated by their lack of concordance with the characteristics of the organic varieties.

Of the neurological amnesic disorders some are transient while others are lasting. *Transient global amnesia* (TGA) was the term used by Fisher and Adams (1964) for a sudden loss or difficulty with memory unaccompanied by any major neurological signs followed shortly after by a return of normal memory function. Characteristically, the period extends over several hours and the patient is permanently amnesic for the duration of the attack. The aetiology, while commonly assumed to be vascular in origin, is by no means clear. Further comment on this condition appears in Chapter 5 and Caplan (1985) has provided a recent review.

Lasting amnesia is much more common than TGA and may be divided into general and specific amnesic disorders.

The principal lasting amnesic syndrome is called by a number of names. Where the unqualified term *the amnesic syndrome* is used in the literature this can be taken to be synonymous with the general amnesic syndrome described by Korsakoff. A translation of his classic paper of 1887 was published by Victor and Yakovlev (1955).

Korsakoff's amnesic syndrome shows (i) an almost complete inability to learn new material despite, (ii) an adequate immediate memory as tested by repetition, with (iii) retrograde amnesia, and (iv) preservation of early established skills and habits. Detailed description of the general amnesic syndrome and its congeners appears at the end of Chapter 5.

While the characteristic pathology of the general amnesic syndrome is bilateral damage to certain structures around the central core or axis of the brain, *material specific amnesias* are caused by *unilateral* lesions. The crucial areas are the same structures which are affected in general amnesic syndromes namely parts of the hippocampus-fornix-mamillary body complex (Fig. 3.15). However, the amnesia is restricted to one class of material, either verbal or nonverbal, and this follows the rule of hemispheric specialization of function. Dominant hemisphere lesions affect verbal memory but spare the nonverbal while non-dominant lesions produce the reverse pattern. Again, these material specific amnesias are discussed further in Chapter 5.

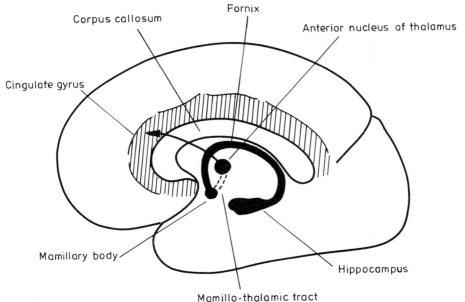

Fig. 3.15 Hippocampus-fornix-mamillary body complex.

Dementia

Dementia is a generic term which refers to a complex set of changes of known or unknown aetiology which are reflected in widespread dissolution of human mental capabilities and social functions. 'The presence of dementia should be suspected whenever mental changes of insidious onset emerge without sufficient situational stress and gradually interfere with the daily living activities that are appropriate for age and background. Dementia can be reversible or irreversible, precipitously progressive or indolent, bristling with multiple cognitive deficits, or characterized almost exclusively by disturbances of affect, motivation, and personality' (Mesulam, 1985 p. 2559).

The dementias have been divided into primary types due to parenchymatous cerebral degeneration and secondary types associated with known conditions. The secondary dementias may be further divided into those associated with systemic or neurological disease. In the primary type, of which Alzheimer's disease is by far the most common, the dementia is the only evidence of disease, while in the secondary type features of neurological or other systemic disorder may manifest themselves before the onset of intellectual decline. Many of the causes of dementia can now be identified (Table 3.3).

Table 3.3   Diagnosis in 417 patients fully evaluated for dementia (from Wells, 1979)

Diagnosis	
Dementia of unknown cause	47.7
Alcoholic dementia	10.0
Multi-infarct dementia	9.4
Normal pressure hydrocephalus	6.0
Intracranial masses	4.8
Huntington's chorea	2.9
Drug toxicity	2.4
Post-traumatic	1.7
Other identified diseases	6.7
Pseudodementia	6.7
Uncertain 1.7	1.7

A detailed discussion of the neuropsychology of intellectual decline is outside the scope of the present volume. Further material is presented in the companion volume (Walsh, 1985).

4

The frontal lobes

Anatomy and functional organization   117
The frontal lobe controversy   122
The frontal lobe syndrome   126
Psychosurgery   158
The frontal lobes and personality   161
Cognitive changes with modified leucotomy   164
Frontal lobe syndrome: one or many?   168

ANATOMY AND FUNCTIONAL ORGANIZATION

The frontal lobes are the most recently developed parts of the brain. In man they make up about one-third of the mass of the cerebral hemispheres. It is only in the past three decades or so that we have begun to come to an understanding of the basic role which the frontal lobes play in many forms of human behaviour especially with regard to the regulation of complex activities. Much of this work has been greatly advanced by Aleksandr Luria and his Russian colleagues and the brief summary in this section owes much to this source (Luria, 1969, 1973a, 1973b). Other contributions are dealt with in later sections of this chapter.

The frontal lobes lie anterior to the central sulcus and may be subdivided into four major subdivisions: (i) the motor area which occupies the precentral gyrus; (ii) the premotor area which lies anterior to the motor area and includes Brodmann's area 6 and part of area 8; (iii) the prefrontal area (9, 10, 45, 46); (iv) the basomedial portion of the lobes (9 to 13, 24, 32). These latter two divisions are often considered together as one 'prefrontal' region.

A specialized area termed the *frontal eye field* is situated in the middle zone of the dorsolateral surface taking in prefrontal as well as premotor cortex (parts of areas, 9, 8, and 6; Fig. 4.1). Stimulation, particularly in area 8, causes eye movements most often to the contralateral side. The area is thought to be the mediator of voluntary and involuntary eye movements and it is strategically situated to receive information from the prefrontal (planning) cortex for relay to the motor system.

117

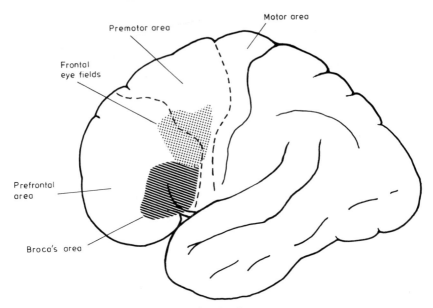

Fig. 4.1 Dorsolateral frontal cortex with functional areas.

In Chapter 2 mention was made of the study of cytoarchitecture. This leads to a distinction in terminology which is often used in relation to the frontal regions. Some anatomists have grouped the finer subdivisions of cytoarchitecture as depicted by workers such as Brodmann into a small number of fundamental types which share common characteristics. Departure from the 'typical' six-layered cortex allows a broad division first of all into cortex in which the granular layers (layers II and IV) are well represented or markedly absent. Cortex termed *agranular cortex* shows a lack of granular layers II and IV whereas layers III and V are very well developed. This agranular cortex is seen in the posterior parts of the frontal lobes anterior to the central sulcus and is characteristic of the motor cortex. Areas 4 and 6 together with portions of Brodmann's areas 8 and 44 belong to this type. Anterior to this the cortex may be divided into a number of fundamental types but as the granular layers are present in varying degree it might loosely be characterized as frontal granular cortex. This term gave its name to a symposium in 1964 and studies of frontal granular cortex might be said to be concerned with those frontal lobe functions which are not purely motor. The relative development of this type of cortex in different species is shown in Figure 4.2.

The frontal regions have well-developed systems of efferent nerve cells leading from the cortex to lower brain centres and peripheral parts of the nervous system. The efferent projections from the frontal areas pass to the ventral and dorsomedial nuclei of the thalamus as well as to numerous other structures (Fig. 4.3). Afferent fibres reach the frontal cortex over the thalamo-frontal radiation (Fig. 4.4).

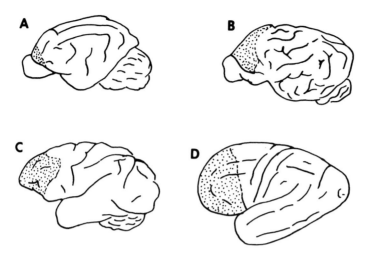

Fig. 4.2 Frontal granular cortex. A, cat; B, dog; C, Rhesus monkey; D, man. (Not drawn to scale).

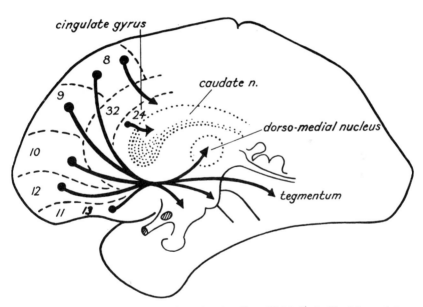

Fig. 4.3 Efferent connections in the frontal region (from Walsh E. G. Physiology of the nervous system (Courtesy of Churchill Livingstone). Figure has been modified by Le Gros Clark, the Lancet, 1948; by courtesy of the editors).

Parallel to his division of the posterior zones into primary (sensory), secondary (association), and tertiary (supramodal or integrative) cortex, Luria perceives the organization of the frontal regions in a similar hierarchical arrangement, viz. motor cortex, premotor cortex (motor organization), and prefrontal cortex (higher integration). This leads to the concept

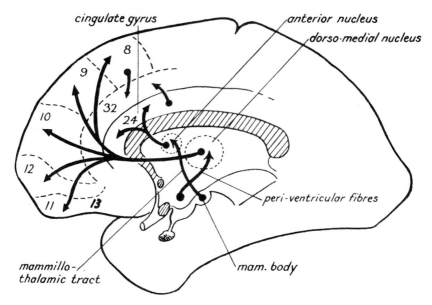

Fig. 4.4 Afferent connections in the frontal region (from Walsh E. G. Physiology of the nervous system. Figure has been modified from Le Gros Clark, the Lancet, 1948; courtesy of the editors).

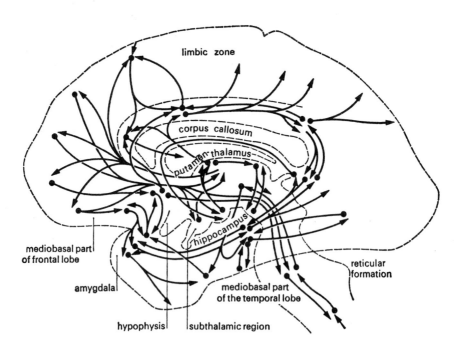

Fig. 4.5 Complete ramification of frontal lobe connections (In: Luria A. R. 1973 The working brain. Allen Lane Penguin after Polyakov; courtesy of VAAP, Moscow, USSR)

of two types of syndrome (i) premotor and (ii) prefrontal. This chapter is principally concerned with the latter.

Luria also points out that the prefrontal regions serve as tertiary zones for the limbic system as well as the motor system. They have rich connections with (i) the upper parts of the brain stem and thalamus and (ii) all other cortical zones. The richness of these connections is shown in Figure 4.5. Through the first set of connections the prefrontal areas particularly the basal and medial aspects of the lobes are intimately concerned with the state of alertness of the organism while the rich connections with the posterior receptor areas and motor cortex allow the lateral prefrontal regions to organize and execute the most complex of man's goal-directed or purposive activities.

From a clinical point of view the division of prefrontal cortex into lateral and basomedial (orbitomedial) regions may serve as a useful first approximation in the search for brain-behaviour relationships. This would accord well with the known projections from the thalamus. The medial part of the dorsomedial nucleus projects to the ventromedial aspects of the prefrontal cortex while the lateral part projects to the dorsolateral aspect.

In the lateral (convexity) portions of the frontal lobes the character of the disturbances alters according to the placement of the lesions in the antero-posterior direction. With posterior frontal lesions adjacent to the motor cortex the disturbances are those of the organization of movements. As the lesions move forward they lead firstly to the disintegration of motor programmes and then to a disturbance of comparison of motor behaviour with its original plan. This latter disruption reminds us that not only must a programme of movement be organized and initiated, it must also be continuously monitored and necessary adjustments made in the light of feedback from the activity for the sequence to be smooth and effective. 'All these disturbances are particularly marked in patients with lesions of the lateral zones of the left (dominant) frontal lobe which are closely connected with the cerebral organization of speech, and the disorganization of *speech activity* and of those *behavioural acts* which are especially dependent upon the participation of speech for their regulation' (Luria, 1973b, p. 222).

Speech disorders are particularly associated with lesions of the lower parts of the lateral cortex of the dominant hemisphere. Disturbance of speech from lesions of the posterior inferior area (Broca's area) is termed motor or expressive aphasia. Though the term *Broca's area* has been widely used it is impossible to define its limits precisely from the early descriptions and material of Broca. It approximates Brodmann's area 44 and part of 45.

There are other speech disturbances of a more subtle nature found with lesions anterior to Broca's area which are seen in patients who are not considered clinically to be suffering from aphasia. Reference is made to these in later parts of this chapter. Luria includes the following in such disorders of the left inferolateral frontal cortex: (i) inability to make a spontaneous discursive statement; (ii) difficulty in expressing a thought in discursive speech and (iii) 'verbal adynamia' or 'frontal dynamic aphasia' (see below).

In the other major functional subdivision, the basomedial frontal cortex, the disorders are related to the state of activation of the subject and his affective responses. Luria (1973a, 1973b) pointed to the research of the British and Russian workers on 'expectancy waves' in the electroencephalogram which, together with other evidence, shows 'that the frontal parts of the brain-cortex play an essential role in the regulation of the state of activation that arises as a result of some task given to the subject' (Luria 1973b, p. 6.). Extensive experience with psychosurgical lesions isolating the basomedial areas has confirmed earlier thought that these areas are concerned with the emotional life of the individual and with the control of inhibitions. A complete account of the functional anatomy of the prefrontal cortex is given by Fuster (1980).

THE FRONTAL LOBE CONTROVERSY

Perhaps the most vexatious question regarding the frontal lobes has been the question as to whether they are more important for man's intellectual life than other portions of the brain. Since the introduction of psychological tests in the area of brain impairment around the 1930s much evidence has accumulated on both sides. This evidence is worth reviewing since it provides a number of lessons about making inferences based on incomplete information.

It seemed natural to some in view of the great development of the prefrontal regions in man that these regions should be concerned with his highest integrative functions. Many neurologists in the era before the introduction of psychological testing, had supported the notion of the paramount importance of the frontal lobe (Jackson, 1874; Phelps, 1897; Dana, 1915; Goldstein & Gelb, 1918; Dew, 1922; Papez, 1929; Worster-Drought, 1931) though there were those who were opposed to this notion (Feuchtwanger, 1923; Jefferson, 1937). Jefferson's six cases of frontal lobectomy not only appeared to demonstrate no apparent loss after operation but an improvement in some cases: 'those who showed no mental alteration before the operation were unaffected by partial removal of the anatomical frontal lobe . . . those who had mental symptoms were much better after the lobe had been excised.' Jefferson was opposed to the notion that the higher functions were 'localized' within the confines of the frontal lobes.

The care which must be exercised in making inferences from clinical material with 'presumptive' evidence of localization was given in a case reported several times by Brickner and one on which he based an interpretation of frontal lobe function. This patient who had undergone a partial bilateral frontal lobectomy for a meningioma, was found at autopsy very much later to have had multiple meningiomas including a very large parieto-occipital tumour. Brickner's case was also important as the author claimed that the patient did not appear to show any marked impairment of abstract thought, one of the higher intellectual functions which some writers, particularly Kurt Goldstein, felt was likely to be most affected by lesions in the frontal lobes. Commenting on Brickner's case Goldstein (1944) pointed to an important distinction which should be borne in mind. 'The underlying reason for this difference is seen in the fact that Brickner considered the use of abstract words as an expression of the ability to think in abstract terms or as a sign of abstract attitude. This is an assumption made very often, and I, myself, had the greatest difficulty in differentiating abstract thinking on the one hand and the concrete use of words with abstract meaning on the other'. Goldstein (1936a) had also been at pains to point out that the changes seen with frontal damage may be elusive to traditional examinations.

> . . . the personality changes characteristic of the frontal lobes are of a definite type and may easily be overlooked, because the methods of examination usually employed are unsuited to disclosing them . . . For these reasons the greater part of the literature is useless for answering the questions whether psychic disturbances occur in cases of lesion of the frontal lobe and if so, what these disturbances are.

The first large study of intellectual changes with frontal lesions was that of Rylander (1939) who examined 32 cases of partial excision for either tumour or abscess. The tests of higher intellectual function, which included some which would be classified as tests of abstract thinking, were also given to 32 control subjects. There were highly significant differences between the operated subjects and the controls on most measures. The intellectual changes occurred in 21 of the 32 cases. This underlines the importance of not basing conclusions on a single case or small samples though it does provoke the question as to why some patients showed changes while others did not. In a second study of 16 cases with brain resections in the temporal, parietal, and occipital lobes, Rylander (1943) found very few of the symptoms he had described in his earlier frontal series, e.g. there were no difficulties with 'abstract thinking, the power of combination, and acts involving judgement'. At a time when psychosurgical procedures were becoming popular he warned of the risk of mental invalidism after extensive frontal surgery particularly in those doing intellectual or other complicated work.

An early study of Halstead (1940) on the sorting behaviour of patients with frontal versus non-frontal locations disclosed a poorer performance on the part of frontal subjects.

Against this emerging support for the importance of the frontal lobes, Hebb accumulated impressive evidence that frontal patients were not in fact inferior on intellectual tasks when compared with posterior lesions (Hebb, 1939a, 1941, 1945; Hebb & Penfield, 1940). The cases were made up of two right frontal cases, four left frontal cases and one with extensive bilateral frontal lobectomy. Examination of the latter case (Hebb & Penfield, 1940) before and after operation failed to show post-operative deficits, in fact there was a striking improvement both clinically and psychometrically in this patient as well as lack of the traditional frontal lobe signs. They commented: 'It becomes evident that human behaviour and mental activity may be more greatly impaired by the positive action of an abnormal area of brain than by the negative effect of its complete absence' (Hebb & Penfield, 1940, p. 431). Hebb (1945) considered there was evidence in some of the reported cases showing deficits after frontal lobe surgery that 'the deterioration they describe(d) may have been due to pathological complication and not to surgical lesion at all'. He did not deny that loss of frontal tissue might have important effects on behaviour merely that such changes had not been adequately demonstrated (Hebb, 1949). Goldstein felt that the frontal lobes were the structures which were most concerned with that complex set of behaviours which he termed taking up the abstract attitude. Because of the extensive nature of the controversy over abstract thinking and brain damage it is dealt with separately below. Speaking of Hebb's cases he remained sceptical. 'However, I think these cases are not convincing because in none of them are such tests used by which the characteristic frontal lobe symptom can be disclosed' (Goldstein, 1944). Although we have learned a good deal about the frontal lobe syndrome in the ensuing four decades it remains a truism of clinical practice that patients with frontal lobe lesions often appear essentially normal until they are examined with appropriate tests. Hebb's counterclaim (1945) was that Goldstein was placing emphasis on cases which supported his interpretations while disregarding those which were opposed.

In 1947 Halstead published his theory of 'biological intelligence'. This was based on factor analysis of a number of tests which appeared sensitive to the effects of cerebral impairment. One of the factors was a factor of abstraction. Among the tests in Halstead's battery, the Category Test had a particularly high loading on this factor. In keeping with earlier claims of lowered abstract ability after frontal lesions, Halstead and his colleagues reported that abstraction loss in the form of high error scores on the Category Test was indeed greater with frontal involvement (Halstead, 1947; Shure & Halstead, 1958). Neither of these sources presents strong evidence upon which to make the general claims that were put forward. The first study presented only a small amount of data and both studies accepted levels of significance well short of those which have become conventional. An examination of Shure and Halstead's data shows that it is largely derived from Shure (1954) and that a direct test of the effect of size of lesion, laterality and locus of lesion (frontal versus non-frontal) in this original study revealed that all three main effects failed to reach significance in a $2 \times 2 \times 2$ Analysis of Variance. Using Shure and Halstead's data Chapman and Wolff (1959) employed their own method for re-estimating the mass of tissues removed in the 1958 study. To this they added other cases of their own where the extent and site of tissue removed could be clearly specified and where each case was restricted to one of the lobar divisions of the brain and where there was neither evidence of progressive disease nor other disorders. The findings showed that 'impairment was independent of site or side of the defect in the cerebral hemispheres but was directly related to the mass of hemisphere tissue loss. No one of the categories of highest functions was significantly or predictably impaired in relation to the site of defect, whereas all functions were progressively impaired with increasing mass of defect.'

During the 1950s Teuber and his associates accumulated a good deal of data, mainly but not exclusively on penetrating missile wounds, concerning the relative performance of frontal versus posterior lesions. Deficits were greater in frontal cases for a small number of visual tasks discussed below but the remainder of the tasks showed equal or greater impairment with posterior lesions. These visual tasks comprised: (i) complex visual tasks including sorting tasks (Teuber Battersby & Bender, 1951; Weinstein et al, 1955); (ii) complex tactual tasks (Semmes et al, 1954; Teuber & Weinstein, 1954); (iii) visual and tactile discrimination learning (Battersby, Krieger, & Bender, 1955); (4) practical problem solving (Battersby, Teuber & Bender, 1953); and (5) the Army General Classification Test, a general intelligence test (Weinstein and Teuber, 1957: Teuber & Weinstein, 1958; Teuber, 1959). The poorer performance of the posterior group could not be explained on the basis of primary visual defects. Much of this and other evidence is comprehensively summarized in Teuber (1964). Supporting evidence against the pre-eminence of the frontal lobes in intellectual functions came from Birkmayer (1951) and Pollack (1960). Recently Black (1976) has confirmed Teuber's findings using subjects with penetrating missile wounds with the damage presumably restricted to one frontal lobe. The principal measures employed were the Wechsler intelligence and memory scales.

A good deal of insight into the reasons for the contradiction in the literature was provided by the two well-designed studies reported by Reitan (1964). The studies used a wide variety of psychological measures and included the Halstead-Reitan group of tests, an Aphasia Screening Test, Reitan's Trail Making Test, an examination for sensory imperception, and the Wechsler-Bellevue Intelligence Scale. These tests were administered to 64 patients with focal lesions and 48 with diffuse cerebral involvement.

The first study required the psychologist to draw inferences from the psychological data in the absence of the neurological diagnosis. These inferences concerned the questions: (i) is the disorder focal or diffuse? (ii) what is the location of the lesion? (left anterior, right anterior, left posterior, right posterior, diffuse). There was a fairly satisfactory degree of concurrence between the psychological and neurological ratings. For the purposes of the present section this means that the psychological test results must have been differentially influenced by the locus of the lesion, e.g. frontal versus non-frontal as well as the laterality and other factors.

The second study looked at the local cases only and employed the formal comparison of test results between the *known* groups, i.e. intergroup mean comparisons using analysis of variance. Virtually no important differential features were revealed by this analysis. Reitan commented: 'Since the results of Study 1 could not have occurred unless the necessary information for the inferences was present in the data, the conclusion seems inescapable that the analysis was inadequate in Study 2'. It follows that the failure of other studies to show differential features between frontal and non-frontal patients cannot be taken to mean that such differential features do not exist. More sophisticated statistical techniques such as multiple discriminant function analysis or cluster analysis may prove of greater value since they permit the most advantageous use of the pattern of results. On the other hand, such methods are probably less flexible than the use of qualitative features of the patient's behaviour on specially selected tests, some of these features being almost pathognomonic of lesions in particular locations. The features which appear to be most characteristic of frontal behaviour are discussed in the remaining sections of this chapter.

THE FRONTAL LOBE SYNDROME

Changes in personality after brain injury are most often noted after damage to the frontal lobes. These changes have been reported for well over a century and no description of what has come to be called the frontal lobe syndrome would be complete without reference to the case of Phineas Gage. The following summary which has appeared in many places is quoted by Kimble (1963).

> Phineas P. Gage, an 'efficient and capable' foreman, was injured on September 13, 1848, when a tamping iron was blown through the frontal region of his brain. He suffered the following change in his personality according to the physician, J. M. Harlow, who attended him. 'He is fitful, irreverent, indulging at times in the grossest profanity (which was not previously his custom), manifesting but little deference to his fellows, impatient of restraint or advice when it conflicts with his desires, at times pertinaciously obstinate yet capricious and vacillating, devising many plans for future operation which no sooner are arranged than they are abandoned in turn for others appearing more feasible. His mind was radically changed so that his friends and acquaintances said that he was no longer Gage.'

Such gross changes are usually seen only with severe bilateral frontal damage but the lack of inhibition, impulsivity and lack of concern of such patients can be seen to a lesser degree in others whose injury is less severe. In its milder forms it could be taken to be within the extreme range of 'extraversion' if the examiner were not familiar with the patient's prior personality. Another of the characteristic features of the frontal syndrome is the mania for making puerile jokes referred to as 'Witzelsucht'.

Many of these signs seen in the early months after head injuries fade with the passage of time though the more severe the injury the more likely it is that some personality change will remain. Both war injuries (Hillbom, 1960) and psychosurgery have provided potent evidence of the personality changes which accompany bilateral frontal damage.

The complex set of changes with bilateral frontal damage which comprise the frontal lobe syndrome is concisely expressed by Benton (1968). The first set of changes is related to what may be loosely termed personality: 'diminished anxiety and concern for the future; impulsiveness, facetiousness and mild euphoria; lack of initiative and spontaneity. (However, it may be noted that, while they are not mentioned prominently in group studies, anxiety states have been described occasionally in clinical case reports as a presenting symptom in patients with frontal lobe disease.)'

The second set of changes may be termed intellectual: 'impaired integration of behaviour over a period of time, a deficit which for want of a better term has been called impairment in recent memory; loss of the capacity to think in abstract terms; finally, inability to plan and follow through a course of action and to take into account the probable future consequence of one's actions, a deficit which is perhaps closely related to some of the observed personality changes as well as to the impairment in recent memory' (Benton, 1968, p. 53). These various changes will be considered separately in the sections which follow though there is obviously a good deal of interaction between them. There is some evidence from lesion studies both in animals and man that there is at least a partial dissociation between the two major groups of symptoms (Warren & Akert, 1964). This is supported by the extensive literature on psychosurgery suggesting that the intellectual changes are more associated with damage to the dorsolateral connections while the personality changes are more associated with damage to the orbitomedial (or basomedial) regions (Girgis, 1971).

Confabulation

Confabulation refers to the tendency of the patient with amnesia to produce erroneous material on being questioned about the past, either recent or remote. It may accompany amnesia associated with a wide variety of pathological disorders e.g. Korsakoff's psychosis, hypoxic brain damage, posttraumatic states, normal pressure hydrocephalus, and anterior communicating artery aneurysms. It was earlier thought to be a necessary part of the diagnosis of Korsakoff's psychosis but, this is no longer considered to be the case (Victor Adams & Collins, 1971). Certainly, confabulation appears to be more common in the early stages, disappearing as the condition becomes chronic (Moll, 1915). Our own experience agrees with that of Zangwill (1978) that the presence of confabulation in Korsakoff's psychosis appears to be inversely related to the presence of insight.

In his literature review and study of cases of confabulation in Korsakoff patients and an unselected group with dementia, Berlyne (1972) pointed to the distinction between two forms of confabulation, a division made many years before by Bonhoeffer (1904). The first and more common type termed *momentary confabulation* consists of the production of autobiographical material often of an habitual nature (e.g. war service or occupation) in response to questioning. The responses are brief but not stereotyped. The second type is much less common and consists of material around a grandiose theme, often arising spontaneously and frequently repeated. It bears no relation to prior experience. Again after Bonhoeffer, Berlyne termed this *fantastic confabulation*.

The latter type of spontaneous, impulsive confabulation appears to be related to the loss of the subject's self critical faculty, with inability to inhibit responses. The common underlying pathology probably lies in frontal lobe dysfunction (Mercer et al, 1977; Stuss et al, 1978; Kapur & Coughlan, 1980). The most common association appears to be with perseveration of response set and this is frequently accompanied by such 'frontal' signs as inability to inhibit incorrect responses, and faulty self-monitoring (Shapiro et al, 1981).

Lesion studies and cognitive change

Abstract thinking

The question of the importance of the frontal lobes for abstract thinking is intimately connected with the controversy over whether these regions are more crucial than others for the highest integrative functions of man. The summary on theoretical formulations of abstraction in the monograph by Pikas (1966) would form an excellent background to research and reading in this area. This work also provided a summary of empirical studies to that time.

The central questions appear to be whether damage to the cerebrum leads to qualitative versus quantitative changes in what we might loosely term abstract thought processes and, if so, whether these are exclusive to frontal lobe involvement.

The foremost advocate of the qualitative position was Kurt Goldstein. In a large number of publications he put forward the notion that there are two qualitatively different modes of thought and behaviour, the abstract and the concrete. The normal person is said to be capable of exercising both modes according to the demands of the situation while the brain damaged patient is restricted to use of the concrete (Goldstein 1936a, 1936b, 1939a, 1939b, 1940, 1942a, 1942b, 1943, 1944, 1959; Goldstein & Scheerer, 1941; Hanfmann, Rickers-Ovsiankina, & Goldstein, 1944). Several of these publications put forward the claim that impairment of abstraction was maximal with lesions of the frontal lobe.

Goldstein's central concept was that of taking up the 'abstract attitude'. There is no doubt that he conceived of the concrete and abstract attitudes as being a dichotomy although there are instances where he admits to degrees of abstraction and concreteness. Examples from his writings make this clear: 'In the concrete attitude we experience and recognize a given thing or situation immediately. Our thinking and acting are directly determined by the present claims upon us. In the abstract attitude we go beyond the current claims of objects or of sense impressions. Specific properties or situations are overlooked. We are oriented in our actions by a conceptual point of view which takes into consideration the demands of the entire situation' (Goldstein, 1943). Or, again '. . . abstraction is separate in principle from concrete behaviour. There is no gradual transition from one to the other. The assumption of an attitude toward the abstract is not more complex merely through the addition of new factor of determination; it is a totally different activity of the organism' (Goldstein, 1940). 'There is a pronounced line of demarcation between these two attitudes which does not represent a gradual ascent from more simple to more complex mental sets. The greater difficulty connected with the abstract approach is not simply one of greater complexity, measured by the number of separate, subservient functions involved. It demands the behaviour of the new emergent quality, generically different from the concrete' (Goldstein & Scheerer, 1941, p. 22.).

Operationally the 'abstract attitude' was defined by performance on a series of tests. These included the Weigl Colour-Form Sorting Test, and an object sorting test together with a block design test of the Kohs' type and the Goldstein-Scheerer Stick Test. In the monograph which gives the method of administration of the tests (Goldstein & Scheerer, 1941), Goldstein presented a detailed treatment of his meaning of the term abstract attitude.

The abstract attitude is the basis for the following *conscious* and *volitional* modes of behaviour:

1. To detach our ego from the outerworld or from inner experiences.
2. To assume a mental set.
3. To account for acts to oneself; to verbalize the account.
4. To shift reflectively from one aspect of the situation to another.
5. To hold in mind simultaneously various aspects.
6. To grasp the essential of a given whole; to break up a given whole into parts, to isolate and to synthesize them.
7. To abstract common properties reflectively; to form hierarchic concepts.
8. To plan ahead ideationally; to assume an attitude towards the 'mere possible' and to think or perform symbolically.

Concrete behaviour has not the above-mentioned characteristics (Goldstein & Scheerer, 1941, p. 4.).

A reading of the examples provided in the monograph to explain these eight modes of behaviour reveals that Goldstein incorporated under one term many of the features of frontal behaviour which are considered under other headings in the remainder of the chapter. As some of these are considered characteristic of frontal behaviour by other workers, it is regrettable, as Battersby and his colleagues (1956) pointed out, that 'Even in a comprehensive monograph describing details of the sorting test (and other allied procedures), no quantitative data were presented which would enable the reader to compare the relative effects of cerebral lesions in different locations'.

There is also a fundamental theoretical difficulty involved:

> The question of whether a more abstract level of functioning is only a quantitative extension of a more concrete level, and the two levels are hence continuous . . . or is so qualitatively different from the more concrete functioning that it is discontinuous from it . . . is indeed an old and yet unresolved one. It is, among other questions, the problem of reductionism versus holism, or relatedly of quantity versus quality, issues with which psychology — indeed all of science — has spent much effort . . . (Harvey, Hunt, & Schroeder, 1961)

Quantitative versus qualitative change. A number of studies by Reitan and his colleagues addressed themselves to the question of qualitative versus quantitative changes following brain damage. Reitan (1955) established the presence of striking group differences between brain damaged and control subjects on the ten tests of Halstead's Impairment Index and the Wechsler-Bellevue Scale. He felt that 'if different kinds of abilities were used by the brain damaged subjects, the interrelationships or correlations between various tests would differ from the interrelationships between tests shown by the group without brain damage' (Reitan, 1958). Correlation coefficients were computed between each pair of variables for each group. A correlation of 0.85 was obtained between the matrices for brain damaged and control groups. Thus, while the brain damaged subjects showed definite impairment their abilities remained essentially of the same kind as nondamaged subjects. In a second study Reitan (1959), using the Halstead Category Test found no significant differences in kind of response to subtests between the two groups though there was a clear difference in the mean error scores. This finding was extended by Doehring and Reitan (1962) again using the Category Test. Taking the ratio of errors on each subtest to total errors on the test they found no difference in the pattern of responding between left hemisphere, right hemisphere and control groups. Earlier Simmel and Counts (1957) in examining the errors of temporal lobe cases and control subjects on the Category Test had reported that both groups reacted essentially alike to the stimulus material choosing the erroneous alternatives in much the same way.

Goldstein, (G), Neuringer, and Olson (1968) pointed out that a difficulty with Kurt Goldstein's (qualitative) and Reitan's (quantitative) positions has been their failure to evaluate the possibility that *both* observations may be correct depending upon the kind of brain damaged patients and the abilities being evaluated. They employed concept identification problems both simple and complex of the type reported in Bourne (1966). They comment:

> The issue of quantitative versus qualitative impairment of abstract reasoning in the brain damaged is not independent of the subject's status, perhaps particularly his age, type of deficit, locus of lesion and problem to be solved. Some brain-damaged individuals behave as do the patients in Goldstein and Scheerer's case presentations. They seem to be completely incapable of adopting the abstract attitude. Others behave as did the typical subject in the 1959 Reitan study. They can apparently adopt the abstract attitude, but not as effectively as the non-brain damaged individual.

It is obviously important in the resolution of this problem to take the suggested factors into consideration. While the study just cited supported the importance of age and task complexity, the role of location of the lesion has been insufficiently explored.

Frontal locus and abstraction. There is a good deal of evidence that patients with frontal lesions perform poorly on so-called tests of abstraction. Many studies after psychosurgery in the forties and fifties showed such loss on a variety of tests (Fleming, 1942; Kisker, 1944; Rylander, 1947; Malmo, 1948; Yacorzynski, Boshes & Davis, 1948; Petrie, 1949; Grassi, 1950). That these changes might be more subtle with less radical operations has already been mentioned. One large study (Mettler, 1949; Landis, Zubin, & Mettler, 1950) reported only transient loss after psychosurgery.

Studies based on the examination of cases with other frontal lesions including excision of small and large portions of the frontal lobes have often described poor abstract ability defined by poor performance on one or more tests (Goldstein, 1936a, 1939, 1944; Rylander, 1939; Halstead, 1947; Shure, 1954; Shure & Halstead, 1958; Milner, 1963). These studies have often concentrated on the behaviour of individuals with frontal lesions without any comparable examination of patients with lesions in other locations or, where this has been done, e.g. in the Halstead studies, the evidence of a major difference is unconvincing. Teuber (1964) has cited several studies where patients with posterior lesions have performed at least as poorly as frontal patients even where sorting or categorizing tests have been used.

The unsatisfactory nature of this area of research lies in the nature of many of the tests used and the unwarranted assumptions which have been made about the abilities which are felt to be central to their solution. *A patient may fail on a test of abstract thinking for a number of reasons other than alteration in the ability to think abstractly.* Milner's argument that the frontal patient may fail because of his inability to inhibit preferred modes of responding would appear to account for many of the failures described in the literature. When one looks at a complex test such as the Category Test one is not surprised at the failure of brain damaged patients in general since so many factors appear to be crucial for good performance on this test. This point of view is supported by studies such as that of Messerli and his colleagues (1979). One of their tasks required the subject to abstract the rule underlying the presentation of series using coloured counters, e.g. Red Green Red Green (RGRG); RRGG; RGGRGG. Frontal patients were significantly poorer than all other lesion groups on complex 'asymmetrical' series such as RGGRGG but individual subjects failed for different reasons. Some perseverated by adhering to an earlier successful programme while others persevered with a newly devised hypothesis even though it proved obviously wrong. Some gave two or more successful sequences and then disregarded the rule. Yet others could verbalize the rule but not execute it.

While the present author feels that there is little doubt about the frontal patient's poor performance on abstraction tasks, it is inaccurate to ascribe the reason for failure to loss of abstract ability.

Planning and problem-solving

One of the most helpful of Luria's contributions to neuropsychology lies in his conception of the frontal lobes at the summit of the brain's hierarchy. His point of view is nowhere more clearly expressed than in *The Working Brain* (1973b).

> Man not only reacts passively to incoming information, but creates *intentions*, forms *plans* and *programmes* of his actions, inspects their performance, and *regulates* his behaviour so that it conforms to these plans and programmes; finally, he verifies his conscious activity, comparing the effects of his actions with the original intentions and correcting any mistakes he has made (pp. 78–80)

This higher form of man's activity has been referred to in other areas of psychology largely under the heading of thought processes, e.g. 'Thinking is a form of problem solving behaviour which involves the correlation and integration of critical events in time and space. It is characterized by (i) a period of preliminary exploration, (ii) a pre-solution period of search, (iii) a period of vicarious testing of tentative solution, (iv) an act of closure and registry of a memory trace, and (v) appropriate action' (Halstead, 1960). It has been the task of neuropsychology to demonstrate the dependence of each of these major steps upon the integrity of the frontal lobes. This is not to say that there were no early contributions of worth, merely that converging lines of evidence in recent years have given us a better total picture of the complex functioning of the prefrontal regions. Some of the complexity can be gained from an examination of three areas: (i) maze behaviour, (ii) visuoconstructive activities, and (iii) problem solving. This is merely a convenient illustrative sample since planning and programming activities permeate virtually everything which man does.

Maze behaviour. As far back as 1914, in the days when mental testing was in its infancy, Porteus introduced a set of pencil and paper maze problems which have been in widespread use since that time and with which he worked in a variety of situations and with a variety of the world's peoples (Fig. 4.6). One of the reasons for the continued use of the test must be that it measures some characteristic which is basic to man's intelligent behaviour. Porteus himself referred to this in a number of ways, e.g. as 'planfulness', 'planning capacity', or at another time as 'prerehearsal', i.e. a mental rehearsal of the act that the individual is about to perform. If we retain the simple term 'planning', it was this which Porteus considered was measured by the Maze Test and which he felt was *a prerequisite to every intelligent act* (Porteus, 1950, 1958, 1959, 1965). Moreover, he was to come to the conclusion based on his own studies and those of others that this factor was maximally represented in the frontal lobes. One of the earliest reports of extensive frontal lobectomy has remarked 'In so far as final conclusions from the first two cases . . . are justifiable it may be stated that maximal amputation of right or left frontal lobe has for its most detectable sequel impairment of those mental processes which are requisite to planned initiative' (Penfield & Evans, 1935).

The advent of psychosurgery allowed Porteus to validate his long standing claim that the Mazes were a measure of planfulness. Patients undergoing classical lobotomy procedures showed a clear loss in this area when investigated clinically. Such patients also showed loss on the Mazes (Porteus & Kepner, 1944; Porteus & Peters, 1947). This finding was soon

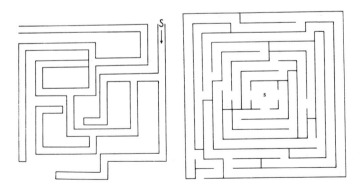

Fig. 4.6 Two examples from the Porteus Maze Test. (By kind permission of D. Hebden Porteus).

confirmed by others (Malmo, 1948; Mettler, 1949, 1952; Petrie, 1949, 1952a, 1952b; Robinson & Freeman, 1954).

That losses on the Maze test are dependent on the location of the lesion within the frontal lobe has been shown by Crown (1952) and Lewis et al (1956). These authors demonstrated that posterior and superior lesions affected performance on the tests more consistently than did lesions in other sites. The work of Robinson on the other hand suggested that the extent of the loss might be related to the amount of the frontal lobe disconnected.

A different type of maze was introduced by Elithorn (1955) which appears sensitive to cerebral impairment. Examples of different degrees of difficulty are shown in Figure 4.7. The subject is instructed to find his way from the bottom to the top passing through the maximum number of dots, this number being printed on the form. The subject is instructed to keep to the dotted lines, told not to cross the white diamonds and that reversing direction is not permitted. Though a later study showed the sensitivity of the Elithorn Maze Test to brain damage there was no indication that frontal patients were differentially impaired (Benton et al, 1963). However, we have noted that same disregard for the rules in the face of their correct repetition by the subject and admonition by the examiner already noted for the electrical stylus maze. A binary form of the maze for experimental work was developed by Elithorn and his colleagues (1963) while Gregson & Taylor (1975) used a computer programme to generate a series of similar mazes where the dot density in the lattice has been controlled.

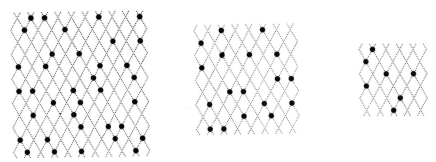

Fig. 4.7 Examples of Elithorn Maze Test.

Visuoconstructive activities. These tasks are often performed poorly by patients with brain damage. Perhaps the most frequently used has been the Block Design task of the Koh's type which has found its way into popular aggregate measures of intelligence such as the Wechsler Scales. The Block Design test failed to live up to expectation as a universal indicator of brain damage but recent reappraisal would suggest that careful analysis of qualitative features of the patient's performance could reveal valuable indicators of brain impairment if the lesion is situated in the frontal or parietal regions.

Constructional difficulties are often all loosely referred to as 'constructional apraxia' (Ch. 6). In posterior lesions the difficulties arise because of a loss of spatial organization of the elements. Luria and Tsvetkova (1964) have demonstrated that frontal constructional difficulties arise through disruption of one or more of the steps mentioned at the beginning of this section, namely, *intention, programming, regulation* or *verification*. Lhermitte, Derousené and Signoret (1972) provided confirmation of this viewpoint by demonstrating how the performance of the frontal lobe patient may be facilitated by means of a programme provided by the examiner. As in the case cited in the section on psychosurgery, a patient who was unable to execute a block design problem could do so immediately and without error when presented with a model or design where each constituent block was clearly delimited. In the words of Barbizet (1970), the examiner is here acting as the patient's frontal lobes by generating part of the programme for solution.

Other tasks are also improved when partial programmes are provided for frontal patients. This does not appear to be the case with lesions in other parts of the brain.

Lhermitte et al also employed the Complex Figure of Rey (Fig. 4.8, Rey, 1941, 1959; Osterrieth, 1944). The frontal patients' copying was much more adequate than reproduction from memory. This was not, however, due to a primary disorder of memory. Following their poor reproduction from memory, the patients were given a structured sequence of the figure to copy.

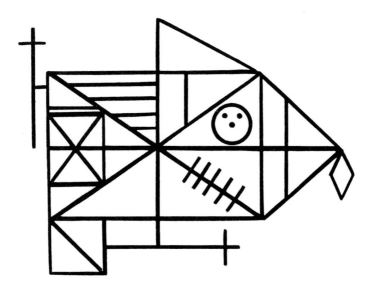

Fig. 4.8 The Complex Figure of Rey (Rey, 1959). Courtesy of Les Editions du Centre de Psychologie Appliquée.

This began with copying the basic rectangle. They then had to copy a version consisting of the rectangle plus other features and more and more complete figures were given until the full figure was reached. The patients copied each of the more and more complete versions from the beginning so that by the time they had reached the full design, they had experienced a sequential programme for its execution on a number of occasions. Their later reproduction from memory was much improved. The improvement appears to be due more to the provision of a programme than to the sheer weight of practice. This is borne out by our own experience where the provision of extra experience alone leads to little or no improvement. Moreover, the patient is just as poor with any new figure for which he does not have a programme. It is painfully evident that one can teach frontal patients specific programmes but not how to generalize even to activities which seem to the observer to be very similar.

Superficially, the Rey Figure copies of frontal patients look like constructional apraxia. However, the spatial relationships of many key elements are preserved, e.g., the crossed hatched lines on the diagonal are at right angles, the lines in the upper left quadrant are horizontal and other features are correctly reproduced (Messerli, Seron & Tissot 1979). It is the failure to organize or integrate the components into the whole which is at fault.

Arithmetical problem solving. With frontal lobe lesions there do not appear to be significant disturbances of well established operations such as addition and subtraction and none of the 'spatial' mathematical difficulties seen in parietal patients (Ch. 6). The essential difficulties are better described as those of problem solving or of 'discursive intellectual activity' (Christensen, 1975). Once again patients may be able to repeat the problem but their actions suggest a form of amnesia. They seem to have forgotten how to generate and execute even a simple two or three step programme which would have presented no difficulty prior to their lesion. As in other areas of behaviour much of their difficulty arises through incomplete analysis and an inability to inhibit the first tendency aroused by the problem (Luria, 1966). A detailed analysis of the arithmetical problem solving ability of patients with frontal (and other) lesions is given in the French monograph of Luria and Tsvetkova (1967). Three sample problems likely to elicit difficulties are as follows (from Luria, 1966):

> 'A. There were 18 books on two shelves, and there were twice as many books on one as on the other. How many books were on each shelf?
> B. A son is 5-years-old; in 15 years his father will be twice as old as he. How old is the father now?
> C. A pedestrian takes 30 minutes to reach the station, while a cyclist goes 3 times as fast. How long does the cyclist take?'

Christensen (1975) gives a succinct summary of the behaviour of the frontal patient confronted with these problems. 'The patient only grasps one particular fragment of the problem; he does not make any plans but starts to carry out disconnected arithmetical operations with this fragment. The whole process of solution may be transformed into a series of impulsive, fragmentary arithmetical operations, frequently unconnected with the ultimate goal' (p. 188).

The patient often construes 'twice as many' and similar expressions as meaning 'multiply' without any regard for the context and so arrives at what appear ludicrous answers, e.g. in problem C (termed 'conflict' problems by Christensen) he arrives at the answer 90 minutes for the cyclist.

Another problem solving task which is performed more poorly by frontal patients than any other group is cognitive estimation (Shallice & Evans, 1978). Here the subject must generate a plan and execute it while checking it against his store of common knowledge. Examples are: 'What is the length of the average man's spine?'; 'What is the length of a pound note?' Frontal patients produced numerous bizarre estimates, i.e. those which exceeded the estimates of all or most normal subjects.

Error utilization. One of the major changes in behaviour with frontal lobe cases is the patient's apparent lack of full awareness of his deficits. Luria has referred to this as a 'lack of self-criticism' or 'lack of critical attitude towards one's own action' (Luria & Homskaya, 1963, 1964). He feels that this 'can be regarded as the result of a general loss of some feedback mechanism, a disturbance in signals of error, or an inadequate evaluation of the patient's own action. It can be reduced to a deficit in matching of action carried out with the original intention . . .' (Luria & Homskaya, 1964, p. 355). In discussing their patient's inability to carry out compounded or symbolic instructions, Luria, Pribram, and Homskaya (1964) stress what has been pointed out several times already, namely that the failure is not one of understanding what is required. 'These incapacities seem not to depend on any difficulty in apprehending the instructions per se: they may however, be related to an inability, shown by our patient, to evaluate errors, especially self-produced errors' (p. 278).

A most important contribution to conceptualizing the nature of the frontal defect has been made by Konow and Pribram (1970). They describe a patient who made errors and, at the same time, gave clear indication that she was aware of making them. She was not, however, able to correct them. 'We therefore confronted her with a test in which one of us carried out the commands of the other, sometimes correctly and sometimes erroneously. The patient usually had no difficulty in spotting our errors. This was true even when they were embedded in rather complex serial performances' (p. 490). The important feature was the patient's inability to use such information to modify her ongoing programme of action. This analysis leads to an important distinction which should have marked implications for attempts to rehabilitate patients with frontal injury, i.e. the distinction between error recognition and *error evaluation* on one hand and *error utilization* on the other. The latter term is a clear expression of the dissociation between thought and action mentioned by many neuropsychologists in a variety of ways.

The problem of error utilization can be subtle but very disruptive and can be easily overlooked unless appropriate tests are used. We have found it a common disability after closed head injury and chronic alcoholism. Serial maze learning of the length and complexity of the Milner pathway (Milner, 1965) using the Austin Maze (Walsh, 1985) or similar apparatus brings out the difficulty very well. The subject may rapidly learn the general plan of the maze, reducing errors to a small number in a few trials, only to have difficulty in eradicating errors completely. Even when the subject has reached an errorless trial subsequent trials may show recurrence of errors. This highlights the point that measures such as trials to criterion (e.g. one errorless trial) may be quite misleading as a measure of the patient's capacity to work effectively. Wherever there is suspicion of frontal lobe involvement the criterion of learning should be the execution of a *stable, error-free performance*. One has only to think of the consequences of even one error in the programme of operating machinery, preparing a recipe or flying a plane to see the importance of excluding the difficulty of error utilization when examining patients for rehabilitation.

Luria argued that the basic factor contributing to the frontal patient's difficulties was lack of the 'verbal regulation of behaviour'. In other words the patient's verbalizations (both internal and external) do not command his actions. Drewe (1975a, b) specifically tested this proposition and found that while it might fit some of the findings it was unable to explain a good deal of the experimental findings in frontal subjects.

The 'Tower of London' problems. This set of problems is the first of a series of tasks intended by the originator (Shallice, 1982) to examine frontal lobe processes. The test has the great advantage that it is derived from the author's general model for thought and action which will allow predictions about frontal deficits to be examined systematically. There are a series of novel problems of graded difficulty in which the most efficient solution depends on breaking down of the goal into subgoals which must then be tackled in an appropriate order. Figure 4.9 illustrates a problem of moderate difficulty. On each problem the subject is presented with a standard array of coloured beads on sticks and must achieve a given arrangement *in a stated number of moves* by shifting the beads one at a time from stick to stick.

In the seminal study patients with left anterior lesions showed a specific deficit compared with right anterior and both posterior groups. The 'Tower' problems seem more highly loaded on a planning factor than most others in common use and are a welcome addition to research and clinical method.

Rigidity and cerebral impairment

One of the most frequently mentioned features of the behaviour of brain

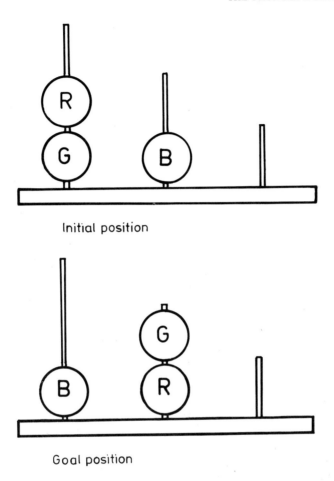

Initial position

Goal position

Fig. 4.9 One of the Tower of London problems (Shallice, 1982).

damaged patients is a lack of flexibility in their approach to many situations. This has been noted in both clinical and psychological test situations. Particular studies express this in different ways, e.g. (i) lessening of the ability to shift from one concept to another when compared with normal subjects (Goldstein & Scheerer, 1941; Weigl, 1941; Aita et al, 1947; Ackerly & Benton, 1948; Gleason, 1953; Halstead, 1959; Milner, 1963, 1964); (ii) inflexibility, rigidity, perseveration or stereotyped behaviour (Nichols & Hunt, 1940; Rosvold & Mishkin, 1950; Appelbaum, 1960; Allison, 1966; Mackie & Beck, 1966; Allison & Hurwitz, 1967); (iii) sensitivity to the effect of set or *Einstellung* (Kauffman, 1963). This list is by no means exhaustive but points to the common occurrence of a mode of behaviour we will term inflexible. There is no convincing evidence that all these descriptions refer to a unitary disability.

This condition has been described most frequently in association with tests of abstract thinking but has been found also in a variety of other test situations involving learning and problem solving as well as being reflected in the patient's everyday behaviour. Among the various tests which have brought out the brain damaged subject's inflexibility have been the Goldstein-Scheerer tests, parts of the Halstead battery, the Wisconsin Card Sorting Test, stylus maze problems, pegboard discrimination, paired associate learning, problem solving, and word association tests. The notion of inflexibility of behaviour in the brain damaged finds one of its clearest and most extensive expressions in the monograph of Goldstein and Scheerer (1941).

One fruitful experimental approach which has received little attention is to examine flexibility under the paradigm of negative transfer. The only direct examination appears to be that of Gleason (1953) who defined negative transfer as 'retardation in the acquiring of an activity as a result of being engaged in a prior activity'. Gleason found support for an increase in negative transfer in brain damaged subjects on several tasks — a pegboard discrimination task, a card sorting task and a rotated stylus maze. He demonstrated that there was 'an application of old responses in new situations where such responses are inappropriate'.

There is considerable evidence that inflexibility is particularly marked after lesions of the prefrontal regions (Nichols & Hunt, 1940; Halstead, 1947; Ackerly & Benton, 1948; Rosvold & Mishkin, 1950; Luria, 1963, 1965, 1966, 1973b; Luria & Homskaya, 1963; Luria, Pribram, & Homskaya, 1964; Milner, 1963, 1964). Milner's findings suggest that such deficits may be more associated with lesions affecting the dorsolateral aspect of the frontal lobes rather than the orbitomedial regions. Such a finding may be in keeping with the reports of a number of psychosurgical studies which show little or no intellectual alteration when division of fibre pathways is restricted to the ventromedial quadrant of the frontal lobes (Malmo, 1948; Petrie, 1952a, b; McIntyre, Mayfield & McIntyre, 1954; Bradley, Dax & Walsh, 1958; Smith & Kinder, 1959; Walsh, 1960; Hohne & Walsh, 1970).

Despite this accentuation of the frontal lobe there is clear evidence that inflexibility is found with lesions in other parts of the brain (Critchley, 1953; Allison, 1966; Allison & Hurwitz, 1967). The latter authors point out that perseveration 'is not an occasional accompaniment of aphasia but . . . occurs in the majority of cases'. In fact, 16 out of their 24 patients showed the symptom. The perseveration was linked to each patient's specific deficit, being elicited by tests related to the deficit but not by tests related to preserved language functions. Like many authors, they comment that perseveration was facilitated by anxiety but was also seen in its absence. They also noted that in their series, absence of spontaneous talk was a frequent accompaniment of perseveration. In line with what is said below on the verbal adynamia with frontal lesions one might suspect that the frontal lobes were affected in at least some of these cases. However, in a few cases where autopsy proof was available, perseveration existed in temporal lesions. With Critchley's observation of perseveration with parietal lesions one can be sure that inflexible behaviour is not seen solely with frontal lesions.

Perseveration or inflexibility appears to be most prominent when the task is difficult or the patient is fatigued. This is not surprising since these are the conditions under which such lapses are likely to appear in normal adults. It is when it becomes constant and pervasive that it provides one of the most valuable signs of early cerebral impairment.

In a number of communications Luria provided evidence of motor perseveration with frontal lobe damage (Luria, 1963, 1965, 1966, 1973b; Luria & Homskaya, 1963; Luria, Pribram, & Homskaya, 1964). In 1965 he distinguished between two kinds of perseveration seen with frontal lobe damage which he considered to be associated with two different neuronal systems. The first type involves compulsive repetition of a movement that has been initiated but the patient is able to shift from one action to another. The second type represents what Luria terms an inertia of the programme of action itself: 'the patient, having once performed the required task, is incapable of switching to the fulfilment of any other task but continues even when instructed otherwise, to perform the first task on which he has "stuck"' (Luria, 1965, p. 1). Type 1 is thought to be associated with deep seated lesions of the premotor zones involving the subcortical ganglia while the second type is associated with massive involvement of the anterior or baso-medial portions of the frontal lobes. 'The only significant difference is that, whereas in lesions of the premotor zones the pathological inertia extends only to the effector components of the action, and performance of the programme as a whole is undisturbed, in massive lesions of the frontal lobes it extends to the scheme of the action itself, with the result that perform-ance of the programme becomes impossible' (Luria, 1973b, p. 206). The validity of Luria's 'premotor syndrome' as a separate distinct entity has been strongly supported by the study of Derouesné (1973) of five cases of frontal tumour restricted largely to the rolandic/prerolandic area. Luria makes it clear that the patient who perseverates when given a verbal instruc-tion does not fail through lack of understanding but because the verbal instruction does not regulate his behaviour as it does in normal subjects, 'it is not a matter of forgetting the instructions (the patient can reproduce its correct wording) but rather the loss of its regulatory role and replace-ment of the required programme by an inert motor stereotype' (Luria, 1973b, p. 206). This apparent disregard of instructions has already been mentioned. An extensive and detailed description of the tasks designed by Luria to elicit this behaviour together with examples of a typical patient's responses is provided by Luria, Pribram, and Homskaya, (1964). Luria's complete neuropsychological examination with explanatory texts was prepared by Christensen (1975).

As mentioned above, the question of inflexibility has been inextricably interwoven with the question of abstract thinking. A striking confirmation of the difficulty which frontal patients have with conceptual shifts was provided by Milner (1963). Using the Wisconsin Card Sorting Test she examined patients with static lesions in the frontal and temporal regions before and after cortical excision for the relief of epilepsy. Patients with dorsolateral frontal excisions were more impaired in their ability to shift than those with temporal excisions or those with orbitofrontal excisions even when combined with temporal lobectomy. There were no laterality effects shown in this study, but a long term follow-up (Milner, 1975) showed more lasting and consistent deficits on the WCST after *left* frontal lesions than with right, such deficits being dissociable from language functions. Teuber et al, (1951) using the same task had found that anterior missile wound patients were less impaired than posterior patients though in this study Teuber did not allow the prior mode of responding to be built up strongly before alternating the principle so that Milner's study is more conclusive for the effect of perseveration or inability to dissolve a prior mental set. As early as 1948, Grant and Berg showed that the 'amount of perseveration' shown on the Wisconsin Card Sorting Test is a function of the amount of reinforcement of original modes of response. Since then numerous studies have shown the effects of reinforcement on reversal learning, i.e. alteration of response set. It must also be remembered that behaviour on complex tasks of abstract thinking is determined by a number of factors some of which are affected more by frontal and others by posterior lesions. Milner (1964) has commented.

> It would be a mistake to attribute the failure of the frontal lobe patients on the sorting task to a defect of abstract thought. Such patients frequently surprise the examiner by telling him that there are three possibilities: 'colour, form and number', yet seem unable to recognize the possibility of change, once a particular mode of responding has become established. Thus they show a curious dissociation between their ability to verbalize the requirements of the test and the ability to use the verbalization as a guide to action (p. 86).

She considers that the difficulty of the frontal patients on the WCST 'should perhaps be regarded as a special instance of a more general inability to change response set readily in accordance with varying environmental signals (1964, p. 323).

The performance of frontal patients on related tests are consistent with the hypothesis that they find it difficult to suppress inappropriate hypotheses (Cicerone Lazar & Shapiro, 1983).

Malmo (1974) extended Milner's (1963) findings and others have confirmed the presence of poorer performance with more perseverative errors on the WCST (Nelson, 1976; Robinson et al, 1980). Nelson's modified version of the test has removed ambiguities from the administration and made it more widely acceptable to patients.

Despite fairly wide acceptance of the notion that set-shifting difficulty is characteristic of brain damaged subjects, particularly of frontal lesions, the nature of the difficulty has remained unclear. Johnson et al (1973) suggest that this is largely due to the use of tasks varying in complexity both of stimulus and response as well as different types of abstraction task such as the Weigl Sorting Test (see above) or the reversal shift paradigm as exemplified by the study of Phelan and Gustafson (1968). Their study suggests the need to study attentional and other general factors which may influence the performance of patients on tests used to elicit inflexible behaviour.

Intellectual loss and inflexibility. It has often been inferred that intelligence and behavioural inflexibility may be more closely related among brain damaged subjects than among normals. Mackie and Beck (1966) examined this proposition in a study employing 20 brain damaged subjects and an equal number of controls. Their results showed that a brain damaged subject may suffer intellectual loss without increased inflexibility and that inflexibility may exist in brain damaged subjects without general intellectual loss.

No examination of test inflexibility in brain damaged subjects would be complete without taking into consideration factors which have been shown to influence the nature, extent, and frequency of such behaviour in normal subjects. Goldstein (1943), in offering a comprehensive treatment of the problem of rigidity, emphasized that it is a normal phenomenon. He distinguished two types of rigidity: (i) primary rigidity where the stimulus aroused a response system so strongly that the individual became incapable of altering his response set, and (ii) secondary rigidity when the subject was faced with a situation with which he could not cope, and which enabled the subject to avoid difficult tasks which gave him an overwhelming feeling of helplessness — the so-called 'catastrophic reaction' (Goldstein, 1936). When Goldstein emphasized the fact that rigidity simply becomes exaggerated with brain damage he was referring to both these reactions. If these two areas are to be evaluated, then not only must we study traditional learning theory which examines factors influencing primary rigidity but also study the effects of the person's perceptions of his own successes and failures as exemplified in studies such as Feather (1966) and Nuttin and Greenwald (1968).

Inflexibility, general considerations. The psychological literature on rigidity or inflexibility should form a background for its study in brain damaged subjects. Reviews of aspects of rigidity are given by Cattell, Dubin & Saunders (1954), Chown (1959), Fisher (1949), and Schaie (1955, 1958). Baer's (1964) factor analysis of a number of rigidity scales and other personality, perceptual, and aptitude tests suggested that rigidity cannot be represented by a unitary factor. This multidimensionality of the concept of rigidity is discussed in detail by Chown who cites the following definitions.

> The difficulty with which old established habits may be changed in the presence of new demands. (Cattell & Tiner, 1949)

The inability to change one's set when the objective conditions demand it. (Rokeach, 1948)

Resistance to shifting from old to new discriminations. (Buss, 1952)

Adherence to a present performance in an inadequate way. (Goldstein, 1943)

Lack of variability of response. (Werner, 1946)

Chown points out that while tests of rigidity can be classed under general headings, e.g. (i) tests of *Einstellung* or set, (ii) concept formation tests, (iii) tests of personality rigidity or dispositional rigidity and (iv) tests of perceptual rigidity, there is a need for a study of the relationship between tests in these areas especially as there is a good deal of overlap apparent between some measures.

Since the presence of these several factors has been neglected or over-looked in many brain damage studies, it is not surprising that the relation between brain damage and inflexible behaviour is yet to be clarified.

Frontal amnesia

Clinical writers have stressed the frequency of memory impairment in patients with tumours of the frontal lobes. This is generally considered to be more marked for recent memory. Hećaen (1964) recorded an incidence of 20% of isolated memory disorder in his own series of 131 frontal tumours while his survey of the literature revealed figures ranging from 29–73% in other series. Unfortunately, there is little if any psychometric detail provided in this material nor is there adequate information about the presence of memory disorder with regard to the relative location of the lesion within the frontal lobe. With the increase in knowledge of the neuropathology of memory disorders reported in the next chapter it seems possible that some of the memory defects seen with frontal lesions may be due to encroachment on connections between the frontal regions and the limbic or 'axial' structures. Certainly some patients with frontal lesions appear to have difficulty with learning new verbal paired associates though a true Korsakoff type of amnesia is rare (Hećaen, 1964).

Some writers consider that there is no true amnesia in frontal patients, i.e. no inability to register or to retrieve material given the proper conditions. In their views the memory disorder is only apparent, and the poor performance of frontal patients on some memory tasks is better seen as a disruption of complex forms of behaviour which reflects itself in numerous ways. One of the foremost advocates of such a theory is Luria: 'a lesion of the frontal lobes leads to gross disturbances of the formation of intentions and plans, disturbance of the formation of behaviour programmes and disturbances of the regulation of mental activity and the verification of its course and results. In other words, while leaving the operative part intact, it leads to a profound disturbance of the whole structure of human conscious activity' (Luria, 1973b, p. 300). Thus the features of 'frontal amnesia' can be readily distinguished from amnesic disorders associated with temporal lobe lesions (Luria, Sokolov & Klimkowski, 1967). In these latter cases the whole programme or general meaning is preserved so that 'patients who are unable to retain separate elements often can grasp the general meaning of a sentence or paragraph'. Frontal patients, on the other hand, suffer from a change in the total structure of behaviour which Luria (1971) believes is due to 'high distractibility on one hand and pathological inertia (of traces) on the other, resulting in a loss of programmed forms of activity. In such cases, there is no true amnesia, general or partial, and good retention of a series of items in any modality after 'free' intervals of two minutes or more is seen.

'The defect of retrieval in these patients results from *an inability to create a stable intention to remember with failure to 'shift' their recall from one group of traces to another*' (Luria, 1971, pp. 372–373).

Other writers have commented on the atypical nature of the memory difficulty of the frontal patient, Benton (1968) calling it 'impaired integration of behaviour over a period of time, a deficit which for want of a better term has been called impairment in "recent memory". . .' Barbizet (1970) agrees that simple registration and recall of both visual and verbal material is largely unaffected by 'frontal lesions'. 'In fact, only by means of memory tests in which the frontal patient must retain several facts simultaneously before he can accomplish a specific task are difficulties in recall and learning revealed, and these are often severe. . .' (Barbizet, 1970, p. 83). The frontal patient, while possessing the information necessary to solve a problem often acts as if he has forgotten the (correct) way to proceed. Barbizet recounts the following difficulty in a patient with resection of portion of the right frontal lobe for trauma.

> Q. What is the length of one quarter of the Eiffel Tower?
> A. After long hesitation, he said he did not know.
> Q What is the height of the Eiffel Tower?
> A. 300 meters
> Q What is half of 300?
> A. 150
> Q. What is half of 150?
> A. 75
> Q What is the length of one quarter of the Eiffel Tower, which measures 300 meters?
> A. (after long cogitation) . . . 200 meters (and despite many attempts he failed each time) (Barbizet, 1970, pp. 84–85).

Barbizet considers that the frontal memory defect is of a specific type, affecting particularly the use of previously acquired information. There is also a great similarity between his descriptions of the disorder and that of Luria. 'The evidence seems to suggest that frontal lesions suppress the programs that govern the execution of the mental strategies that bring recall and memorization into play during the operation of any new task, whether it be the resolution of a problem or the learning of a piece of poetry' (Barbizet, 1970, p. 87).

Frontal patients seem to have difficulty with voluntary learning or memorizing but when they are made to repeat material frequently by the examiner they show that they are quite able to acquire new information which they can also retain.

One specific study has been addressed to the question as to whether frontal patients, like retrorolandic patients, have specific short term memory deficits. Ghent and his colleagues (1962) found consistent negative results for frontal patients when they compared them with control and non-frontal cases on a number of tasks with both immediate recall and delayed recall after 15 seconds. There were no significant differences between frontal and control subjects on conventional tasks in the form of recall of digits or recall of simple visual geometric forms or on specially devised memory for position tasks. These latter were created in an attempt to find, for use with human subjects, suitable tasks which might create an analogous situation to the delayed response paradigm which has presented such striking difficulty for frontal monkeys. With this in mind, stimulus material was chosen which 'could not be categorized readily with reference to a verbal or other framework' (Ghent et al, 1962). Once again the frontal patients were not significantly different from controls.

Milner (1965) studied the effects of visually-guided maze learning in patients with variously located lesions, both unilateral and bilateral. This stylus maze approximates the 'visible path, invisible stops' type of maze devised many years ago by Carr (Woodworth & Scholsberg, 1954). The patient had to find his way from start to finish by touching the boltheads with a stylus, moving one step at a time, errors being signalled by a click from the error counter. After working his way across the board once, he was required to repeat the procedure in blocks of 25 trials twice daily until the criterion of three successive errorless trials had been made. Parietal and left temporal groups were close to the performance of normal subjects but the right temporal, right parieto-temporo-occipital, and frontal groups were markedly impaired. It is highly likely that these various groups performed poorly on this task for quite different reasons.

Although the frontal patients were not more impaired on this task than some other groups, certain aspects of test behaviour were specific to the frontal lobe group. They acted on occasion as if they were unaware of the test instructions by frequently breaking the rules such as failing to return to the previous correct choice after making an error, moving diagonally against repeated instructions and back tracking towards the starting point. This latter type of behaviour led to frontal patients making the same error on the one trial. These qualitative differences may reflect the frontal patient's difficulty in inhibiting aroused response tendencies but it is interesting to note that Milner described a dissociation in some of her frontal patients on the WCST (above) and the stylus maze. One patient had many 'qualitative' errors on the maze but showed normal flexibility on the card sorting task. Two other frontal patients gave the reverse pattern.

In an earlier study Walsh (1960) had used a very similar maze in an examination of patients who had undergone modified frontal leucotomy in the orbitomedial quadrant. One of the most frequently reported changes reported after classical prefrontal lobotomy had been the inability of the patients to benefit from past experience. This was noticed not only in the clinical and social settings but had been remarked many times in studies using the Porteus Maze Test. 'Patients tended to make the same mistake repeatedly after the operation which did not happen before the operation, suggesting a loss in the ability to learn from errors' (Petrie, 1952). Fourteen clinically improved patients tested over a year after modified leucotomy were significantly inferior to an equal number of control subjects on both the stylus maze and the Porteus Mazes. The operated patients also had a greater number of the qualitative errors described by Milner though this comparison failed to reach significance.

Since the study mentioned above there have been many opportunities to observe this disregard of instruction on various forms of the stylus maze which have been used in our clinic. They are seen to a marked degree only in frontal cases and are particularly evident after frontal trauma particularly if this is bilateral.

Verbal behaviour

Two major forms of aphasia occur with frontal lobe lesions. These are Broca's aphasia and transcortical motor aphasia. Treatment of aphasic disorders is beyond the scope of the present text and readers are referred to standard texts on the subject (e.g. Benson, 1979; Kertesz, 1979). However, there are certain verbal disorders which may be observed in the frontal patient who is not demonstrably aphasic and which should be familiar to the neuropsychologist.

Repetition and verbally directed behaviour. Patients with lesions of the left frontal lobe often appear to have intact speech on superficial examination. However, careful examination will often bring out evidence of perseveration or, in severe cases, echolalia. Since some of the features may come out only on detailed examination it is advisable to follow a regular programme of examination in non-aphasic patients suspected of having localized cerebral pathology. Detailed descriptions of such examination have been given in Luria, Pribram & Homskaya (1964), Lhermitte, Derouesne & Signoret (1972) and Christensen (1975).

The following precis is taken from these sources:

The patient typically has no difficulty in repeating isolated words or simple sentences. He may also manage quite well with an unconnected series of words but often has much more difficulty if the word order is changed, e.g. he may repeat the set CAT-FOREST-HOUSE but have difficulty with the rearranged sets CAT-HOUSE-FOREST and FOREST-TABLE-CAT, showing perseveration of the earlier order. When asked to name objects, the patient names single objects readily but may have difficulty if the objects to be named are presented in various pairings, e.g. the series WATCH-PEN, SCISSORS-THERMOMETER, WATCH-THERMOMETER, SCISSORS-PEN may produce perseveration of earlier elements as the test proceeds. Such difficulties are exaggerated if the pairs are presented with only a small temporal separation.

Such difficulties are coupled with reduction of 'verbal fluency' described in the next section and with difficulties in what Luria has termed the verbal regulation of behaviour. These latter are brought out most clearly when a sequence of behaviour is called for. Two examples will suffice.

1. The patient is instructed to place in a line one black counter followed by two white counters and to continue doing this. Two attempts from a patient with a left frontal meningioma are shown (from Luria, et al, 1964).

B.W.W.B.B.W.W.W.W.W.W. . . . . .
B.W.W.B.W.B.W.W.B.W.

These incorrect attempts were made despite the fact that the patient was able to repeat the instructions perfectly. Though he appears to understand, neither his own internal language nor the verbal behaviour of others is capable of regulating his behaviour.

2. The patient has particular difficulty where there is apparent conflict in the instructions, e.g. 'Tap your hand once on the table when I tap twice and tap twice when I tap once'. He may be unable to do so or may begin correctly only to deteriorate rapidly into producing a random series or, more commonly, a rigid stereotype of tapping irrespective of the number of taps given by the examiner. The patient has no difficulty with echo-praxis, i.e. simple repetition of movements in imitation of the examiner and, again, he is able to repeat the instructions signifying that he appre-hended what was required of him.

Verbal fluency. Frontal patients' behaviour is often characterized by a general lack of spontaneity and voluntary action to which the term 'adynamia' has been applied. There is frequently an associated impoverish-ment of spontaneous speech and a reduction in the patient's conversational replies which often shrink to passive responses to questions put to him. These responses often have an echolalic quality, e.g. 'Have you had your lunch?' 'Yes, I've had my lunch.' This verbal adynamia is often more marked after left prefrontal damage than elsewhere in the brain including the right frontal region. Luria (1973b) stresses that this form of reduction of speech cannot be regarded as an aphasic disorder.

Milner (1964) employed Thurstone's Word Fluency Test in a comparison of left frontal, right frontal and left temporal lobectomies. This test requires the patient to *write* as many words as possible in 5 minutes which begin with the letter S and then as many four-letter words which begin with C. Milner found that left frontal cases were much poorer than the other two groups. Since there was a marked difference between the left frontal and left temporal groups the effect would appear to be specific to the left frontal region and not due solely to involvement of the left (language dominant) hemisphere. Moreover, she found a double dissociation between the left frontal and left temporal groups on the task of verbal fluency versus two tasks of verbal recall. Left frontal patients performed poorly on verbal fluency but adequately on verbal recall of prose passages and paired associates while the reverse was true of the left temporal patients.

Benton (1968) confirmed and expanded these findings. His test of verbal associative fluency has been used in other studies and has become part of the Standardized Neurosensory Center Comprehensive Examination for Aphasia (Spreen & Benton, 1969). The patient is asked to say as many words as possible in one minute for each of the letters F, A and S with the proviso that names and other capitalized words are to be avoided and words with different endings but the same stem are not acceptable, e.g. eat, eaten, eating. Benton restricted his examination to the frontal regions, the lesions being mainly tumours classified in three groups, left frontal, right frontal and bilateral. On the verbal fluency test, left frontal and bilateral cases were both inferior to right frontal cases though there was no significant difference between the first two groups. Benton pointed out that the left hemisphere patients were 'ostensibly non aphasic' and felt that since the impairment was seen both in speaking as well as in writing (Milner, 1964) that it was a rather general higher-level language loss. Ramier and Hécaen (1970) confirmed the verbal fluency loss with left frontal lesions. They felt that the defect depended on 'the interaction of two factors: frontal lobe damage (defective initiation of an action) and left-sided lateralization of the lesion (verbal domain).' There is now strong support for the usefulness of scores on verbal fluency tests as an indicator of frontal lobe dysfunction (Pendleton et al, 1982; Miller, 1984).

Benton Word Fluency Test

'F'	'A'	'S'
force	add	skin
fool	a	scoot
fiddle	alphabet	school
fink	adjective	skin (I said skin)
find	account	skittle
fool	advance	sun
Friday	answer	son
fink	animal	sound
fool		skin
find		skittle
fink		sun
fool		
Friday		

The preceding case from our files shows the responses of a young woman of good education who had suffered severe left hemisphere damage with major accent on the frontal region. There were no obvious clinical signs of aphasia at the time of this examination.

The case typifies the frequent occurrence of difficulty in this form of word finding together with perseverations and failure to comply with the instructions. Lhermitte et al (1972) point out that the semantic and morphological perseverations which characterize the performance of frontal patients on this task are also seen in their attempt to define words.

Luria and his colleagues (1967) described a case with a deep left mesial frontal tumour which was also affecting the right side. In this case a disturbance of language became more evident as the tumour increased in size and the authors suggest that careful examination in the early stages of such tumours might reveal certain 'pre-aphasic' signs. One of these is that psychological processes lose what the above authors termed their selective character. When asked to reproduce a sentence or word series the patient would intrude additional associations which he was unable to inhibit. He also had difficulty in naming objects. Luria et al (1967) comments. . .'the naming of an object is a complex process, which includes singling out some leading features of the article, and also assignment to a certain category. This process necessarily includes the suppression of inappropriate alternatives, and a selective choice of proper designations. . .Often this symptom showed itself in a certain excess of detail in the replies indicating an impairment of inhibition of extraneous associations' (p. 111).

The present author has frequently observed this symptom in post-traumatic cases along with other obvious signs of frontal involvement. It is nicely demonstrated during psychological testing where a Vocabulary Test, such as that in the WAIS, is used. Here the patient has to give an appropriate definition of a series of words. If one can consider that in order to produce the correct definition the patient must at the same time inhibit competing response tendencies, the impairment of inhibition leads to many inappropriate responses. To the untrained observer these may appear to have the idiosyncratic quality of some psychotic verbalizations. However the patient may demonstrate during the examination that he is well aware of the correct definition, his difficulty being the inability to inhibit the competitors, some (but not all) of which may appear on association by sound with the word to be defined, i.e. what are referred to in the psychiatric literature as 'clang' associations. The inability in inhibiting aroused response tendencies is often evident in other aspects of the patient's behaviour. The following vocabulary responses are taken from one of the author's post-traumatic cases. The patient also showed impulsiveness, facetiousness and fluctuating euphoria.

DESIGNATE   ..... blow up something (detonate).
REMORSE   .... woman singing a real sad song and she starts crying.

CALAMITY .... man is overcome with stone, rocks, everything.

FORTITUDE ...... where all the soldiers are all going back to the fortitude because all the Indians attack.

TIRADE .... here the patient gave a long rambling description of disaster at sea, shipwreck etc. and finished by announcing. . .'and this was all about a tirade wave.'

Many of this patients' other responses were perfectly acceptable.

Perret (1974) has extended and clarified Ramier and Hécaen's hypothesis utilizing the concept of loss of control of inhibition. He found left frontal patients were significantly poorer than other patients both on a word-fluency test and on a modified version of the Stroop Test (Stroop, 1935) where the subject must make a response in which one category of response is pitted against another, e.g. name the colour in which a word is printed, the word itself being the name of a colour. The words BLUE, GREEN, RED and YELLOW were presented randomly in this way with the print in green, red, or yellow ink.

Right frontal patients performed more poorly than right posterior patients on the modified Stroop Test though the difference was small. The sensitivity of the Stroop Test to frontal lesions has been confirmed in other studies (Golden, 1976).

Perret considered that the basic difficulty which accounted for the exceedingly poor response by left frontal patients lay in the fact that for successful performance the patient must resist the habit of using words according to their meaning. In the word fluency test the subject is asked to search for words according to the beginning letter and not to the usual method of word finding related to meaning. 'Thus the tests may not have measured the ability to find words, but rather to *suppress the habit of using words according to their meaning.*' 'These results corroborate the hypothesis of the role of the frontal lobe in the adaption of behaviour to unusual situations, the left frontal lobe being of fundamental importance when verbal factors are involved' (Perret, 1974, pp. 323–324).

Anterior alexia. This term is growing in favour to describe what some consider a separate syndrome (Benson, 1977, 1979; Kirshner & Webb, 1982; Rothi, McFarling & Heilman, 1982). Benson (1977) used the term *the third alexia* to distinguish it from the other two major forms which occur with centrally placed and occipital lesions respectively. More detailed treatment of the alexias is given by Greenblatt (1983) and Benson (1985).

Patients with anterior alexia most often have a non-fluent aphasia and right-sided hemiplegia or hemiparesis. Other signs of posterior involvement such as hemianopia and auditory comprehension difficulty are characteristically absent. Anterior alexics may be able to read some words, particularly nouns and action verbs but are unable to read some words, such as prepositions and terms of relationship which are syntactically important. They are also unable to read single letters even where they can read the whole word. Thus this form of reading difficulty has been termed syntactic or literal alexia. The syntactic difficulty has been studied as part of the investigation of non-fluent aphasia (Zurif, Caramazza & Myerson, 1972; Caramazza & Berndt, 1978; Samuels & Benson, 1979). Because of the variability of the lesions and the frequent accompanying non-fluent dysphasia the establishment of a separate alexia syndrome is still incomplete.

Perceptual difficulties

In 1861 Aubert described the following phenomenon which bears his name. When a subject is asked to align a luminescent rod to the vertical in a dark room he is usually able to do so with a fair degree of accuracy. However, if the subject's head is tilted (or both his head and body) the perceived vertical is displaced to the side opposite to the direction of body tilt and in proportion to the degree of head or body tilt.

Teuber and Mishkin (1954) examined the Aubert effect in subjects with penetrating missile wounds in various locations. They found a 'double dissociation' on this task with regard to anterior (frontal) and posterior (parieto-occipital) lesions. Frontal patients had difficulty in setting the rod to the vertical with their head and body tilted (the visual-postural condition, Fig. 4.10). Posterior lesion subjects had little difficulty on this task. On the other hand posterior subjects performed much more poorly on a visual-visual condition where the subject is required to set a black thread to the apparent vertical against an interfering background of visual stripes while their body was upright. On the simple visual condition for setting the rod and also on a simple postural task where the patient had to set his own chair to the vertical there were no major group differences.

Visual search and analysis of complex material. Teuber's laboratory was also the first to demonstrate experimentally a 'subtle but lasting deficit in visual searching' (Teuber, Battersby & Bender, 1949). Patients were required to point as quickly as possible to the matching stimulus when one of the 48 stimuli was displayed on a circular centre area (Fig. 4.11). Frontal patients were much poorer on this task than either control subjects or non-frontal lesion cases. Unilateral frontal cases, unlike the other subjects, also were disproportionately slower in finding objects on the side opposite the lesion.

An analysis of eye-movements in frontal subjects has appeared in a number of recent publications. Luria et al (1966) examined eye movements in a patient with a large right frontal tumour and demonstrated a disturbance in the complex process of exploration of complex pictures. Chedru, Leblanc & Lhermitte (1973) reported increased identification time for pictures in the contralateral visual half-field but found that the searching activity was similar in the two visual half-fields. They considered that the longer identification time might be accounted for by assuming that some alerting value was lost on the affected side by an alteration or disruption

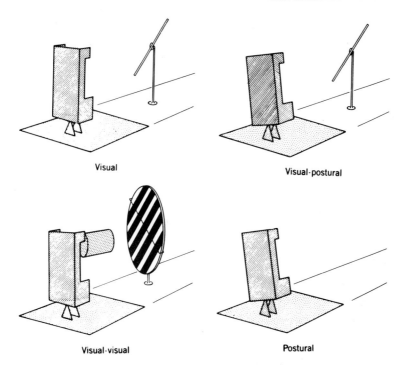

Fig. 4.10 Aubert experiments (Fig 20.6, Teuber, 1964. In: Warren J. M., Akert K (eds) The frontal granular cortex and behavior. Used with permission of McGraw-Hill Book Company).

Fig. 4.11 Field of search test (Fig 20.4, p. 425 from Teuber, 1964. In: Warren J. M., Akert K (eds) The frontal granular cortex and behavior. Used with permission of McGraw-Hill Book Company).

of occipitofrontal connections, an explanation similar to the disconnection hypothesis invoked elsewhere. Eye movements of the four patients studied were normal on verbal command and in following a moving target but differed from normals when complex pictorial material was used. Here preliminary visual exploration was reduced and almost compulsive fixation given to one or two details required for answering specific questions about the picture.

Luria sees the failure of preliminary analysis as a basic reason why frontal patients fail to grasp the meaning of what he terms 'thematic' pictures. The type of behaviour deficit shown by frontal patients in this situation is very similar to that provoked by other problem solving situations. 'To understand the meaning of such a picture the subject must distinguish its details, compare them with each other, formulate a definite hypothesis of its meaning, and then test this hypothesis with the actual contents of the picture, either to confirm it or to reject it, and then resume the analysis' (Luria, 1973b, pp. 213–214). The frontal patient will form an 'hypothesis' based on very little preliminary analysis, what Luria calls the 'impulsive hypothesis.' Since he fails to complete the other steps in the programme of action the patient will also be satisfied with his explanation, e.g. he does not carry out further exploration which would bring forth added information which would then confirm or disconfirm his hypothesis. Luria points out that the recording of eye movements in normal subjects reveals an alteration in the searching process when the subject is asked to answer different questions about a thematic picture such as the period of the picture, the age of the people depicted, their relationship to each other and so on. The frontal patient fixes on any point and impulsively gives the first hypothesis which comes into his mind. The non-analytical nature of the patient's behaviour is reflected graphically in his eye-movement record.

This type of behaviour with thematic pictures is often seen on the Picture Arrangement sub-test of the Wechsler intelligence scales. In this test the subject is given in random order a number of cards which when placed in the correct sequence will tell a logical story.

We have observed frontal patients to be uncritical in their arrangement, making few alterations in the positions of the cards and then telling a loosely connected story in which only one or two salient features are mentioned and the logical links between elements of the picture series are missing. On occasion the patient may state that he is quite satisfied with the random order as presented to him and then proceeds to tell a story which lacks the richness one would expect from his background or from an estimate of his intelligence based on tests of stored information which are relatively resistant to cerebral insult. At other times he describes some salient features of each card as though it were a separate unit and not part of a series. McFie and Thompson (1972) analysed the Picture Arrangement test in 143 adults with circumscribed cerebral lesions and found that, while patients with variously located lesions performed poorly on this test, the

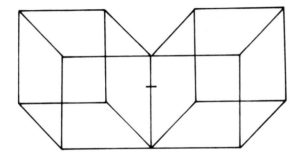

Fig. 4.12 Reversible double Necker cube.

tendency to leave pictures in the presented order (in whole or in part) occurred more frequently with frontal than non-frontal lesions particularly on the right side. They felt that this tendency reflected 'a specific inability to correct a response in spite of evidence that it is wrong' (McFie & Thompson, 1972, p. 551).

There is little doubt that Luria's explanation of the frontal patient's difficulty with thematic pictures would apply equally well to performance on the Picture Arrangement test.

Reversible perspective. Cohen (1959) working in Teuber's laboratory with penetrating missile cases found that unilateral frontal cases experienced much fewer reversals of a double Necker cube (Fig. 4.12) than patients with lesions in other areas though all unilateral brain damaged individuals were inferior to controls. The average number of reversals was smallest for the right frontal group. Rather unexpectedly, bilateral frontal cases showed the reverse phenomenon, reporting many more reversals than normal control subjects. The significance of these findings is uncertain.

Laterality and the frontal lobes

As far back as Jackson (1874) some writers have remarked on the greater disturbance of behaviour by left frontal lesions than by right though some studies, e.g. Rylander (1939) have found no difference associated with the laterality of lesion. Zangwill (1966b) pointed out that Feuchtwanger and Kleist had described certain higher level verbal difficulties in left frontal lesions which were not seen in right-sided cases. These he summarized as: '(1) A certain loss of spontaneity of speech in the absence of articulatory disorder; (2) Difficulty in evoking appropriate words or phrases, amounting on occasions to frank agrammatism; (3) In some cases, definite impairment of verbal thought processes.' More recently attention has been addressed to the question as to whether the asymmetry of function of the two hemispheres is reflected in the frontal lobes as it is in the posterior parts of the brain (Ch. 8). A large study of unilateral frontal tumour cases by

Smith (1966b) using the Wechsler-Bellevue Scale appeared at first to agree with Teuber's evidence that frontal lesions have less effect on test intelligence than lesions in other areas. Thirty one frontal cases had a mean I.Q. of 95.55 whereas 68 posterior cases had a mean I.Q. of 91.46. However, a division into left frontal (14 cases) and right frontal (17 cases) revealed a significant mean I.Q. difference between the left (90.1) and right (99.5) cases. Smith re-examined Pollack's data on the Wechsler-Bellevue Scale for the latter's reported tumour cases and found a mean I.Q. of 86.25 for his 4 left frontal cases and a mean I.Q. of 103.5 for his 6 right frontal cases. Thus by grouping together all frontal cases an important difference had been concealed.

Smith also examined the ages of left and right frontal cases reported in several studies (Rylander, 1939; Halstead, 1947; McFie & Piercy, 1952a, 1952b) and found consistently younger ages for those with left frontal tumours. Together with clinical evidence that left frontal tumours appear to declare themselves earlier than right frontal tumours, Smith finds this a strong argument against the proposition that the disruptive effect of frontal tumours can be attributed to their larger size since the most disruption clearly comes from those of earlier onset, i.e. left frontal.

Benton (1968) looked at the question of laterality effects in frontal lesions by utilizing tests meaningfully related to evidence of hemispheric asymmetry. He chose the following tests:

1. Two 'left hemisphere' tests (i) verbal associate fluency (see above) and (ii) paired associate verbal learning.

2. Two 'right hemisphere' tests (i) three dimensional constructional praxis test (Benton & Fogel, 1962, Ch. 6) and (ii) copying designs, Benton Visual Retention Test.

3. Two 'bilateral' tests (i) Gorham Proverbs and (ii) temporal orientation. Although only a small sample was available (8 right, 10 left and 7 bilateral cases) the findings strongly suggest that interhemispheric differences are reflected in the frontal lobes. Left frontal patients were inferior to right on the word fluency test while right frontal patients were inferior to left frontal on both the constructional praxis and copying tasks. Somewhat unexpectedly the right frontal group was inferior to the left on the proverbs task.

While the data on verbal fluency has been interpreted as showing poorer performance by left frontal cases, Jones-Gotman and Milner (1977) found a right frontal bias on their test of design fluency in which subjects had to generate nonsense designs. The nature of the task and particularly its evaluation has made this finding difficult to replicate.

The care which must be taken in interpretation of unequal test performance of two lesion groups is shown by the experiments on recency judgments carried out by Milner's group. Two early studies (Milner 1971, 1974) asked subjects to judge which of two stimuli inserted in a series had been presented more recently. Patients with left frontal lesions were impaired on verbal material but not on non-verbal material (representational drawings and abstract designs) while those with right frontal lesions were impaired on all three tasks, their performance on the verbal task being nearly as poor as the left frontal group. Similarly Làdavas, Umilta and Provinciali (1979) found a material specific recency effect for patients with epileptic foci in the left frontal region.

In a second set of experiments (Milner, 1982; Petrides & Milner, 1982) despite the use of similar material there was a strong bias towards poorer performance by the left frontal group when the subject was required to choose his own order of responding. The finding comports well with the data which argues for a greater role for the left hemisphere in planning and programming behaviour.

Frontal adynamia

This condition is seen predominantly with bilateral lesions affecting the medial aspects of the frontal lobes and hence may be seen most clearly with lesions of the anterior cerebral arteries. It ranges from a mild state where the patient is less active than usual with little spontaneous speech to the fully blown *akinetic mutism* which accompanies bilateral anterior cerebral artery infarction. In reporting three such cases, Freemon (1971) described that condition as 'a disorder of consciousness characterized by unresponsiveness but with the superficial appearance of alertness. The patient's eyes are open but he neither speaks nor moves, nor is the examiner able to communicate with the patient' (p. 693). Akinetic mutism of frontal origin is seen with bilateral cingulate gyrus lesions (Nielsen & Jacobs, 1951; Buge et al, 1975; Jurgens & Von Cramon, 1982) but the disorder is also seen with periacqueductal lesions.

The milder cases may be described as placidity (Poeck & Kerschensteiner, 1975) and those in our experience have certain common features. Patients are generally akinetic and they will remain in the one situation for long periods of time. No spontaneous conversation or comment is proffered but they will reply cogently to others' conversation and carry out actions without any difficulty even where these are of a high level of complexity. On several occasions we have found that despite their adynamia patients may show a normal reaction time even to a long series of signals occurring randomly over several minutes.

Frontal adynamia presents a serious impediment to rehabilitation since while patients may respond normally to direct external stimuli they lapse back into inactivity on its withdrawal. The problem appears to lie in an inability to generate and sustain one's own motivation, a defect of the *voluntary* regulation of arousal brought about by a break between the neocortical and brainstem components of arousal mechanisms.

PSYCHOSURGERY

Prefrontal lobotomy and its congeners

The birth of modern psychosurgery has been considered to date from November 1935, this being the date when Egas Moniz and Pedro Almeida Lima made the first attempt to alleviate mental suffering by operating on the human frontal lobes (Moniz, 1954). For various reasons, there was at first little interest shown in this new therapy by the medical profession as a whole, and the advent of World War II no doubt contributed to the slow progress made in this field during the ensuing years in Europe.

Following the publication by Freeman and Watts of their book *Psychosurgery* (1942), general interest in these techniques increased rapidly. The classical lobotomy of Freeman and Watts became the standard procedure in most centres, and their finding that the dorsomedial nucleus of the thalamus degenerated when the frontal lobe was isolated provided an interesting and important connection between this work and the suspicions of earlier workers that connections between the frontal lobe and the thalamus provided 'for the addition within the prefrontal fields of affective impulses of thalamic origin' (Herrick, 1963).

The standard early lobotomy consisted of very radical division of the white matter of the frontal lobes in a more or less vertical plane just anterior to the tip of the frontal horn of the lateral ventricle (Fig. 4.13). The extent of destruction of tissue can be seen in Figure 4.14, taken from Freeman and Watts (1948). The term lobotomy used by American and other writers

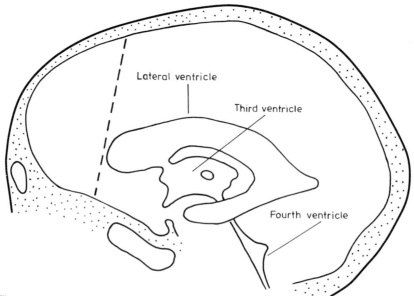

Fig. 4.13 Plane of section in classical pre-frontal lobotomy.

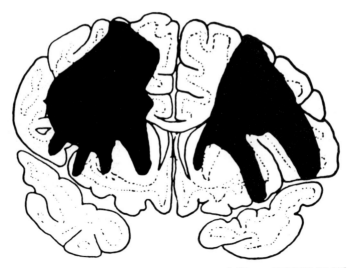

Fig. 4.14 Extensive lobotomy incisions (from Freeman & Watts, ARNMD 27,205, 1948).

means literally an incision into the lobe. English writers on the other hand preferred the term leucotomy, meaning a cutting of the white matter. The two terms can be taken to be synonymous though care should be taken in reading the literature to ascertain the placement and extent of the lesion in any given series.

Neurosurgeons and psychiatrists very soon became aware, following the early radical operations, that a percentage of patients showed a post-lobotomy syndrome which had many undesirable features. Indeed, in many cases where such a syndrome existed after operation, the second state of the patient appeared to be worse or less desirable than the pre-morbid one. Moreover, the mortality rate was considerable in some series as was the incidence of post-operative epilepsy and intellectual deterioration. All this led either to an abandonment of the procedure by some or a search by others for a modified form of operation which would preserve any therapeutic value while minimising the risk of unwanted changes.

In England, Dax and Radley Smith described ventromedial leucotomy in 1943 and in 1945 using a special leucotome (the MacGregor-Crombie leucotome) performed the first selective leucotomies. In these, the upper, middle and lower portions of the frontal lobe were severally divided by sections in a plane parallel to the coronal suture. Other workers also reported that sectioning only the inferior quadrants produced equally good results as those occurring in the more extensive Freeman & Watts operation. From the early forties, the number and types of surgical intervention rapidly multiplied; however, the accumulation of evidence seemed to suggest that the more important thalamo-frontal fibres to be severed were those in close proximity to the tip of the frontal horn of the lateral ventricle, and it was a minor variation of the lower section operation first performed by Dax and Radley Smith which formed the operative technique for a series reported by the present author over a very long period (Hohne & Walsh, 1970; Walsh, 1976).

This operative method would appear to be concerned with the destruction of much the same fibre pathways as the later method of coagulation by Grantham (1951) which also placed its circumscribed lesion just anterior to the frontal horn of the ventricle, in the lower medial quadrant of the frontal lobe. The procedure is described in detail by Bradley, Dax, and Walsh (1958). The placement of the lesions is shown in Figures 4.15 and 4.16.

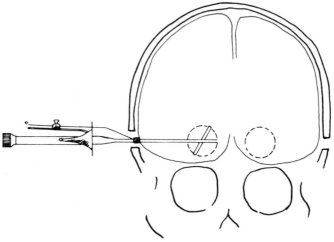

Fig. 4.15 Position of section in orbitomedial leucotomy (from Hohne & Walsh, 1970).

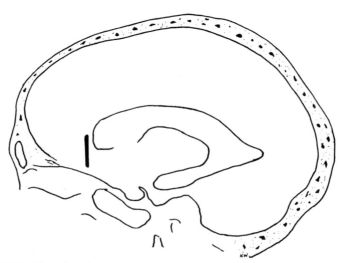

Fig. 4.16 Position of section in orbitomedial leucotomy (from Hohne & Walsh, 1970).

These procedures had much to recommend them. Because of the absence of a large cortical scar, the danger of post-operative epilepsy was minimal. Secondly, if it was felt that further isolation of frontal cortex was necessary, a second operation could be performed to extend the lesion at another time. Thirdly, such operations seemed to be almost free of the type of post-operative change often referred to as the chronic frontal lobe syndrome, while producing equally effective symptomatic relief.

It would seem that if division of this bundle of thalamofrontal fibres was the most important mechanism in producing symptomatic relief, then one would expect most forms of leucotomy to have certain features in common, since the majority of operations interrupted part or all of this radiation.

Since this book is concerned with neuropsychological aspects of lesion studies the reader interested in the clinical effects of the countless psycho-surgical operations may refer to the numerous books and reviews which have appeared on the subject over the past four decades of which the following is a sample (Mettler, 1949; Freeman & Watts, 1950; Greenblatt, Arnold & Solomon, 1950; Mettler, 1952; Petrie, 1952; Freeman, 1953a; Freeman, 1953b, Robinson & Freeman, 1954; Tow, 1955; Freeman, 1958; Robin, 1958; Tooth & Newton, 1961; McKenzie & Kaczanowski, 1964; Hohne & Walsh, 1970; Laitinen & Livingston, 1973).

Some operations aimed at largely sparing the thalamofrontal radiation. Operations which isolated only parts of the frontal cortex have reported good results. The restricted orbital undercutting of Area 13 and part of Area 14 appears to have been as successful as many more radical procedures (Knight & Tredgold, 1955; Sykes & Tredgold, 1964). During the 1960s numerous attempts were made to reduce the size of the lesion and to localize it more accurately by means of stereotactic surgery. These included electrodes, probes used for freezing, and the implantation of radio-active seeds. The latter method was introduced by Knight in 1965 and replaced his previous surgical method while pacing the lesion in the same anatomical site. Results are reported by Knight (1965), Strom-Olsen and Carlisle (1971) and Knight (1972).

In a brief but excellent review of psychosurgery, Sweet (1973) commented on the operations: 'On the assumption that some cerebral component of the limbic system was the appropriate target, lesions have been made in the gyrus-cinguli, in the white matter of the posteromedial orbital cortex just below the head of the caudate nucleus.'

THE FRONTAL LOBES AND PERSONALITY

One of the charges most frequently brought against psychosurgery is the lack of proper scientific rationale. Part of this stems from the relative absence of detailed psychological studies of the effects on the person's internal organization or self. A review of the literature shows that the relatively few studies which have concerned themselves with psychological assessment limit this to an investigation of the effectiveness of operation in reducing anxiety or depression or in demonstrating that psychosurgery, in its 'modified' forms, does not have an adverse effect upon aggregate measures of intelligence such as the Wechsler scales. Remarkably few studies have been addressed to the question of the relation between personality change and a rationale for operation. In 1950 Freeman said: 'In order to establish a satisfactory result by psychosurgery, it is necessary to change the personality of the patient from his pre-operative one or even his premorbid one.' A study of such changes might then not only increase our understanding of brain-behaviour relationships in the sphere of personality but also provide a better understanding of indication and contraindication for psychosurgery.

Early in our own series the rationale for selection was based on the belief that leucotomy becomes the treatment of choice in a patient with the symptom complex of what Arnot (1949) termed 'a fixed state of tortured self-concern', where this has been unrelieved over a long period by other measures. The concept of 'self-concern' as a favourable indication had also been referred to by others (Poppen, 1948; Freeman & Watts, 1950). With this background and knowledge derived from our early cases, a certain picture of the most suitable candidates for leucotomy gradually crystallized, and a constellation of personality features emerged, almost all of which were related to the patient's preoccupation with his self-concept. This was reflected in referrals in numerous ways. Thus, one patient might be referred as suffering 'somatic delusions', of 'hypochondriasis' or even 'paraphrenia' while others were referred for 'persistent painful rumination' or 'anxious depression'. We agree with Robinson and Freeman (1954) that these are all aspects of concern over the self, the continuity of which can be modified by psychosurgery so that guilt-laden rumination about the past and fearful anticipation of the future are reduced in the direction of living more fully and contentedly in the immediate present. In an attempt to assess the personality changes which followed operation, the Minnesota Multiphasic Personality Inventory (MMPI) was administered to 100 consecutive cases before and after operation. The clinical scales of the inventory showed a marked decrease in group means after operation. This effect was differential, the most marked alterations being in the Depression, Hysteria, Psychasthenia, and Schizophrenia scales (beyond 0.001 significance level).

Against the generally favourable improvement on the MMPI one scale moved in an adverse direction. This was the Ego Strength (Es) scale which had been derived from the MMPI by Barron (1953). He felt that this scale reflected the ego strength or latent capacity for integration in the personality, the potential of the personality for coping with situations. The decrease in this scale after operation might support the frequently made claim that leucotomy may lead to a lessening of constructive forces within the personality. It is a reminder that even modified operations may not be carried out with complete immunity. An item analysis showed that many items moved in the 'improved' direction following treatment. The most frequent improvement was in those items related to self-concern expressed either as general painful rumination, brooding or worrying or related to specific areas of dysfunction, most notably concern about mental health or concern over somatic complaints. Accompanying these changes was an improvement in items reflecting introversion. Items expressing depressive mood also showed marked improvement.

If these changes were the the principal cause of improvement there should have been an overlap between the most frequently changed items and those taken from the most improved cases. This was the case, the items being those which expressed the central themes of self-concern, introversion, and depressed psychological mood in the most unambiguous manner.

Item analysis related to particular symptoms showed that anxieties, phobias and painful rumination were most affected, obsessions improved to a lesser degree, while hallucinations and delusions remained unchanged.

Since the main principle of selection was centred around the notion of tortured rumination about the self it follows that we would anticipate alteration in self-concern in successful cases. A comparison of 14 'most improved' with 14 'least improved' cases using Robinson's three tests of self-continuity (Robinson & Freeman, 1954) showed a highly significant difference on all measures when the patients were examined 1–2 years after operation. Those cases classed as improved showed significantly lower scores on the measures of self-concern than those classed as unimproved. One can conclude that a reduction in the capacity for the feeling of self-continuity may be regarded as a central mechanism of psychosurgery.

These findings have several implications: (i) it is only where the particular personality changes described are likely to lead to a better overall state for the patient that a rationale exists for operation; (ii) not only are major frontal sections which produce more drastic changes unjustified, even modified operations may be inimical where decreased self-concern might aggravate rather than help the patient's condition; (iii) selection should be based on symptomatology rather than nosology. This latter point seems particularly important. Reliance on traditional diagnostic categories in selection has often led to disappointing results since the symptom complex most likely to be favourably affected may be present in only few of the cases. The failure of frequently cited 'controlled' studies to show significant improvement after operation is misleading when an examination of the type of case operated shows a remarkable absence of rational principles of selection (Robin, 1958; Vosburg, 1962; McKenzie & Kaczanowski, 1964).

Follow up studies in series like the present suggest that operation is successful to the degree that the symptom complex of tense rumination is present. Where such symptoms form only part of the clinical picture, e.g. in what has been termed pseudoneurotic schizophrenia, only part of the condition will be helped. It would not be logical to expect otherwise.

Finally, the present author had the opportunity of following a small number of patients for almost two decades. Clinical examination supplemented by psychological examination (including the MMPI in a few cases) demonstrates that the changes brought about by operation are still apparent.

The principal feature of modified leucotomy appears to be a modification of the personality in the direction of lessened self-concern. It is probable that this is the central factor by which various forms of prefrontal operation bring about symptomatic relief.

COGNITIVE CHANGES WITH MODIFIED LEUCOTOMY

Less dramatic changes were observed in a small group of 14 patients on whom intellectual measures were taken. However, while these where not marked enough to trouble the patient they are of some theoretical significance in the light of more recent studies.

It has been the general opinion that it was encroachment on the dorso-lateral frontal regions which led to intellectual deficit following radical lobotomy (Malmo, 1948; Petrie, 1952; Smith & Kinder, 1959). The only long term comparison of operation in these two areas strongly supports this notion. Hamlin showed that the long term losses of 'superior topectomy' patients (upper frontal lesions) on intelligence measures was appreciable whereas orbital topectomy examined after the same post-operative period of 14 years showed scores 'remarkably comparable to those of nonoperated controls' (Hamlin, 1970, p. 307). Operation of all types confined to the orbitomedial area seem to have been relatively free of intellectual loss at least as measured by standardized tests. This is now understandable since such tests are greatly dependent upon long-stored information and skills. Most of them are not of the sort to elicit the subtle changes in the regulation of behaviour by the initiation and monitoring of appropriate plans of action which have been demonstrated with such clarity by Luria, Lhermitte, Milner and other neuropsychologists. The following characteristics now recognized by neuropsychologists as typically related to frontal lobe dysfunction were seen in the operated group: (i) lessened ability to formulate an adequate plan for the solution of a problem; (ii) lessened ability to utilize information from their errors to modify subsequent action; (iii) some inflexibility in conceptual behaviour.

The importance of the frontal lobes for the formulation, modification and execution of plans of action has been stressed by Luria and others over many years (Luria, 1973). Difficulties of this kind are well brought out by the Kohs block designs. Though this is a complex task which is also failed by patients with lesions in retrorolandic regions, an examination of the type of performance shows some pathognomonic features in frontal patients. Lhermitte et al (1972) point out that a number of steps are necessary in the solution of the block design problems, namely, preliminary analysis, generation of a programme, implementation and control of the programme and final comparison. Patients with frontal damage may fail at any stage often being blocked in their attempts at solution at the stage of preliminary analysis : *il faut en effet, décomposer le modèle en ses cubes constitutifs de façon à pouvoir choisir le nombre et les faces correctes des ces cubes. Sans cette analyse préalable, la reproduction des modèles est tout à fait impossible'* (Lhermitte et al, 1972, p. 429)

The Goldstein and Scheerer (1941) version of the block design test was given to the operated subjects and a matched control group. If the subject could not complete the design with the small pictured example he was given a design equal in size to the four blocks he was to utilize in his construction. If he failed this he was given a design with the lines of the edges of the blocks superimposed on the design either in a reduced size or a larger version equal to the size of four blocks. No control subject needed any of this assistance whereas the operated subjects often needed a partial programme for the solution, the divided diagram being of particular assistance to most subjects (Fig. 4.17). Design 10 shown in the diagram presented marked difficulty for nine of the fourteen subjects. Qualitative differences were seen in the experimental group. Several subjects expressed puzzlement that a particular design could be reproduced and even after completing the design exhibited uncertainty about it. Several other subjects successfully copied a design, expressed dissatisfaction, broke up the design and commenced again. Subject 14 had no difficulty up to design seven. After great trouble with this design she was given assistance in the form of a large undivided design, then a smaller divided design but still failed. After a long time she succeeded with the aid of the large divided design but volunteered the remark 'You're sure it is possible to get the *other* one right?'. She could see no apparent connection between the original design and the 'assisted' versions which followed. In view of the position and relatively small size of lesions and the apparent preservation of the patients' intelligence, these signs take on added significance. They appear identical in nature though less pronounced than those described with massive frontal

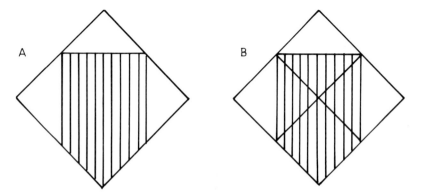

Fig. 4.17 Block design A, undivided (embedded) design; B, divided design.

lesions. Design 10 also proved difficult for the patient described above by Luria and Tsvetkova (1964).

The second area of difficulty was seen on two maze problems. There was a slightly poorer performance by operated subjects than controls on the Porteus Maze Test. Such a loss has been reported frequently with frontal lesions and needs no further documentation. On a second type of maze, an electrical stylus maze (Walsh, 1960), the patient showed more of the qualitative types of error described by Milner (1965) in the section above though the difference between leucotomy and control subjects failed to reach significance. These errors reflected frequent failure to comply with the test instructions though patients showed very clearly on questioning that they understood the rules. Moreover, the knowledge of their errors did not modify the patients' subsequent behaviour or, at least, did not do so as quickly as it did in control subjects. Similarly, the patients often failed on problems of the Porteus Maze Tests by repeatedly entering the incorrect alley while often remarking that their choice *was going to be incorrect*. In a minor way this seems to reflect the difficulty which frontal damaged patients have with inhibiting response tendencies once they have been aroused.

The final example of cognitive impairment comes from the Colour-Form Sorting Test. In this test no control subject experienced difficulty. Again qualitative differences were noted in the experimental group. Only one of thirteen experimental subjects gave a spontaneous verbal account of the correct groupings. Four others were able to complete the two groupings and showed evidence when questioned that they had successfully classified the pieces and were able to shift from one group to the other. All the remaining subjects required further assistance.

Three of the experimental subjects were only able to shift to the second of the groupings after a considerable amount of verbal assistance and a demonstration of the second group by the tester. Two others were able to perform both groupings after explanation as well as documentation on both colour and form groupings.

Three subjects were unable to complete either sorting irrespective of the amount of instruction and assistance given.

The difficulties of scoring such material can be seen in Subject 1 who placed similar forms together and described them in terms of common objects. The request to sort them differently resulted in another grouping described as everyday objects. The subject was then presented with the proper colour groupings. Her response was: 'They don't fit just like that. They don't fit into a pattern according to size. You could have numbers, size, colours.' Despite this verbalization of an apparently high order of abstraction, she was unable to perform the colour groupings, and resorted to several form groupings the last of which was comprised of three groups of forms placed in a row. She explained that the pieces were ordered according to length. Several other examples will demonstrate how difficult to quantify these changes in behaviour may be.

Subject 9 first grouped forms together and gave a correct account. Asked to do it a second way, she persisted in separating the forms; but used them to represent concrete objects. Shown the colour groupings and asked to account for them, she replied: 'One of each shape in each group.'

E: 'What do they have in common?'
S: 'Shape in common. The number in the group.'
E: 'What would you call that group?' (pointing to green pieces)
S: 'The right-hand corner. There are two (groups) in the right-hand corner and two in the left.'

Subject 4 began by turning over the four squares to their white sides to represent a 'tile'. The four circles were placed together as 'rings' while the triangles were 'going to make an octagon; but I need another one.' The request to sort the pieces another way resulted in a more complex pattern. The demonstration of colour sorting seemingly made no sense to her, while the form sorting with the white sides up evoked the following response:

E: 'Does that make sense?'
S: 'Only that you are sorting them out . . into one colour . . white.'

Such subjects cannot be said to have lost all ability to categorize or abstract yet they appear to have great difficutly with a task which normal individuals perform readily. The relatively poor performance of patients on these tasks is in sharp contrast to the fact that these were clinically improved subjects coping with their occupations at their pre-operative level. However, Goldstein (1944) pointed out that in everyday life much thinking runs in such familiar ways, i.e. learned patterns of responses, that frontal impairment may not be evident to the patient's physician or friends.

Over the past few years the Boston group has studied extensively 16 schizophrenics subjected to prefrontal leucotomy over 25 years ago and have compared their results with non-operated schizophrenics and control subjects (Benson et al, 1981; Benson & Stuss, 1982; Stuss & Benson, 1983, 1984; Stuss et al, 1981a, 1981b, 1982a, 1982b, 1983.)

The lesions were variable both in size and extent as well as sometimes being asymmetrical. Although the lesions are described as orbitofrontal it is apparent from the data provided that many of the lesions must have severed portions of the thalamofrontal radiation thus isolating considerable sections of the dorsolateral cortex.

Nevertheless, the general tenor of the results compares well with the summaries in this chapter. The operated subjects differed in being more concrete in their responses, with a difficulty in shifting set and maintaining sequences of correct responses, and a dissociation between verbalization and action. These changes were independent of I.Q. measures from the WAIS. While there was no deficit on one of the abstraction tasks used, the Metaphor Test of Winner and Gardner (1977), the content of the test was familiar and the use of the content not sufficiently demanding to test the 'abstract attitude' in the sense described earlier.

FRONTAL LOBE SYNDROME: ONE OR MANY?

Twenty years ago in speaking of his wide experience with the study of frontal lesion cases, Teuber (1964) remarked: 'I started out by trying to find a unitary concept, but as I moved along, it became clear that no single-factor hypothesis could carry one far enough to cover all the manifestations of frontal lesions. And yet the thing that is so tempting to me after this symposium is to think that there may be a family resemblance among symptoms, even among those which seem in part dissociable.'

As in other areas, the nature of the clinical material available has hindered the development of a theory of the contribution of different frontal areas despite the known anatomic specificity (Hécaen & Albert, 1978). Few unique cases with localized pathology have been studied carefully with appropriate neuropsychological methods. Even the deliberately inflicted lesions of psychosurgery are noted for their variability (see above). Coupled with this, and in order to test the complex functions of the frontal lobes, many of the tests which have been used are themselves complex. This means that there can be sundry reasons for individual failures.

A theoretical system which appears to be capable of incorporating the manifold aspects of frontal lobe dysfunction, both in man and animals is that of Fuster who sees the prefrontal cortex as a kind of superordinate functional system much along the lines of the earlier formulations of Luria. This system is responsible for 'the formation of temporal structure of behavior with a unifying purpose or goal' (Fuster, 1980, p.126). The *temporal structures* endow the organism to deal with the four major characteristics of behaviour if it is to be adaptive: (i) changing demands; (ii) novelty; (iii) complexity; and (iv) integration over time. Fuster sees these component processes as served by the synthetic role of the prefrontal cortex. To be successful the system must be able to anticipate (plan) future outcomes and retain the scheme or plan with the elements executed to date until the goal is attained, and must be able to avert interfering influences that threaten to disrupt it.

A test which is ideal for measuring most of these elements, particularly novelty, complexity, integration over time and interference effects, is the Austin Maze test. Other tests will be seen to have a loading on one or more of these factors.

5

The temporal lobes

Integrative functions of the temporal lobe   169
Complex partial seizures   184
Electrical stimulation of the temporal lobe   187
Temporal lesions and cognitive change   189

INTEGRATIVE FUNCTIONS OF THE TEMPORAL LOBE

The organisation of the temporal lobe is very complex. It is related to the sense systems of olfaction and audition whose primary projection areas and areas of perceptual elaboration lie within its boundaries. It is also related to the visual system and serves to integrate visual perception with the information from the other sensory systems into the unified experience of the world around us. It plays an important role in memory in both its specific and general aspects. It contains systems which help to preserve the record of conscious experience. Finally, it has such an intimate connection with the structures of the limbic system which itself has far reaching connections, that its functional boundaries as well as its morphological boundaries are ill-defined. It is through this system that the temporal lobes help to provide part of the anatomical substrate for the integration of the emotional and motivational aspects of the organism with informational content coming from all those sensory systems situated behind the central fissure and, through its connections with the frontal lobes, with those systems for plans of action which are formulated in these regions. Because of this anatomical and functional complexity one must be cautious of over-simplified conceptions based on an examination of lesions in specific parts of the temporal lobes. Williams says of temporal lobe syndromes: 'it is more true of this part of the nervous system than of any other that disturbances of the part must include consideration of the whole.' (Williams, 1969, p. 700). Therefore, the division of topics in what follows is an arbitrary one. It is particularly oriented to those disorders the examination of which will prove useful in trying to provide a basis for understanding the complex integrative functions which the temporal lobes serve. In the first section, the main areas deal with the effects of unilateral temporal lobe lesions on auditory perception, visual perception, intellectual changes and modality or material specific memory processes while the second section deals with the complex disturbances of behaviour and experience caused by temporal lobe epilepsy and the non-specific disorders of memory which are such a prominent feature of the mesial temporal lobe structures and their connections. For lack of space some areas such as the perception of time and the participation of the temporal lobes in the alerting mechanism will have to be omitted.

ANATOMICAL FEATURES

The temporal lobe lies below the lateral cerebral fissure or fissure of Sylvius. The lateral surface is divided into three convolutions or gyri (superior, middle, and inferior gyri) by two sulci. The superior temporal sulcus runs approximately parallel to the lateral cerebral fissure beginning near the temporal pole in from and running back until, near its end, it turns upward for a short distance into the parietal lobe where it is surrounded by the angular gyrus. On the inner portion of the lateral sulcus the cortex of the superior temporal gyrus dips into the insula in several short horizontal convolutions known as the anterior transverse gyrus of Heschl. The middle temporal sulcus which is often in two disconnected parts, divides the middle from the inferior temporal gyrus, portion of which lies on the inferior or basal portion of the lobe. The artificial lines of demarcation of the boundaries of the lobe with the parietal and occipital lobes are shown in Figure 5.1. The posterior boundary is formed by an imaginary line joining the parieto-occipital sulcus to the preoccipital notch, and the superior boundary runs backwards from the upper end of the lateral sulcus to join the posterior boundary at right angles. Thus the temporal lobe merges into the visual cortex behind and the inferior parietal lobule above. The inferior parietal lobule is made up of the supramarginal and angular gyri. The supramarginal gyrus surrounds the ascending branch of the lateral sulcus.

The inferior parietal lobule lies at the confluence of the parietal, temporal and occipital lobes, i.e. with those posterior or retrorolandic portions of the cerebral cortex which are concerned with the various sensory systems of the body. As this area is rich in multisensory connections it is concerned with the integration of sensory information. Lesions in the lobule particulary in the dominant hemisphere, give rise to symptoms which are characteristically different from lesions in other areas. Whereas lesions in the primary projection areas and the association areas which surround them are modality specific, giving deficit in only one sensory system, lesions in the supramarginal and angular gyri disrupt 'the mnemonic constellations that form the basis for understanding the interpreting sensory signals . . . (which are based on) multisensory perceptions of a higher order' (Carpenter, 1972,

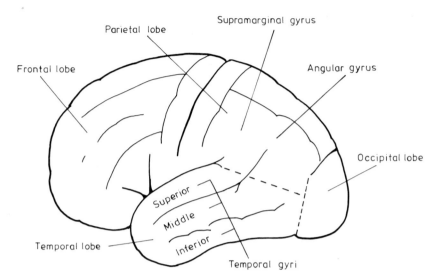

Fig. 5.1 Lateral aspect of the cerebral hemisphere.

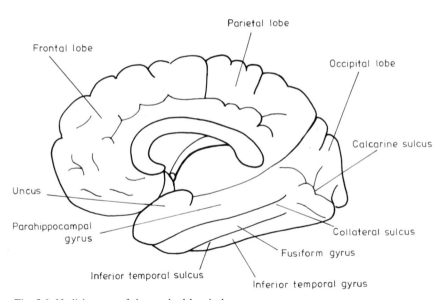

Fig. 5.2 Medial aspect of the cerebral hemisphere.

p. 17). Luria (1973b) has also given prominence to this area considering it as the crowning level of the hierarchically organized systems concerned with gnostic function.

The inferior surface of the temporal lobe (Fig. 2.14) is also divided into three major gyri. Part of the inferior temporal gyrus occupies the lower lateral aspect of the lobe and is separated from the fusiform gyrus by the

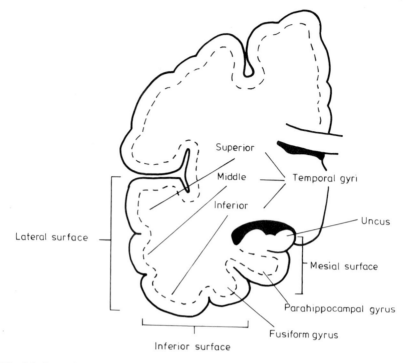

Fig. 5.3 Coronal section through one hemisphere showing the three surfaces of the temporal lobe.

inferior temporal sulcus. The fusiform gyrus is separated from the hippocampal gyrus by the collateral fissure. The anterior portion of the hippocampal gyrus bends around the hippocampal fissure to form the uncus.

The mesial surface, largely the hippocampal gyrus, slopes downwards to the inferior surface (Fig. 5.2).

The cross sectional view (Fig. 5.3) relates the three surfaces to each other and should be of value in understanding descriptions of lesions in this area.

Functional organization

The auditory system

The auditory cortex, like the cortex devoted to other sense modalities, may be divided into two zones: (i) the primary projection area for auditory sensation, and (ii) the secondary or auditory association cortex.

Primary auditory projection. The primary projection area is largely buried in that infolded region of the cortex termed the insula which lies at the junction of the frontal and parietal lobes above the temporal lobes below. This means that a portion of the superior surface of the temporal lobe is hidden from sight when the brain is viewed from its lateral aspect. This insular

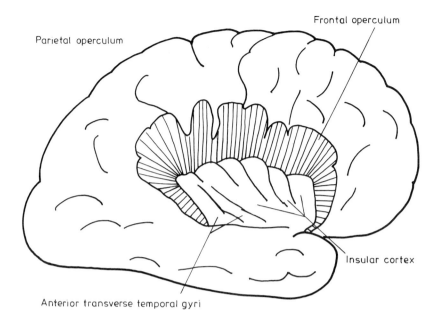

Parietal operculum

Frontal operculum

Insular cortex

Anterior transverse temporal gyri

Fig. 5.4 Insular cortex.

portion of the superior temporal cortex which serves auditory sensation may contain one, or sometimes two anterior transverse temporal gyri, or gyri of Heschl (Fig. 5.4).

Auditory information is transmitted from the sense receptors in the cochlea of the inner ear via the auditory pathways. The pathways for auditory information in the brain stem are exceedingly complex and, even now, some of the details appear to be incomplete. The main features of the pathways (Fig. 5.6) are provided principally to demonstrate the fact that information from one ear may travel via a number of different routes to reach the auditory cortex of both hemispheres. After relaying at several points on the way auditory information reaches its final relay station in the medial geniculate body at the base of the thalamus from which it travels to the primary projection area in Heschl's gyrus.

Damage to the peripheral receptors or acoustic nerve results in deafness on the side of the damage; but damage in the principal auditory pathway in the brain stem, the lateral lemniscus (Fig. 5.5), causes a partial deafness since there are both crossed and uncrossed pathways in this tract.

There are certain similarities and also important differences in the transmission of photo- and phono reception which are important in understanding the effects of lesions in the two sense modalities of vision and audition. Both systems relay their modality-specific information via specialized thalamic nuclei and both auditory and visual cortex have a topological structure, i.e. the relationships of the stimuli as they impinge on the

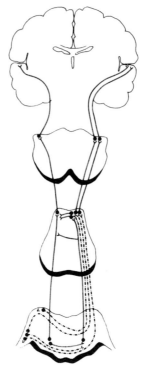

Fig. 5.5 The complex auditory pathways.

organism are preserved from receptor to primary cortex. In the case of audition this is termed tonotopic localization (Fig. 5.5). Fibres carrying impulses produced by high frequency sounds are found in the medial portions of the cortex while the fibres carrying information produced by low frequency sounds terminate in the lateral parts of the auditory cortex.

In the visual system there is a partition of information from each eye, certain fibres from each organ going to one hemisphere and other fibres to the other hemisphere. (See Ch. 7 for further detail). In audition the fibres from the receptor organ (the organ of Corti) in each ear are projected to *both* primary zones of the auditory cortex. This representation is, however, not equal, each ear being represented more strongly in the opposite hemisphere, i.e. the ears are bilaterally but unequally represented in the cortex. Because of this bilateral representation of each organ, complete cortical or cerebral deafness would require lesions affecting the transverse gyri of Heschl bilaterally. Such a situation is exceedingly rare. Unilateral lesions of the primary auditory zones of the cortex do not have a marked effect on auditory acuity but careful testing reveals an elevation of auditory thresholds in the ear contralateral to the lesion.

Auditory association areas. The secondary or association areas of the auditory cortex give clear cut evidence of lateral specialization, the cortex of the hemisphere which is dominant for speech being particularly concerned with the analysis of speech sounds, while the auditory perception of non-verbal material including music appears to be mediated more by the non-dominant hemisphere. This partition or specialization of function is in accordance with what Luria (1973b) calls the law of progressive lateralization and forms an important aspect of the asymmetry of function dealt with in Chapter 8.

Auditory perceptual defects. Lesions in the auditory association cortex of the left side produce sensory or receptive aphasia. The difficulty arises only when the patient has to distinguish speech sounds and the older term, auditory or acoustic agnosia, is in some ways to be preferred since it points to the primary difficulty from which a number of other symptoms flow. However, usage is too well established to allow the change, and the term acoustic agnosia is best preserved for the inability to distinguish non-verbal sounds, which is associated with right hemisphere lesions. The disorder of phonemic hearing is produced largely by lesions affecting the superior temporal gyrus in the region adjacent to the primary auditory cortex of the left hemisphere. A phoneme is the smallest distinctive group of sounds in a language, and one of the principal tasks in learning a language is to distinguish readily between phonemes. The nature of phonemic distinction becomes apparent when we endeavour to learn a new language since the distinctive speech sounds are not the same in all languages and the difficulties which a person may have with learning a new language will depend on the phonemic distinctions which he brings to the task. The ease with which we are able to distinguish *p* and *b* in words such as peach and beach will be difficult for people whose primary language has but a single phoneme for these sounds.

It follows that a person who has an acquired difficulty in discriminating between similar phonemes will have difficulty in understanding spoken speech. Luria expresses this concisely: 'As words in his own language fail to be differentiated his attitude towards words in his native tongue will begin to resemble that to words in a foreign language' (Luria, 1973b). Since the patient's basic difficulty lies in auditory discrimination he is deprived of the regulation of his own speech via the monitoring of his own vocal productions. He is therefore unaware of his own defective speech and hence sees no necessity for correcting it. Moreover, if he has difficulty in producing the correct word to name an object, prompting him is of no avail since he is unable to fit the information into a phonemic system. Structured language disappears and is replaced by very fragmented utterances that have been called a 'word salad'.

The failure to distinguish the vital differences in acoustic content of words means that the patient will be unable to write material that is dictated to him whereas he may be readily able to copy verbal material when it is visually presented. An important exception to the inability to write words from dictation is in the ability to write words which have become so familiar that they no longer require precise analysis of their acoustic content. Prime examples of this conversion of words into motor stereotypes are the patient's signature and the most frequently used words in his trade or profession. Luria and his colleagues have pointed out that this is an example of how the cerebral organization of a process may change over time (Luria et al, 1970). In the process of learning to write words, careful acoustic analysis is needed at first but the motor aspects of writing become more and more automatic with use and less dependent upon auditory discrimination so that the writing of a familiar word comes to have a different neuronal or cerebral organization from a relatively new word. This means that lesions in different sites will have different effects and, once again, a careful qualitative analysis of the precise form of difficulty which the patient has (in this case with some words and not with others) will point more precisely to the location of the lesion.

As one moves away from the area surrounding the primary projection area for audition there is a decrease in phonological disturbances and, in the region of the middle temporal gyrus, the most prominent defect is one of audioverbal memory, an auditory amnesic aphasia. The characteristic feature of these memory disorders is the inability to repeat a series of words which has been presented acoustically despite the fact that the patient may be able to retain and repeat single words. With a series of words the patient may show a primacy effect (the reproduction of the first word given) or a recency effect (the reproduction of the last word given), other members of the series being lost. Luria, Sokolov and Klimkovsky (1967) have analysed these disturbances of audio-verbal memory and suggest that the fault lies in the increased mutual inhibition of the auditory traces. This hypothesis is supported by their finding that increasing the time interval between the presentation of members of the series greatly reduces or eliminates the difficulty. The extension of the time between words is thought to reduce the mutually inhibitory effects which adjacent members of the series have on each other. This type of finding is also relevant to an examination of the amnesic syndrome which follows bilateral mesial temporal lesions discussed below.

Left-sided posterior temporal lesions sometimes lead to a difficulty in using words to name objects, the so-called nominal aphasia. The patient perceives the objects and their significance and can, usually in a roundabout fashion known as circumlocution, describe their use or function. It is the association between the visual apprehension or a particular object and a particular word which is lost.

A second effect of lesions which disrupt the co-ordinated action of vision and audition in this borderland region between the temporal and occipital lobes is an inability to draw objects on verbal request ('Please draw a clock.') while retaining the ability to draw the same object when a copy is presented. It might be assumed that because of disconnection of portions of the auditory and visual regions from each other, that words no longer evoke images which would form the basis for executing a drawing of the object named.

So far we have dealt with difficulties which arise with the understanding of speech sounds. Man must also be able to discriminate and attach meaning to other environmental sounds. The finding of impairment in the recognition of these non-verbal sounds has been described in the literature for many decades under the term acoustic agnosia.

Unfortunately, this term has been used somewhat indiscriminately at times to refer to difficulty with the recognition of any kind of auditory material including speech. In his review of the earlier clinical literature Vignolo (1969) employs the term in its original sense of 'defective recognition of non-verbal sounds and noises'. He and his colleagues have addressed themselves to two major aspects of the problem of auditory agnosia, namely the relationship of auditory agnosia to aphasia, and the relationship of auditory agnosia to hemispheric location of the lesion. The two experiments described by Vignolo (1969) are summarized here in some detail. These experiments demonstrate the value of the clinico-experimental method in neuropsychology for testing hypotheses suggested by clinical findings. They have led to the concept of the double dissociation of auditory functions between the two temporal lobes. The practical diagnostic value of these findings is discussed at the end of this section.

In the first experiment a test of auditory recognition was given to normal subjects and to patients with unilateral temporal lesions both right- and left-sided. Left-sided patients were defined as aphasic if their scores fell below a certain point on one of a number of tests of aphasia. These aphasic patients were then further categorized into types and degrees of aphasia.

The auditory test required the subject to select from four pictures on a card the source of a common environmental sound played to him. The sounds were unambiguous, e.g. baby crying, ambulance siren, yapping dog. Four separate pictures were presented with each sound, each having the following categories of sound source: (i) the correct source (e.g. canary whistling), (ii) acoustically similar source (man whistling), (iii) similar class or semantic category (cock crowing), (iv) unrelated sound source (train). Thus the subjects could have three types of misrecognition; acoustic errors, semantic errors and unrelated errors. The findings supported a distinction made by Vignolo between two different types of auditory agnosia. An inability to discriminate accurately the sound pattern produced a *perceptual-discriminative sound agnosia*, while an inability to associate the auditory stimulation with its meaning resulted in an *associative-sound agnosia*. As might have been anticipated, sound recognition defects were more frequently associated with marked receptive aphasia than they were with other types of aphasia. Thus auditory verbal comprehension and the recognition of non-verbal sound sources were closely related.

An examination of the type of error made by the aphasic and non-aphasic groups showed a highly significant difference with regard to the 'semantic' errors but not to the other types, i.e. 'auditory' or 'unrelated'. This strongly suggests that the difficulties in recognition by the aphasic patients were due, not to any inability to discriminate, but to an inability to associate the sound which had been perceived with its usual meaning. On the other hand, two patients with right hemisphere lesions who performed poorly on this test did so because of an increase in acoustic errors, i.e. their difficulty appeared to be discriminative rather than semantic-associative.

The second experiment strengthened and clarified this distinction. Two tests were employed. One, the Meaninful Sounds Identification Test was similar to the test employed in the first experiment, requiring the subject to select the correct pictorial representation of a well-known environmental sound. The second task, the Meaningless Sounds Discrimination Test, required the subject to discriminate between pairs of complex sounds which had been 'mixed' artificially in a sound studio. Again, groups of left- and right-brain damaged patients, and normal subjects were used.

Each of the brain damaged groups performed poorly on one of the tests the deficit varying according to the hemispheric locus of the lesion. Left-sided damage was related to poor performance on the test of semantic association (Meaningful Sounds) while this group's performance on the discrimination test (Meaningless Sounds) was normal. The right hemisphere group reversed the pattern of deficit having a normal performance on the semantic-associative task and a very poor performance on the perceptual-discriminative test. In keeping with the findings from the first experiment, all patients with an exclusively semantic-associative defect were aphasic.

This double dissociation of function of the two temporal lobes with respect to auditory perception further supports the lateral specialization of function shown by the studies of material-specific memory defects, dichotic listening studies and cortical stimulation of the temporal regions described elsewhere in this chapter, and the finding of asymmetry of auditory recognition is in keeping with the broader notion of cerebral hemisphere asymmetry of function reviewed in Chapter 8. These findings also have a practical application in diagnosis since they appear to make an unequivocal distinction between unilateral lesions of the temporal lobes.

Dichotic listening studies. In 1954 Broadbent described the dichotic listening technique. This consisted of the simultaneous presentation of auditory material to the two ears by means of a stereophonic tape recorder. The material consisted of pairs of digits and when three pairs of these were given in fairly quick succession, the subjects could normally repeat all six digits, usually reporting the three digits which had been presented to one ear followed by the three presented to the other. In right-handed subjects (assumed to be left hemisphere language-dominant) the digits from the right ear were normally reported first. This may be assumed to be in keeping with the verbal nature of the material and stronger contralateral representation of the auditory input mentioned at the beginning of the chapter. This finding is sometimes referred to as ear asymmetry or interaural rivalry. It might be better to avoid such terms since they focus attention on the periphery rather than on the asymmetry of processing by the two hemispheres.

Attention was directed to this area by the early work of Kimura. In her studies with Milner at Montreal (Milner, 1962) it had been found that certain aspects of the Seashore Measures of Musical Talents differentiated between patients who had undergone right or left anterior temporal lobectomy. In particular, right temporal lobectomy produced a marked deficit of tonal memory while left-sided operations had no effect on this subtest. These deficits appeared to be of a higher order or agnostic type since hearing as measured by audiometric testing was apparently unaltered. Following these findings, Kimura (1961a) employed Broadbent's dichotic technique in the assessment of temporal lobe damage. Patients with temporal lobe epilepsy were examined before and after lobectomy. Patients with temporal lobe seizures performed poorly before operation, but following operation the left temporal group became much worse, while the level of performance of the right temporal group remained the same. These right-sided patients, however, now reported more of the right ear digits than they had before the operation. In more general terms, unilateral temporal lobectomy impaired the recognition of material by the contralateral ear. The fact that the left temporal lobectomy group performed very poorly is related to the verbal nature of the material used, i.e. the deficit is a function of the type of material presented. This point of view was strongly supported when Kimura (1964) developed her dichotic test using short melodic patterns instead of verbal material.

Kimura (1961a) assumed that the superiority of the right ear in dichotic listening (verbal) experiments was due to a direct relation between cerebral dominance and the verbal nature of the perception. However, subsequent studies have shown that much of the effect can be accounted for by what has come to be termed the 'ear order effect' (Inglis & Sykes, 1967; Satz et al, 1965; Schuloff & Goodglass, 1969). This effect represents a greater decay related to material reported from the ear which is reported second. The first ear report is closer in time to immediate apprehension of the stimuli while the second report is subject to decay in short-term memory (STM).

Clinical studies of amusia reported in the literature had often given equivocal findings with regard to the question of localization and, as Kimura pointed out, had often confounded any loss of musical recognition with verbal aspects of the test situation such as comprehension of verbal instructions, naming difficulties, and the like. The Kimura test consists of the simultaneous presentation to each ear of melodic patterns of 4 seconds duration. Each pair of melodies was followed by four single melodies and the subject was asked to identify the position of the two dichotically presented patterns in the series, e.g. 'first and third', 'second and third', first and fourth'. Kimura's findings of a left ear (right hemisphere) superiority in the perception of melodies (Kimura, 1964, 1967) was confirmed by Shankweiler (1966) and other workers demonstrated a dichotic superiority for the perception of the intonational aspects of speech, again for the left ear (Blumstein & Cooper, 1974; Zurif, 1974). Kimura (1967) pointed out that this auditory asymmetry for words and music has provided a new technique for the study of cerebral dominance. Her findings were supplemented by others (Schuloff & Goodglass, 1969; Sparks et al 1970) who found a bilateral decrement in auditory recognition with damage to either lobe which varied with the nature of the material presented — left hemisphere lesion cases showed a severe bilateral deficit with words as stimuli while right hemisphere cases showed a marked bilateral deficit with tonal sequences. In each case there was also a falling off in efficiency of the ear contralateral to the lesion for the other class of material, i.e. with left hemisphere lesions there was a right ear loss for tonal sequences while right hemisphere lesions there was a left ear loss of efficiency for digits.

A study by Zurif and Ramier (1972) came close to the same distinction made by Vignolo. Using dichotic digits and dichotic sequences of phonemes they found differences between left- and right-sided lesions suggesting that the left hemisphere is more concerned with the processing of phonological information while the right hemisphere is more concerned with the acoustic parameters of speech.

The question of whether primary sensory deficits contribute to the agnosic or so-called higher order of defects is one which is frequently raised. In some instances there are those who doubt the existence of certain 'pure' syndromes such as visual object agnosia (Ch. 7) in the absence of a primary sensory deficit. As mentioned earlier, primary sensory deficits of cortical origin in audition are difficult to detect because of the bilateral representation of each ear in the cortex. Oxbury and Oxbury (1969) have compared the dichotic findings with digits in groups of cases in each hemisphere where the cortex of Heschl's gyrus was either completely removed or completely spared. Before operation the order of reporting the digits favoured the right ear, i.e. although digits arrived simultaneously the subjects most frequently reported those from the right ear before they reported those from the left. Left temporal lobectomy including Heschl's gyrus increased right ear errors but did not alter the order of report. Left temporal lobectomy sparing Heschl's gyrus reversed the order of report, i.e. left digits were reported before right, but there was no increase in errors. Right temporal lobectomy including Heschl's gyrus did not increase errors and exaggerated the primacy of reporting right ear digits. Right temporal lobectomy sparing Heschl's gyrus led to no alteration on either measure. These data show clearly the importance of loss of the primary auditory cortex in producing the deficits. A recent study of Efron and Crandall (1983) on a small number of temporal lobectomies suggested that operation decreases the perceptual salience of the tone represented to the ear contra-lateral to the lesion.

Finally, dichotic performance has been studied in a few instances where the interhemispheric fibres were interrupted either from agenesis of the corpus collosum or operative division of the fibres for the relief of epilepsy. Two studies (Milner et al, 1968; Bryden & Zurif, 1970) described failure to report digits presented to the left ear when dichotic stimulation was used on commissurotomy patients. Sparks and Geschwind's patient showed complete extinction of digits received by the left ear. The fact that failure to report from the left ear in this patient was so much greater than any right hemisphere cases suggested the importance of the commissural pathways in dichotic stimulation (Sparks & Geschwind, 1968). Two studies of agenesis of the corpus callosum (Saul & Sperry, 1968; Bryden & Zurif, 1970) report no auditory asymmetry nor is there any evidence of marked unilateral auditory effects with hemispherectomy (Curry, 1968; Bryden & Zurif, 1970).

The studies cited above are a sample only of the extensive studies which have been carried out on auditory asymmetry. As extensive review is given in Bradshaw and Nettleton (1983).

Inferring language dominance. It was hoped that dichotic listening results might be used to infer functional asymmetry of the brain in individual cases without having to resort to the Wada technique of intracarotid sodium amytal injection described below. Knowledge of cerebral dominance is desirable in certain neurosurgical procedures and in the application of unilateral electroconvulsive therapy (ECT). However, numerous studies attest to the fact that not only are the differences small but the reliability of the usual method of dichotic *recall* is unacceptably low (Pizzamiglio, De Pascalis & Vignati A, 1974; Blumstein, Goodglass & Tarter, 1975; Berlin, 1977; Fennell, Bowers & Satz, 1977; Colbourn, 1978) while others question the dubious logic employed in drawing inferences from the test results (Satz, 1977; Teng, 1981).

A more robust test termed *dichotic monitoring* was developed by Geffen (1976). This requires the subject to make a manual response on detection of the stimulus rather that using verbal recall. A validation study (Geffen & Caudry, 1981) showed considerably larger measures of ear advantage than for the usual dichotic recall method.

While a more robust non-invasive technique may be helpful even this fails to satisfy requirements in one of the most common situations, namely projected temporal lobe surgery for intractable epilepsy where amytal ablation remains the preferred technique.

Music and the brain. Apart from dichotic listening studies the testing of patients with unilateral lesions (particulary in the temporal lobes) lends general support to a hemispheric asymmetry of function with regard to the perception and execution of music although the evidence as to which particular characteristics relate to the dominant or non-dominant side is still far from clear. Damasio and Damasio (1977) having reviewed the evidence to that time felt the evidence supported a major role for the right hemisphere for musical *execution*. As in the case report of McFarland and Fortin (1982) they felt that this could be dissociated from musical training and experience. The unsatisfactory state of our knowledge is shown by the edited collection of Critchley and Henson (1977) and the very recent review of Henson (1985).

Visual perception

The temporal lobes are neither concerned with the primary reception of visual information nor with its elaboration into meaningful wholes. They are concerned however, with the integration of visual experience with all forms of sensory information coming from the receptors of the other special senses and from the receptors of the bodily senses. Disturbances of all forms of perception of the individual's internal and external worlds are seen in all their complexity in temporal lobe epilepsy examples of which are described below.

The temporal lobes contain portion of the optic radiations which curve forward into the lobe after leaving the lateral geniculate bodies before looping back to their termination in the occipital lobes. Temporal lobe lesions thus produce visual field defects which characteristically affect the upper homonymous quadrants (see Ch. 7) but may sometime produce a complete hemianopia (Falconer & Wilson, 1958). Even in cases where no field loss was apparent to normal examination, changes were detected after temporal lobectomy in the form of raised flicker fusion thresholds for both left- and right-sided cases. Difference between the impact of the lesions according to the side have been demonstrated in a number of studies. Thus, Dorff and his co-workers (1965) found that using the method of presenting two stimuli simultaneously one to each of the visual fields, the left temporal group was impaired in the right (contralateral) visual field, while the right temporal lobe group was impaired in both left and right fields.

Other studies have suggested that lesions of the right temporal lobe might produce disruptions of visual perception that are not shown by comparable lesions on the left side. Milner (1958) found that patients with right temporal lobe lesions had difficulty in recognizing objects from an incomplete pictorial representation of them, a difficulty which was not shown by patients with left-sided lesions. Milner also described an impairment in right-sided cases in the ability to recognize anomalies in pictures, e.g. a picture in which a painting is shown hanging on the wall inside a monkey house. However, using the same test — the McGill Picture Anomalies Test — Shalman (1961) failed to confirm this finding in a small highly selected sample. McFie (1960) described defects in the Picture Arrangement Subtest of the Wechsler Scale, again, restricted to right hemisphere cases. Kimura (1963), using tachistoscopic presentation, found that lesions on the right side impaired subjects' recognition when the material was unfamiliar while left temporal subjects were more impaired when familiar material was being presented.

Warrington and James (1967b) failed to confirm Kimura's general finding of impaired number estimation on tachistoscopically presented material with right temporal damage but did find significantly raised recognition thresholds in the contralateral left visual fields. Rubino (1970) found that right temporal lobe removal rendered the patient less able to identify meaningless visual patterns than did left-sided removals.

Further support to the association of special defects with right temporal lesions was given by Lansdell (1962a) who found right temporal lobectomy patients to be poorer on a design preference test than left lobectomy patients. In a later study, (Lansdell, 1968) he reported that right-sided operations led to poorer performance also on a visuospatial abstract reasoning task that was relatively unaffected by left-sided operations. The more extensive the removals were on the right side the greater were these deficits.

Though both temporal lobes are intimately concerned with perceptual processing it appears that the lateral specialization shown in auditory perception extends also to the visual modality in this area. From the sample of evidence cited the relationship between the side of the lesion and the nature of the perceptual deficit, however, is still far from clear.

Olfactory function

The olfactory receptive area is located in the uncus and adjoining parts of the parahippocampal gyrus. Damage to the olfactory pathways or cortex produces *anosmia*. Olfactory hallucinations are often the signal of irritative lesions in the region and are known as *uncinate fits* sometimes occurring as an epileptic aura.

Following temporal lobectomy Rausch and Serafetinides (1975a, b) described an elevation in the threshold of detection for the quality or identity of an odour. A further study of lobectomy patients (Rausch, Serafetinides & Crandall, 1977) showed more errors in odour recall for operated subjects, with right lobectomy patients performing more poorly than left. Right lobectomy patients only were impaired on matching odours in another study (Abraham & Matthai, 1983) though discrimination as such was not affected. Finally, Eskenazi et al (1983) found no laterality effects though all subjects post-operatively had poorer immediate and delayed odour memory than controls and also showed impairment on a wide range of tests of olfactory functioning.

COMPLEX PARTIAL SEIZURES (TEMPORAL LOBE EPILEPSY)

Behavioural change

This issue has been the subject of heated debate particularly over the past decade. From the 'fifties, epidemiological studies in several countries had suggested a possibly higher frequency of psychopathology in those with temporal lobe epilepsy compared with those with other neurological disorders including other forms of epilepsy. There were also some negative studies. A pivotal report was that of Bear and Fedio (1977) who compared patients with unilateral temporal lobe foci with normal subjects and those with neuromuscular disorders on specific aspects of behaviour. The selected traits were examined both by self-report and close observer rating. Bear and Fedio claim to have demonstrated characteristic patterns in the interictal behaviour of their temporal lobe subjects which were different from the other two groups and, moreover, differences which reflected an asymmetry of the expression of affect between those with right versus left-sided foci. Hermann and Riel (1981) lent partial support to Bear and Fedio's contention by finding characteristic differences between temporal lobe epileptics and those with generalized epilepsy on a self-report questionnaire. In a further study, Bear et al (1982) obtained quantitative ratings from blind interviews of temporal lobe epileptics who had been hospitalized for psychiatric reasons, other epileptics and psychiatric patients with no history of epilepsy. The authors claimed a distinctive profile which included 'desire for social affiliation, circumstantiality, religious and philosophic interests, and deepened affects, among the temporal lobe epileptics.'

Bear (1979) theorized that the connections between sensory cortex and limbic system form the substrate for 'attributing visceral or emotional significance to perceived stimuli' (p. 358). This could lead to an increased connection as the result of heightened electrical activity in temporal lobe epilepsy which might alter the affective experience in this group.

The original article of Bear and Fedio has produced vigorous discussion and at least two negative attempts at replication (Mungas, 1982; Brumback, 1983). The subsequent debate has highlighted the methodological problems inherent in this complex area (Bear, 1983; Mungas, 1983; Silberman, 1983).

A second area of interest is the relationship between temporal lobe epilepsy and psychotic behaviour. In 1969 Flor-Henry made a retrospective case history evaluation of 50 temporal lobe epileptics who had been hospitalized with psychotic episodes and claimed that temporal lobe epilepsy of the dominant hemisphere predisposed to psychosis and that this psychosis was schizophreniform in nature while psychosis accompanying nondominant hemisphere epilepsy tended to be manic-depressive in nature.

Both the major areas mentioned in this section have been ably reviewed by Trimble (1983).

Complex partial seizures arising in the temporal region were outlined in Chapter 3. The term temporal lobe epilepsy was introduced by Lennox

(1951). Part of the complexity of the syndrome no doubt lies in the spread of excitation from the numerous possible sites of origin of the electrical abnormalities though some regions such as the mesial temporal areas are more often involved than others. Williams points out that the way in which the term temporal lobe epilepsy is used 'reflects the difficulty we have in considering disturbance of complex functions in relation to equally complex structures which have a very extensive network of communications throughout the hemisphere. The phrase simply implies that the more evident origins of the disturbances are situated below the sylvian fissure . . .' (1969, p. 700).

The complex symptomatology of temporal lobe epilepsy has been described in detail in its many guises by Lennox and Lennox (1960) and numerous other authors. The following two cases taken from the previously cited work of Williams are particularly illustrative of the multiform nature of the disorder. A woman surgeon developed temporal lobe epilepsy as the result of head injuries caused by being knocked down by a car. The attacks were all heralded by appearance of a human face and shoulders clothed in a red jersey. The figure was intensely and distressingly identified with the patient. The hallucination would then topple sideways and disintegrate into discrete fragments like a jigsaw puzzle, the patient meanwhile experiencing extreme fear with an unnatural quality to it, followed by amnesia in which a general convulsion occurred. The patient had total amnesia for the accident, but it is incidentally interesting that long after the traumatic epilepsy became established she learnt that she had been wearing a read jumper when the car struck her. Here then is a visual hallucination identified with the self, compounded with an emotion, and having in it fragments of memory in time. In another case a woman of 30 had had epilepsy for 15 years. The attacks only happened when she was applying her eye shadow; then, her face close to the mirror attending fixedly to the eyes, the reflected image would change, becoming more intense and dominating her. She would then seem to see a scene with her grandparents and parents, which seemed to be vividly remembered from a former experience. The scene was visualized but was not seen as an hallucination: 'it was in my mind's eye'. This visual memory was accompanied by unremembered words, the whole event being pleasurable and associated with a general sense of sexual excitement. This then is the experience of visual and auditory hallucination inter-mixed, related to past experience, and having visceral sensory and emotional components, induced by a highly specific visual precipitant which must be closely identified with the self and also with sexuality. (Williams, 1969, p. 709)

Hallucinations and illusions of the temporal lobe

Disordered perception in the form of either illusions or hallucinations has been recognized as part of epileptic symptomatology for a very long time.

If the perception refers to a person or object present in the environment we speak of a illusion or false perception. With temporal lobe attacks part or all of the object may be distorted, e.g. everything may appear visually larger or smaller (macropsia, micropsia) or the relative size of parts may appear distorted (metamorphopsia), or sounds louder or softer than usual. These distortions are often accompanied by a feeling that the person is somehow detached from his own body (depersonalization) or that things are unreal (derealization). Though these disorders are common in the visual modality they are by no means restricted to this sense. Hughlings Jackson's case with olfactory hallucinations was described in Chapter 3. These olfactory auras appear to be associated with the anterior and inferior portions of the lobe including the uncus. The odours are always described as being disagreeable or offensive, never pleasant, (Penfield & Jasper, 1954).

Hallucinations refer to perceptual experiences which do not correspond in any way to stimuli in the current environment. The patient is often aware of the 'unreal' nature of the hallucinated objects. The hallucination may be accompanied by emotional experiences which are usually unpleasant, though pleasurable feelings and even short periods of ecstasy have been described infrequently (Lennox & Lennox, 1960). Williams (1956) has examined these emotional experiences in epileptic subjects and related them to specific locations in the temporal lobe. The change in affect at the time of seizure is most commonly that of fear (Williams, 1956; Daly, 1975). Some patients experience unprecipitated fear in the interictal period (Hermann & Chhabria, 1980). While there is as yet no supporting evidence, these interictal phenomena may be associated with abnormal electrical discharges in structures forming the anatomical substrate of emotional experience.

With temporal lobe disturbances there is a fresh interpretation of current experience. Simpson (1969) suggests that, for learning to take place, or to decide whether an object or situation is 'familiar', one must compare the present sensory input with the neural record of past experience. He interprets the data of temporal lobe epilepsy as demonstrating the presence in the temporal lobe of what he terms 'coincidence detection circuits'. If the comparison of the input with the record of the past produces a coincidence or familiarity response, the present stimulation will appear familiar even if nothing similar had occurred in the subject's prior experience. This is the well known phenomenon of *déjà vu* (seen before) which is experienced at times by normal subjects but more frequently and with greater vividness by some patients with temporal lobe epilepsy. On the other hand, a matching which produced a 'no coincidence' response leads to the experience of *jamais vu* or *jamais entendu* (never seen, never heard) even though the stimulus pattern or one very similar has been frequently encountered in the past. Penfield (1954) referred to these alterations in the perception of the present as 'interpretive illusions'.

On some occasions the hallucinations can be shown to be quite clearly related to prior experience and the evidence from cortical stimulation outlined below supports Penfield's contention that they are 'a reactivation of a strip of the record of the stream of consciousness'.

ELECTRICAL STIMULATION OF THE TEMPORAL LOBE

Temporal lobe surgery particulary surgical procedures for the treatment of intractable complex partial seizures presented an opportunity to study the effects of electical stimulation from both the temporal cortex and subcortical regions. Several classes of mental phenomena have been elicited: (i) visceral sensation, fear and anxiety (Jasper & Rasmussen, 1958; Chapman, 1960; Van Buren, 1961; Heath, 1964; Kim, 1971); (ii) complex hallucinations and experiental changes including déjà vu (Mullen & Penfield, 1959; Sem-Jacobsen & Torkildsen, 1960; Penfield & Perot, 1963; Horowitz, Adams & Rutkin, 1968; Weingarten, Cherlow, & Halgren, 1977); (iii) Amnesia (Bickford et al, 1958; Pampiglione & Falconer, 1960; Brazier, 1966; Champman et al, 1967; Serafetinides, Walter & Cherlow, 1975; Halgren et al, 1978). Most of these studies have found a marked inter- and intra-individual variability in response. Only a small proportion of stimulations produce mental phenomena even where evoked potentials and/or after discharges have been recorded (Chapman, 1958; Pampiglione & Falconer, 1960; Walker & Marshall, 1961; Angeleri, Ferro-Milone & Parigi, 1964; Halgren et al, 1978), certainly on less than 10% of occasions. It has also proved difficult to obtain similar experiences on repeated stimulation in the same subject. Halgren et al (1983) have reviewed the stimulation studies of the medial temporal lobe and hippocampal formation.

In 1938 Penfield produced for the first time an evocation of experience by stimulating the temporal cortex in a conscious human subject. These experiences were of two kinds. Firstly, the evocation of an experience which the subject had undergone on a number of previous occasions during his epileptic seizures, and, secondly, the production of previous happenings which had not been seen during the attacks but here also clearly related to specific prior experiences.

Penfield uses the term *experiential hallucination* when the phenomenon occurred spontaneously, and *experiential response* when it was elicited by stimulation.

Several features stand out clearly in the very large number of cases where stimulation of the brain was employed (Penfield & Perot, 1963): (i) despite the stimulation of practically every accessible spot on the cerebral cortex, experiential responses were evoked only from the temporal lobe (a total of 612 patients in Penfield's series were stimulated in non-temporal areas and produced not a single experiential response); (ii) in almost all cases of evoked experiences, the patients were suffering from temporal lobe epilepsy; (iii) only about 8% of temporal lobe cases stimulated gave rise to experiential responses; (iv) responses were evoked from both sides of the

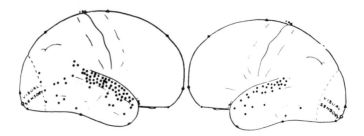

Fig. 5.6 Points on the lateral aspects of the hemispheres where stimulation evoked experiential responses (Penfield & Perot, 1963).

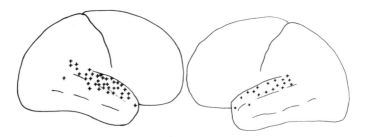

Fig. 5.7 Auditory experiential responses.

brain but there was a marked asymmetry. Figure 5.6 shows the points in the two cerebral hemispheres where electrical stimulation produced an experiential response. The greatest concentration of the responses was in the superior temporal convolution of both hemispheres, with the frequency on the right side greater than that on the left. On the right side, too, the points giving rise to experiential responses extended more posteriorly along the superior temporal convolution and the posterior portion of the whole right lobe is productive while the corresponding regions on the left are almost silent to stimulation.

Auditory responses evoked by stimulation are shown in Figure 5.7. They are concentrated on the superior regions of the lobes with greater frequency on the right. Within this distribution no further finer topographical distribution was discovered, nor did there appear to be any separate effects related to laterality. The responses were most often a voice or voices though sometimes meaningful environmental sounds or music were elicited. The following case is condensed from Penfield and Perot (1963, p. 639). The patient's verbatim responses are reported in full.

A 25-year-old man with 6 year history of epileptic seizures which were at first characterised by vertigo and auditory experiential hallucinations and later changed their character to generalized seizures. Stimulation of a number of points on the cortex of the first or superior temporal convolution produced the following reponses: STIMULATION 'Just like someone whispering, or something, in my left ear, it sounded something like a crowd.' REPEAT STIMULATION 'Again someone trying to speak to me, a single person . . . a man's voice. I could not understand what he said.' ANOTHER POINT STIMULATED 'Something brings back a memory, I could see Seven-Up Bottling Company — Harrison Bakery.' ANOTHER POINT 'I am trying to find the name of a song. There was a piano and someone was playing. I could hear the song, you know. It is a song I have sung before but I cannot find out quite what the title of the song is. That is what I was trying to do when you finished stimulating!' REPEAT STIMULATION 'Someone was speaking to another and he mentioned a name but I could not understand it.' REPEAT STIMULATION "Yes, 'Oh Marie Oh Marie' — someone is singing it." REPEAT 'Someone telling me in *my left (contralateral ear)* (authors italics) Sylvere, Sylvere (the patients's name). It could have been the voice of my brother.' ANOTHER POINT 'It is a woman calling but I cannot make out the name.'

Combined auditory and visual responses were evoked on only very few occasions. Though also few in number experiences of music were more frequently reported from the right side and this is in keeping with clinical reports of amusia and the experimental findings on the greater importance of the right temporal lobe for the perception of music and the melodic elements of speech mentioned in this chapter and elsewhere in the literature.

Temporal lobe stimulation sometimes evoked visual experiences. There was an even greater preponderance of responses from the right side and the experiences were evoked over a much wider range of points in the right temporal lobe than was the case with auditory responses.

TEMPORAL LESIONS AND COGNITIVE CHANGE

Unilateral lesions

Intelligence test differences

There have been frequent assertions that the differential effects of unilateral temporal lobectomy according to the side of the lesion are examples of what Blakemore (1969) calls 'the broad generalization that lesions occurring in the hemisphere of the brain which is dominant for speech produce deficits in performance on tasks which are essentially verbal in nature, while lesions in the non-dominant hemisphere produce performance impairments on essentially non-verbal (visual-spatial and perceptual-motor) tasks'. The question of the hypothesized hemispheric differences both with regard to the temporal lobes and other areas is the special theme of Chapter 8. It will be sufficient here to outline a sample of findings from the temporal lobectomy studies.

Left unilateral anterior temporal lobectomy is often followed by dysphasia which is, however, transient in nature. Though language disturbance may cease to be clinically apparent, there are numerous studies which show that there are verbal deficits which are apparent for some time after operation when appropriate tests are employed. The early studies of Meyer and Yates (1955) and Meyer and Jones (1957) suggest that the decline in verbal intelligence test scores which was found by studies such as Milner (1954a,b; 1958) and Meyer (1959) after left temporal lobectomy were an aggravation of a deficit which patients with a left-sided lesion had before operation. The three latter studies reported no significant change in the Verbal subtests of the Wechsler Scale after operation on the right temporal lobe. Milner's data suggested that there was also no decline on the Wechsler Performance subtests with right-sided operations. However, Miller (1972a) reinterpreted Milner's data in the light of the large practice effect from Form I to Form II of the Wechsler-Bellevue Scale which had been demonstrated by Gerboth (1950) and came to the conclusion that the data did in fact demonstrate a decline in Performance Scale score after right temporal operations. Care must be taken in allowing for practice effects in neurological populations since many such groups fail to show such an effect. (Shatz, 1981). Blakemore and Falconer (1967) also described a lowering of the Performance Intelligence Quotient after right anterior temporal lobectomy. In one of the earliest studies of right temporal lobectomy Hebb (1939b) had noted a lowering of non-language abilities particularly those associated with visual form perception.

The general relation of verbal deficits with left, and performance deficits with right-sided lesions was supported by the studies of Lansdell (1962b), Dennerll (1964) and Blakemore et al (1966). On the other hand the verbal versus non-verbal character of deficits related to the laterality of the lesion was not confirmed by Parsons and Kemp (1960).

A rather different set of findings was reported by Halstead (1958) on 21 epileptic patients subjected to small anterior temporal lobe resections. Firstly, the results of operation of the left versus the right side did not support the contention that important differences exist between the dominant and non-dominant temporal lobes. Secondly, of major interest was the fact that a significant difference between epileptic patients and control subjects which existed on several intellectual measures before operation actually improved though impairment in relation to normal performance was still seen on some tasks. Such results may be due to the smaller nature of the operations compared with the larger temporal excisions in Milner's series and possible differences in the patient populations selected for operation. In discussion of Halstead's (1958) paper Cobb remarked concerning the post-operative improvement on test measures that 'it seems extraordinary, and, if it is true, it must be that the operation removes some noxious influence (if I may speak in very vague terms) that was actually impairing function.' Our own experience would support this position since those with improvement in cognitive measures tend to be those with clinical improvement in their epilepsy. A similar example of 'improvement of function' after removal of cerebral tissue is seen in the discussion of hemispherectomy in Chapter 8.

Several follow-up studies after anterior temporal lobectomy have shown recovery of both the verbal losses which follow left-sided operations (Meyer, 1959; Milner, 1958) and the non-verbal losses which follow right-sided ones within a year of surgery (Blakemore & Falconer, 1967). The latter study covers a period of ten years and it is difficult to reconcile this with the findings of Meier and French (1966) that, while performance scale scores one year after right-sided operations showed no decline over the pre-operative level, the scores at 3 years did show such a decline.

Material specific memory loss

The introduction of anterior temporal lobectomy as a standard treatment for the treatment of intractable complex partial seizures offered a unique opportunity for the study of the role of the mesial temporal structures in memory processes. The resection typically includes the anterior 6 cm or so of the temporal lobe and the underlying structures, the uncus, amygdaloid nucleus, and part of the hippocampus and parahippocampal gyrus. The evidence from this source strongly supports a complementary role for each temporal lobe.

Many studies have reported loss on verbal memory tests post-operatively although this loss is seldom of clinical significance, i.e. it does not inconvenience the patient in everyday life (Meyer & Yates, 1955; Milner, 1958, 1967; Blakemore & Falconer, 1967; Weingartner, 1968; Ládavas, Umilta & Provinciali, 1979; Zaidel & Rausch, 1981). Support for this relationship comes from other unilateral lesion studies, e.g. Coughlan and Warrington (1978) found patients with left hemisphere tasks generally poorer than those with right hemisphere lesions. Of the left-sided group those with temporal lesions were more impaired than those with lesions elsewhere in the hemisphere.

Operations and lesions of the right temporal lobe differentially affect visuospatial and non-verbal pictorial material (Kimura, 1963; Prisko, 1963; Warrington & James, 1967a; Milner & Teuber, 1968; Taylor, 1969; Ladavas, Umilta & Provinciali, 1979). Smith and Milner (1981) also implicated the right temporal lobe in the memory for the location of objects.

This evidence is usually interpreted as showing a *material specificity* of memory loss with unilateral temporal lesions. Milner summarized her point of view in the following way. 'It is now well established that a left temporal lobe lesion in the dominant hemisphere for speech impairs the learning and recognition of verbal material whether aurally or visually presented, and regardless of whether retention is measured by recognition, free recall, or rate of associative learning.' She cites her own work (Milner, 1958, 1962;

Milner & Kimura, 1964) and Meyer and Yates (1955) in support of this view. Further support came from Weingartner (1968) who tested serial verbal learning after both right-sided and left-sided operations and found a learning deficit with left-sided lesions despite the visual presentation of the material.

Some evidence for the opposite point of view came from Meyer (1959). Following an earlier study (Meyer & Yates, 1955) which demonstrated a severe impairment with aurally presented material for left-sided lesions and not right, Meyer specifically tested this proposition. He employed both visual and auditory (and tactile) modalities in an examination of learning with both verbal and non-verbal materials. Right-sided removals produced no post operative deficit, while left-sided removals produced a marked impairment of verbal paired-associate learning only with auditory presentation and not with visual. Several other studies (Luria, Sokolov & Klimkovsky, 1967; Luria & Karasseva, 1968; Warrington & Shallice, 1969) support the view that, while patients with left temporal or left temporo-parietal lesions may have difficulty with verbal memory for all forms of auditory material — words, letters, numbers — they have little or no difficulty with the same material presented via the visual modality. This apparent contradiction over material versus modality specifity still remains to be resolved. There is no doubt of the greater sensitivity of verbal memory to left-sided lesions, the deficit being demonstrable with cerebral tumours (Meyer & Falconer, 1960) and after unilateral ECT on the left side but not on the right (see below).

Finally, Blakemore (1969) questioned the frequent assertion that the deficits after operation should be interpreted as learning deficits as such. He reported an earlier study of his in which he varied the rate of presentation of items by altering the time between words and between pairs in paired-associate learning. Patients after left temporal lobectomy showed the anticipated deficits at normal and rapid rates of presentation but, when the rate was slowed appreciably, the patients demonstrated that they could learn almost as well as before operation. Blakemore argued that the longer time intervals allow verbal mediation to be effective.

While there is a great weight of evidence to support dissociation of function after operative lesions, the evidence for such differences in non-operated subjects with unilateral temporal foci is equivocal. Many comparisons of temporal versus other epileptic groups and with normals have failed to find a signficant difference on memory tests (Mirsky et al, 1960; Scott et al, 1967; Stevens, Milstein & Goldstein, 1972; Silverstein, Schwartz & Rennick, 1973). Others while finding memory impairment in the temporal lobe patients found no relationship between laterality and specificity of memory loss (Schwartz & Dennerll, 1969; Glowinski, 1973).

Unilateral electroconvulsive therapy has provided further evidence for lateral specificity of memory function. Inglis (1970) pointed to a close resemblance between the effects of temporal lobectomy and ECT. Verbal memory is disrupted by left-sided or bilateral treatment but not by right (Zamora & Kaebling, 1965; Gottlieb & Wilson, 1965; Fleminger, de Horne, & Nott, 1970; Pratt, Warrington & Halliday, 1971) while right-sided ECT has a differential effect on non-verbal memory (Cohen et al, 1968; Halliday et al, 1968; Berent, Cohen & Silverman, 1975; d'Elia, 1976; d'Elia et al, 1976).

The demonstration of detrimental effects of bilateral ECT or dominant-side ECT combined with the demonstration of the equal effectiveness of non-dominant ECT has led to fall off in the use of the first two procedures (Squire & Slater, 1978). However, earlier studies in which subjects were randomly assigned to the three modes of treatment strongly support the double dissociation of memory (Cohen et al, 1968; Halliday et al, 1968). With the accumulated evidence to that time Squire and Slater (1978) chose verbal and non-verbal tests known to be sensitive to left and right temporal lobe dysfunction. Their patients with bilateral ECT showed impairment for both classes of material while those with right-sided ECT were impaired on non-verbal material only and this was less than for the bilateral group.

Amytal ablation — the Wada technique

In 1949 Wada developed the method for determining directly the side of the hemisphere which played the major role in subserving speech functions. A temporary cessation or *functional ablation* was effected by injecting a solution of rapidly acting anaesthetic agent into the internal carotid artery which supplies one side of the brain. This intracarotid sodium amytal injection technique produced the following evidence of functional loss: (i) hemiplegia, (ii) hemianaesthesia, (iii) half visual field loss (hemianopia), all on the side opposite the side of the injection. If the hemisphere injected was dominant for language, dysphasia was also produced. These effects cleared within about five minutes though subtle changes in language function may be elicited on careful examination for as long as 30 min after the injection.

The amytal ablation technique has several advantages. Firstly, it allows the neurosurgeon to determine the lateralization of language function quite unequivocally, and to gauge the probable effect on language of operation in either hemisphere, since separate injections can be made on either side on two different occasions. The method has been used extensively to determine the anticipated effects on memory as well as language (Milner, Branch & Rasmussen, 1962, 1964, 1966; Kløve, Grabow & Trites, 1969; Kløve, Trites & Grabow, 1970). The rationale for Milner's test of memory was based on an assumption derived from the findings stated above, namely, that the loss of function in only one temporal lobe does not produce a generalized memory loss. However, if an unsuspected lesion is affecting the hippocampal zone of the opposite hemisphere, then amytal ablation of the temporal lobe should produce transiently the functional effect of a bilateral lesion, namely, the pervasive non-specific amnesic syndrome described in the next section. This generalized memory loss should be apparent for the time of the ablation and clear up as effect of the anaesthetic agent wears off. This reversible functional ablation greatly diminishes the potential risk of producing an undesirable result from surgery. It should be remembered that a non-functioning (atrophic) hippocampus on the side contralateral to proposed surgery may be silent to electroencephalographic examination.

Obviously the short time available, three to five minutes, limits the amount of testing possible. Milner (1966) presented strong evidence for the bilateral basis of the amnesic syndrome, e.g. each of three cases who had already been subjected to anterior temporal lobectomy showed a pronounced memory defect during the injection period when the other hemisphere was chemically ablated. Also, of the 216 injections some 27 cases of anterograde amnesia were produced and, in the 18 cases where the amnesic condition was most clearly produced, *all* occurred after ablation of the hemisphere contralateral to the side of the temporal lobe lesion. The value of pre-operative testing under amytal ablation is one that should recommend itself because of the very drastic changes caused by bilateral lesions. 'The fact that there has been no incidence of post-operative memory loss in patients screened by this method, although the series included a number of cases of bilateral EEG abnormality furnishes some presumptive evidence of its validity' (Milner, 1966). Despite these findings it is difficult to understand the anatomical basis involved. 'Branches of the anterior choroidal artery (which usually arise from the internal carotid) supply the pyriform cortex uncus, posterior medial half of the amygdaloid nucleus, anterior hippocampus, and dentate gyrus. We do not yet understand the reasons for memory dysfunction (in cases with contralateral mesial temporal lobe abnormalities) after injection of amorbarbital into the internal carotid artery, which perfuses only the anterior part of the hippocampal formation.' (Blume et al, 1973).

The carotid amytal ablation technique has also been used in testing for lateralization of functions other than language. Bogen and Gordon (1971) looked at musical ability during depression of activity of the non-dominant (right) hemisphere in six patients. Injection of the right side caused a marked temporary disturbance of singing ability whereas in five of the six patients 'speech remained unaffected except for slight slowing and slurring of words and the presence of some monotonicity; the intelligibility and rhythmicity of speech were hardly affected.' Such a finding is in keeping with the evidence cited elsewhere of the greater importance of the non-dominant hemisphere in certain musical abilities.

On the negative side Serafetinides (1966) noted that visual recognition of geometrical designs was not affected by ablation of either side though he again confirmed the impairment of verbal recall with amytal ablation of the dominant hemisphere.

Opportunities for studying the effects of amytal ablation with special tests occur in only a few centres. Apart from the restriction of time the presence of hemianopia and occasional somnolence of the subject together with aphasia and hemiplegia or hemiparesis makes testing difficult. On occasions we have been defeated by the sudden loss of consciousness especially where both anterior cerebral arteries arise from one side. Furthermore, Rausch et al (1984) found that more sustained disruption occurs with left versus right hemisphere injections and recovery is prolonged if injection is made in the side opposite the seizure focus.

Bilateral lesions and the general amnesic syndrome

Unlike the mild material specific memory losses caused by unilateral lesions the memory difficulties of patients with bilateral lesions affecting the medial temporal regions are profound, pervasive and generally lasting. Several lines of evidence support this relationship.

The first strong line of evidence comes from a prolonged and intensive series of investigations carried out on a patient with bilateral operations which included an extensive amount of medial temporal tissue including the amygdala and much of the hippocampi (Scoville & Milner, 1957). This patient, known as H.M., has had a stable amnesia almost completely free of other cognitive deficits which has persisted for nearly three decades. Many studies are reported in the various summaries (Milner, 1970; Scoville & Correll, 1973; Iversen, 1977).

Immediately after the operation H.M. demonstrated both a retrograde and anterograde amnesia. The retrograde amnesia cleared but the patient was left with some confusion about the chronological order of events particularly with regard to a period of one to two years before the operation. On the other hand, the anterograde amnesia has remained severe with an almost total lack of registration for everyday events. He repeatedly re-reads the same papers and repeats tasks over and over without giving any evidence of having done them before. He fails to learn the location of his house or the location of objects within it. He is unable to learn the name of visitors even after they have been visiting the house frequently over some years and fails to recognize them.

On the other hand, H.M.'s immediate span of attention is normal. He can, provided there is no distraction, repeat a normal span of six or seven digits. This preservation of immediate memory in the clinical testing of amnesic patients had been reported many years earlier by Zangwill (1946) and has been confirmed frequently since. The preservation of intelligence can be seen in a reported Wechsler Intelligence Quotient of 118 some 9 years after operation.

The marked degree of anterograde amnesia in this syndrome has led to a tendency on the part of some writers to overgeneralize and oversimplify the learning and retention deficit. There is now ample evidence that some learning and retention takes place even in such pronounced cases as H.M.

Motor skills do not suffer to the degree shown by many other tasks. H.M. improved his performance with practice on a mirror drawing task even though he was unaware that he had done the task before (Milner, 1962). He also showed improvement on a number of manual tracking and co-ordination tasks (Corkin, 1968.

In 1962 Milner reported H.M.'s complete inability to learn a visually guided stylus maze of the type described in Chapter 4. However, when the number of choice points was reduced so that it fell within his immediate memory span, he demonstrated extensive saving in the number of trials to relearn the maze a week after the initial trials and a comparatively rapid relearning after two years (Milner, Corkin & Teuber, 1968). The learning occurred despite H.M.'s denial of previous experience with the tasks. Milner (1970) also demonstrated that H.M. was able to learn the identity of 20 incomplete outline drawings (Gollin, 1960). When retested 1 hour after first exposure to the stimuli he showed even greater savings than a group of normal subjects.

The amnesic syndrome with unilateral lesions. Despite the weight of evidence in favour of the amnesic syndrome being produced only by bilateral lesions, occasional reports suggest that unilateral lesions may produce the loss. Penfield and Milner (1958) reported two cases of the syndrome after unilateral anterior temporal lobectomy in the hemisphere dominant for language. They attributed this effect to the unsuspected presence of a lesion in the hippocampal region of the non-operated side so that what was a unilateral operation in one sense produced a bilateral lesion in another. Their contention was borne out in one case by the finding of a wasted hippocampal region in the non-operated hemisphere at post mortem and by the presumptive evidence of EEG abnormality in the other case in the side opposite the operation. Baldwin (1956) had previously described similar bilateral effects in unilateral left lobectomies only in cases with bilateral EEG abnormalities. Similarly, less severe amnesia was described by Serafetinides and Falconer (1962) after right lobectomy in cases with added left-sided EEG abnormalities. All these cases appear explicable in terms of the production of a *functionally bilateral* lesion by a unilateral operation.

In 1964 Dimsdale and his colleagues described the occurrence of a case of general amnesia after right lobectomy in which there had been no neurological evidence whatsoever of a lesion on the other side. The authors attributed the memory defect to the extensive nature of the operation. Milner, however, pointed to the authors' report of a verbal memory defect before operation as presumptive evidence of a left temporal lobe lesion which was then compounded with the right-sided lobectomy to produce the effect. In one of our own cases we have had confirmation that in fact clinical, radiological and electrographic evidence may be negative while the hippocampus in the 'silent' temporal lobe may be completely wasted. This patient, who was a candidate in prospect for left-sided lobectomy, died of a cause unrelated to her epilepsy and the *right* hemisphere at autopsy showed wasting in the hippocampal region. Earlier psychological testing in this case had pointed to a lowering of function in certain non-verbal functions usually associated with the 'minor' hemisphere.

Finally the cases described by Stepien and Sierpinski (1964) are quite contrary to all the above findings. These three cases had a general memory defect before the operation and EEG evidence of abnormality on both sides. Removal of one temporal lobe, rather than aggravating the defect as Milner's hypothesis would suggest, resulted in a disappearance of the amnesia. These findings are difficult to reconcile with the numerous studies cited earlier.

A further landmark in the neurological basis of memory disorders was the report of Rose and Symonds (1960) of four cases of severe amnesia occurring after recovery from what may be assumed to be viral encephalitis. Barbizet (1970) points to a similar post-encephalitic case reported by Hillemand in 1931 and whose memory disorder was essentially unchanged when he, Barbizet, examined the patient 36 years later. The features of these cases are essentially those of the general amnesic syndrome, namely, a gross defect of recent memory with difficulty in the registration of ongoing events, some retrograde amnesia, with relatively little impairment of other intellectual functions. A constant feature of these hippocampal amnesias is preservation of immediate memory (Drachman & Arbit, 1966).

Further reports of post-encephalitic amnesia have become almost too numerous to mention, e.g. (Adams, Collins & Victor, 1962; Drachman & Adams, 1962; Leman, Loiseau & Cohadon, 1963; Beck & Corsellis, 1963; Hall, 1963, 1965; Zangwill, 1966a; Barbizet Devic & Duizabo, 1967; Lhermitte & Signoret, 1972). While many of the cases described in the literature have profound, lasting amnesia a few cases of our own who have had a clear-out amnesic syndrome after a viral illness have gone on to complete or almost complete recovery.

The most common cause appears to be a necrotic encephalitis of herpetic origin causing bilateral hippocampal damage and sometimes other lesions. The neuropathological evidence is reviewed in some detail in Brierley (1977).

The third major cause of medial temporal amnesia comes from bilateral compromise of the posterior cerebral arteries. The memory problems may be of a transient or permanent nature. Occasionally, after several transient amnesic episodes the patient may die of a massive cerebrovascular accident as in the case described by Whitty and Lishman (1966).

Typically, the onset is sudden so that the term 'amnesic stroke' is used. Bilateral infarction is common since both posterior cerebral arteries arise from the single parent vessel, the basilar artery. For the same reason patients often suffer a cerebral blindness, which may partially remit. A typical report is that of Victor et al (1961). Their patient who had been followed for a period of 5 years prior to death showed a profound defect in recent memory and inability to learn new facts and skills. His general intellectual functions remained at a 'bright normal' level, although certain mild and relatively inconspicuous abnormalities were disclosed by the tests designed to measure concentration, shifting of mental set, and abstract thinking. He also showed an incomplete retrograde amnesia, covering the two-year period prior to the onset of his illness. His memory for remote events was virtually unaffected (Victor et al, 1961, p. 261).

Post-mortem examination of the brain showed old bilateral infarctions in the inferomedial portions of the temporal lobes. Since that time further studies have described the association of serious memory defect in life with post-mortem evidence of bilateral infarction in the territory of the posterior cerebral arteries (Boudin et al 1967; Boudin et al, 1968; De Jong et al, 1968, 1969). Trillet et al (1980) described 30 cases of vascular origin (17 permanent and 13 transient) with anterograde amnesia as the principal finding. All had cerebral blindness at the outset. These authors reviewed the literature and their own experience and concluded that the typical case closely resembles the original description of the syndrome first described by Dide and Botcazo (1902), namely, cerebral blindness, amnesia and posterior cerebral softening. The latter characteristically includes the fusiform and lingual gyri and cuneus, together with the hippocampus. The thalamus and mamillary bodies may be involved in some cases (Van Buren & Borke, 1972).

Benson et al (1974) reported the acute onset of amnesia in 10 patients, associated with unilateral or bilaterial visual field defects clearly due to posterior cerebral artery territory infarction. In our experience there is always CT evidence of infarction in such cases.

A severe amnesia may be produced by infarction in the dominant hemisphere only (Geschwind & Fusillo, 1966; Mohr et al, 1971). It is possible that, because of the common use of largely verbal or verbal mediated tests of memory, these cases may appear to be instances of the general amnesic syndrome rather than, as we believe, cases of severe verbal specific memory deficits. It is also possible that there may be bilateral by asymmetrical involvement of the posterior regions with pathological emphasis on the dominant side.

Whatever turns out to be the case, severe memory impairment seems more related to the dominant than the non-dominant hemisphere in unilateral cases. The predominant mechanism of production of amnesia may be involvement of the inferomedial parts of the temporal lobes including the hippocampus.

Finally, hypoxic injury to the brain following cardiac or respiratory arrest may result in cognitive loss in which the most prominent feature is a general amnesic syndrome (Muramoto et al, 1979; Volpe & Hirst, 1983a). This may be linked to the known neuronal loss in the hippocampus which accompanies more diffuse cortical damage (Brierley & Cooper, 1962; Adams et al, 1966; Brierley, 1977).

Transient global amnesia

This term was coined by Fisher and Adams (1964) for a condition described earlier by Bender (1956) and Guyotat and Courjon (1956). It is most commonly seen in patients over 50 and is usually a single event lasting a variable time but most commonly 4–8 hours. The attack is characterized by confusion during which the patient has repetitive queries and shows a total inability to form any new memories. There is retrograde amnesia during the attack for events extending back for days, or in some cases even years, before the present but, as the confusion and anterograde amnesia clear, the retrograde anmesia shrinks to leave only amnesia for the period of the attack itself. There are usually no accompanying neurological signs and symptoms. On some occasions the episode or episodes appear to have been precipitated by special circumstances such as immersion in cold or hot water, sexual intercourse or highly emotional experience. There are several reports of TGA after vertebral angiography (see Caplan, 1985) and there is a strong association with migraine with dozens of reports of transient amnesic attacks in *migraineurs*. A less common association is with cerebral tumours and TGA has even been reported in four brothers (Corston & Godwin-Austen, 1982). For reviews see Caplan et al (1981) Fisher (1982), Caplan (1985).

The most common opinion is that the condition is due to temporary ischaemia in the territory of the posterior cerebral arteries though the most experienced writer in the field is strongly opposed to this view (Fisher, 1982). This author believes that the greater part of the evidence is consistent with cerebral seizure. It is possible that the clinical condition may, in fact, have a number of causes. Though it is unusual to find a cause, cases with a proven vascular aetiology support the ischaemic hypothesis (Ponsford & Donnan, 1980).

Though there may be a superficial resemblance between TGA and an hysterical or dissociative amnesia (or fugue) there is little difficulty with differential diagnosis provided the episode has been witnessed and reported by a reliable observer.

Vertebrobasilar insufficiency (VBI). Atherosclerosis is the posterior circulation, namely, vertebral, basilar and posterior cerebral arteries may cause transient attacks of brain stem vascular insufficiency the most common symptoms being those of vestibular and cerebellar disturbance. Very little attention was paid to possible disorders of higher cerebral function. More recently it has been noted that patients showing symptoms of VBI are often forgetful, have poor concentration and occasionally have attacks of transient global amnesia (Rivera & Meyer, 1976). Two small studies (Donnan et al,

1978; Ponsford et al, 1980) suggest that patients with evidence of chronic VBI may show evidence of a mild memory problem which has the characteristics of an axial amnesia.

Neuropsychological characteristics of hippocampal amnesia

There is some evidence to suggest that while general amnesias arising from differently located lesions may share a number of common features such as preserved immediate memory, poor spontaneous recall with relatively better recognition memory that the different locations impress upon the amnesia certain characteristics so that one might think of different amnesic syndromes or, at least, different discriminable sub-types of the overall amnesic syndrome. This comparison is taken up in Chapter 9.

6

The parietal lobes

Anatomical features   201
Sensory and perceptual disturbances   204
Disorders of spatial orientation   212
Constructional apraxia   221
Spatial dyslexia and dyscalculia   231
Spatial disorders   232
Unilateral spatial neglect (USN)   233
Disorders of the body schema   239
The Gerstmann syndrome   243
The parietal lobes and short term memory   244
Postural arm drift   246

The middle third of the cerebral hemispheres strategically situated between the frontal, occipital and temporal lobes, is closely related in function to each of these regions of the brain. Partly as a result of this, a greater variety of clinical manifestations is likely to result from disease of the parietal lobe than from disturbance of any other part of the hemispheres. It must be emphasized, however, that these phenomena require special techniques for their elicitation; otherwise they may be easily overlooked or discounted.

ANATOMICAL FEATURES

The parietal lobe has two main surfaces, one lateral and the other medial. The anterior border or lateral aspect is formed by the central sulcus while the posterior border is formed by the parieto-occipital sulcus and a line drawn from the end of this sulcus to the preoccipital notch on the infero-lateral border of the hemisphere (Fig. 6.1). The lower border separates the inferior part of the partietal lobe from the superior portion of the temporal lobe. It is made up of the lateral sulcus and a line continued back from it to reach the posterior line of demarcation.

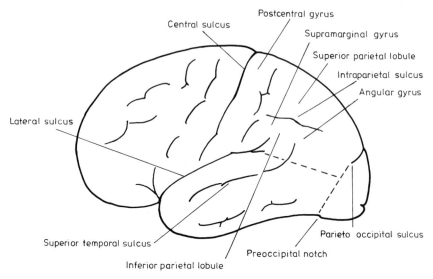

Fig. 6.1 Lateral aspect of the parietal lobe.

Two well-marked sulci lie within the parietal lobe. The post-central sulcus delimits the post-central gyrus which is concerned with somatic sensation. The intraparietal sulcus runs roughly parallel to the lower margin of the lobe about midway in the lobe separating it into a superior and an inferior parietal lobule. The ends of two (sometimes three) sulci invade the inferior parietal lobule. The anterior of these is the posterior branch of the lateral sulcus while just posterior to it is the end of the superior temporal sulcus. The cortex of the inferior parietal lobule around the end of the lateral sulcus is the supramarginal gyrus, that around the superior temporal sulcus is the angular gyrus. Not infrequently the sulci of the supramarginal and angular gyri are independent of the lateral and superior temporal gyri.

The anterior border of the medial aspect of the parietal lobe is formed by a line which extends about midway through the paracentral lobule from the point on the superomedial border of the hemisphere reached by the central sulcus, to the top of the corpus callosum (Fig. 6.2). Thus only the posterior half of the paracentral lobule belongs to the parietal lobe. The posterior border is formed by the parieto-occipital sulcus which is usually very distinct. The region anterior to this sulcus is the precuneus which extends anteriorly to the continuation of the post-central gyrus and is continuous around the subparietal sulcus with the cingulate gyrus. A branch or continuation of the cingulate gyrus, the marginal sulcus, separates the anterior border of the precuneus from the posterior border of the paracentral lobule.

Following this description of the parietal lobe as an empirical convention it would be wise to repeat the warning of Critchley (1953) in his classic monograph on the parietal lobes.

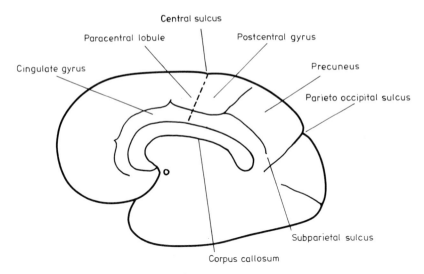

Fig. 6.2 Medial aspect of the parietal lobe.

More than once it has been emphasized that the parietal lobe cannot be regarded as an autonomous anatomical entity. Its boundaries cannot be drawn with any precision except by adopting conventional and artificial landmarks and frontiers. Later, it will also be seen that it is not possible to equate the parietal lobe with any narrowly defined physiological function. In other words, the parietal lobe represents a topographical convenience pegged out empirically upon the surface of the brain. The name serves a mere descriptive role . . . .

Up to 150 years ago, the cerebrum was not divided into lobes or regions by any established figural patterns. In the early nineteenth century Burdach began to speak of the cerebrum as being made up of lobes. These major subdivisions he spoke of anterior, upper and lower lobes, the operculum, and the island of Reil. At a still later date (cf. Quain, 1837) there were three lobes identified, namely, the anterior, posterior and middle lobes, indicating the various positions of the brain as related to the fossae of the base of the skull. This system was adopted and recapitulated in text-books until 1850. Around that time, there developed a tendency to associate regions of the brain with the overlying cranial bones. Thus the anterior lobe became the frontal lobe, while the cortical territory underlying . . . (the) os parietalis became known as the parietal lobe . . .

There is no inherent reason to doubt but that the term parietal lobe . . . and others . . . will eventually be replaced by some other nomenclature. The ideal would be a less narrow terminology, and one which would include the whole retro-rolandic complex, or a three-dimensional temporo-occipital territory as a functional domain. (p. 55).

Later, Critchley came to term this region the 'parieto-temporo-occipital crossroads.' This term had been used also by early European neurologists.

These notions have been reiterated a number of times in the ensuing three decades although no satisfactory nomenclature has as yet emerged. In what follows it is difficult to disentangle the contribution of separate parts of the posterior cortical territory though the division into primary, secondary, (association) and tertiary (supra-modal) cortex proposed by Luria and outlined in brief in Chapter 2 seems of value when considering different degrees of complexity of symptoms in the posterior areas. Many studies employ a heterogeneous collection of variously located lesions while some attempts to separate parietal from non-parietal cases have been made. Certainly some major differences have emerged which are related to the laterality of the lesion in the territory behind the central sulcus.

SENSORY AND PERCEPTUAL DISTURBANCES

The primary reception area for the numerous forms of somatic sensation has its principal locus in the post-central gyrus. The secondary or association cortex posterior to this is thought to deal with the elaboration of the discrete elements into meaningful wholes so that disorders with damage away from the 'somaesthetic' area tend to be more complex, i.e. tend to be perceptual or cognitive in nature rather than simple disturbances of sensation. Further afield in the region of the 'temporo-parieto-occipital crossroads' the disturbances tend to be those which reflect a disruption of intersensory or cross-modal association and integration. Following this 'anatomical' division of deficits according to type of cortex three types of deficit have been selected for treatment: (i) somatosensory discrimination, (ii) disorders of tactile perception, and (iii) disorders of intersensory association. They by no means cover the gamut of parietal disorders.

Somatosensory discrimination

What is commonly called somatic sensation is made up of a number of separate modalities. Among these are touch, pain, temperature, body position sense, kinaesthesis, and vibration. The detailed organization of each of these is dealt with in texts of physiological psychology such as Geldard (1972) as well as in some texts of physiology and neurology. Some major texts do not treat the topic at all!

The somatosensory system is able to combine information from different modalities in different locations and with different temporal relationships. A treatment of these, however, is outside the scope of the present volume which is largely concerned with lesion studies.

The earliest neuropsychological studies of the cerebral basis of somatic sensation in man came from the examination of missile wounds to the head (Head, 1920; Holmes, 1927). The value of these studies suffered from the inability to localize accurately the site of the lesion for correlation with the results of their painstaking examination of sensory-perceptual capacities.

The introduction and increasing use of cortical ablation for the removal of cerebral scars allowed Penfield's group to make the first serious examination of sensory defects following circumscribed ablation of cortical tissue (Evans, 1935). Employing the detailed examination procedure outlined by Head, Evans examined 17 cases, nine posterior and eight anterior.

Evans concluded from the examination of these cases that damage to the extra-parietal areas, the pre- and post-central gyri and the central portion of the parietal lobe led to transient, if any sensory dysfunction 'while limited excisions in the region of the supramarginal gyrus caused extensive and permanent loss of somesthetic sensation.' Such limited case material supplemented by other smaller studies formed the basis for conjecture about the cortical basis of somatosensory function until the studies performed on penetrating missile cases after the Second World War.

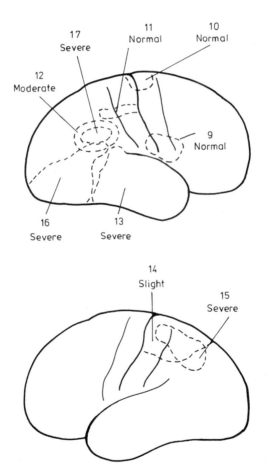

Fig. 6.3 Relation between severity of somatic sensory disturbance and site of lesion (redrawn from Evans (1935). Courtesy of the Association for Research in Nervous and Mental Disease).

Numerous studies on such cases provided increasing evidence that performance on many complex sensory discrimination tasks depended on temporal, posterior parietal or parieto-temporo-occipital areas (Blum, Chow & Pribram, 1950; Teuber, 1950; Battersby, 1951; Teuber, Battersby & Bender, 1951; Teuber & Weinstein, 1954).

In 1956 Hécaen et al in a study of patients with surgical lesions of the minor hemisphere, reported that patients with parietal lesions showed no increase in sensory thresholds unless there was also involvement of the Rolandic region. They also noted difficulties with complex sensorimotor tasks such as using scissors, dressing, and making block constructions in patients with right posterior lesions as well as some of the visuospatial and body image disturbances described below.

One of the most extensive investigations of somatosensory changes after brain injury was that of Semmes et al (1960). This work summarizes a good deal of the work of this group on the effects of penetrating missile wounds and it is difficult to do justice to it in a brief summary. One major finding worth recording is the fact that this group found bilateral deficits on occasion in patients with left hemisphere lesions but only contralateral deficits after lesions of the right hemisphere. The difference was not statistically significant and to date there has been little or no confirmation of this hemispheric asymmetry. Semmes et al, also reported bilateral difficulty in tactually guided learning in patients whose primary sensory deficit seemed restricted to one hand.

Corkin (1964) tested 95 patients who had undergone cortical excision for the relief of epilepsy and compared their performance with that of control subjects on sensory discrimination tasks and tests of tactual learning and problem solving. Her major findings were that sensory deficits and impairment in tactile object recognition were closely related to lesions in the Rolandic region of either side. No lasting sensory impairment was seen in patients whose pre- and post-central gyri were spared. The deficits were usually contralateral though some bilateral effects were produced by unilateral excisions. A wide range of measures such as pressure sensitivity, two-point discrimination threshold, and point localization were used. More complex functions such as tactually guided learning and problem solving showed deficits with removals in the right hemisphere regardless of location of the lesion within the hemisphere. Generalization from these findings is limited since left parietal lesions were not specifically studied.

An extension of this work was reported by Corkin and her colleagues (1970). Tests of pressure sensitivity, two-point discrimination, point localization, position sense, and tactual object recognition were given to 127 cases of limited unilateral cortical removal. Pre-operative, post-operative and follow-up measurements were taken. This study confirmed the earlier report that lasting sensory loss was highly correlated with lesions of the postcentral gyrus and was particularly severe with involvement of the contralateral hand area. Normal scores were reported on patients with precentral lesions which did not encroach upon the post-central hand area. Lesions of the parietal lobe outside the post-central gyrus produced transient loss or no loss at all. Extraparietal lesions produced little or no sign of somatosensory change. Ipsilateral sensory defects were found in 20 of the 50 parietal lobe patients and, unlike the finding of Semmes et al (1960) showed no relation to laterality of the lesion but did appear to be related to the size of the lesion.

For further detail on sensory disorders readers should consult texts on physiological psychology and neurology.

Disorders of tactile perception

Judgment of stimulus orientation

The perception of orientation has been studied in detail by Benton and his colleagues for both tactile and visual perception in normal subjects and those with unilateral lesions (see Chs. 7 and 8). Carmon and Benton (1969) and Fontenot and Benton (1971) tested the perception of the direction of tactile stimulation applied to the palm of the hand. A significant proportion of patients with right hemisphere lesions showed bilateral impairment whereas patients with left hemisphere lesions showed significant impairment only in the contralateral hand. A test of the detection of three dimensional orientation was devised by De Renzi et al (1971) for use in both visual and tactile modalities. Using the hand ipsilateral to the lesion only those with right hemisphere lesions having visual field defects were significantly impaired.

While no sound anatomical data exists on the regions involved there is presumptive evidence that the right parietal lobe may be crucially involved in this basic spatial function.

Astereognosis (Tactile Agnosia)

This term *astereognosis* has been employed to identify a form of *tactile agnosia* in which the patient is unable to recognize objects which he feels. If the disorder is to conform to the general concept of agnosia it should be a higher perceptual disorder in the presence of intact primary sense modalities. Denny-Brown et al (1952) considered the basic disturbance to be a failure to synthesize separate tactile sensations into the perception of form, a process they termed *amorphosynthesis*. Elsewhere they considered the difficulty to be one of inability to carry out a 'summation of spatial impressions' (Denny-Brown & Chambers, 1958).

There has been doubt as to the existence of this as with other forms of agnosia. Several neuropsychological studies have directed themselves in whole or in part to the problem. Corkin (1964) found that impaired tactual recognition was seen only in patients who also had somatosensory deficits.

This was confirmed in the 1970 study previously mentioned: 'Impaired tactual recognition of common objects reflected the sensory status of the hand, and, in this series of patients, there were no object-recognition deficits that were disproportionate to the sensory loss.' (Corkin et al, 1970, p. 57).

Semmes (1965) clarified the relation of sensory status to astereognosis in a study of left hemisphere, right hemisphere and bilateral lesions. She found that impaired performance on tests of tactual shape discrimination was seen both in the absence as well as the presence of sensory defect. An examination of the cases without sensory defect revealed that the impairment was specific to shape, the discrimination of texture, size, and roughness being unaffected. The impairment was, however, related to spatial orientation even when this was measured by a visual task. 'It was suggested, therefore, that impaired shape discrimination after brain injury depends on a general spatial factor as well as on the status of somatic sensation.' (Semmes, 1965, p. 312) Either of these factors seemed capable of producing impairment of tactile form discrimination but when both were present the impairment was more severe suggesting that the factors are independent but additive. Semmes found that they tended to occur together in right hemisphere lesions and she assumed that this was because of the size of the lesion, a large lesion being needed to affect both sensation and orientation. 'Paradoxically, although each of the factors is more localizable in the left hemisphere than the right and the parietal region is implicated for both, these factors show no tendency toward association. One must therefore assume separate foci for the two factors within the left parietal region' (p. 312). Both specific testing of tactual recognition (De Renzi & Scotti, 1969) as well as the wealth of evidence cited later in the chapter would support the idea that the prime representation of the spatial factor which may contribute to astereognosis has its major location in the posterior cerebral areas, particularly of the right hemisphere.

The only standard psychological measure of tactual form perception is the Seguin-Goddard formboard which has been adapted in the much used Halstead-Reitan battery of tests. Teuber and Weinstein (1954) showed that men with posterior lesions performed significantly poorer on this task than those with anterior lesions though all brain damaged subjects were significantly inferior to controls. This latter finding has been replicated many times by Reitan and his co-workers (Reitan & Davison, 1974). For example, Boll (1974) found that apart from tactile object recognition early studies (e.g. Battersby, Krieger & Bender, 1955) suggested that tactile discrimination learning might not be more impaired with posterior lesions than with lesions in other locations though Semmes et al (1954) did find that patients with lesions of the parietal lobe, unlike other patients showed no transfer effect from one modality to another. This may reflect a loss of cross-modal association.

Both Corkin (1965) and Milner (1965) used visually-guided and tactually-guided maze learning in patients with variously located surgical lesions. Small parietal lesions had little effect upon performance while right hemisphere lesions either frontal or temporal produced a marked impairment. However, the complex nature of the tasks makes interpretation difficult.

A study of De Renzi, Faglioni and Scotti (1970) showed that tactile searching like visual searching is poorer for the contralateral field for both left and right hemisphere lesions but that the poorest performances were made by the right posterior group.

Finally, visual object recognition also appears to be related more closely to the right parietal regions than elsewhere. Warrington and Rabin (1970) found that a right parietal group was much inferior to others on a series of perceptual matching tasks of simple perceptual attributes but that this failure was not related to their poor performance on the Gollin incomplete figures test (Gollin, 1960) suggesting that failure of recognition of features (which was required in the matching tasks) could not account for impairment on the test of visual recognition. There was, however, a correlation between the performance on matching tasks and more complex tasks of spatial analysis such as Block Designs suggesting that there was a common spatial element involved in the two types of task but that this differed in complexity. A new test of object recognition was introduced by Warrington and Taylor (1973). This consisted of the recognition of objects photographed from a 'conventional' and an 'unconventional' view. The right posterior group was selectively impaired in this test compared to all other groups, having a very marked deficit whereas the deficit of other brain damaged groups compared with control subjects was much smaller. Right posterior subjects were again inferior on the recognition of Gollin's incomplete figures though not nearly as much as on the new recognition task. Other visuoperceptual tasks such as figure-ground discrimination showed no differences between any of the brain damaged subgroups though all groups were inferior to controls.

Disorders of intersensory association (cross-modal integration)

Studies on intersensory association or cross-modal integration are of interest because such integration or associations between different forms of sense information would appear to be basic to many higher functions. Damage to the region in which such integration is likely to take place, i.e. the area of conjunction of the temporal, parietal and occipital lobes in the dominant hemisphere has often been said to produce the most marked losses of cognitive functions. Few studies relating cross-modal association problems with locus of lesion have appeared to date.

Butters and Brody (1968) found that patients with neurologically confirmed dominant parietal lobe damage were particularly impaired on cross-modal matching tasks (auditory-visual, tactual-visual, visual-tactual) whereas frontotemporal patients were unimpaired either on intramodal or cross-modal tasks. Deficits on the auditory-visual matching task were closely associated with reading difficulties confirming the notion that this cross-modal association is prerequisite for reading. Many of the parietal patients who were impaired on the visual-tactual and tactual-visual matching tasks were also impaired on copying tests which are often used to assess constructional praxis whereas those with mild or absent signs of parietal involvement showed little or no copying impairment. 'The possibility that certain kinds of intersensory associations or integrations may underlie some constructional apraxia disorders and other voluntary motor behaviour is intriguing and certainly deserving of further study.' (Butters & Brody, 1968 p. 342).

Butters et al (1970) found some impairment of cross-modal association (auditory-visual matching) in patients with severe parietal signs but none in those with only mild parietal signs. The care that must be exercised in interpretation of findings was highlighted by the subsequent finding that the impairment of right parietal patients on the auditory-visual task was associated with an auditory decoding problem rather than failure of cross-modal association. The inferred size of the lesions and the propinquity of the auditory association area make it possible that the difficulty arose from disruption of function in this area rather than from parietal damage.

Taking the data from these two studies it does appear that there is some evidence to support the contention that the left parietal area may be dominant for crossmodal associations.

Kotzmann (1972) compared the performance of 10 unilateral left lesion patients with 10 unilateral right and 10 control subjects on a tactile-visual recognition task. Subjects were asked to palpate two classes of objects and to choose the corresponding drawing from a multiple choice visual array. One set of objects was meaningful (pipe, eggcup, bolt etc.) and the other meaningless (moulded nonsense shapes). The brain-damaged groups performed more poorly than control subjects on both tactual recognition tasks. The meaningful/meaningless dichotomy was not related to the laterality of the lesion in any simple way. Left hemisphere subjects had about equal difficulty with the two tactual tasks while right hemisphere subjects performed more poorly on the meaningless task than on the meaningful. An extension of this work might shed further light on the asymmetry of function with regard to tactual perception in the same way that auditory perceptual studies have done for the different classes of auditory information described in the previous chapter.

Symbolic (quasi-spatial) syntheses

Luria in a number of publications has pointed to the importance of the 'tertiary zones' of the left hemisphere in relationships which are logical or symbolic in character. He argues that these relationships are 'quasi-spatial' in nature and this conception provides a basis for understanding what at first appear to be quite separately based disturbances. The first example is acalculia. Although the patient with a dominant parietal lesion can understand and remember a problem and may even think of certain rules which would be appropriate to the solution he is unable to carry out the necessary operations. As outlined below, if the description of the problem contains a number of symbolic relations the patient will have even further difficulty. The simplest examples may be found in the operations of addition and subtraction. The appropriateness of the term 'quasi-spatial' becomes apparent when it is realized that the significance of a number alters according to its spatial relation to other numbers, e.g. the figure 2 in the number 42 has a different significance from the 2 in 24. Luria provides the following example 'To subtract 7 from 31, as a rule we begin by rounding the first number and obtain the result $30 - 7 = 23$. We then add the remaining unit, placing it in the right-hand column, and obtain the result $23 + 1 = 24$. The operation is much more complex when we subtract a number of two digits (for example, $51 - 17$), when, besides observing the conditions just mentioned, we have to carry over from the tens column and to retain the double system of elements in the operative memory.' (Luria 1973b, pp. 154–155).

If one employs a series of mathematical operations of increasing difficulty (e.g. addition or subtraction of one figure numbers, addition or subtraction of two figure numbers, of three figure numbers, multiplication of two or three figure numbers) patients with lesions in this region will break down well below the level which might be expected of them from their educational or occupational level. For the 'spatial' reason mentioned above patients who have no difficulty with a problem such as $796 - 342$ will fail repeatedly on seemingly similar problems, e.g. $534 - 286$ as well as more complex mathematical operations since the 'spatial' or 'carry-over' element is essential for the solution of the second problem but not the first. The rather different characteristics which frontal patients experience with numerical problem solving have been described in Chapter 4.

The other major area of difficulty for patients with lesions of the dominant inferior parietal region is that involving the abstract logical relations of syntax. The communication of such relationships can be greatly affected by the sequence of words, by the introduction of relational terms such as prepositions of space or time, or by more complex syntactical structures. Note the completely different meaning of 'my wife's brother' from 'my brother's wife', or the difference between 'the bridge over the water' and 'the water over the bridge'. Identical words in different situations take on quite different meanings dictated by the structure of the whole. It is this significance of structure that may present difficulties for patients with lesions of the dominant parietal region though they show clear evidence of understanding the individual elements. The Token Test provides excellent opportunity for demonstrating these difficulties and is one of the reasons why this test is so sensitive to dominant hemisphere impairment. The difficulty with logicogrammatical constructions forms part of 'semantic aphasia'.

DISORDERS OF SPATIAL ORIENTATION

It will become obvious that the concept of spatial disorientation as employed in clinical neurology encompasses a variety of different disorders and even some of these, about which there is some consensus as to their validity as distinct entities, may well turn out on further investigation to be more complexly determined than is thought at present. The brief description of the commonly reported spatial disabilities which follows obviously overlaps in part with the preceding section on perceptual disorders and that on disorders of personal space or body schema which follows. The disorders in this section are mainly of the appreciation of spatial relationships between and within objects in extra-personal space. The principal categories are: (i) disorders in the judgment of the location or orientation of stimuli both with respect to each other and to the person; (ii) impairment of memory for location; (iii) topographical disorientation and loss of topographical memory; (iv) route finding difficulties; (v) constructional apraxia; (vi) spatial dyslexia and dyscalculia.

Disorders of location and orientation

Benton (1969b) suggests that a distinction might be made between impairment of localization of a single stimulus which could be termed a difficulty of 'absolute' localization, and difficulty with the perceived spatial relations between two or more stimuli which could be termed a difficulty of 'relative' localization. Paterson and Zangwill (1944) referred to 'defective appreciation of spatial relations in the visual field with or without impairment of visual localization in the strict sense' as *visuospatial agnosia*, in other words, a dissociation between 'absolute' and 'relative' localization. They also confirmed earlier reports of a tendency to overestimate the distance of very near objects and to underestimate the distance of far objects.

Absolute localization may be checked by asking the patient to point to a stimulus placed in different parts of the visual field. This test is usually failed only by grossly impaired patients. Localization difficulty has also been inferred from other tests such as the bisection of lines. The performance of 12 patients with parieto-occipital traumatic lesions on this bisection task and other spatial tests was described by Bender and Teuber (1947) with the addition of a further occipital trauma case a year later (Bender & Teuber, 1948).

Tests of more complex spatial relations often bring out difficulties when none are apparent on simpler tests. The multiple choice version of the Benton Visual Retention Test (Benton, 1950) (Fig. 6.4) would appear

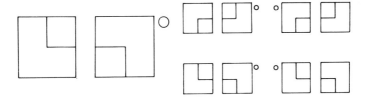

Fig. 6.4 Item 6 from multiple choice version of the Benton Visual Retention Test (Benton, 1956). (Courtesy American Medical Association).

sensitive to the subtler changes in perception of spatial relations and has been relatively neglected in the study of parietal lesions since its introduction as a diagnostic aid (Benton, 1952) though Alajouanine (1960) employed it in his studies of occipital lobe patients. The visuospatial difficulties which many of Alajouanine's occipital patients had on this task remind us of the dangers of dealing rigidly with lobar divisions.

De Renzi et al (1971) have pointed out that spatial perception has been studied very often at a rather complex level, most tests having been derived from tests of intelligence or devised with various neurological symptoms in mind. For this reason they feel that 'it is difficult to disentangle the influence on performance of spatial as compared with praxic, intelligence, and memory factors' (p. 490). They devised a very simple task where two rods jointed together could be placed at various orientations (angles) to each other. The subject's task was to align another pair of rods in the same orientation under the two conditions of visual, and tactile assistance. When tested in this way they found gross impairment was associated almost exclusively with posterior lesions of the non-dominant hemisphere. They contrast this with the less striking asymmetry shown on more complex spatial tasks which are also poorly performed by a proportion of dominant posterior cases. Miller (1972a) comments:

> It may well be that the important factor in determining whether an apparently spatial task is affected by left posterior lesions as well as right is the degree of verbal mediation used by the subject. Although a task may be spatial in nature, this does not prevent a subject from using verbal reasoning in its solution and to the extent that this occurs the task will be more liable to disruption by left-sided lesions even though the task may be particularly difficult to verbalize. (p. 86)

Another simple test used by the Milan group was the reproduction of the location of a number of crosses drawn at random on paper, the measure of performance being taken from the sum of the distances by which the subjects' copies deviated from the originals (De Renzi & Faglioni, 1967). A right hemisphere group was inferior to a left hemisphere group on this task.

The significance of the right hemisphere for localization was again demonstrated by Faglioni and his colleagues (1971). Right posterior lesion patients were most impaired on a visual localization task. The fact that two separate versions of the task, one visual and the other tactile were both poorly performed supports the notion that many deficits produced by parietal lesions are not modality specific.

Perhaps a separate factor in dealing with spatial relations is the ability to carry out reversible operations in space. Two studies (Butters & Barton, 1970; Butters, Barton & Brody, 1970) have employed a number of measures of this type: (i) the Stick Test — patient is shown a simple arrangement of sticks and asked to copy them under the two conditions of sitting alongside or opposite the examiner; (ii) the Pools Reflections Test which is modelled after one of the subtests of Cattell's *A Culture Free Test* (Cattell, 1944). From a number of alternatives the subject must select the one which represents the reflection which the sample would present to the viewer (See Fig. 6.5); (iii) The Village Scene test. Here the subject is shown the model of a village and is asked to choose the correct photograph representing the scene from six photographs one of which is correct and the others are similar views in which the spatial relationships of features of the scene have been altered before being photographed. Both these studies produced data which suggest that this type of task is performed poorly by patients with either left or right parietal lesions. Patients with lesions in other areas showed little or no difficulty with these spatial reversible operations.

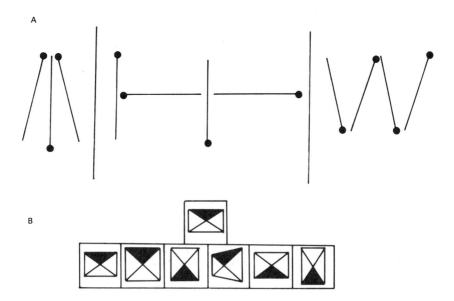

Fig. 6.5 A. Sample designs, Stick Test (from Benson & Barton, 1970).
B. Pool reflection item (from Butters et al, 1970).

There also appears to be a little evidence that a dissociation may exist between localization disorders and the topographical disorders of orientation and memory (Hécaen, Ajuriaguerra & Massonet, 1951; Gilliatt & Pratt, 1952) each type of disorder being seen in isolation in some individuals. Marie and his co-workers (1924) described a right prefrontal tumour which produced marked spatial disorientation in the patient but 'l'absence de troubles dans le fonctions en quelque sort primaires de l'appréciation spatiale, chez ce malade.' (p. 217).

Impaired memory for location

Very little systematic work has been done in this area. Impaired memory for location may form part of a general amnesic disorder or it may be seen in association with other spatial difficulties. However, an occasional patient is seen who performs adequately on the usual spatial tasks but who may encounter difficulty when asked to recall spatial relationships even after a short delay. Such difficulties have been described in occipital cases and right parietal cases by Alajouanine (1960) who used the multiple choice version of the Benton Visual Retention Test as a recognition memory task.

Loosely related to this area was the experiment of De Renzi and his colleagues (1969) who tested a large group of unilateral lesion patients on a simple memory for position task under visual guidance or tactual guidance. Though all brain damaged subjects performed more poorly than controls there was no significant difference between the right and left hemisphere groups. The impairment was greater in those with visual field defects than those without. 'However, the finding that this impairment was significantly more marked on the tactile than on the visual memory tests suggests that it is related to the concomitant injury of posterior areas of the brain rather than to the effect of the visual deficit' (p. 283).

Patients are seen frequently who have a disproportionate difficulty on the memory-for-location aspect of the Tactual Performance Test (TPT) of the Reitan Neuropsychological Test Battery. Though a large number of studies have been reported in which the TPT is demonstrated to be generally sensitive to cerebral impairment (Reitan & Davison, 1974) there is little or no available information on any differential effect of location of lesion on the memory aspect of the task. Since the patient is not advised in advance that he will be asked to recall the location as well as the shapes of the objects which he must place in the formboard (using only tactile information), inferences about individual patient's performances must be limited. It is a striking fact, nevertheless, that after the prolonged experience which this test gives, many patients with cerebral impairment will fail to recall correctly the location of even one of the shapes.

A comparison of differences between the recall and copying versions of the Rey Figure (Rey, 1941, 1959; Osterreith, 1944) might also prove valuable in this regard.

Topographical disorientation and loss of topographical memory

Several different difficulties may be encompassed under this heading; (i) the inability to recall the spatial arrangement of familiar surroundings such as the disposition of rooms within the patient's house, or the disposition of furniture within a room; (ii) the inability to recall and describe well known geographical relationships with which the patient was formerly familiar. These and related areas are beginning to receive attention from neuropsychologists.

Benton (1969) considers the basic defect to be difficulty in calling up visual images. 'We deal here with an impairment in "revisualization", a failure to retrieve long-established visual memories' (p. 219). This is similar to the 'visual irreminescence' of Critchley (1953) which is mentioned in the next chapter in relation to lesions of the occipital lobes, particularly vascular lesions.

Compared with other aspects of spatial ability topographical orientation has received comparatively little attention. Ratcliff and Newcombe (1973) point out that most studies have been concerned with situations in which the patient can explore spatial relationships without gross changes in his own position, i.e. they have been more concerned with spatial agnosia.

In 1955, Semmes and her co-workers described an objective test of spatial orientation. This consisted of 15 diagrams of the type shown in Figure 6.6. The nine dots on each map represented nine circles on the floor of a room, the circles being some 137 cm apart. One wall of the room was designated as North and North was marked on the maps. With the map maintained in constant orientation to his body the subject was required to walk around each designated path. In this way the orientation of the person to the room was constantly changing. Both visual maps and 'tactile-only' versions were provided. Parietal lobe cases were significantly inferior to non-parietal patients and to control subjects. There was no difference between non-

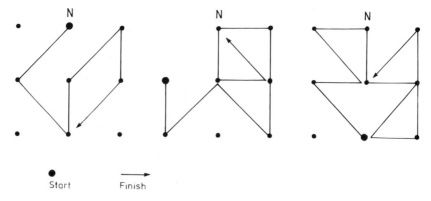

Fig. 6.6 Three items from a locomotor map following test (after Semmes et al, 1955, courtesy of Dr. Josephine Semmes).

parietal cases and controls. Furthermore, as the disorder proved to be unrelated to perceptual modality (visual or tactile) Semmes and her colleagues felt that it was incorrect to label the difficulty as part of visuo-spatial agnosia. A second study (Weinstein et al, 1956) confirmed the poor performance of parietal subjects on the route finding task but, in this study, poor performance was also shown by frontal subjects though to a lesser degree. These frontal subjects also performed poorly on a test of personal orientation.

A later study (Semmes et al, 1963) extended these findings and compared the results on this test of extrapersonal orientation with a test of personal space in which the subject was asked to touch parts of his own body in the order indicated by numbers on diagrams of the human body. Brain injury affected both tasks to an approximately equal degree. Statistical analysis showed that, though the two tasks were significantly related in the brain-injured group studied, there were also independent elements.

With regard to the locus of the lesion, 'both personal and extrapersonal orientation were impaired by lesions of the posterior part of the left hemisphere. Anterior lesions (particularly those of the left hemisphere) tended to impair personal but not extra-personal orientation, whereas the converse was the case for right posterior lesions' (Semmes et al, 1963, p. 769).

Two studies cited in the previous section (Butters & Barton, 1970; Butters, Barton and Brody, 1970) have shown that parietal patients have difficulty with reversible mental spatial operations while other patients do not. Butters, Soeldner and Fedio (1972) extended these findings by including a test which cannot be performed by rotating an external object either at the concrete or the abstract level. In the test, Money's Standardized Road-Map Test of Direction (Fig. 6.7) the patient needs the ability to rotate himself in imagery or on an abstract level. With the road map in a fixed stationary relationship he has to describe the right or left turns which would need to be made while following the route.

A comparison of left frontal and right parietal patients on this task allowed a test of Teuber's hypothesis that the frontal and parietal regions mediate qualitatively different spatial abilities (i) spatial orientation to external objects mediated by the parietal regions, particularly the right, and (ii) spatial discrimination involving the subject's own body mediated particularly by the left frontal region. The study demonstrated a partial double dissociation between the two groups on the test of personal or egocentric space (Money's Test) and a test of extrapersonal space (the Stick Test described above). While the authors mention a number of clinical, statistical and methodological restrictions there appears to be tentative support for Teuber's hypothesis. This difference could, of course, represent the general difficulty frontal patients have with hypothetical ('as if') situations.

Two early studies of Pierre Marie reported disorientation in space with

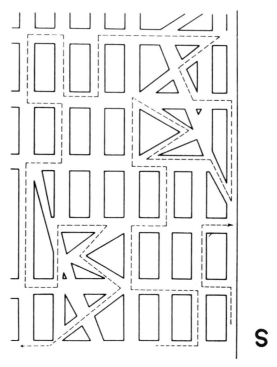

Fig. 6.7 Money's Standardized Road Map Test of Direction Sense.

major lesions of the frontal lobe comprising a traumatic left frontal case, a case of right frontal trauma, and a right frontal tumour (Marie & Behague, 1919; Marie, Bouttier & van Bogaert, 1924).

In testing for difficulties in spatial orientation care should be taken in excluding topographical difficulties on the basis of verbal tests only. 'Long-standing associations of a purely verbal character may enter into the verbal descriptions and give an impression of the appreciation of topographic relationships which in fact the patient no longer possesses' (Benton, 1969, p. 221). Benton reports a case of De Renzi and Faglioni (1962) who was 'completely unable to make localizations on a map of Milan, nevertheless could name the streets and public buildings associated with a given locality as well as all the gates of the city. However, he could not specify the spatial relationships among the gates and his descriptions of routes were schematic and imperfect' (p. 220–221).

Benton and his colleagues (1974) have recently made a more systematic study of this distinction. Geographic orientation was assessed in patients with unilateral cerebral disease using two types of task. The first required the localization of states and cities on a map of the United States while the second was a verbal test of the directional relations between places. Two subtests in this second (verbal) category failed to discriminate between left and right hemisphere cases or brain damaged subjects from controls on the map localization test. A 'vector' score was calculated showing a tendency of the subject to shift localization either toward the right or left part of the map. This score differentiated between the two hemisphere groups and suggested neglect of the visual field contralateral to the side of the lesion in some of the patients. These findings demonstrate the interaction of defects in producing impaired performance on complex tasks.

It has become evident that the relation between locus of lesion and topographical loss is less clear than with some other 'spatial' disorders. However, the most frequent reports have been after posterior lesions, right, left or bilateral (Kliest, 1934; Brain, 1941; Paterson & Zangwill, 1945; Cogan, 1960; De Renzi & Faglioni, 1962; Hécaen, 1969).

Route finding difficulties

The neurological literature has occasionally reported cases where the principal deficit lies in the patients' inability to find their way about in long familiar surroundings or in frequently encountered locations in the recent past. Such patients may be well able to give adequate verbal descriptions of familiar routes but are unable to execute them either by drawing or taking them in real life situations. They become lost in the hospital environs or en route to the hospital.

Perhaps for lack of a more appropriate term such a disorder is often termed *topographical amnesia*. An extensive review is provided by De Renzi (1982). It is impossible to tell in most reported cases just how much of the route finding difficulty is due to memory disturbance because of inadequate examination. Brain (1941) pointed to at least four basic disorders which might lead to route finding difficulties: (i) perceptual disorders of the location and relative position of objects, (ii) failure of recognition of environmental features through object agnosia, (iii) topographical amnesia, (iv) unilateral spatial neglect. This latter cause may result in the patient failing to take appropriate left hand turns with a resulting preponderance of right hand turns (Gloning, 1965).

If one excludes perceptual and attentional defects there remain two basic difficulties to be disentangled, namely *topographical agnosia* and *topographical amnesia*, a distinction first put forward in the classical paper of Paterson and Zangwill (1945).

Topographical agnosia

While some reports suggest that inability to recognize objects that serve as landmarks might be the predominant topographical difficulty in a small number of cases, even these have shown associated perceptual or agnosic difficulties (Pallis, 1955; De Renzi & Faglioni, 1962). It is obvious that even if a separate category of topographical agnosia were to be established it would fail to account for the majority of cases of route finding difficulties produced by brain lesions especially if, as Byrne (1982) suggests, such schemata may be developed by different individuals in different ways. As long ago as 1948 Tolman conceived of the notion of a cognitive map to account for the spatial maze learning of the white rat: 'The alternative possibility (to S–R theory) is that the learner is following signs to a goal, is learning his way about, is following a sort of map — in other words, is learning not movements but meanings. The organism learns sign-significant relations, it learns a behaviour route, not a movement pattern' (Hilgard, 1956, p. 191). Experimental investigation of the development of such 'maps' or schemata might pave the way for more life-related clinical tests of topographical ability.

Topographical amnesia

Cases where amnesia for topography forms the sole or major complaint are likewise rare. The amnesia may include long-stored topographical information as well as material more recently acquired, e.g. Paterson and Zangwill's patient (1945) displayed an inability to describe previously experienced topographical relationships and could not recall whether to turn right or left when leaving the ward doorway to visit the toilet. Both patients described by De Renzi & Faglioni (1962) and Scotti (1968) had a very short forgetting period for spatial information.

However, it is noteworthy that one of these cases (Scotti, 1968) showed a dissociation between recent and long-term topographical memory since he was quite competent in finding his way in previously familiar locations but not in recent ones, such as the hospital. On the other hand the patient of De Renzi et al (1977) who had a right temporo parietal softening showed both topographical amnesia and an inability to learn a visually-guided stylus maze problem over 275 trials although she was free from spatial perceptual disorder and had no apparent verbal or visual memory deficit. Other cases with topographical amnesia as a major feature have been described by Whitty and Newcombe (1973), Whitely and Warrington (1978) and Hécaen and his colleagues (1980).

Clinico-experimental study in this area is hampered by our paucity of knowledge of how geographical knowledge is developed in the normal subject. In a recent review Byrne (1982) makes a number of important distinctions. Prime among these is the difference between spatial information which can be gained from a single viewpoint (visuospatial perception) and the topographical schema of large scale space which is typically acquired by personal locomotor experience. Many of the tasks used in the laboratory and clinic fail to come to grips with the ways in which the dynamically evolved cognitive representation of large scale space is disrupted.

CONSTRUCTIONAL APRAXIA

The first modern description of constructional difficulties in patients with cerebral impairment is usually attributed to Kleist (Strauss, 1924; Kleist, 1934). After first considering certain drawing disabilities of neurological patients to be a form of optic apraxia, he later introduced the term constructional apraxia. Moreover, Benton pointed out that Kleist insisted that this particular disorder was to be distinguished from others that were obviously rooted in visuoperceptual disorders and thought that the basis of the disorder lay in a disruption between visual and kinesthetic processes. This would accord well with what we would call today the general conception of a 'disconnection syndrome' alluded to in earlier chapters.

Many early investigators had felt that the failure of patients on certain tasks such as drawing and route finding reflected a visuospatial disturbance. While many patients with constructional difficulties did have visuospatial problems there were also those who had for example, severe difficulties with drawing without showing a spatial deficit (Lhermitte & Trelles, 1933; Kroll & Stolbun, 1933; Mayer-Gross, 1935.) Strauss (1924) defined a pure case of constructional apraxia as one with adequate form perception, perceptual discrimination and perceptual localization and absence of ideomotor apraxia or motor disability.

Later definitions include those of Critchley (1953), 'an executive defect within a visuospatial domain', and Benton (1967), 'an impairment in combinatory or organizing activity in which details must be clearly perceived and in which the relationships among the component parts of the entity must be apprehended if the desired synthesis of them is to be achieved.'

Constructional apraxia is often said to be the apraxia of the psychologist since it is more often revealed on neuropsychological examination than exhibited clinically. For this and other reasons, numerous studies have been made of constructional disabilities in the past 30 years. The present summary builds on reviews such as those of Benton (1969) and Warrington (1969).

Status of the concept

One of the most frequently asked questions is the following. Is constructional apraxia a single entity or are there separate, distinct types of disorder under this heading? In 1957, Ettlinger and his co-workers reported 10 cases in which right posterior cerebral lesions showed disturbances in spatial perception and manipulation. An investigation of the individual performance suggested the possibility of different varieties of constructional difficulty. Benton and Fogel (1962) pointed to the possible relation with the type of test employed or the activity under examination.

Constructional praxis is a broad concept which has been applied to a number of rather different types of activities. These activities have in common the characteristic that they require the patient to assemble, join or articulate parts to form a single unitary structure. However, they may differ from each other in many respects, e.g. in complexity, in the type of movement and the degree of motor dexterity required in achieving the task, in the demands made on the higher intellectual functions, and in whether they involve construction in two or three spatial dimensions.'

Critchley (1953) had pointed out that three-dimensional construction tasks appeared to be necessary since some patients with parietal lesions who had no difficulty on the commonly employed two-dimensional tests displayed gross abnormalities of construction when the test moved into the third dimension. Such abnormalities could not be elicited by the usual clinical examination. Benton and Fogel confirmed this by demonstrating only a weak positive correlation between the performance of brain damaged subjects on a drawing test (Benton Visual Retention Test) and their newly constructed Three-Dimensional Constructional Praxis task (Figure 6.8). Fourteen patients were adequate on the copying task but defective on the three dimensional task whereas another eight were adequate on the three dimensional task but showed defective copying.

In a later study Benton (1967) addressed himself specifically to the question and, since it appears to be the only such study it is worth referring to in a little detail. Benton employed four apparently dissimilar tests: Benton Visual Retention Test, Stick-construction, Block Designs, Three-Dimensional Constructional Praxis — and measured the concordance between various combinations of tests. The concurrence of failure varied from chance level upward for different pairs of tests but even the highest degree of concurrence fell well below perfect agreement. There was also

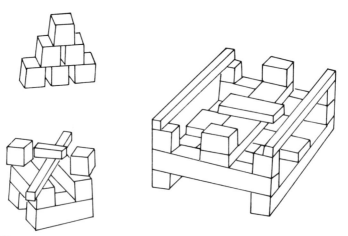

Fig. 6.8 Three dimension constructional praxis test (drawn from Benton & Fogel (1962) courtesy of American Medical Association).

considerable intra individual variation in performance level on these tests. However, there did seem to be more relation between the last three tests than there was between any of these and the drawing test (VRT). Benton concluded that there may be at least two types of tests namely graphic tasks and assembly tasks and that empirical study may well reveal others.

The variety of tests which have been used to elicit constructional apraxia is great.

1. Spontaneous or free drawing. For a careful and detailed description with illustration of the common errors seen with drawing tasks the reader is referred to Warrington (1969).
2. Drawing from a model, e.g. Benton Visual Retention Test (Benton, 1962) as well as simpler clinical versions.
3. Stick pattern constructions, e.g. Stick Test, Goldstein and Scheerer (1941)
4. Block designs, usually modelled on the Kohs test (Goldstein & Scheerer, 1941; Wechsler, 1958)
5. Test of spatial analysis (mentioned above)
6. Three dimensional constructions (Critchley, 1953; Benton & Fogel, 1962)
7. Reconstruction of puzzles, e.g. (Benson & Barton, 1970) and the Object Assembly subtest of the Wechsler Adult Intelligence Scale (WAIS)

In view of the fact that many brain damaged patients fail on some of these and pass on others it is obviously unsatisfactory to use failure on any one as an operational definition of constructional apraxia as some writers have done. Since the WAIS is about the most widely used test in the assessment of higher functions it provides the most frequent opportunity to observe the dissociation which so often occurs between performance on the Block Design and Object Assembly subtests. Obviously many tests, particularly Block Design, are multi-factorial in nature and failure on such a test may arise from a number of causes which need to be explored if the signficance of the failure is to be seen. The failure may rest on inability to analyze the model visually or be made difficult by disruption of the patient's spatial schemata or, as outlined below, be impossible because the patient is uable to initiate, monitor and execute a plan for the solution of the task.

Some of the factors which need to be taken into consideration in interpreting a patient's failure on constructional tasks have been mentioned in the study by Benson and Barton (1970) and are further discussed in relation to clinical assessment in Chapter 10. Benson and Barton suggest that the more general term 'constructional disability' would be more appropriate for most findings, reserving the term 'constructional apraxia' for the case having the features outlined by Kleist. Their study with a variety of tests showed that right hemisphere lesions produced more consistent disturbance than left, while posterior lesions of either hemisphere produced more consistent disturbances than anterior ones.

Laterality and constructional apraxia

Most early cases described as showing constructional apraxia had bilateral posterior lesions. Later, cases were described where constructional apraxia was seen together with one or more symptoms of the Gerstmann syndrome which suggested that the left or dominant parietal area was of importance as part of the substratum of constructional abilities. Still later, attention began to be paid to the role of the minor hemisphere when it was clearly demonstrated that unilateral right hemisphere lesions could produce the symptom (Paterson & Zangwill, 1944; Ajuriaguerra & Hécaen, 1960).

The first large systematic survey of laterality of lesion and constructional apraxia was that of Piercy et al (1960). In 403 consecutive cases with unilateral cerebral lesions 67 cases showed constructional apraxia. Of these 42 had lesions on the right and 25 on the left. This represented 22.3% of the right hemisphere cases and 11.6% of the left. The disproportion between right and left cases was even greater for retrorolandic cases some 37.8% of the right posterior cases showing apraxia against 16.1% of the left. Since that time numerous studies have confirmed the much higher incidence of constructional apraxia with non-dominant hemisphere lesions (e.g. Benton, 1962; Benton & Fogel, 1962; Costa & Vaughan, 1962; Piercy & Smyth, 1962; Arrigoni & De Renzi, 1964; Newcombe, 1969; Black & Strub, 1976).

Many studies have reported that constructional apraxia is not only more frequent with right hemisphere lesions but that it also tends to be more severe, i.e. patients show more grossly defective performances (Benton & Fogel, 1962; Benton, 1967; Gainotti Messerli & Tissot, 1972a).

However, other well controlled studies have not shown hemispheric differences particularly where the severity of general psychological deficit has been taken into account (Warrington James & Kinsbourne 1966; De Renzi & Faglioni, 1967; Benson & Barton, 1970; Dee, 1970; Gainotti Miceli & Caltagirone, 1977).

The assumption of a true relationship between lesions of the non-dominant hemisphere and constructional apraxia has been seriously challenged by the study of Arrigoni and De Renzi (1964). While they also found a higher incidence of difficulties in right-sided lesions on each of three constructive tests in an unselected sample of hospitalized patients they felt that at least part of the difference might lie in the possibility that the lesions of the right hemisphere group were consistently larger. This possiblity has also been alluded to by Costa and Vaughan (1962) and Benton (1965). Wolff (1962) had suggested that one reason for this might be the earlier presentation of dominant lesions because of language disturbances.

From their larger group Arrigoni and De Renzi matched left and right cases for severity of impairment using a reaction time measure which their earlier work had suggested was an index of cerebral impairment that was not affected by the location of lesion. The two groups of 44 patients

Table 6.1 Constructional apraxia and side of lesion

	Present	Absent
Right Hemisphere	27	17
Left Hemisphere	17	27

produced the following findings (Table 6.1).

The difference was in the 'predicted' direction but was no longer significant (when tested by *chi square*). 'This result should make us extremely cautious in attributing a dominance (even if relative) to the right hemisphere with regard to constructive capacities.' (Arrigoni & De Renzi, 1964, p. 190) Benton (1969), in a summary of evidence to that time, pointed out that 'defective performance on the part of patients with left hemisphere disease is not at all rare. Thus, if right hemisphere "dominance" for visuoconstructive performance does exist, it does not appear comparable to the "dominance" for language performance exercised by the left hemisphere'. This does not mean that there are no qualitative differences between the two sides. In fact, Arrigoni and De Renzi describe such differences.

Qualitative differences and laterality

Relation between visuoperceptive and visuoconstructive deficits

Qualitative differences between the two hemispheres is the subject of Chapter 8 but numerous studies, including that of Arrigoni and De Renzi (1964) show characteristic differences in quality of performance on constructional tasks between left and right hemisphere cases (McFie & Zangwill, 1960; Piercy, Hécaen & Ajuriaguerra 1960; Warrington James & Kinsbourne 1966; Gainotti Messerli & Tissot, 1972; Collignon & Rondeaux, 1974). The study of Warrington and her colleagues was directed to an examination of specially designed drawing tests which were rated by independent judges. Though there was no significant difference in degree of disability between the two groups they showed a dissociation of predominant types of error. 'The type of error made by patients with right hemisphere lesions suggest that these patients have difficulty in incorporating spatial information into their drawing performance, leading to disproportion and faulty articulation of parts of the drawing, while the patients with left hemisphere lesions seemed to experience difficulty in planning the drawing process, leading to simplified drawings of the model.' (p. 82) . Similar findings were described by Gainotti and his colleagues (1972) who found left hemisphere cases produced simplified drawings which were helped by the presentation of a model for copying while the visuospatial disturbances of the right hemisphere cases were not helped to any degree by a model. Table 6.2, drawn largely from Warrington (1969), summarizes the main differences.

Table 6.2 Laterality of lesion and characteristics of drawing

Right Hemisphere	Left Hemisphere
Scattered and fragmented	Coherent but simplified
Loss of spatial relations	Preservation of spatial relations
Faulty orientation	Correct orientation
Energetic drawing	Slow and laborious
Addition of lines to try to make drawing correct	Gross lack of detail

Both Warrington (1969) and Benson and Barton (1970) have put forward hypotheses about the relative contributions of the left and right hemispheres to visuoconstructive tasks: ' . . . right hemisphere lesions produce disorders of visuo-spatial perception while left-sided lesions disturb motor function (apraxia)' (Benson & Barton, p. 21) while the 'right hemisphere supplies a perceptual and the left hemisphere an executive component to the task' (Warrington, p. 80). Earlier studies had already suggested this hyopothesis (Hécaen Ajuriaguerra & Massonet 1951; Duensing, 1954b; Ettlinger, Warrington & Zangwill, 1957; Ajuriaguerra & Hécaen, 1960; McFie & Zangwill, 1960; Piercy Hécaen & Ajuriaguerra 1960). Several of these studies are cited by both authors. The argument that the right hemisphere contributes a perceptual element is supported indirectly by studies showing that purely perceptual tasks (without a constructional component) are more poorly performed by patients with right hemisphere lesions (Ch. 8).

Despite the strong clinical evidence of laterality, different experimental studies have given conflicting results. One group of studies supports the contention that a perceptual difficulty usually lies at the root of the trouble. Kleist himself postulated that the left hemisphere was the one mainly implicated in patients with constructional difficulties which were not on the basis of visuoperceptive defects. (Piercy & Smyth, 1962; De Renzi & Faglioni, 1967; Dee, 1970; Gainotti & Tiacci, 1970). Dee (1970) found that 42 out of 46 patients with constructional apraxia had significant visuoperceptive defects and was unable to demonstrate any hemispheric differences apart from the finding that three of the four patients with apraxia and no perceptual deficit had lesions in the left hemisphere. He concluded that most constructional apraxia is due to a disorder of visual perception irrespective of the side of the lesion though he allowed that other explanations must be sought for the minority of cases. Further study of the cases from the 1970 study by Dee and Benton (1970) showed that the patients with constructional apraxia also failed on a haptic-spatial task, supporting the contention of Semmes (1965, 1968) that many spatial disorders extend beyond a single modality and are not determined by primary sensory perceptual defect, i.e. they are multimodal in character. Other studies, e.g.

De Renzi and Scotti (1969) show that posterior lesions may produce spatial difficulties embracing more than one sense modality.

On the other hand, there are studies claiming evidence that the correlation between perceptual and constructional difficulties is higher in right- than left-hemisphere lesion patients (Costa & Vaughan, 1962; Warrington James & Kinsbourne, 1966).

Results of constructional tests in a small number of patients who had undergone cerebral commissurotomy has been cited as additional evidence of the greater role of the non-dominant hemisphere in constructional performance (Gazzaniga Bogen & Sperry, 1965; Gazzaniga, 1970). Though commissurotomy subjects may perform better when using the left hand (right hemisphere) than the right hand, the fact that performance was below par with either hand suggests bilateral but unequal representation of constructional abilities.

Constructional apraxia and locus of lesion

There seems little doubt that, if one can consider frontal constructional difficulties as forming a separate entity, the parietal lobe particularly on the non-dominant side is most closely related with constructional disabilities which have the characteristics of the Kleist-Strauss formulation. Writers not wishing to be limited by the artificial lobar boundaries often relate constructional apraxia to the ill-defined area at the junction of the parietal, temporal, occipital lobes, Luria's zone of overlapping. In a study of 105 cases with tumours of the temporal lobe, Petrovici (1972) found a complete absence of constructional apraxia in the 77 cases which were completely restricted to the temporal lobe, or in 4 frontotemporal cases. On the other hand, the remaining 24 cases with added involvement of the parietal lobe or the parietal and occipital lobes, had 11 cases of constructional apraxia (4 left and 7 right).

A factorial study could be conducted to see whether the parietal, overlapping, and occipital areas contribute separate factors to the 'posterior type' of constructional disability. There are, however, anatomical and pathological reasons why this is difficult if not impossible.

Bilateral parietal or diffuse cerebral lesions lead to very marked disturbances both of constructional praxis and spatial orientation though they are often masked by accompanying organic dementia (Allison, 1962).

Resolving the confusion

This confusing state of affairs can be attributed to the interaction of two factors, namely, the over-inclusive nature of the concept of constructional apraxia together with the great variety of clinical and experimental measures, often of some complexity, which has been used to elicit constructional

difficulties. It might be better to abandon the concept or term constructional apraxia in favour of an examination of the seemingly separate
component functions and their relation to tests as factorially simple as possible. The warning given earlier about the multiple determination of
responses on most tests applies particularly here since even *apparently simple*
perceptual tasks may allow different strategies to be brought into play
(Bryden, 1977; Birkett, 1978).

Studies which have aimed at clarifying the issue by separating out
perceptual and executive functions have emerged in recent years. Arena and
Gainotti (1978) employed two relatively pure measures of perceptual and
constructional ability, the multiple choice version of the Benton Visual
Retention Test and the usual graphomotor version of the same test. No
differences were found between right- and left-hemisphere damaged
subjects on these measures with respect to either incidence or severity of
deficient performance. On the other hand, Mack and Levine (1981) devised
a visuoconstructive task termed the Form Assembly Task which required
the subjects to assemble geometrical pieces with different lengths of lines
and different angles, to form a square (Fig. 6.9).

This test was given together with two visual discrimination tasks to
patients with unilateral lesions. All but one of the right hemisphere subjects
failed on the Form Assembly Task but only 7 out of 19 of the left-hemisphere subjects and the degree of impairment was greater in the former
group. Comparison of the relationship between performance on the three
tests was consistent with the hypothesis already mentioned above that
perceptual deficits may underlie constructional difficulties among those with
right- but not left-hemisphere damage. Further studies of this kind are
clearly necessary.

Fig. 6.9 Form assembly task (from Mack & Levine, 1981).

Associated disabilities

The most widely quoted study of disabilities associated with constructional
difficulties is that of McFie and Zangwill (1960). They compared the visual-
constructive impairment of 8 left hemisphere cases (all in the posterior

Table 6.3 Comparison between left- and right-sided lesion (McFie & Zangwill, 1960).

	Left		Right	
	No. examined	No. with disability	No. examined	No. with disability
Unilateral neglect	8	1	21	14
Dressing disability	8	1	15	10
Cube counting	6	(1)	7	6
Paper cutting	4	0	10	9
Topographical loss	8	1	18	9
Right-left discrimination	8	5	21	0
Weigl's sorting test	6	5	16	1

parietal region) with that of right-sided cases from earlier studies of the Cambridge group. Table 6.3 gives the quantitative features of the study.

It is clear that there is a strong association between the first five symptoms and right-sided lesions while the last two symptoms are seen almost exclusively with left-sided lesions. McFie and Zangwill felt that their left-sided cases corresponded more closely to the classical description of constructional apraxia whereas the difficulties encountered by the right hemisphere patients were more closely associated with visuospatial agnosia. As well as the difference in associated symptoms there also appeared to be qualitative differences in the constructional disabilities of left and right cases. Failure of a high proportion of left-sided cases on Weigl's sorting test appeared to be part of a general intellectual impairment which was not seen with right-sided cases. Gainotti and his colleagues (1972) confirmed this relationship. In right-sided cases there was no relation between constructional apraxia and mental impairment while with left-sided cases there was a significant relationship between constructional apraxia, mental impairment and ideomotor apraxia. A number of studies by Benton (Benton, 1962, 1967; Benton & Fogel, 1962) have shown a generally higher incidence of mental impairment in brain damaged patients with constructional apraxia than those without such apraxia. Despite this general relationship there were both patients with severe mental impairment who showed no defective praxis and patients with severe constructional impairment whose intelligence levels were around the level expected from their educational background. The impairment level was based on the work of Fogel (1962, 1964) using the difference between obtained and expected intelligence scores.

The problems which arise in the interpretation of the significance of associated disabilities are discussed by Warrington (1969).

Frontal apraxia

Constructional difficulties with anterior lesions have been reported sporadically since the early finding of Pollack (1938) that frontal lesions may occasionally disturb constructional praxis. Luria and Tsvetkova (1964) summarized the difference between anterior and posterior lesions:

> In lesions of the parieto-occipital part of the brain the general factor underlying constructive disturbances is a loss of spatial organization of the elements . . . In lesions of the frontal lobes the general factor underlying constructive disturbances is a loss of programming and regulating of sequential behaviour . . . instability of the primary intention or program and to the inability to compare the results with the preliminary intention . . .' (p. 95).

This type of disruption has been considered in Chapter 4.

Constructional apraxia as a disconnection syndrome

In a largely neglected paper Nielsen (1975) drew attention to the marked similarity in the drawing errors of patients with right and left hemisphere lesions and the errors made by the left and right hands of commissurotomy patients. This led him to postulate that the observed constructional difficulties in patients with unilateral lesions might be explained at least partially by a disconnection effect.

Independently, Le Doux and his colleagues (1978) put forward the same argument based on their observations of a patient with complete commissurotomy. This patient, while showing equal perceptual ability of either hemisphere for block design matching (Le Doux, Wilson & Gazzaniga, (1977)), showed a clear inferiority of the right hand (left hemisphere) in executing the block design problems compared with the left hand (right hemisphere).

According to such a model, left-sided lesions may produce constructional difficulties in the right hand (but not the left) since they disconnect the vital right posterior region from the left motor cortex controlling the right hand.

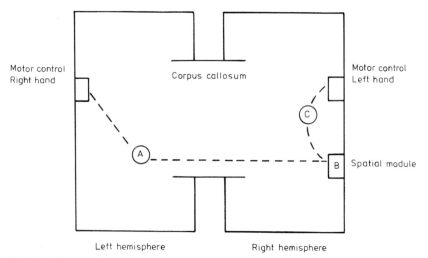

Fig. 6.10 Constructional apraxia as a disconnection syndrome.

It could be postulated that the right posterior cortex contains the basic module for spatial integration (Fig. 6.10, SM) a plausible position in view of accumulated neuropsychological evidence. It would thus be possible to have three situations: (i) a lesion at A would produce only right-handed constructional problems; (ii) a lesion at B would result in constructional difficulty for either hand, while (iii) a lesion at C would produce left-handed difficulties only.

The situation is obviously more complex than this, e.g. constructional apraxia is never seen alone, always in association with other difficulties. However, much has obviously been overlooked in the failure to examine systematically the performance of each hand and the disconnection notion is open to experimental verification.

SPATIAL DYSLEXIA AND DYSCALCULIA

Spatial dyslexia

This form of dyslexia may be clearly distinguishable at times from dyslexia of a symbolic nature. The patient can recognize letters and words but may be unable to read. At least part of this difficulty is attributable to difficulty with the continuous scanning movements necessary for reading. The disorganization in the directional control of eye movements varies a good deal from patient to patient but in severely disabled patients the fixations appear to be made at random so that fixation may jump from one part of a line to another and from part of one line to another line some distance away. Obviously, a patient with this difficulty cannot make sense of printed material. In less severely affected cases the patient may skip only occasional words so that he is able to fill in the sense of what he is reading.

Some patients' reading difficulties appear to depend largely upon unilateral spatial neglect. For this reason spatial dyslexia is seen rather more frequently with right hemisphere lesions. Benton (1969) explains the effect in the following way: 'The patient initially fixates on a point which is at some distance to the right of the beginning of the line, reads to the end of the line and then returns to a point on the next line which is somewhat to the right of the beginning of the line. The result is, of course, that he cannot make any sense of what he reads and he soon becomes confused.' (p. 219) This explanation is very similar to that usually employed in the explanation of reading difficulty of the hemianopic patient (especially those with a left half field loss) which is described in the next chapter.

Spatial dyscalculia (acalculia)

Hécaen and his colleagues divided calculation difficulties into three types each the product of a different mechanism (Hécaen Angelergues & Houillier, 1961; Hécaen, 1969). These are (i) acalculia based on an alexia of figures and numerals; (ii) inability to do arithmetical sums (anarithmia); (iii) dyscalculia of the spatial type. Hécaen and Angelergues (1961) found a predominance of left hemisphere lesions with the first two types and a predominance of right hemisphere lesions with the third. Approximately 24% of 148 right hemisphere cases had this disorder compared with only 2% of 195 left hemisphere cases.

Grafman et al (1982) studied 76 subjects with unilateral damage due to focal haemorrhage having first established the subject's competence to read and write numbers. They were then given a written calculation test together with neuropsychological tests covering perception, construction, and intelligence. Both right and left hemisphere subjects were poorer than controls but those with left posterior lesions were particularly impaired even after the calculation test score had been corrected for the results on the other tests. This would seem to confirm the presence of the type (ii) acalculia and relate it to the left posterior region, and strengthens the notion that, like so many other neurobehavioural disorders, acalculia is not a unitary difficulty.

SPATIAL DISORDERS: GENERAL COMMENTS

The hemispheric asymmetry of function with regard to spatial disorders is summarized in Chapter 8. Bender and Diamond (1970) remind us of the

> extensive interrelationships among the various sensory-motor systems that characterize normal perceptual function . . . cerebellar, oculomotor and vestibular influences are prominent factors in visual function besides the visual projection system itself and the subject's state of alertness. It is not possible therefore to ascribe disturbances in perception of space to disease of the parietal lobe or, more specifically, to disease of the right parietal lobe (p. 184).

While one might agree with this statement if it means *only* to disease of the parietal lobe there is little doubt that the accumulated evidence indicts the right parietal lobe most strongly in certain disorders. There is also some evidence that the presence of residual perceptual and spatial deficits may be the principal reason why recovery after right hemisphere strokes is more difficult to achieve than after seemingly comparable lesions in the left hemisphere (Marquardsen, 1969; Hurwitz & Adams, 1972).

Finally, it is obvious that the concept of 'spatial disorientation' or even 'spatial difficulty' is a very gross one. Dee and Benton (1970) comment that 'assuming that spatial perception may be analyzed into "partial" functions, it would not be surprising to find hemispheric differences in the representations of such functions' (p. 270). It would also be surprising if these partial functions were not closely related to the specific outlying association areas of the different modalities.

UNILATERAL SPATIAL NEGLECT (USN)

As early as 1876 Jackson described a patient who neglected the left side of the page when reading. As with so many later reports the lesion was in the right posterior region. A more complete description of visual inattention came from Holmes (1918) and the phenomenon was confirmed by Poppelreuter (1923) and Riddoch (1935) but it was not until the detailed description by Brain (1941) of inattention for the left half of space in three patients with large right-sided parietal lesions that the condition attracted much attention. It has been variously defined but the essential features are expressed in the following definition of Gainotti and his colleagues (1972b, p. 545). The 'syndrome consists of a tendency to neglect one half of extrapersonal space in such tasks as drawing and reading which require a good and symmetrical exploration of space.'

In everyday activities the patient may neglect food on one side of his plate, may fail to use cutlery on one side, may collide with a wall along a corridor and when asked to read may read portions of the page and even fractions of words. The most striking examples are seen in those with left-sided neglect.

Testing for neglect

Simple clinical tasks include asking the patient to copy a simple symmetrical drawing such as a daisy. The patient will often be satisfied with drawing half the figure, usually the right. Asked to bisect a line drawn on a paper immediately in front of him the patient will place his mark towards the normal side. This test was first devised by Axenfeld in 1894 (De Renzi, 1982). Other 'experimental' measures have been employed, e.g. the omission of items on the neglected side of space with the Poppelreuter overlapping figures test (Critchley, 1953, Hécaen & Angelergues, 1963). Costa et al (1969) devised an empirical position preference score from Raven's Coloured Progressive Matrices. Specially constructed tasks have been produced, e.g. that of De Renzi and Faglioni (1967). The most favoured in recent times is that of Albert (1973). The importance of using several measures in the one patient is shown by the work of Ogden (1985a) where some patients showed clear visual hemineglect on some tasks but not on others.

Laterality of lesion and USN

The first clear statement on a relation between laterality and neglect also came from Brain (1945) who considered that the deficit was very largely restricted to right hemisphere or non-dominant lesions. This point of view has received very wide support though Brain was aware that the apparently low incidence of report of USN in left hemisphere or dominant lesions might be due to the masking effects of other symptoms such as severe aphasia. A direct attempt to test this proposition was made by Battersby et al (1956) during a study of 75 cases with unilateral space occupying lesions. The authors suggest that the apparently high association found between neglect phenomena and the non-dominant hemisphere might be a spurious one. There are a number of factors which make comparison studies exceedingly difficult if not impossible. Chief among these are the characteristics of the groups under study, e.g. (i) the presence and degree of sensory deficits; (ii) the presence and degree of dysphasia; (iii) the presence of intellectual deterioration; (iv) the relative size of the lesion. The sobering effect of the findings of Arrigoni and De Renzi (1964) with regard to laterality and another disorder (constructional praxis) has already been mentioned.

A brief review of studies since 1960 does lend weight to Brain's original hypothesis. In a study of other symptoms associated with constructional apraxia occurring in unilateral cases, McFie and Zangwill (1960) found only one of their 8 left hemisphere cases showed neglect compared with 14 out of 21 right hemisphere cases from previous studies from Zangwill's laboratory (Paterson & Zangwill, 1944, 1945; McFie, Piercy & Zangwill, 1950; Ettlinger, Warrington & Zangwill 1957). The right-sided predominance was also reported by Piercy and his colleagues (1960). Hécaen (1962) reviewed a large number of retrorolandic cases which showed that only 4 out of 206 left hemisphere cases had the deficit as against 52 out of 154 right hemisphere cases. A much higher incidence of qualitative errors suggesting left hemi-inattention was found for right hemisphere cases than left hemisphere cases in Arrigoni and De Renzi's (1964) study of constructional apraxia. A specific test of the laterality hypothesis by Gainotti (1968) using a battery of simple tests showed that unilateral neglect is both significantly more frequent and more severe in patients with lesions of the right hemisphere than of the left. This finding was strongly confirmed in a later study (Gainotti & Tiacci, 1971) and other studies continue to add to the consensus. Oxbury et al (1974) for example, found no cases of neglect in their patients with either left hemisphere or brain stem strokes while 7 of their 17 right hemisphere stroke cases showed the symptom.

In his extensive review of studies relating unilateral neglect to laterality, Hécaen (1982) concludes that prevalence of neglect in right-sided lesions appears established even after factors such as sampling bias have been considered.

Not only has evidence of a quantitative difference between the two hemispheres gained support but the hypothesis has been advanced that qualitative differences also exist. Gainotti and his co-workers (1972) compared patients with unilateral lesions on various tasks of copying drawings. They described for the first time what appears to be a unique feature in the performance of some right hemisphere cases, namely, 'the tendency

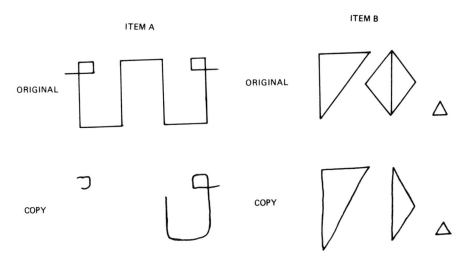

Fig. 6.11 Examples of copying defects in right hemisphere patients, (after Gainotti et al, courtesy of the authors and editors).

to neglect one half of a figure (on the side opposite to the hemispheric locus of lesion), while reproducing designs that are placed even more laterally on the neglected side' (p. 546). Examples of this qualitatively different sign are shown in Figure 6.11.

The majority of references to neglect phenomena have been concerned with visuo-spatial neglect. Recent studies have shown that it can also occur in other modalities. The finding of unilateral neglect in the tactile modality by De Renzi and his co-workers (1970) suggested to those authors 'that hemi-inattention does not depend so much on perceptual and motor factors as on a mutilated representation of space' (p. 202). Heilman and Valenstein (1972a) found 17 cases of auditory unilateral neglect in a 10 month survey. Of 10 cases with positive brain scans, nine were in the right inferior parietal lobule and one in the left frontal region. Though the defect became most apparent in test situations employing simultaneous stimulation it was not restricted to these, being apparent as an abnormal responsiveness when the patients were addressed from the neglected side. There was no loss of auditory acuity in these patients. There may also be an interaction between the nature of the task employed and the laterality of the lesions. Leicester et al (1969) found that not only did neglect appear with lesions of either hemisphere but also that, with particular tasks, neglect occurred predominantly or exclusively with lesions of one hemisphere, e.g. a language related task of matching letters to an auditory sample showed neglect only on the right with dominant left hemisphere lesions. This study also revealed that neglect appeared not 'on every test, but only on those which, for some reason they could not do correctly' (p. 586).

Locus of lesions causing neglect

Although most studies of USN implicate posterior parts of the brain with particular emphasis on the non-dominant parietal lobe neglect phenomena are seen with lesions in other locations both cortical and subcortical.

Parietal lobe

Apart from a large number of case reports, two sources of evidence for a preponderant role for the parietal lobe come from neurosurgical reports and recent localization studies using computed tomography (CT scan).

In patients who had undergone surgery for epilepsy Hécaen et al (1956) found the critical area to be the supramarginal and angular gyri (the inferior parietal lobule) and part of the adjacent superior temporal gyrus. This was confirmed by the study of Heilman and Watson (1977) which showed radionucleotide uptake to be maximal in this region in 14 out of 19 cases with neglect. Similarly the CT scan study of Bisiach et al (1979) implicated the multimodal cortex at the junction of the parietal, temporal and occipital lobes with heavy emphasis on the inferior parietal lobule. Hécaen (1982) points out that not only is this region concerned with multisensory integration but it brings 'into the focus of attention events occurring in the periphery of the visual field' (p. 96). However, caution should be used in inferring the predominant importance of a particular region in view of the studies which follow.

Frontal lobe

The first description of frontal lobe neglect was by Heilman and Valenstein (1972b). All six patients were right-handed and had right-sided lesions, three dorsolateral and three medial. More recently, Damasio and his colleagues (1980) presented five cases of neglect with lesions in the frontal lobe or basal ganglia. In this study four of the five cases were in the *left* hemisphere. That frontal neglect is not uncommon was shown by Ogden (1985a). While contralateral neglect was more severe with right-sided posterior lesions some neglect was also seen with about half her patients with left-sided lesions, being more common with a frontal locus.

Subcortical lesions

A number of reports of neglect and extinction phenomena have been reported recently with subcortical lesions in the thalamus or basal ganglia (Heir et al, 1977; Watson & Heilman, 1979; Damasio, Damasio & Chang Chu, 1980; Valenstein & Heilman, 1981). With one exception all cases have affected the right hemisphere.

Unilateral neglect and perceptual disorders

The higher incidence of impairment of patients with right hemisphere lesions on tasks of complex visual perception (described in Chapter 8) together with the higher incidence of neglect with right-sided lesions has suggested the hypothesis that the two are causally related. Two experiments by Gainotti and Tiacci (1971) add weight to the hypothesis that some perceptual difficulties are due, at least in part, to unilateral spatial neglect. On an overlapping figures test right hemisphere patients made more total errors as well as more errors and omissions for figures lying to one side (left) of the midline than the left hemisphere group while there was no significant difference between the two groups for errors on figures lying to the right of the midline. Furthermore the right hemisphere group with neglect tended to overvalue drawings on the right half of the midline when asked to compare the size of two figures one to the left and one to the right. The authors suggest that the overvaluation may be due to a tendency to gaze to their right (now neglected) side invoking Piaget's theory of the 'fixation effect' (Piaget, 1969): 'the space of visual perception is not homogeneous, but the elements on which the gaze is mostly fixed are systematically overvalued' (Gainotti & Tiacci, 1971, p. 456).

A much higher incidence of visual field defects has been found in right hemisphere groups with a higher incidence of visual spatial neglect (Battersby et al, 1956; McFie & Zangwil, 1960; Hécaen, 1962). There is also a generally poorer performance on visual perceptual tasks by patients with right hemisphere lesions and neglect than by those with right hemisphere lesions without neglect (Oxbury 1974). These authors employed a wide range of tests of visual perception and spatial analysis all of which showed a greater deficit in patients with neglect. However, the fact that some patients with clearly marked perceptual and spatial disorders showed no evidence of neglect suggested that while visuospatial neglect may be an important factor in producing impairments of perception and spatial analysis in patients with non-dominant retrorolandic lesions it certainly cannot be the whole answer.

The role of visual field defects in the disorders of visual perception which are so often associated with unilateral neglect has been the subject of frequent study. The Milan group has produced many studies showing that the perceptual deficits of non-dominant lesions are almost always associated with visual field defects (De Renzi & Spinnler, 1967; De Renzi & Scotti, 1969, 1970, De Renzi, Scotti & Spinnler, 1969; Faglioni, Spinler & Vignolo, 1969. Ratcliff (1973) likewise found greatest impairment on a perceptual task for posterior right hemisphere lesions with visual field defects. Costa et al (1969) inferred that the strong right position preference shown by their right hemisphere cases on Raven's Progressive Matrices was indicative of visual spatial neglect and this was strongly associated in their material with visual field defects.

Nature of the defect

Theories of neglect phenomena are many and no single conception appears adequate to explain the findings. There is also overlap between what appear at first to be separate theories. Three classes of explanation cover most of the opinions.

Sensory synthesis

Denny Brown and his colleagues (1952) considered that a disruption of sensory transmission and synthesis to one hemisphere was the causative process. Battersby et al (1956) felt that mental deterioration needed to be superadded but this was far from universally present in the large scale study of Hécaen and Angelergues (1963) and a later study of Gainotti (1968) though a half to three quarters of subjects did have such impairment.

Attentional deficit

Critchley (1949) in his discussion of tactile inattention argued strongly for an attentional deficit as the basis of the disorder. Heilman and his associates have been the most enthusiastic proponents of this view (Heilman & Watson, 1977; Heilman & Valenstein, 1979; Heilman et al, 1983). They point out that all the anatomical structures described as producing neglect have been shown to be involved in arousal or activation, and attention. They support their argument with experimental studies in animals (Heilman et al, 1983).

Internal representation of space

Neither of the above explanations accounts for the difficulties which some neglect patients appear to have with the internal representation of space. 'This behaviour is suggestive of a deficit not restricted to perception but one also involving also a mutilated mental representation of space.' (De Renzi, 1982, p. 110). This latter expression had also been used earlier by De Renzi Faglioni and Scott (1970) who were impressed by the fact that neglect is not restricted to the visual modality only but affected the tactile modality as well. Some of their subjects confined their tactile exploration to the right (ipsilateral) side as though the left side of space did not exist for them.

Bisiach and Luzzatti (1978) asked two patients with left-sided neglect to describe imagined perspectives (the buildings on either side of the well known piazza outside the Milan cathedral). The subjects failed to allude to buildings on their left as they tried to imagine themselves facing the cathedral. A most impressive fact was that when asked to imagine themselves now faced about, the subjects now omitted buildings on their *imag-*

ined left, buildings which they had only recently reported. Similar support for an inability to deal with the left side of spatial representation came from an experimental study using laboratory apparatus which precluded perceptual scanning as a contributing factor (Bisiach et al, 1981). The study employed only right-lesioned patients and the recent replication with the same test using also left-lesioned subjects demonstrates the same difficulty in both groups. The fact that left-sided lesions showing neglect tend to be anterior conforms with the evidence of the role of this region (as well as the right posterior cortex) in spatial representation cited earlier in the chapter.

Unilateral neglect and recovery of function

The more striking features of hemineglect after cerebrovascular lesions tend to ameliorate in the first few weeks but may remain relatively stable thereafter (Gainotti, 1968; Campbell & Oxbury, 1976). Follow up studies suggest that persistence of neglect may be a key factor in the lesser degree of improvement in independence and social adjustment shown by left hemiplegics compared with right (Denes et al, 1982).

Despite this poor prognosis there are those who feel that neglect may be amenable to rehabilitation (Lawson, 1962) and rehabilitative techniques show some promise of transferring improved scanning, for example, in the training situation to everyday situations (Diller & Weinberg, 1977).

Motor neglect

Many patients with unilateral (sensory) neglect also may fail to use their contralateral arm although they are able to do so when pressed and show no obvious motor defect when they do. However, Laplane and Degos (1983) have described 20 cases of 'pure' motor neglect, i.e. without sensory neglect. The motor neglect was always contralateral. Fifteen cases were frontally located, four were in the parietal region and one was thalamic.

DISORDERS OF THE BODY SCHEMA

Disorders of the body schema are usually attributed to impairment of parietal lobe function. Some observations would suggest that these disorders are more prominent with right parietal lesions than with left. Absence of the disorders of communication seen with left hemisphere lesions at least make the body schema disorders due to right hemisphere damage appear more apparent and striking. There are often associated motor and sensory deficits due to spread of the lesions to somaesthetic, visual and motor pathways. The first systematic studies of disorders of 'the body image' were published by Lhermitte (1942, 1952). Only a sample of the most frequently seen syndromes will be outlined. These are (i) anosognosia, (ii) bodily agnosia and (iii) right-left discrimination, together with a consideration of the Gerstmann syndrome. The related area of unilateral neglect for external space has been treated separately above. Body schema disorders are dealt with more extensively by Frederiks (1969).

Anosognosia

This term means a failure to perceive illness. Its normal clinical usage implies a failure to perceive a defect or the denial of a defect and the term was introduced by Babinski (1914) in describing lack of awareness of hemiplegia. This association between denial or imperception of hemiplegia is a very common finding and in the majority of cases the paralysis is on the left side. In other words, the lesion is in the non-dominant hemisphere. Nathanson and his co-workers (1952) observed that some 70% of patients with denial of unilateral paralysis had damage to the right hemisphere. Patients with this disorder may rationalize about their failure to use the paralysed limbs and sometimes even have the delusion that the limbs do not belong to them, i.e. they are seen as being outside the patient's own body image.

The term anosognosia has also been extended by some writers to the denial or imperception of other deficits so that qualifying terms need to be added. It is interesting to note that these phenomena may sometimes be dissociated, with unawareness or denial of one deficit but not another. Numerous reviews have appeared, e.g. Hécaen and Ajuriaguerra (1952), Critchley (1953), Alajouanine and Lhermitte (1957) and Frederiks (1969).

Anosognosia for hemiplegia (Babinski's syndrome) is almost always associated with acute, massive vascular lesions affecting the retrorolandic area with accompanying hemiplegia, hemianopia, and hemianaesthesia. The middle cerebral artery is most often implicated as the seat of the trouble.

Related, but somewhat less striking, is the symptom of relative inattention to one side of the body. Once again this deficit is mostly for the left half of the body. It is also related in many patients to the neglect of one half of external space already described. It should be stressed that in these cases there is no weakness or paralysis though the patient may fail to move the limbs spontaneously such as not swinging the affected arm when walking. He may neglect the left half of the body when bathing, dressing or combing his hair. Hécaen et al (1956) found that patients with surgical lesions in the right posterior parietotemporal area had marked difficulties with complex sensorimotor activities including dressing. One patient could dress store dummies at his work but had difficulty in dressing himself which may suggest that one of the fundamental deficits in dressing apraxia is unawareness of the position of the limbs. This may be part of the general unawareness of body parts. The so-called 'dressing apraxia' would appear to have a number of determinants only one of which is bodily inattention.

Lack of awareness of body parts

This disturbance of the body image declares itself in the patient's inability to name and localize parts of his own body. Methods of examination have been described in detail by Benton (1959). Common clinical tests include the following: (i) asking the patient to identify parts of the body named by the examiner or to move the named parts; (ii) asking the patient to identify body parts on a diagram or on the examiner; (iii) asking the patient to move parts shortly after the examiner has touched them; (iv) asking the patient to touch one part of his body with another, e.g. 'place your (right) hand on your (left) ear.' This latter task is often known as Head's 'hand-eye-ear' test (Head, 1920) and forms part of many routine screen devices for higher function disorders, such as the Halstead-Wepman Aphasia Screening Test (Russell, Neuringer & Goldstein, 1970). Head's test is also commonly used for determining difficulties with right-left orientation.

One of the most commonly described disorders in this category is finger agnosia, first described by Gerstmann in 1924 (see Gerstmann, 1930). It was defined by him in a later publication in the following way: 'It consists in a *primary* disturbance or loss of ability to recognize, identify, differentiate, name, select, indicate and orient as to the individual fingers of either hand, the patient's own, as well as those of other persons.' (Gerstmann, 1957, p. 886). Some writers would prefer a term like 'faulty finger localization'.

It was as a consequence of his early studies of finger agnosia that Gerstmann described the syndrome which bears his name and which has led to considerable controversy (see below).

Finger agnosia has been studied experimentally by Kinsbourne and Warrington (1962a). They examined 12 patients with this symptom using a number of specially constructed tests most of which require only minimal verbal response. Two of these tests are as follows:

1 *The In-between test.* Two fingers are simultaneously touched. The patient is asked to state the number of fingers between the ones touched. Thus the answer may be 0, 1, 2 or 3 (Fig. 6.12 A).

2 *Two-point finger test.* The fingers are touched in two places. The patient judges whether the two touches are both on the same finger or on different fingers (Fig. 6.12 B). Warrington (1973) considers Test 1 the most clinically useful. Unlike the three studies cited below, Kinsbourne and Warrington maintained that the conjunction of the other Gerstmann symptoms with finger agnosia was more than coincidental.

Warrington cites Lunn's 1948 review of the published cases of finger agnosia . . . 'after excluding cases with widespread lesions and subjects with mixed handedness (they) found no case of finger agnosia with a right hemisphere lesion' (p. 273). There seems little doubt from the accrued evidence that finger agnosia is a sign par excellence of a dominant hemisphere posterior lesion.

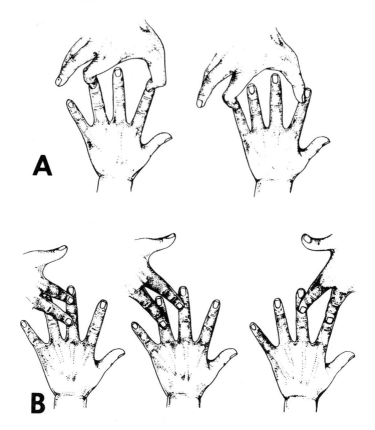

Fig. 6.12 A. The In-Between Test of Finger Agnosia.
B. Two-Point Finger Test (from Kinsbourne & Warrington, 1962a).

Right-left disorientation

This disorientation reflects itself in confusion between left and right for all parts of the body. It is a complex disorder or set of disorders and its significance is still not yet fully understood. Many factors may be involved, apraxic, aphasic and agnosic. Poeck and Orgass (1966) have stressed the role of aphasia though the deficit may be seen in the absence of clinically demonstrable aphasia. The complexity was brought out clearly in a factorial study of Poeck and Orgass (1967). Benton (1959) in a developmental study of lateral orientation in normal children has stressed the dependency of this type of ability on language. Like the other symptoms under discussion of right-left hemisphere malfunction, minor degrees of the disorder are difficult to establish since many normal individuals continue to have lateral confusion in adult life without any signs of cerebral impairment.

THE GERSTMANN SYNDROME

Following his description of finger agnosia in 1924 Gerstmann studied four such cases in the ensuing 6 years all of whom had associated deficits. He considered that four of the features formed a unique constellation to which others gave the title of Gerstmann's syndrome. To the two symptoms mentioned above (finger agnosia and right-left disorientation) must be added agraphia and acalculia. These four deficits formed for Gerstmann a unique constellation reflecting disturbance of the person's knowledge of his hand and its use. Such a constellation appeared to result from dominant hemisphere lesions affecting the region of the angular gyrus and adjacent part of the occipital lobe (Gerstmann, 1930). Many neurologists readily accepted the syndrome as having significant localizing value. However, with the passage of time doubt arose over the validity of the syndrome and the 1960s produced several direct attempts at verification. Critchley in his William Gowers lecture of 1965 commented elegantly upon the evidence to that time (Critchley, 1966).

The first major objective study to find against the validity of the Gerstmann syndrome was that of Benton (1961) whose designation of the syndrome as a 'fiction' attracted wide support. Benton studied the concordance between a number of deficits in a group of patients with cerebral disease arguing that the strength of concordance should be a measure of the viability of the concept of a syndrome. His summary is worth quoting:

> Systematic, objective analysis of the performance of patients with cerebral disease on seven 'parietal' tasks (right-left orientation, finger localization, writing, calculation, constructional praxis, reading, visual memory) indicates that many combinations of deficits, including those known as the 'Gerstmann syndrome', may be observed. The syndrome appears to be no different from the other combinations in respect to either the strength of mutual interrelationships among its elements or the strength of the relationships between its elements and performances not belonging to it. These results hold both for patients with diverse cerebral conditions and for those with focal lesions of the dominant parietal lobe.
>
> The findings are interpreted as indicating that the Gerstmann syndrome is an artifact of defective and biased observation. Further, a review of the pertinent clinical literature offers little support for its alleged focal diagnostic significance (p. 181).

Benton's analysis was soon followed by another large study (Heimburger, Demeyer & Reitan, 1964). Of 456 patients with cerebral disease some 111 showed one or more Gerstmann symptoms. Thirty three cases showed one symptom, 32 two symptoms, 23 three symptoms, and 23 showed all four. These four groups were then related to the nature and extent of pathology. Group I (one symptom only) tended to have small static lesions. An increase in the number of symptoms was paralleled by an increase in the extent and destructiveness of lesions up to Group IV (having all four Gerstmann symptoms). An analysis of Group IV also showed that the angular gyrus does not need to be involved as earlier writers, particularly Gerstmann himself believed. At least 3 of the 23 cases had autopsy confirmation of absence of a lesion affecting the angular gyrus. With regard to the localizing value of the Gerstmann symptoms, Heimburger et al found that the probability of a dominant hemisphere lesion increased with the number of symptoms but that they were of no value for localizing within the hemisphere. They concluded: 'As to localizing significance, Gerstmann's syndrome has approximately the same degree of cogency as dysphasia,' (p. 57).

The results of Poeck and Orgass (1966) supported the contention of the two previous studies that the syndrome does not occur in isolated form. They noted that the complete syndrome was rarely observed without dysphasia which they believed was the 'common denominator of the four symptoms.' 'The performances which are disturbed in the so-called Gerstmann syndrome are closely related to language. However, aphasia also produces other behavioral deficits, appearing as "concurrent" symptoms. It is therefore not justified to regard the four symptoms as a natural syndrome. They are an arbitrary partial grouping of the numerous neuropsychological disturbances resulting from lesion of the leading hemisphere:' (p. 436).

Against this apparently impressive accumulation of negative evidence is the recent description of a pure case of Gerstmann's syndrome, i.e. all four classical features with no associated deficits, following infarction to the left angular gyrus (Roeltgen, Sevush & Heilman, 1983). The authors comment: 'Perhaps the pure Gerstmann syndrome is a rare disorder because the lesions are rarely restricted to the area critical to this syndrome' (p. 47).

Moreover, Strub and Geschwind (1983) point out that most of the contrary evidence is based on a misunderstanding by the opponents of the syndrome of the traditional usage of the term 'syndrome' in clinical medicine and the fact that patients may show other associated neurobehavioural disorders 'in no way negates the utility and certainly not the existence of the syndrome' (p. 315). Certainly the presence of several (not necessarily all) of the four classical features has powerful localizing significance suggesting pathology in the left parietal lobe. Discussion of the different uses of the term 'syndrome' has been presented in Chapter 1.

The review of Strub and Geschwind cited above not only provides an up-to-date appraisal of evidence but also describes methods of examination of the component deficits.

THE PARIETAL LOBES AND SHORT TERM MEMORY (STM)

To date there is only a small amount of evidence about the localization of anatomical systems concerned with short-term memory dysfunction. Much of the work has been carried out by Warrington and her colleagues and reviewed by her in several articles (Warrington, 1971; Warrington & Weiskrantz, 1972; Warrington & Baddeley, 1974). The first report concerned one patient (K. F.) who had many years earlier received an injury to the left parietal region (Warrington & Shallice, 1969). This patient had a marked impairment of the ability to repeat auditory verbal stimuli which contrasted with much less difficulty with comparable visual verbal stimuli. This case suggested the possibility of modality specific short term memory defects. K.F.'s difficulty could not be accounted for by faulty auditory perception or speech defect. A further study of the same patient (Shallice & Warrington, 1970) confirmed the presence of modality specific STM defect. Later Warrington and her colleagues (1971) added two further patients with lesions in the left parietal regions, this time employing 'psychological tests differentially loaded with short term and long term memory components.' Results showed that (i) long term memory functions in audition were relatively intact while auditory STM was impaired and (ii) the disability was specific to the auditory modality, visual STM (as measured by relatively normal decay function) being little affected. Peterson and Peterson techniques were used in all instances. Further testing of K.F. in 1972 confirmed his rapid forgetting in auditory STM compared with relatively normal visual STM (Warrington & Shallice, 1972).

Additional differentiation of the STM defect came with a study of K.F. and one other patient (Shallice & Warrington, 1974). Within the auditory modality two tests were employed, one verbal (letters) and one nonverbal (meaningful sounds). The two patients exhibited a dissociation between these two tasks showing impairment on the verbal task but not on the nonverbal.

Against these studies supporting modal specificity is the study of Butters et al (1970a). These authors compared the performance of frontal and parietal cases, both left and right, on a variety of short term visual and auditory tasks again employing the distractor technique. The right hemisphere group showed more severe impairment on visual STM tasks compared with auditory, while the two left-sided groups (frontal and parietal) showed separate characteristics. Left frontal patients had predominantly registration but not memory deficits. Left parietal patients had memory deficits. However, neither of the left groups showed modal specificity both visual and auditory material being affected. Butters et al consider their results can be interpreted 'as supporting the notion that the right hemisphere, especially the parietal region, is involved in the processing of visual information both verbal and patterned, while the left hemisphere is concerned with verbal material irrespective of sensory modality' (Butters et al, 1970a, p. 458). Further studies are needed to resolve this early apparent difference of findings.

Since a disproportionate impairment in the repetition of verbal stimuli is the most prominent symptoms of 'conduction aphasia', Warrington considers that the results in her three patients with left parietal lesions adds weight to the anatomical basis of this syndrome which has been variously centred in the inferior parietal or temporoparietal region. Many of the studies referring to the anatomical basis of repetition difficulty on conduction aphasia are given in Warrington, Logue and Pratt (1971). Certainly, the obvious clinical feature on which these cases were selected was their marked impairment for repetition of digits on the Digit Span subtest of the WAIS.

POSTURAL ARM DRIFT

A common clinical test used in neurological examination requires the patient to maintain a static position of the outstretched arms in a horizontal position with the eyes closed. In some brain damaged patients there may be considerable drift usually, but not always, towards the midline. Since this drift is so frequently seen with parietal lesions it has come to be called by some clinicians 'parietal drift'. Only one experimental study relating postural arm drift to localization and lateralization appears to have been made (Wyke, 1966). The findings of this study suggest that the more general term postural arm drift should be used since it is by no means uncommon with extraparietal lesions. All Wyke's patients with lesions of the parietal region showed significant drift compared with two-thirds of frontal and one-half of temporal patients. Left hemisphere cases showed some ipsilateral drift plus a more severe drift in the contralateral arm while right hemisphere cases showed only a contralateral drift effect.

7

The occipital lobes

Anatomical features   247
Cerebral blindness   253
Hysterical blindness   257
Visual perception   257
Visual agnosia   260
Alexia without agraphia   269
Visual hallucinations   273
Electrical stimulation   273

ANATOMICAL FEATURES

The occipital lobes form the most posterior portions of the cerebral hemispheres. On the inner or medial aspects there is a natural line of demarcation called the parieto-occipital fissure. On the lateral or convex surfaces there are no such gross landmarks and the occipital lobe merges into the parietal lobe above and the temporal lobe below (Figs. 7.1 and 7.2).

Following the discovery of the fact that the cerebral cortex varied in the cellular composition of its layers from place to place in the hemisphere, numerous attempts were made to map out regions of the cortex having similar distinctive structure. Such studies are termed *cytoarchitecture*, literally the architecture of the cells. One of the best known of such maps is that of Brodmann (1909) (Fig. 7.3). This difference in structure suggested difference in function and, while such a relationship has not been fully established for all areas, it appears to be largely true of the occipital region.

Brodmann's method divided each occipital lobe into three areas having different cellular composition (areas 17, 18, and 19). Area 17 borders on the calcarine fissure which is largely on the medial aspect of the hemisphere and also covers the posterior pole of the hemisphere. This area is known as the striate area because of the striped appearance when it is sectioned. It is in this area that the neural fibres relaying information from the visual receptors in the retina reach their termination. Area 17 is the primary visual

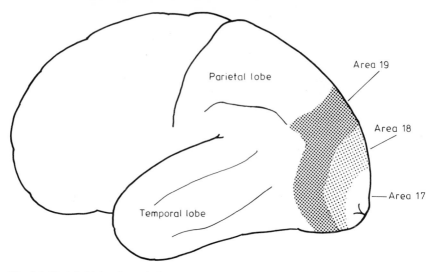

Fig. 7.1 Occipital lobe. Lateral view.

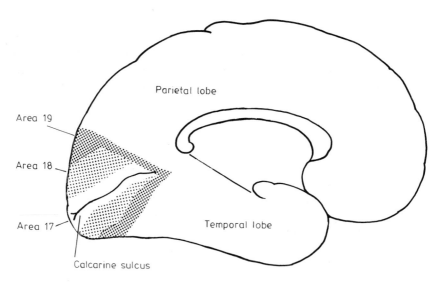

Fig. 7.2 Occipital lobe. Medial view.

cortex. It is surrounded by area 18, the parastriate region, which in turn is surrounded by area 19, the peristriate region which borders on the parietal and temporal lobes (Figs. 7.1 and 7.2).

Area 18 is a secondary sensory area believed to be concerned with the elaboration and synthesis of visual information. This area has numerous interhemispheric or commissural fibre connections with the corresponding area in the other hemisphere.

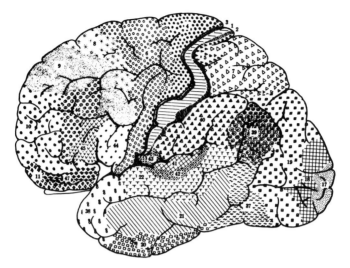

Fig. 7.3 Brodmann's cytoarchitectural map.

Area 19 possesses abundant connections with other regions of the hemispheres so that it appears to be chiefly involved in the integration of visual information with the information gathered by the auditory and other sense systems and it unites visual information with the brain systems subserving speech and other executive functions. It is also concerned, along with areas in the temporal lobes already discussed, with visual memory.

Visual pathways

An understanding of the basic anatomy of the visual pathways allows an understanding of the diagnostic significance of certain common defects of vision brought about by lesions along the pathways from the eye to the visual cortex. Such lesions will cause the patient to have difficulties with a number of psychological test measures, and an awareness of the nature of the visual defect will help in making correct inferences about the patient's performance on visuoperceptive tasks.

The lens of each eye focuses the stimulation from the outer part of each eye's visual field on to the inner half of each retina while stimulation arising in the inner half of the visual fields goes to the outer half of each retina. The terms 'temporal' and 'nasal' have often been used to refer to this division of the half fields of each eye and are included in Figure 7.4 so that the reader may understand texts where these terms occur, but, in what follows, the terms 'left (or right) halves of the visual field' will be used since they are less ambiguous in their reference than the terms 'temporal' and 'nasal'.

The fibres which relay information from the retina are gathered together in the optic nerve which travels back to join its partner in the optic chiasma.

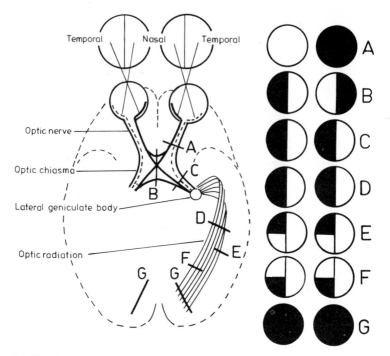

Fig. 7.4 The visual pathways with related field defects.

Here the fibres from the inner half of each retina cross over the midline and go on to enter the contralateral hemisphere while the fibres from the outer halves of each retina enter the hemisphere on the same side as the eye receiving the information. This means that each eye projects visual information to *each* hemisphere. Furthermore, there is a good deal of overlap between the visual fields of the two eyes so that most of the information (i.e. that seen by the two eyes in common) is analysed by both hemispheres (Fig. 7.5).

From the optic chiasma the visual pathways extend backward to the lateral geniculate bodies. These bodies can be considered as special subdivisions of the thalamus. They relay the visual information to the visual cortex while the neighbouring structures, the medial geniculate bodies, relay auditory information to the primary projection area for audition situated in the temporal lobes.

The final part of the optic pathway is known as the optic radiation or geniculocalcarine tract. From the geniculate bodies the pathway passes through an area called the temporal isthmus; then its fibres fan out to cover the upper and outer portions of the lateral ventricles before passing to the calcarine cortex.

A lesion in the temporal isthmus forms a good example of the widespread effects that a small lesion may have if it is strategically placed (see Ch. 1).

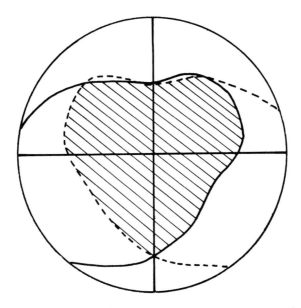

Fig. 7.5 Visual fields with area of overlap.

Not only does a small lesion in this location lead to an interruption of the visual pathways and hence to a visual field defect but also to somatosensory and motor changes since fibre pathways related to these functional systems are in close contiguity in this region (Nielsen & Friedman, 1942). Moreover, because of the asymmetry of function between the two hemispheres of the brain (see Ch. 8) two clinical syndromes are recognizable according to whether the left or right isthmus is damaged. With involvement of the left (dominant) side severe aphasia may accompany the above symptoms while damage to the right (non-dominant) side may produce anosognosia or delusions of the body schema as well as the visual, motor and sensory disturbances.

Visual field defects. Figure 7.4 represents the effect of lesions interrupting the visual pathways at various points. At A, a lesion produces blindness in the right eye. At B, a lesion will produce a loss in the left half of the left visual field and the right half of the right visual field (a bitemporal hemianopia). At C, a lesion in the right optic tract will produce a loss in the left half of the visual field or each eye (an homonymous hemianopia). At D in the optic radiation, complete lesions also give rise to homonymous hemianopia while smaller lesions in the radiation, for example at E in the temporal lobe, may cause loss only in the upper homonymous quadrants while lesions in the parietal lobe (at F) may cause visual defects only in the lower quadrants. Bilateral lesions of the occipital lobe (G1 and G2) produce bilateral homonymous hemianopia or cerebral blindness.

Since it is possible that visual field defects may not be readily apparent due to the capacity for adjustment to the defect which many patients show, they may sometimes be overlooked. Patients with homonymous hemianopia affecting the right halves of their visual fields characteristically have difficulty when asked to read normal print since the habitual scanning pattern is from left to right, while those with left-sided hemianopia have difficulty with reading for a different reason. Here the patient has difficulty in picking up the correct line as his eyes return to the left to begin scanning the next line. He may begin on a line above or below the appropriate one.

Homonymous hemianopia is an unequivocal sign of a unilateral hemispheric lesion. Some would regard hemianopia as the *only* reliable sign of occipital lobe disease (Cogan, 1966; Gloning et al, 1968), since more subtle disturbances of visual perception tend to be associated with lesions spreading into neighbouring regions.

Less regular field defects are produced by partial lesions of the visual cortex or optic radiation such as those produced by penetrating missile wounds in wartime. The blind area in these cases is known as a *scotoma* and, particularly if small, may even pass unnoticed by the patient in much the same way as the normal or physiological blind spot in each eye becomes apparent only when the eye is fixated and visual targets are arranged so that they project into the retinal region of the head of the optic nerve where visual receptors are absent.

These traumatically produced lesions of the visual regions have been extensively studied by Teuber and his collegues (Teuber, 1960).

The borders of scotomata are usually ill-defined and vary with the attitude and attention of the patient and with the particular methods employed in testing.

Examination of the visual fields. The visual fields are routinely checked in the standard neurological examination. The commonly used method of clinical examination is termed *confrontation*. The patient faces the examiner and, with one eye shielded, fixates on the region of the examiner's nose while the latter checks various parts of the visual field by asking the subject to detect the presence or movement of the visual target, usually the examiner's fingers. This method readily picks out the more obvious field defects. More careful systematic examination is made with a tangent screen or retinal perimeter. These methods are described in standard textbooks in medicine and experimental psychology. Two further procedures may be of value.

1. Since it appears that in cases of tumour, field defects for coloured test objects invariably appear before that for black and white objects (Bender & Kanzer, 1941), Walsh & Hoyt (1969) have suggested that coloured targets be employed routinely. Such an examination is simple enough to be included in a small group of 'neurological' tests employed by the neuropsychologist, and may detect some lesions in their early development.

2. Flicker perimetry may also be sensitive to early lowering of visual

efficiency though such testing is time consuming and needs special facilities not normally available in neuropsychological clinics. The method and its implications for localizing the site of brain damage were described by Parsons and Huse (1958).

CEREBRAL BLINDNESS

One of the most common causes of hemianopic defects is cerebral ischaemia produced by narrowing or occlusion of the posterior cerebral artery. The loss of vision for the contralateral half fields is a prominent symptom of a failure of the vertebrobasilar artery system to provide an adequate blood supply to the posterior regions of the cerebrum (Siekert & Millikan, 1955). Where the occipital lobes are affected on both sides a bilateral homonymous hemianopia or complete blindness results.

This blindness has often been termed cortical blindness but the term 'cerebral' is to be preferred since the underlying white matter is usually involved as well as the cortex. The blindness is often accompanied by other neurological signs and, even when the disorder appears to be clinically pure, careful examination will often reveal associated disorders. Since the prime cause is most often vascular in origin, the blindness may follow a period of confusion or even unconsciousness due to the 'vascular accident' and testing of the patient may be rendered difficult because of residual confusion.

In patients with signs of vertebobasilar insufficiency even the diagnostic procedure of arteriography may precipitate cerebral blindness (Silverman, Bergman & Bender, 1961). In our experience this is accompanied on occasions by an amnestic syndrome of marked severity probably due to bilateral ischaemia of the medial temporal regions supplied by the posterior cerebral arteries.

In patients who survive the precipitating vascular episode, recovery of at least some visual function appears to be the rule (Silverman, Bergman & Bender, 1961; Gloning, Gloning & Hoff, 1968). This recovery is so frequent that it has led some workers to doubt the validity of earlier reports of lasting cerebral blindness. Of the 32 surviving cases of cerebral blindness in Gloning, Gloning and Hoff's very large series of occipital lobe cases, all recovered some visual function though many stopped short of full recovery. Recovery of the various components of visual experience shows marked variation from case to case. Warrington (1984a) recently described five patients recovered from the acute stage of cerebral blindness who showed differing patterns of dissociation between the fundamental attributes of visual acuity, spatial location, colour and form perception. Such dissociations had been reported in the early literature (e.g. Holmes, 1918).

Restitution of visual function appears to take place in a typical order. Firstly the sensation of darkness becomes punctuated with elementary visual sensations or photisms. Next, the visual field becomes light but no form perception is possible. This is followed by the appreciation of primitive movement, i.e. the appreciation that the object is moving, or has moved, but not the direction or speed. Contours gradually emerge but are vague and unstable. Colour experience is the last to return. Even at this stage the visual processes may readily fatigue so that the percept appears to blur after some time (*asthenopia*). Some patients go on to recover their normal vision but other remain fixed at a stage of partial recovery.

'Blindsight'

Until recently it has been believed that destruction of the optic radiation leads to a total loss of vision in the related parts (or all) of the visual field. This is true if the measure used is the subject's report of the presence or absence of a target in the affected region. However, recent work has shown that some capacity to detect and localize stimuli within the blind field thus defined, may be demonstrated (Poppel, Held & Frost, 1973; Weiskrantz et al, 1974; Perenin & Jeannerod, 1978) and this visual capacity may be improved by experience or practice (Zihl, 1980). It is assumed that this process is mediated by retinal connections with the brain stem which have been shown to subserve perceptual as well as ocular reflexes in mammals. The improvement with training suggests a possible application in rehabilitation.

Denial of blindness (Anton's syndrome)

It is characteristic of many though not all cases of cerebral blindness that the patient appears indifferent, fails to recognize or even denies the existence of his defect. Post-mortem findings in Anton's case of 1898 showed bilateral softening of the brain in the parieto-occipital regions and he considered that the disconnection of the visual system from other parts of the brain to be the cause of the denial. Denial may also occur for incomplete blindness such as hemianopic defects and it is possible that one explanation may serve to explain both phenomena. There is a strong association between Anton's syndrome and the tendency to confabulate.

While denial may be verbally explicit, some of the patients examined by Gloning and his co-workers admitted their blindness while they were actually under examination but shortly after again denied visual loss. This meant that patients may invent fictions such as 'It is night now and there is no light in this room' or 'I am in a dark cellar' (Gloning, Gloning & Hoff, 1968, p. 13). Though there was a tendency for all patients to confabulate a true Korsakoff's syndrome was rare.

Denial occurs with other disorders such as hemiplegia (*Babinski's syndrome*) and we have also noted it on occasions after prefrontal lobotomy where the patient confabulates or rationalizes about the presence of the operative scars. Numerous psychological explanations have been put forward to explain this denial of illness or disability.

Nathanson, Bergman, and Gordon (1952) reported 28 cases of denial of hemiplegia in a series of 100 cases. The denial occurred with lesions in either hemisphere though more frequently with right hemisphere involvement. These authors considered that the denial of illness closely resembled the mechanism of rationalization or explaining away a defect, found in normal subjects. The difference appeared to be one of degree. In a similar vein Guthrie and Grossman (1952) pointed to the prior use of denial as a defence mechanism in their two neurological subjects, while the denial of operation was considered by Paganini and Zlotlow (1960) to be a continuation of the use of this defence by their schizophrenic subjects. A low level of intellectual function also seems to be related to the production of denial (Fryer & Rich, 1960).

One difficulty in using these explanations for Anton's syndrome lies in the fact that in some cases where blindness and hemiplegia co-exist, there may be denial of one disability with acceptance of the other. Such a dissociation of the denial of one defect and not another needs to be taken into consideration in a theory which endeavours to explain all forms of denial of illness or disability.

Adaptation to visual field defects. At first sight it is a remarkable thing that persons with quite extensive field defects behave in everyday situations as though their vision was close to normal. The fact that patients are little incommoded by homonymous hemianopia has been commented on by numerous authors and is the subject of a study by Gassel and Williams (1963) who found that 'the visual function was little impaired, impaired transiently or defective on few occasions in most patients; and the ability to compensate for the visual field defect was remarkable' (Gassel, 1969, p. 672).

Since the time of World War I when many patients with traumatic damage to the posterior regions of the brain were examined, cases have been described where the patient demonstrates the phenomenon which has been termed *completion*. If a patient with a hemianopic defect is asked to fixate a point and a card is introduced with, say, half an object depicted on it until the border between the 'half drawing' and the blank portion of the card coincides with the division between the patient's visual field and the visual defect he may 'see' the whole object (Fig. 7.6). Similarly he may 'see' the whole of the examiner's face despite the fact that while the patient was looking at the examiner the latter had placed a card in front of a portion of his face. Examination of this completion phenomenon has produced both different findings and different types of explanation to explain the findings (Fuchs, 1938; Lashley, 1941; Pollack, Battersby & Bender, 1957; Warrington, 1962). Gassel and Williams (1963) suggest that the hemianopic field loss functions as an extensive blind spot. 'The hemianopic field is an area of absence which is discovered rather than sensed, its presence is

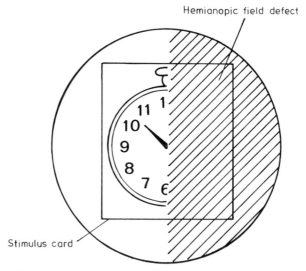

Fig. 7.6 Completion phenomenon.

judged from some specific failure in function rather than directly perceived.' (1963, p. 258). For this reason the deficit may not be discovered by the patient who is often vague about the nature of his impairment.

Gassel further believes that the completion phenomenon is an illusion which is a function of a number of factors which include expectation on the patient's part, his attitude and the testing conditions.

In his discussion of the nature of visual field defects King (1967) points out that incomplete figures (Fig. 7.6) have been as effective as complete figures in eliciting completion (Pollack, Battersby & Bender, 1957), thus disproving the hypothesis that the phenomenon may be accounted for by remaining visual function in the affected area.

With regard to the locus of the lesion Warrington (1962) has pointed out that completion occurs more commonly though not exclusively in patients with parietal lobe lesions.

Apart from being found on routine neurological examination, visual field defects may be discovered on occasions for the first time when a patient has to deal with visual analysis and synthesis of configurations required for successful performance on some psychological tests, e.g. the patient may find difficulty with the Block Design or Object Assembly subtests of the Wechsler Adult Intelligence Scale, one of the most frequently employed tests in neuropsychological assessment. The difficulty with the seemingly easy material of these tests may surprise the patient who has adjusted well to everyday situations in which eye movements and other strategies may have minimized the defect or even rendered him completely unaware of it.

Gassel (1969) argues that the way in which the hemianopic patient adapts to his defect is similar to the operations of visual perception in the normal subject where the imperfections of the eye as an optical instrument do not interfere with the perception of the external world because of rapid eye movements and shifts in attention, both of which are usually carried out without the conscious awareness of the perceiver. 'Thus, in both normal vision and that of patients with homonymous hemianopia what is "seen" is really a conflation of a series of events in space and time, which also involves memory and expectation' (Gassel, 1969, p. 674). In other words, the eye-brain analyzer is able under normal circumstances to convert a less than perfect set of data into a picture of what is 'out there' in the world and has the ability to continue doing so when the information is further reduced or degraded by visual field defects.

HYSTERICAL BLINDNESS

Hysteria or malingering may form a possible problem in differential diagnosis. True cerebral blindness shows a lack of both the menace and optokinetic reflexes where the other conditions do not.

The menace reflex is an eyeblink response produced by rapidly approaching the corner of the eye with a menacing object while the optokinetic reflex consists of jerky eye movements when the patient gazes at a rapidly moving series of objects such as a rotating striped drum.

The electroencephalogram has also proved of use in diagnosis in this situation (Bergman, 1957). Most normal subjects show the characteristic 9–13 cycles per second alpha rhythm in the posterior regions of the brain with the subject relaxed with eyes closed, and this alpha activity disappears from the record when visual stimulation is received. This posterior alpha rhythm is absent in cases of cerebral blindness and is replaced by slow waves, and there is no response in the record to opening and closing the eyes. The presence of a normal, reactive alpha rhythm should contradict a diagnosis of cerebral blindness.

The detection of hysterical disorders using neuropsychological assessment is discussed in Walsh (1985).

VISUAL PERCEPTION

Visual location

Few studies exist where the perceptual ability of brain damaged subjects to assess the visual location of stimuli has not been confounded with other factors. Warrington and Rabin (1970) presented patients with unilateral lesions with the task of comparing the location of a dot on each of two cards presented both simultaneously and successively. On each trial the subject had to judge whether the dots were in identical or different locations. Patients with right hemisphere lesions performed poorly, especially those with parietal lesions. Those with left lesions were not significantly different from controls. This finding was confirmed by Hannay and his colleagues (1976) using a more sophisticated experimental technique.

Visual orientation

The judgment of spatial orientation appears a very basic feature of mammalian perception confirmed by the discovery of specific detection units in cortical area 17 by Hubel and Wiesel (1959). Even before this, clinical studies had shown that brain lesions could disrupt man's perception of the horizontal and vertical. Lenz (1944) tested the ability of subjects with traumatic brain injuries to align a rod to the horizontal or vertical position with and without visual assistance. A systematic deviation was found in subjects with right parietal or bilateral lesions but not with left parietal damage. This finding has been confirmed on several occasions (McFie et al 1950; McFie & Zangwill, 1960; Tzavaras & Hécaen, 1971).

Other tasks of the perception of orientation have shown much poorer performance by subjects with right-sided lesions. The task of copying the alignment of two rods designed by De Renzi (1971) was poorly performed by right posterior subjects for the visual as well as the tactile condition. Tests requiring the subject to compare the slant of two lines show a clearly inferior performance by those with right hemisphere compared with left hemisphere lesions (Warrington & Rabin, 1970; Benton, Hannay & Varney, 1975; Bisiach, Nichelli & Spinnler, 1976; Benton, Varney & Hamsher, 1978). The latter workers have developed a simply administered objective test, the Benton Line Orientation Test, in booklet form. The subject is shown on each item a stimulus line in one of a number of pre-selected orientations and asked to select the corresponding slope from a multiple choice array (Fig. 7.7). The stimulus line is one third of the length of the comparisons and is placed to correspond to the outer, middle, or inner thirds of one of the multiple choice lines. Once again defective performance was associated with right posterior lesions. No defective performance was found for anterior and very few for left posterior lesions.

Stereopsis and depth perception

Cases with acquired disturbances of depth perception have been reported since the early part of this century (for review see De Renzi 1982, p. 141 f). Some patients described their experience of the world as two- rather than three dimensional and were unable to discriminate which of two similar objects was near or far. Most cases had bilateral occipital or parieto-occipital lesions. However, though patients with unilateral lesions may not report such difficulties they may prove inferior on clinical or clinico-experimental tests of depth perception and, as with many other visuospatial abilities, the poor performance is more frequent with right than with left hemisphere lesions (Birkmayer, 1951; Hécaen & Angelergues, 1963). One experimental

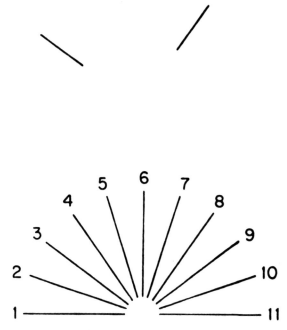

Fig. 7.7 Benton Line Orientation Test.

study (Birch, Proctor & Bortner, 1961) also found differentially poorer performance for right hemisphere lesions but only for monocular viewing. It should be emphasized that these were not selected as posterior hemisphere lesions, the laterality of lesion being arrived at from the presence of either right or left hemiplegia.

The development of random dot stereograms by Julesz (1964) presented us with a technique for the study of depth perception where monocular cues to depth and form could be eliminated as well as the elimination of figure-ground contours. Carmon and Bechtoldt (1969) compared the stereoscopic vision of subjects with unilateral lesions using the Julesz technique. Left hemisphere subjects showed no deficits compared with normal controls. Those with right hemisphere lesions showed significantly more errors and longer reponse times than either of the other two groups. This finding has been replicated by Benton and Hécaen (1970) and Hamsher (1978) although the differences between hemispheres in the latter study were not as pronounced as in the original.

Achromatopsia

This term signifies an acquired difficulty in perceiving colour. The patient perceives well, i.e. has normal acuity, form and depth perception, but sees only shades of grey. The defect may affect only one (hemiachromatopsia) but often both visual fields. The causative lesion damages the inferior visual association cortex (fusiform gyrus) and needs to be restricted to this region since higher lesions affecting the optic radiations will produce field defects in which neither colour nor form are seen (Damasio et al, 1980b; Damasio, 1981; Damasio & Damasio, 1983).

VISUAL AGNOSIA

Visual agnosia refers to a failure to recognize objects through the visual sense where there is neither a primary sensory loss nor mental deterioration. It is a rare clinical occurrence. The essence of the disorder, as outlined by Freud in 1891 when he introduced the term 'agnosia', was a disruption of the relationship between things themselves and the person's concepts of these things ('object concepts') see Freud (1953). This notion distinguished the disorder from the group of aphasias where there was a disruption in the relationship between the concept of the object and the word used to signify it. The essence of these agnosic defects as Williams points out is 'not so much in non-awareness of the stimuli as in misrecognition of their meaning' (Williams, 1970, p. 58).

A number of separate forms of visual agnosia have been described as occurring in a pure form, i.e. in isolation from other defects. The validity of these claims is examined at the end of this section. The forms which have attracted most attention, particularly in recent years are (i) visual object agnosia; (ii) simultaneous agnosia, or simultanagnosia; (iii) visuospatial agnosia; (iv) agnosia for faces, or prosopagnosia; (v) colour agnosia; (vi) pure word blindness, or agnosic alexia.

Whatever the status of these separate forms of visual agnosia or even of the validity of the concept of visual agnosia itself, the deficits described are important indicators of lesions in the occipital lobes, and hence the necessity for understanding the manner in which these forms of recognition disorder may present themselves and the tests which might elicit them.

The impaired recognition of spatial relationships sometimes called spatial or visuospatial agnosia has been described in Chapter 6.

Visual object agnosia

This is a failure to recognize objects when presented via the visual perceptual modality with preservation of recognition by other modalities such as touch. Gassel (1969) notes that there is often some difficulty in drawing objects from memory or in describing them so that defective visualization may play a part in these patients' symptoms.

However, adequate perceptual function can be demonstrated by drawing the object (Rubens & Benson, 1971) or copying a picture of it (Mack & Boller, 1977) or matching objects (Albert, Reches & Silverberg, 1975). Some objects may be recognized but not others and two dimensional representation e.g. photographs, present more difficulty than real objects and complex pictures present marked problems (Rubens & Benson, 1972; Lhermitte et al, 1972).

Sometimes patients with visual object agnosia are able to use objects which they have failed to recognize but are unable to state the function of the object when shown it. This clearly distinguishes the condition from a similar deficit seen in amnesic aphasia where the patient, while unable to find the correct name for a thing, is well able to describe its use. Again, this demonstrates that an examination of the qualitative details of a patient's deficit may prove useful in localizing the causative lesion.

Most authors indict the lateral aspect of the dominant occipital lobe as the source of the difficulty. Kleist (1934) pointed to the importance of area 19 on the left side while Nielsen (1937) felt that, while left-sided lesions were more often the cause, visual agnosia for objects (or mind blindness as it was called earlier) could also occur with lesions of the right occipital region if the lesion lay in the 'cortex of the second and third convolutions'. He later considered that visual agnosia resulted from interruption of fibre connections between both striate areas and the area of the left occipital region depicted. This hypothesis is supported by the fact that cases with lesions of the left occipital lobe and the posterior portions of the corpus callosum — the splenium — do show agnosia. Some patients with a lesion confined mainly to the splenium of the corpus callosum have been found to have a marked visual agnosia for objects which fall in the half-fields contralateral to the so-called minor or non-dominant hemisphere, e.g. right-handed patients with left hemisphere dominance for language have difficulty only in their left visual fields (Trescher & Ford, 1937; Akelaitis, 1942; Gazzaniga, Bogen & Sperry, 1965). Improved experimental techniques of testing since the advent of cerebral commissurotomy in man have clarified and extended the earlier findings (see Chapter 8).

In recent times several well studied cases of visual agnosia have reported post-mortem findings (Lhermitte et al, 1972a; Benson, Segarra & Albert, 1974; Albert et al, 1979) or CT scan (Mack & Boller, 1977). Alexander and Albert (1983) in analysing the anatomical evidence consider the crucial lesions to be the fibre pathways beneath the inferior temporo-occipital junction, in particular the inferior longitudinal fasciculus connecting the occipital association cortex with the medial temporal lobe. They hypothesize that this visual-limbic disconnection is the basis of the various forms of visual agnosia. The lesions are usually bilateral infarcts in the territories of the posterior cerebral arteries.

One of the requirements for a diagnosis of visual agnosia would be the absence of primary sensory defects such as loss of acuity since, in the sense of Freud's definition, the diagnosis depends on a dissociation between levels of visual function, higher order functions being compromized while primary sensory functions remain intact. A review of the literature shows that, while obvious defects of visual acuity may be present, various perceptual disorders are very frequently present in the case of visual object agnosia. In the extensive report of Gloning and his co-workers (1968) which studied 241 cases of occipital lobe disorder, two findings are pertinent here. Firstly, only three cases of visual agnosia for objects were encountered in the total series and, secondly, each of these cases suffered also from a number of other perceptual disorders.

Simultanagnosia

This form of visual agnosia consists of an inability to appreciate more than one aspect of a stimulus configuration at a time. Single aspects can be identified and pointed out from a stimulus array when it is presented again, suggesting clearly that the subject can identify and remember single features or objects, even quite complex ones. Wolpert (1924) first used the term *simultanagnosia* for one of a number of defects in his stroke victim. This patient, while usually able to name correctly objects or drawings, was unable to grasp the meaning of a complex thematic picture nor could he recognize the significance of playing card combinations such as a 'hand' at poker though he recognized the value of each card separately.

There is obvious overlap in the description of cases with simultanagnosia and the relatively rare instances of Balint's syndrome (Balint, 1909; Hécaen & Ajuriaguerra, 1954). Balint's patient showed defective visual scanning and attention. He seemed unable to carry out voluntary search and when an object was at the centre of his attention, he failed to notice other stimuli and, unless pressed, was unable to look to the periphery, the so-called *psychic paralysis of gaze*. If he attempted to attend to the details, he lost the whole. He was also unable to carry out visually guided hand and arm movements (*optic ataxia*) and had displacement of visual attention to the right, and left hemineglect. Balint's cases and others like it showed bilateral parieto-occipital softenings both cortical and sub-cortical.

Luria (1973b) described a case of difficulty in grasping the whole while perceiving the parts. His patient was shown a picture of a pair of spectacles. 'He is confused and does not know what the picture represents. He starts to guess "There is a circle . . . and another circle . . . and a stick . . . and a cross bar . . . why, it must be a bicycle"' (p. 116). Luria points out that these patients have particular difficulty if drawings are overruled with lines or presented against 'optically complex backgrounds'. Such findings suggest that tests of visual figure-ground discrimination such as the Gottschaldt Hidden Figures Test might prove useful in a diagnostic battery. However, Teuber and Weinstein (1956) demonstrated clearly that impairment on hidden figure tasks followed lesions in any lobe of the brain. They concluded from their very extensive studies that the test deficits were a non-specific sequel of the penetrating brain lesions they were studying. Moreover, impairment on the test was significantly related to aphasia since aphasic patients performed more poorly than non-aphasic brain damaged subjects. This latter finding was confirmed by Russo and Vignolo (1967) who found that while visual field defects did not appreciably affect scores on the Gottschaldt Test, the presence and severity of aphasia did to a marked degree. Furthermore, patients with right hemisphere lesions performed at a poorer level than patients with left hemisphere lesions who were not aphasic. They concluded that the type of ability needed on this test may be impaired by lesions affecting at least two separate abilities, one a factor associated with language and the other a visuospatial factor related to the non-dominant hemisphere. This second aspect is in keeping with the accumulation of recent evidence supporting a major role for the non-dominant hemisphere in subserving visuospatial and visuoconstructive abilities.

Kinsbourne and Warrington (1962b; 1963) examined several cases with difficulty in simultaneous form perception with the difficulty of complex figure perception. They recorded the recognition threshold for single and paired stimuli. While the thresholds for single stimuli were close to those of normals, there was invariably a long delay before the second stimulus was perceived. They hypothesized that this slowness in perceiving more than one stimulus at a time might render visual scanning of the whole less efficient, thus lessening the full appreciation of the whole. While there was a delay in recognition, the dual stimuli *did* appear to be adequately apprehended and one would have expected such patients to be even slower with more complex thematic material, but not to have the total inability, which patients with simultanagnosia have no matter how long they are allowed to attend to the stimuli.

It is obvious that the task of analyzing and integrating the information from thematic material is complex indeed, involving as it does the collaboration of visual, perceptual, oculomotor, attentional, and cognitive factors. Any number of these in combination may cause a deficit. If one considers that such complex perceptuo-cognitive acts depend on occipito-frontal connections, it is not surprising that both frontal as well as occipital lesions may disrupt the process. The neuropsychologist needs to determine which of the component processes is affected with lesions in different locations in order to determine the boundaries and connections of this occipito-frontal system.

Prosopagnosia (agnosia for faces)

While patients with this disorder are able to recognize that a face *is* a face and may be able to identify the individual features, they are unable to recognize familiar faces as belonging to a particular friend, acquaintance or family member. In some cases, there is even difficulty with recognition of the patient's own face in the mirror. Charcot described a case in which a patient held out his hand in excuse to another person for having bumped into him when it was, in fact, his own reflection in the mirror (De Romanis

& Benfatto, 1973). Hoff and Poetzl first described the condition in 1937 under the title 'amnesia for faces'. The term 'prosopagnosia' was introduced by Bodamer 10 years later (Bodamer, 1947).

Prosopagnosia rarely, if ever, occurs as an isolated defect being frequently associated with other disorders, particularly achromatopsia and visual object agnosia. However, unlike patients with visual agnosia, who fail to recognize the nature of objects, i.e. the categories to which they belong, patients with prosopagnosia have difficulty with identification within a category they clearly recognize. This may occur not only for faces but also for other perceptual categories such as chairs (Faust, 1955) or cars (Gloning et al, 1966; Lhermitte & Pillon, 1975) or even farm animals (Bornstein et al, 1969; Assal, 1969).

Some patients have difficulties within two or more categories (Alexander & Albert, 1983). The report of Assal et al (1984) described the case of a farmer who was no longer able to recognize the identity of his individual cows. Prosopagnosia for human faces was present at the start of his troubles but recovered completely. CT scan showed bilateral temporo-occipital and occipital lesions on the medial surface of both hemispheres. This location corresponds precisely to the critical lesions postulated on the basis of other autopsy and CT findings (see below). Thus, prosopagnosia sits uneasily under the rubric of the agnosias. The rarity of the condition is shown in the numerous reviews, e.g. only one case occurred in the series of several hundred occipital lesions reported by Gloning and his colleagues (1968). However, some degree of deficit in the recognition of human faces is much more common when tests of this ability are introduced in the examination of patients with posterior lesions. Where facial recognition is poor, visual defects are almost always present in the form of hemianopia or left upper quadrananopia but prosopagnosia can occur without visual field defect (Levin & Peters, 1976).

The failure to distinguish between the clinical syndrome of prosopagnosia and relative difficulty with tests of facial perception and recognition has led to some confusion in the neurological and neuropsychological literature.

Location of the lesions

In most studies, there has been direct (post-mortem) or presumptive evidence of *bilateral* lesions in the occipital lobes. Gloning et al (1970) reviewing six cases concluded that either a bilateral lesion was present or a unilateral lesion was accompanied by involvement of the corpus callosum. They reported post-mortem evidence of bilateral softenings of the brain in the region of the lingual and fusiform gyri in a case which had shown prosopagnosia and other marked signs of visual agnosia, but normal visual acuity. Recently, Damasio and Damasio (1983) reviewed the eight cases in the literature (1892–1976), where adequate autopsy reports were available. All had bilateral infarctions in the territories of both posterior cerebral arteries affecting the lingual and fusiform gyri or their connections. Like-wise, they report three cases of prosopagnosia, where the CT scan showed bilateral lesions in these areas. *They could find no case with autopsy evidence of prosopagnosia caused by a unilateral lesion.*

Other reviewers have suggested the possibility of prosopagnosia without bilateral lesions. De Romanis and Benfatto (1973) reviewed 112 cases described in the literature to that time. Of these, 42 appeared to have lesions in the non-dominant hemisphere, 41 were bilateral, while 29 had dominant hemisphere lesions. Some have even argued for the adequacy of a right parieto-occipital lesion combined with a left-sided lesion elsewhere in the hemisphere (Rondot & Tzavaras, 1969; Lhermitte et al, 1972; Meadows, 1974) and there is even one report of prosopagnosia with abscess of the left frontal lobe (Cole & Perez-Cruet, 1964). However, one would agree with Bornstein that clinical findings alone are insufficient for the purposes of localization (Bornstein, 1963, 1965; Bornstein & Kidron, 1959) even though certain reports of prosopagnosia with right occipital lesions have specifically mentioned the absence of evidence of left hemisphere disease (Lhermitte & Pillon, 1975; Whiteley & Warrington, 1977).

One must agree with Damasio and Damasio (1983 p. 426–427) that the strongest possible argument for the necessity of bilateral lesions in the production of prosopagnosia is 'the normal ability to recognize faces exhibited by patients with either left or *right* hemispherectomy (Damasio, Lima & Damasio, 1975) and by patients with hemispheres isolated by callosal section (Levy, Trevarthen & Sperry, 1972)'.

Nature of the defect

Benton (1980) pointed out that the most obvious explanation to suggest itself was that of a general perceptual impairment, i.e. the patient suffered from an 'impairment in the analysis and synthesis of complex visual stimulus configurations that is most clearly manifested in defective facial recognition, because individual faces present such a formidable discriminative task' (p. 179). Against this, perhaps the strongest piece of evidence is Benton's own study (Benton & Van Allen, 1972) supported by others, (Assal, 1969; Tzavaras, Hécaen & Le Bras, 1970, 1971; Malone et al, 1982), that some patients with prosopagnosia (familiar faces) have no difficulty with the perceptual discrimination of *unfamiliar* faces, which must be considered equally complex perceptually.

Conversely, facial recognition may be preserved in the presence of severe visuoperceptive difficulties as attested by reports, and the rarity of the condition (Meier & French, 1965; Russo & Vignolo, 1967; Warrington & James, 1967a; Tzavaras, Hécaen & Le Bras, 1970; Orgass et al, 1972).

Visual fixation difficulties have been considered important by Gloning and colleagues (Gloning et al, 1966; Gloning, Haub & Quatember, 1967), who felt that the prime difficulty lay in identifying the 'eye region', but they later described a case of severe prosopagnosia, who had no such difficulty (Gloning et al, 1970).

Failure to find a simple unitary cause has lead to a close examination of the performance of patients with unilateral lesions, particularly posterior lesions, on tasks requiring the matching of unfamiliar faces and related tests. Such tasks appear to be performed more poorly by those with right hemisphere damage (De Renzi & Spinnler, 1966b; Warrington & James, 1967a; Benton & Van Allen, 1968; De Renzi, Faglioni & Spinnler, 1968; Milner, 1968b; Tzavaras, Hécaen, & LeBras, 1970; Yin, 1970). Benton (1980) points out that the preponderance of right hemisphere lesions on these tasks holds only if it refers only to patients without significant language comprehension difficulty. The group of left hemisphere patients with comprehension difficulties contains a significant number with difficulties on unfamiliar face matching tasks, and once again there is a tendency for the posterior lesions to have difficulty more frequently than anterior lesions (Hamsher, Levin & Benton, 1979). It seems as though the two hemispheres may contribute different factors to the total process of facial recognition in line with the special properties possessed by each hemisphere discussed in Chapter 8. One would thus expect the findings with unilateral lesions to vary somewhat according to the demands of the tasks used and hence the strategies employed (Galper & Costa, 1980). In summary, unilateral lesions may render the process of facial recognition inefficient, but only bilateral lesions lead to the clinical condition of prosopagnosia.

Prosopagnosia — a disconnection syndrome?

A least some cases of prosopagnosia would fit a disconnection model. Bauer and Trobe (1984) described such a case whose other cognitive functions were intact.

If presented with faces simultaneously, the patient could report correctly whether they were the same or different, but he could *not* recognize faces that had been presented to him 90 seconds earlier. He could read and he could name objects correctly, but he could not recognize any previously viewed objects among members of its own class. He could copy complex figures, but had trouble synthesizing incomplete visual information. These authors suggest that in this case, and probably in many others, that proso-pagnosia 'is part of a more general inability to distinguish among objects within a visual semantic class. It results from impaired visual memory and perception caused by visual association cortex damage and interruption of the inferior longitudinal fasciculus connecting visual association cortex and (the) temporal lobe.' The site of the lesion in this case corresponded with that thought to be crucial in the production of prosopagnosia, namely the junction between medial occipital region and the parahippocampal gyrus (Fig. 7.8) (Damasio, Damasio & Van Hoesen, 1982). Such a lesion could

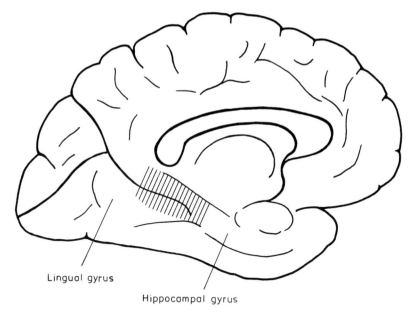

Lingual gyrus

Hippocampal gyrus

Fig. 7.8 Suggested lesion site for the production of prosopagnosia.

dissociate perceptual analysis from memory processes so that the patient would know that a face is a face but fail to establish the identity of a particular individual within the category. For this reason a term such as *amnesia for identity* might be preferable to prosopagnosia at least in those cases where perceptual processes are sufficiently intact for the person to be able to identify the class of object and to be able to discriminate between different examples within the class.

Colour agnosia

Acquired disturbances of colour perception are an important sign of occipital lobe involvement. The basis of the various disturbances of colour sense is still poorly understood but several distinctions are clinically useful. Colour 'agnosia' seems to comprise at least two separate entities namely, visual agnosia for colours and a defect of colour naming.

The patient with agnosia for colours has difficulty in identifying colours in practice. He is unable to match colours or order them in series as in Holmgren's colour sorting test with skeins of wool (Goldstein & Scheerer, 1941) or, if he can manage the task, finds it a good deal more difficult than normal subjects. In keeping with the general philosophy of the term agnosia no primary sense disability is apparent, e.g. on testing with a pseudoisochromatic chart such as that of Ishihara (Lhermitte, Chain & Aron, 1965). As with other visuognostic disorders colour agnosia is often associated with visual field defects particularly right homonymous hemianopia. Disorders of colour recognition have been reported more frequently with lesions of the dominant hemisphere (Kinsbourne & Warrington, 1964).

The colour naming defect is believed by some to be a specific defect (Nielsen, 1962). The patient, who performs normally on the Ishihara and Holmgren tests is unable to name the colour of an object or to recognize it when it is given to him. Though this defect may occur as part of a more general dysphasia it does occur with no observable language difficulty. The failure to recognize the name when given distinguishes it from the amnesic aphasia described earlier. Critchley (1965) has described in detail the features of colour agnosia which distinguish it from other forms of colour blindness.

The relation of colour agnosia to aphasia is one which has to be examined in each case but there is so far little direct support for Geschwind's hypothesis (Geschwind, 1965a, 1965b) that colour naming is secondary to language defect. If they understand the instructions most aphasic patients usually do not show abnormalities on tests of colour vision (Alajouanine, Castaigne & De Ribaucourt-Ducarne, 1960).

The nature of the deficit seems to depend to some degree on the type of test administered. The Milan group developed a test in which the patient is required to colour outline drawings of objects having a definite colour, such as cherries, the national flag, and so on (De Renzi & Spinnler, 1967). They found that difficulty with this task was particularly associated with lesions of the left hemisphere. Their finding was confirmed by Faglioni, Scotti and Spinnler (1970) and Spinnler (1971), both studies showing that the main defect related to this test was receptive aphasia, and in both studies there was a positive relationship with the Weigl test of conceptual thinking. They concluded that this ability to associate a drawing with its colour can be viewed as an aspect of the aphasic's impairment in mastering concepts (Spinnler, 1971). As Gassel (1969) remarks 'colours, separate from coloured objects, involve a degree of intellectual abstraction' so that the relationship with Weigl's test is not surprising.

The greater difficulty with this task for patients with left hemisphere lesions was not found by Tzavaras and Hécaen (1970) though these workers did find a correlation between the degree of deficit in left hemisphere patients and the presence of receptive aphasia.

In 1974, Meadows sought to distinguish three acquired disorders of colour sense. Firstly, achromatopsia as described above, is associated with 'bilateral, inferiorly placed, posterior lesions.' Secondly, disconnection colour anomia, which results from disconnection of colour perception from left hemisphere language function (Geschwind & Fusillo, 1966). Thirdly, aphasic colour anomia exemplified in the paper of Kinsbourne and Warrington (1964). Here colour perception is preserved, but the patient has what Meadows terms 'an aphasia related to colour names'. This term was used since the patient may have difficulty not only with naming colours and colouring drawings appropriately, but may also fail on verbal tests where the characteristic colour of a class of object is sought. Since this description demonstrates clearly that the patient has a disorder of knowing the nature and significance of colour in relation to objects, it would be preferable to retain the term visual agnosia for this type of disorder.

Status of the concept of visual agnosia

There has been a movement in recent years away from the acceptance of visual agnosia in its early accepted sense as a clinical entity to the position that there are patients with varying degrees of difficulty with visual recognition not all of which can be accounted for by a single deficiency. The definition of agnosia as a higher order loss without evidence of disturbance of primary visual functions will depend upon what is accepted as 'primary visual function'. Bay, in a series of papers (e.g. Bay, 1953) put forward the notion that visual agnosia is due to a combination of faulty visual clues due to lowering of visual function plus an ineffective interpretation by the patient of the visual information he has. Bay claims that the lowering of visual function can be demonstrated by refined means of testing where normal tests such as retinal perimetry may show the fields to be normal. His theory has received some support (Critchley, 1964; Bender & Feldman, 1965) though there are also a number of objections. Gassel (1969) points out that the findings such as those of Bergman (1957) and Williams and Gassel (1962) demonstrate that many patients with marked visual field constriction do not have disturbances of visual recognition.

Gloning, Gloning and Hoff (1968) do not believe that dissociation of primary and secondary visual functions exists at all in the sense that Freud first suggested. Their own series of cases gives strong support to this view only three cases with visual recognition difficulties occurring in 241 cases when those with severe visual disturbances or mental deterioration were excluded. As Critchley remarks 'cases of visual agnosia though a commonplace in medical textbooks, represent — let us admit — an extreme rarity in clinical practice' (Critchley, 1964, p. 281).

The rarity of the pure 'syndrome' of visual agnosia should not prevent neuropsychologists from examining the fundamental difficulties which give rise to all forms of visual recognition disorder.

ALEXIA WITHOUT AGRAPHIA

This disorder has been given a number of labels, e.g. *pure alexia, pure word blindness, agnosic alexia*, and recently *word form alexia*. In essence this form of reading difficulty consists of the failure to recognize words without evidence of dysphasia such as speech and writing disorders. Reading difficulties which form part of a written language disturbance are designated *aphasic alexia*.

Agnosic alexia has been termed alexia *without* agraphia since, unlike the dysphasic patient, the patient can write either spontaneously or to dictation. The visual basis of the difficulty becomes apparent when the patient is unable to copy printed material and is unable to read a sentence from a card in front of him which the examiner has just read and the patient has clearly understood. Where the disorder is not very gross the patient may have difficulty only with longer words and a careful search in these cases may reveal elements of simultaneous agnosia. Sometimes the patient can recognize single letters and may even be able to spell whole words without understanding them, the so-called *spelling alexia*.

Alexia without agraphia provides a further example of the explanation of neuropsychological symptoms in terms of a disconnection syndrome. Such an explanation has been used to account for the first case of agnosia without alexia described by Dejerine in 1892 as well as more recent cases (Geschwind, 1965; Walsh & Hoyt, 1969). Several findings make such an explanation more easily understood: (i) there is a highly significant correlation between pure word blindness and colour anomia (Gloning, Gloning & Hoff, 1968). These authors point out that this relationship has been reported frequently since it was first noted by Poetzl in 1928 and suggest the term 'Poetzl's syndrome' for the association; (ii) in some cases (37% of Gloning et al's cases) the reading of numbers is not disturbed; (iii) a right homonymous hemianopia is almost always present.

The concurrence of symptoms is explained by a lesion which damages the left occipital region and the splenium or posterior portion of the corpus callosum which connects both occipital lobes (Fig. 7.9). Both these regions are supplied by the posterior cerebral artery, and infarction in the distribution of this vessel is almost the sole cause of the syndrome since other lesions are most unlikely to affect both areas so completely and exclusively (Walsh & Hoyt, 1969). Since the regions concerned with the non-visual aspects of language are supplied by the other main arteries these latter functions remain unaffected.

Visual information received by the right occipital lobe cannot reach the language hemisphere (left) because of the interruption to the interhemispheric fibres in the splenium. Thus, while they can see, these patients are unable to interpret or speak about what they see. The preservation of the patient's ability to write spontaneously is accounted for by the fact that non-visual stimuli from both hemispheres can reach appropriate language centres over intra- and interhemispheric connections. The patient is, however, unable to transcribe printed material.

The importance of the splenium of the corpus callosum in the production of this syndrome has been emphasized by numerous authors (Kleist, 1934; Alajouanine, Lhermitte & De Ribaucourt-Ducarne, 1960) and is shown by cases where the callosum has been divided in the removal of cysts of the third ventricle (Tresher & Ford, 1937; Maspes, 1948) or in the more recent operation of cerebral commissurotomy for the relief of epilepsy (Gazzaniga, Bogen & Sperry, 1962, 1965; Geschwind, 1962, 1965b, 1965c). These

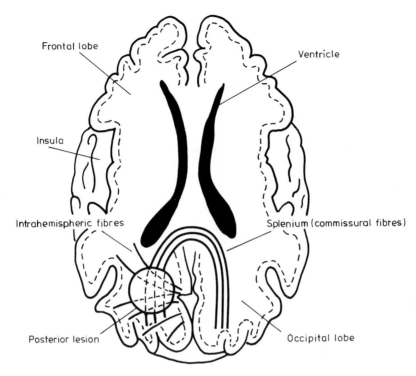

Frontal lobe

Ventricle

Insula

Intrahemispheric fibres

Splenium (commissural fibres)

Posterior lesion

Occipital lobe

Fig. 7.9 Horizontal section with lesion in the left occipital lobe producing alexia without agraphia.

patients showed alexia only in the left visual field since this information is transmitted to the right occipital lobe and cannot reach the language centres in the dominant hemisphere over the severed commissural fibres. For a similar reason removal of the occipital lobe of the language dominant hemisphere has been shown to produce lasting word blindness (Ajuriaguerra & Hécaen, 1951).

Anatomical evidence supporting the suggestion by Geschwind that the lesion in agnosic alexia affects the visual cortex of the dominant hemisphere and the splenium of the corpus callosum without affecting other regions such as the supramarginal gyrus is given by Cumming, Hurwitz and Perl (1969).

The sparing of the reading of numbers may be accounted for by the preservation of associations such as those developed by counting on the fingers. These associations of somatic with visual information could still reach the language hemisphere over the intact interhemispheric pathways anterior to the splenium. By contrast, the naming of colours is not spared since it involves no associations beside the visuo-auditory ones. 'A colour has no feel, smell, or taste and has no fixed associations but its name'. (Geschwind, 1965a, p. 99).

A further refinement in the study of disconnection mechanisms underlying alexia comes from a case of Greenblatt (1973). In this case and a similar one reported by Ajax (1967) the focal lesion involved only the ventromedial aspect of the left occipital lobe and the splenium of the corpus callosum. Greenblatt's patient had alexia without agraphia but no hemianopia, and colour naming was preserved. He put forward the hypothesis that 'within each occipital lobe, the inferior association tracts and the ventro-medial (lingual and fusiform) gyri are necessary for reading. Visual-verbal colour naming, on the other hand, apparently may be served either by the dorsal or by the ventral outflow paths from the calcarine cortex.'

This parcellation of the syndrome has been supported by anatomical evidence from other cases (Ajax, Schenkenberg, & Kosteljanetz, 1977; Vincent et al, 1977; Johansson & Fahlgren, 1979).

Finally, Greenblatt (1983) in his comprehensive examination of the pathological basis of all the alexias has further subdivided alexia without agraphia into a number of sub-types on the basis of functional anatomy. All his evidence fits the disconnection model and provides one of the finest of such arguments in behavioural neurology.

Similarly, the careful symptomatic analysis of a case of agnosic alexia, colour agnosia and severe naming difficulties in a patient with left posterior cerebral artery ischaemia by Lhermitte and Beauvois (1973) has further emphasized the importance of intrahemispheric as well as commissural connections in the production of symptoms in such cases.

Likewise, Albert et al (1973) propose a functional disconnection between the visual, auditory and motor systems used in the understanding of written language as a possible basis for their patient's symptoms.

This patient who had a tumour removed from the left temporo-occipital region showed alexia without agraphia but was able to spell words presented to him orally and was able to recognize words from their letters spelled out to him though he was unable to spell words presented in written form and was unable to carry out written commands. It seems important, as in this case, to establish whether the patient has preservation of capacities which are intramodal (within the auditory-oral system) or intermodal (visual-auditory), or both.

The fact that left hemisphere lesions are paramount in the production of acquired reading disabilities does not imply that the right hemisphere plays no important part in reading. Faglioni, Scotti and Spinnler (1968) have shown that there is a clear dissociation between the effects of left and right hemisphere damage on the subject's performance on visual recognition of verbal material.

Again, as shown for the temporal lobes with regard to auditory material, the dissociation is between the semantic-associative capacities of the left hemisphere and the perceptual-discriminative capacities of the right. An integration of both sets of functions is necessary for effective reading.

Pure alexia has been reported rarely in patients with left homonymous hemianopia and of these only two occurred in clearly right-handed patients (Hirose, Kin & Murikami, 1977; Mochizuki et al 1980). The former case showed an appropriately sited calloso-occipital lesion on CT scan while the latter displayed blockage of the right posterior cerebral artery at arteriography.

Reversible alexia

Reversible alexia without agraphia due to migraine was described by Bigley and Sharp (1983). A second patient who had previously suffered an attack of basilar artery migraine became alexic during the performance of vertebral arteriography (Laurent, Michel & Antoine, 1984). In this case the alexia coincided with the demonstration of spasm in the left posterior cerebral artery. The alexia lasted up to 1 hour and then resolved. Colour naming was spared during the event but he was unable to name well known people from photographs.

VISUAL HALLUCINATIONS

Visual hallucinations are described frequently in conditions affecting the occipital lobes (Allen, 1930; Paillas et al, 1965; Gloning, Gloning & Hoff, 1968). The essential characteristic of these hallucinations is their elementary nature. More organized visual hallucinations of people, objects and scenes usually indicate that the excitation is arising in or has spread to neighbouring regions particularly the temporal lobes. Elementary hallucinations or photisms have been described by a number of authors (Lhermitte, 1951; Ajuriaguerra & Hécaen, 1960; Gloning, Gloning and Hoff, 1968). The latter authors found 55 cases of elementary visual hallucinations in their series. These were almost exclusively projected to the half-field contralateral to the lesion and consisted of points, stars, flames, flashes, wheels, circles and triangles. A few cases of photisms with lesions outside the occipital lobes were reported and each of these seemed to be due to irritation of the visual pathways.

Elementary hallucinations have been well documented with focal epileptic seizures originating in the occipital lobes (Penfield & Jasper, 1954; Russell & Whitty, 1955; Lhermitte, 1951). Again, the sensations are referred to the contralateral half-field.

ELECTRICAL STIMULATION

The findings of studies of spontaneously occurring hallucinations in posterior cerebral lesions have been very strongly confirmed by the results of stimulation, in that complex visual experiences, most frequently that of a person or group of persons, are produced from the temporal, temporo-occipital or parieto-occipital regions but not from the visual cortex itself.

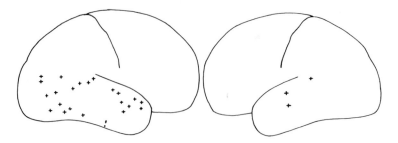

Fig. 7.10 Visual experiential responses evoked by stimulation (from Penfield & Perot, 1963).

Gloning, Gloning and Hoff (1968) reported no hemispheric difference in the incidence of complex visual hallucinations for their lesion cases. This is in marked contrast to the stimulation findings reported by Penfield and Perot (1963) where visual hallucinations of prior experience were elicited overwhelmingly from the right hemisphere (Fig. 7.10).

The content of the hallucinations when complex may be determined by prior experience. A male patient of Gloning and his colleagues who had been a philatelist saw postage stamps in the hemianopic parts of his visual field while one of our patients who had been a forestry officer saw predominantly scenes with trees. As is often the case, the hallucinations were vividly coloured, the patient describing them as colours he had not seen before 'colours such as they bring out for new cars each year'. They were so vivid that they prevented the patient getting to sleep.

Sometimes the experimental hallucination elicited by stimulation is very similiar to that experienced by the patient during an epileptic seizure. The following case is condensed from Penfield and Perot (1963).

> Case 3 — a 12-year-old boy with a 3 year history of seizures. The pattern of his attacks was:
>
>   1. Visual sensation (coloured triangles);
>   2. Experiential hallucination — visual;
>   3. Automatism . . . after the visual sensation usually he would see a robber, or a man with a gun, moving towards him. The man was someone he had seen in the movies or the comic strips . . . (stimulation of several points on the right temporo-occipital cortex produced the following references). 'Oh gee, gosh, robbers are coming at me with guns!. . . Pain in my forehead, and there was a robber. He wasn't in front, he was off to the left side' . . . 'Yes, the robbers, they are coming after me' . . . 'Oh gosh! Here they are, my brother is there. He is aiming an air rifle at me'.

The very wide experience of Penfield and his colleagues with brain stimulation (Penfield & Rasmussen, 1950; Penfield & Jasper, 1954; Penfield & Perot, 1963) show that lights, shadows, colours, movements and other elementary visual sensations occur on stimulation of the occipital lobe (areas 17, 18, 19) and never complex figures or scenes. The fact that Foerster (1936) described the evocation of figures or scenes on stimulation of area 19 might be accounted for by the spread of excitation to regions in front of the occipital lobes.

8

Hemispheric asymmetry

The concept of cerebral dominance   276
Unilateral lesion studies   280
Hemispherectomy   293
Cerebral commissurotomy   298
Agenesis of the corpus callosum   312
Functional asymmetry in normal subjects   314
Dominance revisited   315

THE CONCEPT OF CEREBRAL DOMINANCE

The most significant discovery leading to the notion of cerebral dominance was the finding by Dax, Broca and others of a strong relationship between lesions of the left hemisphere and disorders of language namely disorders of expression, comprehension, reading and writing. For many people the concept of cerebral dominance remained confined to the lateral specialization for language at least until recent times. However, there were notable exceptions. One of these was the great English neurologist Hughlings Jackson. In 1864, that is not long after Broca's first report, Jackson commented 'If, then it should be proved by wider evidence that the faculty of expression resides in one hemisphere, there is no absurdity in raising the question as to whether perception — its corresponding opposite — may not be seated in the other.'

Benton (1965) pointed out that extension of the concept of dominance beyond the sphere of language seemed to be required by the findings of Liepmann and Gerstmann in the early part of the present century. Liepmann had first described *apraxia* 'the inability to perform a skilled act or series of movements, this disability occurring within the setting of preserved comprehension and adequate sensory and neuromuscular capacity.' (Benton, p. 1965, p. 334). A particular form of this disorder termed *ideomotor apraxia* Liepmann found to be associated with lesions of the *left* hemisphere. In this disorder the patient was unable to carry out a skilled act on verbal command. Subsequent reviews have supported Liep-

276

mann's notion that ideomotor apraxia is associated exclusively with lesions of the left hemisphere. Gerstmann's 'syndrome' has been discussed in Chapter 6 but, despite the doubtful status of the syndrome itself, there is no doubt about the strong association of each of the component symptoms or signs with disorders of the left hemisphere and their almost complete absence in right hemisphere disease.

While these findings enriched the range of disorders associated with lesions of the left hemisphere it has been argued that both ideomotor apraxia and the Gerstmann symptoms may be conceptualized as due to a language deficit (Poeck & Orgass, 1966; Brewer, 1969). Brewer reminds us of the evidence showing that many 'ostensibly non-verbal tasks' are verbally encoded by the subject so that failure on such a task is only enlightening when we are sure how the subject normally goes about the task. 'Thus, given the current state of knowledge, it is possible to hold the extreme hypothesis that all tasks showing left-hemispheric dominance are due to an underlying linguistic deficit', (Brewer, 1969).

For a long time many neurologists, while accepting the evidence for laterization of language, were unwilling to admit that the other hemisphere, often termed 'minor' or non-dominant, might also have areas of specialization in which it excelled. Several converging lines of evidence have made it clear that the right hemisphere does, indeed, have such distinctive functions. Zangwill (1961) was one of the first to assemble evidence as to the functions of the minor hemisphere and he defined the principal of cerebral dominance as follows:

> As ordinarily understood, this principle states that certain higher functions, in particular speech, are differentially represented in the two hemispheres and are liable to be disturbed, predominantly if not exclusively, by damage to one alone. Further, it has long been accepted that the dominant hemisphere is typically that contralateral to the preferred hand though many exceptions to this rule are known, particularly among the left handed' (p. 51).

This question of the relationship between lateral hand preference and hemispheric dominance for language has only recently become clarified and will be considered first. This will be followed by the principal lines of evidence which have led to a clearer understanding of the functioning of the two hemispheres. These include (i) the evidence from naturally occurring cerebral lesions including agenesis or absence of the corpus callosum, (ii) commissurotomy studies, and (iii) hemispherectomy. The chapter concludes with a brief consideration of the concept of cerebral dominance in the light of this knowledge.

Hand preference and language dominance

Very soon after the introduction of the concept of dominance with the classic formulation that the left hemisphere was dominant in right-handed individuals and vice versa, numerous exceptions were found to the second half of the formula. Study of right-handed aphasics revealed well over 90% to have lesions in the left hemisphere. On the other hand numerous studies of left-handed aphasics while varying somewhat in their findings have tended to show a much lower proportion of left hemisphere lesions and a higher proportion of right hemisphere lesions than in the right-handed groups. Even in groups of left-handed individuals the left hemisphere appears to be the site of the lesion in 60% or more of the cases. There is also evidence to show that often (but certainly not always) aphasia tends to be less severe and prolonged in left-handed cases (Chesher, 1936; Conrad, 1949).

Such facts have been thought by some to reflect a bilateral representation of speech in left handers (Subirana, 1958; Zangwill, 1960). Support for such a contention comes from the examination of left handers using the Wada technique (see below).

Benton (1965) points out that the category of left handedness poses a number of problems if one is to utilize such a category for correlation with pathology. Some 'left-handers' are indeed more skillful with their left hand than with the right and employ it for preference. Other 'left-handers' in fact both employ the right hand more and are more skilled with it. A third and much larger category is much closer to ambidexterity.

The Wada technique

The introduction of the intracarotid sodium amytal test by Wada (1949) has allowed a more definitive statement to be made on the lateral representation of speech. This technique has been extensively employed at the Montreal Neurological Institute where several hundred cases have been studied, the injections on the right and left sides being carried out on separate days. Most of the subjects have been under consideration for surgery and the greater number were left-handed or ambidextrous patients together with a smaller number of right-handed patients for whom the laterization of language was in doubt (Branch, Milner & Rasmussen, 1964; Milner, Branch & Rasmussen, 1966; Milner, 1974).

In the first report there was a marked difference between the findings for right-handed and non-right-handed patients (Table 8.1).

Several points emerge clearly from these findings. Firstly, there is an absence of bilateral representation in right-handed subjects. Secondly, there is a difference in lateralization between the two non-right-handed groups. The left-handed group has a high percentage of right hemisphere representation and a small percentage of bilateral representation while the ambidextrous group has by far the highest percentage of bilateral representation and a much smaller percentage of right hemisphere speech representation. Grouped together the total non-right-handers showed 48% of left, 38% of right and 14% of bilateral representation.

Table 8.1   Relationship of handedness to speech lateralization (From Branch et al, 1964)

Handedness	No. of Cases	Speech Representation		
		Left	Bilateral	Right
Left	51	22 (43%)	4 (8%)	25 (49%)
Ambidextrous	20	12 (60%)	6 (30%)	2 (10%)
Right	48	43 (90%)	0 —	5 (10%)

A closer examination showed a further difference when the non-right-handed group was divided into those having clinical evidence of early left hemisphere damage (within the first 5 years of life) and those without.

The difference between the two non-right-handed groups seems to imply that in some cases at least the left-handedness is a reflection of early left hemisphere damage. Milner also drew attention to the 'impressive tendency for speech to become organized in the left hemisphere', some two-thirds of normal left-handers having speech representation in the left hemisphere and even 30% of those left-handers with gross early damage to the left hemisphere still have the major representation of language on the left side.

Table 8.2   Handedness and carotid-amytal speech lateralization (From Milner, 1974)

Handedness	No. of Cases	Speech Representation		
		Left	Bilateral	Right
Right	95	87 (92%)	1 (1%)	7 (7%)
Left or ambidextrous *Without* early left hemisphere damage	74	51 (69%)	10 (13%)	13 (18%)
With early left hemisphere damage	43	13 (30%)	7 (16%)	23 (54%)

Warrington and Pratt (1973) in examining transient dysphasia following electroconvulsive therapy applied unilaterally found strong confirmation for predominant language representation in the left hemisphere in about 70% of left-handers, (Lansdell, 1962). Hécaen and Sauguet (1972) have examined the differential characteristics of aphasia in left handers according to the side of the lesion. Left handers with left hemisphere lesions tend to have aphasic disturbances as happens with right-handers. However, they have a lower frequency for comprehension and writing defects and a higher frequency for reading difficulties. Disturbances of other functions from left hemisphere lesions, e.g. disorders of calculation, perception and praxis are similar in the two groups. With right hemisphere lesions left-handed patients, unlike right-handed, have a high frequency of disturbance of language both oral and written, while the disorders of calculation, perception and praxis are again similar in the two groups.

These authors also found a difference between left handers according to the presence or absence of left-handedness in the family history. In those with a positive familial history of sinistrality, language disturbances occurred with similiar frequency with either left or right hemisphere lesions whereas language disturbances were almost absent with right hemisphere lesions where there was no familial history of left-handedness.

The importance of a family history of sinistrality in relation to laterality differences in both right- and left-handers has been reported for both auditory and visual perception (Zurif & Bryden, 1969; Hines & Satz, 1971).

Lansdell (1962) found that not only did the right hemisphere become dominant for speech in some cases of early left hemisphere damage but that this right hemisphere also became involved with the verbal factor in intelligence.

These few facts merely serve to introduce the general question of hand preference and cerebral asymmetry. More extensive treatments are provided by Subirana (1969) and Levy (1974a).

Morphological asymmetry

Morphological asymmetry of the human brain has been observed for nearly a century but with the increasing interest in asymmetry of hemispheric function there has been an acceleration in such reports in the last 15 years (for concise summary see Bradshaw & Nettleton, 1983). These have included architectonic studies as well as gross morphological descriptions from autopsy both in the infant and mature brain. These have been supported by the findings of asymmetries in the living subject by CT scan. The differences are often small enough to need large samples to reach significance and cover a wide range of differences in individuals. Several theories linking asymmetry of structure and function have been put forward but no single explanation is adequate at present. Certainly morphological asymmetry alone seems inadequate to explain the major fact, namely that some 96% of right-handed individuals have language control in their left hemisphere. Moreover, despite anatomic differences, physiological studies of brain activity concurrent with complex psychological functions show increased activity in several areas of *each* hemisphere and this is as true for speech as it is for other functions.

The remainder of the chapter is devoted to a summary of some of the main areas that have extended our knowledge of functional asymmetry between the hemispheres.

UNILATERAL LESION STUDIES

No attempt has been made to present an exhaustive coverage of lesion studies related to asymmetry of hemispheric function. However, most of the principal areas are outlined and these may be supplemented by reviews such as: Mountcastle, 1962; Hécaen, 1969; Subirana, 1969; Milner, 1971; Benton, 1972; Dimond and Beaumont, 1974; Kinsbourne and Smith, 1974; Schmitt and Worden, 1974; Joynt and Goldstein, 1975, and numerous textbooks of neuropsychology.

In reviewing lesion studies there is a tendency to concentrate on lateral differences rather than similarities in function. This often leads to a devaluation of the role of one of the hemispheres in the particular function under scrutiny. Before beginning our review of the evidence for separate functions attributed to each hemisphere it would be wise to remember that there is no convincing evidence for absolute control of any complex psychological process by either hemisphere. 'The idea of cerebral dominance for a function must be revised, since it appears that there may only be a hemispheric preponderance rather than dominance for a certain behaviour. Thus there are relative rather than absolute contributions from the two hemispheres. This makes it more imminent that we categorise behaviour in its component operations if we wish to make sense out of localisation studies on brain behaviour correlations' (Joynt & Goldstein, 1975, p. 172).

Visual perception and asymmetry

The following is a sample of the very large amount of information which has accumulated since the 1960s about the asymmetry of function of the hemispheres with relation to visual perception. A good deal of it tends to support the hypothesis of a special role for the minor hemisphere which is the complement of the left hemisphere's specialization in verbal symbolic processes.

Figure — ground discrimination

In his studies of perceptual deficits after penetrating missile wounds Poppelreuter (1917) developed the overlapping figures test. The subject is required to demonstrate his ability to name or outline a number of figures in overlapping drawings (Fig. 8.1) or to select from a number of alternatives the complex figure in which a simpler figure has been 'embedded' (Fig. 8.2).

A number of studies of soldiers with penetrating missile wounds (Poppelreuter, 1917; Goldstein, 1927; Teuber, Battersby & Bender, 1951) as well as patients with cerebral tumours (Battersby et al, 1953) have shown that difficulty with tasks like the Gottschaldt Hidden Figure Test is a common accompaniment of cerebral lesions. Subsequently, Teuber and Weinstein (1956) and Russo and Vignolo (1967) demonstrated an association of this defect with the presence of aphasia. The latter study compared patients with unilateral right and left lesions with each other and with controls. The presence of aphasia and of visual field defects was checked in each case. While there was a significant association with both the pres-

Fig. 8.1 Overlapping drawings test (after Poppelreuter, 1917).

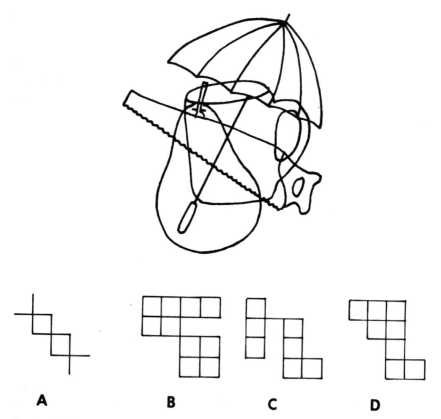

Fig. 8.2 Typical item in embedded figures test. Figure A is embedded in B and D but not C.

ence and severity of language disorders, visual field defects did not affect scores significantly. Furthermore, considered as single groups, the left and right hemisphere cases did not appear to differ. However, right-brain-damaged patients did significantly worse than non-aphasic left-brain-damaged patients, these latter performing very much like the control subjects. Russo and Vignolo suggest that poor performance may be related to the impairment of at least two specific abilities namely a language ability and a perceptual factor, the latter being 'preferentially subserved' by the right hemisphere. Poeck et al (1973) confirmed the finding of a disturbance on the Gottschaldt test with lesions of either hemisphere. They suggest that there is a 'common underlying functional disturbance of the visuospatial type associated with the retrorolandic part of both hemispheres'. They point to the recent evidence from both normal and commissurotomy subjects (see below) which shows that different forms of information processing are utilised by the two hemispheres, i.e. 'non-verbal strategy predominates in visual information processing, unless there is a specific requirement for inner verbalization'. Such complex determination of performance on what appears at first to be a relatively simple perceptual task highlights the care which must be taken in interpreting the findings of lesion studies.

Rubino (1970) extended the knowledge of lateralization in visual perception by greatly reducing the meaningfulness of both 'verbal' and figural material and comparing the performance of left temporal, right temporal and normal control subjects. The verbal material consisted of consonant-vowel-consonant trigrams (CVC) while the non-verbal visual material consisted of randomly generated figures, both sets of stimuli having low association value (meaning). The left temporal group showed a deficit in identification of the nonsense syllables while the right showed a deficit with the unfamiliar figures. Thus there appears to be a relation between efficiency of visual recognition, the nature of the visual material and laterality of the lesion.

Facial recognition

Numerous clinical studies have supported the poorer performance of patients with right posterior lesions on tests of facial recognition. These are cited in Chapter 7 in relation to *prosopagnosia*. It is worth repeating that this latter disorder is seen only with *bilateral* lesions.

Visuospatial perception

Over the past four decades a very large number of studies has produced evidence for the relatively greater importance of the right rather than the left hemisphere for the perception of spatial relationships. The following is a representative sample of such significant papers: Paterson & Zangwill, 1944; McFie, Piercy & Zangwill, 1950; Ettlinger, Warrington, & Zangwill,

1957; Piercy, Hécaen, & Ajuriaguerra, 1960; Whitty & Newcombe, 1965; Milner, 1965; Warrington & James, 1967b; Newcombe, 1969; Warrington & Rabin, 1970. Much of the relevant material has been reviewed in Chapter 6. A few further points might be made.

In order to establish the exact nature of the visuospatial defect which appears to be associated with right posterior lesions it is necessary to show dissociation of the defect from others, e.g. the study of Taylor and Warrington (1973) demonstrates that while patients with right posterior lesions are inferior to other groups on a spatial task of position discrimination they are not inferior on other discrimination tasks such as size and shape. Such studies will help to specify the nature of the defect more precisely.

A second factor which clouds the issue as to what is lateralized is the degree of complexity of the task, hence the degree to which sundry factors dependent on different areas (and hemispheres) may enter into the performance. Many of the tasks mentioned in Chapter 6 involve space perception at a rather complex level. De Renzi, Faglioni and Scotti (1971) point out that this makes it difficult 'to disentangle the influence on performance of spatial as compared with praxic, intelligence and memory factors'. These authors found that with a very simple test such as visual (or tactile) judgment of the orientation of a single rod in space, only the right posterior group performed poorly, other brain damaged groups performing very much like controls. Also the fact that there was no significant difference in effect for the different sense modalities stresses the truly 'spatial' nature of the defect. 'It appears, therefore, that when a spatial perception is tested at a very basic and simple level . . . there is almost a complete dominance of the posterior region of the so-called minor hemisphere. These results must be contrasted with the less striking asymmetry of function shown in more complex spatial tasks — for example, route finding, copying drawings, block designs — that are failed also by patients with damage to the left posterior area' (p. 489). Other studies (Warrington & Rabin, 1970; Benton, Hannay & Verney, 1975) support the importance of the right posterior region in the judgment of orientation and a simple standardized test is now available (Benton, Varney & Hamsher, 1978; Benton et al 1983).

Miller (1972a) reminds us that 'it may well be that the important factor in determining whether an apparently spatial task is affected by left posterior lesions as well as right is the degree of verbal mediation used by the subject. Although a task may be spatial in nature, this does not prevent a subject from using verbal reasoning in its solution and to the extent that this occurs the task will be more liable to disruption by left-sided lesions even though the task may be particulary difficult to verbalize' (Miller, 1972 pp. 86–87).

The issue of task complexity has been handled by Orgass et al (1972) in a different manner. They began by looking at factor analytic studies of visual cognitive processes in normal subjects and then selected tests related to the three most consistently found factors. The three factors were (i) speed of visual closure (Street's Figure Completion Test), (ii) flexibility of visual closure (Gottschaldt Embedded Figures Test) and (iii) perceptual speed (form recognition test). Performance on these tests was then related to the lobar and hemispheric locations of lesions, and the presence of aphasia and visual field defects. The presence of field defects can be taken to indicate the presence of a posterior hemispheric lesion. In keeping with other studies cited above, aphasia was related to factor (ii) (Gottschaldt's Test) while there was no significant relation to laterality, location or presence of field defects. However, the combination of a right-sided lesion with the presence of a visual field defect gave significant impairment of the other two factors, namely, speed of closure and speed of recognition. Since neither laterality nor presence of VFD were alone significant the authors concluded that 'the presence of VFD in the patient with right sided lesions does not act on test performance as a defect in visual function but stands for a critical localization of lesion.'

Finally, Ratcliff and Newcombe (1973) pointed out that a distinction should be made between visuospatial tasks such as those cited above where the subject can explore spatial relations without any major changes in his position and tests such as Semmes' locomotor map-reading task (Ch. 6) which measure the subject's topographical orientation ability in a dynamic situation. Using a 'static' task of the first kind they confirmed the expected inferior performance of those with right posterior lesions. However, on the 'dynamic' map-reading task those with unilateral posterior lesions and bilateral frontal lesions were unimpaired, only bilateral posterior lesions showing a lowered performance. They suggest that while the right hemisphere obviously plays an important role in spatial perception 'it does not bear exclusive responsibility for the maintenance of spatial orientation'. The locus of the lesion related to topographical orientation is unclear and may be clarified by the specification of task variables as well as clarification of concepts of personal or egocentric versus extrapersonal space along the lines of the study by Butters, Soeldner and Fedio (1972). Certainly disorder of topographical orientation has been described after both left and right frontal lesions (Marie & Behague, 1919; Marie, Bouttier & van Bogaert, 1924) as well as with right, left and bilateral posterior lesions (Kleist, 1934; Brain, 1941; Paterson & Zangwill, 1945; Cogan, 1960; De Renzi & Faglioni, 1962; Hécaen, 1969).

Tactile perception

Somatosensory changes

The most extensive study of somatosensory changes after lesions in various parts of the cerebrum is that of Semmes et al (1960). These authors examined a large number of patients with brain injuries caused by penetrating missiles in wartime. The group employed a wide range of measures such as two-point threshold, point localization and pressure sensitivity. One of their findings has relevance to the question of asymmetry of function namely, that they described some bilateral somatosensory deficits after lesions of the left hemisphere but only contralateral deficits after lesions of the right hemisphere. Since this finding has been reported in a number of places it should be pointed out that the differences found were small and did not reach statistical significance and that subsequent workers have not confirmed it though there has been only a small amount of work done in this field.

Sensory dominance

In the study of Semmes et al (1960) right-handed subjects tended to show a differential sensitivity to pressure stimulation, being more sensitive to pressure on the contralateral (left) hand than on the right. In a subsequent study Weinstein and Sersen (1961) showed that this 'sensory dominance' varied in a complex manner with the patient's familial history of handedness. Thus lateral hand preference and 'sensory dominance' are not inextricably related. The situation is analogous to crossed aphasia occurring with right hemisphere lesions in some right-handed subjects. It is important to state the nature of the function being affected when employing the term dominance since the present evidence shows that cerebral dominance cannot be a unitary function.

Size discrimination

Tactual size discrimination was found by Teuber and Rudel (1962) to be affected by lesions in either hemisphere but was more frequent with right-sided lesions. The deficit appeared to be independent of sensory loss though more severe if this was present.

The information from penetrating missile wounds needs to be interpreted with caution because of the somewhat uncertain nature and extent of the lesions. Another major source has been the study of patients undergoing restricted resection of cortical tissue for epilepsy (Corkin, 1964; Corkin, Milner & Rasmussen, 1964). Sensory defects appeared to be strictly related to damage to the pre- and post-central gyri and were mostly for the contralateral side of the body. However, localization by the patient of a point on the patient's body touched by the examiner (point localization) showed bilateral effects with unilateral lesions.

Astereognosis

This defect refers to the inability to appreciate the identity of three-dimensional objects by touch. As with other forms of agnosia this disorder should by definition occur in the absence of sensory loss. The existence of pure astereognosis must be seriously in question in view of Corkin's finding that impairment of tactile object recognition occurred only in those cases with sensory deficits due to lesions in the vicinity of the central sulcus. Semmes' findings on patients with missile wounds was less clear (Semmes, 1965) though she agreed that astereognosis was probably not a clinical entity. She employed tests of roughness, texture and size, together with tests of tactile shape discrimination, in examining patients with right hemisphere, left hemisphere and bilateral lesions. Deficits of shape discrimination were noted with and without the presence of sensory defect. These deficits were related to spatial orientation 'even when this was assessed by a purely visual task'. This finding suggested that shape discrimination may depend on a general spatial factor as well as on the integrity of somatic sensation. Where both factors are affected the disorder is likely to be severe. Semmes' evidence suggested that the factors were organized in a different way in the two hemispheres though this has not been clarified in the ensuing period.

In contrast to the apparently greater impact of left hemisphere lesions on the sensory system than right hemisphere lesions, Weinstein (1965) found the reverse to be true of the motor system. Using a test of finger movement ('finger oscillation') he found that lesions of the right hemisphere near the central sulcus tended to produce bilateral slowing with a more marked contralateral effect whereas left central lesions resulted in contralateral slowing only.

Other recent studies have lent weight to the greater importance of the right hemisphere in tactile perception.

Auditory perception

Asymmetry effects in auditory perception were treated in Chapter 5. The principal thrust of the evidence demonstrates the superior processing of speech sounds by the left hemisphere and of nonlinguistic stimuli by the right. Research with the dichotic listening task proliferated so rapidly that two issues of the journal *Brain and Language* (Volume 1, No. 4 and Volume 2, No. 5) were devoted to this topic. An extensive review of the literature and critical review of theories relating hemisphere specialization for speech and ear advantages was provided recently by Geffen and Quinn (1984).

Temporal order

The perception of temporal order has been the subject of only few studies in brain-damaged individuals (Efron, 1963a, 1963b; Carmon, 1971) and even in these studies, perceptual and amnestic processes were possibly confounded. One study (Carmon & Nachson, 1971) seems to have shown a clear cut difference between lateralized lesion groups. Those with left hemisphere lesions were significantly impaired in the identification of the order of both visual and auditory stimuli as compared with normal controls and those with right hemisphere lesions. Efron speculated that speech might be mediated by the left hemisphere because of its serial rather than its linguistic nature. As Poeck (1985) comments: 'The role of temporal analysis in the aphasic language disturbance is still an open question, as is the clinical significance of the fact that the temporal lobe is the "temporal" lobe' (p. 47).

The left hemisphere particularly the frontal lobe also plays a major role in judging the relative recency of two events and in programming the order of things (see Ch. 4).

The right hemisphere and communication

Discussion of the role of the right hemisphere in language often turns around evidence derived from the capacities of the isolated non-dominant hemisphere following commissurotomy or hemispherectomy (see below). However, a growing source of interest is the disruption of language or language related skills occasioned by lesions of the right hemisphere itself. Subtle deficits have been described in general terms for some 25 years (Critchley, 1962; Eisenson, 1962) but recently more careful experimental studies (e.g. Wapner, Hamby & Gardner, 1981) have begun to specify the difficulties such patients have with complex linguistic or ideational materials. While perfectly adequate on traditional tests of aphasia, patients with right hemisphere lesions may have trouble with processing the extra-linguistic aspects of language. Many of our right hemisphere stroke victims would share some of the features mentioned by Wapner and his colleagues (1981, p. 17):

> Superficially, these patients seem to retain the basics of language. However, while their speech may be literally unexceptionable, clinical inspection reveals that such patients often seem to lack a full understanding of the context of an utterance, the presuppositions entailed or the tone of a conversational exchange. . . . difficulty . . . in dealing with abstract sentences, logical reasoning, and a coherent stream of thought. . . . In addition, the language of such patients is often excessive and rambling; their comments are often off-colour and their humor frequently inappropriate; they tend to focus on insignificant details or make tangential remarks; and the usual range of intonation is frequently lacking.

Such features may present a serious though ill-understood impediment to rehabilitation.

General reviews of the language capabilities of the right hemisphere have been published by Searleman (1977, 1983), Bradshaw and Nettleton (1983) and Ardila (1984).

Memory and learning

Reference has already been made to the effects of unilateral temporal lobectomy on memory and learning in Chapter 5. Dominant temporal lobectomy leads to difficulty in the learning and retention of verbal material whether apprehended via visual or auditory perception and whether tested by recall or recognition (Meyers & Yates, 1955; Milner, 1958, 1967; Blakemore & Falconer, 1967; Milner & Teuber, 1968). Resection of the non-dominant temporal lobe leads to difficulties with non-verbal material both visual and auditory. 'Non-verbal' in this sense can be taken to mean those stimuli which are difficult to encode verbally (Kimura, 1963; Milner, 1968b). Milner has also shown that patients with right temporal removals have difficulty with visually or proprioceptively guided maze learning (Corkin, 1965; Milner, 1965).

Apart from the temporal lobectomy material only a few studies have concerned themselves directly with laterality and memory. De Renzi and Spinnler (1966a) tested patients with lateralized lesions on two tasks of the recognition of familiar figures, one immediate and the other delayed. The registration of familiar visual patterns in this study did appear to be related to the left hemisphere. In the delayed memory test, poor performance was related to the presence of aphasia.

Boller and De Renzi (1967) compared 60 patients with left hemisphere damage with 40 patients with right hemisphere damage on two visual tasks, one easily verbalized (meaningful) and one not easily verbalized (meaningless). The left hemisphere patients were inferior on both tasks though, when the scores were adjusted for the scores obtained on two language tasks the difference between the left and right groups decreased. The importance of aphasia in lowering the scores appeared to be about as great for the meaningless task as for the meaningful. The authors interpret this as showing 'that, whenever possible, patients try to transform meaningless figures into meaningful ones'.

Warrington and Rabin (1971) using a recognition task of recurring figures similar to that devised by Kimura (1963) found no significant difference between left and right hemisphere groups though there was a trend in the predicted direction, right hemisphere patients tending to perform more poorly than left. A consideration of other factors tended to suggest that while temporal and right parietal patients were equally impaired on the recognition memory task, the deficit had an amnesic basis in the temporal group and a perceptual basis in the parietal group.

Emotional functions

Two forms of emotional reaction have been described with lateralized lesions. These are particularly evident during certain examinations when the patient is confronted with failure. The first type of emotional response was termed 'the catastrophic reaction' by Goldstein (1939b) who noted that it was particularly associated with dominant hemisphere lesions. Goldstein noted that these reactions were 'not only "inadequate" but also disordered, inconstant, inconsistent and embedded in physical and mental shock'. The patient appears not only emotionally distressed but develops signs of incipient physical collapse such as pallor and sweating. It is important to recognize the onset of this catastrophic reaction since, apart from the patient's comfort, his performances may be further reduced for some time afterwards and a true picture of his present capacities may not be elicited. '. . . after a catastrophic reaction his reactivity is likely to be impeded for a longer or shorter interval. He becomes more or less unresponsive and fails even in those tasks which he could easily meet under other circumstances. The disturbing after-effect of catastrophic reactions is long enduring' (Goldstein, 1939b p. 37).

The second type of emotional response was originally noted by Babinski (1914) who reported the lack of awareness, indifference, or denial of hemiplegia particularly of the left side (see *anosognosia*, Ch. 6). The reaction is seen more frequently with right-sided lesions though not exclusively (Hécaen, Ajuriaguerra & Massonet, 1951; Denny-Brown, Meyer & Horenstein, 1952). Gainotti (1972) systematically studied a large series of cases, with right and left hemisphere lesions. He lists the following symptoms with their association to laterality: symptoms more frequently seen with left-sided lesions were 'anxiety reactions, bursts of tears, vocative utterances, depressed renouncements, or sharp refusals to go on with the examination'. With right-sided lesions the following were more common: 'anosognosia, minimization, indifference reactions and tendency to joke, and expressions of hate towards the paralysed limb'. Gainotti strongly reinforced what had been said by Goldstein and others, namely that catastrophic reactions were found most often in aphasic subjects after repeated failure of their attempts to communicate. 'They seemed due, as Goldstein argues, to the desperate reaction of the organism, confronted with a task it cannot face'.

Further evidence for a dissociation of emotional functions between the two hemispheres comes from lesion studies and this is supported by evidence in normal subjects.

Using the MMPI Gasparrini et al (1978) found that seven out of 16 patients with left hemisphere lesions had an elevated depression scale but none of the eight patients with right hemisphere lesions.

The evaluation of emotional expression appears poorer for those with right than left hemisphere lesions whether perceived visually (Benowitz et al, 1983) or auditorily (Heilman, Scholes & Watson, 1974; Denes et al, 1984). A retrospective evaluation of the literature by Sackeim et al (1982) revealed that pathological laughter was predominantly associated with right-sided lesions and pathological crying with left-sided lesions. Gelastic epilepsy (laughing outbursts) was more commonly associated with left-sided foci than with right.

The isolated right hemisphere is more efficient than the left in evaluating visually projected emotional expression (Benowitz et al, 1983).

Thus there is a variety of evidence to support a right hemisphere dominance for certain emotional functions. A more complete review is given by Gainotti (1984) who also surveys the methodological issues. Bear (1982) felt that the fundamental deficit for the right hemisphere patient was 'a failure in emotional surveillance' which he links with morphological asymmetries in the brain particularly cortical-limbic connections and the work on personality difference in epileptic patients with unlateral temporal lobe foci (see Ch. 5). Bear's theory converges with the attentional asymmetry theory of Heilman outlined earlier.

Motor impersistence

In 1956, Fisher described a syndrome which he considered 'akin to apraxia' the central features of which were the inability to *maintain* the eyes closed and the tongue protruded though these actions could be carried out adequately for a short period. The disorder was strongly associated with left hemiplegia, i.e. with lesions of the minor hemisphere and, though often transient, persisted in some cases for years. Some degree of mental impairment was always present. Fisher was aware that the groupings of several manifestations as a 'syndrome' needed substantiation. He suggested hypotheses which might explain the several signs, e.g. failure to maintain a motor set, interference with the persistent control of a motor act or distractability.

Though of theoretical interest the value of impersistence as a clinical observation is minimal since it appears to be seen only in the presence of unequivocal lateralizing signs. The disorder is reviewed in Joynt and Goldstein (1975).

Bilateral effects from unilateral lesions

Apart from the effects caused by permanent damage to functional systems, cerebral lesions may often bring about effects due to alteration in neighbouring or remote areas. These effects may alter with time particularly in areas adjacent to the damaged tissue because of resolution of oedema and other reversible changes. The term *diaschisis* was used by von Monakow (1911) to denote functional disturbances in situations anatomically remote from the lesion (Smith, 1974a). Smith points out that the consideration of diaschisis may help to resolve some of the apparently conflicting results described in the literature. His extensive studies of patients with vascular lesions reveal a high percentage of patients with bilateral hemispheric dysfunction and this itself is also affected by the size of the lesion and the age at which it occurs.

Such observations are not rare, e.g. 16 out of 18 patients with left hemiplegia in a study by Belmont, Karp and Birch (1971) showed disruption of movement of the intact side when bilateral function was called for but not when the movement was required only from the intact side.

Bilateral effects from unilateral lesions may involve at least three classes of effect. Firstly, the effect of disconnecting an association area of one hemisphere from the association cortex of the opposite side. Many examples of interhemisphere disconnection effects are provided in the later sections of this chapter. Secondly, the possibility of interference or inhibitory influences is suggested by the improvement in function following removal of pathological tissue as mentioned in the section on hemispherectomy. Thirdly, recent studies have demonstrated that reduction in cerebral function may follow alteration in hemispheric blood flow. A reduction in blood flow and metabolism in *both* hemispheres has been shown to occur following unilateral cerebral lesions both vascular and neoplastic in origin. A summary of evidence on diaschisis has been given by Smith (1975, pp. 70–73).

Attention and the right hemisphere

The concept of attention is a complex one embracing increased physiological responsiveness, preparation for action, and response selectivity. Heilman (1982) has argued that the right hemisphere plays a greater role for these processes and thus can be considered dominant for attention. This would explain why neglect phenomena are seen more frequently and are more severe with right hemisphere lesions. Evidence from studies on patients with hemispheric lesions and on normal subjects are consistent with this hypothesis. The reaction time of brain damaged subjects is generally reduced but right-sided lesions have a greater effect than those in the left hemisphere (De Renzi & Faglioni, 1965; Howes & Boller, 1975). Patients with right parietotemporal lesions and neglect showed less arousal when compared with patients with left hemisphere lesions with aphasia (Heilman, Schwartz, & Watson, 1978). Finally, Heilman and Van Den Abell (1980) tested a measure of attention in normal subjects. This consisted of presenting lateralized visual stimuli to 12 normal subjects and checking alpha desynchronization in the EEG. This phenomenon, formerly called *alpha blocking* has been known to be an indicator of attention or orientation to a stimulus ever since the pioneering work of Berger. These normal subjects showed alpha desynchronization in the left parietal region mainly to right-sided stimuli but the right parietal region showed desynchronization to both right- or left-sided stimuli. Heilman (1982) offers other converging but less direct evidence in support of his proposal.

HEMISPHERECTOMY

The operation of hemispherectomy might more correctly be termed hemi-decortication since not all the hemisphere is removed in most instances. Usually parts of the deep nuclear masses such as the thalamus and striate complex remain untouched. The nature of the operation varies according to the indication for operation. Two major conditions have appeared to date. These are: (i) infantile hemiplegia, and (ii) extensive invasion of the hemisphere by neoplastic disease. Because of the very great difference between these two types of cases they are treated separately here.

Infantile hemiplegia

The earliest report of removal of a very considerable proportion of one hemisphere for the treatment of uncontrollable epilepsy associated with hemiparesis of early onset appears to be that of McKenzie (1938). This was followed by a series reported by Krynauw from Johannesburg (1950a, 1950b). The complex problems posed by using such material to provide evidence about brain function is indicated by the following description of indications for operation given by Carmichael (1966) and cited in Dimond (1972). 'The patient must first of all have a hemiplegia. This should affect the arm more profoundly than the leg, and the patient usually suffers from fits which do not prove amenable to medical treatment. The patient frequently has behaviour disturbances in the nature of being difficult to handle, personality problems, temper tantrums and rages.'

The most striking feature of early reports apart from clinical improvement was the absence of mental deterioration that might be expected on a priori grounds from such massive removal of cortical tissue. Krynauw's first report (1950a) described 12 cases with 'improvement of mentality' as adjudged by clinical evidence though no psychometric evidence was presented in support. Cairns and Davidson (1951) reported three cases with no evidence of intellecual loss but rather an improvement in scores on tests such as the Wechsler-Bellevue and Stanford-Binet scales. Such improvement strongly supported the frequent claim by Hebb and others mentioned earlier (see Ch. 4) that the deficits seen after operations on the brain might often be due to the effect of residual pathological tissue rather than simply due to loss of brain substance. Presumably where the pathological tissue was radically removed as in the present cases of hemispherectomy there was no longer any interference effect so that residual healthy brain tissue was permitted to function at an optimal level thus providing an explanation for the seemingly 'paradoxical' effect that the brain could perform better after hemidecortication than before. In the decade which followed, this point of view received further support in the finding that these cases of infantile hemiplegia seemed to benefit much more from complete hemispherectomy than from partial removal (McFie, 1961).

One of the most influential reports was that of Basser (1962) who described the outcome in 35 cases of hemispherectomy, 17 with the left hemisphere removed and 18 with the right. Twenty five patients had sustained their lesions before the advent of speech and 10 after. This report showed that sensori-motor functions, praxis, and language were largely preserved whichever hemisphere was removed. Thus it seemed that either hemisphere was capable of mediating most functions though mental activity usually remained at a fairly low level with lack of drive and initiative.

Gardner et al (1955) attempted a comparison of residual function following hemispherectomy for tumour in adults and for infantile epilepsy in children claiming more devastating deficits in the adult cases. However, data was supplied on only one infantile case. The study of McFie (1961) using small groups of patients with lesions dating from different ages concluded that patients who sustained their lesions before 1 year of age recovered better than those injured later.

Thus there emerged a piece of neuropsychological dogma which has been endlessly restated without regard to a critical appraisal of the evidence. This dogma states that differentially better recovery can be expected the earlier the onset of injury. While many have left this as a vague generalization others have been more specific. The age beyond which the *plasticity* might be expected can be termed the critical period and estimates have varied from one-year through to 15 years (McFie, 1961; Obrador, 1964; Lenneberg, 1967; Netley, 1972; Krashen, 1973). Contrary evidence, e.g. the data in Griffiths and Davidson's report (1966) which appears to show *better* recovery for those injured after 1 year than those injured before is seldom cited. Two long-term follow-up studies are worth reporting in some detail.

The first is a case of hemispherectomy performed for epilepsy at the age of $5\frac{1}{2}$ years and reported 21 years later by Smith and Sugar (1975). This case provides impressive evidence of the brain's ability to utilize residual tissue in the remaining hemisphere as the basis for high level ability in both the verbal and non-verbal spheres. Before operation at $5\frac{1}{2}$, the patient's mental age was 4 years with marked speech defect but normal verbal comprehension. Four months after operation his mental age was close to his chronological age and his speech 'which earlier had been practically unintelligible, had rapidly become normal'. When tested at 8 years 8 months, his mental age was 7 years 10 months. Since that time further progress has continued and his scores on a wide variety of tests both verbal and non-verbal are now in, and in some cases well above, the normal range. Some extracts from Smith and Sugar's table of his test performances 15 and 21 years after hemispherectomy are shown in Table 8.3.

In addition to these and other good performances on psychometric measures, the patient's performance on all language modalities at these two examinations was normal (speech, comprehension, reading and writing).

The second case is one studied over many years by Damasio, Lima and Damasio (1975). This patient was not a case of infantile hemiplegia but had

Table 8.3 Test performances after left hemispherectomy (Condensed from Smith & Sugar (1975).

Age	21	26 1/2
Post-operative Interval (years)	15 1/5	21
WAIS Weighted Scores		
Information	13	16
Comprehension	19	19
Arithmetic	9	15
Similarities	12	15
Digit Span	7	9
Digit Symbol	8	10
Block Design	11	9
Picture Arrangement	10	9
Object Assembly	8	12
Verbal I.Q.	113	126
Performance I.Q.	98	102
Full Scale I.Q.	107	116
Peabody Picture Vocabulary	125	137+
Benton Visual Retention	7	8

a normal development until the age of 5 at which time she sustained a severe head injury resulting in left hemiplegia. She developed left focal seizures 7 years after injury and these increased in frequency and some thirteen years after injury she was showing aggressive and disturbed behaviour. Two years later right hemispherectomy was performed for the frequent, uncontrollable, seizures. The result of surgical intervention was 'dramatic relief of intractable epilepsy, the recovery of personal independence, and . . . remarkable improvement of motor and sensory capabilities'. Such a case demonstrates that alternative systems may be brought into play even when the lesion had occurred as late as 5 years. Damasio et al comment: 'Removal of the right diseased hemisphere rid our patient of a squalid nuisance, stopping its deleterious effect on the rest of the brain and disclosing a normal, partially duplicated left hemisphere.' The partial duplication of function is evidenced by the patient's normal performance on a number of tasks of a visuoperceptive, visuospatial and visuoconstructive nature normally thought to be dependent upon the integrity of the right hemisphere.

It should be pointed out that the essential difference between this case and those of infantile hemiplegia is the presence of perfectly healthy tissue in both hemispheres for some years prior to a major lesion of one side. The case presents a number of other features in the adaption after operation which need further study but it is obvious that age of occurrence should not in itself be a contraindication to operation.

In recent times St. James-Roberts (1981) re-examined the available hemispherectomy data from a wide range of studies on operated cases who had sustained injury in infancy, childhood or adulthood and found that the data failed to support the plasticity model, being explained more parsimoniously in terms of other factors.

Hemispherectomy for infantile hemiplegia has decreased over the past two decades though most reports have shown improvement after operation (French, Johnson, & Adkins, 1966; Breschi, D'Angelo, & Pluchino, 1970; Wilson, 1970; Verity et al, 1982). A surgical modification (Adams, 1983) which promises to minimize the late complications which lead to abandonment of the operation may result in reintroduction of the procedure.

Adult hemispherectomy

The first reports of removal of most of one hemisphere for tumour were made by Dandy (1928, 1933). A case reported by Zollinger (1935) showed that not all language was lost with dominant hemispherectomy. Zollinger's patient retained an elementary vocabulary which was partially increased by speech training. No other formal neuropsychological examination was carried out partly because of the patient's adynamia or unwillingness. Death of the patient 17 days post-operatively prevented follow-up. A second case of dominant hemispherectomy reported by Crockett and Estridge (1951) survived four months, and although severely impaired, also showed improving capacity for speech as well as verbal comprehension.

These findings were supported by the more detailed examination of a case followed for more than 7 months by Smith (Smith, 1966c; Smith & Burkland, 1966). Immediately after the operation the patient showed the anticipated signs of right hemiplegia, right hemianopia and severe aphasia. On later examinations the patient showed continuing recovery of language functions, not total abolition which might have been expected on the belief that the left hemisphere played the 'dominant' role in such functions. 'Since these functions are not abolished, and since speaking, reading, writing and understanding language show continuing improvement in E.C. after left hemispherectomy, the right hemisphere apparently contributes to all these functions, although in varying proportions (i.e. receptive language functions were initially less impaired and have shown greater recovery than expressive language)'. (Smith, 1966c, p. 470). The patient preserved the ability to sing old songs suggesting that the right hemisphere plays an important role in this area. This finding would be in keeping with evidence from studies of restricted lesions and from brain stimulation mentioned earlier.

Smith's patient also showed preserved learning ability as shown by an increased score of $2\frac{1}{2}$ years on two testings with the Porteus Maze Test at a 10-day interval some 6 months after operation. The patient was also able to solve abstract as well as concrete mathematical problems and was close to normal on non-language tests of higher mental functions. Smith and Burklund (1966) took these good performances to indicate 'either that these functions are not exclusively or predominantly "localized" in the adult dominant hemisphere, or that, following removal of this hemisphere, the right hemisphere has the capacity to amplify previously smaller contributions to these functions . . .'.

A second patient followed by Smith (Burklund & Smith, 1977) showed even more rapid and extensive recovery of language and singing until his rapid decline following recurrence of the tumour and death 18 months postoperatively.

A case of hemispherectomy for epilepsy of late onset described by French, Johnson and Adkins (1966) similarly supports the cases operated for tumour in demonstrating capacity for both language comprehension and some expression.

Hemispherectomy on the right (non-dominant) side has been carried out much more frequently. Early reports such as those of Dandy (1928, 1933) and Rowe (1937) commented on the sparing of intellectual ability at least with clinical tests and the standard intelligence tests of the day. Rowe's case showed a post-operative intelligence quotient on the Stanford-Binet scale in the 'superior adult' range, not greatly different from that which she showed before operation. As with other reports there was also return of considerable motor function and some sensory function on the opposite side of the body. The mental changes noted in this case included impairment of recent memory, emotional instability and loss of inhibition. Mensh et al (1952) were impressed with the extreme variation in performance of their patient with non-dominant hemispherectomy as well as the numerous disturbances reflected in psychological tests. Though verbal facility and vocabulary remained good their patient showed 'concreteness and perseveration of ideas, confused and psychotic-like thinking, clang associations, mingling of old and new information, . . . self-reference . . . and extremely compulsive behaviour.' Smith (1967) also noted extreme variability in one case of right and one of left hemispherectomy and pointed to this as a common finding in the clinical reports of some 40 non-dominant hemispherectomies to that time. Improvement in contra-lateral motor function was also frequently reported. In 1969 Smith reported on three non-dominant cases examined from 1–30 years after operation. All three cases showed specific non-language defects in keeping with similiar reports by Austin and Grant (1955) and Bruell and Albee (1962). Smith notes that while impairment of language functions after dominant hemispherectomy is more severe than the deficits of non-language functions after non-dominant resection, the impairment is still 'sub-total'. 'In all reported cases, no single specialized hemispheric function was totally abolished'. The finding of relatively greater impairment (of speech) with left hemispherectomy than the impairment (non-verbal) after right hemispherectomy suggests a greater degree of specialization for speech functions.

There is a major difference between the effects of partial hemisphere lesions and hemispherectomy which has implications for theories of brain dysfunction. This difference is seen with regard to both motor function and speech. If one assumes that a gain in function is never produced by removal of cerebral tissue, the most plausible explanation seems to be that the improvement is produced by removal of interference or inhibition. One of

Smith's three cases (1969) had been totally unable to lift his leg from the bed and was barely able to move the left arm on command for 1 month before operation. Immediately after recovering from anaesthesia he promptly lifted his left leg on command. His voluntary arm movements were also improved though still impaired. Smith commented: 'This suggests that the more severe or total defects in other specialized hemispheric functions or the presence of unique defects reported in certain cases with lateralized lesions may reflect interference with or inhibition of the role of the opposite hemisphere or of caudally inferior ipsilateral structures in such functions'. The presence of speech after left hemispherectomy demonstrates (though the evidence is scanty) that the non-dominant hemisphere may have limited command over the executive apparatus of speech if the inhibiting influence of the dominant hemisphere is removed. A few hints from the commissurotomy evidence in support of this notion have already been mentioned in the literature.

Finally, the report of Gott (1973) of three hemispherectomy cases all with memory quotients below normal suggests that two communicating hemispheres are probably necessary for normal memory functioning. The similar claim of Sperry with regard to the poor memory of some commissurotomy patients is mentioned below.

CEREBRAL COMMISSUROTOMY

Around the turn of the present century neurologists had described clinical syndromes which they felt were due to lesions of the corpus callosum. The best known of these were the syndromes of alexia without agraphia (Dejerine, 1892) and that of left hand apraxia (Liepmann, 1906). The first disorder has been described in Chapter 7 and the disconnection theory argues that the syndrome is explained by an isolation of the speech areas of the left hemisphere from the right visual cortex. The second disorder was described in Chapter 3 and finds a similar explanation in terms of isolation of the dominant hemisphere language centres from the right motor cortex. Only a few reports of this kind were available until the introduction of surgical division of the corpus callosum for the prevention of the lateral spread of an epileptic discharge (van Wagenen & Herren, 1940). The first commissurotomy operation involved section of the corpus callosum together with bilateral section of the fornix. The operation proved beneficial in some cases and a considerable number of psychological studies of the effect of partial (15 cases) or complete division (9 cases) of the corpus callosum were soon reported by Akelaitis (1940; 1941a, b, c; 1942a, b; 1943; Akelaitis, Risteen, & van Wagenen 1941, 1942, 1943). These were completely negative, i.e. they provided no support for the concept of a hemisphere disconnection syndrome. This state of affairs remained until Myers began his classic studies on callosal section in animals in the early 1950s (Myers, 1955, 1956, 1959, 1961, 1965). Beginning with cats, callosal experiments continued with monkeys and chimpanzees and finally, specially designed tests were applied by Sperry and his colleagues to human patients who had undergone division of the main commissures of the brain for the relief of epilepsy. The principal findings of the Sperry group are set out below.

In keeping with the findings of Akelaitis, split-brain animals behaved quite normally in most of their activities. However, the story was quite different if steps were taken to restrict information to one hemisphere at a time. With tactile information this can be achieved readily because the information is conveyed almost exclusively to the contralateral hemisphere. With vision the fact that each eye presents information to both cerebral hemispheres (Fig. 8.3A) presented a problem if the principal aim is to restrict information to one hemisphere only, for the purpose of studying the single hemisphere's capabilities. In animals, this was simply achieved by dividing the optic chiasma in the midline so that direct transmission of information from each eye to the contralateral hemisphere was no longer possible (Fig. 8.3B).

The first experiments of this kind were carried out by Myers (1955, 1956) and may be described as follows: (i) the chiasma sectioned animals had one eye occluded while it learned a visual discrimination via the other (Fig. 8.3B); (ii) after discrimination training the occluded eye was uncovered and the 'training' eye was occluded; (iii) the animal showed very rapid discrimination learning via the 'untrained' eye.

In a second stage the same procedure was repeated, this time with commissurotomy (callosal division) added to splitting of the optic chiasma (Fig. 8.3C). In this second stage the animal reacted as if it had not seen the problem before, i.e. transfer of memory and learning from one hemisphere to the other was prevented by division of the corpus callosum. It

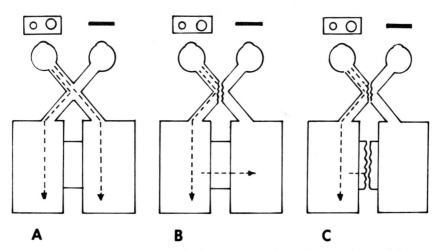

Fig. 8.3 Split brain experiments in animals. A, normal animal; B, optic chiasma divided; C, optic chiasma and commissures divided.

took the animal just as long to learn the discrimination with the second eye as it had with the first.

Of course, splitting the optic chiasma does not form part of the commissurotomy operation in man. The operation is generally restricted to division of the two major forebrain commissures, the corpus callosum and the anterior commissure together with the interthalamic connection (or massa intermedia) where this exists. This latter structure is not a commissure but consists of grey matter. It is a variable structure seen only in a proportion of human brains and its exact role is uncertain.

In man, study of response to visual information by each hemisphere is achieved by taking advantage of the orderly projection of fibres from the two halves of each retina (Fig. 8.4).

It can be seen that with eyes fixated on a central point information to the left of this point is projected by each eye *only* to the right hemisphere (A) while stimuli to the right of the midline project *only* to the left hemisphere (B). This is, of course, true only for the moment of fixation. In normal viewing the presence of both voluntary and involuntary eye movements would mean that stimuli to either side of the midline would be transmitted to *both* hemispheres. In order to prevent this, the technique of half-field (or hemi-retinal) projection has been used. With the subject fixating a central point the stimuli to be studied are projected to either half-field at an exposure so brief (tachistoscopic) that eye movement is not possible. This achieves a functional split of the optic projection in much the same way as achieved by surgical division of the chiasma in animals. It should

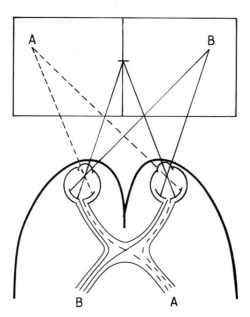

Fig. 8.4 Projection of information from left and right visual fields to the hemispheres.

be stressed that the projection in the studies which follow is to the half-field, left or right (hence to the corresponding contralateral hemisphere) and *not* to the left eye or right eye.

The use of such specialized techniques in the study of commissurotomized man was first reported by Sperry (1961, 1964), Gazzaniga, Bogen and Sperry (1962). The discrepancy between the early studies of Akelaitis and those of Sperry, Bogen, Gazzaniga and their colleagues which are still continuing may be accounted for by a number of factors among which the more important would appear to be difference in completeness of section of the corpus callosum and sophistication of experimental techniques used in post-operative testing. Goldstein and Joynt (1969) carried out a follow-up of one of Akelaitis' patients who had been operated upon some 27 years earlier. They found lasting defects in interhemispheric transfer of information with no evidence of any reorganization of function.

Despite the small number of patients who have been studied with 'split brain' techniques the extensive testing, often ingenious, which has been carried out has led to a fairly consistent picture of the hemisphere disconnection syndrome. The peculiar anatomical condition of the brain has allowed a variety of hypotheses concerning brain function to be tested in a way that would not otherwise be possible.

Visual perception

Using the tachistoscopic half-field technique a marked difference is noted between the two sides. Material which is presented to the right half-field (left hemisphere) can be read or described at about the pre-operative level. Material in the left half-field can *not* be described in speech or in writing. This has held true over hundreds of replications for tachistoscopic presentations of 100 msec or less. 'This is not true if objects are merely held in the left field or shown with longer exposure times, presumably because very rapid eye movements bring stimuli on the left into the right half field. Failure to find the foregoing left field defect in the Akelaitis studies seems best ascribed to the fact that tachistoscopic projection was not used in visual testing.' (Sperry et al, 1969).

Though commissurotomy patients could not speak about what was in the left half-field they could use non-verbal responses such as pointing to a matching stimulus or selecting the name of the object from a list. There is no hemianopia. The right hemisphere is unable to utilize the apparatus of speech for responding.

Earlier experiments revealed the independence of the two visual fields in memory as well as perception. The dissociation between things falling in the two half-fields has been utilized to great effect in the elegant 'chimera' experiments described below.

In the early experiments where two objects were presented simultaneously on the screen, one in each field, the reponse was shown to be dependent on the request made. If the subject was asked to reach behind the screen and retrieve the object from a number of others with his left hand he would select the object presented to the left half-field (right hemisphere/left hand). If asked to name the object he would invariably name that in the right half-field. This occurred even when the subject was still in the process of retrieving the object with his left hand. 'When asked to confirm verbally what item was selected by left hand subject names incorrectly the *right* field stimulus.' (Sperry et al, 1969). Such gross discrepancy attests powerfully to the independence of the two hemisphere-eye combinations.

Chimeric figures

One of the most subtle techniques for testing the perceptual abilities and control of motor response by each hemisphere is the method of chimeric stimuli described by Levy, Trevarthen and Sperry (1972). The technique is based on the observation by Travarthen and Kinsbourne that commissurotomy patients tend to complete material across the midline in a similar way to some hemianopic patients (Ch. 7). For example, when only half a stimulus was presented in such a way that the edge of the half-stimulus coincided with the vertical meridian, the commissurotomy patient often responded as though perceiving a whole stimulus. This completion process was particularly strong in completion to the left when verbal report was used and in completion to the right where the subject was asked to draw the stimulus (Trevarthen, 1974a, b).

Chimeric stimuli consist of a composite joined at the vertical midline comprising the right half of one stimulus and the left half of another, e.g. the left half of one face and the right half of another. Other stimuli constructed by Levy et al were 'antler' patterns, line drawings of common objects, and chain patterns. (Fig. 8.5).

The composite stimuli were exposed briefly in a tachistoscope and the subject was asked to indicate what he had seen. Three modes of response were used: (i) pointing with the left hand, (ii) pointing with the right hand, and (iii) naming the stimulus.

When using pointing responses the subject had in front of him an array of the original stimuli from which the chimeras had been constructed. In the case of naming, the choice stimuli were removed, the subject having been taught assigned names for each of the faces and the different types of 'antlers'.

Levy and her colleagues pointed out that 'recognition of faces appears to be strongly gestalt-like in nature and a face is relatively resistant to analytical verbal description.' They also noted the clinical finding that most patients with difficulty in facial recognition seem to have lesions in the right hemisphere. This suggested that the disconnected right hemisphere might be superior at this type of task. This hypothesis of asymmetry of function

CHIMERIC STIMULI

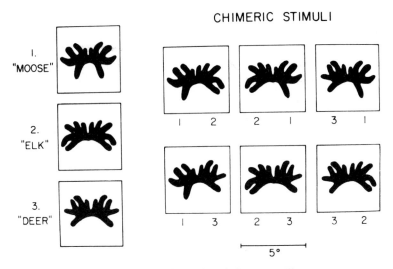

Fig. 8.5 Chimeric figures (from Levy, Trevarthen & Sperry, 1972).

favouring the right hemisphere was strongly supported for all four sets of stimuli (faces, antlers, drawings, and patterns) *irrespective of which hand was used for pointing.* However, when the response was changed to verbal naming there was a reversal in favour of the visual information going to the left hemisphere. When pointing was employed the 'completed' stimulus from the left half of the visual field was favoured, while naming was significantly biased in favour of the right visual field. The assymmetry of function when naming faces, while significant, was not as striking as with pointing and there was a higher proportion of errors. The authors commented: 'It was evident in the hesitancy and incidental comments of the subjects as well, that the left hemisphere found this kind of task extremely difficult and *was inclined to describe the distinctive features of the right field face instead of naming it as a unit.*' (Levy, Traverthen and Sperry, 1972 p. 66, italics added by present author).

The implication of this set of experiments is of such significance that the authors' summary is worth presenting in full:

> Visual testing with composite right-left chimeric stimuli shows that the two disconnected hemispheres of commissurotomy patients can process conflicting information simultaneously and independently. Which hemisphere dominates control of the read-out response was found to be determined primarily by the central processing requirement rather than by the nature of the stimuli or whether the response is ipsilaterally or contralaterally mediated. Where the task needs no more than visual recognition, a visual encoding ensues, mediated by the right hemisphere and based on the form properties of the stimulus as such rather than on separate feature analysis. On the other hand, where some form of verbal encoding is specifically required, the left hemi-

sphere takes over and attempts a visual recognition based on nameable analytical features of the stimulus. Stimuli having no verbal labels stored in longterm memory and which are resistant to feature analysis were found to be extremely difficult for the left hemisphere to identify. We conclude that each of the disconnected hemisphere has its own specialized strategy of information processing, and that whether a hemisphere is dominant for a given task under the test conditions depends upon which strategy is the more proficient (Levy, Traverthen, & Sperry 1972 pp. 75–76).

Visuospatial functions

One of the striking pieces of information supporting the notion of lateral differences in visuospatial functions came from early reports of studies on two commissurotomy patients (Gazzaniga, Bogen & Sperry, 1962; Bogen & Gazzaniga, 1965; Bogen, 1969a). Both these patients were able to write with either hand before surgery, the left being the non-preferred hand. After commissurotomy both patients lost the ability to write with the left hand but preserved the ability to write with the right hand. There was, however, a dissociation between their writing and drawing abilities. Though both patients could copy drawings better with the right hand before operation, after surgery they were each better at this task when using the left hand. This visuospatial superiority of the so-called minor hemisphere was also seen in better performance of Block Design problems with the left hand. Where verbal instructions were used superiority reverted to the right hand.

To make clear the distinction between drawing to instructions (dysgraphia) Bogen (1969a) coined the parallel term *dyscopia*. He defined dyscopia as a difficulty in following a 'visual instruction (that is copying from a model) rather than drawing from verbal instructions.'

Further insight into the nature of the right hemisphere's superiority has been provided by three experiments by Nebes which demonstrated that the effect extends to the tactile modality as well as the visual and also to the synthesis of information between these modalities. Nebes (1974a) put forward the hypothesis that the right hemisphere 'attends to the overall configuration of the stimulus situation, synthesizing the fragmentary chunks of perceptual data received from sampling of the sensory surround into a meaningful percept of the environment. The right hemisphere is thus viewed as giving spatial context to the detailed analysis carried out by the major hemisphere' (p. 156).

In his first experimental test of this hypothesis (Nebes, 1971) the subject was required to judge from visual or tactile appreciation the size of circle from which arcs of various size (80°, 120°, 180°, 280°) had come. Tactile-visual, visual-tactile and tactile-tactile conditions were employed. Four of the five commissurotomized patients tested performed significantly better with their left hand on all three versions, i.e. both on intramodal and cross-modal tasks. In a second experiment (Nebes, 1972) the subject was required to select from a number of tactually presented shapes the one which would be formed from a visually presented fragmented figure. These visual figures each depicted a geometric shape that had been cut up and the pieces drawn apart, maintaining, however, their original orientations and relative positions. Once again commissurotomized subjects proved far more accurate with their left hand than with their right. Control experiments showed that neither difficulty with tactile discrimination nor the intermodal nature of the tasks were significant factors determining the poor performance but rather the 'Gestalt' requirement of the task. The third experiment (Nebes, 1973) utilized the well known Gestalt principal of proximity. Here an alteration in the spacing of the uniform stimulus units gives rise to two differing percepts, e.g. in Figure 8.6 the figure on the left is perceived as columns of dots whereas the figure on the right is seen as rows. Commissurotomy subjects (three in number) were presented tachistoscopically with one of these figures to either the left or right half-field of vision and were required to signal either vertical or horizontal organization by finger movements. All three subjects were more accurate with displays in the left half of the visual field 'suggesting that in man the right hemisphere is more competent than the left in perceiving the overall stimulus configuration inherent in the spatial organization of its parts' (p. 285).

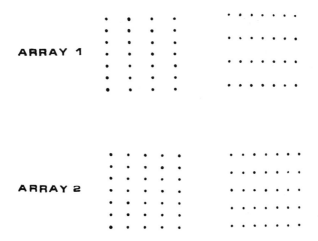

Fig. 8.6 Gestalt figure (Fig. 1, p. 286 Nebes 1973, by courtesy of Pergamon Press).

Such experiments provide strong support for the position that the right hemisphere functions much more efficiently in situations where synthesis of configurations is required from fragmentary information. Nebes (1974b) considered that this ability of the right hemisphere 'can be viewed as a spatial function in which, from limited data, we infer the structure and organization of our environment without having to submit the whole sensory array to a detailed analysis' (p. 12). He pointed out that the results of his experiments taken together with the data from the chimera experiments suggest that it is the type of information processing required in a given situation which determines whether one hemisphere or the other will be 'dominant' or function in a superior manner. 'If only visual recognition is called for, even if the material is verbal, it is the right hemisphere which acts. If, however, a verbal transformation is demanded, even if the material is non-verbal it is handled by the left hemisphere.' If this suggestion is true, (and there is much experimental support for it) then it will enable us to understand why certain contraindications in the lesion literature have arisen on the basis of patients' performance on verbal versus non-verbal tasks. It will also enable tests to be designed which should have greater value in the prediction of laterality of localized lesions in either hemisphere.

Tactile perception

Here the task of object recognition (stereognosis) gave similar results to that in vision. Objects felt with the right hand (but not seen) could be named and described. Using the left hand the patient could recognize the presence of an object but was never able to name or describe it. Experimenters found that it was important to control for auditory cues such as those arising from moving the object on the table surface thus producing information which could alert the left hemisphere to the nature of the object which could then be named, the so-called *cross cueing*.

As with vision, a variety of tests demonstrated that the object felt with the left hand had been perceived and remembered by the right hemisphere. The subject could retrieve an object previously felt by the left hand from a mixed group of objects even after several minutes. The problem then is not one of stereognosis or tactile object agnosia but a unilateral anomia. 'This deficit has been present and persistent in every right-handed patient with complete commissurotomy' (Bogen, 1985, p. 104).

The commissurotomy patient is also unable to copy with one hand a configuration of the fingers of the other hand which has been arranged by the examiner.

The independence of the two hemispheres for tactile information is shown clearly where integration is required for solution of a problem such as the simple jig-saw puzzles of Gazzaniga (1970) (Fig. 8.7).

The subjects could fit together simple two piece jigsaw puzzles with either hand separately but not when intermanual collaboration was required by placing one piece in each hand. It is noteworthy that when stylus maze learning problems were used there was complete intermanual transfer.

When information has to be integrated between two modalities such as vision and touch the commissurotomy patient only succeeds where the information is processed in the same hemisphere. The subject cannot

INTERMANUAL TACTILE COMPARISON

JIGSAW PATTERN	ONE PATTERN IN EACH HAND		BOTH IN L H	BOTH IN R H
	L H	R H		
1	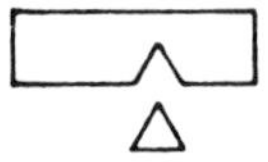 Not Completed		Correct	Correct
2 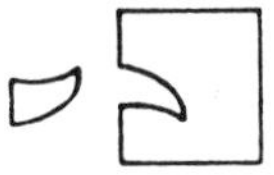	"		"	"
3 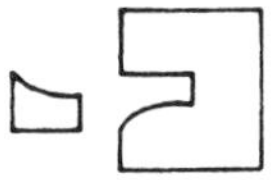	"		"	"

Fig. 8.7 Intermanual tactile comparison (Fig. 28, p. 87, Gazzaniga MS 1970 The bisected brain, by courtesy of Plenium Publications.)

retrieve an object with his right hand if it is flashed to his left visual field. This tactile-visual match is not possible since the information from the two sense modalities is divided between the two hemispheres. For the same reason, other forms of intermodal association are impossible.

The alien hand

Brion and Jedynak (1972) have reported a new sign of callosal disconnection which they termed *la main étrangère*. 'The patient who holds his hands one in the other behind his back does not recognize that his left belongs to him.' They stress that this is not a matter of failed tactile recognition but a failure on the patient's part to recognize that the hand he is holding actually belongs to himself. Two patients when asked to write with their left hand were able to do so but expressed amazement and were unwilling to believe that they themselves had done the writing.

Auditory perception

Differences have been noted in the testing of commissurotomy subjects under dichotic conditions. Firstly, there is a marked lowering in the number of digits correctly reported from the left ear (Milner, Taylor & Sperry, 1968; Sparks & Geschwind, 1968). This difference is also seen after right temporal lobectomy though to a less marked degree. On monaural stimulation subjects showed equal efficiency for the two ears. Milner and her co-workers extended this finding by presenting pairs of competing instructions simultaneously to each ear. The subject was told, for example, to pick up an object from a group of objects hidden from view but on each occasion separate objects were named to the left and right ears. Under these conditions the subjects showed a strong preference to pick up objects named through the left ear with a relative neglect of items named in the right ear. This suppression or neglect of information coming to the right ear varied from subject to subject and with the conditions of testing. Subjects also had some difficulty with naming the objects picked up with the left hand. They tended to misname them and often gave the name which had been simultaneously presented to the right ear. The authors conclude that the 'dissociation between verbal and left-hand stereognostic response indicates a right-left dichotomy for auditory experience in the disconnected hemispheres'.

The suppression of ipsilateral signals under dichotic presentation which is so marked for speech sounds does not occur for dichotically presented pure tones (Efron, Bogen & Yund, 1977). It is likely that pitch information is combined at some central subcortical site.

Language

Language comprehension

Much interest has centred on the non-dominant hemisphere's capacity for language comprehension. The use of auditory material is complicated by the fact that both ears present information almost equally to both hemi-spheres and it is not possible to devise an auditory procedure analogous to the half-field visual tecnhique. It is possible that since the dominant hemisphere hears the same material as the non-dominant hemisphere it may facilitate the latter by some means other than the major commissures.

With this reservation in mind it does seem that the non-dominant hemisphere possesses a fair degree of language comprehension. Patients are able to retrieve with their left hand objects named or even described by function. They may also be able to indicate which name read aloud corre-sponds to an object flashed in the left half-field.

Comprehension of written material has also been tested by the split-field technique. The right hemisphere appears to comprehend limited word classes particularly concrete nouns.

Gazzaniga (1970) noted that while object nouns appeared to be the best comprehended of any of the words flashed in the left visual field, nouns derived from verbs were not comprehended at all. Words containing more than one morpheme also presented difficulty for the right hemisphere. Caplan, Holmes, and Marshall (1974) failed to confirm this hypothesis, namely, that while simple nouns are represented in the right hemisphere agentive (verb-derived) nouns or bi-morphemic nouns are not.

One of Sperry's patients was studied by Sugishita (1978) some 12 years after operation. The subject was given a series of objects to feel with the left hand and then asked to select from a visual array of words a corresponding word using the left hand. She was able to do so if the words were related by category or by function or even by an occupation associated with the object but she could not select words representing abstract concepts related to the object. Patients did not comprehend verbs in the left half-field nor were they able to act upon simple one-word verbal commands such as 'nod'.

Recently, Bogen (1985) reported considerable increase in the number of single words recognized by the right hemisphere with the passage of years but this is rarely accompanied by speech and the syntactic capabilities remain rudimentary at best (Zaidel, 1978). There are a few exceptions. One 15-year-old, normally right-handed, male patient with total callosotomy (but sparing of the anterior commissure) could carry out verbal and pictorial commands presented visually and could write clumsily with his left hand the name of objects presented to the right hemisphere (Gazzaniga, Le Doux & Wilson, 1977).

The major hemisphere always shows normal comprehension of all orally and visually presented material in the commissurotomy subjects.

At first sight, the commissurotomy evidence appears to be at variance with large numbers of lesion studies, e.g. left hemisphere lesion cases with aphasia often seem to have less verbal comprehension than one might expect from the commissurotomy studies.

Relatively small lesions confined to the left hemisphere have been described as producing word-blindness or word-deafness (Geschwind, 1965a, 1970; Luria, 1970; Gazzaniga, 1972). It might have been expected that if the right hemisphere was intact the patient should show at least the amount of comprehension shown by the right hemisphere in commissurotomy subjects. Two explanations have been offered. The first and more plausible explanation suggests interference with right hemisphere function from the left-sided lesion by way of the commissural pathways. The second explanation suggests that, because of their long-standing epilepsy commissurotomy subjects may have developed a stronger biateral representation of language.

Language expression

Extensive examinations of commissurotomy patients seemed to give very strong support to the contention that the right hemisphere is mute. 'Information perceived exclusively or generated exclusively in the minor (right) hemisphere could be communicated neither in speech nor in writing; it has to be expressed entirely through nonverbal responses' (Gazzaniga, 1970, p. 125). This led Levy and her colleagues to ask the question, 'Does the minor hemisphere suffer from expressive aphasia because it cannot wrest control of the linguistic expressive mechanisms from the left hemisphere, or is it the right hemisphere simply incapable of thinking of words?' (Levy, 1974, p. 165).

In an attempt to answer such a question Levy, Nebes and Sperry (1971) tested the ability of the surgically-separated right hemisphere to spell out words. Two commissurotomy patients were asked to use their hidden left hand to rearrange plastic letters to form a meaningful word. Both patients were able to arrange the letters into words but were unable to name the word they had 'spelled out'. They performed very poorly when asked to write the name of an object felt with the left hand whereas they were able to draw the object readily. These patients were also inferior in left-handed writing of verbs as compared with nouns. Levy and her colleagues considered that there were two major factors accounting for poor perform- ance in expression (here written expression) by the right hemisphere: (i) dominance by the major hemisphere over the motor mechanisms for expression and, (ii) an intrinsic limitation in the processing of language. They comment: 'Our results suggest that though there are two aspects of language expression — central conceptual dominance and peripheral motor dominance — there is a fairly direct relationship between the two. When a hemisphere is intrinsically better equipped to handle some task, it is also easier for that hemisphere to dominate motor pathways' (Levy, Nebes and Sperry, 1971, p. 58). When the effect of the dominant hemisphere is removed as in dominant hemispherectomy the positive but limited power of the minor hemisphere over expression becomes apparent.

Until quite recently evidence for vocalization originated by the minor hemisphere in commissurotomy patients was almost non-existent. Butler and Norrsell (1968) reported one patient tested 3 years after total section of both major commissures who was able at times to name simple words presented in the left visual field. Other workers (Trevarthen, 1969; Milner & Taylor, 1970; Teng & Sperry, 1973) have mentioned situations in which the right hemisphere has appeared to initiate fragmentary utterances in split-brain testing. Gazzaniga and Hillyard (1971) could find no confir- mation for expressive capacity in the right hemisphere. There was, more- over, virtually no syntactic ability shown by their tests, even the limited amount of comprehension by the right hemisphere on pictorial-verbal matching tasks being limited to the affirmative-negative dimension.

Two cases of complete callosotomy with the anterior commissure intact have shown limited speech apparently controlled from the right hemisphere (Gazzaniga et al, 1979; Sidtis et al, 1981; Gazzaniga, 1982; Gazzaniga et al, 1982; McKeever et al, 1982). Both patients showed right hemisphere comprehension but no speech for approximately 1 year. Then utterances of one word were noted. At this stage if both hemispheres were shown stimuli simultaneously and asked to name them the left hemisphere dominated but the right hemisphere could write (but not speak) the name of the stimulus presented to it. By about 3 years, instances occurred of the reverse phenomenon, i.e. the left hemisphere could write but not name while the right hemisphere responded with speech. These two patients developed the ability to integrate verbal material presented separately to *either* hemisphere. Gazzaniga gives the following example: 'If two pictures or two words are sequentially flashed to the left or right visual field and the choice available requires an inference to be made from the two words, both hemispheres of P.S. and V.P. can perform the task . . . In one study, for example, if the words "pin" and "finger" are to be assessed, the correct response would be the word "bleed"' (Gazzaniga, 1982, p. 17). This inference capability has been seen only in the *left* hemisphere of other commissurotomy patients including the small number who have developed a fair degree of semantic competence though no speech.

Two conclusions flow from these observations: (i) there is the possibility of paracallosal transfer of language information, and (ii) 'when a right hemisphere does acquire the capacity to speak, it appears to be remarkably like the left brain in general cognitive capacity' Gazzaniga (1982, p. 16).

Unilateral agraphia

The ability to write with the left hand is lost after commissurotomy though the patient may be able to carry out other skilled fine movements such as drawing or copying with the same hand (Bogen & Gazzaniga, 1965; Zaidel & Sperry, 1977). It is noteworthy that a patient of Sugishita et al (1980) had unilateral agraphia after section of only the posterior half of the corpus callosum during removal of an arteriovenous malformation. This patient showed no unilateral apraxia or tactile anomia.

Hemialexia

This refers to the loss of the ability to read in one half of the visual field where there is no concurrent homonymous hemianopia. It follows section of the splenium of the corpus callosum for whatever reason and is a rare occurrence (Trescher & Ford, 1937; Maspes, 1948; Gazzaniga, Bogen & Sperry, 1965; Gazzaniga & Sperry, 1967; Sugishita et al, 1978). Sugishita et al (1978) found their three patients with division of the splenium for pineal tumours had hemialexia post-operatively for both versions of the Japanese language, i.e. Kana (syllabograms) and Kanji (ideograms). Two or three years later the hemialexia was relatively restricted to Kana with improvement in the ability to read the ideograms.

Unilateral apraxia

All of Bogen's patients showed unilateral (left-sided) apraxia after operation (Bogen, 1985). There was some improvement with time but even many years later some degree of apraxia could still be elicited (Zaidel & Sperry,

1977). This disorder is included here since, strictly speaking, it is a language related disorder being in essence a unilateral ideomotor apraxia.

Memory

Numerous studies by Sperry and his associates have demonstrated that each hemisphere has the capacity to store information for subsequent retrieval and this capacity is directly related to the specialization of each hemisphere. However, this does not mean that the memory abilities of split-brain subjects remain normal. Milner and Taylor (1972) tested commissurotomy patients' tactile recognition memory by asking them to feel an object then select it tactually from a group of four after delays of up to two minutes. Two classes of objects were used: (i) everyday objects to which verbal labels could be readily attached, rubber band, key, coin, scissors, and (ii) 'non-verbal' tactile nonsense shapes. In six out of the seven subjects there was a marked superiority for the left hand. This was taken to mean that complex perceptual information can be remembered without the necessity for verbal encoding and it is the right hemisphere which specializes in this regard.

The combination of these two findings seems to imply that 'both cerebral hemispheres normally participate in such tasks, but with the right playing the preponderant role'. Milner (1974) pointed out that concentration on the evidence of hemispheric specialization derived from commissurotomy studies and the parallel studies of asymmetry in normal subjects using similar experimental techniques may lead to an overemphasis of the functional differences between the two hemispheres. She reminds us that unilateral lesion studies have demonstrated that there is a parallel organization of function on the two sides of the brain which is in danger of being overlooked. Zaidel and Sperry (1974) examined a total of 10 commissurotomy patients on six standardized tests of memory. An examination of the data suggested that the processes which mediate the initial encoding as well as the retrieval of contralateral engrams involve co-operation between the hemispheres and so depend upon the commissural connections.

The present selection of commissurotomy evidence has focused on those areas which have been most closely examined. Other areas which have been less systematically explored include emotion, volition and consciousness. Incidental reports related to these have occurred throughout many of the studies mentioned. Much of the material to that time was reviewed by Lishman (1971).

AGENESIS OF THE CORPUS CALLOSUM

On rare occasions the major neocortical commissure, the corpus callosum, fails to develop, a condition termed agenesis. A summary of the literature with representative cover of much of the literature in neuropsychological studies has been provided by Dimond (1972). Apart from the rarity of the condition the usefulness of this material in the study of hemispheric asymmetry is restricted by a number of factors such as the completeness or otherwise of the agenesis and the presence of associated abnormalities of the cerebrum. The fact that no dramatic manifestations may be present during life is demonstrated by the cases where the agenesis is revealed for the first time at post-mortem. Furthermore, most of the cases described in the literature until recently have failed to use sophisticated examination procedures (such as those developed in the study of commissurotomy) which would allow disconnection effects to be demonstrated if present. Some authors (e.g. Russell & Reitan, 1955) have felt that this was probably the case for most of the earlier studies which claimed an absence of symptoms unless the callosal agenesis was associated with other brain anomalies. The question of clinicopathological correlation in these cases was re-examined by Loeser and Alvord (1968a, b).

Since the 1960s, detailed examination of a small number of cases of agenesis has been carried out. Jeeves (1965a) examined three acallosal cases with particular reference to tasks requiring bimanual manipulation and co-ordination. He found all three subjects inferior to suitably matched controls on a variety of such tasks and the ante-mortem evidence including radiological studies seemed to suggest that absence of the callosum was the major anomaly present. Other cases of partial or complete agenesis studied by Jeeves (1965b) varied in their ability on motor co-ordination tasks. Even where the everyday level of motor ability of some of these subjects was close to the norm for their age, sensitive tests involving integration of the two hands showed a poorer performance for acallosal subjects.

A single case studied by Solursh et al (1965) confirmed the difficulty of integrating tactile or proprioceptive information across the midline. Like commissurotomy subjects, this boy could identify by touch with the corresponding (contralateral) hand, objects presented to either hemisphere (i.e. to either half visual field) but was unable to do so with the ipsilateral hand. Despite this, fairly clear indication of transfer of information presented solely to one hemisphere was obtained in other situations. Incomplete compensation for the lack of the major organ of transfer of learning seems to have taken place. Extracallosal pathways appear to be limited in the ability to which they can enter into the transmission of information from one side to the other.

In another patient with complete absence of the corpus callosum Saul and Sperry (1968) could find no evidence of callosal symptoms despite the use of tests developed in the study of split-brain subjects. However, they also found indications that absence of the callosum hampered the patient 'in those activities in which the specialized non-verbal and spatial facilities of the minor hemisphere would normally reinforce, complement and enhance the verbal and volitional performances of the major hemisphere.' (Sperry, Gazzaniga & Bogen, 1969, p. 288).

Ettlinger et al (1972, 1974) in a comparison of patients having partial or total developmental absence of the corpus callosum with control subjects found a conspicuous lack of impairment in the acallosal subjects. Their tests included the following: intermanual tactile matching; depth perception; tachistoscopic visual identification and matching; spatial localization and dichotic listening. Further negative studies support these findings (Ferriss & Dorsen, 1975; Gott & Saul, 1978; Jeeves, 1979). The absence of a pronounced laterality effect which had been found in commissurotomy subjects had also been reported by Bryden and Zurif (1970). The fact that their subject performed in a manner very similar to a group of normal subjects suggested that alternative pathways for adequate listening could be developed in cases of agenesis.

Because of the heterogeneous nature of the clinical material it would be unwise to speculate about the mechanisms and alternate pathways used for compensation. However, the observed enlargement of the anterior commissure in a small number of callosal subjects led some authors (Saul & Sperry, 1968; Ettlinger et al, 1974) to speculate that at least some of the tasks such as cross-matching might utilize this tract. The principal argument against this is that most of the total split-brain picture is seen after callosotomy in which the anterior commissure is spared (Gazzaniga & Le Doux, 1978; McKeever et al, 1981).

The intelligence of callosal subjects covers a wide range. The majority are below the norm on intellectual measures with a few cases at or above normal. Once again it is difficult to disentangle the contribution of any associated cerebral abnormalities and there does not appear to be any common pattern in the small amount of psychometric data available. The common depression of intellectual measures would lead many to agree with Dimond's suggestion that 'in the early stages of development the absence of the corpus callosum places the individual at a disadvantage for which it is difficult subsequently to compensate. This condition does depress intellectual function and the employment of subsidiary pathways cannot totally compensate for this disadvantage' (Dimond, 1972).

Critical reviews covering numerous aspects of callosal agenesis has been given by Ferriss and Dorsen (1975), Jeeves (1979), Milner and Jeeves (1979) and Chiarello (1980).

FUNCTIONAL ASYMMETRY IN NORMAL SUBJECTS

The hemispheric asymmetry of function demonstrated in lesions studies and after commissurotomy has been supported by studies, particularly of auditory and visual perception, in normal subjects. In the years since the first edition of this book this area has stimulated such a proliferation of studies that one eminent neuropsychologist has referred to it as 'a PhD industry'. Students might refer to the following recent books and review articles on cerebral asymmetry which deal comprehensively with studies and theories of brain function based on normal subjects (Beaumont, 1982; Bryden, 1982; Bradshaw & Nettleton, 1983; Corballis, 1983; Hellige 1983; Segalowitz 1983; Young, 1983; Springer & Deutsch, 1985).

DOMINANCE REVISITED

As evidence has accumulated regarding the specialized functions of the two hemispheres, attempts have been made to characterize the different contributions of each hemisphere. Bogen (1969b) traced the emergence of the various dichotomies from the time of Hughlings Jackson up to his own classification. His table is produced below.

Table 8.4 Some dichotomies distinguishing between the two hemispheres (From Bogen, 1969b)

	Dominant (left) Hemisphere	Minor (right) Hemisphere
Jackson (1864)	Expression	Perception
Jackson (1874)	Audito-articular	Retino-ocular
Jackson (1876)	Propositioning	Visual Imagery
Milner (1958)	Verbal	Perceptual or non-verbal
Zangwill (1961)	Symbolic	Visuospatial
Bogen and Gazzaniga (1965)	Verbal	Visuospatial
Levy-Agresti and Sperry (1968)	Logical or analytic	Synthetic perceptual
Bogen (1969b)	Propositional	Appositional

Bogen pointed out the difficulty which we have in the present state of our knowledge in characterizing the ability of the right hemisphere. His earlier dichotomy (a combination of those of Milner and Zangwill) was abandoned because of the evidence of some verbal capacity in the right hemisphere. He proposed the use of the provisional term 'appositional' for right hemisphere function. 'This term implies a capacity for opposing or comparing of perceptions, schemas, engrams, etc. but has, in addition, the virtue that it implies very little else. If it is correct that the right hemisphere excels in capacities as yet unknown to us, the full meaning of "appositional" will emerge as these capacities are further studied and understood' (Bogen, 1969b, p. 149). Though much more information has accumulated since then it is still difficult to select a pair of terms to epitomize the lateral differences in function. Perhaps this is just as well since, as Milner (1974) points out it would be wrong in studying hemispheric differences in function to overlook the large amount of evidence from both neurological and neuropsychological studies which demonstrate that 'similarities as well as differences exist between corresponding areas, in the two hemispheres', i.e. there is what she aptly terms a complementary specialization of the two hemispheres with regard to psychological functions. The question then is one of relative rather than absolute dominance. Benton expressed this in the following way: 'Dominance denotes *asymmetry* in hemispheric function, i.e. the two hemispheres subserve particular functions to an unequal degree.

Theoretically the degree of inequality with respect to a particular function might be either *absolute* (one hemisphere exclusively mediating the function) or *relative* (one hemisphere being the more important in the mediation of the function). All available evidence suggests that absolute inequality is rare, the more common relationship being one of relative inequality' (Benton, 1975, p. 9). Some authors would prefer to specify the particular function being considered rather than speak of one hemisphere as 'the dominant one' (e.g. Poeck, 1975).

Finally, the evidence from some commissurotomy studies coupled with studies of normal subjects has supported the notion that one of the major difference between the functioning of the two hemispheres lies not so much in the specialization for different types of information or for different psychological functions but rather in the different strategies and modes of central processing which each hemisphere employs.

In summarizing the evidence on asymmetry of function in the brain, Levy (1974a, p. 167) concluded that the human cerebral hemispheres exist in a symbiotic relationship in which both the capacities and motivations to act are complementary. Each side of the brain is able to perform and chooses to perform a certain set of cognitive tasks which the other side finds difficult or distasteful or both. In considering the nature of the two sets of functions, it appears they may be logically incompatible. The right hemisphere synthesizes over space. The left hemisphere analyzes over time. The right hemisphere notes visual similarities to the exclusion of conceptual similarities. The left hemisphere does the opposite. The right hemisphere perceives form, the left hemisphere, detail. The right hemisphere codes sensory input in terms of images, the left hemisphere in terms of linguistic descriptions. The right hemisphere lacks a phonological analyser; the left hemisphere lacks a Gestalt 'synthesizer'. This description of hemispheric behaviour suggests that the Gestalt Laws of Perceptual Organisation pertain only to the mute hemisphere. If so, the adaptive functions served by these organisational principles are likewise restricted to the mute hemisphere, just as the adaptive functions served by language are restricted to the verbal hemisphere.

In the past decade the *analytic versus holistic* processing model has received widespread support and writers such as Bradshaw and Nettleton (1983) have drawn attention to the body of evidence in psychology in support of two distinctly different forms of mental organization which have arisen quite independently of any consideration of cerebral asymmetry. These have been given very similar names to those employed in the asymmetry literature.

The concept of cerebral dominance or laterality has come a long way since the days of Paul Broca. Nothing illustrates the way in which the concept has permeated every aspect of brain-dependent functions than the recent comprehensive, and at times, speculative, reviews of Geschwind and Galaburda (1985a, b, c). Le Doux (1983) reminds us that many have been so carried away by work on the differential capacities of the separate and separated hemispheres that they 'treat the normal brain as though it were split', an almost tacit disregard of interhemispheric integration. His caution is a fitting conclusion to this chapter. 'No one cognitive function is completely dependent on one hemisphere or the other. Complex psychological processes reflect the functioning of both sides of the brain at all levels of the neuraxis, and a theory of how these processes relate to brain mechanisms must account for the integrated functioning of the nervous system. Any model which focuses on cerebral compartmentalisation at the expense of integration would seem to be misdirected' (Le Doux, 1983, p. 212).

9

The interbrain

The diencephalon   319

During embryological development three major subdivisions of the brain emerge. These are termed the forebrain or *prosencephalon*, the midbrain or *mesencephalon*, and the hindbrain or *rhombencephalon*. The latter is continuous with the spinal cord. The forebrain itself becomes subdivided into two divisions, the cranial portion being termed the *telencephalon*, and the caudal portion the *diencephalon*. The side walls of the *telencephalon* produce the two cerebral hemispheres each with a lateral ventricle. In broad terms, the *diencephalon* corresponds to the third ventricle and the structures which bound it. Thus the *diencephalon* stands at the junction of the *prosencephalon* and the *mesencephalon* and so merits the title the 'interbrain'. The term *thalamencephalon* has also been used for this region.

The preceding chapters have been concerned exclusively with the major derivatives of the *telencephalon*, namely the cerebral hemispheres, especially the neocortical areas and their connections. In quite recent times it has become obvious that the functional anatomical systems subserving at least certain important higher functions extend deep into the diencephalon. This helps to reinforce the central concept of this text which might be stated as follows: *every complex psychological process has as its neural substrate aggregations of nerve cells both cortical and subcortical joined together by a three-dimensional set of nerve fibres.* Studies of psycho-anatomical relationships in cases where the points of disruption are clearly known help to establish the details of such networks.

In particular two major sets of functional disruptions are known to be produced by diencephalic lesions and the crucial sites needed to produce such changes are emerging. Before outlining briefly these disorders, namely, *diencephalic amnesia* and *thalamic aphasia* it will be helpful to review the general structure of the region.

THE DIENCEPHALON

The diencephalon is a midline structure with symmetrical right and left halves. Crossing the lateral wall of the third ventricle is a groove, the *hypothalamic sulcus* which varies in its prominence and extends from the *interventricular foramen* to the *cerebral aqueduct*. This divides the diencephalon into a dorsal or upper part and a ventral or lower part (Fig. 9.1).

The dorsal part of the diencephalon consists of three parts: (i) the *dorsal thalamus* which is commonly called simply the thalamus by many anatomists and most clinicians; (ii) the *metathalamus* made up of the medial and lateral geniculate bodies and (iii) a collection of structures, including the pineal gland, in the caudal part of the roof which are termed the *epithalamus*.

The ventral part of the thalamus includes (i) the *hypothalamus* and (ii) the *ventral thalamus*. The hypothalamus extends from the *lamina terminalis* to a vertical plane just caudal to the *mamillary bodies* and downwards from the hypothalamic sulcus to include the structures in the side wall and floor of the third ventricle. These include the mamillary bodies themselves. One of the major tracts from the mamillary bodies terminates in the anterior nucleus of the thalamus and is called the *mamillothalamic tract*.

The nuclei of the thalamus were described in Chapter 2 and the relationships of the main components of the diencephalon are shown in Figures 9.1 and 9.2. It must be stressed that the above is an anatomical description and all of the structures in the diencephalon have connections which cross these

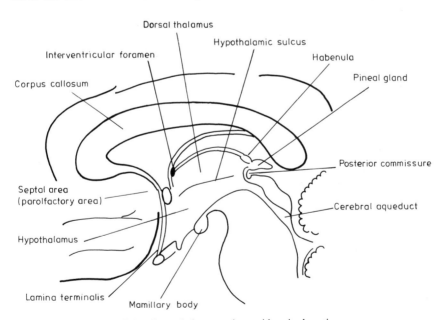

Fig. 9.1 Lateral view of the diencephalon seen in a mid-sagittal section.

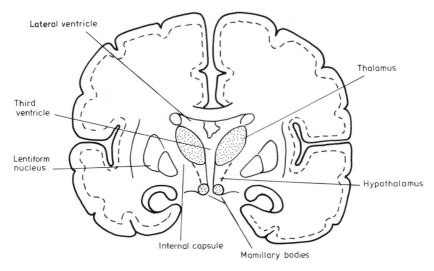

Fig. 9.2 Coronal section of the brain at the level of the mamillary bodies showing the principal features of the diencephalon.

descriptive boundaries into other areas. Thus while some structures in the diencephalon form important nodal points and connections in the neural substrate of memory and learning, the latter includes most subdivisions of the forebrain.

Diencephalic amnesia

Korsakoff's amnesia

In 1881 Wernicke first described three cases of the syndrome which bears his name. The salient features were ataxia, ocular symptoms and mental confusion. Two of the cases were alcoholic. It was later established that the condition was related to poor nutrition the specific deficiency being that of thiamine or vitamin B1. This accounts for its frequent appearance in undernourished alcoholics though it also appears in other circumstances which produce thiamine avitaminosis.

In a series of reports from 1887 to 1891 Korsakoff reported the association of various mental disorders with polyneuritis. Sometimes the patient retained clear consciousness but was agitated, while in others the agitation was part of a confusional state. In most of the patients an amnesic disorder was a prominent feature. Soon after these initial observations Korsakoff, along with others, noted that the amnesic syndrome could be seen without the polyneuritis. As with Wernicke's encephalopathy the most common association was with alcoholism and malnutrition.

Although a close association between Wernicke's disease and Korsakoff's psychosis was recognized by a number of writers at the turn of the century, the intimate clinical relationship was established by Bonhoeffer (1904) though pathological confirmation was not established firmly for about a further three decades (see Victor et al, 1971). Following resolution of the acute episode of Wernicke's encephalopathy, patients were found to be suffering from the Korsakoff amnesic syndrome. Moreover, the pathological lesions appear to be identical in the two conditions. Because of the nature of the populations studied it is not always possible to ascertain whether Korsakoff patients have suffered from one or more episodes of Wernicke's disorder though this is usually the case. Most workers would agree with Victor (1976) that Korsakoff's psychosis is the psychic manifestation of Wernicke's disease.

Neuropathology. The pathology of the Korsakoff and related amnesic syndromes has been reviewed by Brierley (1977) and Horel (1978) together with the classical description of the Wernicke-Korsakoff lesions by Victor et al (1971) and Victor (1976). In the Wernicke-Korsakoff group the mamillary bodies are affected in virtually every case (Harper, 1982). This is in keeping with numerous earlier studies which implicated these structures (Gamper, 1928; Grunthal, 1939; Remy, 1942; Gruner, 1956; Hecaen & de Ajuriaguerra, 1956; Malamud & Skillicorn, 1956). In some cases with mamillary body lesions cited by Victor et al (1971) there had been no amnesia in life. Victor favours the dorsomedial nuclei as the vital site. However, the two cases of Mair, Warrington and Weiskrantz (1979) showed mamillary body lesions but no major thalamic pathology. Also the claim that amnesia followed operative lesions of the dorsal thalamus (Ojemann, 1971) is not borne out by the evidence (Orchinik, 1960). All argument is confounded by the widespread pathology (Harper, 1982; Harper, Kril & Holloway, 1985).

Clinical features

1. There is a profound difficulty or total inability in acquiring new material. This deficit encompasses both verbal and non-verbal material and is also independent of the sense modality through which the material is presented. For this reason, the term *general* amnesic syndrome is used to distinguish it from the material-specific amnesias seen with unilateral lesions of the temporal lobes. Clinical tests demonstrate that material which appears to have been apprehended cannot be recalled after the passage of an unusually brief period which, in severe cases, may be down to minutes. As nothing new is learned there develops an increasing period of anterograde anmesia.

2. There is less complete agreement about the presence of retrograde amnesia but all agree that the Korsakoff patient has a profound difficulty of spontaneous recall of prior events. In endeavouring to extract a personal chronology from the patient several things are noticeable:

a. Much more information can be elicited by direct questioning than the patient can recall spontaneously;

b. The amount of information decreases as questions move closer in time to the present;

c. Some of the information has no 'time tags', i.e. its temporal relations to other happenings appears to have been lost. The 'achronogenesis' has been stressed by several writers (see Barbizet, 1970) and its presence should suggest very strongly an alcoholic aetiology.

Apart from these difficulties the patient will in the advanced stages tend to wander off the subject. Janet (1928) referred to the core of this difficulty as the 'problem of narration'.

Many clinical writers have described a temporal gradient in the sparing of memories, with those of childhood and early adult life being less affected than those of later periods. A test of the temporal gradient hypothesis by Sanders and Warrington (1971) found that the duration of the retrograde defect was very long indeed. However, more recent studies with larger samples and improved methodology have tended to give strong support to a temporal gradient theory (Seltzer & Benson, 1974; Marslen-Wilson & Teuber, 1975; Albert et al, 1979). It may be that the severity of the condition plays a major role. Korsakoff himself noted that while remote sparing was often seen, in other cases 'even the memory of remote events may be disturbed' (Victor & Yakovlev, 1955). Victor (1976) agreed that 'memories of the distant past are impaired in practically all cases of Korsakoff's psychosis and seriously impaired in most of them'.

3. An essential feature is the preservation of immediate memory, the audioverbal and visual spans being around seven.

4. Many aspects of learned behaviour are preserved. Clinical examination reveals no difficulties with speech, language, gesture and well-practised skills. There are no problems with the basic activities of daily living. However, outside a familiar environment, Korsakoff patients will get into difficulties especially if they need to incorporate new information for their behaviour to become adapted to a novel situation.

5. Confabulation had earlier been considered as necessary for the diagnosis of Korsakoff's psychosis but it is by no means a constant feature. It appears to be seen mainly in the acute state together with some confusion. Confabulation has been defined by Berlyne (1972) as 'a falsification of memory occurring in clear consciousness in association with an organically derived dementia'. It appears to be as common in dementia as it is in Korsakoff's disease and is also seen in other neurological disorders. There is some evidence that at least one form of confabulation may be related to marked deficit in frontal lobe dysfunction (Stuss et al, 1978; Kapur & Coughlan, 1980). A study by Mercer et al (1977) using objective tests found that confabulation 'proved to be strongly related to the inability to withhold responses, to monitor one's own responses and to provide verbal self-corrections'. Such a description would fit well with what is known of acute frontal lobe dysfunction. This is closely akin to the observation of experi-

enced clinicians that confabulation is directly related to the absence of insight (Zangwill, 1978). Certainly, confabulation is not a marked feature of the chronic state.

6. The patient often exhibits a lack of initiative and spontaneity together with a blunting of affect.

With regard to terminology, preoccupation in recent years with clinical and experimental studies of general anmesic syndromes has led many to write as if the terms *Korsakoff amnesic syndrome* and *Korsakoff psychosis* were synonymous. This is far from the case. While Korsakoff patients preserve many aspects of learned behaviour they demonstrate other cognitive deficits particularly those of adaptive behaviour (Bolter & Hannon, 1980; Walsh, 1985). On the other hand patients with amnesia from diencephalic lesions not related to alcohol may be free of other cognitive deficits.

Bilateral thalamic lesions

Amnesia has often been reported with tumours around the third ventricle (Smythe & Stern, 1938; Delay, Brion & Derousné, 1964; Kahn & Crosby, 1972; McEntee et al, 1976; Ziegler, Kaufman & Marshall, 1977; Lawrence, 1984; Lobosky, Vangilder & Damasio, 1984). More widespread cognitive deficits are often seen with complicating hydrocephalus as well as pressure on the diencephalon. Because of their complex physiological effects these cases are unhelpful in differentiating brain-behaviour relationships.

More helpful are a number of recent single case reports of bilateral paramedian thalamic infarcts in which severe non-specific anterograde amnesia has dominated the clinical picture (Mills & Swanson, 1978; Cramon & Zihl, 1979; Schott et al, 1980; Barbizet et al, 1981; Walsh, 1982, 1985; Winocur et al, 1984). CT scan has confirmed the presence of symmetrical infarcts and, in the author's case, autopsy evidence was available. It is probable that the bilateral infarcts arise because of the origin in some cases of the two paramedian thalamosubthalamic arteries from a common trunk (Percheron, 1976; Castaigne et al, 1981). Except in two or three cases neuropsychological evidence is scanty. The free recall of one case (Winocur et al, 1984) was nil at 5 minutes over many testings but recognition on a multiple choice test was always 'rapid and perfect' even after delays exceeding 24 hours. A second case followed over several years (Walsh, 1982, 1985) demonstrated marked dissociation between free recall and cued recall suggestive of relatively spared recognition memory. However, the patient performed differently on sundry measures of recognition memory compared with normals though not nearly as severe as the modal Korsakoff patient.

Thalamic dementia. Extensive bilateral damage to the thalamus usually from infarction may result in a drastic reduction in the patient's ability to function intellectually. The sudden onset of coma is followed by a period of stupor and confusion which after a further period is followed by a devastating combination of marked disorders of attention, memory, language, movement and affect (for review, see Cambier & Graveleau, 1985).

Aneurysmal amnesia

Amnesia following subarachnoid haemorrhage has been reported in a small percentage of cases since 1921 (Flateau, 1921; Tarachow, 1939; Walton, 1953) but its specific association with anterior communicating artery aneurysms came much later (Norlén & Olivecrona, 1953; Lindqvist & Norlén, 1966; Logue et al, 1968; Sengupta, Chiu & Brierly, 1975; Luria, 1976). After a period of confusion and subsequent anterograde amnesia many patients go on to complete recovery. A few are left with lasting severe amnesia. Detailed specification of the form of amnesia has been attempted in only a few instances (Luria, 1976; Talland, Sweet & Ballantine, 1967; Brion et al, 1968) the clearest being two recent cases (Volpe & Hirst, 1983b). Apart from the 'core' symptoms of preserved immediate memory and a non-specific anterograde amnesia the cases are marked by great susceptibility to proactive interference and differentially better recognition memory than free recall with some benefit from cued recall. However, a study of seven such patients (Kinsella & Clausen, 1982) employing the material and methods of a previous study of Korsakoff amnesics (Cermak, Butters & Moreines, 1974) showed a clear qualitative difference between the two groups. Unlike the Korsakoff patients the aneurysmal cases employed semantic encoding in much the same way as normal subjects.

This form of amnesia is considered here for convenience although the lesions may lie in part or in whole outside the diencephalon. The review of Gade (1982) implicates the penetrating vessels which supply deep midline structures as the probable mechanism. It may be that both septal and diencephalic structures are involved.

Amnesic syndrome — one or many?

It must now be apparent that lesions in several sites in the brain can cause difficulty with memory and learning. While these cases of differing aetiologies and different lesion sites share the core features of a general amnesia there is growing evidence that the Gestalt of deficits varies significantly with the locus of lesion (Whitty & Zangwill, 1977; Moscovitch, 1982; Butters et al, 1984). 'The unitary character of the organic amnesic syndrome was always a rather dubious assumption and it is now seriously in question' (Piercy, 1977, p. 145). The fact that different aspects of memory and learning processes may be dissociated by lesions in different locations is the clearest evidence for such a position. It will not be practicable to review all the evidence but some of the highlights will be presented. This will do a disservice to the complexity of the evidence especially as it refers to different theoretical positions regarding the amnesic syndrome or syndromes. For the latter, such reviews as that of Meudell and Mayes (1982) are recommended. The following brief sketch will outline only some of the major features of clinicopathological relationships.

The problem of classification of amnesias has much in common with the classification of other disorders, e.g. aphasia, where many cases share common features but characteristic patterns of the basic disorder vary with different anatomical lesion sites. Whether the different configurations should be designated as independent syndromes or as sub-types of a general amnesic disorder is perhaps a matter of terminology. Knowledge of these emerging differences will not only inform us about the regional contributions to different processes in the complex acts of memorization and recall but might also suggest appropriate strategies for management and remediation of amnesic patients. This biological factor analysis depends on detailed examination of cases with 'anatomically clean' lesions, an unfortunately rare event.

The first important difference between amnesic groups was reported by Lhermitte and Signoret (1972). Following Zangwill's early suggestion (1943) that different forms of the amnesic syndrome might exist according to the locus of lesion they compared post encephalitic patients (hippocampal damage) with Korsakoff patients (mamillo-thalamic damage) on a series of tasks. Two of these required the learning of the position of nine stimuli in a three by three array. In the first form of the tasks (Spatial Arrangement) the stimuli were pictures of common objects while the second (Logical Arrangement) consisted of geometrical shapes ordered according to a logical matrix of colour, shape and number. The two groups showed clear differences which we have replicated on numerous occasions. On the first task both groups showed poor acquisition and virtually no free recall even with a short delay. However, the alcoholic subjects benefited markedly with the type of cued recall used while the encephalitic subjects showed no benefit. On the other hand the encephalitic subjects learned the logical matrix with the ease of normal subjects whereas the alcoholic subjects were totally unable to do so and there were further differences on the other tasks used.

While it was suggested that the differences were related to the two major anatomical sites, it is just as plausible to link the observed differences to the presence of associated pathology in the Korsakoff group which gives rise to the difficulty with conceptual operations which form an essential part of the requirements for the Logical Arrangement task and other tasks employed (Talland, 1965; Bolter & Hannon, 1980; Walsh, 1985).

The encephalitic group being free of such pathology had no difficulty with the conceptual tasks. This proposal is strengthened by our observation that the Logical Arrangement task presents great difficulty for alcoholic subjects in the absence of clinical or experimental evidence of memory disorder.

Other studies have confirmed the presence of simultaneous deficits in two or more independent psychological processes in the alcohol-related amnesic disorder (Mattis, Kovner & Goldmeier, 1978; Kovner et al, 1981; Squire, 1981).

Perhaps the most consistent group difference has been with measures of forgetting. Huppert and Piercy (1979, 1982, 1983) compared the speed of forgetting of H.M., whose lesions were wholly or largely hippocampal, with Korsakoff patients. The latter group showed that once the material was learnt subsequent forgetting was at a normal rate whereas H.M. showed a higher rate of forgetting. Squire (1981) confirmed the normal forgetting rate of Korsakoff patients and reported the same for the stab wound case N.A., mentioned below, also with diencephalic damage. His study of patients following ECT, however, showed rapid forgetting for which he postulated hippocampal dysfunction. More recently, Butters et al (1984) described a patient, R.B., with aneurysmal amnesia who showed a 'precipitous decline' in recall on a STM task between 15 and 30 seconds though he had actually been superior to the controls at 15 seconds.

Finally, different groups of amnesic subjects differ in the degree to which remote memory is affected. H.M. showed only a limited deficit (Scoville & Milner, 1957; Milner, 1966; Milner, 1970) as did patients following ECT (Cohen & Squire, 1981; Squire, 1981; Squire & Cohen, 1982) and cases N.A., R.B. and L.N. (Walsh, 1985) with localized diencephalic lesions. Post-encephalitic patients vary greatly, some showing little and others marked retrograde amnesia. Thus lesions restricted to the diencephalon or hippocampus may produce relatively short retrograde amnesia and the longer retrograde amnesia of the Korsakoff patient and some post-encephalitics may reflect more widespread pathology in these conditions. As yet there is little anatomical information on the few unusual cases claiming prolonged retrograde amnesia in the absence of any considerable anterograde deficit (Goldberg et al, 1981).

The multiple dissociations within the amnesias are further reviewed by Moscovitch (1982). The general tenor of the evidence would support a distinction between two patterns of amnesic disorder one hippocampal which may affect storage of information and the other diencephalic which may affect encoding or acquisition (Winocur et al, 1984). This point of view is well supported by the comprehensive review of Parkin (1984).

It appears that memory may be affected differently by lesions in different locations and that we are still far from clear as to which structures, or sets of structures, form the essential substrate for particular aspects of the total process. Though it has been argued that certain structures such as the hippocampus, mamillary bodies and thalamic nuclei are vital there are enough negative instances, i.e. where damage to these structures did *not* produce amnesia, to hold a simplistic view (for review, see Markowitsch, 1984). All we may say with certainty is that lasting amnesia commonly follows bilateral damage to certain of the structures shown in the crude

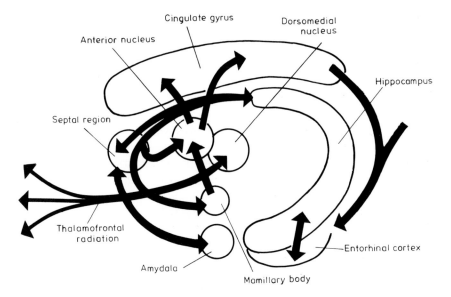

Fig. 9.3 Some of the structures which are involved in the neural substrate of memory.

diagram (Figure 9.3). What is perhaps most surprising is the absence of amnesic disorder with bilateral severing of such major fibre pathways as the fornix.

Preserved learning in amnesia

It has been known for two decades (Corkin, 1965, 1968) that motor learning may be intact in amnesia after bi-temporal lesions. Other tasks without a significant motor component may also be preserved (Cohen & Squire, 1980; Cohen & Corkin, 1981; Wood, Ebert & Kinsbourne, 1982). The evidence is reviewed by Parkin (1982).

Unilateral thalamic damage

Specific memory loss

Memory disturbance often accompanies thalamic aphasia the usual cause of which is intracerebral haemorrhage (see below). Discrete lesions may also produce amnesia and this follows the material specificity shown with unilateral medial temporal lobe lesions outlined in Chapter 5.

Speedie and Heilman (1982) reported a case of unilateral infarction in the left thalamus in a 33-year-old man. Following the sudden onset of confusion and disorientation the patient was unable to remember anything. The confusion cleared leaving him with a severe verbal anterograde amnesia with normal visual recognition memory. Another case with right unilateral thalamic infarction affecting most of the dorsomedial nucleus (Speedie & Heilman, 1983) showed an anterograde amnesia for visuospatial material with preserved verbal acquisition. Both cases also showed some 'frontal' signs.

Five cases of thalamic infarction, three left-sided and two right-sided, reported by Graff-Radford et al (1984) support the differential role of the two thalami in memory functions though the cases were all accompanied by other abnormalities of intellect and personality and best fit into the category of thalamic dementia.

A unique case of a stab wound involving the left dorsal thalamus has been reported over many years (Teuber & Milner, 1968; Squire & Slater, 1978; Squire & Moore, 1979). The evidence of location is derived from CT scan so that precise anatomical definition is not possible. Nevertheless, the case shows sparing of perception, cognition and vigilance in the presence of a largely verbal-specific amnesia. This patient also showed paralysis of upward gaze as reported in many bilateral thalamic infarcts with memory loss, arguing for a similar location of lesion. This case and that of Speedie and Heilman (1982) showed difficulty with complex non-verbal material (the Rey Figure) but not with simple material. Such a difficulty has also been described with amnesia arising from left posterior cerebral artery lesions (Signoret & Lhermitte, 1976). It may be due largely to a deficit in verbal encoding used when the material becomes complex.

The study of patients undergoing thalamotomy for movement disorders provides added support for dissociation of function between the two sides of the thalamus (Krayenbuhl et al, 1965; Ojemann, Hoyenga & Ward, 1968; Shapiro et al, 1973). Likewise stimulation at the time of operation lends further support (Ojemann & Fedio, 1968; Ojemann, 1971, 1977, 1979; Ojemann, Blick & Ward, 1971; Fedio & Van Buren, 1975). A comprehensive review is provided by Mateer and Ojemann (1983).

Thalamic aphasia

There had been a number of early reports of language disturbance with thalamic haemorrhage but the systematic examination of thalamic aphasia possibly dates from the paper of Fisher (1959). In the past two decades numerous studies of *left* thalamic haemorrhage have confirmed the presence of aphasia (which is not normally seen with *right* thalamic haemorrhage) and clarified the characteristics of the disorder (Ciemens, 1970; Fazio, Sacco & Bugiani, 1973; Samarel et al, 1976; Walshe, Davis & Fischer, 1977; Elghozi et al, 1978; Cappa & Vignola, 1979; Mazaux et al, 1979; Mazaux & Orgogozo, 1982). One case of aphasia with right thalamic haemorrhage occurred in a left-handed person (Kirschner & Kistler, 1982).

It has been argued that haemorrhagic lesions have widespread effects which might be responsible for the aphasia rather than just the thalamic disruption and this is supported by the observation that aphasia in these cases improved markedly with time. More convincing are the cases of ischaemia or infarction in the left thalamus though these instances are rare (Elghozi et al, 1978; Speedie & Heilman, 1982, 1983; Graff-Radford et al, 1984).

In thalamic aphasia the emphasis is on expressive speech. While comprehension may be affected it is seldom a major feature. At the outset there may be complete arrest of speech but this soon disappears to leave a condition where the patient has difficulty with volume control. The patient speaks softly and there is verbal adynamia whereby the patient volunteers little or nothing replying only to direct questions. There are semantic paraphasias both in spontaneous speech and on attempting to name objects. Disruption of the ordering of ideas coupled with perseveration of words and phrases may render speech incoherent.

Improvement of language is the rule but verbal adynamia and sometimes the associated verbal memory deficit may persist.

Thalamic neglect

Although unilateral neglect has been studied over a long period (see Chapter 6) contralateral neglect was first reported in three cases with *right* thalamic haemorrhage by Watson and Heilman (1979). The patients also showed limb akinesia, visuospatial disorders, anosognosia and emotional flattening. Shortly after Cambier, Elghozi and Strube (1980) reported three more cases, two with haemorrhage and one with infarction of the right thalamus, all of whom had 'massive left visual neglect' without aphasia. The cases did, however, show 'excessive spontaneous verbalization and . . . luxuriant answers to the most trivial question' (Cambier & Graveleau, 1985, p. 88). We have observed this phenomenon in some right hemisphere cases with lesions affecting the right cerebral artery territory.

Cambier et al, (1982) attribute the multimodal neglect seen with infarction from right posterior cerebral artery occlusion to the thalamus.

In summarizing this brief review one might say that there is emerging evidence that the asymmetry of function so characteristic of the cerebral hemispheres extends to embrace the interbrain and thus lend further support to the notion of extended functional systems. It still remains to learn more about the role of corticosubcortical connections.

10

Neuropsychological assessment

General considerations   330
The neuropsychological syndrome   338
Case examples   340

GENERAL CONSIDERATIONS

The search for single tests of 'organicity' or 'brain damage' is now only of historical interest to most neuropsychologists. Earlier reviews dealt adequately with the shortcomings of this approach (Yates, 1954; Meyer, 1957; Smith, 1982a; Yates, 1966; Kinsbourne, 1971; Reitan & Davison, 1974). This is not to say that cerebral lesions do not have generalized or non-specific effects. Long ago Yates (1966) pointed out that brain damage may produce different types of effect in any individual: (i) a general deterioration in all aspects of functioning; (ii) differential (group) effects, depending on the location, extent etc. of the damage and (iii) highly specific effects in certain locations. It is sometimes forgotten that each of these needs to be taken into account when inferring the reason for poor test performance.

Another uncritically accepted notion, and one that has died hard, is the assumption that a test validated on clearly defined groups must be useful for the everyday task of clinical diagnosis. Tests validated in this way may have low predictive validity. If it can identify 'only those subjects whose brain damage is obvious, then the test serves no useful purpose, since it confirms what needs no confirmation' (Yates, 1966). Study of the literature had led Heilbrun (1962) to observe that a significant proportion of predictive hits seemed to come from those instances in which the neurological symptoms were fairly clear. 'A crucial study would be one in which the neurological group is made up entirely of subjects for whom neurologists disagree as to diagnosis or are unable to make a diagnostic statement at all at the time the psychological measure is obtained and for whom retrospective diagnosis is possible' (Heilbrun, 1962, p. 513). Such predictive validity studies are few in number. One such study is that of Matthews, Shaw and Klove (1966). These workers tested the predictive validity of a number of measures from the Halstead-Reitan Battery and the Wechsler scales on a group of subjects all of whom were initially suspected of neurological disease but in whom only half were subsequently confirmed as neurological, the other half being allotted to a non-neurological diagnosis. The authors rather nicely refer to the latter group as 'pseudoneurologic'. Even in this more difficult diagnostic situation, some of the measures discriminated at a high level. Further treatment of this topic with illustrative cases is given in Walsh (1985).

Another shortcoming of psychological studies in this area might be termed the principle of multiple determination. 'Behavioural deficits are defined in terms of impaired test performance. But impaired test performance may be a final common pathway for expression of quite diverse types of impairment.' (Kinsbourne, 1972). Smith (1975) takes as an example what is probably the test most frequently reported as showing decrement with brain damage in sundry forms and locations, namely the Digit-Symbol Substitution Test, 'the responses are the end product of the integration of visual perceptual, oculomotor, fine manual motor and mental functions.' It is therefore important to be aware that low scores on this test may be due to disturbance in any of the functions involved or any combination of them. It is unfortunate that not only are so many tests in common use in neuropsychology multifactorial in nature but, in most cases, the nature of the functions which determine a successful outcome is unknown. Two methods suggest themselves if we are constrained to use factorially complex tests. These are (i) to observe the sharing of variance between a patient's performance on sundry tests, and (ii) the 'experimental' testing of hypotheses about the various possible reasons for failure. In the latter instance the practitioner will be helped by a sound knowledge of the corpus of knowledge in neuropsychology.

Closely allied to the notion of multiple determination is that of multiple pathways to the goal. Many psychological tests are concerned solely with whether or not the subject can reach the goal. 'The flexibility of cerebral mechanisms is such that the solution of most test items can be reached by many devious routes. The method the subject uses in tackling a problem will in general provide more information as to the character of a skill or of a psychological deficit than will the knowledge as to the subject's success or failure' (Elithorn, 1965). Qualitative observations are of paramount value and no amount of quantification will, at times, override the importance of the psychologist as an observer of behaviour.

Roles for neuropsychological assessment

The two major roles of the clinical neuropsychologist, namely diagnosis and evaluation, are difficult to separate. It should be remembered that the clinical neuropsychologist is seldom in the position of being asked to provide a definitive diagnosis. However, it will be argued that if he accepts the role of applied scientist rather than technician he will be in the position of offering what at times is crucial information with regard to diagnosis. The neuropsychological examination is an integral part of the neurological examination and must be seen in this context. It would be valuable if sensitive behavioural measures could be refined so as to promote the earlier diagnosis of some cerebral lesions. There is encouraging evidence that behavioural measures may be able to detect impairment which is too subtle to be detected by many current neurological procedures, e.g. CT scan which depends on the detection of *structural* alterations in the brain.

The second role lies in the assessment of cases where the diagnosis has already been verified. A systematic and comprehensive documentation of the patient's mental functions is of value in following the progress of patients suffering from craniocerebral trauma, cerebrovascular disorders and the numerous other neurological conditions in which mental symptoms form a prominent part. This role should not be thought of simply as a mechanical documentation but rather the examinations should be seen as providing *understanding* of the ways in which the neurological condition has affected the individual patient. This understanding forms the basis for advice on medical management and rehabilitation and for counselling the patient and relatives about the effects of the disorder.

Neuropsychological assessment also provides an important method of evaluating various forms of medical, surgical, and psychological treatment including cognitive rehabilitation.

Symptoms and syndromes

The significance of a patient's symptoms and signs can be understood in the context of the notion of a functional system (Ch. 1). A functional system in the brain consists of a number of parts of the brain, particularly but not exclusively cortical together with their fibre connections. The system operates in a concerted manner to form the substratum of a complex psychological function. This systemic concept allows a new approach to the use of psychological tests in the diagnosis or assessment of neurological conditions, an approach which parallels the study of other bodily systems.

It will be apparent that if a psychological process is served by an anatomical system which is spread out in the brain then the psychological process will be vulnerable at a number of different points some of which may be widely separated. Such a finding was, in fact, one of the seemingly powerful arguments used against the early localizationists. If, for example, speaking or writing or perceiving could be altered by lesions in sundry locations, then these functions could not be localized. The argument turns, of course, on what is meant by 'localized'.

The modern notion of a functional system also incorporates the notion of regional specialization within the system and it is this which increases its value both in theoretical explanation as well as application to the individual case. While damage anywhere in the system will lead to some change in the function which the system subserves, the *nature* of the change will be dependent upon the particular part of the system which is damaged or the set of connections which has been disrupted since each part contributes something characteristic to the whole. It is thus necessary to look carefully at the *nature* of the changes in a psychological function to determine how they are related to the location and character of the lesion.

This multiple significance of what appears at first to be the same symptom or symptom complex begins to render meaningful the apparently conflicting findings of many early studies and, at the same time, allows symptoms or signs to have localizing value. To take a common example, psychologists have long observed that the Kohs block design test is often performed poorly by many, but certainly not all, brain-damaged subjects. Poor performance on this test could result from a disruption of what might rather loosely be termed constructional praxis. It could also be performed poorly because of visual and other difficulties but if these are excluded and poor performance of the block design task is taken as an operational definition of constructional apraxia, the regional significance still remains to be determined. Here *qualitative* observations are of help. For example, constructional deviations where the patient fails to conform to the square framework are observed most strikingly in patients with posterior lesions, particularly right sided. Constructional deviations are particularly prominent in right hemisphere lesions and markedly so where there is a posterior locus. Ben Yishay et al (1971) have described these errors in terms of deviation from the square format of the design to be copied: 'broken squares; rectangles; linearly placed horizontally, vertically, diagonally; irregular shapes — patterns wherein the individual blocks are improperly aligned with respect to one another and with the horizontal and vertical planes.'

An equally poor score on the block design test may be obtained by a second patient with a frontal lesion. However, such a patient will usually show few constructional deviations and his difficulty may be shown to be dependent upon incomplete preliminary investigation of the problem as in the case examined by Luria and Tsvetkova (1964) cited in Chapter 4. In this case the frontal patient is helped by the provision of a design card upon which the outlines of the four (or more) constituent blocks have been drawn. On the other hand the right parietal patient tends to benefit little from this procedure. The 'partially solved' block design problem apparently has no more meaning in his shattered visuospatial world than the original. As mentioned elsewhere the nature of the observations which will be of value and the tests which will be applied must rest on a knowledge of the findings emerging from research studies.

Face validity and the seductive inference

There is a danger in assuming that if a patient fails on a test then that patient has a deficiency in the psychological function stated by the manual to be what the test measures.

A simple example of making the wrong inference might be as follows: the patient produces a poor score on a memory for designs test, e.g. the Benton Visual Retention Test and this is often reported as a 'visual memory deficit'. On occasion we have seen this extended to the further inference that 'the patient shows poor visual memory suggesting impairment of the right hemisphere' or, even more specifically, 'the patient shows differentially poor visual memory with normal verbal memory suggesting impairment of the right temporal region'. However, in the form given the memory for designs test may have relied on the patient drawing the remembered stimulus. Thus one of the possible reasons for failure could be an executive or graphic difficulty, i.e. the reason for failure is the same as the reason the patient fails on other tasks with a constructional element. Awareness of such a possibility would prompt the use of a task where the constructional element has been removed, e.g. the multiple choice version of the BVRT. Here the subject is shown a design and then must select it some time later from a multiple choice array which contains the item plus three distractors. The same logic applies, *mutatis mutandis*, to the examination of other possible causes for poor performance, e.g. perceptual difficulties.

Another example might be termed *the right hemisphere hypothesis*. Some have claimed, for example, that because chronic alcoholics perform poorly on tests usually considered sensitive to right hemisphere pathology, alcohol has a greater effect on the right hemisphere than the left. Miller (1983) cites two similar examples in the literature, one of which was very similar to the hypothesis about alcohol-related brain damage, namely that since normal aged subjects did less well on tests sensitive to right hemisphere pathology, the right hemisphere ages more rapidly than the left.

This *paralogical thinking* is exploded nicely by Miller:

> If damage to structure X is known to produce a decline in performance on test T it is tempting to argue that any new subject or group of subjects, having a relatively poor performance on T must have a lesion at X. In fact, the logical status of this argument is the same as arguing that because a horse meets the test of being a large animal with four legs that any newly encounterd large animal with four legs must be a horse. The newly encountered speciman could of course be a cow or hippopotamus and still meet the same test. Similarly, new subjects who do badly on T *may do so for reasons other than having a lesion at X* (Miller, 1983, p. 131. Emphasis added).

Sharing of variance

What at first may appear to be a broad pattern of failures may, on closer examination turn out to be the reflection of a common disorder which contributes to failure on seemingly disparate tests. The magnitude of the failure on separate tests will be a reflection of the degree to which the disturbed function is represened in their composition. It is for this reason that emphasis has been placed on the importance of the quality of responses as well as their level since the former will give valuable clues as to which factor (or factors) has led to the poor performance. In most situations only a small number of functional disturbances will account for the many observed deficits in performance. In attempting to explain them it is wise to remember that the law of parsimony has never been repealed.

Hypothesis testing in the single case

One serious drawback to almost every purely quantitative approach to neuropsychological evaluation is the loss of information. Shapiro (1951) quoted Schafer: 'A test response is not a score; scores, where applicable, are abstractions designed to facilitate intra-individual and inter-individual comparisons, and as such they are extremely useful in clinical testing. However, to reason — or do research — only in terms of scores or score patterns is to do violence to the nature of the raw material. *The scores do not communicate the reponses in full*' (emphasis added). Reitan's (1964) study mentioned in Chapter 4 shows clearly that, utilizing the same test data, clinical prediction can be superior to formal or psychometric methods. This may have been due to loss of qualitative features in individual responses or complex *intra-individual* patterns of response lost when only levels of performance were used. Shapiro has also pointed out some of the major difficulties and limitations inherent in the application of standardized validated tests in the clinical diagnostic setting. His comments are as pertinent today as they were 30 years ago though, as he pointed out more recently (Shapiro, 1973), very few serious attempts have been made in the intervening period to overcome these difficulties by application of his recommended solution, namely, the experimental investigation of the single case. It may be that the few published studies cited by Shapiro do not represent fully the clinical use of the method. The fact that it lends itself particularly well to the neuropsychological elucidation of syndromes was shown in the work of Luria and other European workers.

The whole process was summarized succinctly by Shapiro (1973). After reminding us of the scientific concept of error in psychological measurement, he argued that this should prevent us from making unwarranted generalizations from the data but should not prevent us from using observations in a systematic way to advance our understanding of the individual case.

The awareness of error makes us look upon any psychological observation not as something conclusive but as the basis of one or more hypotheses about the patient. One's degree of confidence in any hypothesis suggested by an observation would depend upon the established degree of validity of that observation and upon other information about the patient concerned.

If one or more hypotheses are suggested by an observation, then steps must be taken to test them. In this way further observations are accumulated in a systematic manner. It should then become possible to arrive at a psychological description in which we can have greater confidence. The additional observations may in turn suggest new hypotheses which have in turn to be tested. We are thus led to the method of the systematic investigation as a means of improving the validity or our conclusions about an individual patient (Shapiro, 1973, p.651).

Working hypotheses may arise from generalizations which have emerged from the research literature. Clinical neuropsychology is becoming very rich in this regard as evidenced by the sample provided in Chapters 4–9 which, while representative, is far from exhaustive. As this work grows, converging lines of evidence make the generalizations more secure and thus facilitate the implementation of crucial tests of the various hypotheses, e.g. the evidence on asymmetry of hemispheric function has made the testing of laterality of lesions more open to systematic investigation.

Despite his strong advocacy, even Shapiro considered that this method might not have strong appeal since it could tend to be time consuming. In practice however, it tends to be more economical than the application of a fixed battery of tests since many of these prove irrelevant to the questions being asked. Since in clinical practice certain questions tend to recur frequently, trainees quite soon recognize the most likely hypotheses and the most productive tests to be used in particular situations. Subsequent case evaluation in the light of neurological or neurosurgical knowledge continually improves the process.

In busy clinical practice, time is an expensive commodity and on some occasions the clinician has to tender an opinion after less than an ideal examination of the patient. In this situation his report should make it clear to the referring source that the opinion consists 'of the hypotheses which the applied scientist thinks best account for the data at his disposal, and which he would choose to test next time if he had sufficient time and suitable means' (Shapiro, 1973, p. 652). The term *suitable means* often takes the form of appropriate tests. In some cases these do not exist but this situation is becoming rare as neuropsychology develops and clinicians working in a particular field are likely to acquire the tests which prove useful in answering the most common hypotheses. Very popular standardized tests such as the Wechsler Memory Scale may well provide the central hypothesis which can then be tested by other procedures. Sometimes the whole or part of the answer lies in testing that has already been carried out on the standardized tests. Psychologists trained in one of the psychometric traditions often ask what are the newest or latest tests for brain damage. It can be pointed out that they already have signficant information in the tests they commonly employ but, being largely unaware of the developments in neuropsychology, they are unable to recognize its significance.

As Ley (1970) comments, the criticism that the method is time-consuming is valid 'only in so far as one thinks that: (i) the method will produce findings of sufficient value, and (ii) that there are more valuable things for clinical psychologists to do.' Economy of time must be seen in relation to the importance of the question being asked.

As referring agencies become more sophisticated neuropsychologically they are more likely to present quite specific hypotheses for investigation. The following example from the companion volume (Walsh, 1985) illustrates such a referral. The neurologist wrote: 'Does this patient have an amnesia to which she is not entitled?' Though not expressly stated, the neuropsychologist is being asked to study the patient's hospital file. Perusal of this record revealed the following: A 56-year-old housewife had a history of episodes of sudden detachment from reality, staring eyes and lack of awareness of her surroundings, each episode lasting about 2 minutes. The episodes had commenced shortly after a head injury 15 years before when she was struck on the right temple. EEG recordings had consistently shown the presence of a left temporal focus with no electrical abnormality on the right side. All attempts to control the attacks with drug therapy had failed and the patient was proposed as a candidate for left unilateral temporal lobectomy. Depth electrodes strongly confirmed the presence of a left medial temporal focus. It was at this stage that the referral question was put.

The question thus placed in its context assumes that the neuropsychologist is familiar with the literature related to the question. The neurologist will not be surprised if the patient shows a differentially weaker verbal than non-verbal memory performance in line with the proven double dissociation shown with lateralized temporal lobe lesions between verbal and non-verbal material. This would be a deficit to which the patient would be 'entitled' by virtue of a left medial temporal lesion. However, a 'non-entitled' deficit of *non-verbal* memory would signal possible dysfunction in the right temporal region. This dysfunction might be silent to neurological examination since in the case of an atrophic lesion, the area may be electrically silent, i.e. a normal EEG on the right side would not exclude pathology.

The import of finding a non-entitled neuropsychological deficit would have the utmost significance since surgical ablation of the electrically active focus in the left temporal lobe would be added to the atrophic damage in the previously unsuspected right side. Functionally, this would be equivalent to bilateral medial temporal damage, a condition which produces a general, profound and lasting amnesic syndrome. Hence, the finding of a amnesia to which the patient was not entitled would be a clear contraindication to surgery.

In this case the neuropsychological examination did show minor difficulty with one aspect of new verbal learning though verbal short term memory,

memory for prose material and other verbal intelligence measures were at an appropriate level. However, the patient clearly had much more difficulty with non-verbal memory together with evidence of constructional dyspraxia due to more widespread right hemisphere disruption of function. It seemed that the proposed surgery ran the risk of producing a general amnesic syndrome. At this stage the patient died suddenly and at autopsy the site of the left-sided irritative focus was of normal appearance while the electrically-silent right side was atrophic in the hippocampal region. To operate would have been to produce a devastating amnesic disorder.

Such a fruitful collaboration can only be achieved by effective communication via carefully written reports, case discussions and didactic presentations.

THE NEUROPSYCHOLOGICAL SYNDROME

Deriving as it does largely from the broad base of clinical neurology, the concept of a syndrome plays a central role in the thinking of clinical neuropsychology. Central to the concept of the syndrome is the sense of a unique constellation of signs and symptoms which occur together frequently enough to suggest a particular underlying process. The signs and symptoms, it is inferred have a greater mutual concordance than each possesses in relation to other signs and symptoms. Thus a true syndrome should be capable of being confirmed by appropriate statistical analysis on the strength of the mutual interrelationships. Not all the signs and symptoms are of equal importance and the weighting of the different elements is often an idiosyncratic process 'being unformulated outcome of the interaction of medical instruction and clinical experience' (Kinsbourne, 1971).

It is now several decades since English workers suggested that the syndrome concept should be used in the area of cerebral impairment:

> The assessment of intellectual deterioration calls, not for single valid standardization test, but rather for a flexible test procedure and awareness of the relevant syndromes. This view is justified by a consideration of the multiform effects on intellectual performance of focal and diffuse cerebral lesions and also by a consideration of the focal disturbance of intellectual function already recognized by neurologists and utilized in diagnosis (Piercy, 1959).

> As far as cases of suspected cerebral lesion are concerned, the psychologist can tell the neurologist whether or not the patient's performances resembles that of a typical case of a lesion in one of the major cerebral lobes; the neurologist can then combine the information with evidence from other procedures in arriving at his assessment (McFie, 1960).

Neuropsychologists should be concerned with pattern of impairment and as their knowledge of syndromes increases they will, when confronted with certain symptoms and signs, look for the association of other features to confirm or disconfirm the presence of a particular syndrome.

This is the medical model of *differential diagnosis*. For the method to work effectively in clinical practice knowledge is required in three areas: (i) the corpus of fact in human neuropsychology; (ii) an acquaintance with relevant principles and details of allied clinical neurosciences especially clinical neurology, neuroanatomy and neuropathology; (iii) psychological test theory and practice.

Syndromes also vary a good deal in their degree of specificity or vagueness. The frontal lobe syndrome is a much more general working term than, say, the general amnesic syndrome. One of the reasons for this generality may be the grouping together of a number of functionally different areas particularly if these are affected simultaneously by one pathological process. However, if the term syndrome is used in an extremely broad sense then it fails to have meaning. One such usage was the term 'chronic brain syndrome'. Geschwind (1978) commented: 'My objections to the term is that is carries an implication, however many qualificiations are put on it, that there is such a thing as a single organic brain syndrome, something for which there is no evidence. The brain is the most complicated organ in the body, and thus one can expect many syndromes with different manifestations.'

Finally, it is essential to stress that it is the total configuration or *Gestalt* which imparts significance. A syndrome is, indeed, more than (or other than) the sum of its individual constituents. It is useful working fiction which allows us to create some order out of the complexity of the patient's subjective complaints and the findings of our examinations. Knowledge of a variety of syndromes allows us to generate hypotheses about the nature of the disruptions of function in the individual case.

The method of extreme cases

The method employed in our own unit is essentially what Kraepelin called 'the method of extreme cases' (Zangwill, 1978). In the early stages of training emphasis is placed on introducing the developing neuropsychologist to a wide variety of syndromes in their clear-cut form both in terms of clinical presentation and in deficits on test performance, i.e. classical or *extreme* cases. When these can be recognized with ease more subtle and more complex cases are introduced to teach the range of variation that might be encountered in clinical practice. We have found that this method facilitates the recognition of syndromes in their less dramatic or latent forms and makes it possible to detect characteristic patterns of neuropsychological deficit in their early stages of development.

Selecting the tools

Knowledge of syndromes and brain-behaviour relationships will be the principal factor in determining the selection of tools. Certain of these will be employed on an almost daily basis in answering commonly occurring questions. However, there will be questions or hypotheses which will require 'special' tools which will produce pathognomonic data. Test selection should be germane to the questions asked so that the experienced neuropsychologist will gradually develop quite a large armamentarium from which to choose. While developing this arsenal trainee practitioners will find an encyclopaedic source of test data and wisdom in Lezak (1983). To this and other textual sources they should add a personal store of further qualitative observations. Such test familiarity is necessary for the rapid and economic evaluation associated with the branching decision-making process which is the basis of clinical evaluation using a flexible or individualized method.

The selection of tests may entail a one-step process, i.e. a group of tests is chosen in the belief that these will provide the information needed to answer the questions. Sometimes the issues will remain unresolved but observations derived from the primary set of tests may suggest that further specific tests may provide the answer, i.e. a stepwise approach will be used by many. Much of the efficacy of this method turns on the selection of the primary group of tests since the use of tests which do not touch the problem at all will give apparently negative results. In reporting such negative results it is important to inform the referral agency that 'nothing abnormal was detected with the tests used'. It is of help to colleagues familiar with psychological tests to specify exactly which were used. They should certainly be documented in hospital practice and in medicolegal cases. Unfortunately, negative reports are often written which contain the implication that no impairment is present. We should bear in mind Teuber's dictum 'absence of evidence is not evidence of absence' (of impairment). Russell (1982) points out that the entire controversy between fixed versus flexible tests hinges on a single rather obvious principle that is axiomatic to neuropsychology: *'one cannot determine whether a certain function of the brain is impaired unless that function is tested.'*

CASE EXAMPLES

For the purpose of exposition in a general textbook the following case extracts are of necessity brief. They are included to exemplify just a few of the wide range of questions currently being asked of neuropsychologists. In each case the presented data is restricted mostly to a few widely known tests. It is difficult to do justice to even the most straightforward case in a brief span but each case has a point to make. As such experience accumulates the clinician develops an ever widening and consolidating frame of reference against which to make future judgments.

Korsakoff psychosis

Case: YW
Age: 49
Education: Teaching certificates
Occupation: Primary school principal

A year before his assessment, YW had suffered a 'nervous breakdown' when he was unable to remember certain commitments as head of a rural school. Soon after hospitalization a CT scan revealed cerebral atrophy and a diagnosis of Korsakoff psychosis was made and he was hospitalized for treatment of his alcoholism and had been abstinent since that time. Neuropsychological assessment was requested as part of the decision as to whether he might be able to return to work or whether he should be retired.

YW began drinking in his early twenties and gradually increased his consumption of beer on a daily basis in the rural towns where he spent his professional life. He had never appreciated that he was drinking to excess and managed to obtain higher teaching certificates over the years. He was never absent from work until the final episode which brought him under attention. At this time he was consuming more than 2 litres of wine per day.

He presented as an alert co-operative man well aware of his condition over which he showed realistic concern. He said he was strongly motivated to return to work but knew that his memory was poor though somewhat improved since be became abstinent. He writes down everything he has to remember but there was no evidence of how effective this strategy had been.

The Wechsler Memory Scale (WMS) and the Wechsler Adult Intelligence Scale (WAIS) immediately revealed the extent of his difficulties.

WMS Form I

Information	3	Digits Total	13 (7,6)
Orientation	5	Visual Reproduction	8
Mental Control	9	Associate Learning	9
Memory Passages	4.5 (5,4)		(5,0; 6,0; 5,1)
M.Q.	94		

This revealed the features of a general amnesic syndrome. YW was well oriented though confused on questions of current political leaders. In

Note: The designation 5,0; 6,0; 5,1 refers to performance on the learning of the 10 pairs of the verbal paired associate learning task where six pairs have logical associations requiring the relearning of old associations (e.g., baby — cries) and four pairs require the learning of novel associations (e.g. crush — dark). Thus a perfect score would be '6,4'. In the present case, *which is quite typical of verbal-specific or general amnesic syndromes*, the patient shows a marked dissociation between the 'old' and 'new' learning.

keeping with preservation of insight into his deficits he showed no confabulation. Automatic mental operations were performed speedily without error
and immediate memory span was normal. However, there was a clear
anterograde amnesia (Memory Passages, Visual Reproduction, Associate
Learning).

The amnesic difficulty was strongly confirmed by the Rey Auditory
Verbal Learning Test (RAVLT). This consists of five learning trials of a
15 word list followed by one recall and one recognition trial after a single
trial of an interpolated list of the same length.

List A		List B	List A	List A
Trials	1 2 3 4 5	Recall	Recall	Recognition
Correct	5 7 8 8 11	5	3	14

Patient YW performed a little better on the fifth trial than many with
alcohol-related memory deficits but considerably below that expected from
his background. The results also show a characteristic retroactive inhibition
or interference effect shown by a score of only three after the interpolated
list. He also showed interference by intruding words from the previously
administered associate learning subtest. As with most Korsakoff patients
the recognition trial was significantly better than any of the recall trials.

The complex Figure of Rey showed a very good copy followed by an
attempt at recall which rated a score of zero when the patient attempted
to draw the figure from memory *only 3 minutes later*. (Fig. 10.1)

WAIS Scaled Scores

Information	12	Digit Symbol	12
Comprehension	18	Block Design	8
Similarities	14	Object Assembly	7

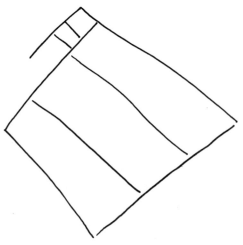

Fig. 10.1 Case YW. Recall of Rey Figure at 3 minutes.

An indication of YW's premorbid intellectual ability can be gained from the three verbal subtests. These would suggest a prior level in the vicinity of 130 I.Q. In contrast the two tests requiring planning and problem solving were significantly inferior. On Block Design he showed inappropriate strategies attempting to solve the problems using faces of the blocks having only one colour, rotating them at odd angles to achieve a diagonal effect. There was also a disinclination to alter placements which he clearly recognized as being incorrect. He was, however, upset with not being able to succeed on tasks which he knew would clearly have been well within his ability.

Three months later another examination was requested before the final decision was taken on his re-employment or retirement. No measurable improvement had taken place and the testing was terminated after he became distressed after failing totally to make the slightest improvement after 10 trials on the Milner pathway of the Austin Maze.

Trial	1	2	3	4	5	6	7	8	9	10
Errors	19	10	15	17	11	19	15	15	23	15

This case not only illustrates most of the commonly found features of an alcohol-related disorder but also shows how advanced cognitive deficit may become in certain situations before action is prompted.

YW shows a general amnesic syndrome together with other non-amnesic cognitive deficits. These latter have been termed 'the adaptive behaviour syndrome' (Walsh, 1985) and may predate the emergence of an amnesic disorder by years or may be seen without amnesia in the well nourished alcoholic.

Amnesia complicating arteriography

Case: DD
Age: 54
Education: 12 years
Occupation: Accountant

Following an adverse reaction to angiography at another centre, this middle-aged man was admitted to the emergency ward of our hospital in a semi-comatose condition. Over the preceding 8 weeks he had suffered a number of sudden attacks of dizziness and inco-ordination with weakness of the left arm and leg, each attack lasting 2–3 minutes. On occasion he also reported numbness of the left side of the face. Apparently the examining physician felt that carotid arteriography was indicated but for reasons which never became clear, a *vertebral* injection was made instead and a large dose of contrast material was used. Shortly after the injection the patient lost consciousness for a few minutes then roused sufficiently to realise that he was blind. He was confused and showed retrograde amnesia for events over the preceding few days. Neurological examination revealed no other localizing signs but it was apparent that DD also had a severe anterograde amnesia. At this stage he was transferred to our large metropolitan hospital's department of neurology. As with idiopathic cases of transient global amnesia (without blindness) he continually posed the same questions about what had happened to him. Over the next 12 hours he slowly improved but was confused, irritable and disoriented and constantly complained of poor vision but was unaware of his recent episode of blindness.

The first neuropsychological examination was carried out 18 hours after angiography. By this time he was able to distinguish objects and could describe a person at 4 feet. His memory had improved sufficiently for him to recall an interview with the psychologist which took place 1 hour before. The Wechsler Memory Scale was administered at this time and comparisons are given when he was re-examined at 72 hours and 4 weeks after the event.

WAIS Scaled Scores	18 Hours	72 Hours	4 Weeks
Information	6	6	6
Orientation	3	5	5
Mental Control	9	8	9
Memory Passages	6	12	10
Digits Total	13	15	15
Visual Reproduction	1	10	11
Associate Learning	7.5	10	14
	5,0;5,0;5,0	4,0;6,1;6,1	6,0;6,3;6,2
M.Q.	89	122	132

At 18 hours: The WMS suggested a general amnesic syndrome though it was difficult to interpret the poor performance on Visual Reproduction because of his visual problem. Associative verbal fluency was given but he was able to give only two words on the letter F in 60 seconds and zero on the letters A and S. He was able to read words, and name objects and colours and showed no other difficulties.

At 72 hours: This examination showed marked improvement in DD's memory. The improvement in Visual Reproduction was confirmed by the Benton Visual Reproduction Test where he scored seven correct with only four errors. Despite this, DD's recall of the Rey Figure fell to only eight, 3 minutes after he had scored 32 out of a possible 36 for his copy. His vision had returned to normal but he was very anxious about a possible return of his blindness. Once again he found it very difficult to find words according to their beginning letter. He managed only four for F, five for A, and seven for S despite a Verbal Intelligence Quotient (WAIS) of 131 and he had had much difficulty with the paired associate learning subtest of the WMS. His memory weakness hampered his acquisition of the Milner pathway on the Austin Maze Test where there was no signficant reduction of errors from the third to the eleventh trial. In sharp contrast DD's performance on the Spatial and Logical Arrangement Tasks of Lhermitte were performed perfectly on the first trial. There were no conceptual difficulties on several other tests.

At 5 Days: CT scan revealed no evidence of cerebral infarction.

At 4 Weeks: Further improvements were shown though, once again, his difficulty with paired associate learning was apparent and he managed to reach only the 40th percentile on the word fluency task, a considerable deficit for a very intelligent man as shown by an extended examination. The parallel form of the Rey Figure (Taylor Figure) was recalled almost perfectly after 3 minutes. Finally, as it was considered that there was still some verbal memory difficulty the Rey Auditory Verbal Learning Test was given.

List A		*List B*	*List A*	*List A*
Trials	1 2 3 4 5	Recall	Recall	Recognition
Correct	8 11 13 9 11	6	9	4

This was thought to be well below par and the poor recognition memory was somewhat surpising.

DD had returned to work and was not concerned about his memory but remained very apprehensive about having another attack of blindness and was still concerned over this when he visited the hospital a year later with another unrelated complaint.

Amnesic stroke

Case: XD
Age: 65
Education: 10 years
Occupation: Business Manager

This successful businessman was in good health until 6 months prior to his present admission. On that occasion he suddenly became blind while driving his car but stopped the vehicle without mishap. The blindness was total but resolved after 10 minutes. During this time XD noted difficulty with his memory.

Following this episode XD had many attacks of blurring of vision, associated vertigo and memory loss lasting 15–30 minutes. Although he improved greatly after each attack he felt that there had been a general deterioration in his memory and he had become very tired in recent months.

Neurological examination revealed no observable deficits and no carotid bruits were noted. The strong history prompted angiographic examination. The main abnormality was a very hypoplastic right vertebral artery and a smooth walled left vertebral with a gross stenosis at its origin. There was also a plaque on the right internal carotid artery.

Neuropsychological examination was requested prior to vertebral endarterectomy since poor vertobrobasilar perfusion appeared to be the likely cause of his troubles.

On examination he was alert, oriented and co-operative with a clear insight into the presence of his stable memory disorder.

WMS Form 1

Information	4	Digits Total	9 (6,3)
Orientation	5	Visual Reproduction	5
Mental Control	9	Associate Learning	6.5
Memory Passages	2		(3,0;5,0;5,0)
M.Q.	87		

There was no confabulation despite the extreme poverty of his verbal recall and on the second card of the Visual Reproduction he failed to gain even one point. The RAVLT showed the same features as in the preceding case of the general amnesic syndrome though much more severe, namely, poor acquisition, retroactive inhibition, and good recognition score.

RAVLT

List A		*List B*	*List A*	*List A*
Trials	1 2 3 4 5	Recall	Recall	Recognition
Correct	4 4 4 4 7	4	0	15

A perfect copy of the Rey Figure was followed by a much impoverished recall at 3 minutes with only the basic outline retained (Fig. 10.2).

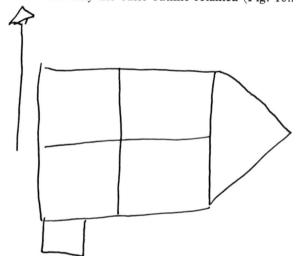

Fig. 10.2 Case XD. Recall of Rey Figure at 3 minutes.

Sundry subtests of the WAIS were performed in the normal to bright normal range with no qualitative features suggestive of disorder other than the amnesia.

Re-examination: 5 weeks after endarterectomy XD was re-examined with parallel forms of the tests given before operation. There was no change in either direction and added memory tests only served to confirm the presence and severity of the amnesic disorder.

A final examination after the lapse of another 6 months showed the condition to be stable. XD was anxious and frustrated because of the pervasive nature of his memory loss and the retention of full insight into his condition. He had suffered no further attacks of visual difficulty and his visual fields were normal.

An open verdict

Case: IJ
Age: 64
Education: 8 years
Occupation: Motor Mechanic

IJ was admitted after experiencing several episodes of recurrent 'surges' of sensation which commenced in the legs, progressed rapidly up the trunk and reached a climax in the head. The sensory experience was accompanied by unusual smells. The episodes typically lasted from 30–60 seconds and were followed by a brief period of confusion but there was no loss of consciousness. His memory was defective for some time after the events but returned to normal a few hours later. There were no abnormal movements, auditory or visual hallucinations, or feelings of derealization or depersonalization. He had never been incontinent. There was no clear precipitating event and he had sometimes had attacks while driving.

The attacks had begun 1 year before but had become more frequent recently. His medications had included aspirin and trifluoperazine.

During the 2 days prior to admission he had had seven attacks. He volunteered the information that his memory had deteriorated over the past 2 years, having to rely constantly on his notebook, and it is possible that memory difficulty pre-dated the onset of the sensory episodes. Over the past year he admitted to an examining psychiatrist that he was disturbed by certain recurring thoughts but there was no detail as he requested them not to be recorded.

At the time of our examination the reason for the attacks remained unclear. Differential diagnosis had included: transient ischaemic attacks, temporal lobe epilepsy, psychosis and early dementia. Clinical examinations made the diagnosis of transient ischaemia or psychosis most unlikely and neuropsychological assessment was sought as an aid to diagnosis.

It was evident from his account of his past history that his remote memory was intact and a screening of his immediate and recent memory was made.

WMS Form 1

Information	4	Digits Total	11 (7,4)
Orientation	4	Visual Reproduction	6
Mental Control	7	Associate Learning	6
Logical Memory	4		(1,0;5,0;6,0).
M.Q.	89		

Despite a good immediate memory, IJ did poorly on the three tests of new learning (Logical Memory, Visual Reproduction, Associate Learning). He recalled little of either memory passage and was unable to recall any more when asked specific questions. The pattern of performance was strongly suggestive of a general amnesic disorder.

As one of the possibilities raised was an early dementing process it was necessary to find out if his memory disorder was accompanied by other signs of intellectual decline. The WAIS was administered over two sessions and the high level and quality of his performances overall threw the poor memory performance into sharp contrast. Dementia was now excluded.

WAIS Scaled Scores

Information	13	Digit Symbol	10
Comprehension	16	Picture Completion	12
Arithmetic	15	Block Design	12
Similarities	12	Picture Arrangement	11
		Object Assembly	10
V.I.Q. prorated	128	P.I.Q.	123

Further evidence of IJ's memory problem was revealed by the Complex Figure of Rey. His copy was well planned and executed with a maximum score of 36 while the recall at 3 minutes was rudimentary (Fig. 10.3).

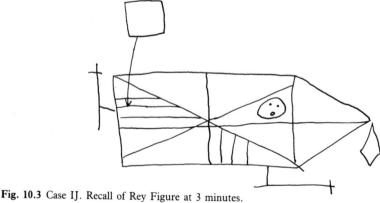

Fig. 10.3 Case IJ. Recall of Rey Figure at 3 minutes.

Following this assessment CT scan revealed no abnormalities. EEG scalp recordings showed normal alpha activity present bilaterally. There was bilateral excess of theta components which was considered to be more marked on the left but there was no clear lateralization. At this stage a diagnosis of temporal lobe epilepsy was made and the patient was commenced on carbamazepine.

The relationship of what appears to be a clear cut and quite severe *general* amnesic syndrome and temporal lobe epilepsy remains unclear. Certainly, in a large number of younger cases we have not seen instances of an axial amnesia though material specific deficits are not uncommon. IJ's epilepsy may have had a more sinister cause but he has not presented again at our hospital in the ensuing 4 years. As is not infrequently the case an open verdict must be entered.

The silence of the right frontal lobe

Case: WS
Age: 14
Education: 8 years
Occupation: Student

The following case illustrates that there is at least one area of the brain where extensive damage may take place without significant change on the wide range of cognitive tests currently employed in neuropsychological assessment. The following résumé covers only part of the detailed investigation of this case.

WS was admitted to hospital with multiple injuries when a home-made bomb he was constructing exploded with a devastating result. He remained conscious despite a penetrating wound above the right eye into the cranial vault, a penetrating chest wound; a penetrating abdominal wound with protruding bowel, lacerations to the hands and minor injuries to the legs and genitalia.

Among numerous emergency surgical procedures fragments of bone and metal were removed from the right frontal lobe though other fragments remained deep in the lobe (Fig. 10.4). The extent of damage can be gauged from this scan.

WS remained conscious, alert and orientated most of the time. Apart from the primary surgery a mediastinal abscess was later drained together with a pericardial effusion. Despite these harrowing experiences WS was able to be moved to a general ward only 2 weeks after admission. At this time he was grossly uninhibited in a fluctuating manner, at times being polite and accommodating, and at others grossly uncooperative, abusive, manipulative and carrying out numerous unsavoury acts such as throwing faeces at the staff. This behaviour moderated sufficiently over the next 2 weeks to enable efforts at rehabilitation to commence though he lacked

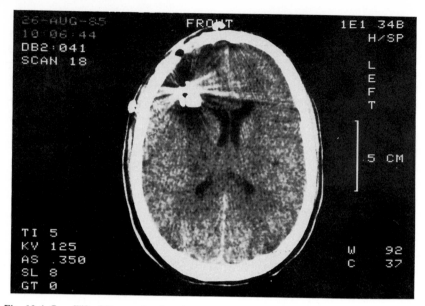

Fig. 10.4 Case WS. CT scan showing shrapnel in the right frontal lobe.

motivation and varied in his concentration span. His first neuropsychological assessment was carried out 3 weeks after his admission. Because of
his many injuries which caused pain and discomfort and a tendency either
to fatigue or become bored, the examination was carried out in several short
sessions. Each time he was pleasantly co-operative though flat in affect and
at times mildly adynamic. At other times he was highly distractable.

By this time it was known that WS had had a long history of antisocial
conduct disorder though little detail was to be had from the parents who,
however, felt that there had been little personality change since the
explosion.

WISC-R Age Scaled Scores

Information	10	Picture Completion	10
Similarities	12	Picture Arrangement	7
Arithmetic	12	Block Design	7
Vocabulary	9	Object Assembly	8
Comprehension	10	Mazes	13
Digit Span	9		
V.I.Q.	114	P.I.Q.	92

Much of the poor performance on the three performance items was due
to slowness resulting from lack of dexterity resulting from his hand lacerations. A minor analytical difficulty was apparent on the Block Design
subtest.

WMS Form I

Information	4	Digits Total	10 (6,4)
Orientation	4	Visual Reproduction	13
Mental Control	9	Associate Learning	19
Memory Passages	11 (13,9)		(6,2;6,4;6,4)

No suggestion of memory deficit was seen in this excellent set of performances which was commensurate with his V.I.Q.

Corsi Block Tapping Test: Immediate memory span: 8.

Complex Figure of Rey: A complete but somewhat careless copy was made which was well planned. At this stage WS appeared bored and his poor recall was difficult to interpret.

Austin Maze (Milner pathway): WS enjoyed this game-like test mastering it in only five trials, a very superior performance, (for further information see Walsh, 1985). He then insisted on being allowed to try it backwards making only one error at his first attempt and zero on his second. Next day he asked to do it again with exactly the same result. Complex learning of this type was clearly unaffected.

Tower of London Test (Shallice, 1982): This recently described test was included in a series of tests usually shown to be sensitive to *left* frontal lobe damage since it was possible that damage might have been sustained in areas other than the primary site of impact. Here again WS turned in a first rate performance:

Average preparation time	5.7 seconds
Average execution time	11.5 seconds
Correct	10 out of 12 problems with three errors two of which were recognised and corrected.

Several other tests suggested intact cognitive processes at a level in keeping with his above average intelligence.

Finally, this case provided an opportunity to check the finding that design fluency might prove a sensitive measure of right frontal lobe function comparable to that of verbal fluency for the left frontal lobe (Jones-Gotman & Milner, 1977). Data from this study are shown in comparison to WS who appeared to have no difficulty in generating drawings under both conditions.

	WS	Normal	Right Frontal
Free condition	17	16.2	8.0
Fixed condition	15	19.7	7.0

When seen at 5 months post-injury, extensive examinations revealed some improvement in speed of information processing but an otherwise stable set of cognitive performances. On the Taylor version of the Rey

Figure his recall score reached the 100th percentile. The analytical problem on the Block Design items was still in evidence but only on the most difficult items.

Unfortunately WS was still causing concern because of his anti-social conduct. He still retained his old group of friends and mixed well with his peer group. It was impossible to tell whether his psychosocial difficulties had been exacerbated by his injuries. His mother at this stage described him as 'a deviant little brat' who had not been worsened by the event.

Carbon monoxide poisoning

Case: QT
Age: 45
Education: 10 years
Occupation: Bank Manager

This man was admitted to hospital following a suicide attempt involving motor vehicle exhaust fumes. He was confused and disoriented for 4 days and his first clear memories were of a family visit 5 days after admission though he subsequently recalled isolated events from the third and fourth days. He was amnesic for the incident but recalled setting out in his car. EEG and CT scan on the third day were both normal. The reason for his attempt remained unclear but may have been related to difficulties with his second marriage.

On examination on the sixth day he was pleasantly co-operative and seemingly unconcerned with the fact that he had tried to commit suicide. He complained of a severe memory difficulty.

As amnesic deficit looms large in many cases of carbon monoxide poisoning testing commenced with the Wechsler Memory Scale, Form I.

WMS Form I

Information	5	Digits Total	14 (7,7)
Orientation	5	Visual Reproduction	12
Mental Control	7	Associate Learning	8
Memory Passages	7		(2,0; 4,2; 6,0)

QT had particular difficulty with new verbal learning. We have found the 'difficult' items on Paired Associate learning particularly sensitive in these cases. However, we have usually found a general amnesia in previous instances of carbon monoxide poisoning so that the good performance on Visual Reproduction was unexpected though we have seen such a sparing in cases of alcohol related amnesia which have all the features of Korsakoff psychosis (see Ch. 2; Walsh, 1985).

RAVLT

List A					*List B*	*List A*	*List A*
Trial	1 2 3 4 5				Recall	Recall	Recognition
Correct	6 5 7 8 8				6	3	7

The RAVLT performance was marked by virtually no extension beyond his immediate memory span (7), marked interference effect, and poor recognition.

Copy of the complex figure of Rey was complete and well organized but only the main outline was recalled at 3 minutes (score 10/36).

Finally, four subtests of the WAIS-R showed only a relatively poor performance on Object Assembly.

Similarities	11	Block Design	12
Digit Symbol	12	Object Assembly	8

Testing was terminated through lack of time with the impression of an amnesic disorder largely uncomplicated with more widespread intellectual loss. Prognosis was reserved as we have seen varying degrees of recovery in amnesic disorders following carbon monoxide poisoning and hypoxic events.

Second neuropsychological assessment was done at 1 month. With one exception the repeated WMS (Form 2), RAVLT, and Rey Figure produced almost identical results. There was still a discrepancy between a good peformance on Visual Reproduction and measures of verbal learning. This dissociation was confirmed by the Benton Visual Retention Test given with a 15 second delay. QT had no difficulty; 8 out of 10 correct with only two errors. The clear difference noted was on the RAVLT. While the poor acquisition and interference effect were identical to the early examination, the Recognition score had risen from 7 to 13 out of a possible 15.

Other subtests of the WAIS-R produced a level of performance as before.

Arithmetic	14	Picture Completion	10
Digit Symbol	12	Picture Arrangement	12

Third examination was at 3 months. The patient said his memory was still poor but had improved somewhat as he was now able to recall some telephone numbers and addresses. Testing was restricted to memory as there had been no indication of other cognitive deficits. In keeping with his subjective report there were slight gains over the 2 month period though a sizeable memory deficit still remained.

WMS Form I

Memory Passages	6
Visual Reproduction	14
Associate Learning	12

(6,0; 6,1; 6,2)

RAVLT

List A Trial	1 2 3 4 5	List B Recall	List A Recall	List A Recognition
Correct	4 7 8 9 9	6	5	13

Taylor Figure
Recall   19/36

The great difficulty with spontaneous recall and the marked interference effect remained as serious as before and the prognosis began to look gloomy. In an endeavour to see whether logical structure of the material to be learned influenced learning and retention two of the tests of Lhermitte and Signoret (1972) were given (see Walsh, 1985). The test of Spatial Arrangement was mastered in four trials, a normal performance and an even better performance of only two trials to criterion on the test of Logical Arrangement suggested that memory retraining might be advantageous in this case since there was reason to believe that visual memory was relatively spared and the ability to benefit from logical structure to aid learning was clearly present. Follow-up was suggested but the patient failed to keep the next appointment.

Alzheimer's disease — or is it?

Case: QW
Age: 53
Education: 11 years
Occupation: 'Retired' car salesman

Extracts from a letter from the referring neurologist give a picture of this man's presentation:

> QW was not entirely sure of the reason for his attendance here. He admitted that he tended to get confused and when I asked specifically he admitted to poor memory. He could not state the day or date but knew that it was July 1985. He could name the present Premier and Prime Minister (but not prominent political figures) ... He was unable to respond when I asked him to interpret proverbs. With serial seven subtraction he could not proceed beyond 93.

QW's wife said that he had been forgetful for 2 years but felt that signs could date back as far as 7.

Neurological examination was normal and CT scan showed mild diffuse cerebral atrophy and the neurologist felt that he almost certainly had Alzheimer's disease and he was referred for neuropsychological assessment to confirm the diagnosis. However, QW rang to defer his examination for

2 months while he took his holidays. When he returned his wife was interviewed prior to the testing session.

Mrs. W stated that Q's difficulties first became apparent 7 years before when he seemed unable to cope with jobs when promoted to management level. She said that he had been quite a heavy drinker in his early years but would not elaborate further. She gave several examples of his forgetfulness some of them having a histrionic flavour. She also said that he would sometimes surprise her by remembering something which she felt he would surely have forgotten.

Finally, Mrs. W indicated that both she and her husband had read a great deal about Alzheimer's disease though she tried to limit the amount of information her husband read as she felt he would find out soon enough about the course of the disease. By the end of the interview some doubt about the provisional diagnosis had already arisen. The differential diagnosis included psychiatric conditions, alcohol-related brain damage, Alzheimer's disease or other degenerative conditions as well as sundry combinations of these.

The assessment was lengthy and wide ranging to elicit data relative to the hypotheses. Only a small portion is presented below.

QW's behaviour at interview reinforced further the doubts over a diagnosis of Alzheimer's disease. He was a very pleasant amiable person who was perfectly oriented in time and place. He conversed in a bright, fluent, logical and sophisticated manner, utilizing and responding to humour appropriately. His only subjective complaint was of a memory disturbance. He stated with an air of smiling indifference that he had Alzheimer's disease.

If his conversation was articulate and intelligent his test performances were uniformly disastrous. Some test examples follow.

WMS Form 1

Information	4	Digits Total	12 (8,4)
Orientation	5	Visual Reproduction	0
Mental Control	0	Associate Learning	1.5
Memory Passages	0		(2,0; 0,0; 1,0)

Despite being alert, attentive and well oriented, he failed on the simple tasks of counting backwards and reciting the alphabet. On serial addition he stated that he was unable to proceed beyond the examples given by the psychologist. Despite a span of eight digits he produced nothing from either prose passage even when directly cued with questions. On Paired Associate learning there was an absence of the pattern of dissociation usually found in organically based amnesias where the patient is capable of recalling most of the old associations but none of the new ones. The responses themselves were revealing;

Baby   — (Cries)   : 'snotty nose'
Metal   — (Iron)   : 'cold'
School — (Grocery) : 'awful'

As soon as tests were put aside he reverted to his normal conversation which included recall of recent events. This difference between test behaviour and everyday behaviour is highly characteristic of pseudoneurological disorders.

Several subtests of the WAIS-R produced the following age scaled scores:

| Picture Completion | 4 | Block Design | 0 |
| Object Assembly | 4 | Digit Symbol | 0 |

He was successful on only three items of Picture Completion, either offering no response or, on other items, drawing attention to trivial omissions. On Block Design not only did he express inability to understand the task instructions but even when presented with a design made up of four white faces he fumbled with the blocks, turning them over and over and only under pressure produced a copy.

QW's attempts at copying the Complex Figure of Rey were illuminating. His first attempt was abandoned after he indicated that he did not have his glasses. He attempted a second copy when they were obtained 15 minutes later producing only parts of the left side of the figure drawing the examiner's attention to his poor effort (Fig. 10.5). He then light-heartedly

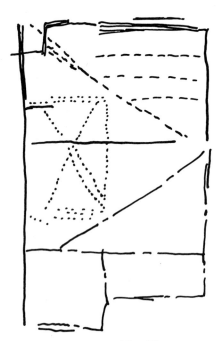

Fig. 10.5 Case QW. Second attempt at copy of Rey Figure.

requested that the figure be taken away as it had been on the first occasion — an interesting statement given his appalling performance on memory tasks.

Numerous tests of different types were all failed dismally with the same air of indifference. These even included tasks done easily by a child of three.

If the scores could be taken at face value this patient would seem to be in the last throes of cerebral dissolution. This was obviously not the case and the opinion was given that the poor performance represented a 'role enactment' in the test situation and that psychological rather than neurological factors were largely or solely responsible. For further examples of role enactment, see Walsh (1985).

Alcohol and error utilization

Case: ZS
Age: 50
Education: 9 years
Occupation: Labourer

This man had always worked as an unskilled labourer and had a long history of alcohol abuse dating back at least 20 years. His own (possibly conservative) estimate was at least 12 standard drinks per day. His alcoholism had caused the breakdown of his marriage seven years before and he was reduced to relying on charitable institutions for lodging and support. At this stage he realised that he needed professional help and entered a recovery project for those with alcohol problems. He had been sober for 5 months when he was sent for an evaluation of his cognitive abilities, such assessment forming part of the planning of his rehabilitation. ZS also stated his concern to this doctor that he was unintelligent but his doctor did not consider this to be the case. He was highly motivated to attend for assessment and to do well. He saw it as a means of finding out whether he had any worthwhile abilities. He was also quite worried about the possibility of brain damage after such a long period of alcohol abuse.

Tests of memory and new learning were carried out first.

WMS Form 1			
Information	5	Digits Total	10 (6,4)
Orientation	5	Visual Reproduction	11
Mental Control	6	Associate Learning	16
Logical Memory	9		(6,1; 6,2; 6,4)
M.Q.	114		

The relative ease with which he handled the tasks sensitive to disorders of new learning (Logical Memory, Visual Reproduction and Associate Learning) was immediately reinforcing to ZS.

RAVLT

List A Trials		*List B* Recall A	*List A* Recall A	*List A* Recognition
	1 2 3 4 5 5 7 7 9 9	6	8	13

This performance was surprisingly unexpected in view of his good performances on the WMS but it is not uncommon in such patients where the pathological process or processes resulting from alcohol abuse often result in difficulty with complex learning especially where subjects must generate strategies of learning and recall for themselves.

A short version of the WAIS-R was used to estimate current levels of functioning in a variety of areas and an estimate of probable premorbid ability based on subtests such as Information and Comprehension which appear relatively stable in the face of years of heavy drinking. It was thought that after a long period of abstinence ZS's intellectual functioning would be stable.

WAIS-R Scaled Scores

Information	11	Block Design	9
Comprehension	11	Object Assembly	10
Similarities	9	Digit Symbol	5

Apart from a non-specific slowing affecting the Digit-Symbol Substitution subtest there were no quantitative or qualitative features to suggest unsuspected cognitive deficits.

Despite the apparent preservation of memory and intellectual abilities at a level consonant with premorbid expectations we have found that patients with a history such as that of ZS often have a serious problem with any degree of new learning that involves benefiting from experience (see Ch. 4 and Walsh, 1985).

Austin Maze (Milner pathway)

Trial	1	2	3	4	5	6	7	8	9	10
Errors	22	30	15	14	11	10	12	6	7	5

Trial	11	12	13	14	15	16	17	18	19	20
Errors	5	5	5	4	5	6	4	5	5	4

Trial	21	22	23	24	25	26	27	28	29	30
Errors	2	1	3	3	4	2	1	1	1	1

Trial	31	32	33	34	35	36	37	38	39	40
Errors	2	1	1	2	1	1	1	1	1	1

Discontinued after 40 trials.

ZS applied himself diligently to the task, insisting that he would 'get it right' eventually. A stable, error-free performance might be expected in 15 trials or less in someone of his estimated premorbid ability. His perform- ance exemplifies very clearly the problem of 'error utilization' or inability to perfect the learning of a novel, relatively complex procedure requiring integration over time. In this case the single error on each of the last six trials was made at a different choice point.

This learning difficulty may easily escape notice unless appropriate tests are used. Such tests need to have the following characteristics: (i) novelty; (ii) complexity; (iii) self-direction and (iv) integration over time.

We have found this *imperfect learning* disorder to correlate highly with success or failure in job retraining and getting back into stable employment in individuals such as ZS and the prognosis in these cases should be guarded.

Further examination usually reveals the presence of other indices of reduction in adaptive behaviour.

Verbal memory problem with a right hemisphere lesion

Case: IX
Age: 25
Education: 12 years
Occupation: Clerical Supervisor, Stock Exchange

At the age of 19 IX experienced a period of several months of headaches accompanied by a throbbing sensation behind the right eye. The headaches ceased spontaneously only to recur some 5 years later when a CT scan revealed a mass in the right frontal lobe with a calcified centre, thought to be an arteriovenous malformation. Examination was carried out before operation and 24 days post-operatively.

At the first session, IX told of deteriorating memory over the preceding 3 months, forgetting people's names, telephone messages and stock exchange codes.

WMS Form 1

Information	6	Digits Total	12 (8,4)
Orientation	5	Visual Reproduction	13
Mental Control	7	Associate Learning	9
Memory Passages	5.5		(5,0; 5,1; 6,0)
M.Q.	90		

This first test was marked by a very poor performance on the three tests of new verbal learning but a near perfect performance on Visual Reproduction.

RAVLT

List A		*List B*	*List A*	*List A*
Trials	1 2 3 4 5	Recall	Recall	Recognition
Correct	7 7 5 7 10	6	5	14

The RAVLT clearly substantiated the verbal learning difficulty.

A sample of intellectual abilities was made using the Naylor-Harwood Adult Intelligence Scale, an Australian approximation to the WAIS.

Information	11	Letter Symbol	12
Comprehension	12	Picture Completion	15
Arithmetic	7	Block Design	14
Similarities	12	Picture Arrangement	10
Digit Span	11	Object Assembly	17
Vocabulary	10		

Apart from the poor performance on Arithmetic there were no qualitative features to suggest lowering of verbal subtests from premorbid levels so that there appeared to be a marked difference between *Verbal* and *Performance* items in favour of the latter. At this juncture the patient was found to be left-handed.

On the later items of the Arithmetic subtest IX appeared to obey the first 'impulsive hypothesis' that came to mind. Simple three-step operations appeared to be beyond his ability. The quality of his performance seemed characteristic of some patients with frontal lobe lesions.

There were no major qualitative features of note although his perform-ance on Picture Arrangement was considerably lower than other tasks, a finding not uncommon with right anterior lesions.

In view of the known location of the lesion, several tests which are frequently performed poorly with frontal lesions were administered. None of these revealed signs of compromise of frontal lobe functions. The two following tests represent this generally intact performance.

Complex Figure of Rey: A well planned and executed copy gave a maximum score of 36 with a score of 30 for recall after 7 minutes.

Austin Maze (Milner pathway): IX's performance was thought to be close to his estimated premorbid ability with no examples of rule breaking, perseverations or other signs associated with frontal pathology.

Trial	1 2 3 4 5 6 7 8 9 10 11 12 13
Errors	18 6 5 5 4 2 2 1 1 1 0 0 0

In summary, IX showed only minor signs of disruption of functions dependent upon the frontal lobes but a clear cut verbal memory difficulty. Second neuropsychological assessment was carried out 24 days after uneventful removal of the AV malformation and portion of the right frontal

lobe. In essence this showed some slight gains on the memory tests probably within the range of the practice effect for these tasks.

WMS Form 2

Information	6	Digits Total	10 (6,4)
Orientation	5	Visual Reproduction	14
Mental Control	8	Associate Learning	12
Memory Passages	11		(3,0; 5,2; 6,3)
M.Q.	103		

RAVLT

List A						*List B*	*List A*	*List A*
Trials	1	2	3	4	5	Recall	Recall	Recognition
Correct	8	9	13	12	11	5	8	14

IX had the same difficulty as before with arithmetical problem solving
(WAIS) but preserved his other abilities at the pre-operative level.

This case reinforces the relative silence of right frontal lesions on a wide
range of cognitive measures. The presence of a verbal specific memory
difficulty with a *right* hemisphere lesion may reflect differences in this
individual's lateralization of functions (in a left-hander). Such a hypothesis
must be tempered with the observation that we have occasionally noted
a similar verbal memory difficulty in right-handed patients with lesions
restricted to the right frontal region. We are still far from a simple equation
between lesion location and neuropsychological performance.

Hysterical pseudodementia

Case: XW
Age: 60
Education: 12 years
Occupation: Laboratory Assistant

This woman had worked as a technical assistant in a laboratory until a few
years before her present referral for possible dementia.

The difficulties began in 1981 when she suddenly became unable to write
and when seen in 1983 was unable to write even her own name. The onset
of this difficulty was not accompanied by any other signs of neurological
deficit. Neither she nor her husband reported any major medical or psychological problems prior to this sudden onset. She did have a history of
hypertension but this was well controlled on medication. There had been
no history of other neurological symptoms apart from left-sided headaches
particularly during times of stress.

Since the onset of her writing difficulties, XW reported that she had
experienced increasing difficulties with her memory and in carrying out

daily tasks. She reported rapid forgetting, being unable to remember where she put things and hanging up the telephone and immediately forgetting the message or reason for the call. She stated that she was unable to remember day to day events or even what day it was. She was unable to cook a simple meal, do the shopping, handle money, knit or sew her own clothes, tasks she had previously performed with ease. Her husband reported that if his wife attempted any routine tasks she would just 'dither' and become upset. Consequently, he had taken over the majority of the domestic responsibilities.

XW described herself as a perfectionist. She stated that she found it extremely distressing, frustrating and even frightening when she found herself unable to perform everyday tasks. Her degree of insight seemed surprising in view of the described severity of her complaint. During the assessment she was pleasantly co-operative but this was punctuated by periodic bouts of uncontrolled weeping. After each of these she rapidly regained her composure and was quite willing to carry on. Throughout the session she displayed apparent comprehension and word finding difficulties.

WMS Form 1

Information	4	Digits Total	4 (4,0)
Orientation	0	Visual Reproduction	0
Mental Control	2	Associate Learning	4
Memory Passages	0.5		(3,0; 3,0; 2,0)
M.Q.	57		

The validity of what appears a very severe amnesic difficulty was called into question since the level of performance was out of keeping with her presentation during examination. Despite scoring zero on Orientation she showed clear evidence of recording ongoing events. While unable to give her date of birth and other well learned information she was able to recall the names of current and recent political figures with ease. Of the two prose passages she produced only one piece of information and questioning

Fig. 10.6 Case XW. Recall of the three cards of the Visual Reproduction of the Wechsler Memory Scale, Form 1.

produced no additions. Fragments of the three cards of Visual Reproduction produced another score of zero (Fig. 10.6). Finally, unlike most
patients with moderate dementia she was unable to produce even a modest
number of responses to the 'Easy' associations of the Paired Associate
subtest.

It seemed to the examiner that this might reflect an attempt to enact the
role of 'sicker than the sickest' and a possible differential diagnosis of
hysterical pseudodementia was entertained. This very simple examination
took over an hour because of extreme slowness, complaints of not being
able to understand the simplest instructions and time out for bouts of
weeping.

Next an attempt was made at supraspan learning using only five digits.
Despite 10 trials XW showed no evidence of even approximating the series.
Testing was then abandoned.

During the second examination, despite the passage of 4 weeks without
significant change, XW spontaneously recalled the examiner's name. When
asked to write her name and a simple sentence to dictation she produced
a small amount of illegible scrawl (Fig. 10.7).

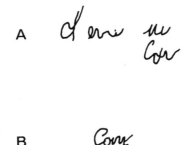

Fig. 10.7 Case XW. Writing to dictation: A. Attempts to write her name. B. The sentence
'The cat ate the fish'.

To check the presence of a pseudoneurological memory disorder XW was
given the 15 item 'memory' task of Rey cited in Lezak (1976, p. 476f). 'The
principle underlying it is that the patient who consciously or unconsciously
wishes to appear impaired will fail at a task that all but the most severely
brain-damaged or retarded patients will perform easily.' Her performance
seemed consistent with a pseudodementia (Fig. 10.8).

Finally, XW's reading was characterized not only by dysfluency but also
by the insertion of material that was not in the original text.

During this second visit further evidence came to hand of inconsistencies
in her behaviour. For example, while she was unable to knit or cook a
simple meal she was quite able to drive herself into the country to visit
friends.

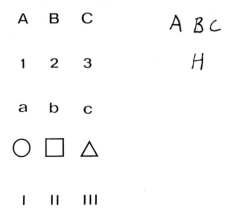

Fig. 10.8 Case XW. Response to Rey's 15 item memory test.

Psychiatric opinion concurred with the diagnosis of hysterical pseudo-dementia and treatment was commenced. Neurological examination and CT scan carried out between the two testing sessions had been normal.

The case of the elderly parachutist

Case: YQ
Age: 60
Education: Post-graduate diploma
Occupation: Property management consultant

Following the death of his wife this successful businessman had taken up parachuting. Several of his jumps were not well executed and on one of them he was badly shaken though apparently not unconscious.

Following this incident (28 December 1983), YQ developed severe left-sided headaches, drowsiness, vomiting, poor concentration and photophobia. During the next two weeks, however, he continued his parachute jumping despite persistent headaches and concentration difficulties. He was involved in three minor car accidents on 2 January 1984. On 3 January 1984 he eventually sought medical attention, and was admitted to hospital where CT scan revealed a left sub-dural haematoma. At operation, a mixture of old and fresh blood was evacuated from the fronto-temporal region.

Post-operatively, there was expressive dysphasia and mild right arm weakness but these were almost normal on discharge 2 weeks later.

At neuropsychological assessment at 2 months, YQ was co-operative although somewhat flippant and facetious. He said that his memory which was poor for some weeks had returned to normal but he still had mild word-finding difficulties when tired.

WMS Form 1
Information   6   Digits Total   13 (8,5)

Orientation	5	Visual Reproduction	12
Mental Control	7	Associate Learning	8.5
Memory Passages	13		(4,0; 5,1; 6,0)
M.Q.	122		

The principal finding of marked difficulty with the 'hard' pairs of Asssociate Learning was further investigated with the Rey Auditory Verbal Learning Test.

RAVLT

List A		*List B*	*List A*	*List A*
Trials	1 2 3 4 5	Recall	Recall	Recognition
Correct	5 5 7 7 7	5	3	12

This test highlighted a verbal learning difficulty of some severity. Apart from the very low level of acquisition, the unsystematic order of recall over successive trials suggested a 'frontal amnesia' (see Ch. 4)

Because of this deficit and the known location of the lesion the ensuing assessment included several tests often found sensitive to frontal lobe dysfunction together with several subtests of the WAIS-R.

WAIS-R Scaled Scores

Information	14	Object Assembly	10
Similarities	10	Digit Symbol	8
Block Design	10		

Apart from a generalized slowing on all tests which robbed him of time credits, YQ showed a concept level on the Similarities sub-test lower than expected for his educational and occupational background.

Verbal Fluency Test 1: (F − = 11; A = 10; S − 12). This was well below expectation and thought to be consistent with residual dysfunction in the left frontal region.

Complex Figure of Rey

Copy: Score 34/36 but poorly organized.
Recall: Score 19/36. A considerable reduction in keeping with the provisional diagnosis of frontal amnesia.

Austin Maze (Milner pathway)

Trial	1	2	3	4	5	6	7	8	9	10	11	12
Errors	26	21	7	12	6	6	4	5	7	5	5	2

Trial	13	14	15	16	17	18	19	20	21	22	23	24
Errors	3	3	1	1	2	4	1	2	3	2	1	1

Trial	25	26	27	28	29	30	31	32	33	34
Errors	1	1	1	2	2	1	1	1	0	0

YQ's performance strongly supported the hypothesis of residual frontal lobe dysfunction. After making only four errors on trial seven a person of his premorbid competence should have reached a stable error-free performance in the next few trials yet it took him more than 25 further trials to reduce his errors to zero and there is no guarantee in such a case that he would be able to maintain this error-free condition. The difficulty demonstrates very clearly what was termed in Chapter 4 *the problem of error utilization.*

Advice was given on the possible disruptive effects of his brain injury on his work performance.

At second assessment at 8 months YQ had returned to his former position as national manager of a major corporation. He described a number of personality changes which he dated to the time of his injury. He described himself as more 'laid back' at work and less committed, preferring to delegate work. He reported being more forthright and outspoken than before. Apart from some minor difficulty recalling names he reported no significant memory problems. His minor word finding difficulty persisted.

To check any recovery of cognitive functioning parallel forms of tests previously used were employed where possible.

WMS Form 2
Despite a rise in M.Q. from 122 to 132 due to small improvements on several subtests, YQ still showed no facility in learning the new or difficult pairs of the Associate Learning subtest. Score 11 (6,0; 6,1; 6,1). There was modest gain on the RAVLT but this was still considerably below par for a man of his premorbid ability.

RAVLT

List A		List B	List A	List A
Trials	1 2 3 4 5	Recall	Recall	Recognition
Correct	5 7 7 10 11	5	9	15

Complex Figure of Rey
The copy score was again 34 but the organization poor. The recall score was even less than before and showed several features described with frontal lobe lesions (see Messerli, Seron & Tissot, 1979). YQ could not resist the impulse to draw a house (possibly aroused by the figure) which he then scribbled out (Fig. 10.9).

Verbal fluency: increased only marginally from a mean of 11 to a mean of 12.3.

Austin Maze (Milner pathway)

Trial	1	2	3	4	5	6	7	8	9	10	11
Errors	37	18	15	14	9	13	10	4	4	4	7

Trial	12	13	14	15	16	17	18	19	20	21	22
Errors	7	3	3	1	2	5	3	1	1	0	0

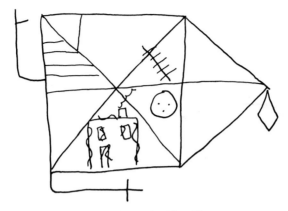

Fig. 10.9 Case YQ. Frontal dysfunction in recall of Rey Figure.

Once again while there might be some improvement there was still a significant problem of error utilization some considerable time after injury. It also became clear at this second examination that YQ had little or no insight into the nature and extent of his deficits.

Postscript: At neurosurgical review 2 months later YQ expressed a strong desire to retire from work as he felt that he was not able to perform intellectually as well as he had prior to his accident. His superior obviously aware of the subtle but pervasive changes wrought by the frontal injury supported the suggestion of immediate retirement. The patient was still keen, however, to continue his parachute jumping. One can only surmise why he took this on in the first place.

Cognitive deficit and the sub-cortex

Case: PS
Age: 56
Education: Teaching diploma
Occupation: Technical College teacher

In July 1984 PS suffered a small spontaneous intracerebral haemorrhage in the region of the genu of the left internal capsule. His physical symptoms resolved satisfactorily in a few weeks and he returned to his position as a teacher in February 1985. Here, a word-finding difficulty became noticeable and he also found that he became unable to construct appropriate sentences. This resulted in disruption of his lectures which was made more marked by his loss of memory for concepts used in his teaching.

Despite his obvious inefficiency he was encouraged by his principal to continue teaching and was still in the same post when he sought assistance in April 1986, some 21 months after his cerebrovascular event. He was depressed over his lasting cognitive difficulties.

On neurological examination PS did not demonstrate any residual sensory or motor deficit. His speech was a little hesitant, but conversational speech was otherwise unremarkable. A CT scan found no evidence of recent pathology.

Neuropsychological assessment was made in April 1986. Because of his professed word finding and memory difficulties the examination began in this area.

WMS Form 1

Information	6	Digits Total	10 (6,4)
Orientation	4	Visual Reproduction	11
Mental Control	9	Associate Learning	10.5
Memory Passages	8.5		(5,0; 6,0; 6,2)
M.Q.	112		

Despite the level of his Memory Quotient he had obvious difficulty with recall of the prose passages and found the unusual pairs on the Associate Learning subtest particularly difficult.

The verbal memory difficulty was less marked on the Rey Auditory Verbal Learning Test but still below his expected premorbid level.

RAVLT

List A		List B	List A	List A
Trials	1 2 3 4 5	Recall	Recall	Recognition
Correct	7 9 12 14 12	7	10	13

Certain subtests of the WAIS-R were then used to sample a range of other intellectual activities. (Age scaled scores)

WAIS-R

Information	18	Block Design	9
Arithmetic	14	Object Assembly	8
Similarities	12	Digit Symbol	9
Digit Span	8		

These performances of general cognitive ability reflected a dissociation between his premorbid capacity and his present functioning. A perfect score on a test of general knowledge, as well as other high scores on tests of well-learnt material, contrasted dramatically with low scores on measures requiring adaptive functioning and organisation of novel material. In the Block Design subtest, for example, the correct placement of blocks often appeared to be performed by chance rotation of the blocks rather than by any deliberate understanding of which block was required in a particular position. This qualitative feature suggested that his scaled score did not fully reflect the pervasive nature of his difficulties.

It was hypothesized that the old haemorrhage may have disrupted the thalamus and/or its projection to the frontal lobes via the thalamofrontal radiation. This led to the use of several tests often shown to be sensitive to frontal lobe involvement.

Austin Maze (Milner pathway)

Trial	1	2	3	4	5	6	7	8	9	10	11	12
Errors	13	9	8	6	4	4	5	3	2	4	4	3

Trial	13	14	15	16	17	18	19	20	21	22	23
Errors	1	2	2	2	3	1	2	2	1	0	0

Despite reaching only four errors on the fifth trial indicating that he clearly understood the task, PS took a further eighteen trials to reach the criterion of two consecutive errorless trials. Although he had great difficulty in eliminating the last few errors there were no instances of rule breaking, impulsivity or perseveration. The performance had a characteristic 'frontal' flavour.

Tower of London Test (Shallice 1982): Here PS managed the first seven items with ease but when the items became more difficult, i.e. required more complex planning, he failed several items and was unable to develop a successful strategy. It was thought that this task would have been well within his premorbid capacity.

Complex Figure of Rey: Both the copy (score 35, 90th percentile) and the Recall (score 27, 80th percentile) were marked by a poorly organized, piecemeal performance.

Verbal fluency: (F = 7; A = 8; S = 11) As expected he performed very poorly on this task. In contrast he was somewhat better in finding names in categories (animals, 16; fruits, 18), though probably poorer than premorbid estimation.

Throughout the interview and cognitive examination PS showed no apparent word-finding difficulty. Oral naming of objects and colours, sentence comprehension, repetition and left-right orientation were all preserved.

Comment: The first stage of this examination is presented as it shows the disruptive nature of even relatively small strategically placed subcortical lesions. We have seen this pattern of disruption frequently enough to warrant further study. Subcortical lesions in a similar location in the right hemisphere seem less disruptive of function but the opportunity for detailed study is restricted as they are less likely to be referred for examination.

A major right hemisphere syndrome

Case: KH

Age: 60

Education: 12 years
Occupation: Hotel keeper

One week after a myocardial infarct KH suffered a right hemisphere stroke thought to be due to an embolus from an intramural clot. He was hemiplegic and hemianaesthesic on the left side and had a left homonymous hemianopia. CT scan showed a large area of decreased attenuation extending throughout the posterior half of the lateral aspect of the right temporal and parietal lobes. This was associated with some swelling and compression of the third ventricle and a 2–3 cm shift in the midline to the left. His hemiplegia resolved rapidly although his left upper limb remained essentially non-functional because of left neglect. He was referred for neuropsychological assessment in order to document higher cortical deficits and assess his potential for ongoing rehabilitation.

At interview it was learned that KH had various business interests which included the hotel which he had acquired in recent years. He had never been a heavy drinker. He was pleasantly co-operative and anxious to do well but it became obvious that he was emotionally very labile. He was extremely talkative so that it was difficult at times to proceed with the assessment. This garrulity which is noted not infrequently in patients with large right hemisphere lesions has not been explained satisfactorily at this time.

WMS Form 1

Information	5	Digits Total	11 (7,4)
Orientation	5	Visual Reproduction	—
Mental Control	9	Associate Learning	18
Memory Passages	12.5		(6,1;6,4;6,4)

The Visual Reproduction subtest was confounded by visuospatial agnosia. Verbal learning and recall were intact on other tests while verbal fluency was not significantly impoverished.

Colour-form Sorting Test: KH was somewhat slow on this test because of a tendency to neglect tokens on the left side. He had some difficulty switching between the two concepts of colour and shape but did eventually shift without assistance.

WAIS-R Age Scaled Scores

Information	13	Comprehension	9
Vocabulary	13	Similarities	11
Arithmetic	9	Picture Completion	11

Much of his performance was in keeping with an estimate of his premorbid ability based on the Nelson Adult Reading Test though he was somewhat rigid in some of his responses to tests involving reasoning. Because of his

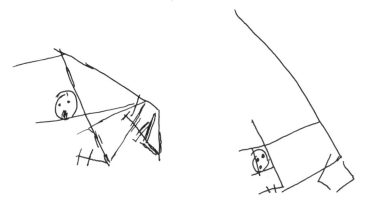

Fig. 10.10 Case KH. Copy and recall of the Rey Figure.

obvious spatial problems other Performance items were not attempted.

Complex Figure of Rey: Copy and recall are shown in Figure 10.10. These drawings show classical neglect of the left side of space and in the manner of some patients with right posterior lesions he tended to draw energetically with the addition of extra lines and tracing and retracing of existing lines. Neglect was also evident in simple drawings (Fig. 10.11) and he showed some perseveration in his writing but not in any other context.

Visual Imagery: In 1978 Bisiach and Luzzatti showed that some patients may neglect the left side of space even when they are describing familiar scenes from memory. On the basis of this finding they hypothesized that unilateral neglect is related to the internal representation of space (see Ch. 6).

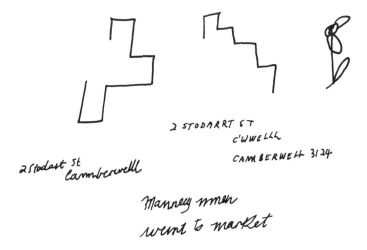

Fig. 10.11 Case KH. Above: attempts at copying a cross, a stepped pyramid and a flower. Below: perseverative elements in writing.

Since KH presented such a clear neglect an attempt was made to check this hypothesis: He was asked to imagine himself standing at various points around a well-known city intersection and to describe what he would see. In his responses he showed no tendency to omit features in the left part of represented space. We have found other negative instances in patients with marked neglect so that a representational explanation does not fit all cases.

Difficulties possibly related to language: It was hoped that relatively-preserved memory and learning skills might have been of help to KH in his rehabilitation but he was unhappy at the centre and soon discharged himself. When seen six months later there was only little improvement and he showed many of the features cited in the review of Wapner, Hamby and Gardner (1981) of the communication disorder of many patients with right hemisphere lesions (see Ch. 8). He was verbose, emotionally labile with a poor sense of humour. It seemed probable that he comprehended poorly what was implied in the contextual aspects of some statements though comprehension of sentences themselves seemed intact, i.e. he had difficulty with the extra-linguistic aspects of language.

He voiced dissatisfaction with his situation and his wife stated that he was demanding and difficult to live with. Some months later he was hospitalized having taken a multi-drug overdose in front of his wife during an argument. Psychiatric help was sought and attempts made at counselling KH and his wife. The outcome is in doubt since contact was lost at this stage.

The prognosis for successful adjustment in these cases is relatively poor and seems to have more to do with the paralinguistic and related factors rather than the better known deficits to do with the world of space.

Monitoring treatment: transcranial anastomosis

Case: ZT
Age: 57
Education: 8 years
Occupation: Mailman

Two months before admission ZT had the first of a series of attacks of dysphasia. Arteriography at another centre showed a 95% stenosis of the intracranial portion of the left internal carotid artery and he was given aspirin on a continuing basis. On the morning of admission he had another episode of speech disturbance which his family described as 'gibberish'. There was no headache or other neurological symptoms and the dysphasia was resolving by the time he reached hospital but an expressive difficulty was still apparent with particular difficulty in naming objects. Neurological examination was otherwise normal. During his admission procedure there were a number of episodes of fluctuating right arm and leg weakness with worsening of his dysphasia.

Left carotid arteriography confirmed the previous finding and a CT scan showed areas consistent with previous infarction in the corona radiata and left parietal lobe.

After several days delay occasioned by unrelated medical conditions an anastomosis was made between the superficial temporal and middle cerebral arteries. At neuropsychological assessment 8 days post-operatively ZT was willing and co-operative, despite an obvious frustration and understandable distress about his language difficulties. An attempt to administer the Wechsler Memory Scale immediately elicited severe expressive difficulties. However, when asked directly whether the year was 1985 he responded with a definite affirmative. While unable to name the hospital spontaneously he correctly identified the name from several choices given to him. The memory examination was abandoned and the Boston Diagnostic Aphasia Examination (BDAE) was introduced. This revealed a 'mixed' dysphasia characterized by agrammatic and dyspraxic speech, receptive difficulties at a complex level, marked word finding and naming difficulties, together with a writing difficulty which resembled that typically associated with Broca's aphasia, namely, poorly-formed graphemes and marked spelling difficulty. Samples from the patient's notebook are shown in Figure 10.12.

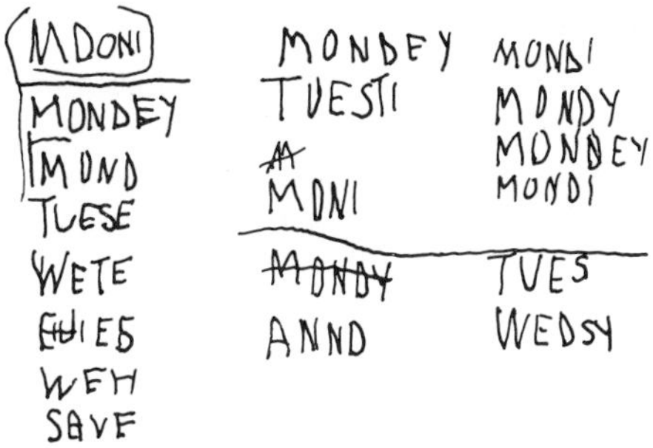

Fig. 10.12 Case ZT. Early attempts to write the days of the week.

Attempts were made to assess other functions, with varying degrees of success.

WAIS-R Age Scaled Scores

Block Design	4
Object Assembly	5
Picture Arrangement	5
Digit-Symbol	5

ZT appeared to grasp the requirements of the tasks but there was marked psychomotor retardation and what appeared to be both analytical and integrative difficulties.

Colour-Form Sorting Test: ZT sorted by shape without difficulty but was unable to shift to the concept of colour. Rather, he resorted to sorting the pieces into patterns.

In summary, at this early stage after operation there was widespread disruption of cognitive function apart from the obvious aphasia.

At second assessment, 1 month later, it was clear from the outset that considerable improvement had taken place. The patient was alert, and well oriented and conversed in a logical, fluent manner. He clearly remembered the contents and requirements of the earlier examination 1 month before, together with the identity of the examiners on that occasion. He was in obvious high spirits and delighted with the degree of his recovery.

It was then discovered that ZT had undergone a cognitive examination at his rehabilitation centre only the previous day so that the projected examination was abbreviated.

The BDAE showed marked improvement but there were still some areas of weakness such as the auditory comprehension of complex ideational material. In contrast to the previous severe word-finding difficulty, receptive deficits, agrammatic speech and dysgraphia, ZT's spontaneous speech was essentially intact. While the quality of his speech output was subject to a fatigue effect, slowly regressing to a mild telegrammatic format and simplistic grammatical constructions by the completion of the session a marked recovery was clearly apparent. There was still an isolated word-finding difficulty and mild residual dyspraxic disturbance. His handwriting had returned to a fluent, sophisticated cursive script (see Fig. 10.13).

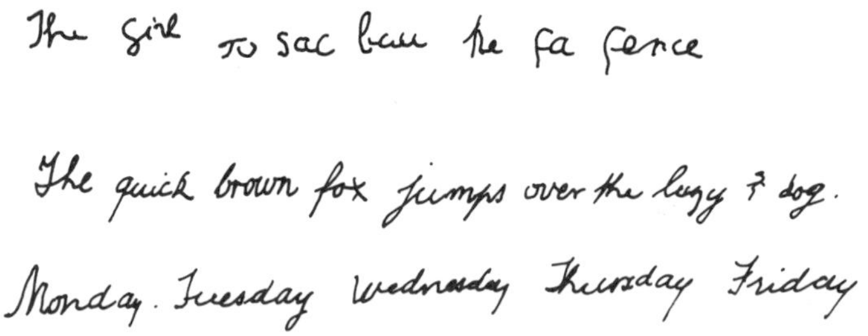

Fig. 10.13 Case ZT. Writing to dictation. Above: 'The girl sat by the fence' written at session one. Below: writing at session two.

The marked psychomotor retardation noted previously had disappeared. On the Letter-Symbol substitution test of the Naylor-Harwood Adult Intelligence Scale which is roughly comparable to the WAIS he managed a scale score of 11 and there was comparable improvement in the remainder of this brief examination. The results from the rehabilitation centre confirmed the overall improvement. Further resolution might be expected.

References

Abraham A, Mathai K V 1983 The effect of right temporal lobe lesions on matching of smells. Neuropsychologia 21: 277–281

Ackerly S S, Benton A L 1948 Report of a case of bilateral frontal lobe defect. Research Publications, Association for Research in Nervous and Mental Disease 27: 479–504

Adams C B T 1983 Hemispherectomy — a modification. Journal of Neurology, Neurosurgery and Psychiatry 46: 617–619

Adams J H 1975 The neuropathology of head injuries. In: Vinken P J, Bruyn G Handbook of clinical neurology, vol 23, North-Holland, Amsterdam ch 3, p 35

Adams J H, Brierley J B, Connor R C T, Treip C S 1966 The effects of systemic hypotension upon the human brain. Clinical and neuropathological observations in 11 cases. Brain 89: 235–268

Adams R D, Collins G H, Victor M 1962 Troubles de la mémoire et de l'apprentissage chez l'homme. In: Centre National de la Recherche Scientifique (eds) Physiologie de l'hippocampe. Centre National de la Recherche, Paris p 273–291

Adams R D, Victor M 1977 Principles of neurology. McGraw-Hill, New York

Adams R D, Victor M 1981 Principles of neurology, 2nd edn. McGraw-Hill, New York

Aimard G, Devic M, Lebel M, Trouillas P, Boisson D 1975 Pure (dynamic?) agraphia of frontal origin. Revue Neurologique 131: 505–512

Aird R B, Masland R L, Woodbury D M (eds) 1984 The epilepsies: A critical review. Raven Press, New York

Aita J A, Armitage S G, Reitan R M, Rabinowitz A 1947 The use of certain psychological tests in the evaluation of brain injury. Journal of General Psychology 37: 25–44

Ajax E T 1967 Dyslexia without agraphia. Archives of Neurology 17: 645–652

Ajax E T, Schenkenberg T, Kosteljanetz M 1977 Alexia without agraphia and the inferior splenium. Neurology 27: 685–688

Ajuriaguerra J de, Hécaen H 1951 La restauration fonctionelle aprés lobectomie occipitale. Journal de Psychologie Normale et Pathologique 44: 510–546

Ajuriaguerra J de, Hécaen H 1960 Le cortex cerebral. Masson, Paris

Akelaitis A J 1940 A study of gnosis, praxis and language following partial and complete section of the corpus callosum. Transactions of the American Neurological Association 66: 182–185

Akelaitis A J 1941a Psychobiological studies following section of the corpus callosum. American Journal of Psychiatry 97: 1147–1157

Akelaitis A J 1941b Studies on the corpus callosum. VIII. American Journal of Psychiatry 98: 409–414

Akelaitis A J 1941c Studies on the corpus callosum. II. Archives of Neurology and Psychiatry 45:788

Akelaitis A J 1942a Studies on the corpus callosum. V. Archives of Neurology and Psychiatry 47: 971–1008

Akelaitis A J 1942b Studies on the corpus callosum. VI. Archives of Neurology and Psychiatry 48: 914–937

Akelaitis A J 1943 Studies on the corpus callosum. VII. Journal of Neuropathology and Experimental Neurology 2: 226–262

Akelaitis A J, Risteen W A, Van Wagenen W P 1941 A contribution to the study of dyspraxia following partial and complete section of the corpus callosum. Transactions of the American Neurological Association 67: 75–78

Akelaitis A J, Risteen W A, Van Wagenen W P 1942 Studies on the corpus callosum. III. Archives of Neurology and Psychiatry 48: 914–937

Akelaitis A J, Risteen W A, Van Wagenen W P 1943 Studies on the corpus callosum. IX. Archives of Neurology and Psychiatry 49: 820–825

Alajouanine T 1960 Les grandes activités du lobe occipital. Masson, Paris

Alajouanine T, Castaigne P, DeRibaucourt-Ducarne B 1960 Valeur clinique de certains tests perceptifs et perceptivo-moteurs. In: Alajouanine T (ed) Les grandes activites du lobe occipital. Masson, Paris

Alajouanine T, Lhermitte F 1957 Des agnosognosies électives. Encephale 46: 509–519

Alajouanine T, Lhermitte F 1964 Non-verbal communication in aphasia. In: DeReuck A V S, O'Connor M (eds) Disorders of language. Churchill, London

Albert M L 1972 Auditory sequencing and left cerebral dominance for language. Neuropsychologia 10: 245–248

Albert M L 1973 A simple test of visual neglect. Neurology 23: 658–664

Albert M L 1978 Subcortical dementia. In: Katzman R, Terry R D, Bick K L (eds) Alzheimer's disease. Senile dementia and related disorders. Raven, New York p 173–179, 194–196

Albert M S, Butters N, Levin J 1979 Temporal gradients in the retrograde amnesia of patients with alcoholic Korsakoff's disease. Archives of Neurology 36: 211–216

Albert M L, Reches A, Silverberg R 1975 Associative visual agnosia without alexia. Neurology 25: 322–326

Albert M L, Soffer D, Silverberg R, Reches A 1979 The anatomic basis of visual agnosia. Neurology 29: 876–879

Albert M L, Yamadori A, Gardner H, Howes D 1973 Comprehension in alexia. Brain 96: 317–328

Alexander M P, Albert M L 1983 The anatomical basis of visual agnosia. In: Kertesz A (ed) Localization in neuropsychology. Academic Press, New York p 393–415

Allen J M 1930 Clinical study of tumours involving the occipital lobes. Brain 53: 194–243

Allen R M 1948 The test performance of the brain diseased. Journal of Clinical Psychology 4: 218–284

Allen R M 1949 A comparison of the test performance of the brain injured and the brain diseased. American Journal of Psychiatry 106: 195–198

Allison R S 1962 The senile brain: a clinical study. Arnold, London

Allison R S 1966 Perseveration as a sign of diffuse and focal brain damage. British Medical Journal 2: 1095–1101

Allison R S, Hurwitz L J 1967 On perseveration in aphasics. Brain 90: 429–448

Angeleri F, Ferro-Milone F, Parigi S 1964 Electrical activity and reactivity of the rhinencephalic, pararhinencephalic and thalamic structures: Prolonged implantation of electrodes in man. Electroencephalography and Clinical Neurophysiology 16: 100–129

Appelbaum S A 1960 Automatic and selective processes in the word associations of brain damaged and normal subjects. Journal of Personality 28: 64–72

Ardila A 1984 Right hemisphere participation in language. In: Ardila A, Ostrosky-Solis F The right hemisphere: neurology and neuropsychology. Gordon and Breach, New York

Arena R, Gainotti G 1978 Constructional apraxia and visuoperceptive disabilities in relation to laterality of cerebral lesions. Cortex 14: 463–473

Armitage S G 1964 An analysis of certain psychological tests used for the evaluation of brain injury. Psychological Monographs 60 No. 1 (whole No. 277)

Arnot R E 1949 Clinical indications for prefrontal lobotomy. Journal of Nervous and Mental Disease 109: 267–269

Arrigoni G, DeRenzi E 1964 Constructional apraxia and hemispheric locus of lesion. Cortex 1: 170–197

Artiola i Fortuny L, Briggs M, Newcombe F, Ratcliff G, Thomas C 1980 Measuring the duration of post-traumatic amnesia. Journal of Neurology, Neurosurgery and Psychiatry 43: 377–379

Assal G 1969 Régression des troubles de la reconnaisance des physionomies et de la mémoire topographique chez un malade opéré d'un hematome intracérébral pariéto-temporal droite. Revue Neurologique 121: 184–185

Assal G, Favre C, Anderes J P 1984 Non-reconnaissance d'animaux familiers chez un paysan. Zoo-agnosie ou prosopagnosie pour les animaux. Revue Neurologique 140: 580–584

Austin G M, Grant F C 1955 Observations following total hemispherectomy in man. Surgery 38: 239–258

Babinski J 1914 Contribution a l'étude des troubles mentaux dans l'hémiplégie organique cérébrale. Revue Neurologique 1: 845–848

Baer D J 1964 Factors in perception and rigidity. Perceptual and Motor Skills 19: 563–570

Baldwin M 1956 Modifications psychiques survenant aprés lobectomic temporal subtotale. Neurochirurgie 2: 152–167

Balint R 1909 Seelenlähmung des 'Schauens', optische Ataxie, raümliche Störung der Aufmerksamkeit. Monatsschrift für Psychiatrie und Neurologie 25: 51–81

Barbizet J 1970 Human memory and its pathology. Freeman, San Francisco

Barbizet J, Degos J D, Louarn S, Nguyen J P, Mas J L 1981 Amnésie par lésion ischémique bi-thalamique. Revue Neurologique 137: 415–424

Barbizet J, Devic J M, Duizabo P 1967 Etude d'un cas d'encéphalite amnésiante d'origine hérpetique. Societe medicale des hôpitaux de Paris 118: 1123–1132

Barron F 1953 An ego strength scale which predicts response to therapy. Journal of Consulting Psychology 17: 327–333

Basser L S 1962 Hemiplegia of early onset and the faculty of speech with special reference to the effects of hemispherectomy. Brain 85: 427–460

Battersby W S 1951 The regional gradient of critical flicker frequency after frontal or occipital injury. Journal of Experimental Psychology 42: 59–68

Battersby W S, Bender M B, Pollack M, Kahn R L 1956 Unilateral 'spatial agnosia' ('inattention') in patients with cerebral lesions. Brain 79: 68–93

Battersby W S, Krieger H P, Bender M B 1955 Visual and tactile discriminative learning in patients with cerebral tumors. American Journal of Psychiatry 70: 703–712

Battersby W S, Krieger H P, Pollack M, Bender M B 1953 Figure ground discrimination and the abstract attitude in patients with cerebral tumors. Archives of Neurology and Psychiatry 70: 703–712

Battersby W S, Teuber H L, Bender M B 1953 Problem solving behavior in men with frontal or occipital brain injuries. Journal of Psychology 35: 329–351

Bauer R M, Trobe J D 1984 Visual memory and perceptual impairment in prosopagnosia. Journal of Clinical Neuro-Ophthalmology 4: 39–46

Bay E 1953 Disturbances of visual perception and their examination. Brain 76: 515–550

Bear D M 1979 Temporal lobe epilepsy — a syndrome of sensory-limbic hyperconnection. Cortex 15: 357–384

Bear D M 1982 Hemispheric specialization and human emotional functions. In: Katsuki S, Tsubaki T, Toyokura Y (eds) Neurology. Proceedings of the 12th world congress of neurology, Kyoto, Japan. Excerpta Medica, Amsterdam, p 63–82

Bear D M 1983 Behavioral symptoms in temporal lobe epilepsy (letter). Archives of General Psychiatry 40: 467–468

Bear D M, Fedio P 1977 Quantitative analysis of interictal behavior in temporal lobe epilepsy. Archives of Neurology 34: 454–467

Bear D, Levin K, Blumer D, Chetham D, Ryder J 1982 Interictal behaviour in hospitalised temporal lobe epileptics: relationship to idiopathic psychiatric syndromes. Journal of Neurology, Neurosurgery and Psychiatry 45: 481–488

Beaumont J G (ed) 1982 Divided visual field studies of cerebral organization. Academic Press, London

Beck E, Corsellis J A 1963 Das Fornixsystem des Menschen im Lichte anatomischer und pathologischer Untersuchungen. Zentralblatt fur die gesamte Neurologie und Psychiatrie 173: 220–221

Beckner M 1959 The biological way of thought. University Press, New York

Bell D S 1968 Speech functions of the thalamus inferred from the effects of thalamotomy. Brain 91: 618–638

Belmont I, Karp E, Birch H G 1971 Hemispheric inco-ordination in hemiplegia. Brain 94: 337–348

Bender M B 1952 Disorders in perception. Thomas, Springfield, Illinois

Bender M B 1956 Syndrome of isolated episode of confusion with amnesia. Journal of the Hillside Hospital 5: 212–215

Bender M B 1977 Extinction and other patterns of sensory interaction. In: Weinstein E A, Friedland R P (eds) Hemi-inattention and hemisphere specialization. Raven, New York, p 107–110

Bender M B, Diamond S P 1970 Disorders in perception of space due to lesions of the nervous system. Research Publication, Association for Research in Nervous and Mental Disease 48: 176–185

Bender M B, Feldman M 1965 The so-called 'visual agnosias'. Proceedings 8th International Congress of Neurology (Vienna) 3: 153–156

Bender M B, Kanzer M M 1941 Dynamics of homonymous hemianopsias and preservation of central vision. Archives of Neurology and Psychiatry 45: 481–485

Bender M B, Teuber H L 1947 Spatial organization of visual perception following injury to the brain. Archives of Neurology and Psychiatry 58: 721–738

Bender M B, Teuber H L 1948 Spatial organization of visual perception following injury to the brain. Archives of Neurology and Psychiatry 59: 39–62

Benowitz L I, Bear D M, Rosenthal R, Mesulam M M, Zaidel E, Sperry R W 1983 Hemispheric specialization in nonverbal communication. Cortex 19: 5–11

Benson D F 1977 The third alexia. Archives of Neurology 34: 327–331

Benson D F 1979 Aphasia, alexia and agraphia. Churchill Livingstone, Edinburgh

Benson D F 1985 Alexia. In: Vinken P J, Bruyn, Klawans H L (eds) Handbook of clinical neurology, New Series 1, vol. 45. Elsevier, Amsterdam

Benson D F, Barton M I 1970 Disturbances in constructional ability. Cortex 6: 19–46

Benson D F, Greenberg J P 1969 Visual form agnosia. Archives of Neurology 20: 82–89

Benson D F, Marsden C D, Meadows J C 1974 The amnesic syndrome of posterior cerebral artery occlusion. Acta Neurologica Scandinavica 50: 133–145

Benson D F, Metter E J, Kuhl D E, Phelps M E 1983 Positron-computed tomography in neurobehavioral problems. In: Kertesz A (ed) Localization in neuropsychology. Academic Press, New York, p 121–139

Benson D F, Segarra J, Albert M L 1974 Visual agnosia-prosopagnosia. Archives of Neurology 30: 307–310

Benson D F, Stuss D T 1982 Motor abilities after frontal leukotomy. Neurology 32: 1353–1357

Benson D F, Stuss D T, Naeser M A, Weir W S, Kaplan E F, Levine H L 1981 The long-term effects of pre-frontal leucotomy. Archives of Neurology 38: 165–169

Benton A L 1950 A multiple choice type of the Visual Retention Test. Archives of Neurology and Psychiatry 64: 699–707

Benton A L 1955 The Visual Retention Test. The Psychological Corporation, New York

Benton A L 1959 Right-left discrimination and finger localization. Hoeber, New York

Benton A L 1961 The fiction of the 'Gerstmann syndrome'. Journal of Neurology, Neurosurgery, and Psychiatry 24: 176–181

Benton A L 1962 The visual retention test as a constructional praxis task. Confinia Neurologica 22: 141–155

Benton A L 1965 The problem of cerebral dominance. Canadian Psychologist 6: 332–348

Benton A L 1967a Constructional apraxia and the minor hemisphere. Confinia Neurologica 29: 1–16

Benton A L 1968 Differential behavioral effects of frontal lobe disease. Neuropsychologia 6: 53–60

Benton A L 1969a Constructional apraxia; some unanswered questions. In: Benton A L (ed) Contributions to clinical neuropsychology. Ch 5. Aldine, Chicago

Benton A L (ed) 1969b Contributions to clinical neuropsychology. Aldine, Chicago

Benton A L 1969c Disorders of spatial orientation. In: Vinken P J, Bruyn G W (eds) Handbook of clinical neurology. Vol 3 Ch 12 North Holland, Amsterdam p 212–228

Benton A L 1972 The 'minor' hemisphere. Journal of the History of Medicine and Allied Sciences 27: 5–14

Benton A L 1975 July On cerebral localization and dominance. Bulletin of the International Neuropsychological Society.

Benton A L 1979 Visuoperceptive, visuospatial and visuoconstructive disorders. In: Heilman K M, Valenstein E (eds) Clinical neuropsychology. Oxford University Press, Oxford

Benton A L 1980 The neuropsychology of facial recognition. American Psychologist 35: 176–186

Benton A, Elithorn A, Fogel M, Kerr M 1963 A perceptual maze test sensitive to brain damage. Journal of Neurology, Neurosurgery and Psychiatry 26: 540–544

Benton A L, Fogel M L 1962 Three dimensional constructional praxis. Archives of Neurology 7: 347–354

Benton A L, Hamsher K de S, Varney N R, Spreen O 1983 Contributions to neuropsychological assessment. Oxford University Press, New York

Benton A L, Hannay J, Varney N R 1975 Visual perception of line direction in patients with unilateral brain disease. Neurology 25: 907–910

Benton A L, Hécaen H 1970 Stereoscopic vision in patients with unilateral cerebral disease. Neurology 20: 1084–1088

Benton A L, Joynt R J 1960 Early descriptions of aphasia. Archives of Neurology 3: 205–221

Benton A L, Levin H S, Van Allen M W 1973 Constructional apraxia and aphasic disorder. Communication at the 1973 annual meeting of the Academy of Aphasia Albuquerque, New Mexico

Benton A L, Levin H S, Van Allen M W 1974 Geographic orientation in patients with unilateral cerebral disease. Neuropsychologia 12: 183–191

Benton A L, Van Allen 1968 Impairment in facial recognition in patients with cerebral disease. Cortex 4: 344–358

Benton A L, Van Allen M W 1972 Prosopagnosia and facial discrimination. Journal of Neurological Science 15: 167–172

Benton A L, Van Allen M W, Fogel M L 1964 Temporal orientation in cerebral disease. Journal of Nervous and Mental Disease 139: 110–119

Benton A L, Varney N R, Hamsher K de S 1978 Visuospatial judgment. A clinical test. Archives of Neurology 35: 364–367

Ben-Yishay Y, Diller L, Mandelberg I, Gordon W, Gerstman L J 1971 Similarities and differences in Block Design performance between older normal and brain-injured persons. A task analysis. Journal of Abnormal Psychology 78: 17–25

Berent S, Cohen B D, Silverman A J 1975 Changes in verbal and non verbal learning following a single left or right unilateral electroconvulsive treatment. Biological Psychiatry 10: 95–100

Bergman P S 1957 Cerebral blindness. Archives of Neurology and Psychiatry 78: 568–584

Berlin C I 1977 Hemispheric asymmetry in auditory tasks. In: Harnad S, Doty R W, Goldstein L, Jaynes J, Krauthamer G (eds) Lateralization in the nervous system. Academic, New York p 303–323

Berlyne N 1972 Confabulation. British Journal of Psychiatry 120: 31–39

Beyn E S, Knyazeva G R 1962 The problem of prosopagnosia. Journal of Neurology, Neurosurgery, and Psychiatry 25: 154–158

Bickford R G, Mulder D W, Dodge H W, Svien H J, Rome H P 1958 Changes in memory function produced by electrical stimulation of the temporal lobe in man. Research Publications, Association for Research in Nervous and Mental Disease 36: 227–243

Bigley G K, Sharp F R 1983 Reversible alexia without agraphia due to migraine. Archives of Neurology 40: 114–115

Birch H G, Proctor F, Bortner M 1961 Perception in hemiplegia: III. The judgment of relative distance in the visual field. Archives of Physical Medicine and Rehabilitation 42: 639–644

Birkett P 1978 Hemispheric differences in the recognition of nonsense shapes. Cortex 14: 245–249

Birkmayer W 1951 Hirnverletzungen Mechanismus, Spaetkomplitationen Funktions Wandel. Springer, Vienna

Bisiach E, Capitani E, Luzzatti C, Perani D 1981 Brain and conscious representation of outside reality. Neuropsychologia 19: 543–551

Bisiach E, Luzzatti C 1978 Unilateral neglect of representational space. Cortex 14: 129–133

Bisiach E, Luzzatti C, Perani D 1979 Unilateral neglect nonrepresentational schema and consciousness. Brain 102:609

Bisiach E, Nichelli P, Spinnler H 1976 Hemispheric functional asymmetry in visual discrimination between univariate stimuli: An analysis of sensitivity and response criterion. Neuropsychologia 14: 335–342

Black F W 1976 Cognitive deficits in patients with unilateral war-related frontal lobe lesions. Journal of Clinical Psychology 32: 366–372

Black F W, Strub R L 1976 Constructional apraxia in patients with discrete missile wounds of the brain. Cortex 12: 212–220

Blakemore C B 1969 Psychological effects of temporal lobe lesions in man. In: Herrington R N (ed) Current problems in neuropsychiatry: schizophrenia, epilepsy, the temporal lobe. British Journal of Psychiatry, Special publication No. 4, Ch. 10, p 60–69

Blakemore C B, Ettlinger G, Falconer M A 1966 Cognitive abilities in relation to frequency of seizures and neuropathology of the temporal lobes in man. Journal of Neurology, Neurosurgery, and Psychiatry 29: 268–272

Blakemore C B, Falconer M A 1967 Long-term effects of anterior temporal lobectomy on certain cognitive functions. Journal of Neurology, Neurosurgery, and Psychiatry 30: 364–367

Blum J S, Chow K L, Pribram K H 1950 A behavioral analysis of the organization of the parieto-temporo-preoccipital cortex. Journal of Comparative Neurology 93: 53–100

Blume W T, Grabow J D, Darley F L, Aranson A E 1973 Intracarotid amobarbital test of language and memory before temporal lobectomy for seizure control. Neurology 23: 812–819

Blumstein S, Cooper W 1974 Hemispheric processing of information contours. Cortex 10: 146–158

Blumstein S, Goodglass H, Tartter V 1975 The reliability ear advantage in dichotic listening Brain and Language 2: 226–236

Bodamer J 1947 Die Prosop-Agnosie Archiv für Psychiatrie und Nervenkrankheiten 179: 6–53

Bogen J E 1969a The other side of the brain. I. Dysgraphia and dyscopia following cerebral commissurotomy. Bulletin of the Los Angeles Neurological Societies 34: 73–105

Bogen J E 1969b The other side of the brain II. An appositional mind. Bulletin of the Los Angeles Neurological Societies 34: 135–162

Bogen J E 1969c The other side of the brain. III. The corpus callosum and creativity. Bulletin of the Los Angeles Neurological Societies 34: 191–220

Bogen J E 1985 Split-brain syndromes. In: Vinken P J, Bruyn G W, Klawans H L (eds) Handbook of clinical neurology, New Series 1, vol. 45. Elsevier, Amsterdam, p 99–106

Bogen J E, Gazzaniga M S 1965 Cerebral commissurotomy in man: minor hemisphere dominance for certain visuospatial functions. Journal of Neurosurgery 23: 394–399

Bogen J E, Gordon H W 1971 Musical test for functional lateralization with intracarotid amobarbital. Nature 230: 524–525

Boll T J 1974 Right and left cerebral hemisphere damage and tactile perception: Performance of the ipsilateral and contralateral sides of the body. Neuropsychologia 12: 235–238

Boller F, DeRenzi E 1967 Relationship between visual memory defects and hemispheric locus of lesion. Neurology 17: 1052–1058

Bolter J F, Hannon R 1980 Cerebral damage associated with alcoholism: A re-examination. The Psychological Record 30: 165–179

Bonhoeffer K 1904 Der Korsakowsche Symptomenkomplex in seinen Beziehungen zu den verschieden Krankheitsformen. Allgemeine Zeitschrift fur Psychiatrie 61: 744–752

Boring E G 1929 A history of experimental psychology. Appleton Century Crofts, New York

Borkowski J G, Benton A L, Spreen O 1967 Word fluency and brain damage. Neuropsychologia 5: 135–140

Bornstein B 1963 Prosopagnosia. In: Halpern L (ed) Problems in dynamic neurology. Hadassah Medical Organization, Jerusalem

Bornstein B 1965 Prosopagnosia. Proceedings of the 8th International Congress of Neurology (Vienna) 3: 157–160

Bornstein B, Kidron D P 1959 Prosopagnosia. Journal of Neurology, Neurosurgery, and Psychiatry 22: 124–131

Bornstein B, Sroka H, Munitz H 1969 Prosopagnosia with animal face agnosia. Cortex 5: 164–169

Borod J, Caron H 1980 Facedness and emotion related to lateral dominance, sex and expression type. Neuropsychologia 18: 237–241

Boudin G, Barbizet J, Derouesné C, Van Amerongen P 1967 Cécité corticale et problème des 'amnésies occipitales'. Revue Neurologique 116: 89–97

Boudin G, Brion S, Pepin B, Barbizet J 1968 Syndrome de Korsakoff d'étiologie artèriopathique. Revue Neurologique 119: 341–348

Bourne L E 1966 Human conceptual behavior. Allyn and Bacon, Boston

Bowsher D 1970 Introduction to anatomy and physiology of the nervous system. 2nd edn. Blackwell, Oxford

Bradley K C, Dax E C, Walsh K W 1958 Modified leucotomy: report of 100 cases. Medical Journal of Australia 1: 133–138

Bradshaw J L, Nettleton N 1983 Human cerebral asymmetry. Prentice-Hall, Englewood Cliffs, NJ

Bradshaw J L, Sherlock D 1982 Bugs and faces in the two visual fields: the analytic/holistic processing dichotomy and task sequencing. Cortex 18: 211–226

Brain R 1941 Visual disorientation with special reference to lesions of the right hemisphere. Brain 64: 244–272

Brain R, Walton J W 1969 Brain's Diseases of the nervous system. 7th edn. Oxford University Press, London

Branch C, Milner B, Rasmussen T 1964 Intracarotid sodium amytal for the lateralization of cerebral speech dominance. Journal of Neurosurgery 21: 399–405

Brazier M A B 1968 The electrical activity of the nervous system. 3rd edn. Pitman, London

Breasted J H 1930 The Edwin Smith surgical papyrus. University of Chicago Press, Chicago

Breschi F, D'Angelo A, Pluchino F 1970 Resultat a distance de l'hémisphèrectomie dans 13 cas d'hémiatrophie cérébrale infantile épileptogene. Neurochirurgie 16: 397–411

Brewer W F 1969 Visual memory, verbal encoding and hemispheric localization. Cortex 5: 145–151

Bridgers S L, Ebersole J S 1985 The clinical utility of ambulatory cassette EEG. Neurology 35: 166–173

Brierley J 1977 The neuropathology of amnesic states. In: Whitty C W M, Zangwill O L (eds) Amnesia, 2nd edn, Butterworths, London, p 199–223

Brierley J B, Cooper J E 1962 Cerebral complications of hypotensive anaesthesia in a normal adult. Journal of Neurology, Neurosurgery, and Psychiatry 25: 24–30

Brion S, Derome P, Guiot G, Teitgen Mme 1968 Syndrome de Korsakoff par anevrysme de l'artère communicante antérieure: le probleme des syndromes de Korsakoff par hémorragie méningée. Revue Neurologique 118: 293–299

Brion S, Jedynak C P 1972 Troubles du transfert interhémisphèrique. Le signe de la main étrangere. Revue Neurologique 126: 257–266

Brodal A 1980 Neurological anatomy in relation to clinical medicine. 3rd edn. Oxford University Press, New York

Brodmann K 1909 Vergleichende Lokalisationslehre der Grosshirnrinde. Barth, Leipzig

Bruell J H, Albee G W 1962 Higher intellectual functions in a patient with hemispherectomy for tumors. Journal of Consulting Psychology 26: 90–98

Brumback R A 1983 Personality analysis of epileptics. Archives of Neurology 40:658

Bryden M P 1977 Strategy effects in the presence of hemispheric asymmetry. In: Underwood G (ed) Strategies of information processing. Academic Press, London

Bryden M P 1982 Laterality: Functional asymmetry in the intact brain. Academic Press, New York

Bryden M P, Zurif E B 1970 Dichotic listening performance in a case of agenesis of the corpus callosum. Neuropsychologia 8: 371–377

Buge A, Escourolle R, Rancurel G, Poisson M 1975 Mutisme akinétique et ramollissement bi-cingulaire. Revue Neurologique 131: 121–137

Bugiani O, Conforto C, Sacco G 1969 Aphasia in thalamic hemorrhage. Lancet 1:1052

Burklund C W, Smith A 1977 Language and the cerebral hemispheres. Neurology 27: 627–633

Buss A H 1952 Some determinants of rigidity in discrimination reversal learning. Journal of Experimental Psychology 44: 222–227

Butler S R, Norrsell W 1968 Vocalization possibly initiated by the minor hemisphere. Nature 220: 793–794

Butters N, Barton M 1970 Effect of parietal lobe damage on the performance of reversible operations in space. Neuropsychologia 8: 205–214

Butters N, Barton M, Brody B A 1970 Role of the right parietal lobe in the mediation of cross-modal associations and reversible operations in space. Cortex 6: 174–190

Butters N, Brody B A 1968 The role of the left parietal lobe in the mediation of intra- and cross-modal associations. Cortex 4: 328–343

Butters N, Milliotis P, Albert M S, Sax D S 1984 Memory assessment: evidence of the heterogeneity of amnesic symptoms. In: Goldstein G (ed) Advances in clinical neuropsychology, vol 1. Plenum, New York, p 127–159

Butters N, Soeldner C, Fedio P 1972 Comparison of parietal and frontal lobe spatial deficits in man: extra-personal vs personal (egocentric) space. Perceptual and Motor Skills 34: 27–34

Byrne R W 1982 Geographical knowledge and orientation. In: Ellis A W (ed) Normality and pathology in cognitive functions. Academic Press, London p 239–264

Cairns H, Davidson M A 1951 Hemispherectomy in the treatment of infantile hemiplegia. Lancet 2: 411–415

Cambier J, Elghozi D, Strube E 1980 Lesions du thalamus droit avec syndrome de l'hémisphère mineur. Discussion du concept de negligence thalamique. Revue Neurologique 136: 106–166

Cambier J, Graveleau T 1985 Thalamic syndromes. In: Vinken P J, Bruyn G W, Klawans H L (eds) Handbook of clinical neurology, New series 1, vol 45. Elsevier, Amsterdam, p 87–9

Cambier J, Masson M, Graveleau T, Elghozi D 1982 Sémiologie de négligence lors de lésions ischemiques dans le territoire de l'artère cérébrale postérieure droite. Revue Neurologique 138: 631–648

Campbell A L, Bogen J E, Smith A 1981 Disorganization and reorganization of cognitive and sensorimotor functions in cerebral commissurotomy. Brain 104: 493–511

Campbell D C, Oxbury J M 1976 Recovery from unilateral visual-spatial neglect. Cortex 12: 303–312

Caplan D, Holmes J M, Marshall V C 1974 Word classes and hemispheric specialization. Neuropsychologia 12: 331–337

Caplan L, Chedru F, Lhermitte F, Mayman F 1981 Transient global amnesia and migraine. Neurology 321: 1167–1170

Caplan L B 1985 Transient global amnesia. In: Vinken P J, Bruyn G W, Klawans H L (eds) Handbook of clinical neurology. New series 1, vol 45. Elsevier, Amsterdam, p 205–218

Cappa S F, Vignolo L A 1979 'Transcortical' features of aphasia following left thalamic hemorrhage. Cortex 15: 121–130

Caramazza A, Berndt R S 1979 Semantic and syntactic processes in aphasia. A review of the literature. Psychological Bulletin 85: 898–918

Carmichael A E 1966 The current status of hemispherectomy for infantile hemiphegia. Clinical Proceedings of the Children's Hospital D.C. 22: 285–293

Carmon A 1971 Sequenced motor performance in patients with unilateral cerebral lesions. Neuropsychologia 9: 445–449

Carmon A, Bechtoldt H P 1969 Dominance of the right cerebral hemisphere for stereopsis. Neuropsychologia 7: 29–39

Carmon A, Nachson I 1971 Effect of unilateral brain damage on perception of temporal order. Cortex 7: 410–418

Carmon A, Nachson I 1973 Ear asymmetry in perception of emotional non-verbal stimuli. Acta Psychologica 37: 351–357

Carpenter M B 1972 Core text of neuroanatomy. Williams and Wilkins, Baltimore

Castaigne P, Lhermitte F, Buge A, Escourolle R, Hauw J J, Lyon-Caen O 1981 Paramedian thalamic and midbrain infarcts: clinical and neuropsychological study. Annals of Neurology 10: 127–148

Cattell R B 1944 A culture-free test. The Psychological Corporation, New York

Cattell R B, Dubin S S, Saunders D K 1954 Verification of hypothesized factors in one hundred and fifteen objective personality tests. Psychometrika 19: 209–230

Cattell R B, Tiner L B 1949 The varieties of structural rigidity. Journal of Personality 17: 321–341

Cermak L S, Butters N, Moreines J 1974 Some analyses of the verbal encoding deficit of alcoholic Korsakoff patients. Brain and Language 1: 141–150

Chapman L F, Wolff H F 1959 The cerebral hemispheres and the highest integrative functions of man. Archives of Neurology 1: 357–424

Chapman W P 1958 Studies of the periamygdaloid area in relation to human behavior.

Research Publications, Association for Research in Nervous and Mental Disease 36: 258–277

Chapman W P 1960 Depth electrode studies in patients with temporal lobe epilepsy. In: Ramey E R, O'Doherty D S (eds) Electrical studies on the unanesthetized brain. Hoeber, New York p 334–350

Chedru F, Leblanc M, Lhermitte F 1973 Visual searching in normal and brain-damaged subjects (contribution to the study of unilateral inattention). Cortex 9: 94–111

Cherlow D G, Serafetinides E A 1976 Speech and memory assessment in psychomotor epileptics. Cortex 12: 21–26

Chesher E D 1936 Some observations concerning the relatedness of handedness to the language mechanism. Bulletin of the Neurological Institute of New York 4: 556–562

Chiarello C 1980 A house divided? Cognitive functioning with callosal agenesis. Brain and Language 11: 125–158

Chown S H 1959 Rigidity — a flexible concept. Psychological Bulletin 56: 195–223

Christensen A L 1975 Luria's neuropsychological investigation. Munksgaard, Copenhagen

Cicerone K D, Lazar R M, Shapiro W R 1983 Effects of frontal lobe lesions on hypothesis sampling during concept formation. Neuropsychologia 21: 513–524

Ciemins M D 1970 Localized thalamic haemorrhage: a cause of aphasia. Neurology 20: 776–782

Clarke E, Dewhurst K 1972 An illustrated history of brain function. Sandford, Oxford

Clarke E, O'Malley C D 1968 The human brain and spinal cord. University of California Press, Berkeley

Cogan D G 1960 Hemianopia and associated symptoms due to parieto-temporal lobe lesions. American Journal of Ophthalmology 50: 1058–1066

Cogan D G 1966 Neurology of the visual system. Thomas, Springfield, Illinois

Cohen L 1959 Perception of reversible figures after brain injury. Archives of Neurology and Psychiatry 81: 765–775

Cohen N J, Corkin S 1981 The amnesic patient HM: learning and retention of a cognitive skill. Society for Neuroscience Abstracts 7:235

Cohen N J, Squire L R 1980 Preserved learning and retention of pattern analyzing skill in amnesia: dissociation of knowing how and knowing what. Science 210: 207–209

Cohen N J, Squire L R 1981 Retrograde amnesia and remote memory impairment. Neuropsychologia 19: 337–356

Colbourn C J 1978 Can laterality be measured? Neuropsychologia 16: 283–289

Cole M, Perez-Cruet J 1964 Prosopagnosia. Neuropsychologia 2: 237–246

Collignon R, Rondeaux J 1974 Approche clinique des modalités de l'apraxie constructive secondaire aux lésions corticales hémisphèriques gauches et droites. Acta Neurologica Belgica 74: 137–146

Commission on Classification and Terminology of the International League Against Epilepsy 1981 Proposals for revised clinical and electroencephalographic classification of epileptic seizures. Epilepsia 22: 489–501

Conrad K 1949 Uber aphasische sprachtochungen bei hirnverletzen Linksaendeia. Nervenarzt 20: 148–154

Corballis M C 1983 Human laterality. Academic Press, New York

Corkin S H 1964 Somesthetic function after cerebral damage in man. Unpublished doctoral dissertation, McGill University

Corkin S 1965 Tactually-guided image learning in man. Effect of unilateral cortical excisions and bilateral hippocampal lesions. Neuropsychologia 3: 339–351

Corkin S 1968 Acquisition of motor skill after bilateral medial temporal-lobe excision. Neuropsychologia 6:255

Corkin S, Milner B, Rasmussen T 1964 Effects of different cortical excisions on sensory thresholds in man. Transactions of the American Neurological Association 89: 112–116

Corkin S, Milner B, Rasmussen T 1970 Somatosensory thresholds-contrasting effects of postcentral-gyrus and posterior parietal lobe excisions. Archives of Neurology 23: 41–58

Corston R N, Godwin-Austen R B 1982 Transient global amnesia in four brothers. Journal of Neurology, Neurosurgery, and Psychiatry 45: 375–377

Costa L, Vaughan H 1962 Performance of patients with lateralized cerebral lesions. 1: Verbal and perceptual tests. Journal of Nervous and Mental Disease 134: 162–168

Costa L D, Vaughan H G Jr, Horwitz M, Ritter W 1969 Patterns of behavioral deficit associated with visual spatial neglect. Cortex 5: 242–263

Coughlan A K, Warrington E K 1978 Word-comprehension and word-retrieval in patients with localized cerebral lesions. Brain 101: 163–185

Courville C B 1942 Coup-contrecoup mechanism of cranio-cerebral injuries: some observations. Archives of Surgery 55: 19–43

Courville C B 1945 Pathology of the nervous system. 2nd edn. Pacific Press, Mountain View, California

Cramon D von, Zihl J 1979 Roving eye movements with bilateral symmetrical lesions of the thalamus. Journal of Neurology 221: 105–112

Critchley M 1949 The phenomenon of tactile inattention with special reference to parietal lesions. Brain 72: 538–561

Critchley M 1953 The parietal lobes. Arnold, London

Critchley M 1962 Speech and speech-loss in relation to the duality of the brain. In: Mountcastle V B (ed) Interhemispheric relations and cerebral dominance. Johns Hopkins University Press, Baltimore

Critchley M 1964 The problem of visual agnosia. Journal of Neurological Science 1: 274–290

Critchley M 1965 Acquired anomalies of colour. Brain 88: 711–724

Critchley M 1966 The enigma of Gerstmann's syndrome. Brain 89: 183–198

Critchley M, Henson R A 1977 Music and the brain: Studies in the neurology of music. Heinemann, London

Crockett H G, Estridge N M 1951 Cerebral hemispherectomy. Bulletin of the Los Angeles Neurological Society 16: 71–87

Crosby E C, Humphrey T, Lauer E W 1962 Correlative anatomy of the nervous system. Macmillan, New York

Crown S 1952 An experimental study of psychological changes following prefrontal lobotomy. Journal of General Psychology 47: 3–41

Cumming W J K, Hurwitz L J, Perl N 1969 A study of a patient who had alexia without agraphia. Journal of Neurology, Neurosurgery, and Psychiatry 33: 34–39

Curry F K W 1968 A comparison of the performance of a right hemispherectomized subject and 24 normals on four dichotic listening tasks. Cortex 4: 144–153

Daly D D 1975 Ictal clinical manifestations of complex partial seizures. In: Penry J K, Daly D D (eds) Advances in Neurology. vol II. Raven, New York p 57–84

Damasio A 1981 Central achromatopsia. Neurology 31: 920–921

Damasio A R, Damasio H 1977 Musical faculty and cerebral dominance. In: Critchley M, Henson R A (eds) Music and the brain. Heinemann, London, p 141–155

Damasio A R, Damasio H 1983 Localization of lesions in achromatopsia and prosopagnosia. In: Kertesz A (ed) Localization in neuropsychology. Academic Press, New York p 417–428

Damasio A R, Damasio H, Chang Chui H 1980 Neglect following damage to frontal lobe and basal ganglia. Neuropsychologia 18: 123–132

Damasio A R, Damasio H, Rizzo M, Varney N, Gersh F 1982 Aphasia with nonhemorrhagic lesions in the basal ganglia and internal capsule. Archives of Neurology 29: 15–20

Damasio A R, Damasio H, Van Hoesen G W 1982 Prosopagnosia: anatomic basis and behavioral mechanisms. Neurology 32: 331–341

Damasio A R, Lima P A, Damasio H 1975 Nervous function after right hemispherectomy. Neurology 24: 89–93

Damasio A R, Yamada T, Damasio H, Corbett J, McKee J 1980 Central achromatopsia: Behavioral, anatomical and physiologic aspects. Neurology 30: 1064–1071

Dana C L 1915 Textbook of nervous diseases. 8th edn. Wood, New York

Dandy W E 1928 Removal of right cerebral hemisphere for certain tumours with hemiplegia. Journal of the American Medical Association 90: 823–825

Dandy W E 1933 Physiological studies following extirpation of the right cerebral hemisphere in man. Johns Hopkins Hospital Bulletin 53: 31–51

Dee H L 1970 Visuoconstructive and visuoperceptive deficit in patients with unilateral cerebral lesions. Neuropsychologia 8: 305–314

Dee H L, Benton A L 1970 Visuoconstructive and visuoperceptive deficit in patients with unilateral cerebral lesions. Neuropsychologia 8: 305–314

Dee H L, Fontenot D J 1973 Cerebral dominance and lateral differences in perception and memory. Neuropsychologia 11: 167–173

Dejerine J 1892 Contribution a l'étude anatomo-pathologique et clinique des différents variétés de cécité verbale. Comptes Rendus, Societe de Biologie 4: 61–90

Dejerine R, Roussy G 1906 Le syndrome thalamique. Revue Neurologique 14: 521–536

De Jong R N, Itabashi H H, Olson J R 1968 'Pure' memory loss with hippocampal lesions: a case report. Transactions of the American Neurological Association 93: 31–34

De Jong R N, Itabashi H H, Olson J R 1969 Memory loss due to hippocampal lesions. Report of a case. Archives of Neurology 20: 339–348

De Kosky S T, Heilman K M, Bowers D, Valenstein E 1980 Recognition and discrimination of emotional faces and pictures. Brain and Language 9: 206–215

Delay J, Brion S, Derouesné C 1964 Syndrome de Korsakoff et étiologie tumorale: étude anatomo-clinique de trois observations. Revue Neurologique 111: 97–133

d'Elia G 1976 Memory changes after unilateral electroconvulsive therapy with different electrode positions. Cortex 12: 280–289

d'Elia G, Lorentzson S, Raotma H, Widepalm K 1976 Comparison of unilateral dominant and non-dominant ECT on verbal and non-verbal memory. Acta Psychiatrica Scandinavica 53: 85–94

Demeurisse G, Derouck M, Cockaerts M J, Deltenre P, Van Nechel C, Demol O, Capon A 1979 Study of two cases of aphasia by infarction of the left thalamus. Acta Neurologica Belgica 79: 450–459

Denes G, Caldognetto E M, Semenza C, Vagges K, Zettin M 1984 Discrimination and identification of emotions in human voice by brain-damaged subjects. Acta Neurologica Scandinavica 69: 154–162

Denes G, Semenza C, Stoppa E, Lis A 1982 Unilateral spatial neglect and recovery from hemiplegia. A follow-up study. Brain 105: 543–552

Dennerll R D 1964 Prediction of unilateral brain dysfunction using Wechsler test scores. Journal of Consulting Psychology 28: 278–284

Denny-Brown D 1958 Nature of apraxia. Journal of Nervous and Mental Disease 126: 9–32

Denny-Brown D, Chambers R A 1958 The parietal lobe and behavior. Research Publications, Association for Research in Nervous and Mental Disease 36: 35–117

Denny-Brown D, Meyer J S, Horenstein S 1952 The significance of perceptual rivalry resulting from parietal lesions. Brain 75: 433–471

De Renzi E 1982 Disorders of space exploration and cognition. Wiley, New York

De Renzi E, Faglioni P 1962 Il disorientamento spatiale da lesione cerebrale. Sistema Nervoso 14: 409–436

De Renzi E, Faglioni P 1965 The comparative efficiency of intelligence and vigilance tests in detecting hemispheric cerebral damage. Cortex 1: 410–433

De Renzi E, Faglioni P 1967 The relationship between visuo-spatial impairment and constructional apraxia. Cortex 3: 327–342

De Renzi E, Faglioni P, Scotti G 1969 Impairment of memory for position following brain damage. Cortex 5: 274–284

De Renzi E, Faglioni P, Scotti G 1970 Hemispheric contribution to exploration of space through the visual and tactile modality. Cortex 6: 191–203

De Renzi E, Faglioni P, Scotti G 1971 Judgment of spatial orientation in patients with focal brain damage. Journal of Neurology, Neurosurgery, and Psychiatry 34: 489–495

De Renzi E, Faglioni P, Scotti G, Spinnler H 1972a Impairment in associating colour to form, concomitant with aphasia. Brain 95: 293–304

De Renzi E, Faglioni P, Scotti G, Spinnler H 1972b Impairment of colour sorting behavior after hemispheric damage: an experimental study with the Holmgren Skein Test. Cortex 8: 147–163

De Renzi E, Faglioni P, Sorgato P 1982 Modality-specific and supramodal mechanisms of apraxia. Brain 105: 301–312

De Renzi E, Faglioni P, Spinnler H 1968 The performance of patients with unilateral brain damage on face recognition tasks. Cortex 4: 17–34

De Renzi E, Faglioni P, Villa P 1977 Topographical amnesia. Journal of Neurology, Neurosurgery and Psychiatry 40: 498–505

De Renzi E, Scotti G 1969 The influence of spatial disorders in impairing tactile recognition of shapes. Cortex 5: 53–62

De Renzi E, Scotti G, Spinnler H 1969 Perceptual and associative disorders of visual recognition. Neurology 19: 634–642

De Renzi E, Spinnler H 1966a The influence of verbal and non-verbal defects on visual memory tasks. Cortex 2: 322–335

De Renzi E, Spinnler H 1966b Facial recognition in brain-damaged patients. Neurology 16: 145–152

De Renzi E, Spinnler H 1967 Impaired performance on color tasks in patients with hemispheric damage. Cortex 3: 194–217

De Romanis F, Benfatto B 1973 Presentazione e discussione di quattro casi di prosopagosia. Rivista di Neurologia 43: 111–132

Derouesné C 1973 Le syndrome 'pré-moteur'. Revue Neurologique 128: 353–363

Dew H R 1922 Tumours of the brain: their pathology and treatment; an analysis of 85 cases. Medical Journal of Australia 1: 515–521

Dide M, Botcazo M 1902 Amnésie continue, cécité verbale pure, perte du sens topographique, ramollissement double du lobe lingual. Revue Neurologique 10: 676–686

Diller L, Weinberg J 1977 Hemi-inattention in rehabilitation: the evolution of a rational remediation program. Advances in Neurology 18: 63–82

Dimond S J 1972 The double brain. Churchill Livingstone, London

Dimond S J, Beaumont J G 1974 Hemispheric function in the human brain. Elek Science, London

Dimsdale H, Logue V, Piercy M 1964 A case of persisting impairment of recent memory following right temporal lobectomy. Neuropsychologia 1: 287–298

Donnan G A, Walsh K W, Bladin P F 1978 Memory disorder in vertebrobasilar disease. Journal of Clinical and Experimental Neurology 15: 215–220

Dorff J E, Mirsky A F, Mishkin M 1965 Effects of unilateral temporal lobe removals on tachistoscopic recognition in the left and right visual fields. Neuropsychologia 3: 39–51

Drachman D A, Adams R D 1962 Acute herpes simplex and inclusion body encephalitis. Archives of Neurology 7: 45–63

Drachman D A, Arbit J 1966 Memory and the hippocampal complex. Archives of Neurology 15: 52–61

Drewe E A 1974 The effect of type and area of brain lesion on Wisconsin Card Sorting Test performance. Cortex 10: 159–170

Drewe E A 1975a Go-No-Go learning after frontal lobe lesions in humans. Cortex 11: 8–16

Drewe E A 1975b An experimental investigation of Luria's theory on the effects of frontal lobe lesions in man. Neuropsychologia 13: 421–429

Duensing F 1954a Zur Frage der optisch-raumlichen Agnosie. Archiv fur Psychiatrie und Nervenkrankheiten 192: 185–206

Duensing F 1954b Raumagnostische und ideatorischapraktische Storung des gestaltenden Handelns. Deutsche Zeitschrift fur Nervenheilkunde 170: 72–94

Durnford M, Kimura D 1971 Right hemisphere specialization for depth perception reflected in visual field differences. Nature 231: 394–395

Ebell B 1937 The papyrus Ebers. Levin and Munksgaard, Copenhagen

Efron R 1963a The effect of handedness on the perception of simultaneity and temporal order. Brain 86: 261–284

Efron R 1963b Temporal perception, aphasia, and deja vu. Brain 86: 403–424

Efron R, Bogen J E, Yund E W 1977 Perception of dichotic chords by normal and commissurotomized human subjects. Cortex 13: 137–149

Efron R, Crandall P H 1983 Central auditory processing II. Effects of anterior temporal lobectomy. Brain and Language 19: 237–253

Efron R, Crandall P H, Koss B, Divenyi P L, Yund E W 1983 Central auditory processing III. The 'cocktail party' effect and anterior temporal lobectomy. Brain and Language 19: 254–263

Eisenson J 1962 Language and intellectual modifications associated with right cerebral damage. Language and Speech 5: 49–53

Elghozi D, Strube E, Signoret J L, Cambier J, Lhermitte F 1978 Quasi-aphasie lors de lésions du thalamus. Revue Neurologique 134: 557–574

Elithorn A 1955 A preliminary report on a perceptual maze test sensitive to brain damage. Journal of Neurology, Neurosurgery, and Psychiatry 18: 287–292

Elithorn A 1965 Psychological tests. An objective approach to the problem of task difficulty. Acta Neurologica Scandinavica, Supplementum 13 Part 2: 661–667

Elithorn A, Kerr M, Jones D 1963 A binary perceptual maze. American Journal of Psychology 76: 506–508

Escourolle R, Poirier J 1973 Manual of basic neuropathology. Saunders, Philadelphia

Eskenazi B, Cain W S, Novelly R A, Friend K B 1983 Olfactory functioning in temporal lobectomy patients. Neuropsychologia 21: 365–374

Ettlinger E G (ed) 1965 Functions of the corpus callosum. Churchill, London

Ettlinger G, Blakemore C B, Milner A D, Wilson J 1972 Agenesis of the corpus callosum: A behavioural investigation. Brain 95: 327–346

Ettlinger G, Blakemore C B, Milner A D, Wilson J 1974 Agenesis of the corpus callosum: A further behavioural investigation. Brain 97: 225–234

Ettlinger G, Warrington E, Zangwill O L 1957 A further study of visual-spatial agnosia. Brain 80: 335–361

Evans J P 1935 A study of the sensory defects resulting from excision of the cerebral substance in humans. Research Publications, Association for Research in Nervous and Mental Disease 15: 331–370

Fabbri W 1956 Leucotomia transorbitaria di Fiamberti e rispetto della personalita individuale nei rilievi psicometrici con il test di Porteus. Note e Riviste di Psichiatria 45: 311–332

Faglioni P, Scotti G, Spinnler H 1968 Impaired recognition of written letters following unilateral hemispheric damage. Cortex 5: 120–133

Faglioni P, Scotti G, Spinnler H 1970 Colouring drawings impairment following unilateral brain damage. Brain Research 24: 546

Faglioni P, Scotti G, Spinnler H 1971 The performance of brain-damaged patients in spatial localization of visual and tactile stimuli. Brain 94: 443–454

Faglioni P, Spinnler H, Vignolo L A 1969 Contrasting behavior of right and left hemisphere damaged patients on a discriminative and a semantic task of auditory recognition. Cortex 5: 366–389

Falconer M A, Wilson J L 1958 Visual changes following anterior temporal lobectomy: their significance in relation to 'Meyer's loop' of the optic radiation. Brain 81: 1–14

Faust C 1955 Die zerebralen Herderscheinungen bei Hinterhauptsverletzungen und ihre Beurteilung. Thieme Verlag, Stuttgart

Fazio L, Sacco G, Bugiani O 1973 The thalamic haemorrhage. An anatomo-clinical study. European Neurology 9:30–43

Feather N T 1966 Effects of prior success and failure on expectations of success and subsequent performance. Journal of Personality and Social Psychology 3: 287–298

Fedio P 1980 Thalamo-cortical mediation of perception and memory in man. Proceedings of the International Union of Physiological Sciences 14:111

Fedio P, Van Buren J M 1974 Memory deficits during electrical stimulation of the speech cortex in conscious man. Brain and Language 1: 29–42

Fedio P, Van Buren J M 1975 Memory and perceptual deficits during electrical stimulation in the left and right thalamus and parietal subcortex. Brain and Language 2: 78–100

Fennell E B, Bowers D, Satz P 1977 Within-modal and cross-modal reliabilities of two laterality tests. Brain and Language 4: 63–69

Ferriss G S, Dorsen M M 1975 Agenesis of the corpus callosum: 1. Neuropsychological studies. Cortex 11: 95–122

Feuchtwanger E 1923 Die Funktionen des stirnhirnes, ihre Pathologie und Psychologie. Springer, Berlin

Fisher C M 1959 The pathological and clinical aspects of thalamic hemorrhage. Transactions of the American Neurological Association 84: 56–59

Fisher C M 1982 Transient global amnesia. Precipitating activities and other observations. Archives of Neurology 39: 605–608

Fisher C M, Adams R D 1964 Transient global amnesia. Acta Neurologica Scandinavica 40 (supp. 19): 1–83

Fisher M 1956 Left hemiplegia and motor impersistence. Journal of Nervous and Mental Disease 123: 201–218

Fisher S 1949 An overview of trends in research dealing with personality rigidity. Journal of Personality 17: 342–351

Flateau E 1921 Sur les hemorragies meningees idiopathiques. Gazette des Hopitaux 94: 1077–1081

Fleming G W T H 1942 Some preliminary remarks on prefrontal leucotomy. Journal of Mental Science 88: 282–284

Fleminger J J, de Horne D J, Nott P N 1970 Unilateral electroconvulsive therapy and cerebral dominance: effect of right- and left-sided electrode placement on verbal memory. Journal of Neurology, Neurosurgery, and Psychiatry 23: 408–411

Flor-Henry P 1969 Schizophrenic-like reactions and affective psychosis associated with temporal lobe epilepsy: etiological factors. American Journal of Psychiatry 126: 400–403

Foerster O 1936 Cited in Gloning, Gloning, Hoff 1968 p 34

Fogel M L 1962 Intelligence Quotient as an index of brain damage. American Journal of Orthopsychiatry 32: 338–339

Fogel M L 1964 The Intelligence Quotient as an index of brain damage. American Journal of Orthopsychiatry 34: 555–562

Fontenot D J, Benton A L 1971 Tactile perception of direction in relation to hemispheric locus of lesion. Neuropsychologia 9: 83–88

Frederiks J A M 1969 Disorders of the body schema. In: Vinken P J, Bruyn G W (eds) Handbook of clinical neurology. vol 4, ch 11 North-Holland, Amsterdam

Frederiks J A M 1985 Disorders of the body schema. In: Vinken P J, Bruyn G W, Klawans H L (eds) Handbook of clinical neurology, Revised series 1, vol. 45, Elsevier, Amsterdam, p 373–393

Freeman W 1953a Level of achievement after lobotomy: a study of 1000 cases. American Journal of Psychiatry 110: 269–276

Freeman W 1953b Hazards of lobotomy: report on 200 operations. Archives of Neurology and Psychiatry 69: 640–643

Freeman W 1958 Frontal leucotomy and its congeners. Diseases of the Nervous System 19: 11–15

Freeman W, Watts J W 1942 Psychosurgery Thomas, Springfield, Illinois

Freeman W, Watts J W 1948 The thalamic projection to the frontal lobe. Research Publications, Association for Research in Nervous and Mental Disease 27: 200–209

Freeman W, Watts J W 1950 Psychosurgery. 2nd edn. Thomas, Springfield, Illinois

Freemon F R 1971 Akinetic mutism and bilateral anterior cerebral artery occlusion. Journal of Neurology, Neurosurgery, and Psychiatry 34: 693–698

French L A, Johnson D R, Adkins G A 1966 Cerebral hemispherectomy for intractable seizures. A long-term follow-up. The Journal-Lancet 81: 58–65

Freud S 1953 Zur Auffassung der Aphasien. 1891 International Universities Press, New York

Fried I, Mateer C, Ojemann G, Wohns R, Fedio P 1982 Organization of visuospatial functions in the human cortex. Brain 105: 349–371

Fryer D G, Rich M P 1960 Denial of illness in relation to intellectual functions. Journal of Nervous and Mental Disease 131: 523–527

Fuchs W 1938 Pseudo-fovea. In: Elliss W D (ed) A source book of Gestalt psychology. Kegan Paul, London

Fuller G B 1967 Revised Minnesota Percepto-Diagnostic Test. Psychological Corporation, New York

Fuster J M 1980 The prefrontal cortex. Raven, New York

Gade A 1982 Amnesia after operations on aneurysms of the anterior communicating artery. Surgical Neurology 18: 46–49

Gaffan D 1972 Loss of recognition memory in rats with lesions of the fornix. Neuropsychologia 10: 327–341

Gainotti G 1968 Les manifestations de negligence et d'inattention pour l'hemispace. Cortex 4: 64–91

Gainotti G 1969 Reactions 'catastrophiques' et manifestations d'indifférence au cours des atteintes cérébrales. Neuropsychologia 7: 174–187

Gainotti G 1972 Emotional behaviour and hemispheric side of lesion. Cortex 8: 41–55

Gainotti G 1984 Some methodological problems in the study of the relationships between emotions and cerebral dominance. Journal of Clinical Neuropsychology 6: 111–121

Gainotti G, Miceli G, Caltagirone C 1977 Constructional apraxia in left brain damaged patients: a planning disorder? Cortex 13: 109–118

Gainotti G, Messerli P, Tissot R 1972a Troubles du dessin et lesions hemispheriques retrorolandiques unilaterales gauches et droites. Encephale 61: 245–264

Gainotti G, Messerli P, Tissot R 1972b Qualitative analysis of unilateral spatial neglect in relation to laterality of cerebral lesions. Journal of Neurology, Neurosurgery, and Psychiatry 35: 545–550

Gainotti G, Tiacci C 1970 Patterns of drawing disability in right and left hemispheric patients. Neuropsychologia 8: 379–384

Gainotti G, Tiacci C 1971 The relation between disorders of visual perception and unilateral spatial neglect. Neuropsychologia 9: 451–458

Galaburda A M, LeMay M, Kemper T L, Geschwind N 1978 Right-left asymmetries in the brain. Science 199: 852–856

Galaburda A M, Sanides F, Geschwind N 1978 Human brain. Cytoarchitectonic left-right asymmetries in the temporal speech region. Archives of Neurology 35: 812–817

Galper R E, Costa L 1980 Hemispheric superiority for recognizing faces depends upon how they are learned. Cortex 16: 21–38

Gamper E 1928 Zur Frage der Polioencephalitis der chronischen Alkoholiker. Deutsche Zeitschrift fur Nervenheilkunde 102: 122–129

Gardner W J, Karnosh L J, McClure C C, Gardner A K 1955 Residual function following hemispherectomy for infantile hemiplegia. Brain 78: 487–502

Gasparrini W G, Satz P, Heilman K, Coolidge F L 1978 Hemispheric asymmetries of affective processing as determined by the Minnesota Multiphasic Personality Inventory. Journal of Neurology, Neurosurgery, and Psychiatry 41: 470–473

Gassel M M 1969 Occipital lobe syndromes (excluding hemianopia). In: Vinken P J, Bruyn G W (eds) Handbook of neurology. vol 2, ch 20 North-Holland, Amsterdam

Gassel M M, Williams D 1963 Visual function in patients with homonymous hemianopia. Part III. The completion phenomenon; insight and attitude to the defect; and visual functional efficiency. Brain 86: 229–260

Gastaut H 1970 Clinical and electroencephalographical classification of epileptic seizures. Epilepsia 11: 102–113

Gastaut H, Broughton R 1972 Epileptic seizures. Clinical and electrographic features, diagnosis and treatment. Thomas, Springfield, Illinois

Gazzaniga M S 1970 The bi-sected brain. Appleton-Century-Crofts, New York

Gazzaniga M S 1972 One brain-two minds? American Scientist 60: 311–317

Gazzaniga M S 1982 Cognitive functions of the left hemisphere. In: Katsuki S, Tsubaki T, Toyokura Y (eds) Neurology. Proceedings of the 12th world congress of neurology, Kyoto, Japan. Excerpta Medica, Amsterdam, p 11–19

Gazzaniga M S, Bogen J E, Sperry R W 1962 Some functional effects of severing the cerebral commissures in man. Proceedings of the National Academy of Science 48: 1765–1769

Gazzaniga M S, Bogen J E, Sperry R W 1965 Observations on visual perception after disconnexion of the cerebral hemispheres in man. Brain 88: 221–236

Gazzaniga M S, Bogen J E, Sperry R W 1967 Dyspraxia following division of the cerebral commissures. Archives of Neurology 16: 606–612

Gazzaniga M S, Freedman H 1973 Observations on visual processes after posterior callosal section. Neurology 23: 1126–1130

Gazzaniga M S, Hillyard S A 1971 Language and speech capacity of the right hemisphere. Neuropsychologia 9: 273–280

Gazzaniga M S, Le Doux J E 1978 The integrated mind. Plenum, New York

Gazzaniga M S, Le Doux J E, Wilson D H 1977 Language, praxis, and the right hemisphere: clues to some mechanisms of consciousness. Neurology 27: 1144–1147

Gazzaniga M S, Sidtis J J, Volpe B T, Smylie C, Holtzman J Wilson D H 1982 Evidence for paracallosal verbal transfer after callosal section. A possible consequence of bilateral language organization. Brain 105: 53–63

Gazzaniga M S, Sperry R W 1967 Language after section of the cerebral commissures. Brain 90: 131–148

Gazzaniga M S, Volpe B J, Smylie C S, Wilson D H, Le Doux J E 1979 Plasticity in speech organization following commissurotomy. Brain 102: 805–815

Geffen G 1976 The development of hemispheric specialization for speech perception. Cortex 12: 337–346

Geffen G, Caudrey D 1981 Reliability and validity of the dichotic monitoring test for language laterality. Neuropsychologia 19: 413–423

Geffen G, Quinn K 1984 Hemispheric specialization and ear advantages in processing speech. Psychological Bulletin 96: 273–291

Geldard F A 1972 The human senses, 2nd edn. Wiley, New York

Gerboth R 1950 A study of the two forms of the Wechsler-Bellevue Intelligence Scale. Journal of Consulting Psychology 14: 365–370

Gerstmann J 1924 Fingeragnosie: Ein unschriebene Störung der Orientierung am eigenen Korper. Wiener Klinische Wochenschrift 37: 1010–1012

Gerstmann J 1930 Zur Symptomatologie der Hirnläsionen im Uebergangsgebeit der unteren Parietal und mittleren Occipitalwindung. Nervenarzt 3: 691–695

Gerstmann J 1957 Some notes on the Gerstmann syndrome. Neurology 7: 866–869

Geschwind N 1962 The anatomy of acquired disorders of reading. In: Money J (ed) Reading disability. Johns Hopkins Press, Baltimore

Geschwind N 1965a Alexia and colour-naming disturbance. In: Ettlinger G (ed) Functions of the corpus callosum. Churchill, London p 95–101

Geschwind N 1965b Disconnection syndromes in animals and man. Part I. Brain 88: 237–294

Geschwind N 1965c Disconnection syndromes in animals and man. Part II. Brain 88: 585–644

Geschwind N 1966 Carl Wernicke, the Breslau School and the history of aphasia. In: Carterette E C (ed) Language and communication. University of California Press, Berkeley

Geschwind N 1967 Brain mechanisms suggested by studies of hemispheric connections. In: Darley F L (ed) Brain mechanisms underlying speech and language. Grune and Stratton, New York

Geschwind N 1969 Problems in the anatomical understanding of the aphasias. In: Benton A L (ed) Contributions to clinical neuropsychology. Aldine, Chicago

Geschwind N 1970 The organization of language and the brain. Science 170: 940–944

Geschwind N 1974 The anatomical basis of hemispheric differentiation. In: Dimond S J, Beaumont J G (eds) Hemispheric function in the human brain. Elek, London

Geschwind N 1978 Organic problems in the aged: Brain syndromes and alcoholism. Journal of Geriatric Psychiatry 11: 161–166

Geschwind N, Damasio A 1985 Apraxia In: Vinken P J, Bruyn G W, Klawans H L (eds) Handbook of clinical neurology, New series 1, vol 45. Elsevier, Amsterdam p 423–432

Geschwind N, Fusillo M 1966 Color naming defects in association with alexia. Archives of Neurology 15: 137–146

Geschwind N, Galaburda A M 1985a Cerebral lateralization Biological mechanisms, associations and pathology: I. A hypothesis and a program for research. Archives of Neurology 42: 428–459

Geschwind N, Galaburda A M 1985b Cerebral lateralization II. Archives of Neurology 42: 521–552

Geschwind N, Galaburda A M 1985c Cerebral lateralization III. Archives of Neurology

Geschwind N, Kaplan E 1962 A human cerebral deconnection syndrome. Neurology 12: 675–685

Geschwind N, Levitsky W 1968 Human brain: left-right asymmetries in temporal speech region. Science 161: 186–187

Ghent L, Mishkin M Teuber H L 1962 Short-term memory after frontal lobe injury in man. Journal of Comparative and Physiological Psychology 55: 705–709

Gibson W C 1962 Pioneers of localization in the brain. JAMA 180: 944–951

Gibson W C 1969 The early history of localization in the nervous system. In: Vinken P J, Bruyn G W (eds) Handbook of clinical neurology. Vol 2, ch 2 North-Holland, Amsterdam

Gilliatt R W, Pratt R T C 1952 Disorders of perception in a case of right-sided cerebral thrombosis. Journal of Neurology, Neurosurgery and Psychiatry 15: 264–271

Girgis M 1971 The orbital surface of the frontal lobe of the brain. Acta Psychiatrica Scandinavica, Supplementum 222: 1–58

Glaser J S 1978 Neuro-ophthalmology. Harper and Row, New York

Gleason W J 1953 Rigidity and negative transfer effects in patients with cerebral damage. Unpublished doctoral dissertation, Northwestern University.

Gloning K 1965 Die zerebral bedingten Storungen des Raumlichen Schens und des Raumerlebens. Maudrich, Wein

Gloning I, Gloning K, Haub G, Quatember R 1969 Comparison of verbal behavior in right-handed and non-right-handed patients with anatomically verified lesions of one hemisphere. Cortex 56: 43–52

Gloning I, Gloning K, Hoff H 1968 Neuropsychological symptoms in lesions of the occipital lobes and adjacent areas. Gauthier-Villars, Paris.

Gloning I, Gloning K, Hoff H, Tschabitscher H 1966 Zur Prosopagnosie. Neuropsychologia 4: 113–132

Gloning I, Gloning K, Jellinger K, Quatember R 1970 A case of 'prosopagnosia' with necropsy findings. Neuropsychologia 8: 199–204

Gloning K, Haub G, Quatember R 1967 Standardisierung einer Untersuchungsmethode der sogenannten 'Prosopagnosie' Neuropsychologia 5: 99–101

Gloning K, Hoff H 1969 Cerebral localization of disorders of higher nervous activity. In: Vinken P J, Bruyn G W (eds) Handbook of clinical neurology. Vol 2, ch 3. North-Holland, Amsterdam

Glosser G, Butters N, Kaplan E 1977 Visuoperceptual processes in brain damaged patients on the digit symbol substitution test. International Journal of Neuroscience 1: 59–66

Glosser G, Butters N, Samuels I 1976 Failures in information processing in patients with Korsakoff's syndrome. Neuropsychologia 14: 327–334

Glowinski H 1973 Cognitive deficits in temporal lobe epilepsy: an investigation of memory functioning. Journal of Nervous and Mental Disease 157: 129–137

Goldberg E, Antin S P, Bilder R M, Gerstman L J, Hughes J E O 1981 Retrograde amnesia: possible role of mesencephalic reticular activation in long-term memory. Science 213: 1392–1394

Golden C J 1976 Identification of brain disorders by the Stroop color and word test. Journal of Clinical Psychology 32: 654–658

Goldstein G, Neuringer C, Olson J 1968 Impairment of abstract reasoning in the brain-damaged: Qualitative or quantitative? Cortex 4: 372–388

Goldstein K 1927 Die lokalisation in der grosshirnrinde. In: Bethe A, Fischer E (eds) Handbuch der Normalen und Pathologischen Psysiologie. Springer, Berlin

Goldstein K 1936a The significance of the frontal lobes for mental performance. Journal of Neurology and Psychopathology 17: 27–40

Goldstein K 1936b The modification of behavior consequent to cerebral lesions. Psychiatric Quarterly 10: 586–610

Goldstein K 1939a Clinical and theoretical aspects of lesions of the frontal lobes. Archives of Neurology and Psychiatry 41: 865–867

Goldstein K 1939b The organism. American Book, New York

Goldstein K 1940 Human nature. Harvard University Press, Cambridge, Massachusetts

Goldstein K 1942a After effects of brain injuries in war. Grune and Stratton, New York

Goldstein K 1942b The two ways of adjustment of the organism to central defects. Journal of the Mount Sinai Hospital 9: 504–513

Goldstein K 1943 Brain concussion: Evaluation of the after effects by special tests. Diseases of the Nervous System 4: 3–12

Goldstein K 1944 Mental changes due to frontal lobe damage. Journal of psychology 17: 187–208

Goldstein K 1959 Functional disturbances in brain damage. In: Arieti S (ed) American handbook of psychiatry. vol. 1. ch. 39. Basic Books, New York

Goldstein K, Gelb A 1918 Psychologischen Analysen Hirnpathologischer Falle auf Grund von Untersuchungen Hirnverletzer. Zeitschrift fur die gesamte Neurologie und Psychiatrie 41:1

Goldstein K, Scheerer M 1941 Abstract and concrete behavior: An experimental study with special tests. Psychological Monographs 43: 1–151

Goldstein M N, Joynt R J 1969 Long-term follow-up of a callosal-sectioned patient. Archives of Neurology 20: 96–102

Gollin E S 1960 Development studies of visual recognition of incomplete objects. Perceptual and Motor Skills 11: 289–298

Gordon H W, Bogen J E, Sperry R W 1971 Absence of disconnexion syndrome in two patients with partial section of the neocommissures. Brain 94: 327–336

Gott P S 1973 Cognitive abilities following right and left hemispherectomy. Cortex 9: 266–274

Gott P S, Saul R E 1978 Agenesis of the corpus callosum: limits of functional compensation. Neurology: 28: 1272–1279

Gottlieb G, Wilson I 1965 Cerebral dominance: temporary disruption of verbal memory by unilateral electroconvulsive shock treatment. Journal of Comparative and Physiological Psychology 60: 368–372

Graff-Radford N R, Eslinger P J, Demasio A R, Yamada T 1984 Non-hemorrhagic infarction of the thalamus. Behavioral, anatomic, and physiological correlates. Neurology 34: 14–23

Grafman J, Passafiume D, Faglioni P, Boller F 1982 Calculation disturbances in adults with focal hemispheric damage. Cortex 18: 37–50

Graña F, Rocca E D, Graña L 1954 Los trepanaciones craneanas en el Peru en la época pre-Hispanica. Santa Maria, Lima, Peru

Grant A D, Berg E A 1948 A behavioral analysis of degree of reinforcement and ease of shifting to new responses in a Weigl-type card sorting. Journal of Experimental Psychology 38: 404–411

Grantham E C 1951 Prefrontal lobotomy for the relief of pain with a report of a new operative technique. Journal of Neurosurgery 8:405

Grassi J R 1950 Impairment of abstract behavior following bilateral prefrontal lobotomy. Psychiatric Quarterly 24: 74–88

Greenblatt M, Arnold R, Solomon H C 1950 Studies in lobotomy. Grune and Stratton, New York

Greenblatt S H 1973 Alexia without agraphia or hemianopsia. Anatomical analysis of an autopsied case. Brain 96: 307–316

Greenblatt S H 1983 Localization of lesions in alexia. In: Kertesz A (ed) Localization in neuropsychology. Academic Press, New York p 323–356

Gregson R A M, Taylor G M 1975 An administrative manual for the Patterned Cognitive Impairment Test Battery. University of Canterbury, New Zealand

Gruner J E 1956 Sur la pathologie des encéphalopathies alcooliques. Revue Neurologique 94: 682–689

Grunthal E 1939 Über das Corpus mamillare und den Korsakowschen symptomencomplex. Confinia neurologica 2: 64–95

Grunthal E 1947 Uber das Klinischer Bild nach unschreibenem beiderseitige Ausfall der Ammonschornrinde. Monatsschrift fur Psychiatrie und Neurologie 113: 1–16

Gurdjian E S 1973 Head injury from antiquity to the present with special reference to penetrating head wounds. Thomas, Springfield, Illinois

Gurdjian E S 1975 Impact head injury. Thomas, Springfield Illinois

Gurdjian E S, Lissner H R, Hodgson V R, Patrick L M 1966 Mechanisms of head injury. Clinical Neurosurgery 12: 112–128

Gurdjian E S, Webster J E, Arnkoff H 1943 Acute craniocerebral trauma. Surgery 13: 333–353

Gurdjian E S, Webster J E, Lissner H R 1955 Observations on the mechanism of brain concussion contusion and laceration. Surgery Gynaecology and Obstetrics 101: 680–690

Guthrie T C, Grossman E M 1952 A study of the syndrome of denial. Archives of Neurology and Psychiatry 68: 362–371

Guyotat J, Courjon J 1956 Les ictus amnésiques. Journal de médicine de Lyon 37: 697–701

Haggard M P, Parkinson A M 1971 Stimulus and task factors as determinants of ear advantages. Quarterly Journal of Experimental Psychology 23: 168–177

Halgren E, Engel J, Wilson C L, Walter R D, Squires N K, Crandall P H 1983 Dynamics of the hippocampal contribution to memory: Stimulation and recording studies in humans. In: Seifert W (ed) Neurobiology of the hippocampus. Academic, New York p 529–572

Halgren E, Walter R D, Cherlow D G, Crandall P H 1978 Mental phenomena evoked by electrical stimulation of the human hippocampal formation and amygdala. Brain 101: 83–117

Hall P 1963 Korsakov's syndrome following herpes zoster encephalitis. Lancet i: 752–753

Hall P 1965 Subacute viral encephalitis amnesia. Lancet 2: 1077

Halliday A M, Davison K, Browne M W, Kreeger L C 1968 A comparison of the effects on depression and memory of bilateral ECT and unilateral ECT to the dominant and non-dominant hemispheres. British Journal of Psychiatry 114: 997–1012

Halstead W C 1940 Preliminary analysis of grouping behavior in patients with cerebral injury by the method of equivalent and non-equivalent stimuli. American Journal of Psychology 96: 1263–1294

Halstead W C 1947 Brain and intelligence. University of Chicago Press, Chicago

Halstead W C 1958 Some behavioral aspects of partial temporal lobectomy in man. Research Publications, Association for Research in Nervous and Mental Disease

Halstead W C 1959 The statics and the dynamics. In: Beck S J, Molish H B (eds) Reflexes to intelligence. The Free Press, Glencoe, Illinois

Hamlin R M 1970 Intellectual function 14 years after frontal lobe surgery. Cortex 6: 299–307

Hamsher K De S 1978 Stereopsis and unilateral brain disease. Investigative Ophthalmology 17: 336–343

Hamsher K de S, Levin H S, Benton A L 1979 Facial recognition in patients with focal brain lesions. Archives of Neurology 36: 837–839

Handfield-Jones R M, Porritt A E 1949 The essentials of modern surgery. Livingstone, Edinburgh

Hanfmann E, Rickers-Ovsiankina M, Goldstein K 1944 Case Lanuti: extreme concretization of behavior of the brain cortex. Psychological Monographs 57, No 4, Whole No 264

Hannay H J, Varney N R, Benton A L (1976) Visual localization in patients with unilateral brain disease. Journal of Neurology, Neurosurgery, and Psychiatry 39: 307–313

Harper C 1982 Neuropathology of brain damage caused by alcohol. Medical Journal of Australia 2: 277–282

Harper C G, Kril J J, Holloway R L 1985 Brain shrinkage in chronic alcoholics: a pathological study. British Medical Journal 290: 501–504

Harvey O J, Hunt D E, Schroeder D M 1961 Conceptual systems and personality organization. Wiley, New York

Hatfield F M, Zangwill O L 1974 Ideation in aphasia: the Picture-Story method. Neuropsychologia 12: 389–393

Hayward R J, Naeser M A, Zatz L M 1977 Cranial computed tomography in aphasia. Correlation of anatomical lesions with functional deficits. Radiology 123: 653–660

Head H 1920 Studies in neurology. Oxford University Press, Oxford

Heath R G 1964 Pleasure response of human subjects to direct stimulations of the brain. In: Heath R G (ed) The role of pleasure in behavior. Harper and Row, New York p 219–243

Heathfield K W G, Croft P B, Swash M 1973 The syndrome of transient global amnesia. Brain 96: 729–736

Hebb D O 1939a Intelligence in man after large removals of cerebral tissue: report of four left frontal lobe cases. Journal of General Psychology 21: 73–87

Hebb D O 1939b Intelligence in man after large removals of cerebral tissue: defects following right temporal lobectomy. Journal of General Psychology 21: 437–446

Hebb D O 1941 Human intelligence after removal of cerebral tissue from the right frontal lobe. Journal of General Psychology 25: 257–265

Hebb D O 1942 The effect of early and late brain injury upon test scores and the nature of normal adult intelligence. Proceedings of the American Philosophical Society 85: 275–292

Hebb D O 1945 Man's frontal lobes: a critical review. Archives of Neurology and Psychiatry 54: 10–24

Hebb D O 1949 The organization of behavior. Wiley, New York

Hebb D O, Penfield W 1940 Human behavior after extensive bilateral removal from the frontal lobes. Archives of Neurology and Psychiatry 44: 421–438

Hécaen H 1960a Les agnosies visuelles pour les objets animés. In: Alajouanine T (ed) Les grandes activites du lobe occipital. Masson, Paris, p 281–284

Hécaen H 1960b Les apraxies. Revue Neurologique 102: 541–550

Hécaen H 1962 Clinical symptomatology in right and left hemispheric lesions. In: Mountcastle V B (ed) Interhemispheric relations and cerebral dominance. Ch 10 Johns Hopkins Press, Baltimore

Hécaen H 1964 Mental symptoms associated with tumors of the frontal lobe. In: Warren
J M, Akert K (eds) The frontal granular cortex and behavior. Ch 16. McGraw Hill, New
York

Hécaen H 1969 Aphasic, apraxic and agnosic syndromes in right and left hemisphere
lesions. In: Vinken P J, Bruyn G W (eds) Handbook of clinical neurology. vol. 4. ch. 15
North-Holland, Amsterdam

Hécaen H 1972 Introduction a la neuropsychologie. Larousse, Paris

Hécaen H, Ajuriaguerra J de 1952 Méconnaissances et hallucinations corporelles. Masson,
Paris

Hécaen H, Ajuriaguerra J de 1954 Balint's syndrome (psychic paralysis of visual fixation)
and its minor forms. Brain 77: 373–400

Hécaen H, Ajuriaguerra J de 1956 Les encéphalopathies alcooliques subaiguees et
chroniques. Revue Neurologique 94: 528–555

Hécaen H, Ajuriaguerra J de, Massonet J 1951 Les troubles visuo- constructifs par lésion
parieto-occipitale droite. Encephale 40: 122–179

Hécaen, H Albert M L 1978 Human neuropsychology. Wiley, New York

Hécaen H, Angelergues R 1961 Etude anatomo-clinique de 280 cas de lésions rétro-
rorolandiques unilatérales des hémisphères cérébraux. Encephale 6: 533–562

Hécaen H Angelergues R 1962 Agnosia for faces (prosopagnosia) Archives of Neurology
7: 92–100

Hécaen H, Angelergues R 1963 La cécité psychique. Masson, Paris

Hécaen H, Angelergues R, Douzenis J A 1963 Les agraphies. Neuropsychologia
1: 179–208

Hécaen H, Angelergues R, Houillier S 1961 Les variétés cliniques des acalculies au cours
des lesions rétrorolandiques: aproche statistique du problème. Revue Neurologique
105: 85–103

Hécaen H, Assal G 1970 A comparison of constructive deficits following right and left
hemispheric lesions. Neuropsychologia 8: 289–303

Hécaen H, Penfield W, Bertrand C, Malmo R 1956 The syndrome of apractognosia due to
lesions of the minor cerebral hemisphere. Archives of Neurology and Psychiatry
75: 400–434

Hécaen H, Sauguet J 1972 Cerebral dominance in left handed subjects. Cortex 8: 19–48

Hécaen H, Tzortzis C, Rondot P 1980 Loss of topographic memory with learning deficits.
Cortex 16: 525–542

Heilbrun A B 1962 Issues in the assessment of organic brain damage. Psychological Reports
10: 511–515

Heilman K M 1973 Ideational apraxia: a redefinition. Brain 96: 861–864

Heilman K M 1979a Neglect and related disorders. In: Heilman K M and Valenstein E
(eds) Clinical neuropsychology. Oxford University Press, New York, p 268–307

Heilman K M 1979b Apraxia. In: Heilman K M, Valenstein E (eds) Clinical
neuropsychology. Oxford Press, New York p 159–185

Heilman K M 1982 Right hemisphere dominance for attention. In: Katsuki S, Tsubaki T,
Toyokura Y (eds) Neurology. Proceedings of the 12th world congress of neurology,
Kyoto, Japan. Excerpta Medica, Amsterdam, p 20–26

Heilman K M, Rothi L, Kertesz A 1983 Localization of apraxia-producing lesions. In:
Kertesz A (ed) Localization in neuropsychology. Academic Press, New York,
p 371–390

Heilman K M, Scholes R, Watson R T 1975 Auditory affective agnosia. Journal of
Neurology, Neurosurgery and Psychiatry 38: 69–72

Heilman K M, Schwartz H D, Watson R T 1978 Hypoarousal in patients with the neglect
syndrome and emotional indifference. Neurology 28: 229–232

Heilman K M, Valenstein E 1972a Auditory neglect in man. Archives of Neurology
26: 32–35

Heilman K M, Valenstein E 1972b Frontal lobe neglect in man. Neurology 22: 660–664

Heilman K M, Valenstein E 1979 Mechanisms underlying hemispatial neglect. Annals of
Neurology 5: 166–170

Heilman K M, Valenstein E, Watson R T 1985 The neglect syndrome. In: Vinken P J,
Bruyn G W, Klawans H L (eds) Handbook of clinical neurology, Revised series 1,
vol. 45, Elsevier, Amsterdam, p 153–183

Heilman K M, Van Den Abell T 1980 Right hemisphere dominance for attention: The mechanism underlying hemispheric asymmetries of inattention (neglect). Neurology 30: 327–330

Heilman K M, Watson R T 1977 The neglect syndrome — a unilateral defect of the orienting response. In: Harnad S et al (eds) Lateralization in the nervous system. Academic, New York p 285–302

Heilman K M, Watson R T, Schulman H M 1974 A unilateral memory defect. Journal of Neurology, Neurosurgery and Psychiatry 37: 790–793

Heilman K M, Watson R T, Valenstein E, Damasio A R 1983 Localization of lesions in neglect. In: Kertesz A (ed) Localization in neuropsychology. Academic Press, New York p 471–492

Heimburger R F, Demeyer W, Reitan R M 1964 Implication of Gerstmann's syndrome. Journal of Neurology, Neurosurgery and Psychiatry 27: 52–57

Hellige J B 1983 Cerebral hemisphere asymmetry: method, theory, and application. Praeger, New York

Henson R A 1985 Amusia In: Vinken P J, Bruyn G W, Klawans H L (eds) Handbook of clinical neurology, new series 1, vol. 45. Elsevier, Amsterdam, p 483–490

Hermann B P, Chhabria S 1980 Interictal psycho-pathology in patients with ictal fear. Archives of Neurology 37: 667–668

Hermann B P, Riel P 1981 Interictal personality and behavioral traits in temporal lobe and generalized epilepsy. Cortex 17: 125–128

Herrick C J 1963 Brains in rats and men. (Reprinted from 1926) University of Chicago Press, Chicago

Hier D B, Davis K R, Richardson E P 1977 Hypertensive putaminal haemorrhage. Annals of Neurology 1: 152–159

Hilgard E R 1956 Theories of learning, 2nd edn. Appleton-Century-Crofts, New York p 185–222

Hillbom E 1960 After effects of brain injuries. Acta Psychiatrica et Neurologica Scandinavica 35, Supplementum 142: 5–195

Hines D, Satz P 1971 Superiority of right visual half-fields in right handers for recall of digits presented at varying rates. Neuropsychologia 9: 21–25

Hirose G, Kin T, Murakami E 1977 Alexia without agraphia associated with right occipital lesion. Journal of Neurology, Neurosurgery, and Psychiatry 40: 225–227

Hirst W 1982 The amnesic syndrome: Descriptions and explanations. Psychological Bulletin 91: 435–460

Hoff H, Poetzl O 1937 Uber eine optisch-agnostische Storung des 'Physiognomie-Gedachtnisses'. Zeitschrift fur die gesamte Neurologie und Psychiatrie 159: 367–395

Hohne H H, Walsh K W 1970 Surgical modification of the personality. Mental Health Authority, Victoria, Special Publications No. 2. Victorian Government Printer, Melbourne

Holmes G 1918 Disturbances of visual orientation. British Journal of Ophthalmology 2: 449–469

Holmes G 1927 Disorders of sensation produced by cortical lesions. Brain 49: 413–428

Hooper R S 1966 Head injuries — past, present and future. Medical Journal of Australia 2: 45–54

Hooper R 1969 Patterns of acute head injury. Edward Arnold, London

Horowitz M J, Adams J E, Rutkin Bb 1968 Visual imagery on brain stimulation. Archives of General Psychiatry 19: 469–486

Howes D 1962 An approach to the quantitative analysis of word blindness. In: Money J (ed) Reading disability: progress and research in dyslexia. Johns Hopkins Press, Baltimore

Hubel D H, Wiesel T N 1959 Receptive fields of single neurones in cat's striate cortex. Journal of Physiology 148: 574–591

Huppert F A, Piercy M 1976 Recognition memory in amnesic patients: effects of temporal context and familiarity of material. Cortex 12: 3–20

Huppert F A, Piercy M 1978 Dissociation between learning and memory in organic amnesia. Nature 275: 317–318

Huppert F A, Piercy M 1979 Normal and abnormal forgetting in organic amnesia: effect of locus of lesion. Cortex 15: 385–390

Huppert FA, Piercy M 1982 In search of the functional locus of amnesic syndromes. In: Cermak L S (ed) Human memory and amnesia. Erlbaum, Hillsdale, NJ

Hurwitz L J, Adams G F 1972 Rehabilitation of hemiplegia: indices of assessment and prognosis. British Medical Journal 1: 94–98

Inglis J 1970 Shock, surgery, and cerebral asymmetry. British Journal of Psychiatry 117: 143–148

Inglis J, Sykes D H 1967 Some sources of variation in dichotic listening in children. Journal of Experimental Child Psychology 5: 480–488

Isaacson R L, Pribram K H (eds) 1976 The hippocampus. vol 1 Structure and development, vol 2 Neurophysiology and behavior. Plenum Press, New York

Iversen S D 1977 Temporal lobe amnesia. In: Whitty C W M, Zangwill O L (eds) Amnesia, 2nd edn., Butterworths, London, p 136–182

Iwata M, Sugishita M, Toyokura Y, Yamada R, Yoshioka M 1974 Etude sur le syndrome de disconnexion visuo-linguale apres la transection du corps calleux. Journal of the Neurological Sciences 23: 421–432

Jackson J H 1864, 1874, 1876 See Selected writings of John Hughlings Jackson. Taylor J (ed) Basic Books, New York, 1958

Jackson J H 1890 Case of tumour of the right temporosphenoidal lobe bearing on the localization of the sense of smell and on the interpretation of a particular variety of epilepsy. Brain 12: 346–357

Jackson J H 1958 Selected writings of John Hughlings Jackson. Taylor J (ed) Basic Books, New York

Jamieson K G 1971 A first notebook of head injury, 2nd edn. Butterworth, Sydney

Janet P 1928 L'évolution de la memoire et la notion du temps. Chahine, Paris

Jasper H H, Rasmussen T 1958 Studies of clinical and electrical responses to deep temporal stimulation in man with some considerations of functional anatomy. Research Publications, Association for Research in Nervous and Mental Disease 36: 316–334

Jeeves M A 1965a Psychological studies of three cases of congenital agenesis of the corpus callosum. In: Ettlinger E G (ed) Functions of the corpus callosum. Churchill, London p 73–94

Jeeves MA 1965b Agenesis of the corpus callosum: physiopathological and clinical aspects. Proceedings of the Australian Association of Neurology 3: 41–48

Jeeves M A 1979 Some limits to interhemispheric integration in cases of callosal agenesis and partial commissurotomy. In: Russell I S, Van Hof M W, Berlucchi G (eds) Structure and function of cerebral commissures, ch. 37. University Park Press, Baltimore

Jefferson G 1937 Removal of right or left frontal lobes in man. British Medical Journal 2: 199–206

Johansson T, Fahlgren H 1979 Alexia without agraphia: Lateral and medial infarction of the left occipital lobe. Neurology 29: 390–393

Johnson G, Parsons O A, Holloway F A, Bruhn P 1973 Intradimensional reversal shift performance in brain-damaged and chronic alcoholic patients. Journal of Consulting and Clinical Psychology 40: 253–258

Jones B 1979 Lateral asymmetry in testing long-term memory for faces. Cortex 15: 183–186

Jones G V 1983 On double dissociation of function. Neuropsychologia 1983: 397–400

Jones-Gotman M, Milner B 1977 Design fluency: the invention of nonsense drawings after focal cortical lesions. Neuropsychologia 15: 653–674

Joynt R J 1964 Paul Pierre Broca: His contribution to the knowledge of aphasia. Cortex 1: 206–213

Joynt R J, Goldstein M N 1975 Minor cerebral hemisphere. In: Friedlander W J (ed) Advances in Neurology vol. 7. Raven Press, New York

Joynt R J, Honch G W, Rubin A J, Trudell R G 1985 Occipital lobe syndromes. In: Vinken, P J, Bruyn G W, Klawans H L, Frederiks J A M Handbook of Clinical Neurology, Revised series 1, vol 45 1985 ch 5 p 49–63

Julesz B 1964 Binocular depth perception without familiarity cues. Science 145: 356–363

Jurgens U, Von Cramon D 1982 On the role of the anterior cingulate cortex in phonation: a case report. Brain and Language 15: 234–248

Kahn E A, Crosby E C 1972 Korsakoff's syndrome associated with surgical lesions involving the mamillary bodies. Neurology 22: 117–125

Kaplan H A, Ford D H 1966 The brain vascular system. Elsevier, Amsterdam

Kapur N, Coughlan A K 1980 Confabulation and frontal lobe dysfunction. Journal of Neurology, Neurosurgery and Psychiatry 43: 461–463

Kauffman I 1963 Some aspects of brain damage as related to Einstellung. Journal of Neuropsychiatry 4: 143–148

Kertesz A 1979 Aphasia and associated disorders: taxonomy, localization and recovery. Grune and Stratton, New York

Kertesz A 1983 Localization in neuropsychology. Academic Press, New York

Kertesz A, Hooper P 1982 Praxis and language: the extent and variety of apraxia in aphasia. Neuropsychologia 20: 275–286

Kim Y K 1971 Effects of basolateral amygdalectomy. In: Umbach W (ed) Special topics in stereotaxis. Hippokrates-Verlag p 69–81

Kimble D P 1963 Physiological psychology. Addison-Wesley, Reading, Massachusetts

Kimura D 1961a Some effects of temporal lobe damage on auditory perception. Canadian Journal of Psychology 15: 156–165

Kimura D 1961b Cerebral dominance and the perception of verbal stimuli. Canadian Journal of Psychology 15: 166–171

Kimura D 1963 Right temporal lobe damage: perception of unfamiliar stimuli after damage. Archives of Neurology 8: 264–271

Kimura D 1964 Left-right differences in the perception of melodies. Quarterly Journal of Experimental Psychology 16: 355–358

Kimura D 1966 Dual functional asymmetry of the brain in visual perception. Neuropsychologia 4: 275–285

Kimura D 1967 Functional asymmetry of the brain in dichotic listening. Cortex 3: 163–178

Kimura D 1969 Spatial localization in left and right visual fields. Canadian Journal of Psychology 23: 445–448

Kimura D 1973 The asymmetry of the human brain. Scientific American 228: 70–80

King E 1967 The nature of visual field defects. Brain 90: 647–668

Kinsbourne M 1971a The minor cerebral hemisphere as a source of aphasic speech. Archives of Neurology 25: 302–306

Kinsbourne M 1971b Cognitive deficit: experimental analysis. In: McGaugh J L (ed) Psychiobiology. Academic, New York ch 7

Kinsbourne M 1972 Contrasting patterns of memory span decrement in ageing and aphasia. Journal of Neurology, Neurosurgery, and Psychiatry 35: 192–195

Kinsbourne M 1976 The neuropsychological analysis of cognitive deficit. In: Grenell R G, Gabay S (eds) Biological foundations of psychiatry. Raven, New York

Kinsbourne M, Smith W L 1974 Hemisphere disconnection and cerebral function. Thomas, Springfield, Illinois

Kinsbourne M, Warrington E K 1962a A study of finger agnosia. Brain 85: 47–66

Kinsbourne M, Warrington E K 1962b A disorder of simultaneous form perception. Brain 85: 461–486

Kinsbourne M, Warrington E K 1963 The localizing significance of limited simultaneous visual form perception. Brain 86: 697–702

Kinsbourne M, Warrington E K 1964 Observations on colour agnosia. Journal of Neurology, Neurosurgery, and Psychiatry 27: 296–299

Kinsella G, Clausen H 1982 Amnesia following rupture of an anterior communicating artery aneurysm. In: Stanley G V, Walsh K W (eds) Brain Impairment. Proceedings of the seventh brain impairment conference, University of Melbourne, p 121–130

Kirschner H S, Kistler K H 1982 Aphasia after right thalamic haemorrhage. Archives of Neurology 39: 667–669

Kirshner H S, Webb W G 1982 Word and letter reading and the mechanism of the third alexia. Archives of Neurology 39: 84–87

Kisker G W 1944 Abstract and categorical behaviour following therapeutic brain surgery. Psychosomatic Medicine 6: 146–150

Kleist K 1934 Gehirnpathologie. Barth, Leipzig

Kløve H, Grabow J D, Trites R L 1969 Evaluation of memory functions with intracarotid sodium amytal. Transactions of the American Neurological Association 94: 76–80

Kløve H, Reitan R M 1958 The effects of dysphasia and spatial distortion on Wechsler-Bellevue results. Archives of Neurology and Psychiatry 80: 708–713

Kløve H, Trites R L, Grabow J D 1970 Intracarotid sodium amytal for evaluating memory function. Electroencephalography and Clinical Neurophysiology 28: 418–419

Knight G 1965 Stereotractic tractotomy in the surgical treatment of mental illness. Journal of Neurology, Neurosurgery, and Psychiatry 28: 304–310

Knight G 1972 Psychosurgery today. Proceedings of the Royal Society of Medicine 65: 1099–1108

Knight G, Tredgold R F 1955 Orbital leucotomy. A review of 52 cases. Lancet 1: 981–985

Konow A, Pribram K H 1970 Error recognition and utilization produced by injury to the frontal cortex in man. Neuropsychologia 8: 489–491

Kotzmann M 1972 Tactile discrimination of three-dimensional form in brain-damaged patients. Unpublished Masters thesis, University of Melbourne

Kovner R, Mattis S, Gartner J, Goldmeier E 1981 A verbal semantic deficit in the alcoholic Korsakoff syndrome. Cortex 17: 419–426

Kovner R, Mattis S, Goldmeier E, Davis L 1981 Korsakoff amnesic syndrome: the result of simultaneous deficits in several independent processes? Brain and Language 12: 23–32

Krashen S 1973 Lateralisation, language learning and the critical period: some new evidence. Language and learning 23: 63–74

Krayenbuhl H, Siegfried J, Kohenhof M, Yasargil M G 1965 Is there a dominant thalamus? Confinia neurologica 26: 246–249

Kroll M B, Stolbun D 1933 Was ist konstructive Apraxie. Zeitschrift fur die gesamte Neurologie und Psychiatrie 148: 142–158

Krynauw R A 1950 Infantile hemiplegia treated by removing one cerebral hemisphere. Journal of Neurology, Neurosurgery, and Psychiatry 13: 243–267

Kuhl D E, Engel J, Phelps M E, Selin C 1980a Epileptic patterns of local cerebral metabolism and perfusion in man determined by emission computed tomography of 18 FDG and 13 NH3. Annals of Neurology 8: 348–360

Kuhl D E, Phelps M E, Kowell A P et al 1980b Effects of stroke on local cerebral metabolism and perfusion: Mapping by emission computed tomography of 18 FDG and 13 NH3. Annals of Neurology 8: 47–60

Làdavas E, Umiltà C, Provinciali L 1979 Hemisphere-dependent cognitive performances in epileptic patients. Epilepsia 20: 493–502

Laitinen L V, Livingston K E (eds) 1973 Surgical approaches to psychiatry. Medical and Technical Publishing Company, Lancaster

Landis C, Zubin J, Mettler F A 1950 The functions of the human frontal lobe. Journal of Psychology 30: 123–138

Lansdell H 1962a A sex difference in effect of temporal lobe neurosurgery on design performance. Nature 194: 852–854

Lansdell H 1962b Laterality of verbal intelligence in the brain. Science 135: 922–923

Lansdell H 1968 The use of factor scores from the Wechsler-Bellevue Scale of Intelligence in assessing patients with temporal lobe removals. Cortex 4: 257–268

Laplane D, Degos J D 1983 Motor neglect. Journal of Neurology, Neurosurgery, and Psychiatry 46: 152–158

Lashley K S 1941 Patterns of cerebral integration indicated by the scotomas of migraine. Archives of Neurology and Psychiatry 46: 331–339

Lashley K S, Clark G 1946 The cytoarchitecture of the cerebral cortex of Ateles. Journal of Comparative Neurology 82: 233–306

Laurent B, Michel D, Antoine J C, Montagnon D 1984 Migraine basilaire avec alexie sans agraphie: spasme artériel a l'artériographie et effet de la naloxone. Revue Neurologique 140: 663–665

Lawrence C 1984 Testing for memory disorder. Editorial comment. Australian and New Zealand Journal of Psychiatry 18: 207–210

Lawson I R 1962 Visual-spatial neglect in lesions of the right cerebral hemisphere: a study in recovery. Neurology 12: 23–33

Le Doux J E 1983 Cerebral asymmetry and the integrated function of the brain. In: Young A W (ed) Functions of the right cerebral hemisphere. Academic Press, New York

Le Doux J E, Wilson D H, Gazzaniga M S 1977 Manipulo-spatial aspects of cerebral lateralization: Clues to the origin of lateralization. Neuropsychologia 15: 743–750

Le Doux J E, Wilson D H, Gazzaniga M S 1978 Block design performance following callosal sectioning. Archives of Neurology 35: 506–508

Leicester J, Sidman M, Stoddard L T, Mohr J P 1969 Some determinants of visual neglect. Journal of Neurology, Neurosurgery, and Psychiatry 32: 580–587

Leman P, Loiseau P, Cohadon F 1963 Sur deux cas d'encéphalite rappelant cliniquement les encéphalites nécrosantes temporales mais d'évolution favorable. Revue Neurologique 198: 798–806

Le May M 1976 Morphological cerebral asymmetries in modern man, fossil man, and non human primates. In: Harnad S R, Steklis H, Lancaster J (eds) Origins and evolution of language and speech. Annals of the New York Academy of Sciences 280: 349–366

Le May M, Culebras A 1972 Human brain morphologic differences in the hemispheres demonstrable by carotid arteriography. New England Journal of Medicine 287: 168–170

Le May M, Kido D K 1978 Asymmetries of the cerebral hemispheres on computed tomograms. Journal of Computer Assisted Tomography 2: 471–476

Lenneberg E H 1967 Biological foundations of language. Wiley, New York

Lennox W G 1951 Phenomena and correlates of the psychomotor triad. Neurology 1: 365–371

Lennox W G, Lennox M A 1960 Epilepsy and related disorders. Little Brown, Boston

Lenz H 1944 Rauminnstörungen bei Hirnverletzungen. Deutsche Zeitschrift fur Nervenheilkunde 156: 22–64

Levin H S, Peters B H 1976 Neuropsychological testing following head injuries: Prosopagnosia without field defect. Diseases of the Nervous System 37: 68–71

Levin H S, Peters B H, Hulkonen D A 1983 The early concepts of anterograde and retrograde amnesia. Cortex 19: 427–440

Levy J 1974a Psychobiological implications of bilateral asymmetry. In: Dimond S J, Beaumont J G (eds) Hemisphere function in the human brain. Elek Science, London ch 6

Levy J 1974b Cerebral asymmetries as manifested in split-brain man. In: Kinsbourne M, Smith W L (eds) Hemisphere disconnection and cerebral function. Thomas, Springfield, Illinois ch 9

Levy J, Nebes R D, Sperry R W 1971 Expressive language in the surgically separated minor hemisphere. Cortex 7: 49–58

Levy J, Trevarthen C B, Sperry R W 1972 Perception of bilateral chimeric figures following hemispheric deconnection. Brain 95: 61–78

Levy-Agresti J, Sperry R W 1968 Differential perceptual capacities in major and minor hemispheres. Proceedings of the National Academy of Science 61:1151

Lewis N D C, Landis C, King H E 1956 Studies in topectomy. Grune and Stratton, New York

Ley P 1970 Acute psychiatric patients. In: Mittler P (ed) The psychological assessment of mental and physical disorders. Tavistock Publications, London ch 7

Ley R G, Bryden M P 1979 Hemisphere differences in processing emotions and faces. Brain and Language 1: 127–138

Lezak M D 1976 Neuropsychological assessment. Oxford University Press, New York

Lezak M D 1976 Neuropsychological assessment. 2nd Edn Oxford University Press, New York

Lhermitte F 1951 Les hallucinations. Doin, Paris

Lhermitte F 1983 'Utilization behaviour' and its relation to lesions of the frontal lobes. Brain 106: 237–255

Lhermitte F 1984 Autonomie de l'homme et le lobe frontal. Bulletin de l'Academie National de Médecine (Paris) 168: 224–228

Lhermitte F, Beauvois M F 1973 A visual-speech disconnexion syndrome. Brain 96: 695–714

Lhermitte F, Chain F, Aron D 1965 10 cas d'agnosie des couleurs. Proceedings of the 8th International Congress of Neurology, Vienna 3: 217–221

Lhermitte F, Chain F, Escourolle R, Ducarne B, Pillon B 1972 Etude anatomo-clinique d'un cas de prosopagnosie. Revue Neurologique 126: 329–346

Lhermitte F, Chedru F, Chain F 1973 A propos d'un cas d'agnosie visuelle. Revue Neurologique 128: 301–322

Lhermitte F, Derouesné J, Signoret J L 1972 Analyse neuropsychologique du syndrome frontal. Revue Neurologique 127: 415–440

Lhermitte F, Pillon B 1975 La prosopagnosie: Rôle de l'hémisphère droit dans la perception visuelle. Revue Neurologique 131: 791–812

Lhermitte F, Signoret J L 1972 Analyse neuropsychologique ed différenciation des syndromes amnésiques. Revue Neurologique 126: 161–178

Lhermitte J 1942 De l'image corporelle. Revue Neurologique 74: 20–38

Lermitte J 1952 L'image corporelle en neurologie. Schweizer Archiv fur Neurologie und Psychiatrie 69: 213–236

Lhermitte J, Trelles J O 1933 Sur l'apraxie pure constructive. Encephale 28: 413–444

Lichtheim L 1885 On aphasia. Brain 7: 433–484

Liepmann H 1906 Der Weitere. Krankheitsverlauf bei dem einsitig Apraktischen und der Gehirnbefund auf Grund von Serienschnitten. Monatsschrift fur Psychologie und Neurologie 19: 217–243

Liepmann H 1908 Drei Aufsatze aus dem Apraxiegebiet. Karger, Berlin

Liepmann H Maas O 1907 Fall von linksseifigen Agraphie und Apraxie bei rechtsseifigen Lahmung. Journal fur Psychologie und Neurologie 10: 214–227

Lindenberg R, Freytag E 1957 Morphology of cortical contusions. Archives of Pathology 63: 23–42

Lindenberg R, Freytag E 1960 The mechanisms of cerebral contusions. A pathologic-anatomic study. Archives of Pathology 69: 440–469

Lindqvist G, Norlén G 1966 Korsakoff's syndrome after operation on ruptured aneurysm of anterior communicating artery. Acta Psychiatrica Scandinavica 42: 24–34

Lishman W A 1971 Emotion, consciousness and will after brain bisection in man. Cortex 7: 181–192

Little J R, Furlan A J, Medic M T, Weinstein MA 1982 Digital subtraction angiography in cerebrovascular disease. Stroke 13: 557–566

Lobosky J M, Vangilder J C, Damasio A R 1984 Behavioural manifestations of third ventricular colloid cysts. Journal of Neurology, Neurosurgery, and Psychiatry 47: 1075–1080

Loeser J D, Alvord E C 1968a Agenesis of the corpus callosum. Brain 91: 553–570

Loeser J D, Alvord E C 1968b Clinico-pathological correlations in agenesis of the corpus callosum. Neurology 18: 745–756

Logue V, Durward M, Pratt T R C et al 1968 The quality of survival after rupture of an anterior cerebral aneurysm. British Journal of Psychiatry 114: 137–160

Luria A R 1963 Restoration of function after brain injury. Macmillan, New York

Luria A R 1964 Factors and forms of aphasia. In: de Reuck A V S, O'Connor M (eds) Disorders of language. Churchill, London

Luria A R 1965 Two kinds of motor perseveration in massive injury of the frontal lobes. Brain 88: 1–10

Luria A R 1966 Higher cortical functions in man. Basic Books, New York

Luria A R 1969 Frontal lobe syndromes in man. In: Vinken P J, Bruyn G W (eds) Handbook of clinical neurology. vol 2, ch 23 North-Holland, Amsterdam

Luria A R 1970a The functional organization of the brain. Scientific American 222: 66–78

Luria A R 1970b Traumatic aphasia. Mouton, The Hague

Luria A R 1971 Memory disturbances in local brain lesions. Neuropsychologia 9: 367–376

Luria A R 1972 Aphasia reconsidered. Cortex 8: 34–40

Luria A R 1973a Towards the mechanisms of brain disturbance. Neuropsychologia 11: 417–421

Luria A R 1973b The working brain. Allen Lane, The Penguin Press, London

Luria A R 1976 The neuropsychology of memory. Winston and Sons, Washington

Luria A R, Homskaya E D 1963 Le trouble du role regulateur de langage au cours des lesions du lobe frontal. Neuropsychologia 1: 9–26

Luria A R, Homskaya E D 1964 Disturbance in the regulative role of speech with frontal lobe lesions. In: Warren J M, Akert K (eds) The frontal granular cortex and behavior. ch 17 McGraw Hill, New York

Luria A R, Homskaya E D, Blinkov Ş M, Critchley M 1967 Impaired selectivity of mental processes in association with a lesion of the frontal lobe. Neuropsychologia 5: 105–117

Luria A R, Karasseva T A 1968 Disturbances of auditory speech memory in focal lesions of the deep regions of the left temporal lobe. Neuropsychologia 6: 97–104

Luria A R, Karpov B A, Yarbuss A L 1966 Disturbances of active visual perception with lesions of the frontal lobes. Cortex 2: 202–212

Luria A R, Pribram K H, Homskaya E D 1964 An experimental analysis of the behavioral disturbance produced by a left frontal arachnoidal endothelioma (meningioma) Neuropsychologia 2: 257–280

Luria A R, Simernitskaya E G, Tubylevich B 1970 The structure of psychological processes in relation to cerebral organization. Neuropsychologia 8: 13–20

Luria A R, Sokolov E N, Klimkovsky M 1967 Towards a neuro-dynamic analysis of memory disturbances with lesions of the left temporal lobe. Neuropsychologia 5: 1–12

Luria A R, Tsvetkova L D 1964 The programming of constructive activity in local brain injuries. Neuropsychologia 2: 95–108

Luria A R, Tsvetkova L S 1967 Les troubles de la résolution des problemes. Analyse neuropsychologique. Gauthier-Villars, Paris

Mack J L, Boller F 1977 Associative visual agnosia and its related deficits. The role of the minor hemisphere in assigning meaning to visual perceptions. Neuropsychologia 15: 345–349

Mack J L, Levine R N 1981 The basis of visual constructional disability in patients with unilateral cerebral lesions. Cortex 17: 515–532

Mackie J B, Beck E C 1966 Relations among rigidity, intelligence, and perception in brain-damaged and normal individuals. Journal of Nervous and Mental Disease 142: 310–317

Magoun H W 1958 Early development of ideas relating the mind with the brain. Wolstonholme G E W, O'Connor C M (eds) The neurological basis of behaviour. Churchill, London

Malamud N, Skillicorn S A 1956 Relationship between the Wernicke and Korsakoff syndrome. Archives of Neurology and Psychiatry 76: 585–596

Malmo H P 1974 On frontal lobe functions: psychiatric patient controls. Cortex 10: 231–237

Malmo R B 1948 Psychological aspects of frontal gyrectomy and frontal lobotomy in mental patients. Research Publications, Association for Research in Nervous and Mental Disease 27: 537–564

Malone D R, Morris H H, Kay M C, Levin H S 1982 Prosopagnosia: a double dissociation between the recognition of familiar and unfamiliar faces. Journal of Neurology, Neurosurgery, and Psychiatry 45: 820–822

Marie P, Behague P 1919 Syndrome de désorientation dans l'espace consécutif aux plaies profondes du lobe frontal. Revue Neurologique 26: 1–14

Marie P, Bouttier H, van Bogaert L 1924 Sur un cas de tumeur préfrontale droite. Troubles de l'orientation dans l'espace. Revue Neurologique 31: 209–221

Markowitsch H J 1984 Can amnesia be caused by damage to a single structure? Cortex 20: 27–45

Marquardsen J 1969 The natural history of acute cerebrovascular disease: a retrospective study of 769 patients. Acta Neurological Scandinavica 38: 1–192

Marslen-Wilson W D, Teuber H L 1975 Memory for remote events in anterograde amnesia: recognition of public figures from news photographs. Neuropsychologia 13: 347–352

Maspes P E 1948 Le syndrome expérimental chez l'homme de la section du splenium du corps calleux. Revue Neurologique 80: 100–113

Mateer C A, Ojemana G A 1983 Thalamic mechanisms in language and memory. In: Segalowitz S J (ed) Language functions and brain organization. Academic Press, New York p 171–191

Matthews C G, Shaw D J, Kløve H 1966 Psychological test performances in neurologic and 'pseudo-neurologic' subjects. Cortex 2: 244–253

Mattis S, Kovner R, Goldmeier E 1978 Different patterns of mnemonic deficits in two organic amnesic syndromes. Brain and Language 6: 179–191

Mayer-Gross W 1935 The question of visual impairment in constructional apraxia. Proceedings of the Royal Society of Medicine 29: 1396–1400

Mazaux J M, Orgogozo J M 1982 Étude analytique et quantitative des troubles du langage par lésion du thalamus gauche: l'aphasie thalamique. Cortex 18: 403–406

Mazaux J M, Orgogozo J M, Henry P, Loiseau P 1979 Troubles du langage au cours des lésions thalamiques. Revue Neurologique 135: 59–64

McFarland H R, Fortin D 1982 Amusia due to right temporoparietal infarct. Archives of Neurology 39: 725–727

McFie J 1960 Psychological testing in clinical neurology. Journal of Nervous and Mental Diseases 131: 383–393

McFie J 1961 The effects of hemispherectomy on intellectual functioning in cases of infantile hemiplegia. Journal of Neurology, Neurosurgery, and Psychiatry 24: 240–249

McFie J, Piercy M F 1952a Intellectual impairment with localized cerebral lesions. Brain 75: 292–311

McFie J, Piercy M F 1952b The relation of laterality of lesions to performance on Weigl's Sorting Test. Journal of Mental Science 98: 299–305

McFie J, Piercy M F, Zangwill O L 1950 Visual spatial agnosia associated with lesions of the right cerebral hemisphere. Brain 73: 167–190

McFie J, Thompson J A 1971 Variation with age of the effects of cerebral lesions in man. Brain Research 31:363

McFie J, Thompson J A 1972 Picture arrangement: A measure of frontal lobe function? British Journal of Psychiatry 121: 547–552

McFie J, Zangwill O L 1960 Visual-constructive disabilities associated with lesions of the left cerebral hemisphere. Brain 83: 243–260

McHenry L C 1969 Garrison's history of neurology. Thomas, Springfield, Illinois

McIntyre H D, Mayfield F H, McIntyre A P 1954 Ventromedial quadrant coagulation in the treatment of the psychoses and neuroses. American Journal of Psychiatry 111: 112–120

McKeever W F, Huling M D 1971 Lateral dominance in tachistoscopic word recognition performances obtained with simultaneous bilateral output. Neuropsychologia 9: 15–20

McKeever W F, Sullivan K F, Ferguson S M, Rayport M 1981 Typical cerebral hemisphere disconnection deficits following corpus callosum section despite sparing of the anterior commissure. Neuropsychologia 19: 745–755

McKeever W F, Sullivan K F, Ferguson S M, Rayport M 1982 Right hemisphere speech development in the anterior commissure-spared commissurotomy patient. A second case. Clinical Neuropsychology 4: 17–22

McKenzie K G 1938 Cited in Williams D J, Scott J W 1939 The functional response of the sympathetic nervous system of man following hemidecortication. Journal of Neurology and Psychiatry 2: 313–322

McKenzie K G, Kaczanowski G 1964 Prefrontal leucotomy. A 5 year controlled study. Canadian Medical Journal 91: 1193–1196

Meadows J C 1974 The anatomical basis of prosopagnosia. Journal of Neurology, Neurosurgery, and Psychiatry 37: 489–501

Meier M J, French L A 1965 Lateralized deficits in complex visual discrimination and bilateral transfer of reminiscence following unilateral temporal lobectomy. Neuropsychologia 3: 261–272

Meier M J, French L A 1966 Longitudinal assessment of intellectual functioning following unilateral temporal lobectomy. Journal of Clinical Psychology 22: 22–27

Mensh I N, Schwartz H G, Matarazzo R R, Matarazzo J D 1952 Psychological functioning following cerebral hemispherectomy in man. Archives of Neurology and Psychiatry 67: 787–796

Mercer B, Wapner W, Gardner H, Benson D F 1977 A study of confabulation. Archives of Neurology 34: 429–433

Messerli P, Seron X, Tissot P 1979 Quelques aspects de la programmation dans le syndrome frontal. Archives Suisses de Neurologie, Neurochirurgie et de Psychiatrie 125: 23–35

Mesulam M M 1985 Dementia: its definition, diagnosis, and subtypes. Journal of the American Medical Association 253: 2559–2561

Mettler F A (ed) 1949 Selective partial ablation of the frontal cortex. Hoeber, New York

Mettler F A (ed) 1952 Psychosurgical problems. Blakiston, New York

Meudell P, Mayes A 1982 Normal and abnormal forgetting: some comments on the human amnesic syndrome. In: Ellis A W (ed) Normality and pathology in cognitive function. Academic Press, London p 203–237

Meyer V 1957 Critique of psychological approaches to brain damage. Journal of Mental Science 103: 80–109

Meyer V 1959 Cognitive changes following temporal lobectomy for temporal lobe epilepsy. Archives of Neurology and Psychiatry 81: 299–309

Meyer V, Falconer M A 1960 Defects of learning ability with massive lesions of the temporal lobe. Journal of Mental Science 106: 472–477

Meyer V, Jones H G 1957 Patterns of cognitive test performances as functions of the lateral localization of cerebral abnormalities in the temporal lobe. Journal of Mental Science 103: 758–772

Meyer V, Yates A J 1955 Intellectual changes following temporal lobectomy for psychomotor epilepsy. Journal of Neurology, Neurosurgery, and Psychiatry 18: 44–52

Miller E 1972 Clinical neuropsychology. Penguin Books, Harmondsworth, Middlesex

Miller E 1983 A note on the interpretation of data derived from neuropsychological tests. Cortex 19: 131–132

Miller E 1984 Verbal fluency as a function of a measure of verbal intelligence and in relation to different types of cerebral pathology. British Journal of Clinical Psychology 23: 53–57

Mills R P, Swanson P D 1978 Vertical oculomotor apraxia and memory loss. Annals of Neurology 4: 149–153

Milner A D, Jeeves M A 1979 A review of behavioural studies of agenesis of the corpus callosum. In: Russell I S, Hof M W, Berlucchi G (eds) Structure and function of the cerebral hemispheres. Macmillan, London

Milner B 1954a Intellectual function of the temporal lobe. Psychological Bulletin 51: 42–64

Milner B 1954b Psychological defects produced by temporal lobe excision. Research Publications, Association for Research in Nervous and Mental Disease 36: 244–257

Milner B 1958 Psychological defects produced by temporal lobe excision. Research publications, Association for Research in Nervous and Mental Disease 36: 244–257

Milner B 1959 The memory defect in bilateral hippocampal lesions. Psychiatric Research Reports 11: 43–58

Milner B 1962 Laterality effects in audition. In: Mountcastle V B (ed) Interhemispheric relations and cerebral dominance. ch 9 John Hopkins Press, Baltimore

Milner B 1963 Effects of different brain lesions on card sorting. Archives of Neurology 9: 90–100

Milner B 1964 Some effects of frontal lobectomy in man. In: Warren J M, Akert K (eds) The frontal granular cortex and behavior, ch 15 McGraw Hill, New York

Milner B 1965 Visually-guided maze learning in man: effects of bilateral hippocampal, bilateral frontal and unilateral cerebral lesions. Neuropsychologia 3: 317–338

Milner B 1966 Amnesia following operations on the temporal lobes. In: Whitty C W M, Zangwill O L (eds) Amnesia. Butterworth, London

Milner B 1967 Brain mechanisms suggested by studies of temporal lobes. In: Darley F L (ed) Brain mechanisms underlying speech and language. Grune and Stratton, New York

Milner B 1968a Disorders of memory after brain lesions in man. Neuropsychologia 6: 175–179

Milner B 1968b Visual recognition and recall after right temporal lobe excision in man. Neuropsychologia 6: 191–209

Milner B 1970 Memory and the medial temporal regions of the brain. In: Pribram K H, Broadbent D E (eds) Biology of memory. Academic Press, New York p 29–50

Milner B 1971 Interhemispheric difference in the localization of psychological processes in man. British Medical Bulletin 27: 272–277

Milner B 1972 Disorders of learning and memory after temporal lobe lesions in man. Clinical Neurosurgery 19: 421–446

Milner B 1974 Hemispheric specialization scope and limits. In: Schmitt F O, Worden F G (eds) The neurosciences third study. ch 8 MIT Press, Cambridge, Massachusetts

Milner B 1975 Report on section on the 'Frontal Lobes' at the 17th International Symposium of Neuropsychology. Neuropsychologia 13: 129–133

Milner B 1982 Some cognitive effects of frontal lobe lesions in man. Philosophical Transactions of the Royal Society of London. Series B: Biological Sciences 298: 211–226

Milner B, Branch C, Rasmussen T 1962 Study of short term memory after intracarotid injection of sodium amytal. Transactions of the American Neurological Association 87: 224–226

Milner B, Branch C, Rasmussen T 1964 Observations on cerebral dominance. In: de Reuck A V S, O'Connor M (eds) Disorders of language. Churchill, London

Milner B, Branch C, Rasmussen T 1966 Evidence for bilateral speech representation in some non-right handers. Transaction of the American Neurological Association 91: 306–308

Milner B, Corkin S, Teuber H L 1968 Further analysis of the hippocampal amnesic syndrome: 14 year follow-up study of H.M. Neuropsychologia 6:215

Milner B, Kimura D 1964 Dissociable visual learning defects after temporal lobectomy in man. Paper read at the 35th Annual Meeting of the Eastern Psychological Association, Philadelphia

Milner B, Taylor L B 1970 Somesthetic thresholds after commissural section in man. Paper presented at the American Academy of Neurology meeting, Miami

Milner B, Taylor L 1972 Right-hemisphere superiority in tactile pattern-recognition after cerebral commissurotomy: evidence for nonverbal memory. Neuropsychologia 10: 1–15

Milner B, Taylor L, Sperry R W 1968 Lateralized suppression of dichotically-presented digits after commissural section in man. Science 161: 184–186

Milner B, Teuber H L 1968 Alteration of perception and memory in man: reflections on methods. In: Weiskrantz L (ed) Analysis of behavioral change. ch. 11. Harper and Row, New York

Milner P 1970 Physiological psychology. Holt, Rinehart and Winston, New York

Mirsky A, Primac D, Marsan C, Rosvold H, Stevens J 1960 A comparison of the psychological test performance of patients with focal and non-focal epilepsy. Experimental Neurology 2: 75–89

Mochizuki H, Sugishita M, Tohgi H Satoh Y 1980 Alexia without agraphia associated with right occipital lobe lesion in a right-hander. Rinsho Shinkeigaku 20: 750–756

Moll J M 1915 The amnestic or 'Korsakov's syndrome' with alcoholic aetiology: an analysis of thirty cases. Journal of Mental Science 61: 424–443

Moniz E 1954 How I succeeded in performing the prefrontal leucotomy. Journal of Clinical and Experimental Psychopathology 15: 373–379

Moscovitch M 1982 Multiple dissociations of function in amnesia. In: Cermak L S (ed) Memory and amnesia. Erlbaum, Hillsdale, N J

Mountcastle V B (ed) 1962 Interhemispheric relations and cerebral dominance. Johns Hopkins Press, Baltimore

Mullan S, Penfield W 1959 Illusions of comparative interpretation and emotion. Archives of Neurology and Psychiatry 81: 269–284

Mungas D 1982 Interictal behavior abnormality in temporal lobe epilepsy. Archives of General Psychiatry 39: 108–111

Mungas D M 1983 Behavioral symptoms in temporal lobe epilepsy (letter). Archives of General Psychiatry 40: 468–469

Muramoto O, Kuru Y, Sugishita M, Toyokura Y 1979 Pure memory loss with hippocampal lesions. Archives of Neurology 36: 54–56

Myers R E 1955 Interocular transfer of pattern discrimination in cats following section of crossed optic fibres. Journal of Comparative and Physiological Psychology 48: 470–473

Myers R E 1956 Functions of corpus callosum in interocular transfer. Brain 79: 358–363

Myers R E 1959 Interhemispheric communication through the corpus callosum: Limitations under conditions of conflict. Journal of Comparative and Physiological Psychology 52: 6–9

Myers R E 1961 Corpus callosum and visual gnosis. In: Fessard A et al (eds) Brain mechanisms and learning. Blackwell, Oxford

Myers R E 1965 The neocortical commissures and interhemispheric transmission of information. In: Ettlinger E G (ed) Functions of the corpus callosum. Churchill, London

Myers R E, Sperry R W 1953 Interocular transfer of a visual form discrimination habit in cats after section of the optic chiasma and corpus callosum. Anatomical Record 115: 351–352

Nathanson M, Bergman P S, Gordon G G 1952 Denial of illness. Archives of Neurology and Psychiatry 68: 380–387

Nebes R D 1971 Superiority of the minor hemisphere in commissurotomized man for the perception of part-whole relations. Cortex 7: 333–349

Nebes R D 1972 Dominance of the minor hemisphere in commissurotomized man on a test of figure unification. Brain 95: 633–638

Nebes R D 1973 Perception of spatial relationships by the right and left hemispheres in commissurotomized man. Neuropsychologia 11: 285–289

Nebes R D 1974a Dominance of the minor hemisphere for the perception of part-whole relationships. In: Kinsbourne M, Smith W L (eds) Hemispheric disconnection and cerebral function. ch. 7. Thomas, Springfield, Illinois

Nebes R D 1974b Hemispheric specialization and commissurotomized man. Psychological Bulletin 81: 1–14

Nelson H E 1976 A modified card sorting test sensitive to frontal lobe deficits. Cortex 12: 313–324

Netley C 1972 Dichotic listening performance of hemispherectomized patients. Neuropsychologia 10: 233–240

New P F J, Scott W R, Schnur J A, Davis K R, Taveras J M 1974 Computerized axial tomography with the EMI scanner. Radiology 110: 109–123

Newcombe F 1969 Missile wounds of the brain. Oxford University Press, Oxford

Nichols I C, Hunt JMcV 1940 A case of partial bilateral frontal lobectomy: A psychopathological study. American Journal of Psychiatry 96: 1063–1087

Niedermeyer E, Lopes da Silva F H 1982 Electro-encephalography: Basic principles, clinical applications and related fields. Urban and Schwarzenberg, Baltimore

Nielsen H 1975 Is constructional apraxia primarily an interhemisphere disconnection syndrome? Scandinavian Journal of Psychology 16: 113–124

Nielsen J M 1937 Unilateral cerebral dominance as related to mind-blindness. Minimal lesion causing visual agnosia for objects. Archives of Neurology and Psychiatry 38: 108–115

Nielsen J, Jacobs L 1951 Bilateral lesions of the anterior angulate gyri. Bulletin of the Los Angeles Neurological Society 16: 231–234

Nielsen J M, Friedman A P 1942 The temporal isthmus and its clinical syndromes. Bulletin of the Los Angeles Neurological Societies 7: 1–11

Norlén G, Olivecrona H 1953 The treatment of aneurysms of the circle of Willis. Journal of Neurosurgery 10: 414–415

Nuttin J, Greenwald A G 1968 Reward and punishment in human learning. Academic Press, London

Obrador S 1964 Nervous integration after hemispherectomy in man. In: Schaltenbrand G, Woolsey C N (eds) Cerebral localization and integration. University of Wisconsin Press, Madison p 133–146

Ogden J A 1985a Anterior-posterior interhemispheric differences in the loci of lesions producing visual hemineglect. Brain and Cognition 4: 59–75

Ogden J A 1985b Contralateral neglect of constructed visual images in right and left brain-damaged patients. Neuropsychologia 23: 273–277

Ojemann G 1971 Alteration in nonverbal short-term memory with stimulation in the region of the mamillothalamic tract in man. Neuropsychologia 9: 195–201

Ojemann G A 1975 Language and the thalamus: object naming and recall during and after thalamic stimulation. Brain and Language 2: 101–120

Ojemann G 1976 Subcortical language mechanisms. In: Whitaker H Neurolinguistics. vol. 1. Academic Press, New York p 103–138

Ojemann G 1977 Asymmetric function of the thalamus in man. Annals of the New York Academy of Science 299: 380–396

Ojemann G 1979a Individual variability in cortical localization of language. Journal of Neurosurgery 50: 164–169

Ojemann G 1979b Altering human memory with human ventrolateral thalamic stimulation. In: Hitchcock E, Ballantine H, Myerson B (eds) Modern concepts in psychiatric surgery. Elsevier, Amsterdam, p 103–109

Ojemann G 1980 Brain mechanisms for language: observations during neurosurgery. In: Lockhard J, Ward A A (eds) Epilepsy: a window to brain mechanisms. Raven, New York, p 243–260

Ojemann G 1981 Interrelationship in the localization of language, memory and motor mechanisms in human cortex and thalamus. In: Thompson R (ed) New perspectives in cerebral localization. Raven, New York, p 157–175

Ojemann G, Blick K, Ward A 1971 Improvement and disturbance of short-term verbal memory with ventrolateral thalamic stimulation. Brain 94: 225–240

Ojemann G, Fedio P 1968 Effect of stimulation of the human thalamus and temporal white matter on short term memory. Journal of Neurosurgery 29: 51–59

Ojemann G A, Fedio P, VanBuren J M 1968 Anomia from pulvinar and subcortical parietal stimulation. Brain 91: 99–117

Ojemann G, Hoyenga K, Ward A 1968 Prediction of short-term memory disturbances after ventrolateral thalamotomy. Journal of Neurosurgery 29: 51–59

Ojemann G, Mateer C 1979a Human language cortex: localization of memory, syntax, and sequential motorphoneme identification systems. Science 205: 1401–1403

Ojemann G, Mateer C 1979b Cortical and subcortical organization of human communication: evidence from stimulation studies. In: Steklin H, Raleigh M (eds) The neurobiology of social communication in primates. Academic, New York, p 111–131

Ojemann G A, Ward A A 1971 Speech representation in the ventrolateral thalamus Brain 94: 669–680

Orchinik C W 1960 Some psychological aspects of circumscribed lesions of the diencephalon. Confinia neurologica 20: 292–310

Orgass B, Poeck K, Kerschensteiner M, Hartje W 1972 Visuo-cognitive performances in patients with unilateral hemispheric lesions. Zeitschrift fur Neurologie 202: 177–195

Osterrieth P A 1944 Le test de copie d'une figure complexe. Archives de Psychologie 30: 206–353

Oxbury J M, Campbell D C, Oxbury S M 1974 Unilateral spatial neglect and impairments of spatial analysis and visual perception. Brain 97: 551–564

Oxbury J M, Oxbury S M 1969 Effects of lobectomy on the report of dichotically presented ligits. Cortex 5: 1–4

Paganini A E, Zlotlow M 1960 Denial of lobotomy as a continuation of the defense mechanism of denial in schizophrenia. Psychiatric Quarterly 34: 260–268

Paillas J E, Cossa P, Darcourt G, Naquet R 1965 Etude sur l'epilepsie occipital. Eighth International Congress of Neurology, Vienna vol. 3: 193–196

Pallis C A 1955 Impaired identification for faces and places with agnosia for colours. Journal of Neurology, Neurosurgery, and Psychiatry 18: 218–224

Palmer J 1985 Advances in imaging technology and their applications. Medical Journal of Australia 142: 3–4

Pampilgione G, Falconer M A 1960 Electrical stimulation of the hippocampus in man. In: Field J, Magoun H W, Hall V E (eds) Handbook of physiology, Section 1, neurophysiology, vol. 2 American Physiological Society, Washington p 1391–1394

Papez J W 1929 Comparative neurology. Crowell, New York

Parkin A J 1982 Residual learning capability in organic amnesia. Cortex 18: 417–440

Parkin A J 1984 Amnesic syndrome: a lesion-specific disorder? Cortex 20: 479–508

Parsons O A, Huse M M 1958 Impairment of flicker discrimination in brain-damaged patients. Neurology 8: 750–755

Parsonage M 1983 The classification of epileptic seizures (ILAE). In: Rose F C (ed) Research progress in epilepsy. Pitman, London, p 22–38

Parsons O A, Kemp D E 1960 Intellectual functioning in temporal lobe epilepsy. Journal of Consulting Psychology 24: 408–414

Paterson A, Zangwill O L 1944 Disorders of visual space perception associated with lesions of the right cerebral hemisphere. Brain 67: 331-358

Paterson A, Zangwill O L 1945 A case of topographical disorientation associated with a unilateral cerebral lesion. Brain 68: 188–212

Pendleton M G, Heaton R K, Lehman R A W, Hulihan D 1982 Diagnostic utility of the Thurstone word fluency test in neuropsychological evaluation. Journal of Clinical Neuropsychology 4: 307–317

Penfield W 1938 The cerebral cortex in man. Archives of Neurology and Psychiatry 40: 417–442

Penfield W 1954 Temporal lobe epilepsy. British Journal of Surgery 41: 337–343

Penfield W, Evans J 1935 The frontal lobe in man: a clinical study of maximum removals. Brain 58: 115–133

Penfield W, Jasper H 1954 Epilepsy and the functional anatomy of the human brain. Little, Brown, Boston

Penfield W, Milner B 1958 Memory deficit produced by bilateral lesions of the hippocampal Zone. Archives of Neurology and Psychiatry 79: 475–497

Penfield W, Perot P 1963 The brain's record of auditory and visual experience. Brain 86: 595–697

Penfield W, Rasmussen A T 1950 The cerebral cortex of man. Macmillan, New York

Penfield W, Roberts 1959 Speech and brain mechanisms. Princeton University Press, Princeton, New Jersey

Percheron G 1976 Les artères du thalamus humain. 11. Artèes et territoires thalamiques paramédians de l'artère basilaire communicante. Revue Neurologique 132: 309–324

Perenin M T, Jeannerod M 1978 Visual function within the hemianopic field following early cerebral decortication in man — 1. Spatial localization. Neuropsychologia 16: 1–13

Perret E 1974 The left frontal lobe of man and the suppression of habitual responses in verbal categorical behavior. Neuropsychologia 12: 323–330

Petrides M, Milner B 1982 Deficits on subject-ordered tasks after frontal- and temporal-lobe lesions in man. Neuropsychologia 20: 249–262

Petrie A 1949 Preliminary report of changes after prefrontal leucotomy. Journal of Mental Science 95: 449–455

Petrie A 1952a Personality and frontal lobes. Routledge and Kegan Paul, London

Petrie A 1952b A comparison of the psychological effects of different types of operation on the frontal lobes. Journal of Mental Science 98: 326–329

Petrovici I N 1972 Schlafenlappen und Apraxie. Fortschritte der Neurologie und Psychiatrie 40: 656–672

Phelan J A, Gustafson C W 1968 Reversal and nonreversal shifts in acute brain-injured with injury diffusely organized. Journal of Psychology 70: 249–259

Phelps C 1897 Traumatic injuries of the brain and its membranes. Appleton, New York

Piaget J 1969 The mechanisms of perception. Routledge and Kegan Paul, London

Piercy M F 1959 Testing for intellectual impairment — some comments on tests and testers. Journal of Mental Science 105: 489–495

Piercy M F 1977 Experimental studies of the amnesic syndrome. In: Whitty C W M, Zangwill O L (eds) Amnesia, 2nd ed, Butterworth, Woburn, Massachusetts, p 1–52

Piercy M, Hćaen H, Ajuriaguerra J de 1960 Constructional apraxia associated with unilateral cerebral lesions — left and right sided cases compared. Brain 83: 225–242

Piercy M F, Smyth V 1962 Right hemisphere dominance for certain non-verbal intellectual skills Brain 85: 775–790

Pizzamiglio L, De Pascalis C, Vignati A 1974 Stability of dicholic listening test. Cortex 10: 203–205

Poeck K 1975 July In editorial — On cerebral localization and dominance. Bulletin of the International Neuropsychological Society.

Poeck K 1985 Temporal lobe syndromes. In: Vinken P J, Bruyn G W, Klawans H L (eds) Handbook of clinical neurology, New Series 1, vol. 45. Elsevier, Amsterdam p 43–48

Poeck K, Kerschensteiner M 1975 In: Zulch K (ed) Cerebral localization. Springer-Verlag, Heidelberg

Poeck K, Kerschensteiner M, Hartje W, Orgass B 1973 Impairment in visual recognition of geometric figures in patients with circumscribed retrorolandic brain lesions. Neuropsychologia 11: 311–317

Poeck K, Lehmkuhl G 1980 Ideatory apraxia in a left-handed patient with right-sided brain lesion. Cortex 16: 273–284

Poeck K, Orgass B 1966 Gerstmann's syndrome and aphasia Cortex 2: 421–437

Poeck K, Orgass B 1967 Uber Storungen der Recht-links Orientierung. Nervenarzt 38: 285–291

Pollack F 1938 Zur Pathologie und Klinik der Orientierung. Schweizer Archiv fur Neurologie und Psychiatrie 42: 141–164

Pollack M 1960 Effect of brain tumor on perception of hidden figures, sorting behavior and problem solving performances. Dissertation Abstracts 20: 3405–3406

Pollack M, Battersby W S, Bender M B 1957 Tachistoscopic identification of contour in patients with brain damage. Journal of Comparative and Physiological Psychology 50: 220–227

Ponsford J L, Donnan G A 1980 Transient global amnesia — a hippocampal phenomenon? Journal of Neurology, Neurosurgery, and Psychiatry 43: 285–287

Ponsford J L, Donnan G A, Walsh K W 1980 Disorders of memory in vertebrobasilar disease. Journal of Clinical Neuropsychology 2: 267–276

Poppel E, Held R, Front D 1973 Residual visual function after brain wounds involving the central visual pathways. Nature 243: 295–296

Poppelreuter W 1917 Die psychischen schadigungen durch kopfschuss im Kriege 1914–1916. Voss, Leipzig

Poppelreuter W 1923 Zur Psychologie und Pathologie der optischen Wahrnemung. Zeitschrift fur die gesamte Neurologie und Psychiatrie 83: 26–152

Poppen J L 1948 Prefrontal lobomy: technique and general impression based on results in 470 patients subjected to this procedure. Digest of Neurology and Psychiatry 17: 403–408

Porteus S D 1950 The Porteus Maze Test and intelligence. Pacific, Palo Alto, California

Porteus S D 1958 What do the Maze Tests measure? Australian Journal of Psychology 10: 245–256

Porteus 1959 Recent maze test studies. British Journal of Medical Psychology 32: 38–43

Porteus S D 1965 Porteus Maze Test: 50 years' application. Pacific, Palo Alto, California

Porteus S D, Kepner R DeM 1944 Mental changes after bilateral prefrontal lobotomy. Genetic Psychology Monographs 29:4

Porteus S D, Peters H N 1947 Psychosurgery and test validity. Journal of Abnormal and Social Psychology 42: 473–475

Post F 1975 Dementia, depression and pseudodementia. In: Benson D F, Blumer D (eds) Psychiatric aspects of neurological disease. ch. 6. Grune and Stratton, New York

Pratt R T C, Warrington E K, Halliday A M 1971 Unilateral ECT as a test for cerebral dominance, with a strategy for treating left handers. British Journal of Psychiatry 119: 78–83

Prisko L H 1963 Short-term memory in focal cerebral damage. Unpublished doctoral dissertation, McGill University

Ramier A M, Hécaen H 1970 Role respectif des atteintes frontales et de la latéralization lésionelle dans les déficits de la fluence verbale. Revue Neurologique 123: 17–22

Ratcliff G, Newcombe F 1973 Spatial orientation in man: effects of left, right, and bilateral posterior lesions. Journal of Neurology, Neurosurgery, and Psychiatry 36: 448–454

Rausch R, Fedio P, Ary C M, Engel J, Crandall P H 1984 Resumption of behavior following intracarotid sodium amobarbital injection. Annals of Neurology 15: 31–35

Rausch R, Serafetinides E A 1975a Specific alterations of olfactory function in humans with temporal lobe lesions. Nature 255: 557–558

Rausch R, Serafetinides E A 1975b Human temporal lobe and olfaction. In: Denton D A, Coghlan J P (eds) Olfaction and taste. Academic Press, New York p 321–324

Rausch R, Serafetinides E A, Crandall P H 1977 Olfactory memory in patients with anterior temporal lobectomy. Cortex 13: 445–452

Reitan R M 1955 Certain differential effects of left and right cerebral lesions in human adults. Journal of Comparative and Physiological Psychology 48: 474–477

Reitan R M 1958 Qualitative versus quantitative changes following brain damage. Journal of Psychology 46: 339–346

Reitan R M 1959 Impairment of abstraction ability in brain damage: Quantitative versus qualitative changes. Journal of Psychology 48: 97–102

Reitan R M 1964 Psychological deficits resulting from cerebral lesions in man. In: Warren J M, Akert K (eds) The frontal granular cortex and behavior. ch. 14. McGraw Hill, New York

Reitan R M, Davison L A (eds) 1974 Clinical neuropsychology: current status and applications. Wiley, New York

Remy M 1942 Contribution a l'étude de la maladie de Korsakow. Monatsschrift fur Psychiatrie und Neurologie 106: 128–144

Rey A 1941 L'examen psychologique. Archives de Psychologie 28: 112–164

Rey A 1959 Le test de copie de figure complexe. Editions Centre de Psychologie Appliquee, Paris

Riddoch G 1935 Visual disorientation in homonymous half-fields. Brain 58: 376–382

Rivera V M, Meyer J S 1976 Dementia and cerebrovascular disease. In: Meyer J S (ed) Modern concepts of cerebrovascular disease, Eighth Internation Congress, Salzburg. Thieme, Stuttgart

Robin A A 1958 A controlled study of the effects of leucotomy. Journal of Neurology, Neurosurgery, and Psychiatry 21: 262–269

Robinson A L, Heaton R K, Lehman R A, Stilson D W 1980 The utility of the Wisconsin Card Sorting Test in detecting and localizing frontal lobe lesions. Journal of Consulting and Clinical Psychology 48: 605–614

Robinson M F, Freeman W 1954 Psychosurgery and the self. Grune and Stratton, New York

Rochford G 1971 A study of naming errors in dysphasic and in demented patients. Neuropsychologia 9: 437–443

Roeltgen D P, Sevush S, Heilman K M 1983 Pure Gerstmann's syndrome from a focal lesion. Archives of Neurology 40: 46–47

Rokeach M 1948 Generalized mental rigidity as a factor in ethnocentrism. Journal of Abnormal and Social Psychology 43: 259–278

Rondot P A, Tzavaras A 1969 La prosopagnosie après vingt années d'études cliniques et neuropsychologiques. Journal de Psychologie Normale et Pathologique 66: 133–166

Rondot P, Tzavaras A, Garcin R 1967 Sur un cas de prosopagnosie persistant depuis quinze ans. Revue Neurologique 117: 424–428

Rose F C, Symonds C P 1960 Persistent memory defect following encephalitis. Brain 83: 195–212

Rosvold H E, Mishkin M 1950 Evaluation of the effects of prefrontal lobotomy on intelligence. Canadian Journal of Psychology 4: 122–126

Rothi L J, McFarling D, Heilman K M 1982 Conduction aphasia, syntactic alexia and the anatomy of syntactic comprehension. Archives of Neurology 39: 272–275

Rowbotham G F 1964 Acute injuries of the head, 4th edn. Livingstone, Edinburgh

Rowe S N 1937 Mental changes following the removal of the right cerebral hemisphere for brain tumor. American Journal of Psychiatry 94: 605–614

Rubens A B 1977 Anatomical asymmetries of human cerebral cortex. In: Harnad S, Doty R W, Goldstein L, Jaynes J, Krauthamer G (eds) Lateralization in the nervous system. Academic, New York

Rubens A B, Benson D F 1972 Associative visual agnosia. Archives of Neurology 24: 305–316

Rubens A B, Mahowald M W, Hutton J T 1976 Asymmetry of the lateral (sylvian) fissures in man. Neurology 26: 620–624

Rubino C A 1970 Hemispheric lateralization of visual perception. Cortex 6: 102–130

Russell E W 1982 Theory and developments of pattern analysis methods related to the Halstead-Reitan Battery. In: Logue P E, Shear J M (eds) Clinical neuropsychology: a multidisciplinary approach. Thomas, Springfield, Illinois.

Russell W, Nathan P 1946 Traumatic amnesia. Brain 69: 280–300

Russell E W, Neuringer C, Goldstein G 1970 Assessment of brain damage: a neuropsychological key approach. Wiley, New York

Russell J R, Reitan R M 1955 Psychological abnormalities in agenesis of the corpus callosum. Journal of Nervous and Mental Disease 121: 205–214

Russell R W 1932 Cerebral involvement in head injury. Brain 55: 549–503

Russell R W, Smith A 1961 Post-traumatic amnesia in closed head injury. Archives of Neurology 5: 4–17

Russell W R, Whitty C W M 1955 Studies in traumatic epilepsy. III. Visual fits. Journal of Neurology, Neurosurgery, and Psychiatry 18: 79–96

Russo M, Vignolo L A 1967 Visual figure-ground discrimination in patients with unilateral cerebral disease. Cortex 3: 113–127

Rylander G 1939 Personality changes after operations on the frontal lobes: clinical study of 32 cases. Acta Psychiatrica et Neurologica Scandinavica, Supplement 20: 5–81

Rylander G 1943 Mental changes after excision of cerebral tissue. Acta Psychiatrica et Neurologica Scandinavica, Supplement 25: 1–81

Rylander G 1947 Psychological tests and personality analysis before and after frontal lobomy. Acta Psychiatrica et Neurologica Scandinavica Supplement 147: 383–398

Sackeim H A, Greenberg M S, Weiman A L, Gur R C, Humgerbuhler J P, Geschwind N 1982 Hemispheric asymmetry in the expression of positive and negative emotions. Archives of Neurology 39: 210–218

Samarel A, Wright T L, Sergay S, Tyler R H 1976 Thalamic hemorrhage with speech disorder. Transactions of the American Neurological Association 101: 283–285

Samuels J A, Benson D F 1979 Some aspects of language comprehension in anterior aphasia. Brain and Language 8: 275–286

Sanders H I, Warrington E K 1971 Memory for remote events in amnesic patients. Brain 94: 661–668

Satz P 1977 Laterality tests: an inferential problem. Cortex 13: 208–212

Satz P, Aschenbach K, Fennell E 1965 Order of report, ear asymmetry, and handedness in dichotic listening. Cortex 1: 377–396

Saul R, Sperry R W 1968 Absence of commissurotomy symptoms with agenesis of the corpus callosum. Neurology 18:307

Schachter D L, Tulving E 1982b Memory, amnesia and the episodic semantic distinction. In: Isaacson R L, Spear N E (eds) Expression of knowledge. Plenum, New York

Schaie K W 1955 A test of behavioral rigidity. Journal of Abnormal and Social Psychology 51: 604–610

Schaie K W 1958 Rigidity-flexibility and intelligence. Psychological Monographs 72, No. 9 Whole No. 462

Schmitt F O, Worden F G 1974 (eds) The neurosciences third study program. The MIT Press, Cambridge, Massachusetts

Schott B, Mauguiere F, Laurent B, Serclerat O, Fischer C 1980 L'amnésie thalamique. Revue Neurologique 136: 117–130

Schulhoff C, Goodglass H 1969 Dichotic listening: side of brain injury and cerebral dominance. Neuropsychologia 7: 149–160

Schwartz M, Dennerll R 1969 Immediate visual memory as a function of epileptic seizure type. Cortex 5: 69–74

Scott D, Moffett A, Matthews A, Ettlinger G 1967 Effects of epileptic discharges on learning and memory in patients. Epilepsia 8: 188–194

Scotti G 1968 La perdita della memoria topografica: descrizione di un caso. Sistema Nervoso 20: 352–361

Scotti G, Spinnler H 1970 Colour imperception in unilateral hemisphere-damaged patients. Journal of Neurology, Neurosurgery, and Psychiatry 33: 22–28

Scoville W B, Correll R E 1973 Memory and the temporal lobe. A review for clinicians. Acta Neurochirurgica 28: 251–258

Scoville W B, Milner B 1957 Loss of recent memory after bilateral hippocampal lesions. Journal of Neurology, Neurosurgery, and Psychiatry 20: 11–21

Searleman A 1977 A review of right hemisphere linguistic abilities. Psychological Bulletin 84: 503–528

Searleman A 1983 Language capabilities of the right hemisphere. In Young A W (ed) Functions of the right cerebral hemisphere. Academic Press, New York

Segalowitz S J 1983 Two sides of the brain: brain lateralization explored. Prentice-Hall, Englewood Cliffs, New Jersey

Seifert W (ed) 1983 Neurobiology of the hippocampus. Academic Press, New York

Seltzer B, Benson D F 1974 The temporal pattern of retrograde amnesia in Korsakoff's disease. Neurology 24: 527–530

Sem-Jacobsen C W, Torkildsen A 1960 Depth recording and electrical stimulation in the human brain. In: Ramey E R, O'Doherty D S (eds) Electrical studies on the unanesthetized brain. Hoeber, New York p 275–290

Semmes J 1965 A non-tactual factor in astereognosis. Neuropsychologia 3: 295–315

Semmes J 1968 Hemispheric specialization: a possible clue to mechanism. Neuropsychologia 6: 11–26

Semmes J, Weinstein S, Ghent L, Teuber H L 1954 Performance on complex tactual tasks after brain injury to man: analyses by locus of lesion. American Journal of Psychology 67: 220–240

Semmes J, Weinstein S, Ghent L, Teuber H L 1955 Spatial orientation in man after cerebral injury — 1: Analysis by locus of lesion. Journal of Psychology 39: 227–244

Semmes J, Weinstein S, Ghent L, Teuber H L 1960 Somatosensory changes after penetrating brain wounds in man. Harvard University Press, Cambridge, Massachusetts

Semmes J, Weinstein S, Ghent L, Teuber H L 1963 Correlate of impaired orientation in personal and extra-personal space. Brain 86: 747–772

Sengupta R P, Chiu J S P, Brierly H 1975 Quality of survival following direct surgery for anterior communicating artery aneurysms. Journal of Neurosurgery 43: 58–64

Serafetinides E A 1966 Auditory recall and visual recognition following intracarotid amytal. Cortex 2: 367–372

Serafetinides E A, Falconer M A 1962 Some observations on memory impairment after temporal lobectomy for epilepsy. Journal of Neurology, Neurosurgery, and Psychiatry 25: 251–255

Shallice T 1979 Case study approach in neuropsychological research. Journal of Clinical Neuropsychology 1: 183–211

Shallice T 1982 Specific impairments of planning. Philosophical Transactions of the Royal Society of London 298: 199–209

Shallice T, Evans M E 1978 The involvement of the frontal lobes in cognitive estimation. Cortex 14: 294–303

Shallice T, Warrington E K 1970 Independent functioning of verbal memory stores: a neuropsychological study. Quarterly Journal of Experimental Psychology 22: 261–273

Shallice T, Warrington E K 1974 The dissociation between short-term retention of meaningful sounds and verbal material. Neuropsychologia 12: 553–555

Shalman D C 1961 The diagnostic use of the McGill Picture Anomalies Test in temporal lobe epilepsy. Journal of Neurology, Neurosurgery, and Psychiatry 24: 220–222

Shankweiler D P 1966 Effects of temporal lobe damage on the perception of dichotically presented melodies. Journal of Comparative and Physiological Psychology 62:115

Shapiro B E, Alexander M P, Gardner H, Mercer B 1981 Mechanisms of confabulation. Neurology 31: 1070–1076

Shapiro D Y, Sadowsky D, Henderson W, Van Buren J 1973 An assessment of cognitive function in post-thalamotomy Parkinson patients. Confinia neurologica 35: 144–166

Shapiro M B 1951 Experimental studies of a perceptual anomaly. 1. Initial experiments. Journal of Mental Science 97: 90–100

Shapiro M B 1973 Intensive assessment of the single case: an inductive deductive approach. In: Mittler P (ed) The psychological assessment of mental and physical handicaps. ch. 21. Tavistock Publications, London

Shatz M W 1981 WAIS practice effects in clinical neuropsychology. Journal of Clinical Neuropsychology, 3: 171–179

Sherrington C S 1951 Man on his nature, 2nd edn. Cambridge University Press, Cambridge

Sherwood M, McNamee 1967 Psychological study of the amnesic syndrome: Effects of interference on recall. Cortex 4: 359–371

Shure G H 1954 Intellectual loss following excision of cortical tissue. Unpublished doctoral dissertation, University of Chicago

Shure G H, Halstead W C 1958 Cerebral localization of intellectual processes. Psychological Monographs 72: Whole No. 465

Sidman M, Stoddard L T, Mohr J P 1968 Some additional quantitative observations of immediate memory in a patient with bilateral hippocampal lesions. Neuropsychologia 6: 245–254

Sidtis J J, Volpe B T, Wilson D H, Rayport M, Gazzaniga M S 1981 Variability in right hemisphere language function after callosal section. Evidence for a continuum of generative capacity. Journal of Neuroscience 1: 323–331

Siekert R G, Millikan C H 1955 Syndrome of intermittent inefficiency of the basilar arterial system. Neurology 5: 625–630

Signoret J L, Lhermitte F 1976 The amnesic syndrome and encoding process. In: Rosenzweig MR, Bennett E L (eds) Neural mechanisms of learning and memory. MIT Press, Cambridge, Massachusetts, p 67–75

Silberman E K 1983 Behavioral symptoms in temporal lobe epilepsy (letter). Archives of General Psychiatry 40:468

Silverman S M, Bergman P S, Bender M B 1961 The dynamics of transient cerebral blindness. Report of nine episodes following vertebral angiography. Archives of Neurology 4: 333–348

Silverstein M L, Schwartz M, Rennick p 1973, Recall of verbal material in temporal lobe epilepsy and schizophrenia. Diseases of the Nervous System 34: 234–240

Simmel M B, Counts S 1957 Some stable response determinants of perception, thinking and learning: A study based on the analysis of a single test. Genetic Monographs 56: 3–157

Simpson J A 1969 The clinical neurology of temporal lobe disorders. British Journal of Psychiatry. Special Publication No. 4: 42–48

Smith A 1962a Ambiguities in concepts and studies of 'brain damage' and 'organicity'. Journal of Nervous and Mental Disease 135: 311–326

Smith A 1962b Psychodiagnosis of patients with brain tumors. Journal of Nervous and Mental Disease 135: 513–533

Smith A 1965 Verbal and nonverbal test performances of patients with 'acute' lateralized brain lesions (tumors). Journal of Nervous and Mental Disease 141: 517–523

Smith A 1966a Certain hypothesized hemispheric differences in language and visual functions in human adults. Cortex 2: 109–126

Smith A 1966b Intellectual functions in patients with lateralized frontal tumours. Journal of Neurology, Neurosurgery, and Psychiatry 29: 52–59

Smith A 1966c Speech and other functions after left (dominant) hemispherectomy. Journal of Neurology, Neurosurgery, and Psychiatry 29: 467–471

Smith A 1967 Nondominant hemispherectomy: Neuropsychological implications for human brain functions. Proceedings of the 75th Annual Convention, American Psychological Association

Smith A 1969 Nondominant hemispherectomy. Neurology 19: 442–445

Smith A 1973 Symbol Digit Modalities Test. Western Psychological Services, Los Angeles

Smith A 1974a Diaschisis and neuropsychology. Bulletin of the International Neuropsychological Society p 2–3

Smith A 1974b Dominant and nondominant hemispherectomy. In: Kinsbourne M, Smith W L (eds) Hemisphere disconnection and cerebral function. Thomas, Springfield, Illinois p 5– 33

Smith A 1975 Neuropsychological testing in neurological disorders. In: Friedlander W J (ed) Advances in neurology. vol 7. Raven Press, New York p 49–110

Smith A 1981b On the organization, disorganization and reorganization of language and other brain functions. In: Lebrun Y, Zangwill 0 (eds) Lateralization of language in the child. Proceedings of an international symposium held at St. Ode, Belgium, Oct 1–3, 1979. Swets Publishing Service, Lisse, Holland

Smith A, Burklund C W 1966 Dominant hemispherectomy: preliminary report on neuropsychological sequelae. Science 153: 1280–1282

Smith A, Kinder E F 1959 Changes in psychological test performances of brain-operated schizophrenics after eight years. Science 129: 149–150

Smith A, Sugar O 1975 Development of above normal language and intelligence 21 years after left hemispherectomy. Neurology 25: 813–818

Smith K U, Akelaitis AJ 1942 Studies of the corpus callosum. I. Laterality in behavior and bilateral motor organization in man before and after section of the corpus callosum. Archives of Neurology and Psychiatry 47: 519–543

Smith M L, Milner B 1981 The role of the right hippocampus in the recall of spatial location. Neuropsychologia 19: 781–793

Smythe G E, Stern K 1938 Tumours of the thalamus — a clinico-pathological study. Brain 61: 339– 374

Sokal R R, Sneath P H 1963 Principles of numerical taxonomy. Freeman, San Francisco

Solursh L P, Margulies A I, Ashem B, Stasiak E A 1965 The relationship of agenesis of the corpus callosum to perception and learning. Journal of Nervous and Mental Disease 141: 180–189

Sparks R, Geschwind N 1968 Dichotic listening in man after section of the neocortical commissures. Cortex 4: 3–16

Sparks R, Goodglass H, Nickel B 1970 Ipsilateral versus contralateral extinction in dichotic listening from hemisphere lesions. Cortex 6: 249–260

Speedie L J, Heilman K M 1982 Amnestic disturbance following infarction of the left dorsomedial nucleus of the thalamus. Neuropsychologia 20: 597–604

Speedie L J, Heilman K M 1983 Anterograde memory deficits for visuospatial material after infarction of the right thalamus. Archives of Neurology 40: 183–186

Sperry R W 1961 Cerebral organization and behavior. Science 133: 1749–1757

Sperry R W 1964 The great cerebral commissure. Scientific American 210: 42–52

Sperry R W 1974 Lateral specialization in the surgically separated hemispheres. In: Schmitt F O, Worden F G (eds) Neuroscience, third study program. MIT Press, Cambridge, Massachusetts

Sperry R W, Gazzaniga M S, Bogen J E 1969 Interhemispheric relationships: the neocortical commissures; syndromes of hemispheric disconnection. In: Vinken P J, Bruyn G W (eds) Handbook of clinical neurology. vol. 4. North-Holland, Amsterdam ch 14.

Spinnler H 1971 Deficit in associating figures and colours in brain damaged patients. Brain Research 31: 370–371

Spreen O, Benton A L 1969 Neurosensory Centre examination for aphasia. Neuropsychology Laboratory, University of Victoria, Canada

Springer S P Deutsch G 1985 Left brain, right brain. Revised edn. Freeman, New York

Squire L R 1974 Recent memory as affected by ageing. Neuropsychologia 12: 429–435

Squire L R 1981 Two forms of human amnesia: an analysis of forgetting. Journal of Neuroscience 1: 635–640

Squire L R, Cohen N 1982 Remote memory, retrograde amnesia and the neuropsychology of memory. In: Cermak L (ed) Human memory and amnesia. Lawrence Erlbaum, Hillsdale, New Jersey p 275–303

Squire L R, Moore R Y 1979 Dorsal thalamic lesion in a noted case of human memory dysfunction. Annals of Neurology 6: 503–506

Squire L R, Slater P C 1978 Bilateral and unilateral ECT: effects on verbal and nonverbal memory. American Journal of Psychiatry 135: 1316–1320

Starr A, Phillips 1970 Verbal and motor memory in the amnestic syndrome. Neuropsychologia 8: 75–88

Stepien L, Sierpinski S 1964 Impairment of recent memory after temporal lesions in man. Neuropsychologia 2: 291–303

Stevens J, Milstein V, Goldstein S 1972 Psychometric test performance in relation to the psychopathology of epilepsy. Archives of General Psychiatry 26: 532–538

St. James-Roberts 1981 A reinterpretation of hemispherectomy data without functional plasticity of the brain. Brain and Language 13: 31–53

Strauss H 1924 Uber Konstruktive Apraxie. Monatsschrift fur Psychiatrie und Neurologie 63: 739–748

Strich S J 1969 The pathology of brain damage due to blunt head injuries. In: Walker A E, Caveness W F, Critchley M (eds) The late effects of head injury. Thomas, Springfield, Illinois

Strom-Olsen R, Carlisle S 1971 Bi-frontal stereotactic tractotomy. British Journal of Psychiatry 118: 141–154

Stroop J R 1935 Studies of interference in serial verbal reactions. Journal of Experimental Psychology 18: 643–662

Strub R L, Geschwind N 1983 Localization in Gerstmann syndrome In: Kertesz A (ed) Localization in neuropsychology. Academic, New York p 295–321

Stuss D T, Alexander M P, Lieberman A, Levine H 1978 An extraordinary form of confabulation. Neurology 28: 1166–1172

Stuss D T, Benson D F 1984 Neuropsychological studies of the frontal lobes. Psychological Bulletin 95: 3–28

Stuss D T, Benson D F 1983 Frontal lobe lesions and behavior. In: Kertesz A (ed) Localization in neuropsychology. Academic Press, New York, p 429–454

Stuss D T, Benson D F, Kaplan E F, Weir W S, Della Malva 1981a Leucotomized and nonleucotomized schizophrenics: Comparison on tests of attention. Biological Psychiatry 16: 1085–1100

Stuss D T, Benson D F, Kaplan E F, Weir W S, Naeser M A, Lieberman I, Ferrill D 1983 The involvement of Orbitofrontal cerebrum in cognitive tasks. Neuropsychologia 21: 235–248

Stuss D T, Kaplan E F, Benson D F 1982a Long-term effects of prefrontal leucotomy: Cognitive functions. In: Malatesha R N, Hartlage L C (eds) Neuropsychology and cognition, vol 2. Martinus Nijhoff, The Hague, p 252–271

Stuss D T, Kaplan E F, Benson D F, Weir W S, Chiuli S, Sarazin F F 1982b Evidence for the involvement of orbitofrontal cortex in memory functions: An interference effect. Journal of Comparative and Physiological Psychology 6: 913–925

Stuss D T, Kaplan E F, Benson D F, Weir W S, Naeser M A, Levine H L 1981b Long-term effects of prefrontal leucotomy — an overview of neuropsychologic residuals. Journal of Clinical Neuropsychology 3: 13–32

Subirana A 1958 The prognosis in aphasia in relation to cerebral dominance and handedness. Brain 81: 415–425

Subirana A 1969 Handedness and cerebral dominance. In: Vinken P J, Bruyn G W (eds) Handbook of clinical neurology. vol 4. North-Holland, Amsterdam ch 13

Sugishita M 1978 Mental association in the minor hemisphere of a commissurotomy patient. Neuropsychologia 16: 229–232

Sugishita M, Iwata M, Toyokura Y, Yoshioka M, Yamada R 1978 Reading of ideograms and phonograms in Japanese patients after partial commissurotomy. Neuropsychologia 16: 417–426

Sugishita M, Toyokura Y, Yoshioka M, Yamada R 1980 Unilateral agraphia after section of the posterior half of the truncus of the corpus callosum. Brain and Language 9: 215–225

Sunderland S 1940 The distribution of commissural fibres in the corpus callosum of the macaque monkey. Journal of Neurology and Psychiatry 3: 9–18

Sweet W H 1973 Treatment of medically intractable mental disease by limited frontal leucotomy justifiable? New England Journal of Medicine 289: 1117–1125

Sweet W H, Talland G A, Ervin F R 1959 Loss of recent memory following section of fornix. Transaction of the American Neurological Association 84: 76–82

Sykes M K, Tredgold R F 1964 Restricted orbital undercutting. British Journal of Psychiatry 110: 609–640

Talland G 1965 Deranged memory. Academic Press, New York

Talland G A, Sweet W H, Ballantine H T 1967 Amnesic syndrome with anterior communicating artery aneurism. Journal of Nervous and Mental Disease 145: 179–192

Tallent N 1963 Clinical psychological consultation. Prentice Hall, Englewood Cliffs, New Jersey

Tarachow S 1939 The Korsakoff psychosis in spontaneous subarachnoid haemorrhage. Report of three cases. American Journal of Psychiatry 95: 887–899

Taylor A M, Warrington E K 1973 Visual discrimination in patients with localized cerebral lesions. Cortex 9: 82–93

Taylor J 1958 Selected writings of John Hughlings Jackson. Basic Books, New York

Taylor L 1969 Localization of cerebral lesions by psychological testing. Clinical Neurosurgery 16: 269–287

Teasdale G, Jennet B 1974 Assessment of coma and impaired consciousness: A practical scale. Lancet 2: 81–84

Teng E L 1981 Dichotic ear difference is a poor index for the functional asymmetry between the cerebral hemispheres. Neuropsychologia 19: 235–240

Teng E L, Sperry R W 1973 Interhemispheric interaction during simultaneous bilateral presentation of letters or digits in commissurotomized patients. Neuropsychologia 11: 131–140

Teszner D, Tzavaras A, Gruner J, Hécaen H 1972 L'asymmetrie droite-gauche du planum temporale: a propos de l'étude anatomique de 100 cerveaux. Revue Neurologique 126: 444–449

Teuber H L 1950 Neuropsychology. In: Harrower M R (ed) Recent advances in diagnostic psychological testing. Thomas, Springfield, Illinois ch 2

Teuber H L 1955 Physiological psychology. Annual Review of Psychology 6: 267–296

Teuber H L 1959 Some alterations in behavior after cerebral lesions in man. In: Bass A D (ed) Evolution of nervous control from primitive organisms to man. American Association for the Advancement of Science, Washington

Teuber H L 1964 The riddle of frontal lobe function in man. In: Warren J M, Akert K (eds) The frontal granular cortex and behavior. McGraw Hill, New York ch 20

Teuber H L 1975 Recovery of function after brain injury in man. Ciba Foundation Symposium (new series) 34: 159–190 Elsevier, Amsterdam

Teuber H L, Battersby W S, Bender M B 1949 Changes in visual searching performance following cerebral lesions. American Journal of Physiology 159: 592 abstract

Teuber H L, Battersby W S, Bender M B 1951 Performance of complex visual tasks after cerebral lesions. Journal of Nervous and Mental Disease 114: 413–429

Teuber H L, Battersby W S, Bender M B 1960 Visual field defects after penetrating missile wounds of the brain. Harvard University Press, Cambridge, Massachusetts

Teuber H L, Liebert R S 1958 Specific and general effects of brain injury in man; evidence of both from a single task. Archives of Neurology and Psychiatry 80: 403–407

Teuber H L, Milner B, Vaughan H G 1968 persistent anterograde amnesia after stab wound of the basal brain. Neuropsychologia 6: 267–282

Teuber H L, Mishkin M 1954 Judgement of visual and postural vertical after brain injury. Journal of Psychology 38: 161–175

Teuber H L, Rudel R G 1962 Behavior after cerebral lesions in children and adults. Developmental Medicine and Child Neurology 4: 3–20

Teuber H L, Weinstein S 1954 Performance on a formboard task after penetrating brain injury. Journal of Psychology 38: 177–190

Teuber H L, Weinstein S 1956 Ability to discover hidden figures after cerebral lesions. Archives of Neurology and Psychiatry 76: 369–379

Teuber H L, Weinstein S 1958 Equipotentiality versus cortical localization. Science 127: 241–242

Tolman E C 1948 Cognitive maps in rats and men. Psychological Review 55: 189–208

Tooth G C, Newton M P 1961 Leucotomy in England and Wales, 1942–1954. HMSO, London

Tow P M 1955 Personality changes following frontal leucotomy. Oxford University Press, London

Trescher J H, Ford F R 1937 Colloid cyst of the third ventricle. Archives of Neurology and Psychiatry 37: 959–973

Tress B M, Stimac G K, Brant-Zawadski M 1985 Nuclear magnetic resonance imaging.

Applications in the diagnosis of cerebrospinal diseases. Medical Journal of Australia 142: 25–28

Trevarthen C B 1969 Cerebral midline relations reflected in split-brain studies of the higher integrative functions. Paper presented at the 19th International Congress of Psychology, London

Trevarthen C 1974a Analysis of cerebral activities that generate and regulate consciousness in commissurotomy patients. In: Dimond S J, Beaumont J G (eds) Hemispheric function in the human brain. Paul Elek, London ch 9

Trevarthen C 1974b Functional relations of disconnected hemispheres with the brain stem and with each other: monkey and man. In: Kinsbourne M, Smith W L (eds) Hemisphere disconnection and cerebral function. Thomas, Springfield, Illinois ch 10

Trillet M, Fischer C, Serclerat D, Schott B 1980 Le syndrome amnésique des ischemies cérébrales posterieures. Cortex 16: 432–434

Trimble M R 1983 Interictal behaviour and temporal lobe epilepsy. In: Pedley T A, Meldrum B S (eds) Recent advances in epilepsy 1. Churchill Livingstone, Edinburgh, p 211–229

Tzavaras A, Hécaen H 1970 Color vision disturbances in subjects with unilateral cortical lesions. Brain Research 24: 546–547

Tzavaras A, Hécaen H 1971 Etude des coordinées visuelles subjectives au cours des lesions corticales unilatérales. Revue Neurologique 125: 458–461

Tzavaras A, Hécaen H, Le Bras H 1970 The problem of specificity of deficit of human face recognition in unilateral hemispheric lesions. Neuropsychologia 8: 403–416

Tzavaras A, Hécaen H, Le Bras 1971 Disorders of color vision after unilateral cortical lesions. Revue Neurologique 124: 396–402

Tzavaras A, Merienne L, Masure M C 1973 Prosopagnosie, amnésie et troubles du langage par lésion temporale gauche chez un sujet gaucher. Encephale 62: 382–394

Tzavaras A, Tzavaras H 1975 Cited as personal communication by Howes and Boller (1975)

Valenstein E, Heilman K M 1981 Unilateral hypokinesia and motor extinction. Neurology 31: 445–448

Van Buren J M 1961 Sensory, motor and autonomic effects of mesial temporal lobe stimulation in man. Journal of Neurosurgery 18: 273–288

Van Buren J M, Borke R C 1969 Alterations in speech and the pulvinar. A serial section study of cerebro-thalamic relationships in cases of acquired speech disorders. Brain 92: 255–284

Van Buren J M, Borke R C 1972 The mesial temporal substratum of memory. Anatomical studies in three individuals. Brain 95: 599–632

Van Wagenen W P, Herren R Y 1940 Surgical division of the commissural pathways in the corpus callosum; relation to spread of an epileptic attack. Archives of Neurology and Psychiatry 44: 740–759

Verity C M, Strauss E H, Moyes P D, Wada J A, Dunn H G, Lapointe J S 1982 Long-term follow-up after cerebral hemispherectomy: Neurophysiologic, radiologic, and psychological findings. Neurology 32: 629–639

Victor M 1976 The Wernicke-Korsakoff syndrome. In: Vinken P J, Bruyn G W (eds) Handbook of clinical neurology. North-Holland, Amsterdam, vol 28, ch 9

Victor M, Adams R D, Collins G F 1971 The Wernicke-Korsakoff syndrome. Davis, Philadelphia

Victor M, Angevine J B, Mancall E L, Fisher C M 1961 Memory loss with lesions of the hippocampal formation. Report of a case with some remarks on the anatomical basis of memory. Archives of Neurology 5: 244–263

Victor M, Yakovlev P I 1955 S.S. Korsakoff's psychic disorder in conjunction with peripheral neuritis. A translation of Korsakoff's original article with brief comments on the author and his contribution to clinical medicine. Neurology 5: 394–406

Vignolo L A 1969 Auditory agnosia. A review and report of recent evidence. In: Benton A L (ed) Contributions to neuropsychology. Aldine, Chicago ch 7

Vincent F M, Sadowsky C H, Saunders R L, Reeves A G 1977 Alexia without agraphia, hemianopia, or color-naming defect: a disconnection syndrome. Neurology 27: 689–691

Vinken P J, Bruyn G W (eds) 1969 Handbook of clinical neurology. North-Holland, Amsterdam

Vinken P J, Bruyn G W, Klawans H L (eds) 1984 Handbook of clinical neurology, Revised series 1, vol 45 Elsevier, Amsterdam

Volpe B T, Hirst W 1983a The characterization of an amnesic syndrome following hypoxic ischemic injury. Archives of Neurology 40: 436–440

Volpe B T, Hirst W 1983b Amnesia following the rupture and repair of an anterior communicating artery aneurysm. Journal of Neurology, Neurosurgery, and Psychiatry 46: 704–709

Von Bonin G 1962 Anatomical asymmetries of the cerebral hemispheres. In: Mountcastle V B (ed) Interhemispheric relations and cerebral dominance. Johns Hopkins, Baltimore

Von Monakow C 1911 Lokalisation der Hirnfunktionen. Journal fur Psychologie und Neurologie 17: 185–200

Vosburg R 1962 Lobotomy in Western Pennsylvania: looking back over ten years. American Journal of Psychiatry 119: 503–510

Wada J 1949 A new method for the determination of the side of cerebral speech dominance. A preliminary report on the intracarotid injection of sodium amytal in man. Igaku to Siebutsugaku 14: 221–222

Wada J A, Clarke R, Hamm A 1975 Cerebral hemispheric asymmetry in humans. Archives of Neurology 32: 239–246

Walker A E, Marshall C 1961 Stimulation and depth recording in man. In: Sheer D E (ed) Electrical stimulation of the brain. University of Texas Press, Austin, p 514–518

Walsh F B, Hoyt W F 1969 The visual sensory system: anatomy, physiology, and topographic diagnosis. In: Vinken P J, Bruyn G W (eds) Handbook of clinical neurology. Vol 2. North-Holland, Amsterdam ch 19

Walsh K W 1960 Surgical modification of the personality. Unpublished Master's thesis, University of Melbourne

Walsh K W 1976 Neuropsychological aspects of modified leucotomy. In: Sweet W H (ed) Neurosurgical treatment in psychiatry, pain, and epilepsy. University Park Press, Baltimore ch 11

Walsh K W 1982 Thalamic amnesia: A key to the problem of memory disorders? In: Stanley G V, Walsh K W (eds) Brain Impairment. Proceedings of seventh brain impairment workshop, University of Melbourne p 96–120

Walsh K W 1985 Understanding brain damage. A primer of neuropsychological evaluation. Churchill Livingstone, Edinburgh

Walshe J M, Davis K R, Fischer C H 1977 Thalamic haemorrhage a computed tomographic clinical correlation. Neurology 27: 217–222

Walton J N 1953 The Korsakov syndrome in spontaneous subarachnoid haemorrhage 99: 521–530

Wapner W, Hamby S, Gardner H 1981 The role of the right hemisphere in the apprehension of complex linguistic materials. Brain and Language 14: 15–33

Warren J M, Akert K 1964 The frontal granular cortex and behavior McGraw Hill, New York

Warrington E K 1962 The completion of visual forms across hemianopic field defects. Journal of Neurology, Neurosurgery, and Psychiatry 25: 208–217

Warrington E 1969 Constructional apraxia. In: Vinken P J, Bruyn G W (eds) Handbook of clinical neurology. vol 4 North-Holland. Amsterdam ch 4

Warrington E K 1971 Neurological disorders of memory. British Medical Bulletin 3: 243–247

Warrington E K 1973 Neurological deficits. In: Mittler P (ed) The psychological assessment of mental and physical handicaps. Tavistock Publications, London ch 9

Warrington E K 1984a Visual deficits associated with occipital lobe lesions. Paper presented to advanced course in neuropsychology, British Postgraduate Medical Federation, Institute of Neurology, London 10–13 July

Warrington E K, Baddeley A D 1974 Amnesia and memory for visual location. Neuropsychologia 12: 257–263

Warrington E K, James M 1967a An experimental investigation of facial recognition in patients with cerebral lesions. Cortex 3: 317–326

Warrington E K, James M 1967b Tachistoscopic number estimation in patients with unilateral cerebral lesions. Journal of Neurology, Neurosurgery, and Psychiatry 30: 468–474

Warrington E K, James M, Kinsbourne M 1966 Drawing disability in relation to laterality of cerebral lesion. Brain 89: 53–82

Warrington E K, Logue V, Pratt R T C 1971 The anatomical localization of selective impairment of auditory short-term memory. Neuropsychologia 9: 377–387

Warrington E K, Pratt R T C 1973 Language laterality in left-handers assessed by unilateral E C T. Neuropsychologia 11: 423–428

Warrington E K, Rabin P 1970 Perceptual matching in patients with cerebral lesions. Neuropsychologia 8: 475–487

Warrington E K, Rabin P 1971a A preliminary investigation between visual perception and visual memory. Cortex 6: 87–96

Warrington E K, Rabin P 1971b Visual span of apprehension in patients with unilateral cerebral lesions. Quarterly Journal of Experimental Psychology 23: 423–431

Warrington E K, Shallice T 1969 The selective impairment of auditory verbal short-term memory Brain 92: 885–896

Warrington E K, Shallice T 1972 Neuropsychological evidence of visual storage in short-term memory tasks. Quarterly Journal of Experimental Psychology 24: 30–40

Warrington E K, Taylor A M 1973 The contribution of the right parietal lobe to object recognition. Cortex 9: 152–164

Warrington E K, Weiskrantz L 1972 An analysis of short-term and long-term memory defects in man. In: Deutsch J A. The physiological basis of memory. Academic Press, New York p 365–395

Watson R T, Heilman K M 1979 Thalamic neglect. Neurology 29: 690–694

Watson R T, Heilman K M, Cauthen J C, King F A 1973 Neglect following cingulectomy. Neurology 23: 1003–1007

Watson R T, Heilman K M, Miller B D, King F A 1973 Neglect following mesencephalic reticular formation lesions (Abstract). Neurology 23:395

Wechsler D 1958 The measurement and appraisal of adult intelligence, 4th edn. Williams and Wilkins, New York

Weigl E 1941 On the psychology of the so-called process of abstraction. Journal of Abnormal and Social Psychology 36: 3–33

Weingarten S M, Cherlow D G, Halgren E 1977 Relationship of hallucinations to the depth structures of the temporal lobe. In: Sweet W H, Obrador S, Martin-Rodriguez (eds) Neurosurgical treatment in psychiatry, pain, and epilepsy. University Park Press, Baltimore, p 553–568

Weingartner H 1968 Verbal learning in patients with temporal lobe lesions. Journal of Verbal Learning and Verbal Behavior 7: 520–526

Weinstein S 1965 Deficits concomitant with aphasia or lesions of either hemisphere. Cortex 1: 154–169

Weinstein S, Semmes J, Ghent L, Teuber H L 1956 Spatial orientation in man after cerebral injury. 11. Analysis according to concomitant defects. Journal of Psychology 42: 249–263

Weinstein S, Sersen E A 1961 Tactual sensitivity as a function of handedness and laterality. Journal of Comparative and Physiological Psychology 54: 665–669

Weinstein S, Teuber H L 1957 Effects of penetrating brain injury on intelligence test scores. Science 125: 1036–1037

Weinstein S, Teuber H L, Ghent L, Semmes J 1955 Complex visual test performance after penetrating brain injury in man. American Psychologist 10:408

Weiskrantz L 1968 Some traps and pontifications. In: Weiskrantz L (ed) The analysis of behavioral change. Harper and Row, New York ch 15

Weiskrantz L (ed) 1968 Analysis of behavioral change. Harper and Row, New York

Weiskrantz L, Warrington E K, Sanders M D, Marshall J 1974 Visual capacity in the hemianopic field following a restricted occipital ablation 97: 709–728

Werner H 1946 The concept of rigidity: a critical evaluation. Psychological Review 53: 43–52

Whiteley A M, Warrington E K 1977 Prosopagnosia: A clinical, psychological and anatomical study of three patients. Journal of Neurology, Neurosurgery, and Psychiatry 40: 395–403

Whiteley A M, Warrington E K 1978 Selective impairment of topographical memory. Journal of Neurology, Neurosurgery and Psychiatry 41: 575–578

Whitty C W M, Lewin W 1960 A Korsakoff syndrome in the post-cingulectomy confusional state. Brain 83: 648–653

Whitty C W M, Lishman W A 1966 Amnesia in cerebral disease. In: Whitty C W M, Zangwill O L (eds) Amnesia. Appleton Century-Crafts, New York

Whitty C W M, Newcombe F 1965 Disabilities associated with lesions in the posterior parietal region of the nondominant hemisphere. Neuropsychologia 3: 175–186

Whitty C W M, Newcombe F 1973 R C Oldfield's study of visual and topographic disturbances in a right occipito-parietal lesion of 30 years duration. Neuropsychologia 11: 471–475

Whitty C W M, Zangwill O L (eds) 1966 Amnesia. Butterworth, London

Whitty C W M, Zangwill O L 1977 Amnesia, 2nd edn. Butterworth, London

Wilkins R H 1965 Neurosurgical classics. Johnson Reprint Corporation, New York

Williams D 1956 The structure of emotions reflected in epileptic experiences. Brain 79: 28–67

Williams D 1969 Temporal lobe syndromes. In: Vinken P J, Bruyn G W (ed) Handbook of clinical neurology. vol 2. North-Holland, Amsterdam ch 22

Williams D, Gassel M M 1962 Visual function in patients with homonymous hemianopia. I. The visual fields. Brain 85: 175–250

Williams M 1970 Brain damage and the mind. Penguin, Harmondsworth, Middlesex

Wilson P J 1970 Cerebral hemispherectomy for infantile hemiplegia, a report of 50 cases. Brain 93: 147–180

Winner E, Gardner H 1977 The comprehension of metaphor in brain-damaged patients. Brain 100: 717–729

Winocur G, Kinsbourne M 1978 Contextual cueing as an aid to Korsakoff amnesics. Neuropsychologia 16: 671–682

Winocur G, Oxbury S, Roberts R, Agnetti V, Davis C 1984 Amnesia in a patient with bilateral lesions to the thalamus. Neuropsychologia 22: 123–143

Witelson S F 1977 Anatomic asymmetry in the temporal lobes. In: Dimond S J, Blizard D A (eds) Evolution and lateralization of the brain. Annals of the New York Acadamy of Sciences 299: 328–354

Witelson S F, Pallie W 1973 Left hemisphere specialization for language in the newborn. Neuroanatomical evidence of asymmetry. Brain 96: 641–646

Wolff H G 1962 Discussion of Teuber's paper. In: Mountcastle V B (ed) Interhemispheric relations and cerebral dominance. Johns Hopkins Press, Baltimore

Wolpert I 1924 Die Simultanagnosie. Storung der Gesamtauffassung. Zeitschrift fur die Gesamte Neurologie und Psychiatrie 93: 397–415

Wood F, Ebert V, Kinsbourne M 1982 The episodic-semantic distinction in memory and amnesia. In: Cermak L (ed) Human memory and amnesia. Erlbaum, Hillsdale, New Jersey p 167–193

Woodworth R S, Schlosberg H 1954 Experimental psychology, 3rd edn. Metheun, London

Woollam D H M 1958 Concepts of the brain and its functions in classical antiquity. In: Poynter F N L (ed) The history and philosophy of knowledge of the brain and its functions. Blackwell, Oxford

Worster-Drought C 1931 Mental symptoms associated with tumours of the frontal lobes. Proceedings of the Royal Society of Medicine 24: 1007

Wyke M 1966 Postural arm-drift associated with brain lesions in man. Archives of Neurology 15: 329–334

Wyke M, Holgate D 1973 Colour-naming defects in dysphasic patients. Neuropsychologia 11: 451–461

Yacorzynski G K, Boshes B, Davis L 1948 Psychological changes produced by frontal lobotomy. Research Publications, Association for Research in Nervous and Mental Disease 27: 642–657

Yates A 1954 The validity of some psychological tests of brain damage. Psychological Bulletin 51: 359–380

Yates A J 1966 Psychological deficit. Annual Review of Psychology 17: 111–144

Yin R K 1970 Face recognition by brain-injured patients: dissociable ability. Neuropsychologia 8: 395–402

Young A W 1983 functions of the right cerebral hemisphere. Academic Press, New York.

Zaidel D W, Rausch R 1981 Effects of semantic organization on the recognition of pictures following temporal lobectomy. Neuropsychologia 19: 813–817

Zaidel E 1978 Lexical organization in the right hemisphere. In: Buser P, Rougeul-Buser A (eds) Cerebral correlates of conscious experience. Elsevier, Amsterdam

Zaidel E 1978 Lexical organization in the right hemisphere. In: Buser P, Rougel-Buser A (eds) Cerebral correlates of conscious experience. INSERM symposium series, No. 6 Elsevier, Amsterdam, p 177–197

Zaidel D, Sperry R W 1974 Memory impairment after commissurotomy in man. Brain 97: 263–272

Zamora E N, Kaelbling R 1965 Memory and electro-convulsive therapy. American Journal of Psychiatry 122: 546–554

Zangwill O L 1943 Clinical tests of memory impairment. Proceedings of the Royal Society of Medicine 36: 576–580

Zangwill O L 1946 Some qualitative observations on verbal memory in cases of cerebral lesions. British Journal of Psychology 37: 8–19

Zangwill O L 1960 Cerebral dominance and its relation to psychological function. Thomas, Springfield, Illinois

Zangwill O L 1961 Asymmetry of cerebral hemisphere function. In: Garland H (ed) Scientific aspects of neurology. Livingstone, London

Zangwill O L 1966a The amnesic syndrome. In: Whitty C W M, Zangwill O L (eds) Amnesia. Butterworths, London, p 77–91

Zangwill O 1966b Psychological deficits associated with frontal lobe lesions. International Journal of Neurology 5: 395

Zangwill O L 1978 Personal communication

Ziegler D K, Kaufman A, Marshall H E 1977 Abrupt memory loss associated with thalamic tumor. Archives of Neurology 34: 545–548

Zihl J 1980 'Blindsight': Improvement of visually guided eye movements by systematic practice in patients with cerebral blindness. Neuropsychologia 18: 71–77

Züllinger R 1935 Removal of left cerebral hemisphere: report of a case. Archives of Neurology and Psychiatry 34: 1055–1064

Zulch K J 1971 Some basic patterns of the collateral circulation of the cerebral arteries. In: Zulch K J (ed) Cerebral circulation and stroke. Springer, New York

Zurif E B 1974 Auditory lateralization: Prosodic and syntactical factors. Brain and Language 1: 391–404

Zurif E B, Bryden M P 1969 Familial handedness and left-right difference in auditory and visual perception. Neuropsychologia 7: 179–187

Zurif E B, Caramazza A, Myerson R 1972 Grammatical judgments of agrammatic aphasics. Neuropsychologia 10: 405–417

Zurif E B, Ramier A M 1972 Some effects of unilateral brain damage on the presentation of dichotically presented phoneme sequence and digits. Neuropsychologia 10: 103–110

Index

Ablation, animal, 19
Abstract thinking, 128–132
Acalculia, *see* Dyscalculia
Achromatopsia, 259–260, 268
Adynamia, 148
  see also Frontal, adynamia
Agenesis, corpus callosum, *see* Corpus callosum, agenesis
Agnosia, 107–111, 180
  acoustic, 175, 177
  anosognosia, 111, 240
  associative-sound, 177
  astereognosis, *see* Agnosia, tactile
  auditory, 108, 175
  body, (corporeal), 110
  colour, 109, 267–269
  finger, 110
  perceptual-discriminitive, 177
  prosopagnosia, 109, 263–276
    a disconnection syndrome?, 266–267
    locus of lesion, 264–265, **267**
    nature of defect, 265–266
  simultanagnosia, 262–263
  spatial, 109
  tactile, 109, 207–209
    astereognosis, 109
    topographical, 219–220
  visual, 109, 260–269
    and temporal lobe, 182–183
  visual object, 105, 109, 260–262
  visuospatial, 109, 212
Agnosic alexia, *see* Alexia, agnosic
Agranular cortex, *see* Cytoarchitecture
Agraphia, *see* Dysgraphia
Akinesia, 110
Akinetic mutism, 157
Alexia, 105
  agnosic, 106, 107, 269–273, **271**
  anterior, 151–152
  reversible, 273
  spelling, 270
  without agraphia, *see* agnosic
  see also, Dyslexia
  see also, Syndrome, disconnection

Alien hand, 307
Alveus, **48**
Amaurosis fugax, 95, 96
Amnesia, 113–115
  affective, 114
  anterograde, 19, 91, 114–115
  audioverbal, 176
  diencephalic, 320–327
  frontal, 144–147
  global, 114, 199
  Korsakoff (the amnesic syndrome),
      18–19, 47, 115, **115**, 128, 144,
      195–200, 320–323
    bilateral lesions and, 195–196
    different forms, 200
    specific features, 115
    unilateral lesions and, 196–197
    vascular lesions and, 197–198
  material-specific, 115, 191–193, 198
  post-traumatic, 3, 91, 92, 114
    see also, anterograde
  post-encephalitic, 197
  psychogenic, *see* affective
  retrograde, 19, 91, 114
  temporal lesions and, 195–200
  thalamic, 323–328
  topographical, 219
  transient global, *see* global
Amnesic syndrome, *see* Amnesia, korsakoff
Amorphosynthesis, 207
Amusia, *see* Agnosia, auditory
Amygdaloid nucleus, *see* Basal ganglia
Amytal ablation, 193–195, 278–280
  memory, 193–194
  speech representation, 193–194
Aneurysm, 97
Anastomoses, vascular, 76–77, **76**
Anastomosis, transcranial, 95
Anatomical terms, *see* Terms, anatomical
Angiography, *see* Arteriography
Anomia, colour, 105, 268
Anosmia, 183
Anosognosia, *see* Agnosia
  see also Body schema

Anton's syndrome, *see* Syndrome, Anton's
Aphasia, 103–107, 176
　abstraction and,
　agrammatism, 104–105
　amnesic, 106, 176
　auditory, amnestic, 176
　auditory receptive, 105
　Broca's, *see* expressive
　conduction, 28, **104**, 106
　disconnection model, 106–107
　expressive (Broca's), 16–17, 103–105
　frontal dynamic, 121–122
　global, 106
　jargon, 105
　latent (minimal)
　motor, *see* expressive
　nominal, *see* amnesic
　related disorders,
　receptive, *see* sensory
　semantic, 212
　sensory (Wernicke's), 17–18, 105, 175
　thalamic, 328–329
　transcortical, 107
　visual receptive, 105
　Wernicke's, *see* sensory
Apraxia, 111–113
　callosal, *see* left-sided
　constructional, 112–113, 221–231
　　associated disabilities, 113, 228–229
　　disconnection syndrome and, 230–231
　　frontal lobes and, 134–136, 229–230
　　laterality and, 224–227
　　locus of lesion and, 113, 227
　　status of concept, 221–223
　　tests, 113, 223
　　visuoperceptive difficulties and,
　　　225–227
　dressing, 113
　ideational, 112
　ideomotor, 111, 112
　dominance and, 111
　left-sided, 112, 311–312
　motor, 111
　unilateral limb, *see* left-sided
Aqueduct, cerebral, **54**
Arachnoid granulations, **37**, 38, **39**
　mater, 35, 38, **39**
Archipallium, 47
Aristotle, *see* Localization, history of
Arm drift, postural, 246
Arterial circle, *see* Circle, arterial
　occlusion, 76, **76**, 77
　supply, brain, 77
Arteries
　anterior cerebral, 69–71, **69**, **70**, **73**
　anterior choroidal, 68, 69, **73**
　anterior communicating, 69, **69**
　basilar, **69**
　internal carotid, 68, **68**, **69**
　meningeal, 35, 92

midddle cerebral, **69**, **70**, 71, **71**, 73
opthalamic, 68
posterior cerebral, **69**, 72, **72**, 73
　posterior choroidal branch, 73
posterior communicating, 68, 69, **69**, **73**
vertebral, **69**, 72
vertebrobasilar system, 72–73
Arteriography, 82, **83**
　Digital subtraction, 82, 83
Arteriosclerosis, **76**, 95, 96
Arteriovenous malformation (AVM), 97
Atheroma, 94, 95
Assessment, neurological
　see Neurology, examination
Assessment, neuropsychological, 330–340
　roles, 331–332
　single case method, 335–338
　syndrome and, 338–339
Association cortex, *see* Cortical zones
　　secondary
　fibres, *see* Fibres, association
Associationism, 19
Asrereognosis, *see* Agnosia, tactile
Asthenopia, 254
Asymmetry, hemispheric, 276–317
　language dominance, 276–280
　　handedness, 277–278
　morphological, 280
　unilateral lesions, 280–292
　　auditory perception, 287
　　bilateral effects, 291–292
　　emotion, 289–291
　　memory, 289
　　motor impersistence, 291
　　tactile perception, 285–287
　　visual perception, 281–285
Ataxia, optic, 262
Auditory cortex, *see* Cortex, auditory
Auditory radiation, **66**
Aura, epileptic, 183, 186
Austin maze, *see* Maze, Austin
Automatisms, 101
Autopagnosia, *see* Agnosia, body
Axial amnesia, *see* Amnesia, Korsakoff
Axial structures, 45

Babinski's syndrome, *see* Syndrome,
　　Babinski's
Basal ganglia, 39, 40, 65, 66–67, **66**, **67**,
　　236
　amygdaloid nucleus, **40**, 45, **46**, 47, 67,
　　67
　caudate nucleus, **40**, **48**, **49**,, 65, 66, **66**,
　　67
　globus pallidus, **40**, 65, 66, **66**
　putamen, **40**, 65, 66, **66**, **67**
Blindness, cerebral (cortical), 253–257
　denial of *see* Syndrome, Anton's
　hysterical, 257

Blindsight, 254
Blood supply, 67–77, **67, 69, 70, 71, 72, 73, 76**
Body image
  anosognosia, 111, 240
  see also Body schema
  parts, lack of awareness, *see* Body schema
  schema, disorders, 239–242
  lack of awareness, 111, 241
Bouillaud, *see* Language, localization
Brain contusion, *see* Contusion, cerebral
  coverings, *see* Meninges
  damage,
    intellectual changes, 130–132
    unitary concept, 21
    see also Lesion, unilateral
  scan, *see* Tomography
    computerized axial,
    positron emission;
    see also Magnetic resonance imaging
  stem, 52–59, **53, 54, 58**
Broca's aphasia, *see* Aphasia, expressive; *see also*, Language, localization
Brodmann, *see* Cytoarchitecture

Calculation difficulties, *see* Dyscalculla
Carotid syphon, 68, **68**
Catastrophic reaction, 143
Caudate nucleus, *see* Basal ganglia
Cell doctrine, *see* Localization, ventricular theory
Centrencephalic epilepsy, *see* Epilepsy
Cerebellum, 35, 39
Cerebral contusion, *see* Contusion, cerebral
Cerebrospinal fluid, system, 3, 35–39, **36, 37, 38**
  production, 37, 38
Cerebrovascular disorders, 94–98
Chimeric figures, 302–303, **303**
Choroid plexus, *see* Plexus, choroid
Cingulum, 61, **61, 62**
Circle, arterial (Willis), 73–77, **75**
Circuit of Papez, *see* Papez circuit
Circumlocution, 176
Cistern
  cerebellomedullary, 36
  interpenduncular, **37**
  pontine, **37**
Colliculi, 54
  inferior, 57
  superior, 57
  see also Midbrain, tectum;
  see also Brain, stem
Colour anomia, *see* Anomia, colour
Colour-form sorting test, 129, 166, 167
Coma, 91
Commissures,
  anterior, 49, **54**, 62, **62**, 63

  hippocampal, 49, **49**, 62, 63, **64**, 65
  posterior, 53, 54
  see also, Corpus callosum, Fibre arrangement
Commissurotomy, 28, 29, 298–312
  animal studies, 28, 299–300
  apraxia, unilateral, 311–312
  language, 308–312
  memory, 312
  partial, 30
  perception,
    auditory, 307–308
    tactile, 306–307
    visual, 300–306
  see also Syndrome, Disconnection
Completion, visual 255–257, **256**
Complex Figure of Rey, **135**, 136
Computerized axial tomography, *see* Tomography, computerized, axial
Confabulation, *see* Frontal lobe, confabulation
Concussion, 91
Confabulation, 127–128
Conflict reaction, 148
Constructional apraxia, *see* Apraxia constructional
Contre coup, *see* Injuries
Contusion, 89–91, **90, 91**
Convolution, *see* Gyrus
Corona radiata, *see* Fibres projection
Corpus callosum, **48**
  agenesis, 312–314
  anterior forceps, 63, **64**
  as cerebral organ, 14
  body of, **44**, 63, **64**
  fibre arrangement, 62, **62**, 63, **64**
  genu, 43, **44**, 63
  posterior forceps, 63, **64**
  rostrum, 43, **44**
  section of, 28, 29
  splenium, 35, 43, **44, 48**, 63, 270
Cortex, 49–52,
  archipallium, 47
  auditory, 51, 172–175, **173**
  cellular layers, *see* Cytoarchitecture
  definition of, 35, 39
  early, 18
  motor, 51
  neocortex, 50
  paleocortex, 50
  prefrontal, 121
  premotor, 121
  sensory (somaesthetic), 51
  structure, *see* Cytoarchitecture
  visual, 51
Cortical localization, *see* Localization
  maps, 19
  zones, 51–52
    primary, 51–52, 107, 118, 172–173

Zone (cont'd)
  secondary (association), 29, 52, 107, 118
  tertiary (zones of overlapping), 52, 107, 118, 210
Cranial nerves,
  early, **10, 53, 57**
Cranioscopy, see Phrenology
Craniotomy, early, 4–5
Cross-model integration, 209–210
Crus cerebri, see Midbrain
Cuneus, 44, **44**
Cytoarchitecture, 19–20, 49–51, 247–249
  agranular cortex, 118
  Brodmann's areas, 20, 249
  frontal lobe, 118, **119**
  granular cortex, 118, **119**
  history, 19–20
  occipital lobes, 247–249, **248, 249**

Dax, see Language localization
Déjà vu, 101–186
Denial, see Anosognosia
  blindness, see Syndrome, Anton's
  hemiplegia, see Syndrome, Babinski's
Depersonalization, 186
Derealization, 186
Diagnosis, differential, 22–23
Diaschisis, 291
Dichotic listening, 178–181
  and language dominance, 181
Dichotic monitoring, 181
Diencephalon, 318–320, **320**
Digital Subtraction, see Arteriography, Digital Subtraction
Disconnection syndrome, see Syndrome, disconnection
Disorders, neurological, 88–103
Disorientation, right-left, 242
  topographical, 216–219
Dissociation, double, 24–27,
  example of, 26, 152
  auditory perception, 177–178
  congruent, 26
  example of, **26**
Dominance, cerebral, 276–317
  music, 181–182
  see also, Asymmetry, hemispheric
  see also, Hemispherectomy,
  see also, Language, localization
Double simultaneous stimulation, 110
Drawing disability, see Dysgraphia
Dvra mater, 34–35, **34**, 38, **39**
Dysarthria, 103
Dyscalculia, 211, 231–232
Dysgraphia, 105
Dyslexia, spatial, 231
Dysphasia, 103

Echopraxis, 148
Edwin Smith sugical papyrus, 1–3
Einstellung, see Rigidity
Electroconvulsive therapy (ECT),
  memory, 192, 193
Electro encephalography (EEG), 85–87, **85**, 257,
  and epilepsy, 86, 87
Elithorn maze, see Maze, Elithorn
Embolus, 94
Endarterectomy, see Stenosis, arterial
Epilepsy, 6, 98–103
  absences, 99–100
  centrencephalic, 99
  generalized, 99, **102**, 103
  partial (focal), 100, 102
    complex, 100, 184–187
    simple, 100
  petit mal, see absences
  status epilepticus, 99
  temporal lobe, 100, 101, 102, **102**, 184–187
  unilateral, 102–103
Epithalamus, 54
Equipotentiality, 15
Error evaluation, 137–138
  utilization, 137–138
Expectancy waves, 122
Extinction, see Sensory suppression

Faces, agnosia, see Agnosia, prosopagnosia
Faculty, psychology, see Localization, theories
Falx cerebri, 34–35, 39
Fasciculus,
  arcuate, **60**, 61, **61, 62**, 106
  inferior longitudinal, 61, **62**
  inferior occipitofrontal, **60, 61**
  superior longitudinal, 60, **61**
  superior occipitofrontal, **60, 61**
  uncinate, 61
Fibres,
  association, 18, 30, 59–61, **60, 61, 62**, 174, 175
  comissural, 30, 47, 60, 62, **62**, 63, **64**
  projection, 47, **48**, 60, **65**, 172–173
    corona radiata, 65, **65**
    internal capsule, 65, **66**
  see also, Basal ganglia
  see also, Syndrome, disconnection
Fimbria, 49, **49**
Finger agnosia, see Agnosia, finger
Fissure, see Sulcus
Flourens, 15, 16
Foramen, interventricular, 37, **37, 48**, 49, **54**
  magnum, 72
Foramina, fourth ventricle, 59

Forceps, anterior, *see* Corpus callosum
    posterior, *see* Corpus callosum
Fornix, **46**, 47, **48, 49, 64**
    anterior columns, **48**, 49, **64**
    body, **48**, 49, **49, 64**
    crura, 47, **49, 64**
    see also, Commissure, hippocampal
Fossa, anterior cranial, 40
    interpeduncular, 57
    middle cranial, 40, 44
Frontal lobe, **42**, 117–168
    abstract thinking, 123, 124, 128–132, 166
    adynamia, 157
    anatomy, and functional organization,
        117–122, **118, 119, 120**
    apraxia, 229–230
    asymmetry (laterality), 155–157
    basomedial cortex, 121
    confabulation, 127–128
    connections, **119, 120**, 121
    controversy, 122–126
    intellectual changes, 127, 164–168
    neglect and, 236
    perceptual disorders, *see* Perception,
        disorders
    personality, 126, 127, 161–164
    planning, 132–138
    problem solving, 132–138
    syndrome, *see* Syndrome, frontal
    verbal behaviour, 147–152
    visual search, *see* Perception, disorders
Function, concepts of, 23
Functional, asymmetry, *see* Asymmetry,
        hemispheric
    localization, *see* Localization, functional
    plasticity, *see* Plasticity, functional
    systems, *see* Systems, functional

Galen, *see* Localization, theories
Gall, *see* Phrenology
Ganglia, basal, *see* Basal ganglia
Geniculate bodies,
    lateral, 57
    medial, 57
Geographical orientation, *see* Spatial,
        orientation
Gerstmann syndrome, *see* Syndrome,
        Gerstmann
Globus pallidus, *see* Basal ganglia
Grand mal seizures, *see* Epilepsy,
        generalized
Granular cortex, *see* Cytoarchitecture
Grey matter, 39
Gyri, 35, 40–41
    early description, 3
    insular, **42**
    occipitotemporal, 44
    orbital, 44, *45*
    transverse temporal (Heschl), 42, 51

Gyrus
    angular, 170, **202**
    cingulate, 43, **44, 45, 46**, 61, **61, 203**
    dentate, 45, **46**, 47, **48**
    fasciolus, 47, **48**
    fusiform, **45, 171**
    Heschl, 170, **172**, 173, **173**
    hippocampal, *see* parahippocampal
    lingual, 44, **44**, 45, **45**
    parahippocampal, 43, 44, **45, 46**, 47, **48,**
        171, 172, **172**
    precentral, **43**, 44
    postcentral, **43**, 44, **202**
    rectus, **45**
    subcallosal 45, **46**
    supracallosal, 47
    supramarginal, 170, **202**
    temporal, inferior, **45, 48**, 170, 171, **171**,
        172
    temporal middle, **43**, 170, **171, 172**
    temporal, superior, 17, 42, **43**, 170, **171,**
        172

Haematoma
    extradural, 92
    intracerebral, 97
    subdural, 5, 92, **93**
Haemorrhage
    intracerebral, 96–97
    traumatic, 92
Hallucinations,
    occipital (visual), 273
    temporal, 183, 185–187
Handedness, *see* Asymmetry, hemispheric
Head injury, *see* Injuries, brain
Hemianopia, *see* Visual field defects
Hemidecortication, *see* Hemispherectomy
Hemi-inattention, *see* Neglect, unilateral
Hemiparesis, early description, 3
Hemiplegia, denial, *see* Syndrome,
        Babinski's
    infantile, *see* Hemispherectomy
Hemisphere, nondominant, *see*
        Nondominant hemisphere
Hemispheres, cerebral 39–49
    superolateral surface, 40–43, **40, 41**
    medial surface, 43–44, **43**
    inferior surface, 44, **45**
Hemispherectomy, 293–298
    adult, 296–298
    infantile hemiplegia, 193–296
Heschl's gyri, *see* Gyri, transverse temporal
Hewson ratios,
Hippocampal formation, 45, 47, **48**; *see also*
        commissure, hippocampal; *see also*
        system, hippocampal
Hippocampal lesions, *see* Amnesia,
        Korsakoff; *see also*, Amnesia, post-
        encephalitic

Hippocampus, 47, **48, 49, 64**
and memory loss, 195–200
Hippocrates, 6, 11
History
Egyptian, 1–4
Greece, 6
Holistic theory, see Flourens
Homonymous hemianopia, see Visual field
defects
Hydrocephalus, 38, 97
Hypothalamus, 57
Hypothesis testing, 18
Hysterical fugue, 114

Imaging, see Magnetic Resonance
Impersistence, motor, 291
Inattention, sensory, see Sensory
suppression; see also, Neglect
Indusium griseum, 47, **48**
Infantile hemiplegia, see Hemispherectomy
Infarct, cerebral, see Ischaemia, cerebral
Inflexibility, see Rigidity
Inhibition, loss, 151
Injuries, brain
contre coup, 3, 89, **90**
definition of, 89, **90**
early descriptions, 1–3
severity of, 91–92
Injury, spinal
early description, 3
Insula, 41, **42**, 45, 172–173, **173**
Interbrain, 318–329
Intersensory disorders, see Cross-modal
integration
Interthalamic adhesion, 56
Internal capsule, see Fibres, projection
Intersensory association
see Cross-modal integration
Ischaemia, cerebral, 94–95
cerebral infarct, 96
Isthmus, temporal, 250–251

Jamais-vu, 101, 186

Korsakoff amnesia, see Amnesia, Korsakoff

Language disorders, see Aphasia
Language, localization, 16–17
history, 16–18
Bouillaud, 16
Broca, 16–17
Dax, 16
Wernicke, 17–18

Lateral hand preference, see Handedness
Laterality, see Dominance, cerebral
Lentiform body, see Basal ganglia
Lesion studies, 15–19, 20, 88, 128–157
Lesions, unilateral see Asymmetry,
hemispheric
Leucotomy, see Psychosurgery
Limbic lobe, 45–47
system, see System limbic
Lobar divisions, 42–43, **43**
Lobectomy, see Epilepsy, temporal
Lobes, see e.g. Frontal lobe, Temporal
lobe; see also, Cytoarchitecture
Lobotomy, see Psychosurgery
Lobule, paracentral, 44, **44, 203**
parietal, 44, **202**
inferior, 170–171, **202**
Localization, language, see Language,
localization
Localization, history of, 1–20
Aristotle, 6–7, 10, 11
corpus callosum (Lancisi), 14
corpus striatum (Willis), 14
faculty psychology, 14–15
Galen, 6–11, 13, 15, 16
pineal (Descartes), 13
psychic gas (pneuma), 7–8
ventricular theory, 6–11, 8, 10
white matter (Vieussens), 14
Logico-grammatical disorders, 212
Luria, see Cortical, Localization, zones; see
also, Frontal, planning, problem
solving; see also, Impulsive
hypothesis, 154; see also,
Neuropsychology; see also,
Rigidity, perseveration; see also,
System, functional

Macropsia, 186
Magnetic resonance imaging, 83–85, **84**
Mamillary body, **46, 48**, 49, 53
Mamillothalamic tract, **48**
Massa intermedia, see Interthalamic
adhesion
Maze,
Austin, 138, 168
behaviour, 133–134
Elithorn, 134, **134**
Porteus, 133–134, **133**, 147, 166
Medial structures, see Axial, structures
Medulla oblongata, 52, 53, **54**, 59
Medullary substance, see White matter
Memory disorders, see Amnesia,
for location, 215
short-term
parietal lobes, 244–246
temporal lobes, 191–200
topographical, 216–219, 220

Meninges, 3, 34–35, **34**, 93
  see arachnoid mater, dura mater, pia
    mater
Meningioma, *see* Tumours
Mesencephalon, *see* Midbrain
Metamorphopsia, *see* Epilepsy, temporal
  lobe symptoms
Metastases, *see* Tumours, secondary
Metathalamus, 57
Micropsia, 186
Midbrain, **45**, 53, **53**, 57, **58**
  basis pedunculi (crus cerebri), 57
  cerebral peduncles, 57, 59
  substantia nigra, 57, **58**
  tectum, 57
Mind, *see* Localization, history of
Minor hemisphere, *see* Non-dominant
    hemisphere
Motor impersistence, *see* Impersistence,
    motor
Myleloarchitecture, 19–20

Naming, *see* Aphasia, nominal
Neglect, unilateral, 233–239
  and perceptual disorders, 237
  laterality, 233–235
  locus of lesion, 236
  nature of defect, 238–239
  measures, 233
  recovery of function, 239
  syndrome, 109–110
  thalamic, 329
Neocortex, *see* Cortex
Neoplasm, *see* Tumours
Neurology
  elements of, 78–116
  examination, 78–79
  techniques, *see* e.g., Arteriography
    Imaging, magnetic resonance
    Tomography, computerized axial
Neuropsychology
  nature and development, 19–20
  neuroanatomy and, 24
  approaches of
    qualitative, 24, 130–131
    quantitative, 24, 130–131
Non-dominant hemisphere functions
  attention, 292
  communication, 288
  emotion, 289–291
  perception, 281–287
Nuclei
  hypothalamic, 45
  septal, 45, **46**
  thalamic, 45, **46**, 54, **55**, 56, **56**
Nucleus, amygdaloid, *see* Basal ganglia
  caudate, *see* Basal ganglia
  globus pallidos, *see* Basal ganglia
  Putamen, *see* Basal ganglia

Occipital lobe, 247–275
  anatomy, **42**, 247–253, **248**
  experiential response, **274**
Olfactory bulb, 44, **45**
  sulcus, 44
  tract, 44, **45**, **48**
Opercula, 41–42, **173**
Optic chiasm, **45**, **53**
Optic radiation, 65, **66**, 250
Orbital gyri, *see* Gyri, orbital
Organic mental syndrome, *see* Dementia
Organ of corti, 174
Orientation, *see* Spatial orientation
  topographical

Paleocortex, *see* Cortex
Papez circuit, 46
Paraphasia, 105
Parietal lobe, 201–246
  anatomy, 42, 201–204, **202**, **203**
  sensory disorders, 204–212
  see also, Spatial disorders
Pathognomonic,
  definition of, 23
Peduncles, *see* Midbrain
Perception, disorders
  auditory, 175–178
  depth, 258–259
  frontal, 152–155
  neglect and, 237
  stimulus orientation, 207
  tactile, 207–209
  temporal, 185–187
  visual search, 152–155
Perseveration, *see* Rigidity
Petit mal seizures, *see* Epilepsy
Phoneme, 175
Photisms, 253
Phrenology, 14–15, **15**, 18, 19
Planning, *see* Frontal lobe, planning
Pia mater, 35, 38, **39**
Pineal gland, 43, 54
Plexus, choroid, **9**, 37, **37**, 38, **48**
Pons, 52, **53**, 57
Porteus maze test, *see* Maze, Porteus
Postural arm drift, *see* Arm drift, postural
Precuneus, 44, **44**
Prefrontal cortex
  see Cortex, prefrontal; *see* Psychosurgery,
    leucotomy; *see* Psychosurgery,
    lobotomy
Premotor cortex, *see* Cortex, premotor
Primary cortex, *see* Cortical zones, primary
Problem solving, *see* Frontal lobe, problem
    solving
Programming, *see* Frontal lobe, planning
Projection areas, *see* Cortical zones, primary
  fibres, *see* Fibres, projection

Psalterium, *see* Commissures, hippocampal

Psychomotor seizures, *see* Epilepsy,
  temporal lobe

Psychosurgery, 158–164, **158, 159**
  cognitive changes, 164–168
  maze behaviour, 133–134
  modified operations, 159, 160, **160,**
    161–162, 164–168
  personality changes, 127, 161–164
  radical (classical), 158, 159, **158, 159**

Pulvinar, 54

Putamen, *see* Basal ganglia

Pyramids, decussation, 11, **53,** 59

Quasi-spatial syntheses, *see* Symbolic
  syntheses

Rami, *see* sulcus lateral

Rete mirabile, 9

Reticular formation, 52, 57, 91

Rey Figure, **135,** 136

Rhinencephalon, *see* Cytoarchitecture

Right hemisphere, *see* Non-dominant
  hemisphere

Right-left disorientation, *see* Disorientation
  right-left

Rigidity, 138–144
  abstract behaviour, 140
  Einstellung, 139, 144
  frontal lobe, 139–144
  intellectual loss and, 143
  perseveration, 140–141
  motor, 141
  Wisconsin card sorting test, 140, 142

Scotoma, 252

Seizures, *see* Epilepsy

Sensory extinction, *see* Sensory suppression,
  110

Sensus communis, 9, 11

Sinus superior sagittal, 38, **38, 39,** 74, 75

Sinuses, confluence of, 73
  great venous, **75**

Size discrimination, *see* Perception disorders
  tactile

Somaesthetic disorders, *see* Somatosensory
  discrimination; *see also* Parietal lobe

Somatosensory discrimination, 204–207, **205**

Spatial disorders
  general comments, 232–233
  location, 212–215
  neglect, *see* Neglect, unilateral
  operations, reversible, 214
  orientation, 216–219
  route finding, 219–220

Spatial orientation disorders

  see Spatial disorders

Speech lateralization, *see* Dominance,
  cerebral

Spurzheim, *see* Phrenology

Stenosis, arterial, 94, 95

Stereopsis, 258–259

Stimulation, electrical, 87, 88, **88**
  occipital lobe, 273–275, **274**
  temporal lobe, 187–189

Subarachnoid space, 35, 36, **37, 39**

Subcallosal area, 43, **44**

Subdural haematoma, *see* Haematoma,
  subdural

Subdural space, 35

Substantia nigra, 57, **58**

Subthalamus, 57

Sulci, 35, 140–141

Sulcus
  calcarine 42, 44, **44,** 171
  callosal, 43
  central, **40** 41, 42, 44, **202, 203**
  collateral, 48, 171
  hypothalamic, 48, 54
  inferior temporal, **171**
  intraparietal, **202**
  lateral, **40,** 41, 42, **202**
  longitudinal, 39, **41**
  marginal, 43, **44**
  olfactory, 44
  paracentral, 43–44, **44**
  parieto-occipital, **40,** 42, **44**
  subparietal, **203**

Supramodal, *see* Cortical localization
  zones tertiary

Suppression, *see* Sensory suppression

Symbolic synthesis, 210–212

Syndrome, amnesic, *see* Amnesia, Korsakoff
  advantages of, 22
  Anton's 254–257
  Babinski's, 254–255
  conduction, 27–28, **104,** 106–107
  definition of, 22
  disconnection, 18, 27–31, **30,** 111–112,
    112, 266–267, 270–273, **271**
  agnosic alexia, 270–273
  constructional apraxia, 112–113
  origin, 21–23
see also Commissurotomy
  frontal lobe, 126–128
    syndrome: one or many?, 168
  Ganser
  Gerstmann, 243–244
    and dominance, 276
  premotor, 141

System, hippocampal, 47–49, **48**
  auditory, 172–182
  functional, 23–24, 29
  internal carotid arterial, 68–71, **68**
  limbic, 45–47
  vertebrobasilar, arterial, 72, **72**

Tactile perception, *see* Perception, disorders
Taxonomy, biological, 23
Tectum, *see* Midbrain
Tegmentum, 57
Temporal lobe, 169–200
  anatomy, 42, 170–172, **171**
  defects
    auditory perception, *see* Perception,
      disorders
    olfaction, 183
    visual field, 182
    visual perception, 182–183
  epilepsy, *see* Epilepsy, temporal lobe
  hallucinations, 83, 185–187
  illusions, 185–187
  memory
    material-specific, 191–193
  music and, 181–182
  Organization
    fuctional, 172–183
      auditory system, 172–182
      olfaction, 183
      visual perception, 182–183
    integrative, 169–170
  stimulation, 187–189
    amnesia
      bilateral lesions, 195–196
      unilateral lesions, 196–199
    experiential response, 187–188, **188**
Temporal lobectomy
  intellectual changes, 189–91
Tentorium cerebelli, 34–35, 44
Terms anatomical, 32–33, **33**
Tertiary cortex, *see* Cortical zones, tertiary
Thalamus, **49**, 54, 55, 56, **56, 67**
  see Nuclei, thalamic; and internal capsule,
    65; projections
    lateral, **55**, 121
    medial, **56**, 121
Thrombus, *see* embolus
Tomography
  brain, *see* Hemispheres cerebral
  computerized axial, 79–81, **80, 81**
  positron emission, 81
Topographical disorientation, *see*
  Disorientation, topographical; *see also*
    Agnosia, topographical
  orientation, *see* Orientation, topographical
Tower of London test, 138, **139**
Tracts, *see* Fibres
Transient ischaemic attacks, *see* Ischaemic,
  cerebral
Trauma, cerebral, 88–92
  see also Injuries
Tumours, 92–94
  glioma, 93
  meningioma, 93

primary, 93
secondary, 93

Uncus, 44, **45, 46**, 47
Unilateral lesions, *see* Lesions, unilateral

Veins, cerebral, 73, **74**
  internal jugular, 73, **75**
  great cerebral (Galen), 73, **74**
  see also, sinuses, venous
Velum
  inferior medullary, 59
  superior medullary, 59
Ventricles, 36–38
  fourth, 36, **36**, 37, 38, **38**
  lateral, 36, **36**, 37, **38**
  third, 36, **36**, 37, **38**
Ventricular localization, *see* Localization,
  ventricular
Verbal fluency, 148–149, 156
Verbal regulation of behaviour, 147–148
Vertebrobasilar insufficiency, 199–200
Vesalius, Andreas, 11–13, **12**
Visual field defects, **250, 251**, 251–253
  adaptation, 255–257
  examination of 252–253
  hemianopia, 251, 252
  neglect and, 237
  quadrantanopia, 251
  scotoma, 252
Visual pathways, 249–253, **250**
Visual perception, 257–260
  achromotopsia, 259–260
  location, 257–258
  orientation, 257–258
  stereopsis and depth perception,
    258–259
Visual search, *see* perception, disorders
Visuoconstruction, defects, *see* Apraxia
  constructional
Visuospatial agnosia, *see* Agnosia,
  visuospatial
  neglect, *see* Neglect, unilateral

Wada technique, *see* Amytal ablation
War wounds
  contribution of, 2
Wernicke, connection theory, 17–18, 27–28
White matter, 39, **42**, 59–66
Wisconsin card sorting test, *see* Rigidity
Witzelsucht, 127
Word salad, 175